PROTECTED AREAS
AND
INTERNATIONAL ENVIRONMENTAL LAW

Protected Areas and International Environmental Law

by

ALEXANDER GILLESPIE

MARTINUS NIJHOFF PUBLISHERS
LEIDEN/BOSTON

A C.I.P. record for this book is available from the Library of Congress.

Cover photo: © UNESCO / Forbes, Inez

Printed on acid-free paper.

Layout and camera-ready copy:
Anne-Marie Krens – Oegstgeest – The Netherlands

ISBN 978 9004 16158 0

Koninklijke Brill NV incorporates the imprints Brill, Hotei Publishing, IDC Publishers, Martinus Nijhoff Publishers and VSP.

http://www.brill.nl

Printed and bound in The Netherlands

TABLE OF CONTENTS

ACRONYMS

ACAP	Agreement on the Conservation of Albatross and Petrels
ACCOBAMS	Agreement on the Conservation of Cetaceans of the Black Sea, Mediterranean Sea and Contiguous Atlantic Area
AEWA	African-Eurasian Migratory Birds Agreement
ASCOBANS	Agreement on the Conservation of Small Cetaceans of the Baltic and the North Seas
ASPA	Antarctic Specially Protected Area
ARPA	Amazon Region Protected Areas Programme
APM	Associated Protective Measures
BRIM	Biosphere Reserve Integrated Monitoring
BSPA	Baltic Sea Protected Area
CAFF	Conservation of Arctic Flora and Fauna
CBD	United Nations Convention on Biological Diversity
CCD	United Nations Convention to Combat Desertification in Countries Experiencing Serious Drought and/or Desertification, Particularly in Africa
CEMP	CCAMLR Ecosystem Monitoring Programme
CEP	Committee on Environmental Protection
CEPA	Communication, Education and Public Awareness
CMS	Convention on Migratory Species
CPAN	Circumpolar Protected Area Network
CPD	Centre of Plant Diversity
EBA	Endemic Bird Area
FAO	Food and Agricultural Organisation of the United Nations
GCRM	Global Coral Reef Monitoring Network
HSMPA	High Seas Marine Protected Area
IBP	International Biological Programme
ICC	International Co-ordinating Council
ICDP	Intergrated Conservation and Development Project
ICRI	International Coral Reef Initiative
ICZM	Integrated Coastal Zone Management
IPCC	Intergovernmental Panel on Climate Change
ITTA	International Tropical Timber Agreement
ITTO	International Tropical Timber Organisation
IUCN	International Union for the Conservation of Nature
LME	Large Marine Ecosystems
MAB	Man and the Biosphere
MEA	Multilateral Environmental Agreements

MHT	Major Habitat Type
PACT	Partnerships for Conservation Initiative
SCAR	Scientific Committee on Antarctic Research
SMAs	Specially Managed Areas
SOLAS	Safety of Life at Sea Convention
SPA	Specially Protected Areas
SPAMI	Specially Protected Area of Mediterranean Importance
SRA	Specially Reserved Area
SSSI	Sites of Special Scientific Interest
STRP	Scientific and Technical Review Panel
TBPAs	Trans-boundary Protected Areas
TEV	Total Economic Value
UNFCCC	United Nations Framework Convention on Climate Change
UNICPOLOS	United Nations Open Ended Informal Consultative Process on Oceans and the Law of the Sea
UNCLOS	United Nations Convention on the Law of the Sea
UNEP	United Nations Environment Programme
WCED	World Commission on Environment and Development
WCMC	World Conservation Monitoring Centre
WHC	World Heritage Convention
YBIEL	Yearbook of International Environmental Law

TREATIES REFERRED TO IN THIS BOOK

London Convention for the Preservation of Fauna and Flora in Africa. (1933). *BH*142.txt.

Convention on Nature Protection and Wild Life Preservation in the Western Hemisphere (1940). *BH*175.txt

International Convention For The Prevention Of Pollution Of the Sea By Oil (1954). 327 *UNTS*. 3.

Convention Concerning the Protection of Indigenous and Other Tribal Populations in Independent Countries of the International Labour Organisation (1957). *ILO* 107.
Antarctic Treaty (1959). 402 *UNTS* 71.

Convention for the Regulation of Whaling (1946). 161 *UNTS* 143.

African Convention on the Conservation of Nature and Natural Resources (1968). 1001 *UNTS* 3.

The Convention on Wetlands of International Importance (1971). 996 *UNTS* 245; 11 *ILM* (1972) 963.

Convention for the Protection of the World Cultural and Natural Heritage (1972). *BH*605.txt

Convention on International Trade in Endangered Species of Wild Flora and Fauna. 12 *ILM* (1973) 1055.

Convention for the Protection of the Marine Environment of the Baltic Area (1974). In UNEP (1983). *Selected Multilateral Treaties in the Field of the Environment.* (Ed. A. Kiss, UNEP, Nairobi). 405

Convention on the Conservation of European Wildlife and Natural Habitats (1979). *BH*756.txt; 1284 *UNTS* 209.

Convention on the Conservation of Migratory Species of Wild Animals. 19 *ILM* (1980) 15. BH752.txt

Convention on the Conservation of Antarctic Marine Living Resources (1980). 19 *ILM* (1980) 841.

Kuwait Regional Convention for Co-operation on the Protection of the Marine Environment from Pollution (1980). In UNEP (1983). *Selected Multilateral Treaties in the Field of the Environment.* (Ed. A. Kiss, UNEP, Nairobi). at 486.

Convention for the Co-operation in the Protection and Development of the Marine and Coastal Environment of the West and Central African Region (1981). *ILM* 20 (1988). 746-761.

Convention for the Protection of the Marine Environment and Coastal Area of the South East Pacific (1981). In UNEP. (1991). *Multilateral Treaties in the Field of the Environment.* (ed. Rummel-Bulska, I. Cambridge University Press, Cambridge). 130.

Convention for the Conservation of the Red Sea and Gulf of Aden Environment (1982). In UNEP. (1991). *Multilateral Treaties in the Field of the Environment.* (ed. Rummel-Bulska, I. Cambridge University Press, Cambridge). 144.

Convention for the Protection and Development of the Marine Environment of the Wider Caribbean Region (1983). In UNEP. (1991). *Multilateral Treaties in the Field of the Environment.* (ed. Rummel-Bulska, I. Cambridge University Press, Cambridge). 258.

Protocol Concerning Specially Protected Areas and Wildlife to the Conventon for the Protection and Development of the Marine Environment of the Wider Carribean Region (1985). This is reprinted in Austen, A. (ed). *Basic Legal Document on International Animal Welfare and Wildlife Conservation* (Kluwer, London). 610.

Protocol to the Barcelona Convention on Marine Protected Areas. 84/132/EEC: Council Decision of 1 March 1984.

ASEAN Agreement on the Conservation of Nature and Natural Resources (1985). This is reprinted in Austen, A. (ed). *Basic Legal Document on International Animal Welfare and Wildlife Conservation* (Kluwer, London). 193.

Convention for the Protection, Management and Development for the Marine and Coastal Environment of the East African Region. 1985. (French) *Journal Official* 1989, 7729.

Convention for the Protection of the Natural Resources and Environment of the South Pacific Region (1986). In UNEP. (1991). *Multilateral Treaties in the Field of the Environment.* (ed. Rummel-Bulska, I. Cambridge University Press, Cambridge). 372.

Protocol on Environmental Protection to the Antarctic Treaty (1991). 19 *ILM* (1980) 837. *BH*992.txt.

The United Nations Convention on Biological Diversity (1992). 31 *ILM* (1992). 818.

Statement of Principles for a Global Consensus on the Management, Conservation and Sustainable Use of all Types of Forests. 1992. 31. *ILM.* 1992. 881.

The Habitats Directive. Council Directive 92/43/EECof 21 May 1992.

Convention on the Protection of the Black Sea Against Pollution (1992). *BH*1004.txt. 32 *ILM* 1101.

Convention for the Protection of the Marine Environment of the North-East Atlantic (OSPAR) (1992). *BH*1012.txt. 32 *ILM* 1069.

Convention on the Protection of the Marine Environment of the Marine Environment of the Baltic Sea Area (1992). Reprinted in *United Nations Law of the Sea Bulletin* No. 22.

Convention to Combat Desertification in Those Countries Experiencing Drought and/or Desertification, Particularly in Africa (1994). 33 *ILM* (1994). 1332.

International Tropical Timber Agreement (1994). 33 *ILM* (1994). 1016.

Agreement on the Conservation of Small Cetaceans of the Baltic and North Seas. (1995). *UKTS.* No 52.

Protocol Concerning Specially Protected Areas and Biological Diversity in the Mediterranean (1995). This is reprinted in Austen, A. (ed). *Basic Legal Document on International Animal Welfare and Wildlife Conservation* (Kluwer, London). 213.

African Eurasian Waterbird Agreement (1995). This is reprinted in Austen, A. (ed). *Basic Legal Document on International Animal Welfare and Wildlife Conservation* (Kluwer, London). 617.

The Kyoto Protocol. 37 *ILM* (1998). 22.

Agreement on the Conservation of Cetaceans of the Black Seas, Mediterranean Sea and Contiguous Area. (1997). 36 *ILM.* 777.

The 2003 African Convention on the Conservation of Nature and Natural Resources. This was signed in Maputo, 11 July 2003. As of 2005, it was not yet in force.

ACKNOWLEDGEMENTS

This book would not be possible without the support of a number of people and organizations. First, the process that ended with this book would not have begun were it not for the assistance of the New Zealand Law Foundation, and their granting me the New Zealand Research Fellowship. Their support, and patience, has been remarkable.

Second, to Andrew Bignell, for the friendship, facilitation into key positions in international forums, and challenging me to get involved in thinking about protected areas under an international auspice.

Third, to the staff and management of the World Heritage Centre at UNESCO in Paris, who helped me work through my work as Rapporteur, and Special Advisor to the Chair with humour, friendship and exceptional insights. There are too many highly talented individuals in this organisation to thank, but without their help, I would never have been able to understand the intricacies and workings of the WHC. They are truly, a human group of outstanding universal value.

Finally, special thanks in particular to Tata Lawton, John Paki, and Tumu te Heuheu, Paramount Chief of Ngati Tuwharetoa, for reminding me that successful diversity is what we practice everyday, and that values, are not just things we read about in books.

This book is for my daughter Renee.

Alexander Gillespie March 12, 2007

INTRODUCTION

The goal of this book is to help with the creation of more internationally protected areas, and help ensure the effective conservation of those which already exist. This goal reflects a realization that the international framework by which this objective may be achieved is very difficult to navigate due to its fragmented and ad-hoc nature, and what may an increasing antipathy towards protected areas under international or regional auspices. I have tried to write this book as a map, by which many of these difficulties can be bypassed. A large part of this map is in the details that I have attempted to collect. These details reflect one of the richest areas of international environmental law, with decisions and jurisprudence on international environmental matters going back over three decades. Incredibly, many of these details, to date, have been near invisible outside of each solitary regime. This is a loss to both the regimes which discuss protected areas, and a large number of overlapping regimes in international environmental law and policy that are deprived of this depth of knowledge.

The second reason I decided to write this book was due to what I fear is an increasing antipathy, if not antagonism, to the creation of protected areas under an international auspice. I first discovered this antipathy through my work at the International Whaling Commission (IWC), with regard to attempts by a number of countries to increase the number of international whale sanctuaries. Although the countries seeking this objective were originally successful (although Japan refused to accept the southern ocean sactuary, and continues to practice so called scientific whaling in the area) latter attempts for further sanctuaries in the South Pacific, and the South Atlantic have proved unsuccessful. Moreover, the established protected areas under the IWC, are increasingly under threat, and are the subject to annual attempts to have them delisted.[1] Originally, I assumed that such efforts were specific to the IWC. However, as my experience and knowledge of other international regimes grew, it became apparent that similar initiatives were being undertaken in a number of other forums. For example, within the International Maritime Organisation, attempts to get a series of regional protected areas approved, have run into increasing problems,[2] with Russia (unsuccessfully) calling for a moratorium on

1 See Gillespie, A. (2005). *Whaling Diplomacy.* (Edgar Ellen, London). Chapter 9.

2 Indeed, despite the revised PSSA Guidelines, following the designation of the Western European PSSA (in 2004) and the Baltic PSSA (in 2003), Russia, with the support of Liberia and Panama (the latter being the primary flags of convenience States) and sections of the shipping industry, called for the review of the PSSA Guidelines. Arguing that PSSAs were being used in blunt applications (as in, the nominated areas did not all possess the alleged

all new protected area applications, until a more robust, independent evaluation process was established.[3] Likewise, within the Committee on Fisheries (COFI) from the Food and Agriculture Organisation, despite a late endorsement that marine protected areas may have some utility for stock management areas and that work in this area should be furthered, some members clearly argued against such work, deeming it 'inappropriate'.[4]

A further example of the reticence towards increasing the number of protected areas under international auspices came from the 4th United Nations Open Ended Informal Consultative Process on Oceans and the Law of the Sea (UNICPOLOS) in 2003, when the Netherlands, in good faith, advanced the idea of establishing a new regime to identify and protect ecosystems (such as seamounts, hydrothermal vents, deep-sea trenches, deep-sea coral reefs, cold seeps and pockmarks) beyond national jurisdiction, building on the framework established by the United Nations Convention on the Law of the Sea (UNCLOS).[5] This idea, which had been building up over the previous couple of years, was strongly attacked by a number of other delegations, who spoke clearly against any expansion of the regimes which create protected areas in international law. The arguments against any new regime included fears that the proposals were not necessarily based on scientific justifications, and that they were being justified with hidden agendas in mind, such as closing off parts of the world's resources from countries that need them, without obtaining the necessary State consent for such losses.[6] The depth of feeling was so strong on this issue, that even the suggestion for the formation of a group

characteristics) or that PSSAs added nothing of value to other protection options, or proposed PSSAs did not address the real issues. Such as with the Baltic PSSA, which was already a Special Area and no new APMs were called for, and its primary risk is due to land-based pollution. MEPC. (2004). Report of the MEPC on its 51st Session. MEPC. 51/22. 28-31. With the Western European PSSA, although it was agreed that although the area was unique for its deep water corals, the whole area did not necessarily fulfil the naturalness criteria, not have a universal applicability for the critical spawning and breeding concerns. MEPC. (2003). Report of the MEPC on its 49th Meeting. MEPC. 49/WP.10. For some background on this resistance, see Kiselev, V. (1988). 'Special Areas for Preventing Pollution of the Sea'. Marine Policy. 241-245. See Peet, G. (1994). 'Particularly Sensitive Sea Areas'. *International Journal of Marine and Coastal Law.* 9(4). 469, 475-481.

3 MEPC. (2004). Report of the MEPC on its 51st Session. MEPC. 51/22. 29-33. It was agreed the PSSA Guidelines would again be reviewed, with a view to greater clarity in application, vulnerability analysis, enhanced legal strength, and conceptual application (i.e. are they simply a generic tool for 'sustainable development' or are they to be restricted for only the most unique marine areas, in conjunction with the most detailed of restrictions. United States of America (2004). Proposed Amendments to Assembly Resolution A.927 (22) to Strengthen and Clarify the Guidelines for Identifying PSSAs. 52/8.

4 COFI. (2005). Report of the 26th Session of the Committee of Fisheries. FIPL/R780 (en). xx.

5 Report of the UNICPOLOS at its Fourth Meeting. A/58/95. (2003, June 26). Paragraph 98.

6 Ibid. Paragraph 104.

of international experts be assembled to look further at the issue, was rejected without success.[7]

A final example of restricting the number of protected areas, although by no means as malevolent as the above examples, comes from the World Heritage Convention (WHC). Here, although there is no formal limit on how many sites may be inscribed,[8] the Committee has consistently, since 1978, tried to develop methods by which the growth in the number of sites can be restricted. The primary method, in conjunction with Tentative Lists, comparative and thematic studies, has been by appealing to the Parties to voluntarily limit their nominations, with cultural nominations in particular.[9] It is hoped that such restrictions will defuse the 'ticking time bomb' by which the standards and credibility of the World Heritage List could be destroyed by inscribing sites which do not really possess outstanding universal value. This fear that sites will be inscribed which do not have outstanding universal value has already been noted with some WHC natural sites.[10]

The approach of the WHC is the antithesis of other regimes such as the Man and the Biosphere (MAB) regime, or the Convention on Wetlands of International Importance (Ramsar), from which there is no upper limit on how many sites may be inscribed. For

7 Note, this debate was directly related to the issue of bottom-trawling on the high seas. See Report of the UNICPOLOS at its Fifth Meeting. A/59/122. (2004, July 1). Paragraphs 76-79, 89. Report of the UNICPOLOS at its Sixth Meeting. A/59/122. (2005, July 7). Paragraph 44 and 82.

8 Operational Guidelines. 2002 Edition. Paragraph 6.

9 *Ibid.*

10 Such as with the West National Park of Niger, UNESCO. (1996). 20th Session of the WHC. WHC-96/CONF.201/21. Mar 10, 1997. 41; the Djoudj national bird sanctuary in Senegal, UNESCO. (1979). 3rd Session of the WHC. CC-79/CONF.003/3. Aug 27, 1979. pp.4; and the Pitons in St Lucia. All three of these sites were inscribed against the recommendations of the Advisory Body. UNESCO. (1978). 2nd Session of the WHC. CC-78/CONF.010/10. Oct 9, 1978. pp.8. UNESCO. (1987). 11th Session of the WHC. CC-87/CONF.005/9. Jan 20, 1988. pp 14. UNESCO. (1992). 16th Session of the WHC. WHC-92/CONF.002/12. Dec 14, 1992. Annex II. UNESCO. (1981). 5th Session of the WHC. CC-81/CONF.003/6. Jan 5, 1981. pp.7. UNESCO. (1998). 22nd Session of the WHC. WHC-98/CONF.208/18. Jan 29, 1998. 89-90. UNESCO. (1999). 12th General Assembly of the WHC. WHC-99/CONF.206/7. Nov 8, 1999. 1-2. UNESCO. (1979). 3rd Session of the WHC. CC-79/CONF.003/13. Nov 30, 1978. pp.6. UNESCO. (1980). 3rd General Assembly of the WHC. CC-80/CONF.018/6. Oct 20, 1980. 2. Hales, D. (1984). 'The World Heritage Convention: Status and Directions.' In McNeely, J. (ed). *National Parks, Conservation and Development.* (Smithsonian, Washington). 744, 746-48. UNESCO. (1996) Expert Review on Evaluation of General Principles and Criteria for Nominations of Natural World Heritage Sites. WHC-96/CONF.202/INF.9. Apr 15. 3, 6.

example, in 2006, Mexico alone, presented 21 proposals from within its own borders, to be inscribed to the International Coordinating Council of the MAB.[11]

Although growing lists at the MAB and the Ramsar are not a clear problem (providing the inscription criteria are met), this may be different at the WHC, as the WHC prides itself on the extra-ordinary outstanding universal value of each site it inscribes. As such, having too many sites overall, or too many sites from any one country or region raises debates about whether such sites truly reflect universal outstanding universal value, or not. However, despite appeals to voluntarily limit the nominations coming forward from State Parties, the WHC List has continued to grow exponentially. Accordingly, the WHC Committee has tried to set a maximum number nominations to be examined at each meeting[12] there may be serious legal questions as to whether this can be done under the Convention.[13] Although the above proposals on a cap included an attempt to increase the number of natural sites nominated by suggesting that one of the two nominations from each country should be natural[14] it is clear that a number of Parties are of the belief that the potential number of natural sites on the WHC List is not limitless. Moreover, the IUCN earlier suggested a final number between 250 and 300 natural and mixed sites on the WHC List.[15] Such possible limits are despite the fact that cultural listings have come to rapidly outgrow the number of natural sites both in nominations and inscriptions, by a ratio of about one to four. This is despite the disappearing, but nevertheless endorsed goal, that there should be parity between cultural and natural listings.[16]

---

11 UNESCO. (2006). International Coordinating Council of the MAB. SC-06/CONF.202/16. November 28.

12 The proposed figure was 45 per year, with a maximum of two per Party, with priority being given to under-represented Parties, under-represented categories and trans-boundary nominations. Note, the number has increased. UNESCO. (2004). 28th Session of the WHC. WHC-04/28.COM/26. Oct 29. Decision 29 COM 18 A. Decision 28 COM 13.1. Point 17. 11-14. UNESCO. (2000). 24th Session of the WHC. WHC-2000/CONF.204/21. Feb 16, 2001. 12, 18. UNESCO. (2003). 27th Session of the WHC. WHC-03/27.COM/24. Dec 10. 136-137. UNESCO. (2001). UNESCO. (2004). 7th Extra-Ordinary Session of the WHC. WHC-04/7.EXT.COM/10. Oct 10. Table 1.

13 UNESCO. (2004). Item 4B of the Provisional Agenda. Legal Implications Relating to the Abstention From Proposing Nominations by Members of the World Heritage Committee. WHC/-04/7 Ext.Com/4B.Add. 2004, Nov 26.

14 UNESCO. (2004). 28th Session of the WHC. WHC-04/28.COM/26. Oct 29. Decision 28 COM 13.1. Point 17a. pp. 14.

15 See UNESCO. (2005). Special Expert Meeting of the World Heritage Convention: The Concept of Outstanding Universal Value. (Kazan, Russia). Box 3. pp12.

16 *Operational Guidelines.* 2002 Edition. Paragraphs 6 and 15.. This was due to a growing recognition that it was not a competition, and they were two fundamentally different things. For some debate within the Convention on this point, see UNESCO. (1980). 3rd Session of the WHC. CC-80/CONF.018/6. Oct 20, 1980. 2. UNESCO. (1984). 7th Session of the WHC. SC/83/CONF.009/8. Jan 12, 1984. pp 4. UNESCO. (1980). 4th Session of the WHC.

My concern is not only with the credibility of the World Heritage List, but with what to do with the sites that although not of outstanding universal value, still require protection due to their regional, national, intrinsic or anthropocentric values. In this regard, although the Ramsar, and to a lesser degree, the MAB, are providing valuable forums to create protected areas of international merit, there are clear gaps on what is being created. From the debate on hotspots, to the omissions of a specific regime to cover forests, through to the nascent attempts to cover coral reefs, the international architecture in this entire area is fragmented and in need of supplementation.

Even where the international regimes for the creation of protected areas exist, real difficulties exist in terms of their management, the threats to protected areas, and sovereign compliance with obligations already undertaken to conserve established protected areas.

I am not of the belief that there is some sort of overall conspiracy against protected areas. I am, however, of the belief that the international framework from which protected areas are established, is confusing, ad-hoc, and at times contradictory. Moreover, the differences between the various regimes, on many questions span a divergent range of approaches, and a number of fundamental issues that would make the international network more meaningful and coherent, have not been addressed. It is partly due to this framework, the questions that have not been answered, and an increasing diversity of needs between countries, that differences over protected areas are arising. It would be foolish to suggest that this book could resolve all of these differences. This book does however, seek to provide a map by which interested individuals can navigate between the regimes, understand the terrain, move towards identifying answers for the pressing questions, and work out which are the best practices by which the international community can proceed with what I consider to be one of the most important environmental tasks of the 21st century.

CC-80/CONF.016/10. Sep 29, 1980. pp.9. UNESCO. (2003). 27th Session of the WHC. WHC-03/27.COM/24. Dec 10. 137. UNESCO. (1996). 19th Session of the WHC. WHC-95/CONF.203/16. Jan 31, 1996. 45. UNESCO. (1996) Expert Review on Evaluation of General Principles and Criteria for Nominations of Natural World Heritage Sites. WHC-96/CONF.202/INF.9. Apr 15. 6.

Chapter I

THE HISTORY AND SCOPE OF PROTECTED AREAS

1 From Antiquity to the Twentieth Century.

By definition, sanctuaries are 'holy places or places of refuge'. This definition is commonly applied to sanctuaries of value to animals as well as humans. As such, they may represent, 'a place where birds, wild animals, etc. are bred and protected'.[1] The practice of sanctuaries reaches a long back into the Western (and probably human) psyche. The first established parks were built by the Persians, and were known in Greek as *paradeisoi*, from which the word 'paradise' has evolved.[2] The Classical Greeks, also learnt to embrace the values of nature,[3] and were in large part responsible for the idea of sanctuaries (in multiple forms). The Romans highly valued gardens, and groves of trees and a number of volcanoes were deemed sacred.[4] Around the same period, areas were set aside by Royal Decree in India for the protection of natural resources. From the Dark Ages to the Enlightenment, throughout Europe, vast sections of land were protected for the benefits of the nobility and the pursuits of hunting. At times, the extent of such areas, by which hunting was prohibited to all but Royalty (and those they gave privileges to) was vast. For example, during the reign of Henry II in England, just under a third of the country was included as a type of protected area.[5] The trend of large parks being established continued over the following centuries, with the nobility increasingly establishing their own parks and reserves. In many instances, these were created at the expense of local populations. For example, in Staffordshire alone, in the Eighteenth century, there are four recorded examples where entire villages had to be moved for the creation of protected areas.[6]

In 1791 the first commonly recognized modern environmental sanctuary, as in one that was established by the State, and not an individual, was established on the West Indian

---

1 *The Concise Oxford Dictionary.* (1990. Clarendon, Oxford). 1060.

2 Straus, B. (2005). *Salamis.* (Arrow, London). 45.

3 See generally, Fairclough, B. (1930). *The Love of Nature Among the Greeks and Romans.* (Longmans, London).

4 Geikie, A. (1912). *The Love of Nature Among the Romans.* (Murray, London). 129-161.

5 Poole, A. (1954). *From the Domesday Book to the Magna Carta.* (Oxford University Press, Oxford). 30-32.

6 Thomas, K. (1983). *Man and the Natural World: Changing Attitudes in England, 1500-1800.* (Oxford University Press, Oxford). 202-203.

island of Sant Vincent.[7] This idea quickly took hold, and the English poet illiam Wordsworth was arguing in 1810 for his vision of the Lake District, as, 'a sort of national property'. In 1832, the American poet, explorer and artist, George Catlin, pointed to the need of a, 'national park, containing man and beast, in all the wild and freshness of their nature's beauty'. Within fifty years, various administrations began to respond to these types of calls.

In 1864 the United States Congress gave a small part of the present Yosemite National Park to the State of California, for, 'public use, resort and recreation'. Other notable national protected areas included the Blue Mountains in New South Wales of Australia in 1866, Yellowstone in the United States in 1872, parts of the Canadian Rockies in 1879, and Tongariro in New Zealand. The Tongariro gift of 1877 was particularly notable as it was given by a leader of the indigenous peoples, to all of the people of New Zealand, as presented by the Crown, to be protected indefinitely. Krueger National Park was established in South Africa in 1898, and a few decades later King Albert Park (later known as Virunga National Park), was established in 1925 after the Belgian King sought to ensure protection for the mountain gorillas living on the flanks of the Virunga volcanoes. The first dedicated marine protected area (MPA) followed a decade later in 1935, with the Fort Jefferson National Monument in Florida.[8] By this point, regional and international regimes were just coming into existence, with the purpose of, inter alia, increasing the number and quality of protected areas. Such regimes were coming into existence, because as John F. Kennedy realized in 1962,

> Growth and development of national park and reserve programs throughout the world are important to the welfare of the people of every nation. We must have places where we can find release from the tensions of an increasingly industrialized civilization, where we can have personal contact with the natural environment that sustains us. To this end, permanent preservation of the outstanding scenic and scientific aspects of every country, and of the magnificent and varied wildlife which can be so easily endangered by human activity is imperative. National parks and reserves are an integral aspect of intelligent use of natural resources. It is the course of wisdom to set aside an ample portion of our national resources as national parks and reserves, thus ensuring that future generations may know the majesty of the Earth as we know it today.[9]

---

7 See Grove, R.H. (1992). 'The Origins of Western Environmentalism.' *Scientific American.* July. 22, 25.

8 As noted in IMO General Assembly. 17th Session. A 17/Res.720. Guidelines for the Designation of Special Areas and the Identification of Particularly Sensitive Sea Areas. Page 4.

9 Letter from J.F. Kennedy to the First World Conference on National Parks, 1962. Reprinted in Adams, A. (1962). *First World Conference on National Parks.* (US Department of the Interior, Washington). Pp.1.

2 A Matrix of Protected Areas

In the 21st century there are over a dozen regimes which are directly involved in protected area issues. Collectively, they provide a matrix which has created substantial overlaps, whereby individual sites may be listed under numerous regimes. This is most common at the 'high end', with overlaps between the World Heritage Convention (WHC), Man and the Biosphere (MAB), and the Convention on Wetlands of International Importance (Ramsar). For example, in 2004, 24 Ramsar sites were also part of WHC sites,[10] and at least 84 MAB sites were also Ramsar sites, whilst 76 MAB sites were wholly or partly included within WHC sites.[11] Some of the WHC sites also have International Maritime Organisation (IMO) protected status.[12] When the regional regimes are added on top of the international arrangements, a site may find itself listed under an even greater variety of regimes. The record appears to be a single site in Europe which is involved with seven different international and regional agreements.[13]

With such considerations in mind, it is essential to note that the following chapter is only about the core agreements in this area. This chapter seeks to broadly show where the core agreements came from and what their objectives are. This chapter does not seek to cover all of the regimes which clearly have an influence in this area, if they are not primarily regimes under which protected areas can be inscribed, such as the United Nations Convention on Biological Diversity (CBD) or the Convention on Migratory Species (CMS).

3 International Conventions

A The World Heritage Convention (WHC)

This original event that aroused particular international concern was the decision to build the Aswan High Dam in Egypt, which would have flooded the valley containing the Abu Simbel temples, a treasure of ancient Egyptian civilization. In 1959, after an appeal from the governments of Egypt and the Sudan, UNESCO launched an international safeguarding campaign, from which the temples were dismantled, removed to dry ground and reassembled. Its success led to other safeguarding campaigns.[14] Soon

---

10 UNESCO. (2004). 7th Extraordinary Session of the WHC. WHC-04/7. EXT.COM/9. Nov 25. Annex II.

11 *Ibid.*

12 UNESCO. (2004). 28th Session of the WHC. WHC-04/28.COM/26. Oct 29. Decision 28 COM 15B.31.8pp93. Decision 28 COM 15B.7.pp78 MEPC. (2004). Report of the MEPC on its 51st Session. MEPC. 51/22. 38. Decision 29 COM 7B.5 (on Banc d'Arguin).

13 Harrison, J. (2002). 'International Agreements and Programmes on Protected Areas'. *Parks.* 12 (3): 2, 3.

14 Such as in Venice, Moenjodaro (Pakistan) and restoring Borobodur (Indonesia).

after, at the 1965 White House Conference on International Cooperation it was noted that certain outstanding scenic, historic and national resources, whose survival was a matter of concern to all countries, were under a multiple variety of threats. Accordingly, it was recommended that

> There be established a Trust for the World Heritage that would be responsible to the world community for the stimulation of international cooperative efforts to identify, establish, develop and manage the world's superb natural and scenic areas and historic sites for the present and future benefit of the entire world citizenry.[15]

This idea was actively supported and publicized by the IUCN throughout the late 1960s, and in 1971 the United States became its foremost advocate, arguing for the creation of what then President Nixon called 'a new international initiative'. This initiative entailed the goal that the nations of the world 'agree to the principle that there are certain areas of such unique worldwide value that they should be treated as part of a World Heritage Trust'.[16] The United States presented a draft WHC Convention to the preparatory conference of the 1972 Stockholm Conference on the Human Environment.[17] This draft was strongly supported by a coalition of international NGOs,[18] and notable international organizations such as UNESCO.[19] The final document was concluded and adopted on November 16, 1972. Although this document has allowed the facilitation of strong regional divisions, it is first and foremost an international instrument.

The principle difference of the WHC, compared to all other international instruments, is that the WHC seeks only to inscribe sites of 'outstanding universal value'. Although this goal may be slightly easier to achieve with natural, as opposed to cultural properties[20] (which the WHC also covers), the threshold for inscription is very high,

---

15 White House Conference on International Cooperation, Recommendation 3. Noted in Train, R. (1972). 'An Idea Whose Time Has Come: The World Heritage Trust, A World Need and World Opportunity.' In Elliot, H. (ed). *Second World Conference on National Parks.* (IUCN, Lausanne). 377, 378.

16 President Nixon, noted in Train, R. (1972). 'An Idea Whose Time Has Come: The World Heritage Trust, A World Need and World Opportunity.' In Elliot. *ibid.* 377, 378.

17 UNESCO. (1992). 16th Session of the WHC. WHC-92/CONF.002/12. Dec 14, 1992. 3.

18 Recommendation 8. Conservation of the World Heritage. In Elliot, *ibid.* 444-445. Before the WHC existed, the First World's Park Congress called upon all (pan-American) governments to ratify and implement the Convention on Nature Protection and Wildlife Preservation in the Western Hemisphere. See 'Closing Plenary Session.' In Adams, A. (ed). *First World Conference on National Parks.* (US Department of the Interior, Washington). 385-86 . Recommendation No 26.

19 UNESCO. (1997). 21st Session of the WHC. WHC-97/CONF.208/17. Feb 27, 1998. 2.

20 UNESCO. (1994). The Nara Document on Authenticity. WHC-94/CONF.003/INF.008. Nov 21, 1994. 1-4. UNESCO. (1977). 1st Session of the WHC. CC-77/CONF.001/9. Oct 17, 1977. pp.5.

with less than 1% of all protected areas, being eligible for the WHC List[21] due to their being, 'the most outstanding properties from an international point of view.'[22] This means that the 'failure' rate of attempted nominations for natural properties is particularly high. For example, in 2006, approximately only one in three of the formally nominated natural sites was recommended for inscription by the Advisory Body.[23] Therefore, State Parties should not assume that a site of national and/or regional importance will automatically be included in the World Heritage List, as the Convention is not intended to provide for the protection of all properties of great interest, importance or value, but only for a select list of the most outstanding of these from an international viewpoint.[24] Accordingly, when the Committee has been presented with what it has concluded are not suitable WHC sites, it has recommended that the nominating countries consider having them inscribed within other regimes which do not have the same standards, such as the MAB. This approach has been followed with rejected sites from, inter alia, the Czech Republic,[25] Poland,[26] India,[27] Russia[28] and Uganda.[29]

Although the WHC has a strong set of regional initiatives, it is first and foremost, an international convention, by which all of its Parties have pledged to protect the sites of outstanding universal value of all countries, and not just their own sites.[30] Its international lineage may be seen in its very close connection to UNESCO,[31] (which sees

21 UNESCO. (1981). 5th Session of the WHC. CC-81/CONF.003/6. Jan 5, 1981. pp.8.

22 UNESCO. (1998). *Report of the World Heritage Strategy Natural and Cultural Heritage Expert Meeting.* (UNESCO, Amsterdam). 3.

23 See IUCN (2006). Evaluations of Nominations of Natural and Mixed Properties to the World Heritage List. WHC-06/30.COM/INF.8B2.

24 *Operational Guidelines.* 2002 Edition. Paragraph 6. UNESCO. (1996) Expert Review on Evaluation of General Principles and Criteria for Nominations of Natural World Heritage Sites. WHC-96/CONF.202/INF.9. Apr 15. 1.

25 Czech Tatra national park. UNESCO. (1992). 16th Session of the WHC. WHC-92/CONF.002/12. Dec 14, 1992. 34.

26 The Valley of the Pradnik River. UNESCO. (2003). 27th Session of the WHC. WHC-03/27.COM/24. Dec 10. 112.

27 The Gir Wildlife Sanctuary. UNESCO. (1992). 16th Session of the WHC. WHC-92/CONF.002/12. Dec 14, 1992. 34.

28 The Vodlozero national park in Russia and the Bashkirian Ural. UNESCO. (1998). 22nd Session of the WHC. WHC-98/CONF.208/18. Jan 29, 1998. 60-61.

29 Murchison Falls. UNESCO. (1995). 18th Session of the WHC. WHC-94/CONF.003/16. Jan 31. 1995. 44.

30 The deterioration or disappearance of any item of natural (or cultural) heritage of outstanding universal value constitutes a harmful impoverishment of the heritage of all the peoples (including future generations) and nations of the world. WHC. Preamble. Paragraph 2 and Article 4.

31 WHC. Article 31. States which are not a party to UNESCO can also accede to the Convention but they must be invited by the General Conference of the Organization to accede to it. WHC Article 32.

the WHC as their premier international legal instrument)[32] and the large number of signatories the Convention possess, which have grown from 40 Parties in 1978,[33] to 180 as of 2005. The total sites on the list, as of the end of 2006 was 830 properties, of which 644 are cultural, 162 are natural and 24 are mixed.

Finally, although all WHC sites are a matter of concern for the international community, the overall sovereignty of each State over its own sites cannot be under-estimated.[34] This question on sovereignty, as discussed in the chapter on compliance in this book, is notable by the fact that a number of countries have struggled to reconcile their international obligations (once they have successfully listed a site with the WHC) and national objectives with that site. This conflict was most clearly demonstrated in Australia with the Commonwealth v. Tasmania (the Tasmanian Dams Case).[35] In this case, although it was held that the recommendations of the WHC Committee are not binding on the sovereign government, the broad commitments undertaken by the government when signing the Convention could not be lightly dismissed. Accordingly, plans to construct a hydro-electric dam on the Franklin River in Tasmania (despite being supported by the Tasmanian government) were rejected as it was within a World Heritage site, to which international obligations (voluntarily assumed by the State Party) were paramount.

B The Man and the Biosphere Programme (MAB)

Although having strong regional components,[36] the MAB is primarily an international instrument. Its heritage began in the mid 1960s when the International Biological Programme (IBP) proposed that a series of areas be protected for the systematic in-situ protection of genetic resources. This idea was expanded upon at the 1968 UNESCO Intergovernmental Conference of Experts on the Scientific Basis for the Rational Use

---

32 UNESCO. (1997). 21st Session of the WHC. WHC-97/CONF.208/17. Feb 27, 1998. 2.

33 UNESCO. (1978). 2nd Session for the WHC. CC-78/CONF.010/10. Oct 9, 1978. pp.2. In 1979 it was 48, 61 states in 1981, by 1983 there were 78, in 1988 there were 106 and 111 in 1989, 123 in 1991, 136 in 1993, 152 in 1997, 156 in 1998, 158 in 1999, 161 in 2000, 167 in 2001.

34 UNESCO. (1996). 19th Session of the WHC. WHC-95/CONF.203/16. Jan 31, 1996. 18.

35 (1983). 158 CLR. 1.

36 MAB has a series of regional networks. These include the East Asian Biosphere Reserve Network (EABRN), EuroMAB (with 42 members in 2003 including North America), ArabMAB, AfriMAB and ad IberoMAB. Although there is a need for greater coordination and analysis between regions, many of these networks are achieving important results. UNESCO. (2002). *Biosphere Reserves: Special Places for People and Nature.* (UNESCO, Paris). 142-152. UNESCO. (2001). MAB ICC Bureau Meeting. SC/-01/CONF.211/13. Apr 10. 15.

and Conservation of the Resources of the Biosphere,[37] and the word 'biosphere' entered into the international lexicon, along with the need to protect genetic resources, endangered species, habitats and ecosystems. In the same year, another UNESCO conference argued that conservation must not be the sole objective of resource management.[38] The following year, UNESCO argued for a, 'co-ordinated worldwide network of national parks, biological reserves and other protected areas' which could serve multiple objectives such as scientific research, and by 1970, the parks in the proposed network were known as 'biosphere reserves'.[39] The Man and the Biosphere (MAB) International Coordinating Council first met in 1971, and the idea of a worldwide network of protected areas was concluded.[40]

Despite strong original intentions, the MAB programme had a slow take-up, and was reviewed and reworked at a formal congress in 1983 (in Minsk). Part of the conclusions of the Congress was an independent reappraisal of the concept of biosphere reserves. The reappraisal concluded that the intellectual core of a biosphere reserve was that unlike other forms of protected area, biosphere reserves have three central functions. These are the conservation of genetic resources, an international network for monitoring, and sustainable local development. This reappraisal was finally adopted at the 1995 Seville Conference and the Statutory Framework on Biosphere Reserves.[41] In 2002, the MAB Parties rejected the proposal to strengthen the powers of the Statutory Framework, by drawing up a binding legal instrument, preferring to keep it 'flexible'.[42] As of 2006, there were 507 MAB sites in 102 countries.

---

37 UNESCO. (1970). *Use and Conservation of the Resources of the Biosphere: Proceedings of the Intergovernmental Conference of Experts on the Scientific Basis for Rational Use and Conservation of the Resources of the Biosphere.* (UNESCO, Natural Resources Research Series 10, Paris).

38 UNESCO. (1968). *Use and Conservation of the Biosphere.* (UNESCO, Paris). 144.

39 UNESCO. (1970). Plan for a Long Term Intergovernmental and Interdisciplinary Programme on Man and the Biosphere. (UNESCO, General Conference, 16th Session of the ICC Bureau. Document 16C/78). UNESCO. (2002). *Biosphere Reserves: Special Places for People and Nature.* (UNESCO, Paris). 19.

40 UNESCO. (1971). International Coordinating Council for the Programme on Man and the Biosphere. (UNESCO, MAB Report Series No 1).

41 Seville Strategy. Objective 1.1. UNESCO. (2002). *Ibid.* 21-26.

42 UNESCO. (2002). 17th Session of the ICC Bureau. SC-02/CONF.201/11. Apr 12. 7-8.

C *The Convention on Wetlands of International Importance Especially as Waterfowl Habitat (Ramsar)*

Despite getting off to a strong start, with the 1972 World Congress on National Parks urging all governments concerned to adhere to the newly created Ramsar Convention,[43] by 1974, only 4 States had become Parties to the Convention.[44] To help change this situation, a process began which has continued into the new century. This is that a number of areas or groupings, such as small island developing states,[45] and/or states within Oceania,[46] as well as regional initiatives within the Western Hemisphere,[47] in Africa,[48] (especially Francophile countries),[49] as well as Central and South America, the Caribbean,[50] Asia[51] and the Tropics[52] have been targeted for membership. This process has been successful, as by 1980, there were 28 Parties to Ramsar,[53] and by 2002, the number was 134.[54] Although this figure exceeded the earlier target of membership (120 members by 2002)[55] the longer term goal, which was originally proposed in Agenda 21 (and adopted by the Ramsar itself)[56] is for universal membership.[57] As of the end of 2006, there were 153 Contracting Parties to the Convention, with 1631 wetland sites, totalling 145.6 million hectares. Although having strong regional components,[58] and a noticeably strong recognition of national sovereignty over such pro-

---

43 Recommendation 9. Wetlands Convention. In Elliot, H. (ed). *Second World Conference on National Parks.* (1972, IUCN, Lausanne). 445.

44 Recommendations adopted by the International Conference on the Conservation of Wetlands and Waterfowl at Heiligenhafen, Federal Republic of Germany, 6 December 1974. Recommendation 1. The Ramsar Convention – Ratification.

45 Recommendation 7.2. Small Island Developing States. (1999, San Jose).

46 Resolution 8.42. Small Island Developing States in the Oceania Regions. (2002, Valencia).

47 Recommendation 1.1. Expanding the Conventions Membership. (1980, Cagliari).

48 Recommendation 3.6. Further Contracting Parties in Africa. (1987, Regina).

49 Recommendation 7.4. Wetlands for the Future. (1999, San Jose).

50 Recommendation 3.7. Further Contracting Parties in Central America, the Caribbean and South America. (1987, Regina).

51 Recommendation 3.10. Further Contracting Parties in Asia and the Pacific. (1987, Regina).

52 Recommendation 5.13. The Neotropical Region. (1993, Kushiro).

53 Recommendation 1.1. Expanding the Conventions Membership. (1980, Cagliari).

54 Resolution 8.25. The Ramsar Strategic Plan. (2002, Valencia). Annex I.9.

55 Resolution 7.27. The Convention's Work Plan 2000-02. (1999, San Jose).

56 See Resolution 9.8. Streamlining the Implementation of the Strategic Plan of the Convention 2003-2008. (Kampala, 2005). Goal 5.

57 Resolution 9.7. Regional Initiatives in the Framework of the Ramsar Convention. (2005, Kampala). Resolution 8.30. Regional Initiatives for the Further Implementation of the Convention. (2002, Valencia). Resolution 8.41. Resolution 8.25. The Ramsar Strategic Plan. (2002, Valencia). Annex. Objective 21.

58 Resolution 9.19. The Importance of Regional Wetland Symposia in Effectively Implementing the Ramsar Convention. (2005, Kampala). Establishment of a Regional Ramsar Centre for Training and Research on Wetlands in Western and Central Asia. (2002, Valencia). Resolution

tected wetland areas,[59] the Ramsar is fundamentally global in outlook, as it attempts to protect wetlands of 'international importance'.[60]

D *Antarctica*

Antarctica is somewhat of an anomaly in the debate about protected areas. The need for greater protection of the flora and fauna of Antarctica dates to the First World Conference on National Parks in 1962.[61] Two years later, the Consultative Parties responded with the Agreed Measures which established a procedure for, inter alia, the creation of 'Specially Protected Areas' (SPAs). However, progress in this area was very slow, in both its ambit of coverage and actual listings of protected areas. Despite the Second World Congress on National Parks recommending the need for an enhanced establishment of protected areas in the Polar regions,[62] and argumentation for the designation of Antarctica and its surrounding seas as, 'the first world park' (under the auspice of the United Nations)[63] the issue of the conservation of flora and fauna effectively fell off the agenda of the Antarctica Treaty meetings until 1981.[64] The issue was reactivated the following year at the Third World Conference on National Parks, which brought to the public's attention the possibility of a minerals exploration regime being adopted prematurely,[65] at cost to the Antarctic environment.[66] As the nego-

---

8.43. A Subregional Strategy for the Ramsar Convention for South America. (2002, Valencia). Recommendation 7.4. Wetlands for the Future. (1999, San Jose). Recommendation 5.14. Collaboration for Mediterranean Wetlands. (1993, Kushiro). Recommendation 6.11. Collaboration for Mediterranean Wetlands. (1996, Brisbane). Recommendation 6.6. Regionally Based Ramsar Liaison Officers. (1996, Brisbane). Resolution 7.22. Mediterranean Wetlands. (1999, San Jose).

59 Ramsar. Article 2.3.

60 'And they may incorporate riparian and coastal zones adjacent to the wetlands, and islands or bodies of marine water deeper than six metres at low tide lying within the wetlands, especially where these have importance as waterfowl habitat.' Ramsar. Article 2.1.

61 Although welcoming the attention given to conservation within the ATS the Conference, 'recommended the adoption of more positive measures to prevent the exploitation of the marine life of this habitat on which the entire Antarctic Ecosystem depends'. See 'Closing Plenary Session.' In Adams, A. (ed). *First World Conference on National Parks.* (US Department of the Interior, Washington). 382. Recommendation No 16.

62 Recommendation 3. Conservation of North Polar and Subpolar Ecosystems. In Elliot, H. (ed). *Second World Conference on National Parks.* (1972, IUCN, Lausanne). 377, 378.

63 Recommendation 5. Establishment of Antarctica as a World Park Under United Nations Auspice. In Elliot, *ibid.* 443.

64 See Elliot, L. (1994). *International Environmental Politics: Protecting the Antarctic.* (St Martins Press, London). 66-67.

65 See Elliot. *Ibid.* 69-70.

66 Recommendation 4. Antarctica. Recommendations of the World National Parks Congress. In McNeely, J. (ed). *National Parks, Conservation and Development.* (Smithsonian, Washington). 767.

tiations on the proposed regime progressed, and then unraveled before the adoption of the Madrid Protocol, a rather complex system for protecting areas of 'outstanding interest'[67] or 'outstanding' values'[68] developed. These developments covered eight different types of protected areas.[69] This system was synthesized (and simplified, including an overall renumbering scheme)[70] in the 1991 Madrid Protocol, though Annex V of the instrument.[71] Despite the new regime, the protected areas that are created under the Madrid Protocol auspice, are still inscribed under the 1964 Agreed Measures. Finally, it is important to note that with regard to marine protected areas (effectively areas protected for their scientific value), the inscription process is done in cooperation with the Convention for the Conservation of Antarctic Marine Living Resources (CCAMLR), which allows for the creation of 'closed areas'[72] as part of their possible conservation measures. As of 2006, there were 45 acceding States to the Antarctic Treaty, and 29 of these were Consultative Parties.

E The United Nations Convention on the Law of the Sea (UNCLOS)

As discussed below a number of regional seas agreements have specific protocols in place to enhance the creation of regional marine protected areas. However, most regional seas regimes (with the exception of the somewhat unique Mediterranean and its semi-enclosed status) are clear that their provisions are local, and do not apply to the high seas.[73] Accordingly, the overall practice and belief, is that any MPAs on the high seas, must be constructed through the appropriate international channel. The appropriate international channel is the UNCLOS. However, although the broad obligation imposed on all Parties, via Article 192 of the UNCLOS, 'to protect and preserve the marine

---

67 See Article VIII (1) of the 1964 Agreed Measures. See also Recommendation XV-9. Antarctic Protected Area System: Development of Improved Descriptions and Management Plans for Specially Protected Areas. In Antarctic Treaty: Report of the Fifteenth Meeting (Paris, 1989). 80.

68 See Annex V, Article 3 (1).

69 Specially Protected Areas, SSSIs, Marine Sites of Special Scientific Interest, Historic Sites and Monuments, Specially Reserved Areas, Multiple Use Planning Areas, Areas of Special Tourist Interest, and CCAMLR Environmental Monitoring Protection Sites.

70 See Article 3(3) of Annex V of the Madrid Protocol. See also Resolution V (1996). Revised Renumbering of Antarctic Protected Areas. In Antarctic Treaty: Report of the Twentieth Meeting. (Utrecht, 1996). 43. Decision 1 (2002). Naming and Numbering System for the Antarctic Specially Protected Areas. In Antarctic Treaty: Report of the Twenty-Fifth Meeting. (Warsaw, 2002). 139.

71 See Joyner, C. (1998). *Governing the Frozen Commons: The Antarctic Regime and Environmental Protection.* (South Carolina UP, Carolina). 16-162.

72 CCAMLR. Article 9 (2).

73 See for example, Report of the Working Group on the Development of Guidelines for the Listing of Protected Areas Under the SPAW Protocol. (2005). UNEP (DEC)/CAR WG.29/INF.12. Caribbean Protocol. Article 9.

environment'[74] is reinforced by the possible creation of 'special areas',[75] the application of such areas is not straight forward. On the one hand, the special areas of UNCLOS falls directly under the IMO considerations with regard to international shipping and special areas. On the other hand, the debate has evolved in the forum of the United Nations Open Ended Informal Consultative Process on Oceans and the Law of the Sea (UNICPOLOS).

The UNICPOLOS process began in 1999 when the United Nations General Assembly decided to facilitate the review of developments in ocean affairs. The first UNICPOLOS was held in 2000, and had 13 different topics to examine. Although MPAs were repeatedly recognized as an important topic to discuss,[76] it was not until 2003, following the WSSD and CBD urging, that the issue gained prominence. Despite the fact that the UNICPOLOS has reaffirmed the efforts of States to develop and facilitate the use of marine protected areas, consistent with international law, it has yet to develop a clear platform or the modalities of how this may be achieved.[77]

F The International Maritime Organisation (IMO)

The IMO, which has 167 Member States, has three methods by which areas are effectively protected from the threats that international shipping may represent. These are routing, special areas and particularly sensitive sea areas (PSSAs).

The practice of following predetermined routes for shipping originated in 1898 and was adopted, for reasons of safety, by shipping companies operating passenger ships across the North Atlantic. Related provisions were subsequently incorporated into the original 1960 Safety of Life at Sea (SOLAS) Convention, and by 1966 the IMO was recommending a number of (voluntary) traffic separation schemes and 'areas to be avoided'.[78] These soon became mandatory in the early 1970s, following a series of accidents. By the 21st century, traffic separation schemes and other ship routing systems have been established in most of the major congested, shipping areas of the world, and the number of collisions and groundings in these areas have been reduced. Such traffic management, as designated under Chapter V of the SOLAS Convention, have also been used to contribute to the protection of the marine environment. Aside the creation of precautionary areas (where ships must navigate with particular caution) the most applicable measure

---

74 See also Article 194 (5).

75 UNCLOS. Article 211.

76 Report of the UNICPOLOS At its First Meeting. A/55/274 (2000, July 31). Paragraphs 31-32. Report of the UNICPOLOS At its Second Meeting. A/56/121(2001, June 22).

77 Report of the UNICPOLOS At its Fourth Meeting. A/58/95. (2003, June 26). Paragraph 22. Report of the World Summit on Sustainable Development. A/CONF. 199/20. WSSD. Paragraph 32 (d).

78 IMO Assembly Resolution A.161 (ES.IV) Traffic Routing Measures.

is, 'areas to be avoided'. These are defined as, 'areas within defined limits in which either navigation is particularly hazardous or it is exceptionally important to avoid casualties and which should be avoided by all ships or certain classes of ships.'[79] These 'areas to be avoided'[80] are not regarded as prohibited areas unless specifically stated as such, and each class of ship is dealt with on a case-by-case basis.[81] In a closely related manner, the IMO also possesses the ability to adopt routing measures, whereby a vessel is routed around, or carefully managed through, a sensitive area. The IMO has been adopting such routing measures since the early 1970s.[82]

The idea of establishing 'special areas' which had stricter requirements for the discharge of harmful substances from ships, than in general, was embodied in the 1954 International Convention for the Prevention of Pollution of the Sea by Oil.[83] In its original version the 1954 Convention was based on the concept of so-called 'prohibited zones' extending, as a rule, 50 miles from the coast in which the discharge of oily mixtures was prohibited. The first area specially designated for protection under this Convention was the Great Barrier Reef in 1971.[84] The realization that there may be other special areas in need of extra protection from international shipping was clearly articulated in 1978, at the International Conference on Tanker Safety and the Prevention of Marine Pollution, and the IMO was invited to study with the the other possible 'special areas'. This coincided the International Convention for the Prevention of Pollution from Ships (MARPOL 73/78) and its creation of six different annexes, (oil, noxious liquid substances, packaged harmful substances, sewage, garbage, and air pollutants). Under each annex, a Special Area can be established in which stricter environmental standards apply for ships that would not otherwise be operative.

The IMO can also create PSSAs. Although work on PSSAs under the IMO auspice began in 1986[85] the first Guidelines for the Designation of Special Areas and the

---

79 IMO Assembly Resolution (1985) A.572(14). Safety at Sea. Annex. 2.1.12

80 IMO General Assembly. 17th Session. A 17/Res.720. Guidelines for Designation of Special Areas and the Identification of Particularly Sensitive Sea Areas. 39.

81 Annex. Paragraph 5.7.4.

82 IMO Assembly Resolution A.284 (VIII). Routeing Measures. The original proposals were NAV IV/2/Add 5 and NAV IV/2/Add 7. With the region of the Rochebonne Shelf (France) all oil tankers were banned. With Cape Terpeniya all large (over 1,000 tons) oil or hazardous materials tankers were prohibited for the conservation of 'unique wildlife' (bears and beavers).

83 International Convention For The Prevention Of Pollution Of The Sea By Oil, 1954. 327 *UNTS* 3.

84 IMO General Resolution. 232 (VII). Amendments to the 1954 Convention For the Prevention of Pollution of the Sea by Oil, 1954, as Amended in 1969, Concerning Protection of the Great Barrier Reef. Through a reinterpretation of the words 'nearest land' the Reef came to obtain a greater degree of protection associated with the Annexes of MARPOL special areas.

85 For the encouragement of this process in 1990, See IMO (1990). *Proceedings of the International Seminar on Protection of Sensitive Sea Areas.* (IMO, London). Annex 1. Paragraphs 10 and 25.

Identification of PSSAs did not get concluded, following notable international prompting,[86] until 1991.[87] These were slightly changed in 2000,[88] before a fully revised resolution for the identification and protection of PSSAs was passed in 2001 eclipsing the older 1991 resolution on this subject.[89]

G Species Specific Conventions

A variation on the above approach is where an international legal instrument is crafted to protect a particular species, and the species is the subject of either a controlled or totally prohibited take. Accordingly a moratorium or 'closed season' is an optional conservation measure that can be placed around the species in question, and the areas that they inhabit. This type of policy option is particularly noticeable with birds[90] and fishing arrangements. With the latter, this policy option can be clearly seen in at least 16 bilateral and multilateral agreements between the 1850s and 1940.[91] Post-World

86 See IMO (1990). *Proceedings of the International Seminar on Protection of Sensitive Sea Areas.* (IMO, London). Annex 1. Paragraph 5.

87 IMO General Assembly. 17th Session. A 17/Res.720. Guidelines for the Designation of Special Areas and the Identification of Particularly Sensitive Sea Areas.

88 The some areas such as with areas of historic value were excluded, and expanded others, such as using biogeographical criteria; and international, regional or national significance. Annex 6. Changes to the Guidelines for the Designation of Special Areas Under MARPOL 73/78 and Guidelines for the Identification of Particularly Sensitive Sea Areas. 59-62. MEPC. Report of the MEPC on its 45th Session. 29. MEPC 45/20 (2000). MEPC. Report of the MEPC on its 44th Session. MEPC 44/20 (2000). 29.

89 Resolution A.885 (21). Also, Annex 6. Guidelines for the Designation of Special Areas Under MARPOL 73/78 and Guidelines for the Identification and Designation of Particularly Sensitive Sea Areas. MEPC (2001). Report of the MEPC on its 46th Session. MEPC 46/23.

90 Austria/Hungary/Italy 1875 Declaration for the Protection of Birds Useful to Agriculture. IPE, ibid. IV. 1561. The 1897, 1907, 1914 and 1927 Convention(s) Concerning Hunting (waterbirds) on Lake Constance and the Rhine Between Baden and Switzerland. In IPE, IV. 1599. 1916 Convention Between the United States and Great Britain for the Protection of Migratory Birds. IPE. IV, 1638. Article 2. 1936 Convention Between the United States and Mexico for the Protection of Migratory Birds. IPE. IV. 1723.

91 1858 Fishing Regulations for the Bidassoa River. This is reprinted in Ruster, B and Simma, D. (eds). *International Protection of the Environment.* (IPE). (Oceana, New York). Volume IX. 4321. Convention Between France and Great Britain on Fisheries. 1867. *IPE.* XXI. 1. Article XXIX. Convention Between the Grand Duchy of Baden and Switzerland Concerning Fishing in the Rhine. 1869. IPE. 4695, 4730. The 1880 Convention between Prussia and the Grand Dutchy of Hesse, for the Protection and Promotion of Fishing. 1880. *IPE.* XI. 5399. 1880 Convention Between France and Switzerland Regulating Fishing in the Frontier Waters. *IPE.* 4844. 1882 Convention Between Italy and Switzerland Concerning Fishing in the Frontier Waters. In *IPE.* XI. 5413. 1889 Regulation Between Korea and Japan Respecting Fisheries. *IPE.* XXI. Article 5. Exchange of Notes Between Great Britain and the United States of America Respecting the Preservation of the Fisheries in the Waters Contiguous to Canada

War II, the facility to create closed seasons has been followed in the majority of international fishery agreements,[92] and has become strongly endorsed by a number of high level policy forums including the Rome Consensus on World Fisheries,[93] and the FAO Code of Conduct for Responsible Fisheries.[94]

---

and the United States. *IPE*. XXI. 27. Article 3. The 1897 Regulations Between Spain and Portugal for Fishing the Mino River. *IPE*. XI. 5431. Chapter 3. The 1920 Exchange of Notes Between Finland and Norway on the Subject of Adoption of Rules for Fisheries at the Tana Watercourse. *IPE*. X. Article 2. 1921 Agreement Between Italy, and the Kingdom of Serbs, Croats and Slovenes for the Adriatic. *IPE*. VI. 2582. 1925 Convention Between Estonia and Latvia for the Protection of Fish. *IPE*. VI. 2599. 1927 Convention between Germany and Poland Concerning Fishing. In *IPE*. XI. 5518. Agreement Regarding the Regulation of Plaice and Flounder Fishing in the Baltic Sea. *IPE*. VI 2632. Article 2. Convention Between the United States and Canada for the Preservation of the Halibut Fishery. 1930. *IPE*. VI. 2636 & 1937. *IPE*. VI. 2639, 2651. 1934 Agreement Between Hungary and Czechoslovak Concerning a General Closed Season. *IPE*. IX. 4463.

92 For some examples among many, see North East Atlantic Fisheries Convention. 486 *UNTS*. 157. Article 7.1.c. These broad powers to control the catch on targeted species were reiterated in Article 7 of the 1982 Convention on Future Multilateral Co-operation in North East Atlantic Fisheries. BH794.txt. 1969. 1973 Convention on Fishing and Conservation of Living Resources in the Baltic Sea. In Kiss, A. (ed). *Selected Multilateral Treaties in the Field of the Environment.* (UNEP, Nairobi). 317. Article X. Convention on the Conservation of Antarctic Marine Living Resources.B.H.883.txt A/CONF.129/15 (25 I.L.M 543). Article IX.g. Convention for the Strengthening of the Inter-American Tropical Tuna Commission established by the 1949 Convention between the United States of America and the Republic of Costa Rica. Article VII. Convention on the Conservation and Management of Highly Migratory Fish Stocks in the Western and Central Pacific Ocean. Available from <http:www.oceanlaw.net/texts/westpac.htm> Article 10(2)(d). The 2000 Framework Agreement for the Conservation of Living Marine Resources on the High Seas of the South Pacific, allows for the creation of 'subzones' in which take can be strictly controlled (article 6). The 2001 Convention on the Conservation and Management of Fishery Resources in the South-East Atlantic Ocean allows for the creation of areas and periods in which fishing may occur (article 6). The 2000 Convention on the Conservation and Management of Highly Migratory Fish Stocks in the Western and Central Pacific Ocean, allows the adoption of measures to ensure conservation and management of the targeted species (article 5). The 1994 Convention on the Conservation and Management of Pollock Resources Central Bering Sea also allows for the adoption of conservation measures (article IV). Finally, the South African Development Community Protocol on Fisheries goes so far as to protect key habitats for the relevant fish, and called upon each State to co-ordinate the establishment of marine protected areas (article 14). Convention for the Strengthening of the Inter-American Tropical Tuna Commission established by the 1949 Convention between the United States of America and the Republic of Costa Rica. Article VII allows the development of measures to protect and restore populations.

93 As adopted by the FAO Ministerial Conference on Fisheries, Rome, 14-15 March 1995. Paragraphs 6 and 10 emphasised the importance of protecting fish habitat and overall conservation measures.

94 FAO Code of Conduct. Section 6.8

The most well known example of this type of closed season, is that implemented by the International Convention on the Regulation of Whaling (ICRW). The lineage of this area traces back to the 1937 Convention on the Regulation of Whaling[95] which set aside certain areas from whaling ships. The 1938 Protocol to this Convention created the first whale sanctuary.[96] Similar mechanisms were incorporated into Article V of the 1946 ICRW. Within this provision, it is noted that,

> The Commission may amend from time to time the provisions of the Schedule by adopting regulations with respect to the conservation and utilization of whale resources, fixing... open and closed waters, including the designation of sanctuary areas.[97]

4 Regional Conventions

There are a number of notable regional agreements for, inter alia, the creation of protected areas. These include the 1940 Convention on Nature Protection and Wild Life Preservation In The Western Hemisphere,[98] the 1976 Convention on the Conservation of Nature in the South Pacific,[99] and the 1985 ASEAN Agreement on the Conservation of Nature and Natural Resources.[100] However, it is with the European and African Conventions, and some of the developments under the Regional Seas programmes that some regional developments with regard to protected areas have fully developed.

A The Regional Seas Agreements

The United Nations Environment Programme (UNEP) launched its Regional Seas Programme in 1974. Although there has been an increased attempt to synchronise these documents since the end of the twentieth century,[101] and there is a substantial overlap in terms of the approach of the regional conventions, they remain fundamentally separ-

---

95 The 1937 International Convention for the Regulation of Whaling. (1940) *American Journal of International Law.* Supp. 34:16. Also in *LNTS.* CXE. 79. See Article VII. This prohibition on whaling factory ships was in all seas between South 40 degrees South, and all seas North of 40 degrees North.

96 The 1938 (London) Protocol Amending the International Whaling Agreement. *LNTS.* CXCVI. 131. Article 1 & 2.

97 From the outset this provision was to prove ambiguous, as key terms like 'sanctuary area' were not defined in the 1946 ICRW or its first Schedule.

98 BH175.txt.

99 Reprinted in Austen, M. (ed). *Basic Legal Documents on International Animal Welfare and Wildlife Consideration.* (Kluwer, London). 167.

100 Reprinted in Austen, *ibid.* 193-205.

101 UNEP. (1999). Second Global Meeting of Regional Seas Conventions and Action Plans. The Hague, 5-8 July. Available from the UNEP Regional Seas Program. Paragraphs 118-119, 131.

ated in both their priorities and approach to the management of each regional sea. In total, since 1974, 13 regional conventions and action plans have been established under its auspice. The agreements cover the Wider Caribbean (1983);[102] West and Central Africa (1981);[103] East Africa (1985);[104] Kuwait (1978);[105] the Mediterranean (with the Barcelona Convention), the Red Sea and Gulf of Aden (1982);[106] and the South East Pacific (1981).[107]

In some places where there are no regional conventions, 'Action Plans' exist, such as for the East Asian Seas[108] and the North West Pacific.[109] Outside of the UNEP auspice, other notable regional seas programmes include those with renewed conventions, covering the North-East Atlantic,[110] the Baltic,[111] the Black Sea[112] and the Caspian Sea. All of these regional conventions contain broad obligations to protect and conserve the marine environment, and many of them have a number of protocols attached to them, which are designed to deal with any number of issues, ranging from oil spills to land based pollution.

Despite the large number of regional seas agreements, and recommendations that critical areas of them such as with MPAs receive greater development,[113] only a minority

---

102 The 1983 Convention for the Protection and Development of the Marine Environment of the Wider Caribbean Region. In UNEP. (1991). *Multilateral Treaties in the Field of the Environment (Cambridge University Press, Cambridge).* 258.

103 1981 Convention for Co-operation in the Protection and Development of the Marine and Coastal Environment of the West and Central African Region In UNEP. (1991). *Ibid.* at 118.

104 The 1985 Convention for the Protection, Management and Development of the Marine and Coastal Environment of the Eastern African Region (Nairobi Convention). In UNEP. (1991). *Ibid.* 32.

105 Kuwait Regional Convention for Co-operation on the Protection of the Marine Environment from Pollution; In UNEP. (1983). *Selected Multilateral Treaties in the Field of the Environment.* (Cambridge University Press, Cambridge). at 486.

106 1982 Regional Convention for the Conservation of the Red Sea and Gulf of Aden Environment. In UNEP. (1991). *Ibid*, 144.

107 The 1981 Convention for the Protection of the Marine Environment and Coastal Area of the South East Pacific. In UNEP. (1991). *Ibid.* at 130.

108 East Asian Seas Action Plan, adopted in 1995. See 1995 *YBIEL.* 6: 239.

109 In 1994, the Action Plan for the Protection, Management and Development of the Marine and Coastal Environment of the North West Pacific Region was adopted. See 1994 *YBIEL.* 5: 178.

110 1992 Convention for the Protection of the Marine Environment of the North-East Atlantic (OSPAR). BH1012.txt. 32 *ILM* 1069. The Convention came into effect in 1998.

111 The Preamble recognised that the purpose of the new Convention was to 'extend, strengthen and modernise' the earlier Convention.

112 1992 Convention on the Protection of the Black Sea Against Pollution. BH1004.txt. 32 *ILM* 1101.

113 See IMO (1990). *Proceedings of the International Seminar on Protection of Sensitive Sea Areas.* (IMO, London). Annex 1. Paragraph 9.

of the regional arrangements have specific protocols or policy developments directly relating to marine protected areas. This minority includes the 1990 Protocol Concerning Specially Protected Areas and Wildlife to the Convention for the Protection and Development of the Marine Environment of the Wider Caribbean Region, (the 'Caribbean Protocol'); the 1995 Protocol concerning Specially Protected Areas and Biological Diversity in the Mediterranean (the 'Mediterranean Protocol') and the Protocol for the Conservation and Management of Protected Marine and Coastal Areas of the South-East Pacific.[114] Specific MPA programmes are also present under the auspice of the Helsinki[115] and OSPAR Conventions. In the latter instances, although MPAs are not created under a specific instrument, clear and detailed regimes for the establishment of MPAs have developed. For example, Annex V of the OSPAR Convention obliges its signatories to seek the creation of, 'means, consistent with international law, for instituting protective, conservation, restorative or precautionary measures related to specific areas or sites or related to particular species or habitats'. Protected Marine and Coastal Areas are part of the East African Action Plan,[116] the North West Pacific Action Plan,[117] and the ROPME (Arabia) Regional Seas Programme.[118]

B The African Context

There have been four regional treaties for the creation of protected areas in Africa. These were in 1900,[119] 1933, 1968 and 2003. Theoretically, each of the latter treaties supercedes the earlier ones.[120] As of 2007, the 2003 treaty was not yet in force.[121] In all instances, the scope of the treaties have been restricted to African territories although

114 1989 Protocol for the Conservation and Management of Protected Marine and Coastal Areas of the South East Pacific. Reprinted in Austen, A. (ed). *Basic Legal Document on International Animal Welfare and Wildlife Conservation (Kluwer, London).* 247.

115 HELCOM Recommendation 15/5 (1994). Guidelines for Designating Marine And Coastal Baltic Sea Protected Areas (BSPA) And Proposed Protection Categories, Updated and approved by HELCOM HOD 11/2003 Guidelines for management of Baltic sea protected area.

116 UNEP. (1998). First Inter-Regional Seas Programme Co-ordination. UNEP/WBRS.1/7. June 25. 6.

117 *Ibid.* 7.

118 The ROPME announced its intention to draft a new protocol on Biological Diversity and the Establishment of Specially Protected Areas. UNEP. (1998). First Inter-Regional Seas Programme Co-ordination. UNEP/WBRS.1/7. June 25. 5.

119 1900 Convention Designed to Ensure the Conservation of Various Species of Wild Animals in Africa. *IPE.* IV. 1605.

120 Once the 1968 African Convention came into force, the 1933 London Convention ceased to have effect in States which had signed the African Convention. African Convention (1968). Article XXI (3).

121 If Parties are both signatories to the 2003 Convention, then it applies, but if only one Party is, then only the original 1968 Convention applies. 2003 African Convention. Article XXXIV.

the 1900 and 1933 ones were administered by a number of colonial powers.[122] By 2003, the emphasis was such that accession to the African treaty was only possible for any 'independent and sovereign African State'.[123] Despite this long tradition of such treaties in Africa, all of the above conventions have included protected areas as a subset of their environmental considerations. The exception to this is the 1985 Protocol Concerning Protected Areas of Wild Fauna and Flora in the Eastern African Region,[124] which is the only African instrument specifically designed for the creation of protected areas. It is, however, only applicable for a few East African States, unlike the 2003 African Convention, which is open to signature to any member of the African Union.[125]

C The European Context

The first regional initiative for the creation of protected areas in Europe came with the creation of the European Diploma in 1965.[126] Although the (strictly European)[127] Diploma, has been both renewed, and continues into the 21st century,[128] protecting sites of 'exceptional European interest',[129] the primary instrument in this region is the 1979 Bern Convention on the Conservation of Habitat and Wildlife in Europe.[130] Although the Bern Convention is primarily about European wildlife and habitats, non-European States can be invited to adhere.[131]

The Bern Convention was strongly supplemented by the 1992 Habitats Directive. The Habitats Directive derives from the European Community, which is a member of the Bern Convention. In order to fulfil its obligations arising from the Convention, particularly in respect of habitat protection, it produced the Habitats Directive, and subsequently set up the Natura 2000 network. The Bern Convention and the Habitats Directive have a complete coincidence of objectives. Both are regional legal instruments aimed at the conservation of wild flora, fauna and natural habitats. Their main differences come from

---

122 The territories covered in the 1933 London Convention, were largely set down in Article 1 of the Convention. 1933 London Convention. Article 1.

123 African Convention (1968). Article XXII. The African Convention also applies to areas within the limits of national jurisdiction of any Party, and any activities by that Party, carried out beyond its borders.2003 African Convention. Article 1.

124 Protocol Concerning Protected Areas of Wild Fauna and Flora in the Eastern African Region. Reprinted in Austen, A. (ed). *Basic Legal Document on International Animal Welfare and Wildlife Conservation (Kluwer, London).* 186.

125 2003 African Convention. See articles XXXVI and XXXVII.

126 See Res. 65 (5) of the Committee of Ministers of the Council of Europe.

127 The European Diploma is available for any European State. European Diploma. Article 3.

128 See the Res. 73/4 and amended thereafter and Res. (98):29.

129 European Diploma. Article 3 (4).

130 was partly in fulfilment to European intentions in response to the 1972 United Nations Conference on the Human Environment. Bern Convention, preamble.

131 Bern Convention. Article 19 (1) and 20.

the territory they apply to and to the fact that the Directive is more explicit on the obligations concerning conservation of natural habitats.[132] The Directive is designed to implement, improve the reach and reinforce the application the Bern Convention in the European Community.

The Bern Convention and the Habitats Directive are supplemented by the European Diploma, and the Natura 2000 and the Emerald Networks. The habitat obligations of both the Bern Convention and the Habitats Directive can be met through designations of sites to the Natura 2000 Network. Sites under the Natura 2000 Network are also recognised as sites in the Emerald Network.[133] The Emerald Network, as established under the Bern Convention in 1996,[134] and modalities agreed in 1998,[135] is based on the same principles as Natura 2000. The Emerald Network represents the de facto extension of Natura 2000 to non-Community countries. Since the implementation phase of the Emerald Network has started, pilot projects have been launched in 17 countries of Central and Eastern Europe (Albania, Bulgaria, Croatia, Czech Republic, Estonia, Georgia, Hungary, Latvia, Lithuania, Moldova, Poland, Romania, Russia, Slovenia, Slovakia, the former Yugoslav Republic of Macedonia and Ukraine) and 3 non EC Western States (Cyprus, Malta and Turkey). Iceland and Switzerland have joined in the Emerald process, using their own financial sources. The number of States outside the EC participating in the Network had risen to 19, including 14 in central and Eastern Europe.[136] It also includes a number of African states such as Tunisia, Morocco, Senegal and Burkina Faso. With the inclusion of such States, the Emerald network is commonly seen as an instrument to assist Central and Eastern European states which are candidates to the EC to prepare for Natura 2000 and the Bern Convention (which also has tried to help central and east European countries to implement the Convention).[137] For other states, it is important in the 'standard-setting' perspective.

---

132 See Fernandez-Galiano, E. (2002). 'The Emerald Network: Areas of Special Conservation for the Whole of Europe'. 12 (3) *Parks*. 21, 23.

133 Resolution No. 5 (1998) Concerning The Rules For The Network of Areas of Special Conservation Interest (Emerald Network). Report of the 18th Meeting of the Bern Convention. T-PVS (98) 62. Appendix 3. Article 1.

134 Resolution No. 3. Concerning the Setting Up of a Pan-European Ecological Network. CoE (1996). Report of the 15th Meeting of the Bern Convention. T-PVS (96) 23. Appendix 7. Also, The Recommendation to the Parliamentary Assembly. CoE (1997). Report of the 16th Meeting of the Bern Convention. T-PVS (97) 63. Appendix 3.

135 Resolution No. 5 (1998) Concerning The Rules For The Network of Areas of Special Conservation Interest (Emerald Network). Report of the 18th Meeting of the Bern Convention. T-PVS (98) 62. Appendix 3.

136 Report of the 21st Meeting of the Bern Convention. T-PVS (2001). 89. 11-12

137 Recommendation to the Parliamentary Assembly. CoE (1997). Report of the 16th Meeting of the Bern Convention. T-PVS (97) 63. Appendix 3.

5 Conclusion

Humanity has been creating protected areas since Antiquity. By the twenty first century, this objective was being achieved at the international and regional levels, by a myriad of legal instruments. The most notable international regimes which can actually inscribe protected areas are the WHC, MAB, Ramsar, IMO, and the Antarctica Treaty. The international regimes are supplemented by a strong body of regional regimes, of which the European and African contexts are particularly notable, as are parts of the regional seas agreements. Although there are clear gaps in the system, the system is clearly evolving and collectively, the international community is well en-route to systematically covering many of the areas that need to be addressed.

Chapter II

DEFINITIONS

1 The Debate on Classification

According to the Convention on Biological Diversity (CBD), a 'protected area' is, 'a geographically defined area, which is designated or regulated and managed to achieve specific conservation objectives.'[1] This definition, which broadly reflects the IUCN definition of a protected area,[2] should be viewed as the lowest common denominator for any definition of protected areas. From this lowest common denominator, a further 800 (approximately) variations have been adduced to describe protected areas. These definitions range from those which encompass small parks in suburban neighborhoods,[3] to areas of vast magnitude, some crossing national borders. This proliferation of standards has inevitably resulted in a multitude of national, regional and international regimes, thematic overlaps and clashes, and an ocean of acronyms, sometimes even within individual regimes. For example, the International Maritime Organization has the capacity to create what are commonly known as MPAs. However, these areas are in reality little more than traffic avoidance schemes, rather than resource extraction zones.[4] Nevertheless the IMO can establish, 'Special Areas' or 'Particularly Sensitive Sea Areas,' or it can create areas to be avoided, from which ship traffic is excluded.[5] Although all of these options have a substantial overlap, they are theoretically, different.[6]

---

1 CBD. Article 1. Definitions.

2 The IUCN defines a protected area as, 'an area of land and/or sea especially dedicated to the protection and maintenance of biological diversity, and of natural and associated cultural resources, and managed through legal or other effective means'. Noted in UNEP. (2003). *United Nations List of Protected Areas.* (IUCN/Thanet, UK). 2.

3 IUCN. (2001). 'Cities and Protected Areas.' *Parks.* 11 (3). 1-48.

4 CBD Secretariat. (2004). *Technical Advice on the Establishment and Management of a National System of Marine and Coastal Protected Areas.* (CBD Technical Series No. 13). 7.

5 IMO Assembly Resolution (1985) A.572(14). Safety at Sea. Annex. 2.1.12. IMO General Assembly. 17th Session. A 17/Res.720. Guidelines for the Designation of Special Areas and the Identification of Particularly Sensitive Sea Areas. 39. The term Special Area is defined in Annex I of MARPOL 73/78. Identical definitions are incorporated into Annex II and V.

6 The difference between a Special Area and a PSSA is that a Special Area provides additional protection to a sea area so designated. Its designation results in a direct prohibition of certain type of pollutant. Conversely, identification of a PSSA is nothing more than a qualification and a basis on which measures may be taken through the IMO, such as routing measures and compulsory reporting requirements for ships over a certain size with certain cargoes, (such as with the Canaries); or a PSSA may have exactly the same rules as a Special Areas with regard to the respective MARPOL Annexes such as with Ecuador's Galapagos Archipe-

Likewise, the Antarctic regime at one point provided for eight different types of protected areas, although these were later refined.[7] At a more practical level, a confusion over what is, and is not, permitted in a protected area may result in unsatisfactory results. For example, in 2006, it became apparent that over 25% of Europe's Red Knot bird species had died since 1998 because one of Europe's supposedly protected coasts, was not really protected. That is, necessary inter-tidal habitat and critical food of shellfish for this migratory species, was not off-limts to cockle boats, who were allowed to

---

lago. With the Western European PSSA, the only requirement is extra reporting (although originally the proposal was to ban all oil tankers except those which were double hulled). In some instances, a Special Area and a PSSA can encompass the same place, such as with the Baltic Sea, and no new APM (Associated Protective Measures), beyond those already existing for the Special Area are called for. In some of the above instances, the ships are routed around, or piloted through an area, due to its PSSA status, although in other instances, the areas routed around are neither Special Areas nor PSSAs. For example, with the extension to the Great Barrier PSSA in 2003, although it was already an established PSSA, and already had pre-existing routing measures around it (before it was a PSSA), when it was classified as a PSSA, and subsequently expanded, as part of the package, Australia wanted a particular shipping route through the Torres Strait made compulsory, in addition to an extension of the recommended pilotage scheme (which at this point applied to all vessels over 70 metres in length, and all loaded oil, chemical or gas tankers) made mandatory.
MEPC. (2004). Report of the MEPC on its 51st Session. MEPC. 51/22. 35-36. MEPC. (2003). Report of the MEPC on its 49th Meeting. MEPC. 49/8/1, also 49/WP.7. 45-52. MEPC. (2003). Report of the MEPC on its 49th Meeting. MEPC. 49/WP.7. 43.

7 Specially Protected Areas (SPAs) Sites of Special Scientific Interest (SSSIs) Areas of Special Tourist Interest (ASTIs) Historic Sites and Monuments (HSMs) Tomb Specially Reserved Areas (SRAs) Marine Sites of Special Scientific Interest (MSSSIs) Multiple-use Planning Areas (MPAs) The Madrid Protocol, rationalized the existing protected area system by creating two new designations Antarctic Specially Protected Areas (ASPAs) and Antarctic Specially Managed Areas (ASMAs). All SPAs and SSSIs previously designated were incorporated as ASPAs. All existing SPAs and SSSIs automatically became ASPAs when Annex V entered into force. Other protected areas have been designated under Conventions within the Antarctic Treaty system. Specially Protected Areas, Sites of Special Scientific Interest, Areas of Special Tourist Interest, Historic Sites and Monuments, Tomb Specially Reserved Areas, Marine Sites of Special Scientific Interest, Multiple-use Planning Areas. In 1989, the signatories to the ATS, agreed to review the descriptions of the SPAs already listed on Annex B of the Agreed Measures, to provide a: 'detailed description of the natural ecological system that the area is intended to preserve'. Recommendation XV-9. Antarctic Protected Area System: Development of Improved Descriptions and Management Plans for Specially Protected Areas. In Antarctic Treaty: Report of the Fifteenth Meeting (Paris, 1989). 80. The Madrid Protocol, rationalized the existing protected area system by creating two new designations Antarctic Specially Protected Areas (ASPAs) and Antarctic Specially Managed Areas (ASMAs). All SPAs and SSSIs previously designated were incorporated as ASPAs. All existing SPAs and SSSIs automatically became ASPAs when Annex V entered into force. Other protected areas have been designated under Conventions within the Antarctic Treaty system.

continue to dredge in the protected area, to the overt detriment of a very threatened species.[8]

The problem of understanding the scope and operation of protected areas is magnified when countries come into conflict over the management of such areas. A common manifestation of this problem is with regard to human communities living inside protected areas. Whilst some countries sanction this practice, others consider it the antithesis to the objectives of protected areas.[9] Likewise, there is a substantial divergence of opinion between many countries as to what human activities, such as mining, or forestry, or agriculture, should be permitted in protected areas.[10] Moreover, if a number of regimes are involved in the regulation of such protected areas, desirable goals such as comparisons, benchmarks and standards between protected areas can become lost in a sea of incompatible frameworks and paradigms.[11] Finally, and most importantly, if a robust international classification scheme can be adopted, debates premised on an all or nothing approach to the philosophical construction and practical implementations of protected areas can be avoided, as a wide variety of alternative, more accommodating, options may be presented.

The solution to many of the above problems is an internationally applicable classification scheme that could apply to all protected areas, no matter where, or under what auspice they operate. Investigation into this option was first mooted in 1962 at the First World Park's Congress. The Congress recommended that the International Commission on National Parks and the IUCN establish an internationally applicable classification of terms for national parks and equivalent reserves in different parts of the world.[12] Although, the IUCN began work on this task, and formulated some broad classifications for protected areas,[13] progress was slow, and the Second World Parks Congress in

8 Anon. (2006). 'Protection That Isn't'. *New Scientist.* November 18. 7.

9 IUCN. (2004). *Speaking A Common Language.* (IUCN, Gland). 89. Wells, S. (2004). 'Application of the IUCN Protected Area Management Categories in the Marine Environment'. 14(3) *Parks.* 28-38.

10 IUCN. (2004). 112. Kapila, S. (2004). 'Shell's Perspective on the IUCN Protected Areas Management Category System'. 14(3) *Parks.* 46, 49-50. Business Council for Sustainable Development. (2002). *Breaking New Ground.* (Earthscan, London). 164-168.

11 See IUCN. (2004), *ibid.* (IUCN, Gland). 15. See Recommendation 5.19. IUCN Protected Area Management Categories. (Vth IUCN World Parks Congress). Phillips, A. (2004). 'The History of the International System of Protected Area Management Categories'. 14(3) *Parks.* 4-13.

12 See Brockman, C.F. 'Problems of Nomenclature: The Need for Definitions.' In Adams, A. (ed). *First World Conference on National Parks.* (US Department of the Interior, Washington). 366-367.

13 In 1969, the IUCN General Assembly passed a resolution that sought to define a national park as a, 'relatively large area where one or several ecosystems are not materially altered by human exploitation and occupation'. IUCN, 1969 definition. As noted in IUCN. (2004). *Speaking A Common Language.* (IUCN, Gland). 45. Originally, the IUCN divided protected

1972 urged it to redouble it efforts.[14] Six years later, the IUCN unveiled its first official classification system. This system, which created ten categories of protected areas,[15] was the subject of intense discussion at the Third World Parks Congress in 1982. The primary concerns were that the proposed ten level system did not contain an overall definition of protected areas, the categories overlapped with broad categories of land management, and the system excluded internationally designated protected areas, such as those under the auspices of the WHC or the supplies of the WHC or the MAB.[16] These concerns were highlighted at the Third,[17] and Fourth World Parks Congress. The 4th Congress was notable in calling for a simplified system of six, rather than ten, categories of protected areas. Two years later in 1994, the IUCN issued their six level criteria for classifying protected areas, from which international designations were excluded from the exercise.[18] This six category system was endorsed at the Fifth World Parks Congress in 2003[19] and at the seventh Conference of the Parties of the CBD in 2004. Of note, the CBD recognized,

> [T]he value of a single international classification system for protected areas and the benefit of providing information that is comparable across countries and regions and therefore welcomes the ongoing efforts of the IUCN World Commission on Protected Areas to refine the IUCN system of categories.[20]

Despite the international recognition of this overall protected area schema, the uptake of the IUCN classification scheme has been limited. For example, approximately slightly less than 10% of all national protected area legislation appears to have been influenced

---

areas into three classes (strict protection with no or minimal human interference, directed nature reserves with some secondary – not primary – human utilization, and finally where nature is protected for human recreational values). See Dasmann, R. (1972). 'Development of a Classification System for Protected Natural and Cultural Systems.' In Elliot, H. (ed). *Second World Conference on National Parks.* (IUCN, Lausanne). 388-401.

14 Recommendation 10. Standards and Nomenclature for Protected Areas. In Elliot, *ibid.* 445.

15 These were (i) Strict nature reserves/scientific reserves, (ii) National Parks, (iii) Natural Landmarks or Monuments, (iv) Managed reserves or sanctuaries, (v) Protected landscapes or seascapes) (vi) Resource reserves, (vii) Natural Biotic Areas/Anthropological reserves (viii) Multiple Use Management Areas/Managed Resource Areas, (ix) Biosphere Reserve, and (x) World Heritage Sites.

16 IUCN. (1982). 'Categories, Objectives and Criteria for Protected Areas.' In McNeely, J. (ed). *National Parks, Conservation and Development.* (Smithsonian, Washington). 47-53.

17 Recommendation 1. Information on Protected Areas. Recommendations of the World National Parks Congress. In McNeely, *ibid.* 765.

18 IUCN. (1994). *Guidelines for Protected Area Management Categories.* (IUCN, Gland).

19 See Recommendation 5.19. IUCN Protected Area Management Categories. (Vth IUCN World Parks Congress).

20 CBD. Decision VII/28. Protected Areas. Paragraph 31.

by the IUCN categories.[21] In terms of international influence, only a few instruments have directly utilized the IUCN categories. The forums and regimes that the IUCN categories have had a substantial influence on are the 2003 African Convention,[22] the Helsinki Commission and its Baltic Sea Protected Areas regime,[23] the Arctic Circumpolar Protected Area Network[24] and the 2000 Intergovernmental Forum on Forests, which also encouraged countries to use the IUCN categories when classifying forest protected areas.[25] Finally, in 2005 the Parties to the Ramsar Convention called for the creation of a new data set to be obtained when a wetland site is listed under the Convention, which covers the wetlands protected area category, as classified by the Parties themselves, but also in accordance with the IUCN categories. Moreover, the Convention's scientific body (the STRP) was directed to consider co-ordination efforts in integrating Ramsar sites into other systems of protected areas.[26]

Despite the growing utilization of the IUCN classification schema in some regional and international bodies, the majority of such bodies have not even reviewed the IUCN system, much less adopted it. In some forums, such as the WHC, this omission is perplexing. Exactly why regimes have failed to adopt the schema is a matter of speculation. In some instances, it may be that consideration of the issue has not been undertaken, and there may be no fundamental objections to it. Indeed, in a number of regimes, the protected areas categories they have already established would easily fit within the IUCN schema.

In other instances, however, there is a legitimate concern that unless the designation of category status is conducted in a manner that facilitates inclusiveness, transparency,

---

21 Of 322 relevant pieces of national legislation developed since 1978 from 164 surveyed countries, only 7 % were strongly influenced by the IUCN categories. This figure rose to 10% when the survey was restricted to between 1994 and 2002. With regard to national legislation, a comprehensive review of 192 countries, involving 439 pieces of legislation, showed that seven countries (Argentina, Belize, Cambodia, Guatemala, Philippines, Spain and Turkey) had legislation that directly, or indirectly, utilized the 1978 criteria, and 13 countries (Australia, Brazil, Bulgaria, Cambodia, Cuba, Georgia, Hungary, Kuwait, Mexico, Niger, Uruguay, Vietnam and Slovenia) had criteria directly or indirectly reflecting the 1994 criteria. IUCN. (2004). *Speaking A Common Language.* (IUCN, Gland). 55. Dillon, B. (2004). 'The Use of the Categories in National and International Legislation and Policy'. 14 (3) *Parks.* 15-27.

22 2003 African Convention. Article 5.

23 Helcom Recommendation 15/5 (1994). Guidelines For Designating Marine And Coastal Baltic Sea Protected Areas. The areas recommended were for five (not six) types. These were, Strict Nature Reserve and Wilderness Areas, National Park, Natural Monument, Habitat and Species Management Area and Protected Landscape and Seascapes.

24 See CAFF. (1996). *The Circumpolar Protected Area Network: Principles and Guidelines.* CAFF Habitat Conservation Report, No 4. Principle 7.

25 IUCN. (2004). *Ibid.* 60-68.

26 Resolution 9.22. Ramsar Sites and Protected Areas. (2005, Kampala). Paragraphs 8 and 11.

verification, certification, periodic review and due process, then the schema may be worthless.[27] This is especially true if the classification categories ultimately get caught up in issues related to legislation and/or land use regulations.[28] In this regard, unless the protected area regimes, in conjunction with the countries that have jurisdiction over the protected areas in question, have a direct role in the classification of any protected area (and therefore guarantee its status), the regional and international application of the scheme, may be worthless.

Finally, some protected area regimes appear to have backed away from the classification question when dealing with sensitive questions of extracting resources within protected areas. This problem first became apparent in 1997 with the first approximation report of the Montreal Process, (a grouping of the 12 non-European countries that possess the majority of the world's boreal and temperate forests). In the report, the group concluded that while most of the countries had information on the existence and extent of protected areas, the classification of such areas was 'poorly developed' and it was clear that 'protected areas are used for different purposes by different countries.'[29] In 2000 the United Nations Economic Commission for Europe (UNECE) asked countries to report on the extent of their forest protected areas for its Temperate and Boreal Assessment, to report utilizing the IUCN categories. However, once more, the results were confusing, as it was not clear whether plantations should be classified as 'forest protected areas' or whether forests managed for multiple purposes could constitute protected areas. As a result, the UNECE created an alternative set of definitions, which although compatible with the IUCN categories, also contain many categories that do not meet IUCN's definitions of a protected area.[30] This problem was later replicated in other forestry forums. Accordingly, out of 9 regional criteria and indicator initiatives operating in 2004, only four mentioned (but often in a confused way) IUCN protected area classification categories.[31]

---

27 Dudley, N. (2003). 'Categorising Protected Areas.' World Conservation. 14-15. IUCN. (2004). *Speaking A Common Language.* (IUCN, Gland). 159-161.

28 Stolton, S. (2004). 'Issues that Arise for the Categories in a Changing World'. 14(3) *Parks.* 63-71.

29 The Montreal Process. (1997). *The First Approximation Report.* (Canadian Forest Service, Ottawa). 3, 14-15. For some of the different interpretations in this area, see the Montreal Process. (2000). *Progress and Innovation in Implementing the Indicators for the Conservation and Management of Temperate and Boreal Forests.* (Canadian Forest Service, Ottawa). 4-56.

30 IUCN. (2004). *Ibid.* 120. Stolton, S. (2004). 'Issues That Arise for the Categories in a Changing World'. 14(3) *Parks.* 63, 66.

31 The Montreal, Tarapoto and Lepaterique Processes, as well as the ITTO. See IUCN. (2004). *Ibid.* 123-127.

2 International Practice and the IUCN Categories

With the United Nations List of Protected Areas it is possible to classify many of the sites they vertify within the following IUCN six level criteria. Although 33% of the (33,036) sites have not been classified, much to the consternation of the World Congress on Protected Areas,[32] it has been possible to classify the other 67% (covering 81% of the total area covered) of the world's protected areas.[33] Very broadly, categories I to IV focus on variations of limited human involvement in a protected area. Conversely, category V and VI represent a fundamentally different idea about what a protected area is. The primary difference between more traditional protected areas and category V and VI is that although the original 'wilderness' idea remains in all documents, it has been increasingly supplemented in a number of regimes by a additional considerations.[34] In particular, although small parts of the area may be designed to minimize human influence, the vast majority of the areas are designed to both benefit nature and to further social and economic objectives, such as meeting the needs of local populations.[35] Thus, human populations and their related activities may be compatible with the designation of a protected area, if the overall objectives of the area are not transgressed.[36]

A Category I: Strict Nature Reserves and Wilderness Areas

Category I is divided into parts Ia and part Ib. Category Ia is designated as 'strict nature reserves.'[37] In 2003, 4,731 strict nature reserves were recorded globally. This represents 4.6% of all protected areas, or 5.5 % (1,033,888 km2) of the total area encompassed by protected areas.[38]

All strict nature reserve sites impose strict regulations on any artificial change in the environment or any biological and geological depredation (such as hunting, fishing,

---

32 See Recommendation 5.04. Building a Comprehensive and Effective Protected Area System. (Vth IUCN World Parks Congress).

33 UNEP. (2003). *United Nations List of Protected Areas.* (IUCN/Thanet, UK). 13, 21. There are however a number of uncertainties with the UN list, relating to size, date of establishment, geographical location, management categories etc, for a number of sites. See pages 19-20.

34 Such as the reinvigorated approach to park management in Ethiopia, as supported by a number of European NGOs in the new century, of excluding local peoples from national parks, along the lines of the Kenyan model. Pearce, F. (2005). 'Big Game Losers'. *New Scientist.* Apr 16. 21.

35 IUCN. (2002). Management Guidelines for IUCN Category V Protected Areas. (IUCN, Gland). 14. Phillips, A. (2003). 'A Modern Paradigm.' In *World Conservation* 2: 6-7.

36 See Recommendation 2.82 from the 2000 at the World Conservation Congress in Amman, Jordan.

37 These were formerly known as scientific reserves in the 1978 IUCN criteria.

38 Chape, S. (2003). 'Monitoring Global Commitment.' *World Conservation.* 8-9.

picking, cutting or uprooting), with certain possible exceptions for justifiable scientific purposes aimed at controlling or maintaining certain species and/or environments. Human occupation is not permitted, nor is economic activities such as agriculture, forestry, mining, industry and/or tourism. However, certain traditional activities may be authorised for the sole purpose of maintaining the environment and pre-existing obligations. These activities can continue provided they are localised and controlled and do not interfere with maintaining the biological and landscape diversity of the area. Moreover, efforts should be made to minimise or even eliminate these activities. In addition, human activities in areas contiguous to Ia Reserve sites must be controlled so as not to damage the physical and biological integrity of the protected area. Thus, the site must be closely monitored, and public access minimized. The overarching objective of management for the Ia classification, is to preserve habitats, ecosystems and species in the most undisturbed state that is possible.

The second division of category I is reserved for 'wilderness areas' which are classified as category Ib. In 2003, 1,302 wilderness reserves were recorded globally. Wilderness areas represent 1.3% of all protected areas, or 5.4 % (1,015,512 km2) of the total of internationally recorded protected areas.[39] Unlike strict nature reserves, wilderness areas are a relatively new designation, only appearing in the IUCN categories in 1994, with no equivalent classification in the 1978 IUCN categories. Wilderness areas must be of sufficient size to make practical preservation and use possible. They are unmodified or only slightly modified. As such they retain their natural character and influence, without significant human habitation. However, low density, low impact indigenous communities living in balance with the area may be permissible, as may well controlled public access. However, in both instances, there should be opportunities for solitude. Travel within the area should be non-motorised.

The term, 'strict nature reserve' can be traced back to the 1933 Convention Relative to the Preservation of Fauna and Flora in their Natural State, by which all hunting, extraction, construction or domestication within the identified area was strictly prohibited. Moreover, entry to the area, for any reason, was prohibited without express authority.[40] The term, and its strict exclusion of human activity, was later included in the 1940 Convention on Nature Protection and Wild Life Preservation in the Western Hemisphere, which also sought to maintain the, 'primitive conditions'[41] of the area as 'inviolate.'[42] The 1968 African Convention on the Conservation of Nature and Natural Resources also retained a classification system using strict nature reserves and all of its strongly restrictive caveats on any form of human activity.[43] The European Diploma has created

39 *Ibid.*

40 1933 Africa Convention. Article 2 (2).

41 1940 Western Hemisphere Convention. Preamble, Article I (4).

42 1940 Western Hemisphere Convention. Article III.

43 African Convention (1968). Article III.

one option for protected areas, where the overarching objective is to preserve biological and landscape diversity ecosystems.[44]

Category I objectives are also well reflected within the first category of protected areas established under the Antarctic regime. This regime, which is permeated with an overall ethos to preserve the region as 'inviolate,'[45] has direct application through the long-standing category of 'Specially Protected Areas' (SPAs).[46] With these areas, entry into the site, or the extraction of native flora, cannot be taken without a permit, and permits can only be issued for 'compelling scientific purpose[s],'[47] and in accordance with the management plan for the protected area.[48] In all instances, any permitted action must not jeopardize the natural ecological system existing in that area.[49] Moreover, human activities have to be carefully regulated to such an extent that even the driving of vehicles in SPAs is prohibited.[50] The necessity for permits to enter into SPAs and Sites of Special Scientific Interest (SSSIs),[51] including marine SSSIs,[52] unlike with other protected area categories in Antarctica,[53] has been consistently iterated between 1964[54] and the Madrid Protocol.[55]

The only regime to actively refuse to inscribe areas with no linkages to human interaction is the MAB. This regime has rejected a number of sites, despite their strong biological importance, due to 'the absence of permanent settlements' in the associated buffer zones.[56]

---

44 European Diploma. Annex I. Section I.

45 See Annex V, Article 3 (2)(a).

46 See Article VIII (1) of the 1964 Agreed Measures.

47 See Article VIII (2)(a) of the 1964 Agreed Measures.

48 See Article 7 of Annex V of the Madrid Protocol.

49 See Article VIII (4) (b) of the 1964 Agreed Measures.

50 See Article VIII (2) (b) of the 1964 Agreed Measures.

51 Recommendation XV-10. Antarctic Protected Area System: Establishment of Specially Reserved Areas. In Antarctic Treaty: Report of the Fifteenth Meeting (Paris, 1989). 82. See paragraph 129 in the Report.

52 See Conservation Measure 91-01. (2004) Procedure for According Protection to CEMP Sites.

53 See Annex V, Article 4 (3).

54 Recommendation XV-9. Antarctic Protected Area System: Development of Improved Descriptions and Management Plans for Specially Protected Areas. In Antarctic Treaty: Report of the Fifteenth Meeting (Paris, 1989). 80.

55 Madrid Protocol, Article 3 (4).

56 Archipelago de Revillagigedo and Isla Guadelupe, both in Mexico. UNESCO. (2006). MAB ICC. 19th Session. SC-06/CONF.202/16. Nov 28. 23-24.

B Category II: National Parks

Category II protected areas are classified as 'national parks.' In 2003, 3,881 national parks were recorded globally. National parks represent 3.8% of all protected areas, or 23.6 % (4,413,142 km2) of total protected areas.[57]

The 1994 IUCN classifications of national parks, which are the same as the 1978 IUCN classification on this category, define these areas as being designed for ecosystem protection and tourism. National parks should contain and protect ecosystems that have retained their integrity and exclude any exploitation or occupation inimical to the purposes of the area's designation. For visiting human populations, the national parks should afford spiritual solitude, and educational and recreational opportunities. All of these activities must be conducted in an environmentally and culturally sustainable manner. The management objectives are to protect and perpetuate the natural characteristics of the area (including its geomorphological sites, its biodiversity and associated ecosystems) and scenic areas of national and international significance. The area should be large enough to contain one or more entire ecosystems not materially altered by current human occupation or exploitation.

Within international law, the idea of national parks can be traced to the 1933 Africa Convention. This agreement defined national parks as areas under public control, with clearly delineated boundaries and strict regulation of hunting and extraction activities. The purpose of these areas was for 'the propagation, protection and preservation of wild animal life and wild vegetation, and for the preservation of objects of aesthetic, geological, prehistoric, historical, archaeological, or other scientific interest for the benefit, advantage, and enjoyment of the general public'.[58] Although all settlements ('white' or 'native') were to be controlled to ensure 'as little disturbance as possible,' they were not prohibited outright.[59] The 1940 Western Hemisphere convention largely mirrored these objectives for national parks,[60] but added the restriction (which Argentina objected to)[61] that the resources of national parks shall not be 'subject to exploitation

---

57 Chape, S. (2003). 'Monitoring Global Commitment.' *World Conservation.* 8-9.

58 1933 Africa Convention. Article 2 (1).

59 1933 Africa Convention. Article 4 (1).

60 'Areas established for the protection and preservation of superlative scenery, flora and fauna of national significance which the general public may enjoy and from which it may benefit when placed under public control'.1940 Western Hemisphere Convention. Article I (1). In addition, within national parks, all hunting, killing or capturing of fauna or flora was to be prohibited, unless authorised and supervised by the park authorities, or for duly authorized scientific investigations. Article III.

61 Argentina entered the reservation that, 'Existing resources in national parks may only be exploited for commercial purposes in those regions which, despite their lack of the characteristics necessary to be considered national parks, have been incorporated into the system solely to maintain a uniformity of action in those areas, and when such exploitation will not be

for commercial profit.'[62] The 1968 African convention largely replicated the objectives of the Africa and Western Hemisphere conventions on the designation of national parks.[63] The contemporary regional conventions which also to replicate some of these ideals come from the regimes and protocols designed to facilitate the creation of MPAs. In this regard, the OSPAR,[64] and Helsinki[65] regimes, in addition to the Mediterranean Protocol,[66] all place a high premium on the targeted area being as 'natural' as possible, with low-levels of human induced disturbance.

C *Category III: Natural Monuments*

Category III protected areas are designated as 'natural monuments.' As of 2003, a total of 19,833 natural monuments were recorded globally. This represents 19.4% of all protected areas, or 1.5 % (275,432 km2) of total protected areas.[67] The idea of natural monuments, (also known as natural landmarks) can be traced to the 1940 Western Hemisphere Convention, which defined these areas as,

> Regions, objects, or living species of flora and fauna of aesthetic, historic or scientific interest to which strict protection is given. The purpose of nature monuments is the protection of a specific object, or a species of flora or fauna, by setting aside an area, an object, or a single species, as an inviolate nature monument, except for duly authorized scientific investigations or government inspection.[68]

---

contrary to the general purpose of the law which established them, and the exploitation is sufficient to maintain the principle of regional development according to the needs of each country'.

62 1940 Western Hemisphere Convention. Article III.

63 The 1968 African Convention defined a 'national park' as an area under State control and the boundaries of which may not be altered or any portion alienated except by the competent legislative authority. 2) Exclusively set aside for the propagation, protection, conservation and management of vegetation and wild animals as well as for the protection of sites, landscapes or geological formations of particular scientific or aesthetic value, for the benefit and enjoyment of the general public, and 3) In which the killing, hunting and capture of animals and the destruction or collection of plants are prohibited except for scientific and management purposes and on the condition that such measures are taken under the direction or control of the competent authority. 4) Covering any aquatic environment to which all of the provisions above are applicable.

64 OSPAR Recommendation 2003/3 on a Network of Marine Protected Areas. Appendix 1.

65 Helsinki Commission (2004). *Guidelines for Designating BSPAS.* 2. Guidelines for designating BSPAs

66 Mediterranean Protocol. Article 4. (a)-(c).

67 Chape, S. (2003). 'Monitoring Global Commitment.' *World Conservation.* 8-9.

68 1940 Western Hemisphere Convention. Article I (3).

The later IUCN classifications, whilst retaining the core idea of an area protected because of its specific natural features of rare unique value due to its aesthetic or cultural importance,[69] did not necessarily seek to exclude humans. Rather, in the IUCN category III, it was hoped that the area would deliver benefits (without compromising the integrity of the area) to resident populations.

D Category IV: Habitat/Species Management Areas

'Habitat' is the key areas or factors of the environment, whether natural or modified, needed for species, either migratory,[70] or static,[71] which are connected with the, 'vital biological functions' of the species in question. For example the areas necessary for breeding, nursing, feeding or resting, as well as key areas through which they may transit.[72] The protection of such areas has been recognised as the most critical element for the survival for any endangered species since 1968.[73] The IUCN category system recognises 'habitat/species management areas' as category IV areas. In 2003, 27,641 habitat/species management areas were recorded internationally. These areas represent 27.1% of all protected areas, or 16.1 % (3,022,515 km2) of total protected areas.[74]

Habitat/species management areas were previously denominated as nature conservation reserves, managed nature reserves or wildlife sanctuaries. The term 'Reserves' was originally found in the 1933 Africa Convention.[75] 'National Reserves' were defined in the 1940 Western Hemisphere Convention,[76] and 'special reserves' for the purposes of the 1968 African convention were divided into, game reserves,[77] and 'partial reserves

69 Such as spectacular waterfalls, caves, craters, fossil beds, sand dunes and marine features, along with its unique biodiversity.

70 The Convention on Migratory Species. Article I (g).

71 Resolution No 1. (1989) On the Provisions Relating to the Conservation of Habitats.

72 Note, the additions to the CMS agreement come from the Wadden Sea Seals Agreement. Article I.

73 UNESCO. (1968). Use and Conservation of the Biosphere. (UNESCO, Paris). 151.

74 Chape, S. (2003). 'Monitoring Global Commitment.' *World Conservation.* 8-9.

75 Reserves were defined as areas where the hunting or taking of the natural fauna and flora, exclusive of fish, could only be done for scientific or administrative purposes. 1933 Africa Convention. Article 7 (1).

76 National reserves were defined as, 'Regions established for conservation and utilization of natural resources under government control, on which protection of animal and plant life will be afforded in so far as this may be consistent with the primary purpose of such reserves'. 1940 Western Hemisphere Convention. Article I (2).

77 'Game reserve' shall denote an area: (a) set aside for the conservation, management and propagation of wild animal life and the protection and management of its habitat. (b) within which the hunting, killing or capture of fauna shall be prohibited except by or under the direction or control of the reserve authorities. (c) where settlement and other human activities shall be controlled or prohibited.

or sanctuaries.'[78] In the IUCN context, habitat/species management areas are protected areas managed primarily for conservation through management intervention. They constitute an area of land and/or sea subject to intervention for management purposes so as to ensure the maintenance of habitats and/or to meet the requirements of specific species. Scientific research, monitoring and public education are all important elements to ensuring the viability of these areas. In addition, benefits are to be delivered to people living within the area, to the extent that they are consistent with the other objectives of management. Habitat manipulation, is permissible to achieve conservation. The size of the area is dependent on the habitat requirements of the species to be protected and may range from small to very large.

The strongest international agreement from the perspective of habitat protection is the Convention of Migratory Species and its subsidiary agreements, by which the Parties are obliged to protect the habitat of identified migratory species. Similar commitments are imposed regionally upon the Parties to the Convention on the Conservation of European Wildlife and Habitats, and the 1992 European Habitats Directive. Variations on this obligation have been established in several animal specific conventions (especially fishery related agreements).

E Category V: Multiple Use Areas

According to the IUCN criteria, category V protected areas are protected landscapes and/or seascapes.[79] In 2003, a total of 6,555 protected landscapes/seascapes were recorded internationally. Category V landscapes/seascapes represent 6.4% of all protected areas, or 5.6% (1,056,008 km2) of total protected areas.[80]

Category V areas are managed mainly for conservation and recreation. Category V areas are designed to foster a close relationship between nature and people, with the physical attributes of an area integrated with its associated social, cultural and traditional values. In terms of its natural characteristics, category V areas have landscape values, scenic quality, and possess significant associated habitats and flora and fauna. Such sites must be of international or national significance.[81] Development is not, ipso facto, excluded from such areas. As such, conservation and development projects may become integrated into the area. However, any extraction of resources, including by traditional communities,

---

78 Partial reserve' or 'sanctuary' shall denote an area: (a) set aside to protect characteristic wildlife and especially bird communities, or to protect particularly threatened animal or plant species and especially those listed on the Annex to the [1968 African] Convention, together with the biotopes essential for their survival, (b) in which all other interests and activities shall be subordinated to this end. African Convention (1968). Article III. (c).

79 IUCN. (2002). *Management Guidelines for IUCN Category V Protected Areas.* (IUCN, Gland).

80 Chape, S. (2003). 'Monitoring Global Commitment.' *World Conservation.* 8-9.

81 IUCN. (2002). Management Guidelines for IUCN Category V. *Ibid.* 28.

must be conducted in a carefully planned, participatory, sustainable manner, and the public must be able to enjoy the site.[82] The overriding principle with regard to possible sustainable uses, is that economic activities that do not need to take place within the area should be located outside it. Nevertheless, as a lived in, working landscape, a variety of economic activities are permitted, such as agriculture, forestry, tourism and some forms of industry, commerce and retailing as well as residential areas and some infrastructure. The tests for whether such an activity or use is acceptable within the category Vprotected area is whether it is sustainable, whether it contributes to the aims of the area, and if there are strong reasons for it being retained within the area. If it fails these tests, it should be either redesigned to conform, or taken outside of the site. Accordingly, practices such as farming, fishing and forestry are permissible, but they should be small-scale, traditional forms that support biodiversity and ecosystem concerns and are community-based. Accordingly, the following types of forests would fall outside of the IUCN definitions of category V protected areas. Forests managed for resource protection other than biodiversity (such as for watershed or drinking water protection, avalanche control, firebreaks, windbreaks and/or erosion control), forests primarily used as a community resource (such as for fuelwood) or as a strategic resource (such as for timber supply), forests created by accident and/or forests without clear management objectives (whereby biodiversity protection is not at least equal to other considerations). Plantations typically fail to meet category V areas due to their low value to biodiversity, and minimal provision of the other amenities associated with protected areas.[83]

Within a category V area large scale development, such as mining, should only be accepted if it has been vetted through a full Environmental Impact Assessment process, it meets over-riding national needs and there is no alternative.[84] The meaningful involvement of local people is essential, and the protected area should never be inimical to their long term interests, or designed in isolation from local, regional or possibly even national development and conservation objectives.[85]

Category V areas have been embraced in the 2003 African Convention,[86] the International Tropical Timber Organisation,[87] and indirect application as an option within

---

82 *Ibid.* 23, 39.

83 IUCN (2006). *Forests and Protected Areas: Guidance on the Use of the IUCN Protected Area Management Categories.* (IUCN, Gland). 20-23, 45.

84 IUCN. (2002). *Management Guidelines for IUCN Category V Protected Areas.* (IUCN, Gland). 40-41, 57-70.

85 *Ibid.* 40.

86 And its strong emphasis on ' sustainable development' and the mix of economic, social, [and] cultural' considerations. See 2003 African Convention. Preamble and Article V.

87 Although the ITTO has recognised the value of totally protected areas, they have argued that such areas alone are not necessarily successful in conserving appropriate amounts of biodiversity (especially where it is migratory or transitory), or meeting the needs of local inhabitants (who need 'tangible economic assets'). Accordingly, a midway point is needed

the European Diploma.[88] However, the best exemplar of category V areas is with MAB biosphere reserves.[89]

The overarching objective of a biosphere reserve is 'sustainable development.' The emphasis on sustainable development is not only part of newer conservation conventions authorizing the establishment of protected areas, such as the 2003 African Convention,[90] it was also the underlying theme of the international community in environmental and development debates, from the 1992 Earth Summit, to the World Summit on Sustainable Development and the Millennium Goals. The essence of biosphere reserve concept is that people are not excluded from the protected area, and are an intricate part of the management and conservation of the area and its surroundings, therefore fostering the achievement of sustainable development.[91] As such the MAB is one of the few regimes that does not necessarily view concentrations of humans around the core zone of protected area to be inimical to the goals of species and ecosystems protection.[92]

---

in a number of instances, such as with 'sustainably managed production forests' where both conservation and utilisation objectives are met in the same area, by some areas being specifically related to conservation, whilst others timber extraction, which still protects biodiversity objectives. ITTO. (1993). *ITTO Guidelines on the Conservation of Biological Diversity in Tropical Production Forests.* (ITTO, Yokohama, Policy Development Series 5). 3-4. Note, this idea has also be embraced by a number of commentators. See Kramar, R. (ed). *Last Stand: Protected Areas and the Defence of Tropical Biodiversity.* (Oxford University Press, Oxford).

88 Accordingly, all the land uses (including agriculture, forestry, tourism, leisure activities) must be clearly indicated an appropriately zoned. Any permanent human occupation and socio-economic activities must be conceived in such a way as to uphold the principles of sustainable development and they must not damage the integrity of the natural and cultural values of the protected area. Thus, hunting and fishing may be tolerated providing that it is subject to a strict regulation and supervision to avoid weakening the animal population. Finally, public access must be authorised and regulated and supported by reception centres and educational facilities. European Diploma. Annex I. Section II.

89 IUCN. (2002). *Management Guidelines for Category V. Ibid.* 30.

90 2003 African Convention. Article IV and XIV. The 2003 Convention built on this area on the ideals of the 1968 Convention before it. African Convention (1968). Article XIV.

91 UNESCO. (2002). *Biosphere Reserves: Special Places for People and Nature.* (UNESCO, Paris). 17.

92 MAB. (2000). 16th Session of the ICC Bureau. SC-00/CONF.208/13. 17. UNESCO. (2001). MAB ICC Bureau Meeting. SC/-01/CONF.211/13. Apr 10. 21. UNESCO. (2003). ICC Bureau Meeting. SC/-03/CONF.217/14. July 30. UNESCO. (2002). 17th Session of the ICC Bureau. SC-02/CONF.201/11. Apr 12. 17. Cape West Coast in South Africa MAB. (2000). 16th Session of the ICC Bureau. SC-00/CONF.208/13. 21. Mornington Peninsular very close to Melbourne centre. UNESCO. (2002). ICC Bureau Meeting. SC-02/CONF.210/10. 9

Despite the MAB ideals being characterized in recent years as a 'new paradigm for protected areas,'[93] its roots extend back to 1968.[94] Nevertheless, support for the MAB approach on this question intensified in the 1990s in the wake of the 1992 Earth Summit,[95] the 1995 Seville Strategy[96] and the 2002 World Summit on Sustainable Development.[97] The sustainable development objective is embodied in many protected areas schemes by the division of a biosphere into a core area (which may actually be a higher level protected area, such as one within the categories I to IV)[98] surrounded by a buffer and transition zone. Whilst the core area seeks to achieve conservation objectives, the buffer zone seeks to further development and demonstration values (such as research and monitoring).[99] The objective of development (which is 'socio-culturally and ecologically sustainable' and consistent with the protection of the core area)[100] whilst largely omitted in the original 1974 MAB Criteria,[101] has come to be a defining feature of what a biosphere reserve is, and how it differs from other protected schemas.[102]

Within the MAB framework, it is important to note that the core area is preserved, and not subject to the same type of activities as in the buffer and transition zones.[103] This point has been emphasized with both new applications,[104] including some which have

---

93 CBD Secretariat. (2004). *Biodiversity Issues for Consideration in the Planning, Establishment and Management of Protected Area Sites and Networks.* (CBD Technical Series No 15). 14-23. McNeely, J. (1984). 'Protected Areas Are Adapting to New Realities.' In McNeely, J. (ed). *National Parks, Conservation and Development.* (Smithsonian, Washington). 1-10. Pearce, F. (2001). 'The People Versus Nature.' *New Scientist.* May 12. 12.

94 Droste, B. (1984). 'How UNESCO's Man and the Biosphere Programme is Contributing to Human Welfare.' In McNeely, J. (ed). *National Parks, Conservation and Development.* (Smithsonian, Washington). 689, 690.

95 UNESCO. (1998). *Biosphere Reserves: Myth or Reality?.* (UNESCO, Paris). 3.

96 The Seville Strategy identified BRs as, 'sites of excellence to explore and demonstrate approaches to conservation and sustainable development on a regional scale,' The Statutory Framework of the World Network of Biosphere Reserves. Article 3.

97 UNESCO. (2002). 17th Session of the ICC Bureau. SC-02/CONF.201/11. Apr 12. 14-15. UNESCO. (2004). 18th Session of the ICC Bureau. SC-04/CONF.204/14. Jan 11. 3. UNESCO. (2002). 17th Session of the ICC Bureau. SC-02/CONF.201/11. Apr 12. 2.

98 UNESCO. (2002). Biosphere Reserves: Special Places for People and Nature. (UNESCO, Paris). 161-162.

99 The Statutory Framework of the World Network of Biosphere Reserves. Article 3.

100 Ibid Article 3 (2).

101 UNESCO (1974). *Criteria and Guidelines for the Choice and Establishment of Biosphere Reserves* (UNESCO, Paris MAB Report No 22). For comment, see UNESCO. (2002). *Biosphere Reserves: Special Places for People and Nature.* (UNESCO, Paris). 21.

102 UNESCO. (1998). *Biosphere Reserves: Myth or Reality?.* (UNESCO, Paris). 8-9.

103 Seville Strategy. Objective IV.1.

104 Toliara in Madagascar. UNESCO. (2003). ICC Bureau Meeting. SC/-03/CONF.217/14. July 30. 10.

been deferred until this issue is settled,[105] and sites re-examined in the Periodic Review.[106] Inadequate protection of core areas has resulted in Parties being asked to rectify their omissions.[107] With regard to human interference within the core area of a biosphere reserve, although the MAB programme, generally, does not advocate a 'closed jar' approach to conservation, whereby humans are sealed off from natural areas, it does recommend an overall, 'gradation of human interventions.'[108] With regard to core areas, this means that although human settlements may be established in both the transition and the buffer zones,[109] they should not be permitted in the core zone.[110] Nevertheless, humans should be involved in the other two zones. Indeed, the governing body of the MAB has recommended that while an area without human habitation may be suitable as a protected area with a high level classification, it should be considered to be unsuitable for classification as a biosphere reserve.[111]

The Ramsar Convention also presents a type of protected area regime, which seeks to ensure the conservation of wetlands in conjunction with those who live in close proximity. This embodies the Convention's emphasis on 'wise use,'[112] which seeks to ensure the maintenance of the ecological characteristics of wetlands, which is to be achieved through the implementation of ecosystem approaches, within the context of sustainable development.' Within this definition, two sub-themes are important. The first of these themes is 'sustainable utilization,' which was earlier defined as, 'human use of a wetland so that it may yield the greatest continuous benefit to present generations while maintain-

105 Red River Delta in Vietnam. UNESCO. (2003). ICC Bureau Meeting. SC/-03/CONF.217/14. July 30. 16. Cat ba in Vietnam. UNESCO. (2003). ICC Bureau Meeting. SC-02/CONF.210/10. Jan 7. 16.

106 El Cielo in Mexico. UNESCO. (2003). ICC Bureau Meeting. SC-02/CONF.210/10. Jan 7. 21.

107 Picos de Europa. UNESCO. (2003). ICC Bureau Meeting. SC-02/CONF.210/10. Jan 7. 16. Redes in Spain. UNESCO. (2001). ICC Bureau Meeting. SCI/-01/CONF.217/8. Dec 12, 2. 14.

108 The Statutory Framework of the World Network of Biosphere Reserves. Article 4 (1).

109 *Ibid* Article 4 (7).

110 UNESCO. (2002). *Biosphere Reserves: Special Places for People and Nature.* (UNESCO, Paris). 17. Maya in Guatemala. UNESCO. (2001) ICC Bureau Meeting. SC-01/CONF.217/8. Dec 12. 21.

111 Yathong, Macquarie and Prince Regent Islands of Australia. UNESCO. (2003). ICC Bureau Meeting. SC/-03/CONF.217/14. July 30. 18.

112 The Parties shall, 'formulate and implement their planning so as to promote the conservation of the wetlands included in the List, and as far as possible the wise use of wetlands in their territory'. Ramsar. Article 3.1. Note, the wise use principle inscribed in Article 3.1 of the Convention in 1971, and its definition and application by the Conference of the Contracting Parties, have been established and have evolved completely independently from the so-called 'wise use movement' that has emerged in recent years in North America. The use of the same term does not necessarily indicate that there is a commonality of understanding and/or purpose.

ing its potential to meet the needs and aspirations of future generations.'[113] 'Natural properties of the ecosystem' was defined as 'those physical, biological or chemical components, such as soil, water, plants, animals and nutrients, and the interactions between them.'[114] Although the contours of the wise use definition were revisited in 1990,[115] 1993,[116] and 2005,[117] and the concept has come to embrace a wide variety of considerations,[118] the core of the principle remains that the natural values of the system may be utilised by humanity, so long as the overall system is conserved. For example, the Ramsar Principles and Guidelines for Integrated Coastal Zone Management seek to bring together a multiplicity of users, stakeholders and decision makers in the coastal zone in order to secure more effective ecosystem management while achieving economic development and intra and inter-generational equity through the application of sustainability principles.[119]

The final agreement of note in this category of mixed regimes is the Antarctic Treaty. The parties to this regime possess a category of specially managed areas (ASMAs) within their protected overall area schema. The scope of these areas was initially discussed by the Consultative Parties in 1987 before being adopted in 1989.[120] ASMAs were subsequently incorporated into the 1991 Madrid Protocol,[121] and were finally operationalised in 2004[122] and 2005.[123] The basic idea is that a strong management plan is

---

113 Resolution 9.1. Additional Scientific and Technical Guidance for Implementing the Ramsar Wise Use Concept. (2005, Kampala). Annex A. Paragraph 22.

114 Recommendation 3.3. Wise Use of Wetlands. Annex. Definition of Wise Use. (1987, Regina).

115 Recommendation 4.10. Guidelines on the Implementation of the Wise Use Concept. (1990, Montreux).

116 Additional Guidance for the Implementation of the Wise Use Concept. Annexed to Resolution 5.6. Wise Use of Wetlands (1993, Kushiro).

117 Resolution 9.1. Additional Scientific and Technical Guidance. *Ibid.* 22.

118 The Guidelines called for the establishment of national wetland policies, which should include many of the basics of what is now recognised as good management practices, such as maintaining the ecological integrity of sites, institutional organisation (legal protection and policy co-ordination) for sites, adequate manager support, identification of wetlands suitable for inclusion, monitoring and threat mitigation, local involvement (especially indigenous peoples), public education and utilisation of the precautionary principle. Recommendation 4.10. Guidelines for the Implementation of the Wise Use Concept. Annex. Guidelines for the Implementation of the Wise Use Concept of the Convention.

119 Resolution 8.4. Principles for Incorporating Wetland Issues Into Integrated Coastal Zone Management. (2002, Valencia).

120 Recommendation XV-11. Antarctic Protected Area System: Establishment of Multiple Use Planning Areas: Report of the Fifteenth Meeting (Paris, 1989). 84.

121 See Article 4 of Annex V of the Madrid Protocol.

122 These were ASMA No 2, McMurdo Dry Valleys, and ASMA No 3, Capen Dension. See Antarctic Treaty: Report of the Twenty-Seventh Meeting. (Cape Town. 2004). Measure 1, at 39.

formulated for ecologically important areas, buttressed by clear zoning so that core areas exist within a broader protected regime. Within the buffer zone, the activities that pose potential risks require careful management, so as to not to detract from the values for which the area was designated.[124] Given that the area is actively used, permits to enter the area (unlike the possible core areas within them) are not required.

F Category VI: Managed Resource Area

Category VI areas are sites that are considered to be managed resources, utilized primarily for sustainable use. In 2003, 4,132 managed resource protected areas were recorded globally. This represents 4.0% of all protected areas, or 23.3% (4,377,091 km2) of total protected areas.[125] Category VI areas should be built predominantly on natural conditions, with little modification, as the basis for sustainable livelihoods. The dominant land uses will involve activities such as hunting and gathering, grazing and management of natural resources. The objective is to protect and maintain the biological diversity and other natural values of the area in the long term. The natural resource base must not be alienated from other land use purposes that would be detrimental to the areas biodiversity, and sound management practices must ensure sustainable production purposes. At least two thirds of the area should be in, and is planned to remain in, a natural condition. Although it may contain limited areas of modified ecosystems, large scale human activities, such as modern agriculture or commercial plantations should not be included, if they may compromise the long-term long term natural values. Thus, if the objective is to include a forest as a category VI area, at least two-thirds of the area should be in its natural state, large commercial plantations should not be included, and a management authority must be in place.[126]

3 Conclusion

The CBD has given the international community a broad definition of what a protected area is. However, there is no final definition for protected areas, and there is no agreed international framework for all protected area. This diversity of definitions, both between and often within the various regimes has resulted in a substantial amount of confusion over the thinking surrounding what, how and why a protected area is in existence. Such

---

123 Measure 3. (2005). Antarctic Specially Managed Areas: Designations and Management Plans. Report of the 28th Consultative meeting. (Stockholm, 2005). This encompassed Deception Island.

124 See Antarctic Treaty: Fourteenth Meeting. (Rio de Janeiro, 1987). Paragraphs 91-95.

125 Chape, S. (2003). 'Monitoring Global Commitment.' *World Conservation.* 8-9.

126 IUCN (2006). *Forests and Protected Areas: Guidance on the Use of the IUCN Protected Area Management Categories.* (IUCN, Gland). 22.

difficulties have substantively limited the ability for a coherent international regime that encompasses all regimes to be developed. To help, in part, resolve such difficulties, the IUCN has developed a 6 level classification scheme, which can, theoretically, encompass all types of protected areas. The 6 levels range from strict reserves with no human interference, through to areas which allow types of relatively large scale human activities.

Although some international regimes have begun to utilize the IUCN classifications, many have not. If the regimes in question and the sovereign parties were given a greater buy-in into the classifications for the sites under their auspice, a level of robustness could be added to the classification process could be made. This would allow a greater development of alternative paradigms and management options for protected areas in the international arena, and would avoid otherwise exclusionary debates which may limit the development of a number of types of protected areas, in a world where the original human exclusion values, have increasingly limited utility. Finally, such an adoption would allow a number of regimes which are already, in effect, operating protected area classifications within the IUCN categories, to be fully synchronised with both the categories in general, and other regimes which have similar goals, in particular. Of note, category I and II regimes are already well entrenched in numerous national, regional and international regimes. Category IV is consistently practiced within regimes such as the CMS and Bern Convention, whilst category V is prevalent within the MAB, Ramsar and Antarctic regime.

Chapter III

VALUES

1 The International Facilitation of the Values of Protected Areas

This chapter pertains to the reasons that protected areas are created. Ultimately, these reasons are the ascribed 'values' that are attributed to protected areas. It is with these values that the overlap between philosophy and law becomes most prominent, as countries seek to reflect their contemporary and historical justifications of what they deem most important for the preservation of protected areas. Fundamentally, this discussion is not a science. In many instances, values overlap, conflict or (and most commonly) lack certainty. Moreover, the parameters around what values are important for one country in this area, are not always the same for another country, and within each individual country, the parameters may change over time. Despite these caveats, the international community has, through its different forums, begun to develop some clear recognition of the values which reflect the collective interpretations of why protected areas are important.

2 Cumulative Values

Any potential site may encompass a number of values. Different regimes have their own practices in this area. Thus, whereas some regimes require that a site meets all of the prescribed values (typically identified as a form of inscription criteria) they are trying to protect, more commonly, protected areas regimes only require the nominated site meet only one value. Despite a site only needing to meet one value to be inscribed on a list, it may actually have a number of possible values. This situation is well demonstrated with the WHC, by which although a natural site may be inscribed if it meets only one of the four criteria,[1] the practice is that most sites are usually inscribed for meeting at least two criteria.[2] Although the WHC has rejected the idea that there is a 'greatest of the greatest' which can be derived from the WHC List,[3] it is notable that only a few sites are listed with all four natural criteria being fulfilled. Among these are the Wet Tropics of Queensland, the Tasmanian Wilderness and Shark Bay in Western Australia, the Amistad in Costa Rica/Panama, the Three Parallel Rivers in China, the

---

1 *Operational Guidelines.* 2002 Edn. Paragraph 44.

2 Ibid. Paragraph 45.

3 UNESCO. (1984). 8th Session of the WHC. SC/84/CONF.004/9. Nov 2, 1984. pp 6. UNESCO. (2001). 25th Session of the WHC. WHC-01/CONF.208/24. Feb 8, 2002. 69.

Galapagos in Ecuador, the Rio Platano in Honduras, Gunung Mulu in Malaysia, Te Wahipounamu in New Zealand, Lake Baikal and the Volcanoes of Kamchatka in the Russian Federation, the Vallee de Mai Nature Reserve in the Seychelles, Canaima in Venezuela and Yellowstone, the Grand Canyon and the Great Smokey Mountains in the United States. These sites are typically seen as the first class, 'excellent examples of natural heritage sites that meet the criteria for inclusion on the World Heritage List'.[4]

3 The Wide and Evolving Spectrum

There are dozens of possible reasons for why certain areas should be protected. Most of the conventions in this area recognize a very wide spectrum of values in their preamble. For example, the Madrid Protocol proclaims that protected areas in the Antarctic must reflect, 'outstanding values' with regard to, 'environmental, scientific, historic, aesthetic or wilderness values, any combination of those values, or ongoing or planned scientific research'.[5] This type of general articulation is not uncommon. Many such conventions have not developed clear rules of interpretation related to each possible value. Although some regimes have developed clear rules in this area, many of the others work in a generic sense, through which underlying values are either difficult to identify or blurred between categories. For example, although there are no MPAs under the Antarctic Treaty, marine sites of special scientific interest are permissible, but in practice the scientific focus in these areas is upon the wildlife. Thus, although it is protected for its scientific value, it benefits are clearly to the wildlife, but wildlife is not a recognised category as such, under sites inscribed for scientific value.[6]

It is also important to note that the values for why areas are protected are not static. They are, as the WHC Special Meeting on Outstanding Universal Value concluded, 'evolving'.[7] Sometimes this evolution is through a simple tweaking of the emphasis of existing rules such as with the continual re-writing of a conventions guidelines, as

---

4 UNESCO. (1978). 2nd Session of the WHC. CC-78/CONF.010/3. Sep 5, 1978. pp.4.

5 See Annex V, Article 3 (1).

6 Thus, the Cape Sherreff site (reknown for its large and diverse populations of seabirds and pinnipeds), has been designated, for its valuable long-term studies undertaken on the islands and surrounding waters, and the vulnerability of these studies to accidental or wilful interference. Accordingly, no killing, taking or disturbing of the biodiversity, or entry to the site where the habitats are present, is permissible. See Conservation Measure 91-02. (2004). Protection of the Cape Shirreff CEMP Site. The Seal Islands, are another, very similar, recognized CEMP site. See Conservation Measure 91-03. (2004). Protection of the Seal Islands CEMP Site.

7 UNESOC. (2005). Assessment and Conclusion of the Kazan Meeting. WHC-05/29. COM/9.

with the WHC.[8] Even though the values may be evolving, basic issues over exactly what is 'outstanding universal value' are often far from clear. Accordingly, in 2006 the Committee called for the creation of two compendiums, largely based upon past WHC Committee practice, to show how Outstanding Universal Value has been dealt with in a number of different situations.[9]

In other instances, the emphasis of traditional values may change. For example, with the Ramsar Convention, ecological values of habitat types of wetlands have come to equal, if not overshadow the original emphasis on listing criteria of waterfowl populations.[10] An alternative way of showing this, has happened with the IMO, under which the primary reasons for protection, are now considered secondary. For example, scientific and educational values were the reasons Great Barrier was originally protected from international shipping in 1971, whereas when the site was revisited and enlarged decades later, the emphasis was clearly upon its biological and ecological values.[11] In other instances, new values are added, such as with the Antarctic regime, whereby the protected area justifications were widened to clearly include a new subdivision of ecology,

---

8 The Convention permits the Committee to define the criteria on the basis of which a property belonging to the world heritage may be included in ... the WH List. WHC Article 11 (5). See for example, *Operational Guidelines for the Implementation of the WHC.* CC-77/ CONF.001/8 Rev. Oct 20, 1977. *Operational Guidelines for the Implementation of the WHC* WHC/2 Revised. Oct, 1980. *Operational Guidelines for the Implementation of the WHC.* WHC/2 Revised. Nov, 1983. UNESCO. (1988). 12th Session of the WHC. SC-88/CONF.001/ 13. Dec 23, 1988. 5. UNESCO. (1992). 16th Session of the WHC. WHC-92/CONF.002/12. Dec 14, 1992. 43-44. UNESCO. (1996). 20th Session of the WHC. WHC-96/CONF.201/21. Mar 10, 1997. 77-79.

9 Decision 30 COM 9.

10 For the changing criteria, see Recommendations adopted by the International Conference on the Conservation of Wetlands and Waterfowl at Heiligenhafen, Federal Republic of Germany, 6 December 1974. Annex II. Recommendations for Criteria to be used in identifying Wetlands of International Importance. Recommendation 1.4. Criteria for Identifying Wetlands of International Importance. (1980, Cagliari). Recommendation 2.3. Action Points for Priority Attention. (1984, Groningen). Recommendation 3.1. Criteria for Identifying Wetlands of International Importance. (1987, Regina). Recommendation 4.2. Criteria for Identifying Wetlands of International Importance. (1990, Montreux). Resolution 6.3. Review of the Ramsar Criteria. (1996, Brisbane).

11 IMO General Resolution. 232 (VII). Amendments to the 1954 Convention For the Prevention of Pollution of the Sea by Oil, 1954, as Amended in 1969, Concerning Protection of the Great Barrier Reef. Through a reinterpretation of the words 'nearest land' the Reef came to obtain a greater degree of protection associated with the Annexes of MARPOL special areas. Annex 6. Guidelines for the Designation of Special Areas Under MARPOL 73/78 and Guidelines for the Identification and Designation of Particularly Sensitive Sea Areas. MEPC (2001). Report of the MEPC on its 46th Session. MEPC 46/23. Sections 4.4.15 to 4.4.17.

namely, outstanding geological, glaciological and/or geo-morphological areas.[12] Another example is whereby entirely new categories are created, such as with landscape values, or 'mixed' (cultural and natural) heritage combinations, as with the WHC. Alternately, entirely new conventions, such as the European Landscape Convention may evolve. A final example of 'new values' is the inclusion, or recognition of the non-anthropocentric 'intrinsic value' of protected areas,[13] although no regime has yet attempted to apply such values.

Accordingly, the best way to view the overall situation with regard to values of inscription is that it is cannot be viewed through a coherent, all inclusive schema, by which all international instruments share or interpret the values equally. Rather, there is a very wide spectrum of values for why an area may be protected. These are often weighted differently in each international or regional instrument. The following is the primary collection of such values. They are in no order of precedence.

4 Confidence Building

Protected areas which spill over from national boundaries can be strong tools for confidence building between States. The best example of such co-operative values, in terms of enhanced ecology, management and even general security, is with regards to Trans-boundary Protected Areas (TBPAs). TBPAs are particularly useful for large ecological areas which go over national boundaries, such as barrier reef systems, large scale river basins, large forest areas, critical habitat for endangered species, MPAs and mountain ranges. Mountain ranges are the majority of the ecosystems involved with TBPAs.[14] In such situations, States often agree to cooperate with each other for the benefit of the protected area. Such cooperation also has the value of confidence building between countries. A good example of this value (there are also worst examples where States refused such co-operation)[15] was the commitment that came from the 1974 Brezhnev-Nixon Summit in Moscow, from which the super-powers agreed to cooperate on, inter alia, shared protected areas, as they later came to do within forums such as the WHC.[16] Contemporary examples involves the transboundary peace park in the

---

12 See Antarctic Treaty: Report of the Fourteenth Meeting. (Rio de Janeiro, 1987). Paragraph 88. Annex V, Article 3 (2)(b) and (f). Recommendation XV-10. Antarctic Protected Area System: Establishment of Specially Reserved Areas. In Antarctic Treaty: Report of the Fifteenth Meeting (Paris, 1989). 82. See paragraph 129.

13 See Article 3 of the Madrid Protocol, and the preamble of the Bern Convention.

14 IUCN. (2002). *A Global Overview of Mountain Protected Areas on the World Heritage List.* (IUCN, Gland). 11.

15 Such as with Brazil and Argentina, which both rejected suggestions that their buttressed parks (Iguaçu & Iguaçu) be joined to form one ecological unit.9th Session (1985) of the WHC, at 7. 10th Session (1986) of the WHC, at 4.

16 11th Session (1989) of the WHC, at 18.

demilitarized (protected area) zone on the border of Iraq and Kuwait,[17] or the MAB Marine Peace Park initiative between the Republic of Korea and the Democratic People's Republic of Korea.[18]

5 Science

Protected areas often provide perfect conditions for scientific research, both in terms of the topic of study and the surrounding environment, which often maintains perfect and undisturbed places of study.[19] Due to such importance, practically every regime which creates protected areas, including even the most preserved (such as strict nature reserves or wilderness areas) seek to facilitate exceptions for approved scientific research, over all other human activities.

Scientific research may range from the strictly local, through to the global. For example scientific research within the protected areas of the Arctic is highly regarded in terms of the problems of climate change and long range air pollutants.[20] The recognition of the scientific value of protected areas has been emphasized in the Western Hemisphere Convention,[21] the 1968 African Convention,[22] (and its 2003 successor),[23] the Ramsar Convention,[24] the Bern Convention,[25] and its associated Habitats Directive,[26] the European Diploma,[27] the Convention on Migratory Species, and its subsidiary agreements including, inter alia, ACCOBAMS,[28] ASCOBANS[29] AEWA,[30] and the

17 See Alsidirawi, F. (2004). 'Establishing a Transboundary Peace Park in the Demilitarized Zone on the Kuwait/Iraqi Border'. 14(1). *Parks.* 48-56.

18 UNESCO. (2006). MAB ICC. 19th Session. SC-06/CONF.202/16. Nov 28. 13.

19 See 'Scientific Values of National Parks.' In Adams, A. (ed). *First World Conference on National Parks.* (US Department of the Interior, Washington). 62-98. Godfrey-Smith, W. (1979). 'The Value of Wilderness'. *Environmental Ethics.* 1: 309-319.

20 Conservation of Arctic Flora and Fauna. (2002). *Protected Areas of the Arctic: Conserving a Full Range of Values.* (CAFF Secretariat, in Department of Foreign Affairs, Canada). 21-22.

21 1940 Western Hemisphere Convention. Article VI.

22 African Convention (1968). Article VI (2) and XII.

23 2003 African Convention. Article XII (1) (c). and XVIII.

24 The Ramsar agreement contained the broad commitment for parties to encourage research and the exchange of data and publications regarding wetlands and their flora and fauna. Ramsar. Article 4.3. Accordingly, since this point, the Ramsar has directed and coordinated scientific research with regards to both wetlands, and key species (primarily waterfowl).

25 Bern Convention. Article 11 (1)(b).

26 Habitats Directive. Article 18.

27 European Diploma, Article 1.

28 ACCOBAMS. Article II.3.d.

29 ASCOBANS. Preamble, and Action Plan. Part 2.

30 AEWA. Action Plan. Point 5. Resolution 2.4. International Implementation Priorities. MOP 2 of the AEWA (Bonn, 2002). Available from the AEWA Secretariat.

ACAP;[31] the CBD,[32] and with MPAs regimes in the Mediterranean[33] and Caribbean,[34] and the Baltic.[35] Likewise, the importance of the 'scientific point of view' permeates every category of the WHC natural site criteria.[36]

Despite the common repetition of this goal, only two regimes have actively developed regimes around the scientific value of protected areas. The first is the MAB programme, which aside running promotions such as Young Scientist awards,[37] when originally launched, placed the scientific value of biosphere reserves, above their conservation or utilisation values.[38] Although the scientific values of biosphere reserves are now held equal with their other core justifications, an overall World Network of Biosphere Reserves has been created through which States are expected to co-operatively participate through, inter alia, information exchange on environmental topics relating to global, regional and thematic scientific issues via research, monitoring, environmental education and training.[39] The ultimate objective of the World Network is to help provide scientists, policy makers and the public with access to existing scientific data and facilitate the coordination of integrated biological monitoring and the sharing of management experience for sustainable development. Although there are a number of technical difficulties in the area,[40] the MAB regime has remained strongly committed to the centrality of scientific research. Accordingly, when accepting new sites,[41] or periodically

31 ACAP. Preamble and Article III.d.

32 CBD. Decision VII/28. Protected Areas. Annex. Section IV.

33 Mediterranean Protocol. Articles 4. (d), 16, 17 and 20. See also Annex 1, section 1.B.3. of the Protocol.

34 Caribbean Protocol. Articles 4(2). And 17.

35 OSPAR Recommendation 2003/3 on a Network of Marine Protected Areas. Appendix 2 Practical criteria/considerations. Section 6.

36 WHC Article 2.

37 MAB. (2000). 16th Session of the ICC Bureau. SC-00/CONF.208/13. 6.

38 UNESCO. (2002). *Biosphere Reserves: Special Places for People and Nature.* (UNESCO, Paris). 19. Bridgewater, p. (2002). 'Biosphere Reserves: A Network for Conservation and Sustainability'. 12 (3) *Parks.* 15.

39 The Statutory Framework of the World Network of Biosphere Reserves. Articles 2, 3 (3), 4 (7), 7 & 8. Also, see the Seville Strategy. Objective III.1. Seville + 5 Recommendations. Available from MAB at < http://www.unesco.org/mab/mabicc/2000/eng/SevilleAction.htm> Recommendation 1.

40 Such as the limits of the database, inadequate scientific support in places etc. UNESCO. (1998). *Biosphere Reserves: Myth or Reality ?' (UNESCO, Paris).* 19-23. The goal in this area is articulated in Seville Strategy. Objective IV.2. UNESCO. (2001). MAB ICC Bureau Meeting. SC/-01/CONF.211/13. Apr 10. 15.

41 Yading in China. UNESCO. (2003). ICC Bureau Meeting. SC/-03/CONF.217/14. July 30. 9. Golija in Yugoslavia. UNESCO. (2001). ICC Bureau Meeting. SCI/-01/CONF.217/8. Dec 12, 2. 15.

reviewing existing ones,[42] the Committee has consistently emphasized the importance of enhancing the scientific research in these areas.

The second regime which has placed a premium on scientific research in protected areasis that relating to Antarctica. The emphasis upon international scientific co-operation has always been at the heart of the Antarctic Treaty System,[43] and aside the general ongoing support for scientific endeavours in the Antarctic,[44] this activity has grown in importance, in its linkage with environmental problems. This can be seen clearly with the Madrid Protocol[45] by which the Parties direct support into the study of global environmental problems,[46] such as climatic change and ozone depletion in particular.[47]

The most direct manifestation of this long term support for scientific research within protected areas in the Antarctic, is the creation, since 1964, of a particular class of protected area, justified because of their 'outstanding scientific interest'.[48] Twenty seven years later, the Madrid Protocol reiterated that, 'areas of particular interest to on-going or planned scientific research' could be suitably protected areas in the Antarctic.[49] These areas, which are known as Sites of Special Scientific Interest (SSSI), are protected due to their scientific values and facilitation of scientific research, rather than their

42 El Cielo in Mexico. UNESCO. (2003). ICC Bureau Meeting. SC-02/CONF.210/10. Jan 7. 21. Bogeda in China. UNESCO. (2001). ICC Bureau Meeting. SCI/-01/CONF.217/8. Dec 12. 18.

43 See Articles 2 and 3 of the Antarctic Treaty.

44 See for example, Resolution 2. Support of the ATCM for the International Polar Year. Final Report of the XXVI ATCM, Madrid, 2003. 288.

45 The 'the unique opportunities Antarctic offers for scientific monitoring of and research on processes of global as well as regional importance' were reiterated as clear priorities in need of support in the Madrid Protocol. See the preamble and Articles 3 (3) and 6 (1)(a) of the Madrid Protocol.

46 Recommendation XV-14. Promotion of International Scientific Co-operation: A Declaration. In Final Report of the 15th Antarctic Treaty Meeting (Paris, 1989). 89. Recommendation XV-15. Promotion of International Scientific Co-operation. Also from the 15th Meeting at 92.

47 Declaration on the Ozone Layer and Climate Change. 15th Meeting *ibid.* 119.

48 See Article VIII (1) of the 1964 Agreed Measures. See also Recommendation XV-9. Antarctic Protected Area System: Development of Improved Descriptions and Management Plans for Specially Protected Areas. Fifteenth Meeting *ibid.* 80.

49 See Annex V, Article 3 (2. (e).

conservation values (although they are closely related).[50] SSSIs have also come to encompass marine sites.[51]

6 Economic

It is recommended under the CBD, that each Contracting Party shall, as far as possible and as appropriate, adopt economically and socially sound measures that act as incentives for the conservation and sustainable use of components of biological diversity.[52] Accordingly, the Parties to the CBD have undertaken a number of studies on the economic valuation of biodiversity,[53] and have encouraged all the signatories to ensure adequate incorporation of, 'market and non-market values of biological diversity into plans, policies and programmes'[54] at both local, regional and international levels, where appropriate.[55] Internalization of the economic costs of environmental considerations, so that markets are not distorted, is a foremost consideration in this area.[56] Parties also agreed to, inter alia, identify, study, and voluntarily confront such perverse incentives.[57]

The core of such thinking is that all biological resources should reflect their total economic value (TEV), and perverse incentives, which distort that value, should not be encouraged. The TEV is the cumulative economic values of all aspects of biodiversity, not just the obvious consumptive values. The end result for much biodiversity and its related ecosystems is that its TEV should lend itself to economic justifications for conservation, not blunt traditionally consumptive utilization.[58] For example, the TEV of a forest is not just the value of its extracted timber, but rather, what its value as selectively and sustainably extracted timber, in addition to the economic values of

---

50 See Annex V, Article 3 (2. (e) of the Madrid Protocol. See also, Recommendation VII-3. Sites of Special Scientific Interest. In Report of the Seventh Meeting. (1972, Wellington). 56. Recommendation VIII-3. Sites of Special Scientific Interest. In Report of the Eighth Meeting. (1975, Oslo). 53.

51 Recommendation XIV-6. Marine Sites of Special Scientific Interest. In Antarctic Treaty: Report of the Fourteenth Meeting (Rio de Janeiro, 1987). 119.

52 Article 11.

53 Recommendation II/9. Economic Valuation of Biodiversity. UNEP/CBD/COP/3/3. pp. 47. Decision IV/10. Measures for Implementing the CBD. UNEP/CBD/COP/4/27.pp.115. Decision V/15. Incentive Measures. UNEP/CBD/COP/5/23.pp.137. Decision V/3. Progress Report on the Implementation of… Coastal Biological Diversity. UNEP/CBD/COP/5/23. pp.74.

54 Decision III/18. Incentive Measures. UNEP/CBD/COP/3/38. 101.

55 Decision VI/15. Incentive Measures. UNEP/CBD/COP/6/20.pp.179. Annex I. Recommendation VII/9. Incentive Measures. UNEP/CBD/COP/6/4. pp.75.

56 Ibid. Annex I. Paragraph 16, and Annex II.

57 Incentive Measures. UNEP/CBD/COP/7/L33. Recommendation IX/9. Elaboration of Proposals for the Application of Ways and Means to Remove or Mitigate Perverse Incentives. UNEP/CBD/COP/7/4. pp.81.

58 Parlange, M. (1999). 'Eco-Nomics.' *New Scientist.* Feb 6. 42-45.

non-timber forest products, biodiversity, genetic information, forest land conversion, watershed protection, carbon storage and sequestration, tourism and recreational values, amenity values, option values and existence values. For example, one of the most comprehensive studies to date which examined the marketed and non-marketed economic values associated with eight Mediterranean countries, found that timber and fuel-wood generally accounted for less than a third of the TEV of forests in each country. Indeed, values associated with non-wood forest products, recreation, hunting, watershed protection, carbon sequestration and passive uses accounted for between 25% and 96% of the TEV.[59] Another example is with coral reefs.[60] Initial studies suggest that due to their wide range of functions,[61] globally, coral reefs possess a TEV of nearly 30 billion (USD) per year in terms of the fisheries (5.7), coastal protection (9.0), tourism (9.6), and biodiversity (5.5).[62]

The logic of TEV can be applied to protected areas.[63] This is an important area as the creation and adequate conservation of protected areas can be economically expensive.[64] Accordingly, it is necessary to show that the economic values of protected areas are not only costs, but also benefits. The TEV of protected areas may be divided into use and non-use values. Use values include direct use values, indirect use values and option values. Non-use values include existence values and bequest values. Direct use values of a protected area are values derived from the use of the area for activities such as recreation, tourism, natural resource harvesting, hunting, gene pool services, education and research. Indirect use values are largely comprised of the protected areas ecological functions such as watershed protection, climatic stabilization such as carbon sequestration, and/or natural services such as pollination. Option values of a protected area are derived from the option of using the area at some point in the future.[65] Exist-

---

59 Millennium Ecosystem Assessment. (2005). *Ecosystems and Human Well-Being.* (Island Press, Washington). 40-41. CBD Secretariat. (2001). *The Value of Forest Ecosystems.* (CBD Technical Series No 4, Montreal). Carr, T. (1993). 'Rainforest Entrepreneurs.' *Environment.* 35(7): 12-15.

60 Decision on Determining the Economic Value of Coral Reefs to User Communities. In ICRI (2001). Report of the ICRI Meeting in Cebu, the Philippines, 5-6 April, 2001.

61 Spalding, M. (2001). *The World Atlas of Coral Reefs.* (UNEP/WCMC). 47-56.

62 See Cesar, H. (2004). *The Economics of Worldwide Coral Reef Degradation.* (WWF, Netherlands). 4-5.

63 IUCN. (1998). *Economic Values for Protected Areas.* (IUCN, Gland). Note, this is a current CBD study topic). Munasinghe, M. (1994). 'Protected Area Economics and Policy. (World Bank, IUCN, Washington). See CBD. Decision VII/28. *Protected Areas.* Annex. Paragraph 3.4.9.

64 Pearce, F. (2003). 'Huge Price Tag Put on Protecting Biodiversity.' *New Scientist.* May 24. 7. IUCN. (2000). *Financing Protected Areas: Guidelines for Protected Area Managers.* (IUCN, Gland).

65 See Gillespie, A. (1997). *International Environmental Law, Policy and Ethics.* (OUP, Oxford) chapter 6. CBD Secretariat. (2004). *Biodiversity Issues for Consideration in the Planning,*

ence values are the benefits that accrue to individuals because the park exists, even when it is unlikely the person will ever visit it. For example, a Canadian study found that respondents were willing to pay $ (C) 244.35 per household to establish four additional national parks, which they may never visit.[66]

The only international organizations responsible for protected areas, which have attempted to take a broader view of economic value, are the MAB and the Ramsar. However, although the MAB has tried to develop its own economic criteria to increase acceptable outputs from MAB sites,[67] the primary organization on this point is the Ramsar. In the Ramsar, wetlands are recognized as possessing multiple values,[68] including, inter-alia, water supply, defences against natural disasters,[69] (as was shown with the 2004 Asian tsunami)[70] food security and poverty alleviation.[71] However, such economically significant values have traditionally been downgraded, if not invisible in planning decisions. This is despite the fact that 'wetlands may, directly or indirectly, have a potential value exceeding that obtained from transforming them into other types of land'.[72] Given this difficulty the Ramsar Parties have consistently recommended that in cases of large scale wetland transformation, 'the decision is not taken until an assessment of all the values involved has been made'.[73] The question of 'all values' was furthered in 1984[74] and 1996[75] when the Ramsar Parties identified as a priority, the quantification of both direct (monetary) and indirect (non-monetary) values of wetlands and formulation of criteria to enable both values to be taken fully into account in the planning and conservation of wetlands. Only when the two values are combined,

---

Establishment and Management of Protected Area Sites and Networks. (CBD Technical Series No 15). 23-31.

66 Conservation of Arctic Flora and Fauna. (2002). *Protected Areas of the Arctic: Conserving a Full Range of Values.* (CAFF Secretariat, in Department of Foreign Affairs, Canada). 30.

67 Seville Strategy. Objective 1.1. Seville + 5 Recommendations. Recommendation Number 6. MAB. (2000). 16th Session of the ICC Bureau. SC-00/CONF.208/13. 13. UNESCO. (2001). MAB ICC Bureau Meeting. SC/-01/CONF.211/13. Apr 10. 14. UNESCO. (2001) ICC Bureau Meeting. SC-01/CONF.217/8. Dec 12, 23-24.

68 Wetlands, 'constitute a resource of great economic, cultural, scientific and recreational value. Ramsar. Preamble. Paragraph 5.

69 Resolution 9.9. The Role of the Ramsar Convention in the Prevention and Mitigation of Impacts Associated with Natural Phenomena, Including Those Induced or Exacerbated by Human Activities. (2005, Kampala).

70 Anon. (2005). 'Buffer Zone'. *New Scientist.* Dec 24. 5.

71 Resolution 9.14. Wetlands and Poverty Reduction. (2005, Kampala).

72 Recommendation 1.6. Assessment of Wetland Values. (1980, Cagliari).

73 Recommendation 1.6. *Ibid.*

74 Recommendation 2.3. Action Points for Priority Attention. (1984, Groningen).

75 Recommendation 6.10. Economic Valuation of Wetlands. (1996, Brisbane).

(and economic dis-incentives to their conservation are removed)[76] can the 'true values of wetlands'[77] be meaningfully considered in management decisions.[78]

A Tourism

The most obvious manifestation of direct economic value, in the context of protected areas, is tourism.[79] Tourism[80] is one of the economic powerhouses of the modern global economy. In 2002, tourism was producing 4.4% of the world's GDP, and employed around 200 million people globally. It is expected that this number will grow in the future. This growth in numbers is particularly noticeable with nature tourism.[81] For example, tourist numbers increased by 130% between 1996 and 2001 (to 40,000 per year) to Svalbard, in Norway, one of the key polar bear habitats.[82] Key international institutions, such as the Global Environment Facility (GEF) have actively encouraged such growth. This encouragement can be seen in 76 GEF projects with eco-tourism components, encompassing 542 protected areas (and supported by over 500 (USD) million in GEF financing).[83]

---

76 The Ramsar has followed with approving interest, the CBD debate and decisions with regard to incentive measures. In doing so, the Ramsar parties have recognised the promotion of incentive measures that encourage the wise use of wetlands, and conversely, removal of perverse incentives which are the antithesis of wise use is a clear goal of the Ramsar's future work. Against this broad goal, the Ramsar has urged Parties to ensure that incentive measures are taken into consideration when applying and creating national wetland policies. Conversely, perverse incentives should be removed. The 8th COP took this a little further, calling upon Parties to review their existing legislation and practices in order to identify and remove perverse incentives such as taxes and subsidies, especially with agricultural policies, which may be linked to underlying causes of wetland uses. The target was that 50 parties will have reviewed their national policies with regard to incentives by 2005. Resolution 8.23. Incentive Measures as Tools for Achieving the Wise Use of Wetlands. (2002, Valencia). Resolution 8.40. Guidelines for Rendering the Use of Groundwater Compatible with The Conservation of Wetlands. (2002, Valencia). Resolution 8.25. The Ramsar Strategic Plan. (2002, Valencia). Annex. Operational Objective 8. Resolution 7.15. Incentive Measures. (1999, San Jose). Resolution 8.34. Agriculture, Wetlands and Water Resource Management. (2002, Valencia).

77 Resolution 7.16. Impact Assessment. (1999, San Jose).

78 See principle 2 of Resolution 8.4. Principles for Incorporating Wetland Issues Into Integrated Coastal Zone Management. (2002, Valencia).

79 See 'Economic Values of National Parks.' In Adams, A. (ed). *First World Conference on National Parks.* (US Department of the Interior, Washington). 98-128.

80 As in when someone travels to and stays or visits another place outside of his or her usual environment for not more than one consecutive year for leisure, business and other purposes.

81 Wilkie, D. (1999). 'Can Nature Help Finance Protected Areas in the Congo Basin?' *Oryx.* 33(4): 332-328.

82 Conservation of Arctic Flora and Fauna. (2002). *Protected Areas of the Arctic: Conserving a Full Range of Values.* (CAFF Secretariat, in Department of Foreign Affairs, Canada). 10-11.

83 GEF. (2005). *Making a Visible Difference in Our World.* (GEF, Washington). 29.

At the end of the twentieth century, 63 million people were annually visiting 116 natural WHC sites. 15 sites recorded over one million visitors per year (eight of these in the USA) with the Great Smokey Mountains, having the highest number (9,265,667). Only 14 natural sites had no visitors (due to war, access or government policy to discourage visitation). 31 WHC natural sites in USA, Canada, Australia and New Zealand accommodated over 84% of all WH visitors (52 million annually). For the 30 sites in Africa for which data is available, the average visitation numbers were 22,705 per year, while the average for the 16 sites in Canada and the United States was 2.6 million per year.[84] Even within domestic markets, the numbers of visitors to protected areas can be large. For example, somewhere between 10 and 20 million people visit national parks in the United Kingdom annually.[85] Denali National Park in Alaska, receives over 400,000 visitors per year, whilst Urho in Finland, receives almost 200,000.[86] In 2003 to 2004, Antarctica was visited by 43,000 tourists.[87]

Such numbers are already generating vast amounts of revenue, and these amounts are expected to increase. Consider, in the mid 1990s, nature tourism and visits to national parks in Costa Rica was estimated to generate over $600 million (USD) per annum. By 2001, this figure was over 1 billion,[88] and by 2004, this figure had trebled to 3 billion.[89] In the same period Australia's top 8 national parks were estimated to be bringing in 2 billion (AUD) per year,[90] with about a quarter of this sum coming from the Great Barrier Reef alone.[91] In terms of highest economic worth of an individual site, the Yosemite site in the United States generates approximately 1.3 billion (USD) per year.[92] In poorer countries, the revenue from protected areas, or key species within them, can be pivotal.[93] For example, in the Congo, (prior to the civil war) gorilla

---

84 IUCN. (1998). *Human Use of World Heritage Natural Sites: A Global Overview.* (IUCN, Gland). 4.

85 IUCN. (2002). *Sustainable Tourism in Protected Areas: Guidelines for Planning and Management.* (IUCN, Gland). 62.

86 Conservation of Arctic Flora and Fauna. (2002). *Protected Areas of the Arctic: Conserving a Full Range of Values.* (CAFF Secretariat, in Department of Foreign Affairs, Canada). 28.

87 See the Final Report of the Twenty-Eighth Antarctic Treaty Consultative Meeting. (Stockholm, 2005). Paragraph 156.

88 IUCN. (2002). *Sustainable Tourism in Protected Areas. Ibid.* (IUCN, Gland). 24.

89 Toepfer, K. (2004). 'Protected Areas.' *Our Planet.* 14(2): 1.

90 SBSTTA. Report of the Ad Hoc Technical Expert Group on Protected Areas. UNEP/CBD/SBSTTA/9/INF/3. 22 Sep, 2003. pp.25.

91 In the mid 1990s, visitors to Australia's Great Barrier Reef spend $543 (US) million in the same year. IUCN. (2002). *Sustainable Tourism in Protected Areas. Ibid.* 25.

92 See IUCN (2002). *A Global Overview of Mountain Protected Areas on the World Heritage List.* (IUCN, Gland).11.

93 Wilkie, D. (1999). 'The Potential Role of Safari Hunting as a Source of Revenue'. *Oryx.* 33(4): 339-345.

watching operations were generating over one million (USD) per year in tourist income.[94] By 2001, the global whale-watching industry was worth an estimated $1 billion (USD) per year, and whale-watching was being practiced in 65 countries, attracting more than 9 million participants per year.[95] In some small countries, such as Tonga, whale-watching has become the single most important tourist attraction. In 2003, within Australia more than 1.6 million visits were made to watch whales. This is more than double previous numbers five years earlier. This increase in numbers translates to an annual percentage growth rate of 15% between 1998 and 2003.[96] Likewise, within New Zealand, more than 425,000 visitors and locals went whale-watching in 2004, generating a total expenditure related to whale watching tourism of 120 (NZD) million.[97] Even remote protected areas, with few visitors, like Auyuittuq National Park in Canada, with only 500 visitors per year, still obtained $175,000 (USD) from the process.[98]

Due to such obvious importance, spurred on by the World Summit on Sustainable Development,[99] the CBD has undertaken a number of studies of the potential benefits and costs of tourism upon biodiversity.[100] Although there are clear potential costs, tourism can, if well managed, also create clear benefits. These include, inter alia, revenue creation for the maintenance of natural areas, contribution to economic development, funded infrastructure and services, the provision of employment and funds for sustainable practices, alternative ways for communities to raise revenue from biological diversity, and helping public education and awareness.[101] As such, carefully managed tourism,

94 IUCN. (2002). *Sustainable Tourism in Protected Areas: Guidelines for Planning and Management.* (IUCN, Gland). 25.

95 Hoyt, E. (2001). *Whalewatching 2001: Numbers, Expenditures and Socio-Economic Benefits.* (IFAW, London). 3. Report of the IWC 48 (1998). 19.

96 IFAW. (2004). The Growth of the Whalewatching Industry in Australia. IWC/56/16. IWC. 52nd Report. (2001). 12. Orams, M. (1999). *Economic Benefits of Whale Watching in Vava'u, Kingdom of Tonga.* (Centre for Tourism Research, Massey University at Albany, Auckland).

97 IFAW. (2005). *The Growth of the New Zealand Whale Watching Industry.* (IFAW, Melbourne). 4-5.

98 Conservation of Arctic Flora and Fauna. (2002). *Protected Areas of the Arctic: Conserving a Full Range of Values.* (CAFF Secretariat, in Department of Foreign Affairs, Canada). 29.

99 See paragraph 44 (b) of the Plan of Implementation. The countries agreed to promote the ongoing work under the Convention on the sustainable use on biological diversity, including on sustainable tourism, as a cross-cutting issue relevant to different ecosystems, sectors and thematic areas.

100 Report of the 4th COP to the CBD. UNEP/CBD/COP/4/27. June 15. pp.40. Decision V/25. Biological Diversity and Tourism. UNEP/CBD/COP/5/23.pp.185.

101 Recommendation IV/7. Development of Approaches and Practices for the Sustainable Use of Resources, Including Tourism. UNEP/CBD/SBSTTA/4/14.pp.50.

can be an exemplar of the sustainable use of biodiversity in particular, and sustainable development in general.[102]

Despite the international recognition of the potential value of carefully managed tourism for biodiversity, and despite the fact that most protected areas benefit from tourism,[103] only a few regimes, such as the Caribbean Protocol[104] or the IMO[105] have an obvious consideration of this topic. However, the only protected area regime to actively encourage sustainable tourism is the MAB, which recognizes tourism as a 'golden opportunity' to benefit surrounding local communities,[106] and has actually called upon inscribed MAB sites to develop (carefully) their eco-tourism potential.[107]

7 Values by Species, Ecosystem and Geomorphic or Physio graphical Type

The values of protected areas due to their importance for species and/or ecosystem conservation are the traditional values for the establishment of protected areas. Together, with geomorphic and/or physiographical type, these values represent the 'core' of most international regimes which are empowered to inscribe protected areas.

---

102 Decision V/25. Biological Diversity and Tourism. UNEP/CBD/COP/5/23.pp.185. 102IUCN. (2003). 'Protected Areas as Engines for Development.' *Parks.* 13 (3). 1-71.

103 See IUCN (2002). *A Global Overview of Mountain Protected Areas on the World Heritage List.* (IUCN, Gland).11.

104 Caribbean Protocol. Article 4.2.

105 The economic value of PSSAs is a clear reflection and interpretation of the Article 211 of the UNCLOS with regard to the criteria of 'utilization or the protection of its resources'. This is particularly notable as the Special Areas criteria have no comparable consideration. In the PSSA context, inter alia, economic criteria are defined in terms of the economic benefits of the region, recreation and tourism, and human dependency. Annex 6. Guidelines for the Designation of Special Areas Under MARPOL 73/78 and Guidelines for the Identification and Designation of Particularly Sensitive Sea Areas. MEPC (2001). Report of the MEPC on its 46th Session. MEPC 46/23. Sections 4.4.12-4.4.15.

106 Equitable sharing of all benefits derived from the use of natural resources are distributed with the stakeholders (by such means as sharing the entrance fees, sale of natural products or handicrafts, use of local construction techniques and labour, and development of sustainable activities like agriculture or forestry), were called for. See the Seville Strategy. Objective 1.2. UNESCO. (2003). ICC Bureau Meeting. SC-02/CONF.210/10. Jan 7. 26.

107 Yading in China, Tuscan Islands in Italy. UNESCO. (2003). ICC Bureau Meeting. SC/-03/CONF.217/14. July 30. 9, 10. Selva Pisana in Italy. UNESCO. (2003). ICC Bureau Meeting. SC/-03/CONF.217/14. July 30. 15. Shennongjia in China. UNESCO. (2001). ICC Bureau Meeting. SCI/-01/CONF.217/8. Dec 12. 19.

A Endangered Species

Habitat loss is the primary cause of species extinction. For example, habitat loss impacts upon, inter alia, 86% of all threatened birds, 86% of all threatened mammals and 88% of all threatened amphibians.[108] Accordingly, one of the clearest values of protected areas is that they can be critical in the protection of endangered, threatened or migratory species, as the area can conserve the habitats which are vital for species survival.[109]

The value of habitat preservation as the essential part of species conservation is clearly recognised in the conventions which are directly related to species preservation, such as the CMS with its generic obligation on all of its Parties to, 'endeavour to conserve, and where feasible and appropriate, restore those habitats of the species which are of importance in removing the species from danger of extinction'.[110] This obligation is also transferred to the subsidiary Agreements, developed under the CMS auspice, dealing with individual species.[111]

A very similar recognition of the value of habitat preservation as a crucial step to the protection of endangered species can also be seen with the Bern Convention and its associated Directives on Birds,[112] and Habitats,[113] at both the generic[114] and species specific levels.[115] Accordingly, the Parties are obliged to 'take steps to designate areas of special conservation interest to ensure that necessary and appropriate conservation

108 IUCN. (2004). *A Global Species Assessment.* (IUCN, Gland). xxi.

109 Millennium Ecosystem Assessment. (2005). *Ecosystems and Human Well Being: The Biodiversity Synthesis.* (World Resources Institute, Washington). 10. For the early recognition of this view, see Talbot, L. (1962). 'The International Role of Parks in Preserving Endangered Species.' In Adams, A. (ed). *First World Conference on National Parks.* (US Department of the Interior, Washington). 295-305.

110 Article III. (4)(a). See also Article II (1).

111 CMS. Article V(5)(e)-(g).

112 See With the Birds Directive (79/409/EEC) part of the obligation imposed on members was the duty to preserve natural habitats of these wild birds. Member states were required to classify the most suitable territories in number and size as Special Protection Areas for the conservation of bird species listed in Annex 1 to the Directive and regularly occurring migratory species not mentioned in Annex I. See Simpson, K. (2002). 'The Natura 2000 Network'. 12 (3) *Parks.* 36, 37.

113 Bern Convention. Preamble.

114 Ibid. Articles 1, 3 (1), 4 (1), (2) and (3).

115 Recommendation No. 1. (1982). Concerning the Protection of Gran Sasso (Italy).

measures are taken for each area situated within their territory'[116] of the species being listed on the Appendices.[117]

With regard to the more general protected area agreements, the recognition of the value of protected areas to help conserve endangered, threatened or migratory species is first recorded in the 1933 London Convention.[118] Other notable examples include the 1940 Western Hemisphere Convention,[119] the Antarctic regime[120] (of which species protection is the most commonly utilised protected area justification),[121] the European Diploma,[122] and the 2003 African Convention.[123] The OSPAR[124] and Helsinki regimes,[125] in addition to the Mediterranean,[126] Caribbean[127] and South East Pacific Protocols, cover this area for MPAs.[128]

In all of the above instances, any number of species may be encompassed. For example, the MAB programme, which has a long standing commitment to using its sites to protect 'flagship' species,[129] has come to approve sites which encompass, inter alia, the giant

116 Recommendation No 16. (1989). On Areas of Special Conservation Interest.

117 Ibid. On Areas of Special Conservation Interest.

118 1933 London Convention. Preamble. Paragraph 1.

119 1940 Western Hemisphere Convention. Article I (5) and VII.

120 The second, third and fourth areas of the 1964 Agreed Measures for SPAs all overlapped. These were for 'areas with unique complexes and species', 'areas which are the type locality or only known habitat of any plant or invertebrate species', and 'areas that contain specially interesting breeding colonies of birds or mammals'. The 1991 Madrid Protocol refined this section to only cover, 'areas with important or unusual assemblages of species, including major colonies of breeding native birds or mammals' and areas with, 'the type locality or only known habitat of any species'. Madrid Protocol. Annex V. Article 3 (2) (c)-(d).

121 See New Zealand (2005). A Review of the Antarctic Protected Areas System. CEP Paper WP 11 (Stockholm, 2005). 2.

122 European Diploma. Annex I. Criteria.

123 2003 African Convention. Article XII (1) (c).

124 OSPAR Recommendation 2003/3 on a Network of Marine Protected Areas. Appendix 1.

125 See Helsinki Commission. Guidelines... 2. Guidelines for designating BSPAs. Annex I.

126 Mediterranean Protocol. Articles 4. (a)-(c). 16 and Annex 1.B.

127 Caribbean Protocol. Article 4(2).

128 1989 Protocol for the Conservation and Management of Protected Marine and Coastal Areas of the South East Pacific. Reprinted in Austen, A. (ed). *Basic Legal Document on International Animal Welfare and Wildlife Conservation (Kluwer, London).* Article 11.

129 UNESCO. (1968). *Use and Conservation of the Biosphere.* (UNESCO, Paris). 147, 216. See UNESCO. (ed). *Conservation, Science and Society: The 1983 International Biosphere Reserve Congress.* (UNESCO, Paris). 251-300.

panda,[130] the far east leopard,[131] several well known species of migratory birds,[132] and even the migrating Monarch butterfly.[133]

The generic protected area regime which has the most direct links to threatened species and the most developed and systematic way of dealing with this consideration is the Ramsar. The importance of the conservation, of 'waterfoul'[134] and especially those that are migratory[135] cannot be underestimated.[136] Indeed, the conference from which the Ramsar Convention evolved was billed as the International Conference on the Conservation of Wetlands and Waterfowl, and all of the recommendations from the 1971 Conference were waterfowl related. Moreover, the original inscription ideals placed their primary emphasis upon inscribing wetlands of international importance to waterfowl.[137] This emphasis of wetlands becoming protected areas because of their importance to waterfowl, continued until 1979, when the CMS came into existence and tried to encompass all migratory species, and not just the avian ones.

Since the existence of the CMS with its emphasis on migratory species (and the need to have protected areas for them) has come into existence, other conventions, which traditionally encompassed migratory species, have taken a somewhat harder approach to listing areas of relevance to migratory species (as the primary justification). For example, with the WHC, some sites, such as the Great Right Valley Migration Flyway ('the Hula') which encompasses over one million migratory birds was rejected for nomination in 2006. Moreover, although some World Heritage sites do have notable

---

130 UNESCO. (2002). *Biosphere Reserves: Special Places for People and Nature.* (UNESCO, Paris). 176-177. Baishuijang and Foping in China. MAB. (2000). 16th Session of the ICC Bureau. SC-00/CONF.208/13. 20. UNESCO. (2004). 18th Session of the ICC Bureau Meeting. SC-04/CONF.204/14. Jan 11. 13.

131 Kedrovaya in Russia. UNESCO. (2004). 18th Session of the ICC Bureau Meeting. SC-04/CONF.204/14. Jan 11. 15.

132 Darvinsky in Russian Federation. UNESCO. (2003). ICC Bureau Meeting. SC-02/CONF.210/10. Jan 7. 12.

133 Mariposa Monarca, Mexico. UNESCO. (2006). MAB ICC. 19th Session. SC-06/CONF.202/16. Nov 28. 25.

134 For Ramsar purposes, 'waterfowl are birds ecologically dependent on wetlands.' Ramsar. Article 1.

135 Non-aviary migratory species were not even on the Ramsar radar until 1999. The 7th COP recommended the Guidelines for International Co-operation Under the Ramsar Convention emphasised, inter alia, co-operation on shared wetland-dependent species, including migratory birds and other migratory species. Resolution 7.19. International Cooperation. (1999, San Jose). Annex. The Guidelines for international cooperation under the Ramsar Convention.

136 See Paragraph 2 of the Preamble to the Ramsar Convention.

137 Ramsar. Articles 2.2 and 2.6.

migratory species within them,[138] due to an overlap between the species in focus, and the area they transit through, the IUCN has suggested that,

> the Convention is not well suited for dealing with natural phenomenon such as migration that occurs across different geographical regions... bird migration is a global natural phenomenon that cannot be associated with a single site.[139]

It was not until the mid 1980s, that the primacy of wetlands of international importance for waterfowl was challenged under the assumption that other values may be equally valid for the inscription of wetlands.[140] Thus, although the value of wetlands to avian species remains very important, other inscription justifications based on endangered species in general, have become much more prominent.[141] Therefore, a wetland should be considered internationally important if it supports vulnerable, endangered, or critically endangered species or threatened ecological communities,[142] and/or it supports populations of plant and/or animal species important for maintaining the biological diversity of a particular biogeographic region,[143] and/or it supports plant and/or animal species at a critical stage in their life cycles, or provides refuge during adverse conditions.

Within this criteria, aside the traditional and continuing importance of protecting stocks (20,000 or more[144] or 1% of the individuals in a population of one species or subspecies)[145] of waterbirds,[146] the importance of wetlands with regards to fish is particularly notable.[147] The fish criteria is that a wetland should be considered internationally important if it supports a significant proportion of indigenous fish subspecies, species

---

138 Such as Donana in Spain, Banc d'Arguin in Mauritania, Djoudj in Senegal and Ichkeul in Tunisia.

139 See IUCN (2006). Evaluations of Nominations of Natural and Mixed Properties to the World Heritage List. WHC-06/30.COM/INF.8B2. 47. For the final decision, see 30 COM. 8B.25.

140 In 1984, the Ramsar COP identified as a priority area, the development of common criteria for evaluating the importance of wetlands at local, regional and international levels, and expanding the Cagliari Criteria, to cover also ecological factors, concerning life other than waterfowl. Recommendation 2.3. Action Points for Priority Attention. (1984, Groningen).

141 Resolution 7.10. Improving Implementation of the Strategic Framework and Vision for the List of Wetlands of International Importance. (2002, Valencia).

142 Criterion 2.

143 Criterion 3.

144 Criteria 5. Or half that number of ducks, geese, swans or coots. See Recommendations adopted by the International Conference on the Conservation of Wetlands and Waterfowl at Heiligenhafen, Federal Republic of Germany, 6 December 1974. Annex II. Recommendations for Criteria to be used in identifying Wetlands of International Importance.

145 Criteria 6. Of at least one hundred individuals. Recommendations adopted by the International Conference on the Conservation of Wetlands and Waterfowl at Heiligenhafen, Federal Republic of Germany, 6 December 1974. Annex II. *Ibid.*

146 Ramsar. Articles 2.2 and 2.6.

147 Recommendation 5.9. Ramsar Guidelines On Fish Habitat. (1993, Kushiro). Resolution 6.2. Criteria Based on Fish. (1996, Brisbane).

or families, life-history stages, species interactions and/or populations that are representative of wetland benefits and/or values and thereby contributes to global biological diversity.[148] Alternately, if a wetland is an important source of food for fish, spawning grounds, nurseries and/or migration paths on which fish stocks depend, either within the wetland or elsewhere, then it may be internationally important.[149]

The final convention of note, of which species conservation is a central consideration, is with the World Heritage Convention. The WHC allows site inscription if the area, 'constitute[s] the animals and plants of outstanding universal value from the point of view of science or conservation'.[150] This section, which has morphed into what is currently known as criteria II and IV of the Operational Guidelines. Criteria II stipulates, the nominated site must contain,

> [o]utstanding examples representing significant on-going ecological and biological processes in the evolution and development of terrestrial, fresh water, coastal and marine ecosystems and communities of plants and animals.[151]

Criteria IV stipulates, sites seeking listing under this subsection must,

> Contain the most important and significant natural habitats for in-situ conservation of biological diversity, including those containing threatened species of outstanding universal value from the point of view of science or conservation.[152]

Although these sections are separate, it is important to note that the overlap between them is substantial, and over the years, the inadvertent practice of the WHC Committee has been to blur the distinction between them. This is especially so because whilst criteria II identifies 'plants and animals', criteria IV recognizes the importance of 'threatened species'. Aside this drafting overlap, in ecological terms, the species listed in criteria IV will often be in criteria II areas,[153] and accordingly, in only in a few instances, have listings been on criteria IV alone. When this has happened, it has usually been with due to stand-out species, although in most instances other, secondary stand-out species are also acknowledged.

The instances of one stand-out species, as the primary justification for a criteria IV listing has involved the whale sanctuaries of Peninsular Valdez[154] and El Vizcaino,[155] the

---

148 Criteria 7.

149 Criterion 8.

150 WHC.Article 2,

151 *Operational Guidelines*. 2002 Edn. Paragraph 44 (ii).

152 *Ibid.* Paragraph 44. (iv).

153 UNESCO. (1998). 22nd Session of the WHC. WHC-98/CONF.208/18. Jan 29, 1998. 58.

154 Peninsula Valdes and its global important concentration of breeding southern right whales. UNESCO. (1999). 23rd Session of the WHC. WHC-99/CONF.209/22. Mar 22, 2000. 18.

primate and mountain gorilla sanctuaries of Kahuzi-Biega and Okapi; the Arabian Oryx[156] sanctuary; the Altai Mountains and the snow leopard, Sikhote-Alin and the Amur tiger; and finally Niokolo-Koba with its leopards and elephants. In terms of migratory species, the sites of note, listing just under criteria IV alone, include the Srebarna Nature Reserve, the Keoladeo National Park in India and Ichkeul National Park in Tunisia.[157] Other sites involving migratory species of note, but in conjunction with other criteria, include Lapland, Corsica, Donana, the delta of the Danube in Rumania and Banc d'Arguin in Mauritania.[158]

Instances in which the criteria IV listing has involved threatened species of global importance, in conjunction with other listing criteria include big cats, bears, primates, cetaceans, turtles, rhino and elephants, amongst others. With regard to big cats, the Siberian tiger is in the Central Sikhote-Alin in Russia.[159] Tigers are also in Kaziranga in India, the Royal Chitwan in Nepal and Sundarbans in Bangladesh.[160] The Indo-Chinese tiger is in Thung Yai in Thailand; the puma and lynx are in the Canadian Rockies and in Gros Morne. Lynx are also in Plitvice in Croatia and the Bialowieza Forest. Snow leopards are in the Golden Mountains of Altai in Russia.[161] Sagarmatha in Nepal and Nanda Devi in India are notable with big cats, and leopards are also recorded at Mount Kenya. The clouded leopard is in Wulingyuan. Leopards are also in Sinharaja in Sri Lanka. Cheetah in Ngorongoro in Tanzania. Lynx are in Redwood in America, puma in Yosemite and the panther in the Everglades. Jaguars are in Canaima in Venezuela, Manu in Peru, Noel Kempff in Bolivia, Pantanal and the Atlantic Forests in Brazil. Puma are in the Huascaran in Peru, Guanacaste of Costa Rica[162] and the Iguazu Falls of Argentina and Brazil.[163]

---

155 The El Vizcaino sanctuary. UNESCO. (1993). 17th Session of WHC. WHC-93/CONF.002/14. Feb 4, 1993. 34.

156 The Arabian Oryx. UNESCO. (1995). 18th Session of the WHC. WHC-94/CONF.003/16. Jan 31. 1995. 40-41.

157 UNESCO. (1979). 3rd Session of the WHC. CC-79/CONF.003/13. Nov 30, 1978. pp.11.

158 Cattaneo, M. & Trifoni, J. (2003). *The World Heritage Sites of UNESCO: Nature Sanctuaries* (WhiteStar, Vercelli). 36, 58, 66, 176.

159 Central Sikhote-Alin in Russia. UNESCO. (2001). 25th Session of the WHC. WHC-01/CONF.208/24. Paris 8, Feb 2002. 92.

160 Sundarbans of Bangladesh. UNESCO. (1997). 21st Session of the WHC. WHC-97/CONF.208/17. Feb 27, 1998. 37.

161 The Russian Gold Mountains. UNESCO. (1998). 22nd Session of the WHC. WHC-98/CONF.208/18. Jan 29, 1998. 58. Also in the Uvs Nuur Basin of Mongolia/ Russia. UNESCO. (2003). 27th Session of the WHC. WHC-03/27.COM/24. Dec 10. 102.

162 The Area de Conservacion Guanacaste of Costa Rica. UNESCO. (1999). 23rd Session of the WHC. WHC-99/CONF.209/22. Mar 22, 2000. 20.

163 Cattaneo, M. & Trifoni, J. (2003). *Ibid.* 51, 84, 96, 98, 136, 144, 150, 160, 168, 170, 172, 174, 181, 184, 188, 223, 240, 244, 288, 306, 308, 310, 320

Grizzly bears are in the site of the Kamchatka volcanoes, Yellowstone, Glacier Park, Wood Buffalo and Redwood in Canada. Brown bears are in Yosemite, Lapland, Plitvice in Croatia and Durmitor. The giant panda is in Huanglong, and most significantly, at Wolong, Mount Siguniang and Jiajin mountains in China (the latter includes 30% of the world's pandas).[164] The Himalayan black bear is in Russia[165] and Nepal. The panda with tawny fur is in Sagarmatha in Nepal. The Asiatic Black bear in Wulingyuan and the spectacled bear are in the Huascaran in Peru.[166]

Diurnal primates are in the Rwenzori Mountains in Uganda. Bwindi in Uganda holds mountain gorillas[167] as does Virunga in the Democratic Republic of the Congo. Orang-utans are in Kinabalu in Malaysia. Notable small primates include the Japanese macaque in Shirakami and the wooly spider monkey in the Atlantic Forests in Brazil.[168]

Mount Kenya holds black rhino. Asiatic rhino are in the Royal Chitwan in Nepal. Black and white rhino are in St Lucia in South Africa. Manas holds Indian rhino and Javan rhino are in Sundarbans in Bangladesh and Thung Yai in Thailand.[169] The Asiatic ibex, the Pyrenees ibix and the Abyssinian ibix in Simien Park in Ethiopia are all notable,[170] as is the addax antelope in the Air and Tenere reserves in Niger[171] and the komodo dragon in Komodo National park in Indonesia.[172] Elephants are notable at a number of sites in Africa, Kaziranga and Manas in India, Sinharaja in Sri Lanka and Thung Yai in Thailand.[173]

---

164 See IUCN (2006). Evaluations of Nominations of Natural and Mixed Properties to the World Heritage List. WHC-06/30.COM/INF.8B2. 9-16.

165 Central Sikhote-Alin in Russia. UNESCO. (2001). 25th Session of the WHC. WHC-01/CONF.208/24. Paris 8, Feb 2002. 92.

166 Cattaneo, M. & Trifoni, J. (2003). *The World Heritage Sites of UNESCO: Nature Sanctuaries* (WhiteStar, Vercelli). 18, 51, 52, 136, 154, 160, 168, 211, 218, 232, 238, 240, 245, 257, 297.

167 Bwindi National Park in Uganda. UNESCO. (1995). 18th Session of the WHC. WHC-94/CONF.003/16. Jan 31. 1995. 42.

168 Cattaneo, M. & Trifoni, J. (2003). *Ibid.* 76, 78, 87, 162, 194, 204, 316.

169 Cattaneo, M. & Trifoni, J. (2003). *Ibid.* 84, 116, 164, 174, 185, 188.

170 *Ibid.* 34, 72. For the Asiatic Ibix. The Uvs Nuur Basin. UNESCO. (2003). 27th Session of the WHC. WHC-03/27.COM/24. Dec 10. 102.

171 Cattaneo, M. & Trifoni, J. (2003). *Ibid.* 68.

172 *Ibid.* 204.

173 *Ibid.* 92, 172, 174, 188.

Threatened birds, as recognized under criteria IV, can be found in WHC sites in South Africa,[174] Kenya,[175] the UK,[176] Brazil,[177] Japan,[178] New Zealand,[179] the former Yugoslavia,[180] and Senegal.[181] A few sites are particularly notable for their possession of some avian species. They are the Kamchatka volcanoes and stellers sea eagle, the American bald eagle in Gros Morne in Canada and in Yellowstone and Yosemite in the United States. The white tailed eagle in Lapland and the imperial eagle in Doana are notable. Albatross can be found on WHC sites including the Galapagos, the Macquarie Islands (of Australia) and the Sub Antarctic Islands of New Zealand. The Siberian crane in Keoladeo in India and the desert owl in the Air and Tenere reserves in Niger are also note worthy,[182] as is the snow goose on Russia's Wrangle Island.[183]

Giant tortoises are in the Seychelles and the Galapagos (as are green turtles). *Chelonia mydas* and *Eremochelys embricata* are at Fernando de Noronha in Brazil and *Caretta caretta, Chelonia mydas* and *Eretmochelys imbricata* are at Kakadu. Green and loggerhead turtles are at Fraser Island. Loggerheads are at Shark Bay. Green turtles and common sea turtles are in the Great Barrier Reef site. Green and hawksbills are at Isla de Cocos in Costa Rica. Green, olive ridley and leatherbacks are at Guanacaste in Costa Rica.[184] Hawksbill's are at sites in Brazil[185] and leatherbacks in Costa Rica.[186] Finally, turtles are particularly noted in St Lucia in South Africa.[187]

---

174 Drakensberg in South Africa.

175 UNESCO. (1997). 21st Session of the WHC. WHC-97/CONF.208/17. Feb 27, 1998. 38.

176 Gough Island Wildlife Reserve. UNESCO. (1996). 19th Session of the WHC. WHC-95/CONF.203/16. Jan 31, 1996. 35.

177 UNESCO. (2001). 25th Session of the WHC. WHC-01/CONF.208/24. Paris 8, Feb 2002. 89.

178 Decision 29 COM. 8B6. 264 species of birds, including 9 which are threatened according to the IUCN.

179 The Albatross on the Sub Antarctic Islands.

180 The Srebarna Biosphere and the threatened Dalmatian Pelican.

181 The Djoudj National Bird Sanctuary. UNESCO. (1978). Second Session of the WHC CC-78/CONF.010/3. Sep 5, 1978. pp.4.

182 Cattaneo, M. & Trifoni, J. (2003). *The World Heritage Sites of UNESCO: Nature Sanctuaries* (WhiteStar, Vercelli). 18, 39, 66, 68, 136, 176, 226, 239, 244, 295, 378, 379

183 UNESCO. (2004). 28th Session of the WHC. WHC-04/28.COM/26. Oct 29. Decision 28COM 14B.14. pp23.

184 Cattaneo, M. & Trifoni, J. (2003). *Ibid.* 120, 277, 280, 290, 294, 337, 345, 353..

185 Especially the hawksbill turtle. UNESCO. (2001). 25th Session of the WHC. WHC-01/CONF.208/24. Paris 8, Feb 2002. 89.

186 Leatherbacks. UNESCO. (1999). 23rd Session of the WHC. WHC-99/CONF.209/22. Mar 22, 2000. 20.

187 The Greater St Lucia Wetland Park. UNESCO. (1999). 23rd Session of the WHC. WHC-99/CONF.209/22. Mar 22, 2000. 25.

With regard to large cetaceans, there are finwhales at the site of Banc d'Arguin in Mauritania. Humpback whales can be seen in the Malpelo Islands off Colombia,[188] Gros Morne in Canada, Fraser Island and Great Barrier in Australia as well as off Glacier Park. Right whales, pilot whales, and sperm whales can be seen off the Macquarie Islands of Australia. The El Vizcaino whale sanctuary of Mexico has humpback, Gray and blue whales. The Mexican islands in the Gulf of California is particularly notable, as this site contains 39% of the world's total number of marine mammal species, and a third of the world's total number of marine cetaceans (including the highly endangered vaquita).[189] Russia's Wrangel island[190] is an important breeding ground for the gray whales, which migrate from the El Vizcaino site. Peninsula Valdez off Argentina has right, humpback and the orca. The Sub-Antarctic Islands of New Zealand have right whales.[191] Shiretoko in Japan has 28 species of marine mammal, including minke, sperm, sei and dall's porpoise.[192] 20 species of cetaceans can be found in the Coiba protected area of Panama.[193] Finally the St Lucia Park in South Africa[194] is notable for its large cetaceans.

In terms of small cetaceans, rough toothed and bottle-nosed dolphins are within the site of Banc d'Arguin in Mauritania. Susu are in the Royal Chitwan in Nepal. Bottle-noses are with the Belize barrier reef and Costa Rica's Isla de Cocos. The Great Barrier Reef has bottle-nosed dolphins, irrawaddy, spinner and Indo-Pacific dolphins. Freshwater dolphins are in Noel Kempff in Peru. Dolphins are also noted off Komodo in Indonesia, Fernando de Noronha in Brazil, Shark Bay in Australia and the Atlantic Forests of Brazil.[195]

The last subset under the WHC criteria in the species related section relates to migratory species. This section has been drawn out for attention since 1979.[196] In the contemporary context, it is noted that, 'migratory routes, wherever they are located, should be adequately protected'. The Guidelines then add a few sentences on the need, when considering areas containing migratory species, for consideration to be given to, 'seasonal breeding and nesting sites for an area containing migratory species. Specific sites which

188 See IUCN (2006). Evaluations of Nominations of Natural and Mixed Properties to the World Heritage List. WHC-06/30.COM/INF.8B2. 65.

189 Decision 29 COM 8B.9.

190 UNESCO. (2004). 28th Session of the WHC. WHC-04/28.COM/26. Oct 29. Decision 28COM 14B.14. pp23.

191 Cattaneo, M. & Trifoni, J. (2003). *The World Heritage Sites of UNESCO: Nature Sanctuaries* (WhiteStar, Vercelli). 66, 215, 226, 344, 267-271, 328-331.

192 Decision 29 COM. 8B6.

193 Decision 29 COM 8B.13.

194 The Greater St Lucia Wetland Park. UNESCO. (1999). 23rd Session of the WHC. WHC-99/ CONF.209/22. Mar 22, 2000. 25.

195 Cattaneo, M. & Trifoni, J. (2003). *Ibid.* 66, 215, 226, 344, 267-271, 328-331, 353

196 UNESCO. (1979). 3rd Session of the WHC. CC-79/CONF.003/13. Nov 30, 1978. pp.8.

have been listed, under which the migratory aspect has been directly (and favourably) quoted have been the Ichkeul national park in Tunisia,[197] Donana National Park in Spain,[198] the shared Uvs Nuur Basin between Mongolia and Russia[199] and the Djoudj National Bird Sanctuary in Senegal.[200]

B Ecosystems

The protection of ecosystems can be justified on the grounds that such protection may help the species within them, or the species surrounding them. The ecosystems may also be a storehouse of biodiversity, in terms of materials and services which are directly, or indirectly important to humanity and all other dependent species.[201]

A strong and direct example of the benefits of preserving ecosystems is with what is known as, 'spillover benefits', whereby protected areas provide ecological benefits to surrounding areas outside of the protected area. MPAs are an exemplar of such spillover benefits, or as the Millennium Ecosystem Assessment concluded, 'marine protected areas often provide striking examples of the potential synergies between conservation and sustainable use'.[202] This conclusion is justified (but treated with caution by the FAO)[203] on two grounds. First, well placed, and well policed MPAs which have a no-take/no-catch approach considerably help the recovery of endangered species, threatened habitats and the overall functioning of local (and depending on size) regional ecosystems. MPAs can also produce spectacular increases in abundance, biomass and average size of exploited species in adjacent areas, whilst also helping to sustain biological diversity and ecosystem functioning.[204] For example, within three years of

---

197 UNESCO. (1980). 4th Session of the WHC. CC-80/CONF.016/10. Sep 29, 1980. pp.4.

198 UNESCO. (1995). 18th Session of the WHC. WHC-94/CONF.003/16. Jan 31. 1995. 41.

199 UNESCO. (2003). 27th Session of the WHC. WHC-03/27.COM/24. Dec 10. 102.

200 UNESCO. (1978). 2nd Session of the WHC. CC-78/CONF.010/3. Sep 5, 1978. pp.4.

201 Godfrey-Smith, W. (1979). 'The Value of Wilderness'. *Environmental Ethics.* 1: 309-319.

202 Millennium Ecosystem Assessment. (2005). *Ecosystems and Human Well Being: The Biodiversity Synthesis.* (World Resources Institute, Washington). 11.

203 FAO. Committee on Fisheries. (2005). Marine Protected Areas and Fisheries. COFI/2005/8. 203COFI. (2005). Report of the 26th Session of the Committee of Fisheries. FIPL/R780 (en). XX.

204 CBD. (2004). *Technical Advice on the Establishment and Management of a National System of Marine and Coastal Protected Areas.* (CBD Technical Series No 13). 10-11. MacKenzie, D. (2006). 'Glimmer of Hope for Doomed Fish'. *New Scientist.* November 11. 10. Odum, W. (1984). 'The Relationship Between Protected Coastal Areas and Marine Fisheries Genetic Resources. In McNeely, J. (ed). *National Parks, Conservation and Development.* (Smithsonian, Washington). 648-655. Roberts, C. (1998). *Fully Protected Marine Reserves.* (WWF, Gland). 88-89.

St Lucia's fishing grounds being listed as no take zones in 1995, commercially important stocks in adjacent waters doubled. These increases generated valuable exports for the country and a source of protein for its people.[205] Thus, not only does the area have direct benefits for conservation, it also has strong links with sustainable coastal and marine development.[206] The importance of MPAs in such spillover contexts has been endorsed in the Scientific Consensus Statement on Marine Reserves and Marine Protected Areas,[207] and the CBD.[208]

The importance of conserving ecosystems and representative habitats, especially those which are rare, unique or threatened (and the species therein) as a guiding principle, was first well recognized within the MAB programme in 1969[209] and thereafter.[210] It went on to become a well recognized principle with marine ecosystems in generic documents such as Agenda 21,[211] as well as within specific regimes such as the OSPAR[212] and Helsinki[213] Commissions, in addition to the Mediterranean,[214] Caribbean[215] and East African Protocols.[216]

The MAB regime has maintained a long standing commitment to the importance of ecosystems conservation through protected areas[217] and the Antarctic regime has also come to place a premium on the protection of representative examples of the major

205 Toepfer, K. (2004). 'Protected Areas.' *Our Planet.* 14(2): 1.

206 Agenda 21. Chapter 17.8.

207 As signed by 161 leading marine scientists under the auspice of the American Association for the Advancement of Science. The full statement can be found at: < http://www.nceas.ucsb.edu/Consensus/>

208 CBD. Decision VII/5 Marine and Coastal Biological Diversity. Sections 12 and 19.

209 UNESCO. (1971). *International Coordinating Council for the Programme on Man and the Biosphere.* (UNESCO, MAB Report Series No 1).

210 The Statutory Framework of the World Network of Biosphere Reserves. Article3 (1) and 4 (2). Seville + 5 Recommendations. Recommendation Number 3.

211 Agenda 21. Chapter 17.85.

212 OSPAR Recommendation 2003/3 on a Network of Marine Protected Areas. Appendix 1.

213 See Helsinki Commission (2004). Guidelines for designating BSPAs. Annex II.

214 See Mediterranean Protocol, Article 16 and Annex 1.B. On the particular importance of representativeness, see Annex I of the Protocol, section C.

215 Caribbean Protocol. Article 4(2).

216 Protocol Concerning Protected Areas of Wild Fauna and Flora in the Eastern African Region. Reprinted in Austen, A. (ed). *Basic Legal Document on International Animal Welfare and Wildlife Conservation* (Kluwer, London). Article 8(2)(b).

217 UNESCO. (1971). *Ibid.* The Statutory Framework of the World Network of Biosphere Reserves. Article3 (1) and 4 (2). Seville Strategy. Objective 1.1 & 1.2. Seville + 5 Recommendations. Recommendation Number 3.

land and fresh and salt water ecological systems.[218] Regional regimes, such as those from the 2003 African Convention,[219] and those related to Europe have a similar emphasis. In the later case, affirmation of seeking to protect representative ecosystems is clear under the European Diploma[220] and the Habitats Directive.[221] Moreover, the Parties of the Bern Convention have come to directly identify the type of representative habitats that need to be conserved under their auspice. For example, aside the directed and specific recommendations to individual countries to conserve a particular area, the Parties have also identified nine natural habitats (and their subsidiary forms) as endangered natural habitat types requiring specific conservation measures.[222] These were coastal and halophytic communities,[223] non-marine waters,[224] scrub and grassland,[225] forests,[226] bogs and marshes,[227] inland rocks, certain rock types, sands,[228] wooded grasslands and scrubs.[229]

---

218 Antarctic Treaty: Report of the Fourteenth Meeting. (Rio de Janeiro, 1987). Paragraph 88. See Annex V, Article 3 (2)(b) and (f) of the Madrid Protocol.

219 2003 African Convention. Article XII (1) (a).

220 The European Diploma recognises the importance of conserving representative habitats, especially those which are vulnerable, constituting typical examples of the various kinds of ecosystem in Europe' European Diploma. Annex I. Criteria.

221 Annex I of the Habitats Directive set out the natural habitat types of community interest whose conservation requires the designation of special areas of conservation. This was set out as 9 habitat types and their associated subsets. The overall types were Coastal and Halophytic habitats (32 types identified), coastal sand dunes and inland dunes (12 types), freshwater habitats (19 types), temperate heath and scrub (9 types), sclerophyllous scrub (13 types), natural and semi natural grasslands (29 types), raised bogs and mires and fens (12 types), rocky habitats and caves (14 types), forests (68 types). Habitat Directive. Annex III.

222 Resolution No. 4 (1996) Listing Endangered Natural Habitats Requiring Specific Conservation Measures.

223 With 9 subsets, in addition to sea inlets and coastal features , estuaries and tidal rivers, mud flats and sand flats, saltmarshes, salt steppes, salt scrubs, salt forests (with 16 subsets), coastal sand dunes and sand beaches (2 subsets),. Shingle beaches and coastal agro-systems.

224 Including, coastal lagoons , standing fresh water (and 31 subsets), standing brackish and salt water (and two subsets), running water.

225 Including temperate heath and scrub, sclerophyllous scrub (and 12 subsets), phrygana, steppes and dry calcareous grasslands (and 8 subsets), dry siliceous grasslands (and 3 subsets), humid grassland and tall herb communities (and 11 subsets), mesophile grasslands (and two subsets).

226 Including, broad-leaved deciduous forests (and 8 subsets), temperate coniferous forests (and 63 subsets of different temperate forests in the region), temperate riverine and swamp forests and brush (and 19 subsets) and temperate broad-leaved evergreen forests.

227 Including, raised bogs blanket bogs, water-fringe vegetation, fens, transition mires and springs (and ten subsets).

228 Including screes (and three subsets), inland sand dunes and caves.

229 Including parklands and wooded steppe.

A similar approach has been followed by the Ramsar. In the wetlands instance, although it has been long established that, 'representative, rare or unique example of a natural or near-natural wetland type found within the appropriate biogeographic region' may be suitable for inscription on the Ramsar list, this area was largely undeveloped until the late 1980s.[230] After this point, the Parties rapidly expanded from the official definition of a wetland,[231] to systematically identify, conserve and list, under-represented wetland types, in addition to the traditionally recognized wetlands.[232] The three traditional types of wetlands are inland,[233] coastal[234] or human made.[235] Thus, in an attempt to expand the coverage of wetland types, with regard to inland wetlands, the Ramsar Parties have urged all Parties to expand their focus to both, conserve and list, subterranean cave and karst systems,[236] peatlands[237] wet grasslands,[238] moun-

---

230 Recommendation 2.3. Action Points for Priority Attention. (1984, Groningen). The 1974 criteria suggested that such representative or unique wetlands may, as well as being characteristic of the biogeographical region, they may also/either exemplify a critical stage or extreme in biological or hydromorphological processes and/or represent an integral part of a peculiar physical feature. Recommendations adopted by the International Conference on the Conservation of Wetlands and Waterfowl at Heiligenhafen, Federal Republic of Germany, 6 December 1974. Annex II. Recommendations for Criteria to be used in identifying Wetlands of International Importance.

231 Wetlands are areas of marsh, fen, peatland or water, whether natural or artificial, permanent or temporary, with water that is static or flowing, fresh, brackish or salt, including areas of marine water the depth of which at low tide does not exceed six metres. Article 1, Ramsar Convention.

232 Resolution 8.11. Additional Guidance for Identifying and Designating Under Represented Wetland Types as Wetlands of International Importance. (2002, Valencia).

233 In terms of inland wetlands, these include permanent inland deltas, permanent rivers/streams/creeks, seasonal/intermittent freshwater lakes, permanent saline/brackish/alkaline lakes and flats, permanent saline/brackish/alkaline marshes/pools, permanent freshwater marshes/pools, seasonal/intermittent freshwater marshes/pools on inorganic solids, non forested peatlands, alpine wetlands, tundra wetlands, shrub dominated wetlands, freshwater, tree dominated wetlands, forested peatlands, freshwater springs, oases, geothermal wetlands, inland karst and other subterranean hydrological systems.

234 Marine/coastal wetlands include permanent shallow marine waters; marine sub-tidal aquatic beds; coral reefs; rocky marine shores; sand, shingle or pebble shores; estuarine waters; intertidal mud, sand or salt flats; intertidal marshes; intertidal forested wetlands; coastal brackish/saline lagoons; coastal freshwater lagoons and marine/coastal karst and other subterranean hydrological systems.

235 Human made wetlands include aquaculture ponds; points; irrigated land; seasonally flooded agricultural lands; salt exploitation sites; water storage areas; excavations; wastewater treatment areas; canal and drainage channels/ditches and human made karst and other subterranean hydrological systems. Resolution 8.13. Enhancing the Information on Wetlands of International Importance. (2002, San Jose). Annex I. Ramsar Classification System for Wetland Type.

236 Resolution 6.5. Subterranean Karst Wetlands. (1996, Brisbane). Resolution 7.13. Karst and Other Subterranean Hydrological Systems. (1999, San Jose).

tain wetlands, (especially those with glaciers),[239] temporary pools,[240] and river basins.[241] With regard to coastal wetlands, in addition to the adoption of some general principles for Integrated Coastal Management,[242] the Ramsar Parties have called for general protection of tidal flats,[243] and have emphasised the importance of conserving and listing areas containing mangroves[244] and coral reefs.[245]

---

237 Peatlands include bogs, fens, carrs, and peatswamp forest. Peat is dead and partially decomposed plant remains that have accumulated in situ under waterlogged conditions. An active peatland ('mire') is a peatland on which peat is currently forming and accumulating. The presence of peat or vegetation capable of forming peat is the key characteristic of peatlands. Peatlands can be coastal/marine or inland/fresh. Peatlands contribute to biological diversity, global water issues, wetland functions and climatic change. Resolution 8.11. Additional Guidance for Identifying and Designating Under Represented Wetland Types as Wetlands of International Importance. (2002, Valencia). Annex. Identification and Designation of Peatlands. Resolution 8.17. Guidelines for Global Action on Peatlands (GAP). (2002, Valencia). Annex. Paragraph 14. Recommendation 6.1. Conservation of Peatlands. (1996, Brisbane). Resolution 8.25. The Ramsar Strategic Plan. (2002, Valencia). Annex. Operational Objective 3.2.

238 Wet grasslands are natural and near natural ecosystems with a vegetation characterised and dominated by lower growing perennial grasses, sedges, reeds, rushes and/or herbs. They appear under periodically flooded or waterlogged conditions. They can fall under Ramsar as part of a floodplain component, a human made wetland or as a wet grassland habitat. They have many hydrological and chemical functions, notably, flood alleviation, groundwater recharge and water quality improvement. Resolution 8.11. *Ibid.*

239 Resolution 8.12. Enhancing the Wise Use and Conservation of Mountain Wetlands. (2002, Valencia).

240 Temporary pools are usually small (less than 10 hectares in area) and shallow wetlands which are characterised by an alternation of flooded and dry phases, and whose hydrology are largely autonomous. They tend to occupy depressions, are often endorheic (i.e. no stream or river comes from them) and are flooded over sufficient periods of time allow the development of wetland ecosystems. They often have very unique ecological communities that can be highly dependent upon them. Resolution 8.33. Guidance for Identifying, Sustainably Managing and Designating Temporary Pools as Wetlands of International Importance. (2002, Valencia). Annex. Paragraphs 12-17.

241 The 7th COP adopted the Guidelines for Integrating Wetland Conservation and Wise Use into River Basin Management. See Resolution 7.18. River Basin Management. (1999, San Jose).

242 Resolution 8.4. Principles for Incorporating Wetland Issues Into Integrated Coastal Zone Management. (2002, Valencia). Recommendation 6.8. Strategic Planning in Coastal Zones. (1996, Brisbane).

243 Resolution 7.21. Intertidal Wetlands. (1996, San Jose).

244 Resolution 8.11. Additional Guidance for Identifying and Designating Under Represented Wetland Types as Wetlands of International Importance. (2002, Valencia). Resolution 8.32. Conservation, Integrated Management and Sustainable Use of Mangrove Ecosystems and Their Resources. (2002, Valencia).

245 Recommendation 6.7. Conservation and Wise Use of Coral Reefs and Associated Ecosystems. (1996, Brisbane). Resolution 8.11. *Ibid.*

The IMO has adopted a variant on this approach, by focusing not on the type of ecosystem under its auspice (oceans) but on the qualities of the particular ocean in question. Of the two protected area mechanisms available to the IMO (special areas and PSSAs), the oceanographic and ecological conditions are foremost. In the first instance, drawing directly from the language of UNCLOS,[246] the IMO in its jurisprudence on special areas as come to distinguish between the two criteria. In the first instance, oceanographic conditions relate to factors that would cause the concentration or retention of harmful substances in the waters or sediments of the area, or – to be more direct – how vulnerable the ecosystem is to potential damage. The possible conditions include, circulation patterns (such as convergence zones or gyres) or temperate and salinity stratification, long residence time caused by law flushing rates, extreme ice state, and/or adverse wind conditions. For example, the Baltic sea was designated in 1973 as a special area due to its shallowness, its brackish waters, its interconnected hydrological regimes, low nutrients, and dense surrounding populations of humans, extremely slow and irregular exchanges of deep water with ocean waters, slow chemical and biological degradation of pollutants, and the disproportionately high concentration of pollutants in the Baltic.[247]

The second criteria utilized for IMO special areas is 'ecological conditions'. This section is very species related, as it covers depleted or threatened or endangered marine species, areas of high natural productivity (such as fronts, up-welling areas, or gyres), spawning, breeding or nursery grounds for important marine species and areas representing migratory routes for sea-birds and marine mammals, rare or fragile ecosystems (such as coral reefs, mangroves, seagrass beds or wetlands) and/or critical habitats for marine resources including fish stocks and/or areas of critical importance for the support of large marine ecosystems. However, when dealing with 'ecological conditions' for PSSA applications, the IMO has attempted[248] to distinguish this section by considerably expanding the thinking behind the category to include eight possible subsets, that moves it beyond the more species focused approach of 'ecological conditions' for special areas. The additional categories are uniqueness,[249] dependency,[250] representiveness,[251]

---

246 UNCLOS. Article 211.

247 IMO General Assembly. 17th Session. A 17/Res.720. Guidelines for the Designation of Special Areas and the Identification of Particularly Sensitive Sea Areas. 42-45.

248 Despite the attempt to divide ecological and oceanographic conditions, the overlap is often substantial. Indeed, the Baltic sea was listed as both a special area, and a PSSA, for effectively the same reasons, in both brackets. For the PSSA listing, see MEPC. (2004). Report of the MEPC on its 51st Session. MEPC. 51/22. 34. For the special area listing, examine IMO General Assembly. 17th Session. A 17/Res.720. Guidelines for the Designation of Special Areas and the Identification of Particularly Sensitive Sea Areas. 42-45.

249 As in, it is 'the only one of its kind', such as with habitats of endangered species or rare nurseries or feeding grounds.

250 Such as with highly inter-dependent ecological processes, such as coral reefs, kelp forests, mangrove forests, seagrass beds and migratory routes for fish, reptiles birds and mammals.

productivity,[252] diversity,[253] integrity,[254] vulnerability[255] and finally, its naturalness – or the degree it is unaltered by human influence. The original eight ecological criteria were added to in 2001[256] by the additional possibilities of critical habitat,[257] and bio-geographical importance.[258] Thus, with a PSSA like the Great Barrier Reef, its ecological criteria could be seen in its uniqueness (as the largest single collection of coral reefs in the world and biologically supporting the most diverse ecosystem known to humanity) dependency (a highly dependent ecosystem) its representative nature (the largest and most complex example of a coral reef ecosystem in the world), diversity (the most diverse coral system known), in pristine natural condition, and its complete integrity (as a functioning biological unit).[259]

The final convention of note, which has come to place a clear value on the protection of ecosystems, is the WHC. The WHC, which sets out to conserve, inter alia, 'natural sites or precisely delineated natural areas of outstanding universal value from the point of view of science, conservation or natural beauty'[260] has developed a broad category, which encompasses ecosystems, known as criteria II (and partly criteria IV, as noted above). Criteria II recognises natural sites which are,

---

251 As in areas of highly representative ecological processes, or habitat types or other natural characteristics.

252 As in areas that result in an increase in biomass, such as oceanic fronts, up-welling areas and some gyres.

253 In terms of either species and/or habitats.

254 As in the area is a biologically functional unit, and, at best, an effective self sustaining ecological entity.

255 Its degree of susceptibility to degradation by anthropogenic or non-anthropogenic events, including its particular oceanographic features. This concern overlaps with the consideration of 'natural factors' which covers such hydrographical concerns such as depth, coastal topography etc, meteorological such as typical weather concerns, and oceanographic, such as tidal and ocean streams/currents etc.

256 Annex 6. Guidelines for the Designation of Special Areas Under MARPOL 73/78 and Guidelines for the Identification and Designation of Particularly Sensitive Sea Areas. MEPC (2001). Report of the MEPC on its 46th Session. MEPC 46/23. Section 4.4.2.

257 A sea area may be a critical habitat for fish stocks or rare or endangered marine species, or an area of critical importance for the support of large marine ecosystems.

258 An area that either contains rare bio-geographic qualities or is representative of a biogeographical 'type' or types, or contains unique or unusual geological features. Annex 6. Guidelines for the Designation of Special Areas. *Ibid.* Section 4.4.10.

259 Annex 6. Guidelines for the Designation of Special Areas Under MARPOL 73/78 and Guidelines for the Identification and Designation of Particularly Sensitive Sea Areas. MEPC (2001). Report of the MEPC on its 46th Session. MEPC 46/23. Summary of Existing PSSAs. 17,

260 WHC Article 2.

> [o]utstanding examples representing significant on-going ecological and biological processes in the evolution and development of terrestrial, fresh water, coastal and marine ecosystems and communities of plants and animals.[261]

Despite the apparent clarity of this criterion, it is relatively rare for sites to be inscribed under criteria II alone. The only sites that have been are Shirakami-Sanchi in Japan, East Rennell of the Solomon Islands, and the Hawaiian Volcanoes. Also notable for single listings under criteria II are the Heard and McDonald Islands of Australia,[262] Alejandro de Humboldt Park in Cuba,[263] and the Cerrado protected area in Brazil.[264] All of the other listings under criteria II have been in conjunction with other (typically criteria IV) inscription values.

The core of criteria II is in outstanding, functioning ecosystems. This criterion broadly captures complete ecosystems, such as tropical forests or coral reefs.[265] This criteria, does not, prima facie, focus upon the threatened nature of either the ecosystem or any species that may be within it. However, although the criteria may not focus upon this, multiple ecosystems of such outstanding features typically include such threatened species.

The possibilities for listing under this criterion have broken down into two areas. First, outstanding examples representing significant on-going ecological and biological processes may be listed. These are typically linked to high levels of endemic biodiversity, but this is not always the case. For example, the closed salt lake system in the Uvs Nuur Basin (the site also includes mountains, forests, steppes and deserts) shared between Mongolia and Russia,[266] and the Waterton Glacier park of Canada and the United States[267] were both listed, largely irrespective of considerations relating to the levels of their biodiversity.

The second area, although implicitly linked to the first relates to the, 'ecological and biological processes in the evolution and development of terrestrial, fresh water, coastal and marine ecosystems and communities of plants and animals'. The key words are 'evolution and development' and these have commonly been interpreted to relate to high levels of endemic biodiversity with key ecosystems. This part of criteria IV (which has an obvious overlap with criteria II and threatened species, which are often in exactly

---

261 *Operational Guidelines.* 2002 Edn. Paragraph 44 (ii).

262 UNESCO. (1997). 21st Session of the WHC. WHC-97/CONF.208/17. Feb 27, 1998. 36.

263 UNESCO. (2001). 25th Session of the WHC. WHC-01/CONF.208/24. Feb 8, 2002. 91.

264 Ibid. 90.

265 *Operational Guidelines.* 2002 Edn. Paragraph 44.

266 UNESCO. (2003). 27th Session of the WHC. WHC-03/27.COM/24. Dec 10. 102.

267 Criteria II due to its distinctive climate, physiological setting, mountain prairie interface and tri-ocean hydrographical divide. UNESCO. (1996). 19th Session of the WHC. WHC-95/CONF.203/16. Jan 31, 1996. 34.

the same places as criteria IV considerations) is commonly interpreted to mean sites which are, 'the most biologically diverse'.[268] The words 'most biologically diverse' are often code for 'hotspots'. The idea of protecting hotspots is becoming apparent within the workings of a number of regimes such as the MAB,[269] the East African Protocol,[270] the 2003 African Convention,[271] the regimes surrounding the Arctic,[272] and the WHC.[273]

The recognition of high levels of biodiversity may be seen in terms of either its nature, or the ecosystems it falls within. For a few examples (among dozens) consider the following. Bialowieza Forest has 232 species of bird and 8,500 types of insect within its protected area. St Lucia wetland in South Africa holds 520 species of birds, 129 species of mammals and 110 species of butterfly.[274] Tsingy has 430 species of flora, of which 85% are endemic. Lake Baikal contains over 1,500 species of aquatic fauna of which 80% are endemic. Guanacaste in Costa Rica has terrestrial fauna numbers in excess of 2 million insects, including 500 types of butterfly and 500 bird species. The Galapagos has the highest percentage of endemism in the world (of over 300 fish, 1,600 insects, 80 spiders, 300 coleopteras and 650 molluscs). Pantanal in Brazil has 656 species of bird. The Atlantic Forests in Brazil contain over 50% of its 10,000 trees and 92% of its amphibians are unique to the region.[275] The Coiba site in Panama includes 760 species of marine fish, 33 species of sharks and 20 species of cetaceans.[276] A number of African sites, such as the Bwindi National Park[277] and the

---

268 *Operational Guidelines.* 2002 Edn. Paragraph 44.

269 West Polesie. UNESCO. (2001). ICC Bureau Meeting. SCI/-01/CONF.217/8. Dec 12, 2. 16. Triglav in Slovenia. UNESCO. (2003). ICC Bureau Meeting. SC-02/CONF.210/10. Jan 7. 15. Toliara in Madagascar. Chinchorro and Sierra La Laguna in Mexico. Julian Alps in Slovenia. Socotra in Yemen. UNESCO. (2003). ICC Bureau Meeting. SC/-03/CONF.217/14. July 30. 10-13. Such as Mulanje in Malawi, Bardenas in Spain, and East Usambara in Tanzania. MAB. (2000). 16th Session of the ICC Bureau. SC-00/CONF.208/13. 21-22.

270 'Populations of the greatest number of species of fauna and flora depending on these ecosystems'. Protocol Concerning Protected Areas of Wild Fauna and Flora in the Eastern African Region. Reprinted in Austen, A. (ed). *Basic Legal Document on International Animal Welfare and Wildlife Conservation* (Kluwer, London). Article 8(2)(c).

271 2003 African Convention. Article XII (1) (b).

272 See CAFF. (1996). The Circumpolar Protected Area Network: Principles and Guidelines. CAFF Habitat Conservation Report, No 4. 8-9. Principles 4 and 5.

273 In 2002, in discussing the Global Strategy, the Committee invited the IUCN to give: 'greater emphasis to the analysis of biodiversity both in terms of qualitative and quantitative richness and endemism.' UNESCO. (2002). 26th Session of the WHC. WHC-02/CONF.202/25. Aug 1, 2002.11.

274 'Greater St Lucia Wetland Park'. 40 *World Heritage.* (2005): 45, 48.

275 Cattaneo, M. & Trifoni, J. (2003). *The World Heritage Sites of UNESCO: Nature Sanctuaries* (WhiteStar, Vercelli). 20, 30, 36, 40, 114, 118, 120, 142, 158, 190, 192, 203, 272, 276, 282, 293, 301, 314, 316

276 Decision 29 COM 8B.13.

277 UNESCO. (1995). 18th Session of the WHC. WHC-94/CONF.003/16. Jan 31. 1995. 42.

Rwenzori Mountains (both in Uganda)[278] are particularly notable. The Dong Phayayen-Khao Yai Forest complex contains more than 800 fauna species, 112 species of mammals, 392 species of birds and 200 reptiles and amphibians.[279] With floral diversity, sites in Dominica,[280] the Congo,[281] and China[282] are highlighted. With the Alejandro de Humboldt site in Cuba, listing was due, in part, to being one of the most important sites for conservation of endemic flora in the entire Western hemisphere. This site contains 16 of the 28 plant formations identified in Cuba, including an estimated 1,800 to 2,000 spermatophytes of which nearly 70% are endemic to the park.[283] The Cape Floral region of South Africa claims, as one of the world's 25 biodiversity hotspots, to be one of the richest areas for plants (in terms of species per genus and per family) on Earth. Such floral diversity is often in conjunction with vertebrate diversity.[284] The Cerrado site in Brazil contains over 60% of all floral species and 80% of all vertebrate species of the region.[285] The Mexican Islands in the Gulf of Mexico contain 695 vascular plants, 891 species of fish, 39% of the world's marine mammals and a third of the world's total number of cetacean species.[286]

Specific ecosystems where the high levels of endemic biodiversity were noted by the Committee include some areas which are hard to classify, due to their vast and diverse nature such as the Laponian Area of Sweden,[287] New Zealand's Sub-Antarctic Islands,[288] or the Lorentz National Park in Indonesia.[289]

In other instances, one type of ecosystem and its link to high levels of endemic species is identified as being primary above other ecosystems such as with some sites involving mountains (being included in at least one third of the total of all natural and mixed WHC

---

278 Ibid.

279 Decision 29 COM 8B.11.

280 The Morne Trois Pitons National park. UNESCO. (1997). 21st Session of the WHC. WHC-97/CONF.208/17. Feb 27, 1998. 37.

281 Okapi Wildlife Reserve. UNESCO. (1996). 20th Session of the WHC. WHC-96/CONF.201/21. Mar 10, 1997. 47-48.

282 Mount Emei. UNESCO. (1996). 20th Session of the WHC. WHC-96/CONF.201/21. Mar 10, 1997. 448.

283 UNESCO. (2001). 25th Session of the WHC. WHC-01/CONF.208/24. Paris 8, Feb 2002. 91.

284 UNESCO. (2004). 28th Session of the WHC. WHC-04/28.COM/26. Oct 29. Decision 28 COM 14B12. pp. 21-22.

285 UNESCO. (2001). 25th Session of the WHC. WHC-01/CONF.208/24. Paris 8, Feb 2002. 90.

286 Decision 29 COM 8B.9.

287 UNESCO. (1996). 20th Session of the WHC. WHC-96/CONF.201/21. Mar 10, 1997. 49.

288 The high level of projective, biodiversity, wildlife population densities and endemism were noted, as were several evolutionary processes. UNESCO. (1998). 22nd Session of the WHC. WHC-98/CONF.208/18. Jan 29, 1998. 58.

289 UNESCO. (1999). 23rd Session of the WHC. WHC-99/CONF.209/22. Mar 22, 2000. 21-22.

sites)[290] volcanoes (in Russia[291] and elsewhere)[292] or wetlands (which are the second most common WHC natural site),[293] rivers (in the Philippines,[294] China,[295] and Brazil)[296] and lakes (in Russia).[297] Some coral reefs[298] (such as with the Belize Barrier reef reserve system,[299] and the Tubbataha reef marine park of the Philippines)[300] have been emphasized, as have some coastal areas (often including reefs or other key ecosystems, like sea grasses), such as the Sundarbans of Bangladesh,[301] Ibiza park in Spain,[302] Cocos island national park,[303] Russia's Wrangel island[304] and East Rennel of the Solomon Islands. East Rennel has the largest coral atoll in the world and the largest lake in the insular pacific.[305]

---

290 See IUCN. (2002). *A Global Overview of Mountain Protected Areas on the World Heritage List.* (Gland, IUCN). 3-6. Also, Cattaneo, M. & Trifoni, J. (2003). *The World Heritage Sites of UNESCO: Nature Sanctuaries* (WhiteStar, Vercelli). 16, 34, 52, 68, 76, 83, 96, 150, 154, 160, 168, 170, 212, 220, 230, 242, 258, 296, 301, 369, 382.

291 Kamchatka 'major concentrations of wildlife'. UNESCO. (1996). 20th Session of the WHC. WHC-96/CONF.201/21. Mar 10, 1997. 47.

292 Including Giants Causeway (and the effect of the lava); the Aeolian islands;; Ujung Kulon in Indonesia, the Hawaii Volcanoes, Cattaneo. *Ibid.* 24, 45, 135, 200, 258.

293 UNESCO. (1995). 18th Session of the WHC. WHC-94/CONF.003/16. Jan 31. 1995. 41. UNESCO. (1999). 23rd Session of the WHC. WHC-99/CONF.209/22. Mar 22, 2000. 25. Notably, Lapland, Parque Bacional de Coto Donana in Spain, Delta of the Danube in Rumania; St Lucia Wetland in South Africa, Pantanal in Brazil. Cattaneo, M & Trifoni, J. (2003). The World Heritage Sites of UNESCO: Nature Sanctuaries (WhiteStar, Vercelli). 16, 16, 36, 56, 114.

294 Such as with the Puerto-Princesa River National Park in the Philippines, UNESCO. (1999). 23rd Session of the WHC. WHC-99/CONF.209/22. Mar 22, 2000. 22.

295 The Three Parallel Rivers in China, 'may be the most biologically diverse temperate region on Earth'. UNESCO. (2003). 27th Session of the WHC. WHC-03/27.COM/24. Dec 10. 98-99.

296 The Jau National Park in Brazil, although inclusive of forest also includes the hydrological basin of the Jau river, which is deemed an important area for its interrelated biodiversity. UNESCO. (2001). 24th Session of the WHC. WHC-2000/CONF.204/21. Feb 16, 2001. 63.

297 Lake Baikal in Russia contains an outstanding variety of endemic flora and fauna. UNESCO. (1996). 20th Session of the WHC. WHC-96/CONF.201/21. Mar 10, 1997. 46.

298 Cattaneo, *Ibid.* 120, 190, 192, 203, 272, 276, 345-348, 357

299 UNESCO. (1996). 20th Session of the WHC. WHC-96/CONF.201/21. Mar 10, 1997. 46.

300 UNESCO. (1993). 17th Session of WHC. WHC-93/CONF.002/14. Feb 4, 1993. 35.

301 UNESCO. (1997). 21st Session of the WHC. WHC-97/CONF.208/17. Feb 27, 1998. 37.

302 This Park supports 220 species in the Mediterranean basin. UNESCO. (1999). 23rd Session of the WHC. WHC-99/CONF.209/22. Mar 22, 2000. 27.

303 UNESCO. (1997). 21st Session of the WHC. WHC-97/CONF.208/17. Feb 27, 1998. 37.

304 UNESCO. (2004). 28th Session of the WHC. WHC-04/28.COM/26. Oct 29. Decision 28 COM 14B14. pp. 23.

305 UNESCO. (1998). 22nd Session of the WHC. WHC-98/CONF.208/18. Jan 29, 1998. 60.

Finally, forests need to be considered. Forests are increasingly common as MAB sites,[306] and are also the most common kind of habitat within WHC natural sites. Indeed, forests are present in over 90% of WHC natural sites. As of 2005, there were 87 WHC properties (52 tropical, 9 subtropical, 19 temperate, 7 boreal) that contain significant forest cover, and double this number of sites in total, if the consideration is the inclusion of 'some' forest habitat. Counting only the properties with 'significant' forest cover gives a total of 70,000,000 hectares of WHC protected forest area. This figure represents approximately 17% of the global forest area under protected area status. When the nominations under preparation and countries tentative lists are considered, this figure may increase to around 25% of global forest areas.[307] Within this subset, particular forests which have been highlighted by the Committee in the listing process, due to their high levels of endemic biodiversity include sites listed in China,[308] Russia,[309] Portugal,[310] Switzerland,[311] Australia,[312] Brazil,[313] Kenya,[314]

---

306 Nijegorodskoe in Russia. UNESCO. (2003). ICC Bureau Meeting. SC-02/CONF.210/10. Jan 7. 12. Terras do Mino in Spain. UNESCO. (2003). ICC Bureau Meeting. SC-02/CONF.210/10. Jan 7. 13.

307 See Report of the World Heritage Centre on Implementing Decisions. WHC-05/29.COM/5. UNESCO. (2001). 25th Session of the WHC. WHC-01/CONF.208/24. Paris 8, Feb 2002. 115. For earlier figures, see Cattaneo, M. & Trifoni, J. (2003). *The World Heritage Sites of UNESCO: Nature Sanctuaries* (WhiteStar, Vercelli). 16, 40, 52, 60, 78, 83, 96, 108, 143-153, 162, 181, 188, 190, 198, 200, 216, 220, 226, 236, 240, 252, 285, 310, 316, 325, 337, 340, 364, 372. For the earlier definitive study of forests under the WH auspice, see IUCN. (1997). *A Global Overview of the Forest Protected Areas on the World Heritage List.* (IUCN, Gland).

308 Mount Wuyi in China is the largest, most representative example of a largely intact forest encompassing the diversity of the Chinese Subtropical forest and the South Chinese rainforest. UNESCO. (1999). 23rd Session of the WHC. WHC-99/CONF.209/22. Mar 22, 2000. 26.

309 The Central Sikhote-Alin in Russia has ' high level of endemic plants, invertebrates and animals.' UNESCO. (2001). 25th Session of the WHC. WHC-01/CONF.208/24. Feb 8, 2002. 92. The Virgin Komi Forests, UNESCO. (1996). 19th Session of the WHC. WHC-95/CONF.203/16. Jan 31, 1996. 35 and the Western Caucasus. UNESCO. (1999). 23rd Session of the WHC. WHC-99/CONF.209/22. Mar 22, 2000. 23.

310 The Laurisilva of Madeira of Portugal contains the largest surviving relic of virtually extinct laurisilva forest type that was once widespread in Europe. It is considered to be a center of plan diversity containing numerous rare and endemic species. UNESCO. (1999). 23rd Session of the WHC. WHC-99/CONF.209/22. Mar 22, 2000. 23.

311 The Jungfrau region.

312 The Greater Blue Mountains of Australia contain (wet and dry) eucalypt vegetation (of 90 taxa, representing 13% of the global total). UNESCO. (2001). 24th Session of the WHC. WHC-2000/CONF.204/21. Feb 16, 2001. 62.

313 For the high levels of endemism, see the Brazilian Atlantic forests. UNESCO. (2001). 25th Session of the WHC. WHC-01/CONF.208/24. Feb 8, 2002. 89. See also, Discovery Coast Atlantic Forest Reserves. UNESCO. (1999). 23rd Session of the WHC. WHC-99/CONF.209/22. Mar 22, 2000. 19. The Atlantic Forest Southeast Reserves. UNESCO. (1999). 23rd Session of the WHC. WHC-99/CONF.209/22. Mar 22, 2000. 19.

Malaysia,[315] Surinam,[316] Colombia,[317] Indonesia[318] and Bolivia.[319] The Area de Conservacion Guanacaste in Costa Rica claims an incredible 2.4% of all global biodiversity.[320]

C Geomorphic or Physiographical Areas

Geomorphic and/or physio-graphical areas can be divided into three areas. The first relates to the Earth's history, (including phenomena that record important events in the past development of the planet, such as the record of crustal dynamics, the genesis and development of mountains, plate movements, continental movement, rift valley development, meteorite impacts, and changing climate in the geological past). Second, the record of life (in terms of fossil sites). Finally, significant ongoing geological processes (in the development of landforms, such as processes associated with glaciers, mountains, deserts, active volcanoes, rivers, deltas, islands and coasts). Geomorphic and/or physiographical areas are important because of what they represent in evolutionary terms, with regard to both final products and creation processes.

Although such areas, obviously, contain ecosystems and species, these are not the primary focus of their value. Rather, their value is in protecting intricate parts of the Earth's history and processes, which are not necessarily 'alive,' 'vibrant' or as 'visible' as the other species and ecosystems which surround humanity. Accordingly, a number of international regimes, such as the MAB,[321] and the Bern Convention,[322] have excluded such values from their inscription criteria. Conversely, some other regimes, such as that pertaining to Antarctica have re-orientated their inscription values to include

314 The Mount Kenya National Natural Forest Park. UNESCO. (1997). 21st Session of the WHC. WHC-97/CONF.208/17. Feb 27, 1998. 37-38.

315 Kinabalu with its high diverse biota and high endemism. UNESCO. (2001). 24th Session of the WHC. WHC-2000/CONF.204/21. Feb 16, 2001. 65. Gunung Mulu also has very high biological endemism, including one of the richest areas in the world for palm species. UNESCO. (2001). 24th Session of the WHC. WHC-2000/CONF.204/21. Feb 16, 2001. 66.

316 The Central Suriname Nature Reserve in Surinam has 'high endemic biodiversity'. UNESCO. (2001). 24th Session of the WHC. WHC-2000/CONF.204/21. Feb 16, 2001. 66.

317 Los Katios park listed, due to it being: 'a centre of endemism for flora and fauna.' UNESCO. (1995). 18th Session of the WHC. WHC-94/CONF.003/16. Jan 31. 1995. 40.

318 Sumatra. UNESCO. (2004). 28th Session of the WH Committee. WHC-04/28.COM/26. Oct 29. Decision 28 COM 14B5. pp. 17.

319 Noel Kempff. UNESCO. (2001). 24th Session of the WHC. WHC-2000/CONF.204/21. Feb 16, 2001. 63.

320 UNESCO. (1999). 23rd Session of the WHC. WHC-99/CONF.209/22. Mar 22, 2000. 20.

321 UNESCO. (2001). ICC Bureau Meeting. SC/-01/CONF.211/13. Apr 10. 18.

322 Report of the 21st Meeting of the Bern Convention. T-PVS (2001). 89. 11-12.

such geomorphic or physiographical areas,[323] whilst newer regimes, such as the European Diploma, have come to openly embrace them.[324]

Despite this changing recognition of geomorphic and/or physiographical values, the only regime to have developed a clear jurisprudence in this area is the WHC. The WHC, from its broad coverage which can encompass this area,[325] has sought to inscribe, under criteria I, outstanding examples representing major stages of Earth's history, including the record of life, significant on-going geological processes in the development of landforms, or significant geomorphic or physiographic features.[326]

Although it is common for most sites to fulfil more than one criterion when being inscribed on the WHC List, in some instances, they only fulfil one criterion. In these single criteria instances, it is more common for a site to be justified only under criteria I, than any other criteria. The sites which have utilized this route include the Ischigualasto natural park in Argentina, Miguasha park in Canada, the Messel Pit fossil site in Germany, the Aggtelek and Slovak caves in Hungary and Slovakia, Isole Eolie in Italy, the High Coast of Sweden, Monte San Giorgio in Switzerland, the Dorset and Devon Coast in the United Kingdom and Phong Nha-Ke Bang in Vietnam. In 2006, the site of the High Coast of Sweden, extended under natural criterion I alone, with the 5,600 islands of the Kvarken Archipelago, which is an area of rapid glacio-isostatic uplift with rates that are among the highest in the world.[327]

---

323 The Consultative Parties responded to this recommendation by supplementing the 1964 Agreed Measures on the creation of Specially Reserved Areas (SRAs) in 1989. Although SRAs recognise biological considerations for listing, the category was meant to be primarily used for designating areas of outstanding geological, glaciological, geo-morphological, ... areas. Finally, the Madrid Protocol in 1991, reiterated the emphasis upon SPAs to include, inter alia, 'examples of outstanding geological, glaciological or geomorphological features'. Recommendation XV-10. Antarctic Protected Area System: Establishment of Specially Reserved Areas. In Antarctic Treaty: Report of the Fifteenth Meeting (Paris, 1989). 82. See paragraph 129. For these values in the Madrid Protocol, see Annex V, Article 3 (2)(b) and (f).

324 The European Diploma aimed at conserving remarkable natural phenomena or geological or physiographic formations characteristic of the earth's history. These may include:
a. sites or complexes of major importance for the conservation of significant evidence of the earth's history;
b. noteworthy palaeontological sites;
c. outstanding examples of geological, geomorphological, volcanic, hydrographic, physiographic or bio-geographical phenomena;
d. particularly grandiose or spectacular examples of protected natural features such as waterfalls, caves, rock formations, glacial cirques, glaciers. European Diploma. Annex I. Criteria.

325 The WHC is obliged to protect, inter alia, 'natural features consisting of physical and biological formations or groups of such formations… and/or … geological and physiographical formations and precisely delineated areas…. WHC. Article 2.

326 *Operational Guidelines.* 2002 Edn. Paragraph 44 (i).

327 See Decision 30 COM BB.27.

In addition, to being the most common stand-alone inscription value, criteria I is also one of the single most value for all sites to have listed. As of 2005, two thirds of all WHC natural properties included this criterion in addition to other criteria.[328]

Criteria I, as assisted by some thematic studies,[329] has been broadly interpreted and has come to encompass a number of different areas. With regard to the 'record of life' globally important (stand alone) fossil sites in Australia,[330] Germany,[331] Switzerland,[332] Argentina,[333] the United Kingdom,[334] Canada[335] and Egypt[336] are notable. Sites in which fossil remains were still notable in the nominations (but not stand alone criteria) are also in Indonesia[337] and Kenya.[338] In 2005, the first meteor impact site (Vredefort Dome) in South Africa was inscribed under this criterion.[339]

In terms of 'on-going geological processes' sites including both volcanoes and glaciers are notable,[340] although both could also fit within geomorphic or physio-graphic considerations. The sites inscribed only for their volcanoes are in Italy,[341] and as additional considerations, sites can be found in Australia,[342] Russia,[343] St Lucia[344] and

328 See IUCN. (2005). *Background Paper for the Special Expert Meeting of the World Heritage Convention on the Concept of Outstanding Universal Value.* (IUCN, Gland). 6-7.

329 See IUCN (1996). *Earth's Geological History: A Contextual Framework for Assessment of Fossil Site Nominations.* (IUCN, Gland). As discussed in the 20th (1996) Session of the WHC., at 60.

330 These were the sites Rivereligh/Naracoorte. UNESCO. (1995). 18th Session of the WHC. WHC-94/CONF.003/16. Jan 31. 1995. 40.

331 The Messel Pit Fossil site. UNESCO. (1996). 19th Session of the WHC. WHC-95/CONF.203/16. Jan 31, 1996. 34.

332 Monte San Giorgio. UNESCO. (2003). 27th Session of the WHC. WHC-03/27.COM/24. Dec 10. 100.

333 The Ischigualasto site. UNESCO. (2001). 24th Session of the WHC. WHC-2000/CONF.204/21. Feb 16, 2001. 60.

334 The Dorset and Devon Coast. UNESCO. (2001). 25th Session of the WHC. WHC-01/CONF.208/24. Paris 8, Feb 2002. 93.

335 Miguasha Park. UNESCO. (1999). 23rd Session of the WHC. WHC-99/CONF.209/22. Mar 22, 2000. 20.

336 Decision 29 COM. 8B5 (Whale Valley).

337 Lorentz National Park. UNESCO. (1999). 23rd Session of the WHC. WHC-99/CONF.209/22. Mar 22, 2000. 21-22.

338 Sibiloi Park. UNESCO. (1997). 21st Session of the WHC. WHC-97/CONF.208/17. Feb 27, 1998. 38.

339 Decision 29 COM 8B.4.

340 The Operational Guidelines, with regard to this subset of the criteria, talk of glaciers and volcanoes. *Operational Guidelines.* 2002 Edn. Paragraph 44.

341 Isole Eolie. UNESCO. (2001). 24th Session of the WHC. WHC-2000/CONF.204/21. Feb 16, 2001. 64.

342 Heard and McDonald Islands. UNESCO. (1997). 21st Session of the WHC. WHC-97/CONF.208/17. Feb 27, 1998. 36.

Dominica.[345] Finally, fold-thrust/over-thrust sites are notable. These features are encompassed (but often under different classifications) for the Waterton Glacier park, the Pyrenees, and Te Wahipounamu in New Zealand. The only site to actually seek nomination under criteria I alone, on the basis of over-thrust, was from Switzerland. However, this was removed before the inscription was debated, due to lack of support from the IUCN evaluation.

With regard to glaciers Switzerland,[346] Sweden[347] and Los Glaciers in Argentina,[348] have all been sites listed (in conjunction with other criteria) with an emphasis on their glaciers. The ice-stream of the Ilulissat Icefjord in Denmark, flowing at a rate of 19 meters per day, is obvious under this category.[349] The Fjords of Norway, containing two of the world's longest and deepest fjords are also apparent in this category.[350]

'Significant geomorphic or physiographic features' have also come to encompass caves and karst ecosystems. These sites are also typically in conjunction with criteria II with regard to unique biota.[351] Sites of note in this category include Malaysia,[352] Slovakia,[353] the United States,[354] Vietnam[355] Australia,[356] and Cuba.[357] Finally, a

343 Kamchatka. UNESCO. (1996). 20th Session of the WHC. WHC-96/CONF.201/21. Mar 10, 1997. 47.

344 Pitons. UNESCO. (2004). 28th Session of the WHC. WHC-04/28.COM/26. Oct 29. Decision 28 COM 14B11. pp. 20.

345 UNESCO. (1997). 21st Session of the WHC. WHC-97/CONF.208/17. Feb 27, 1998. 37.

346 The Jungfrau region in Switzerland as one of the most glaciated regions of the Alps, incorporating the largest and longest glacier in Western Eurasia.

347 The High Coast of Sweden. UNESCO. (2001). 24th Session of the WHC. WHC-2000/CONF.204/21. Feb 16, 2001. 67.

348 Cattaneo, M. & Trifoni, J. (2003). *The World Heritage Sites of UNESCO: Nature Sanctuaries* (WhiteStar, Vercelli). 16, 42, 323.

349 UNESCO. (2004). 28th Session of the WHC. WHC-04/28.COM/26. Oct 29. Decision 28 COM 14B8. pp. 19.

350 Decision 29 COM 8B.7.

351 See IUCN. (2001). Karst Ecosystems and World Heritage. (IUCN, Gland). 12-33.

352 Gunung Mulu. UNESCO. (2001). 24th Session of the WHC. WHC-2000/CONF.204/21. Feb 16, 2001. 65-66.

353 The Caves of the Aggtelek & Slovak Karst. UNESCO. (1996). 19th Session of the WHC. WHC-95/CONF.203/16. Jan 31, 1996. 34.

354 Carlsbad Caverns. UNESCO. (1996). 19th Session of the WHC. WHC-95/CONF.203/16. Jan 31, 1996. 35.

355 Phong Nha – Ke Bang National park. UNESCO. (2003). 27th Session of the WHC. WHC-03/27.COM/24. Dec 10. 101.

356 Purnululu National park. UNESCO. (2003). 27th Session of the WHC. WHC-03/27.COM/24. Dec 10. 103.

357 Desembarco del Granma National Park. UNESCO. (1999). 23rd Session of the WHC. WHC-99/CONF.209/22. Mar 22, 2000. 21.

number of other sites have been listed with regard to their geological uniqueness in terms of their exposure of the oceanic plate and tectonic movements;[358] the world's oldest and deepest lake;[359] as well as areas containing classic geological features such as the Laponian area of Sweden[360] and the Pyrenees.[361] The Three Parallel Rivers in China were listed for, inter alia, displaying geological history of the last 50 million years associated with the collision of the Indian plate and the Eurasian plate and the uplifting of the Himalaya range and the Tibetan plateau.[362]

8 Intangible Human Values

In addition to all of the above values there is also a series of more intangible values, from which protected areas are beneficial to humanity. These include, inter alia, values of aesthetics, education, recreation, spiritualism and social context.[363] All of these values are, allegedly, 'separate from political expediencies'.[364] These values were first noted at the First World Parks Conference on National Parks in 1962 as those which come from protected areas, and, 'are necessary to the life of man [as they] provide a powerful physical, moral and regenerative spiritual influence, and contribute to the artistic and cultural life of peoples'.[365] This recognition of the social, philosophical and spiritual value to humanity of wilderness has deep currents in western philosophy, which are traceable to, important theorists such as, inter alia, Rousseau, Madison and Jefferson.[366] Due to such historical lineage, it is not surprising that key legislation

358 With Australia's Macquarie Islands. UNESCO. (1997). 21st Session of the WHC. WHC-97/CONF.208/17. Feb 27, 1998. 798.

359 Lake Baikal in Russia. UNESCO. (1996). 20th Session of the WHC. WHC-96/CONF.201/21. Mar 10, 1997. 46.

360 UNESCO. (1996). 20th Session of the WHC. WHC-96/CONF.201/21. Mar 10, 1997. 49.

361 UNESCO. (1997). 21st Session of the WHC. WHC-97/CONF.208/17. Feb 27, 1998. 39.

362 UNESCO. (2003). 27th Session of the WHC. WHC-03/27.COM/24. Dec 10. 98.

363 See Gillespie, A. (1997). *International Environmental Law, Policy and Ethics.* (OUP, Oxford). Millennium Ecosystem Assessment. (2005). Ecosystems and Human Well-Being. (Island Press, Washington). 40-41.

364 See 'Closing Plenary Session.' In Adams, A. (ed). *First World Conference on National Parks.* (US Department of the Interior, Washington). 378. Recommendation No 8.

365 See 'Closing Plenary Session.' *Ibid.* 377. Recommendation No 4.

366 Nash, R. (1977). 'International Conceptions of Wilderness'. In Hendee, S. (ed). *Wilderness Management.* (US Forest Service, Miscellaneous Publication no 1365). 58. Vest, J. (1987). 'The Philosophical Significance of Wilderness Solitude'. *Environmental Ethics.* 9: 303-315. Simonsen, K. (1981). 'The Value of Wilderness'. *Environmental Ethics.* 3: 260-265. Vanderheiden, S. (2002). 'Rousseau, Cronon and the Wilderness Idea'. *Environmental Ethics.* 24: 169-188. Thomson, J. (2000). 'Environment As Cultural Heritage.' *Environmental Ethics.* 22: 240-258. Hammond, J. (1985). 'Wilderness and Heritage Values'. *Environmental Ethics.* 7: 165-170. Nash, R. (1973). *Wilderness and the American Mind.* (Yale UP, New Haven). xv.

on protected areas in a number of western countries, such as the 1964 (American) Wilderness Act, has come to define wilderness as a place offering 'outstanding opportunities for solitude.'[367]

Such wilderness values, or other values derived from protected areas are not necessarily restricted to any one culture. It would appear (contrary to some popular philosophical debate)[368] that the value of 'wilderness' can be found in many non-western cultures,[369] and even if areas are not valued because of their wilderness, their cultural connections, such as with sacred groves, may justify their protection due to the cultural beliefs of the local/traditional/indigenous peoples. Despite the philosophical interest of the debate, and the fact that a number of international instruments, such as, inter alia, the Bern Convention[370] and the Madrid Protocol,[371] recognize such wilderness values, no regimes have actively developed them. The one exception to the above rule is with regards to the aesthetic value of protected areas.

A Aesthetics

The idea that protected areas may have a high aesthetic value is well recognised in the philosophical literature,[372] and in the preambles of a number of international agreements including, inter alia, the 1968 and 2003 African Conventions,[373] the Madrid Protocol,[374] the Bern Convention,[375] European Diploma,[376] and the Caribbean[377] and Mediterranean Protocols.[378]

---

367 The Wilderness Act (Public Law 88-577). In *US Statutes at Large* 78, pp890-96.

368 Birch, T. (1990). 'The Incarceration of Wilderness: Wilderness Areas as Prisons'. *Environmental Ethics*. 12: 1, 2. Guha, R. (1989). Radical American Environmentalism and Wilderness Preservation: A Third World Critique. 11 *Environmental Ethics*. 71-83. Marnham, p. (1981). *Dispatches from Africa*. (Abacus, London). 8.

369 Burnett, G. (1994). 'Wilderness and the Bantu Mind'. *Environmental Ethics*. 16: 144-160.

370 Bern Convention. Preamble.

371 See Annex V, Article 3 (1) and 3 (2)(g).

372 See Gillespie, A. (1997). *International Environmental Law, Policy and Ethics*. (OUP, Oxford). Godfrey-Smith, W. (1979). 'The Value of Wilderness'. *Environmental Ethics*. 1: 309-319.

373 2003 African Convention. Article XII (1) (c). African Convention (1968). Article VI (2).

374 See Annex V, Article 3 (1) and 3 (2)(g). of the Madrid Protocol.

375 Bern Convention. Preamble.

376 European Diploma, Article 1.

377 Caribbean Protocol. Article 4.2.

378 Mediterranean Protocol. Articles 4. (d). 16 and Annex 1.B.3.

Although aesthetic values are commonly recognized in the debates about protected areas, the only regime to actively engage with aesthetic values is the WHC. The launching point into the discussion of aesthetic values comes from the WHC appreciation of, 'natural features consisting of physical and biological formations or groups of such formations, which are of outstanding universal value from the aesthetic … point of view' and/or 'natural sites or precisely delineated natural areas of outstanding universal value from the point of view of … natural beauty'.[379] This section of the WHC has been interpreted (as criteria III) to allow for the inscription of sites that 'contain superlative natural phenomena or areas of exceptional natural beauty and aesthetic importance'.[380]

Despite the relative simplicity of criteria III, this category has been controversial to apply, as it is very difficult to measure. That is, whereas 'superlative natural phenomena' can be objectively measured and assessed, such as with the tallest mountain, the deepest canyon, the largest cave etc. 'exceptional natural beauty' is harder to assess. Aside from some broad principles, the Committee has continually expressed caution in this area. The broad principles are that the aesthetics criterion is only applied to areas (and not species), and that natural aesthetics should not have a human influence upon them. Accordingly, Venice and its lagoon, as well as Mont-Saint Michel and its bay[381] were rejected under this category. In addition, existing sites should avoid aesthetically disrupting developments such as radio tracking facilities[382] or telecommunications towers.[383]

The foremost example of this caution was the committees recommendation that the aesthetic criterion should only be used in conjunction with other criteria, and singularly, only in exceptional circumstances.[384] This approach has been consistently applied, for as of 2005, although 114 natural properties had been inscribed under this criterion, this is most commonly done in conjunction with other criteria. Nevertheless, a number of sites have been listed, after fulfilling only the aesthetic criteria. These include the Belovezhskaya Forest of Belarus and Poland, three sites in China (Jiuzhaigou Valley, Huanglong Area and Wulingyaun), Sagarmartha in Nepal and Kilimanjaro in Tanzania.

---

379 WHC. Article 2.

380 *Operational Guidelines*. 2002 Edn. Paragraph 44. (iii).

381 Rejected under the natural aesthetics criteria, although they were both inscribed for their cultural values. Pressouyre, L. (1992). *The World Heritage Convention, Twenty Years Later*. (UNESCO, Paris). 24.

382 On St Kilda of the UK. UNESCO. (1986). 10th Session of the WHC. CC-86/CONF.003/10. Dec 5, 1986. pp 6.

383 The Lord Howe Island Group. UNESCO. (1983). 6th Session of the WHC. CC-83/CONF.015/8. Jan 17, 1983. pp.4.

384 UNESCO. (1979). 3rd Session of the WHC. CC-79/CONF.003/13. Nov 30, 1978. pp.8. UNESCO. (1996) Expert Review on Evaluation of General Principles and Criteria for Nominations of Natural World Heritage Sites. WHC-96/CONF.202/INF.9. Apr 15. 3.

Aside these listings solitary under the auspice of criteria III, the more common approach is to list sites of spectacular aesthetic qualities, in conjunction with other considerations. This approach, whereby aesthetic concerns are linked with other criteria, has involved listings from France,[385] Russia,[386] Iceland,[387] Sweden,[388] Switzerland,[389] Malaysia,[390] Cuba,[391] the United States,[392] Australia,[393] the Philippines,[394] the United Kingdom,[395] Indonesia,[396] St Lucia,[397] Belize,[398] South Africa,[399]

---

385 The Pyrenees. UNESCO. (1997). 21st Session of the WHC. WHC-97/CONF.208/17. Feb 27, 1998. 39.

386 The Volcanoes of Kamchatka. UNESCO. (1996). 20th Session of the WHC. WHC-96/CONF.201/21. Mar 10, 1997. 47. Lake Baikal. UNESCO. (1996). 20th Session of the WHC. WHC-96/CONF.201/21. Mar 10, 1997. 46. And the Virgin Komi Forests UNESCO. (1996). 19th Session of the WHC. WHC-95/CONF.203/16. Jan 31, 1996. 35.

387 Ilulissat Icefjord. UNESCO. (2004). 28th Session of the WHC. WHC-04/28.COM/26. Oct 29. Decision 28 COM 14B8. pp. 19.

388 The Laponian Area. UNESCO. (1996). 20th Session of the WHC. WHC-96/CONF.201/21. Mar 10, 1997. 49.

389 The Jungfrau region.

390 Gunung Mulu. UNESCO. (2001). 24th Session of the WHC. WHC-2000/CONF.204/21. Feb 16, 2001. 65-66.

391 Desembarco del Granma National Park. UNESCO. (1999). 23rd Session of the WHC. WHC-99/CONF.209/22. Mar 22, 2000. 21.

392 Carlsbad Caverns. UNESCO. (1996). 19th Session of the WHC. WHC-95/CONF.203/16. Jan 31, 1996. 35.

393 Macquarie Islands. UNESCO. (1997). 21st Session of the WHC. WHC-97/CONF.208/17. Feb 27, 1998. 798. Purnululu National Park. UNESCO. (2003). 27th Session of the WHC. WHC-03/27.COM/24. Dec 10. 104.

394 The Puerto-Princesa River National Park. UNESCO. (1999). 23rd Session of the WHC. WHC-99/CONF.209/22. Mar 22, 2000. 22.

395 Gough Island Wildlife Reserve. UNESCO. (1996). 19th Session of the WHC. WHC-95/CONF.203/16. Jan 31, 1996. 35.

396 Sumatra. UNESCO. (2004). 28th Session of the WHC. WHC-04/28.COM/26. Oct 29. Decision 28 COM 14B5. pp. 17.

397 Pitons. UNESCO. (2004). 28th Session of the WHC. WHC-04/28.COM/26. Oct 29. Decision 28 COM 14B11. pp. 20.

398 The Belize Barrier Reef Reserve system. UNESCO. (1996). 20th Session of the WHC. WHC-96/CONF.201/21. Mar 10, 1997. 46.

399 Drakensberg.

Uganda,[400] Canada,[401] China,[402] Kenya,[403] Vietnam,[404] Norway,[405] Brazil,[406] Columbia[407] and India (with its valley of flowers).[408]

B Cultural Values

The primary reason the WHC Committee has come to urge caution in the application of the aesthetic value of nominated protected areas, is because such values are ultimately subjective, and such subjective values are often laden with cultural baggage. In itself, this is not problematic, as the importance of conserving protected areas, because of their cultural values is well recognized in both philosophy,[409] and the broad intentions of most international and regional protected areas regimes. These regimes include, inter alia, the 2003 African Convention,[410] the Bern Convention,[411] the European Diploma,[412] the Arctic regime,[413] the Mediterranean[414] and Caribbean Protocols.[415]

---

400 Rwenzori Mountains. UNESCO. (1995). 18th Session of the WHC. WHC-94/CONF.003/16. Jan 31. 1995. 42.

401 Waterton Glacier Park, as shared with the US. UNESCO. (1996). 19th Session of the WHC. WHC-95/CONF.203/16. Jan 31, 1996. 34.

402 Mount Wuyi. UNESCO. (1999). 23rd Session of the WHC. WHC-99/CONF.209/22. Mar 22, 2000. 26. The Three Parallel Rivers. UNESCO. (2003). 27th Session of the WHC. WHC-03/27.COM/24. Dec 10. 98.

403 Mount Kenya National Natural Forest Park. UNESCO. (1997). 21st Session of the WHC. WHC-97/CONF.208/17. Feb 27, 1998. 37-38.

404 Ha Long Bay. UNESCO. (1995). 18th Session of the WHC. WHC-94/CONF.003/16. Jan 31. 1995. 43.

405 Geirangerfjord in Norway. Decision 29 COM 8B7.

406 The Atlantic Forest Southeast Reserves, Pantanal and the Brazilian Atlantic forests. UNESCO. (1999). 23rd Session of the WHC. WHC-99/CONF.209/22. Mar 22, 2000. 19. UNESCO. (2001). 24th Session of the WHC. WHC-2000/CONF.204/21. Feb 16, 2001. 64. UNESCO. (2001). 25th Session of the WHC. WHC-01/CONF.208/24. Feb 8, 2002. 89.

407 Decision 30 COM 8B.28.

408 Decision 29 COM 8B.14.

409 See 'Cultural Values of National Parks.' In Adams, A. (ed). *First World Conference on National Parks.* (US Department of the Interior, Washington). 128-145.

410 This places a premium on traditional values. 2003 African Convention. Article IV.

411 Bern Convention. Preamble.

412 European Diploma, Article 1.

413 Conservation of Arctic Flora and Fauna. (2002). *Protected Areas of the Arctic: Conserving a Full Range of Values.* (CAFF Secretariat, in Department of Foreign Affairs, Canada). 24.

414 See Mediterranean Protocol, Article 16 and Annex 1.B (f). An area can be selected, because of, inter alia, the area has a high representative value with respect to the cultural heritage, due to the existence of environmentally sound traditional activities integrated with nature which support the well-being of local populations. Each protected area under the SPAW must fulfil at least one of the criteria for cultural and socio-economic (as in, it is not an option not to). Report of the Working Group on the Development of Guidelines for the Listing of Protected Areas Under the SPAW Protocol. (2005). UNEP (DEC)/CAR WG.29/INF.12.

The Ramsar is notable for its long standing recognition of the cultural value of wetlands.[416] In this regard the Parties to Ramsar have issued a series of Guiding Principles for the Taking Into Account the Cultural Values of Wetlands.[417] In 2005, the Parties to the Ramsar encouraged each other to identify and analyze further case studies of wetlands of significant cultural value, and make them widely known, thus increasing the knowledge and understanding of the relationship between cultural processes and wetland conservation and wise use. Moreover, the Parties agreed that a wetland may be considered of international importance when, in addition to its ecological values, it holds significant cultural values, whether material or non-material, linked to its origin, conservation and/or ecological function.[418]

Even PSSAs under the auspice of the IMO have come to embrace cultural values. For example, extrapolating from Article 211 of UNCLOS, (with regard to 'utilization or the protection of its resources') the PSSA categories have come to embrace, inter alia, human dependency. The term 'human dependency' has been utilized at the IMO to support traditional subsistence and/or cultural needs of the local human population.[419] Thus, when Australia proposed an extension to an existing PSSA in 2003, it was influential that the extension area (the Torres Strait) was the home to 10,000 indigenous Australians and 20,000 Papua New Guinea nationals, who depend on the maritime resources for subsistence purposes.[420]

The final convention of note to deal with the cultural values of protected areas is the WHC. The WHC, which (obviously) has a dual purpose with regard to the protection of cultural heritage, has also come to place a value on the cultural values of natural sites. Their growth of interest in this area is most noticeable with regard to indigenous/

---

415 Caribbean Protocol. Article 4(2). The Caribbean Protocol took a slightly different approach, in allowing areas to be nominated because, inter alia, the area is associated with the productivity of ecosystems and natural resources that provide economic or social benefits and upon which the welfare of local inhabitants is dependent.

416 'Wetlands constitute a resource of great… cultural value… the loss of which would be irreparable'. Preamble, Ramsar.

417 Resolution 8.19 Guiding Principles for Taking Into Account the Cultural Values of Wetlands for the Effective Management of Sites. (2002, Valencia). Paragraph 19. These Guidelines encourage parties, within their national and legal frameworks, to consider compilation and assessment of both material and non-material cultural elements related to wetlands; to promote the appreciation and revitalisation of such cultural values; include relevant cultural heritage into the design and implementation of wetland management plans and to integrate cultural and social impact criteria into environmental assessments.

418 Resolution 9.21. Taking Into Account the Cultural Value of Wetlands. (2005, Kampala). Paragraphs 11 and 12.

419 Annex 6. Guidelines for the Designation of Special Areas Under MARPOL 73/78 and Guidelines for the Identification and Designation of Particularly Sensitive Sea Areas. MEPC (2001). Report of the MEPC on its 46th Session. MEPC 46/23. Sections 4.4.12-4.4.15.

420 MEPC. (2003). Report of the MEPC on its 49th Meeting. MEPC. 49/WP.7. 43.

traditional/local values in which the overlap, of both tangible and intangible values between people and the natural sites they value, is very difficult to disentangle, both institutionally (as there is a new UNESCO Intangible Convention, and its relationship with the WHC is not yet certain)[421] and philosophically. A good example of this is with sacred groves. These areas, which are increasingly under threat, contain areas of obvious biodiversity, which is protected for its cultural values, as much as its natural ones.[422] Thus, when the Osun-Osogbo sacred grove of Nigeria, was inscribed on the WHC list in 2005, it was the art work to the Goddess of fertility, and the symbol is represented for the local peoples, which resulted in its inscription under the cultural, not the natural, criteria of the WHC List.[423]

The WHC has come to recognize local/traditional/indigenous cultural values associated with natural areas as part of a continuum with universal values.[424] Accordingly, as the 2005 Kazan meeting concluded, 'the identification of outstanding universal value of a site needs wide participation by stakeholders including local communities and indigenous people'.[425] This conclusion was in fact, already implicitly recognized by the WHC Committee in its existing debates (although there is a clear debate about how far indigenous/traditional/local values should be taken in the WHC deliberations).[426] For example, with the Tongariro site in New Zealand, the Committee originally deferred its listing, until, inter alia, a new management plan was established which gave, 'better reflection to the Maori cultural values as part of the management concept of the site'.[427] Similar decisions, reflecting the need to incorporate indigenous values within the cultural values criteria, were seen with the Okapi Wildlife Reserve in Zaire and the resident Pygmy population.[428]

---

421 In 2004, the Committee, although welcoming the formation of the Intangibles Convention, urged caution in the links within this Convention. It also emphasized the, 'primacy of the WHC in relation to tangible cultural heritage and where the tangible cultural heritage has a clear link with intangible heritage which cannot be severed'. 2004, 7th Extraordinary Meeting. 7 EXT COM 9. The text of the adopted resolution is from the author.

422 UNESCO. (2003). *The Importance of Sacred Natural Sites for Biodiversity Conservation.* (UNESCO, Paris). 6-7, 153-158. Millennium Ecosystem Assessment. (2005). *Ecosystems and Human Well-Being.* (Island Press, Washington). 44. Anon. (2005). 'Tibet's Mountain God's Have a Way of Preserving Nature'. *New Scientist.* Nov 26. 18.

423 It was inscribed under cultural criteria ii, iii, and iv.

424 UNESCO. (2003). *Linking Universal and Local Values.* (World Heritage Papers 13, Paris). 166.

425 Section 12.d.

426 For example, in 2005 New Zealand insisted, and it was eventually accepted, that as a compilation of past committee decisions and discussions on outstanding universal value should draw out references or obvious omissions relating to the values of indigenous peoples related to world heritage. Decision 29 COM 9.

427 UNESCO. (1987). 11th Session of the WHC. CC-87/CONF.005/9. Jan 20, 1988. pp 8.

428 UNESCO. (1996). 20th Session of the WHC. WHC-96/CONF.201/21. Mar 10, 1997. 47-48.

C Cultural Landscapes

Despite the increasing recognition that natural sites may have a cultural value, independent of their other values, due to the pre-occupation with all of the other values of protected areas listed above, the exact way in which to reconcile cultural and natural values has taken time to evolve. The solution to the problem, so that the above categories are not unnaturally stretched to encompass cultural values, is through the creation of a category known as 'cultural landscapes'.

Cultural landscapes (as first defined in 1925) are, 'fashioned from a natural landscape by a cultural group. Culture is an agent, the natural the medium, the cultural landscape the result'.[429] Despite this early recognition, the idea of cultural landscapes, as an inscription option, has taken a very long time to evolve, and to date, this evolution has been disproportionately in Europe. Indeed, the 2004 European Landscapes Convention,[430] the Alps Convention, and the European Diploma all recognise the value of landscapes, which according to the 2004 European Landscape Convention are areas, 'as perceived by people, the character of which is the result of the action and interaction of natural and/or human factors'.[431] The European Diploma has gone on to identify such areas as, sites or landscapes of outstanding aesthetic or cultural value or of a spectacular nature; complexes conserved as evidence of the history of the countryside or woodlands in Europe; or country or wooded areas which are cultivated using extensive methods and constitute typical examples of European landscapes.[432]

In the international sphere, the only convention which has tried to engage this category of 'cultural landscapes' is the WHC. In part, this interest is due to the dualistic nature of the WHC, in that it also seeks to protect cultural, as well as natural, heritage.[433] Despite these twin objectives, by-and-large, the WHC has kept the two categories separate, with little overlap. This was especially so in the early years of the WHC when there was an assumption that natural heritage was pristine, without the influence of

---

429 This is the definition of Carl Sauer. See UNESCO. (2002). *Cultural Landscapes: The Challenge of Conservation* (UNESCO. World Heritage Papers No 7) 17.

430 Note however, that this (soft) convention values all forms of landscape (and not only the exceptional classes of landscape) as an essential part of peoples lives, and creates processes to enhance and protect it. See Dejeant, M. (2004). 'The European Landscape Convention Enters Force.' *Environmental Policy and the Law*. 34(2): 79-83.

431 European Landscape Convention, 2004. Article 1. Definitions.

432 European Diploma. Annex I. Criteria.

433 Cultural heritage as, 'works of man or the combined works of nature and man, and areas including archaeological sites which are of outstanding universal value from the historical, aesthetic, ethnological or anthropological point of view'. WHC. Article 1.

humanity.[434] Despite this assumption, in the 1980s, a 'mixed' category of nomination began to appear which blurred the traditional dualism between the natural and cultural heritage.[435] However, it was not until 2003 that the four natural and six cultural criteria were combined into a single list, with the view of making them more integrated.[436] The mixed inscriptions, whereby a site was noted for its natural and its cultural values, came to encompass notable areas such as Mounts Wuyi and Emei in China, the Laponian Area of Sweden, the Ibiza Park in Spain, the Pyrenees, and Tongariro national park in New Zealand.

Although mixed sites were accepted, a fusing of natural and cultural criteria was not universally endorsed due to concerns about possible inconsistencies in the listing criteria,[437] a possible dilution of the value of natural properties,[438] and the potential extent of this new category.[439] Despite these concerns, in 1992 the Committee revised their interpretation,[440] as there was no such definition or recognition of cultural landscapes within the actual WHC, of cultural criteria to justify inscription cultural landscapes. The goal was to ensure, 'the combined works of nature and man' of outstanding universal value' were duly appreciated.[441]

Cultural landscapes, as incorporated into the Operational Guidelines,[442] were divided into three parts. The first part is, clearly defined landscapes. These include gardens or park landscapes constructed for aesthetic reasons which are often, but not always

---

434 UNESCO. (1977). 1st Session of the WHC. CC-77/CONF.001/9. Oct 17, 1977. pp.3. UNESCO. (1996) Expert Review on Evaluation of General Principles and Criteria for Nominations of Natural World Heritage Sites. WHC-96/CONF.202/INF.9. Apr 15. 4.

435 UNESCO. (1985). 9th Session of the WHC. SC-85/CONF.008/9. Dec, 1985.4. UNESCO. (1992). 16th Session of the WHC. WHC-92/CONF.002/12. Dec 14, 1992. Annex II.

436 UNESCO. (2003). 6th Extra-ordinary Session of the WHC. WHC-03/6. EXT.COM/8. Paris, May 27, 2003. 8. UNESCO. (1998). *Report of the World Heritage Strategy Natural and Cultural Heritage Expert Meeting.* (UNESCO, Amsterdam).3, 4, 9, 11-13. UNESCO. (1999). 23rd Session of the WHC. WHC-99/CONF.209/22. Mar 22, 2000. 93-94.

437 It became apparent that there was an inconsistency in the operational guidelines for nominations with a combination of cultural and natural elements. Specifically, article 2 defining natural heritage did not refer to cultural aspects of heritage, yet (iii) did. UNESCO. (1988). 12th Session of the WHC. SC-88/CONF.001/13. Dec 23, 1988. 6.

438 UNESCO. (1991). 15th Session of the WHC. SC-91/CONF.002/15. Dec 12, 1991. 17.

439 UNESCO. (1984). 8th Session of the WHC. SC/84/CONF.004/9. Nov 2, 1984. pp 6.

440 Cultural landscapes have possible linkages with Criterion V (an outstanding example of a traditional human settlement, land-use, or sea-use, which is representative of a culture (or cultures) or human interaction with the environment especially when it has become vulnerable under the impact of irreversible change) and Criterion VI (directly or tangibly associated with events or living traditions, with ideas, or with beliefs, with artistic and literary works of outstanding universal significance).

441 UNESCO. (2000). Synthesis Report of the Meeting on Cultural Landscapes: Concept and Implementation. WHC-2000/CONF.204/WEB.3. Oct 13, 2000. Annex III.

442 *Operational Guidelines.* 2002 Edn. Paragraph 57.

associated with religious, monumental buildings or ensembles. The second part includes organically evolved landscapes. These relate to relict (fossil) landscapes, which are historical or continuing landscapes, which retain an active social role in contemporary society closely associated with traditional ways of life, which are still evolving. The third part includes associative cultural landscape. These are landscapes of powerful religious, artistic or cultural associations of the natural element, rather than material cultural evidence which may be insignificant or absent.[443]

To help address some of the earlier concerns, it was decided that next to the Global Study on Cultural Properties, thematic studies on 'cultural landscapes' would be undertaken.[444] These thematic studies covered both specific topics, such as heritage canals,[445] regional themes, such as the Sacred Mountains of Asia,[446] the Asian Rice Culture and its Terraced Landscapes,[447] the European Alps,[448] and generalised studies on cultural landscapes in the Asia Pacific region,[449] the Andes, Africa[450] the Caucus, the Mediterranean and Europe in general.[451] Further thematic meetings on desert and oasis landscapes have also been suggested.[452] These studies have helped facilitate a number of cultural landscapes as being recognized as outstanding universal value by the Committee.[453]

9 Conclusion

The values of why areas protected are changing. This change is not about old values becoming redundant, but rather, that new values are being recognized, and regimes are either being formally remodelled, or tweaking their interpretations in their practice, so as to accommodate (or not) the new values.

---

443 For a full discussion of this area, see UNESCO. (2002). Cultural Landscapes: The Challenge of Conservation (UNESCO. World Heritage Papers No 7)

444 UNESCO. (1988). 12th Session of the WHC. SC-88/CONF.001/13. Dec 23, 1988. 3. UNESCO. (1993). Expert Meeting on Cultural Landscapes. WHC-93/ INF.4. Nov. 1993. 1-4. UNESCO. (1995). 18th Session of the WHC. WHC-94/CONF.003/16. Jan 31. 1995. 38.

445 UNESCO. (1995). 18th Session of the WHC. WHC-94/CONF.003/16. Jan 31. 1995. 43.

446 UNESCO. (1999). 23rd Session of the WHC. WHC-99/CONF.209/22. Mar 22, 2000. 13.

447 UNESCO. (1995). *Asian Rice Culture and Its Terraced Landscapes.* (UNESCO, Paris).

448 UNESCO. (1999). 23rd Session of the WHC. WHC-99/CONF.209/22. Mar 22, 2000. 13.

449 UNESCO. (1995). *The Asia Pacific Regional Workshop on Cultural Landscapes.* (UNESCO, Paris).

450 UNESCO. (1996). 20th Session of the WHC. WHC-96/CONF.201/21. Mar 10, 1997. 60-61.

451 UNESCO. (1996). Report of the Expert Meeting on European Cultural Landscapes. WHC-96/ CONF.202/INF.10. Apr 30, 1996.

452 UNESCO. (2000). Synthesis Report of the Meeting on Cultural Landscapes: Concept and Implementation. WHC-2000/CONF.204/WEB.3. Oct 13, 2000. Annex III.

453 See Fowler, P. (2003). *World Heritage Cultural Landscapes.* (UNESCO, World Heritage Papers No 6).

Scientific values are commonly recognized in all regimes, but the MAB and the Antarctic regime are particularly notable. The latter, having developed a specific classification category for sites of scientific interest. The economic values of biodiversity is an internationally sought goal through the CBD. However, the only regimes which have begun to fully examine this area are the MAB and the Ramsar. With regard to traditional economic values, such as tourism generated income, although most protected areas benefit economically from tourism, only the MAB actively seeks this potential benefit.

The value of protected areas for endangered species is notable with most regimes, and the species related regimes, such as the Bern and the CMS, in particular. With regard to the more generic regimes, the most notable for its thematic endangered species work is the Ramsar, which has evolved to value avian, and non-avian species which rely upon wetlands. The other notable regimes, such as the MAB, and the WHC have tended to focus more on flagship species or megafauna. The protection of ecosystems is found within all protected area regimes. However, there is a diversity of ways in which this has been approached. The work of the Bern convention, in identifying by existing type, Ramsar by expanding type, as opposed to the IMO which has worked more on quality of ecosystems, as opposed to the WHC, which has developed a strong lean towards hotspots are all notable. Geomorphic or physio-graphical protected areas are notable in that whilst some regimes have actively excluded them from consideration, newer regimes have come to embrace them. However, it is only the WHC which has developed a systematic listing and understanding of such values.

Although discussion of intangible values of protected areas have become fashionable, only two areas have really begun to develop. The first area is aesthetics, but this has had a tightly hemmed in development, and only within the WHC. The second is 'cultural values'. Cultural values are recognized in many regimes, but the Ramsar is the most pronounced in their support. However, it is the WHC, which has most obviously begun to grapple with this area, although it has, to date, sent out contradictory messages when dealing with this topic. Nevertheless, the development of the new value of cultural landscape, in a number of other regimes, including the WHC, may help resolve some of the current difficulties.

Chapter IV

OBLIGATIONS AND GAPS

1 The Impetus to Protect

Protected areas are one of the less glamorous areas of international environmental law. They are commonly overshadowed by what are perceived as much more dramatic topics, which capture the public attention to a much greater degree.[1] This is an ironic situation for three reasons. First, protected areas are often the foremost methods by which species and ecosystems are effectively preserved. Second, protected areas are tangible, and are not merely theoretical constructs. Third, the obligation to create protected areas is one of the most long-standing goals in numerous environmental treaties. For a long time this goal was not tied to any specific outcomes, and the numbers of protected areas grew slowly. However, in the new century, due to an increased recognition of the above considerations, the international community has not only iterated the goal to create more protected areas, they also set targets of what they want to achieve. The international interest is this area can be seen with a number of examples, such as marine protected areas and transboundary protected areas. Collectively, such support has lead to the creation, in total, of over 102,000 protected areas spread over the Earth.

Despite the laudable intentions of this goal, and the success to date, fundamental gaps exist in the thinking of how new goals to further increase the numbers and types of protected areas, are to be achieved. These gaps are primarily due to a number of thematic gaps in the international architecture, designed to protect the Earth's ecology. That is, certain key ecological areas, although noted in passing in a number of existing protected areas treaties are not necessarily central concerns. Moreover, in the specific agreements which have the knowledge and capacity to specifically cover such topics as forests, coral reefs, mountains or deserts, the machinery to create and enhance protected areas is missing.

---

1 Indeed, whilst Conventions such the United Nations Framework Convention on Climate Change attract close to three hundred Non-Governmental Organisations (NGOs) per conference of the Parties, or 400 NGOs for the Convention on Biological Diversity, see Report of the 9th COP. FCCC/CP/2003/ 6. March 30, 2004. 35-38, and Report of the 7th COP to the CBD. UNEP/CBD/COP/7/21. Apr 13. pp. 3-7; the premier instruments for protected areas, such as the World Heritage Convention, typically only receive less than a dozen environmentally inclined NGOs. In 2003, there in addition to the advisory bodies, there were 20 NGOs, of which 6 were environmentally inclined. UNESCO. (2003). 27th Session of the WHC. WHC03/ 27.COM/24. 2003. Paris, 10 December. 2.

Given that the problems of the gaps in the architecture will (if ever) take years to solve, a number of international organizations have begun to prioritise what areas they should be seeking to protect via working out where the current gaps are, by using, inter alia, inventories, comparative and thematic analysis. Despite the utilization of tentative lists and comparative and thematic analysis, it is not always clear what the primary conservation objectives should be. This problem is partly due to a number of different approaches to consider and exactly what and where the priority areas are is a matter of debate between four different (but often overlapping) schemas. These schemas are the Udvardy system, the Global 200, Species Focused Approaches, and Hotspots.

Although these schemas are all commendable, it is necessary to note that they are not all seeking to conserve the same areas. Nevertheless, given that the differences between them are philosophical in their priority setting, it is not necessary to try to select which one is best. Rather, I will argue, until the thematic gaps in the international legal architecture are filled by meaningful instruments which can directly list protected areas by specific type, the schemas should be fully utilised by the existing protected areas regimes, as the best way to prioritise what needs areas need to be saved, and thereby meet the goals that the international community has set itself. This chapter discusses the historical progression of the obligation to create protected areas, with a focus on marine protected areas and transboundary protected areas. It also explores the thematic gaps in the current international system for protected areas in the context of marine, forest, dryland, and mountainous areas. Finally, this chapter examines the four different schemas and how each can be utilized to identify priority areas and meet international goals in spite of the current deficiencies in the system.

2 The Obligation to Create Protected Areas

The current international initiatives to increase the numbers and types of protected areas, and enhance their status and management domestically, regionally and internationally are not new. For example, the 1933 African Convention, (and its 1968[2] and 2003 successors)[3] obliged its Parties to, 'explore forthwith the possibility of establishing in their territories national parks and strict natural reserves'.[4][5] This was especially so

2 African Convention (1968). Article X. (1) & X (2).

3 2003 African Convention. Article XII (1). The 2003 African Convention obliges its Parties to, 'establish, maintain and extend, as appropriate, conservation areas'.

4 The 1933 Convention Relative to the Preservation of Fauna and Flora in their Natural State. Reprinted in the *International Protection of the Environment* (IPE). Volume IV: 1693. Article 3 (1). This was to be done within two years of entry into force of the Convention, or as soon as possible thereafter. Article 3 (2).

5 1933 London Convention. Article 7 (2).

for the benefit of endangered species.[6] The 1940 Western Hemisphere Convention had a very similar obligation.[7] This obligation is long standing in both general and specific contexts.

Variations on this obligation (as opposed to the option) existed with the early treaties which were species specific. The first notable occurrence where habitat was protected, so as to protect the targeted species, was the 1911 Convention between the United States, Great Britain, Russia and Japan for the Preservation and Protection of Fur Seals.[8] This approach was adopted with a number of other early species specific agreements, such as those related to the protection of certain birds and their associated habitats,[9] as well as a later collection of species specific agreements ranging from Vicuna[10] to sea turtles[11] and whales.[12]

Despite this relatively early success of international law in furthering the creation of protected areas, from an early point, momentum was building for the creation of more protected areas. For example, the second recommendation from the First World Congress on Protected Areas in 1962 called for the creation of,

> A series of natural reserves providing permanent examples of the many diverse types of habitats, both natural and semi-natural, so as to preserve them permanently for world science.[13]

---

6 This approach was because the purpose of the 1933 London Convention was to stop the risk of: 'extinction or permanent injury' to a number of species of fauna and flora of certain parts of the world, and in particular of Africa, that were, 'in danger'.1933 London Convention. Preamble. Paragraph 1.

7 This Convention obliged its Contracting Governments to, 'explore at once [or 'as soon as possible' or 'circumstances will permit'] 1940 Western Hemisphere Convention. Preamble, Article II(I) and II (2).

8 The 1911 Convention Between The United States, Great Britain, Russia and Japan for the Preservation And Protection Of Fur Seals. *Treaty Series, No.* 564; 37 *Statutes at Large,* 1542. Article 1.

9 Austria/Hungary/Italy 1875 Declaration for the Protection of Birds Useful to Agriculture. *IPE, ibid.* IV. 1561. The 1897, 1907, 1914 and 1927 Convention(s) Concerning Hunting (waterbirds) on Lake Constance and the Rhine Between Baden and Switzerland. In *IPE,* IV. 1599. 1916 Convention Between the United States and Great Britain for the Protection of Migratory Birds. IPE. IV, 1638. Article 2. 1936 Convention Between the United States and Mexico for the Protection of Migratory Birds. IPE. IV. 1723.

10 Convention for the Conservation and Management of the Vicuna, 1979. Article 5.

11 See for example, the Memorandum of Understanding Concerning Conservation Measures for Marine Turtles of the Atlantic Coast of Africa. 39 *ILM.* 1 (2000). Paragraph 1.

12 IWC. 30th Report. (1980) 27. IWC. 46th Report. (1996). 28.

13 See 'Closing Plenary Session.' In Adams, A. (ed). *First World Conference on National Parks.* (US Department of the Interior, Washington). 376. Recommendation No 2.

The Conference went on to argue for the creation of an official world list for each, 'bio-climatic region ... of the most representative habitats' so that such habitats may be, 'selected and legally established at an early date'.[14] The first international response to these calls was the 1968 UNESCO Conference on the Use and Conservation of the Biosphere. From this conference, the MAB program recommended that, inter alia, Member states accelerate the establishment and development of national parks and wildlife sanctuaries.[15]

Three years later in 1971, the Ramsar Convention was concluded, so as to prevent the 'irreparable loss' of wetlands'[16] 'by combining far-sighted national policies with co-coordinated international action'[17] through which the Parties agreed to, 'promote the conservation of wetlands and waterfowl by establishing nature reserves on wetlands'.[18] In furtherance of this objective, aside the obligation upon all Parties to designate at least one wetland when acceding to the Convention,[19] all Parties were invited to increase the designation of their wetlands to the List of Wetlands of International Importance subsequently.[20] The Parties have set themselves the goal of possessing 2,500 sites encompassing 250 million hectares by 2010 (they had 1,555 in 2005).[21] The Ramsar Parties have also directed resolutions to specific Parties, encouraging them to recognise wetlands of international importance within their borders, and the need to specifically conserve them.[22]

---

14 See 'Closing Plenary Session.' *Ibid.* 376-377. Recommendation No 3.

15 UNESCO. (1968). *Use and Conservation of the Biosphere.* (UNESCO, Paris). Recommendation 15. 228.

16 Ramsar. Preamble. Paragraphs 3 and 4.

17 *Ibid.* Paragraph 6.

18 Ramsar. Article 4.1.

19 Resolution 4.5. Accession Requirements. (1990, Montreux).

20 'And they may incorporate riparian and coastal zones adjacent to the wetlands, and islands or bodies of marine water deeper than six metres at low tide lying within the wetlands, especially where these have importance as waterfowl habitat.' Ramsar. Article 2.1. Also, Recommendation 4.4. Establishment of Wetland Reserves. (1990, Montreux).

21 Resolution 9.15. The Status of Sites in the Ramsar List of Wetlands of International Importance. (2005, Kampala). Resolution 9.1. Additional Scientific and Technical Guidance for Implementing the Ramsar Wise Use Concept. (2005, Kampala). Annex B. This goal first appeared in Resolution 8.26. The Implementation of the Strategic Plan 2003-2008. (2002, Valencia). Annex I. Global Implementation of the Targets for the Convention.

22 Final Act of the Ramsar Conference. Annex II. Recommendations adopted by the International Conference on the Conservation of Wetlands and Waterfowl at Ramsar, Iran, 3 February 1971. Recommendation 1. Conservation of the Wadden Sea, northwestern Europe. See also Recommendation 2.5. On the Wadden Sea. Recommendation 10. African Wetlands. Recommendation 4. Conservation of Lakes Ab-i-Istada and Dasht-e-Nawar, Afghanistan. Resolution 8.39. High Andean Wetlands as Strategic Ecosystems. (2002, Valencia). Recommendation 5.1. Ramsar Sites in Specific Contracting Parties. (1993, Kushiro). Recommendation 4.9. Sites in the Territories of Specific Contracting Parties. (1990, Montreux). Recommendation 2.9. Conservation of Unlisted Wetlands. (1984, Groningen).

The MAB and the Ramsar did not satisfy the international appetite for more protected areas, and the 1972 United Nations Conference on the Human Environment, in calling for all natural resources to be safeguarded,[23] specifically added in Recommendation 38 that, 'Governments take steps to set aside areas representing ecosystems of international significance for protection under international agreement'. This point from Stockholm was picked up by the 1972 Second World Congress on Protected Areas which called,

> [U]pon all governments to widen the coverage of their protected areas so as to ensure that adequate and representative samples of natural biomes and ecosystems throughout the world are conserved in a coordinated system of national parks and related protected areas.[24]

The response of the international community to these recommendations was the creation of the World Heritage Convention in 1972, and two habitat related conventions in 1979. The international community's desire to create more protected areas appeared to be in full swing.

The World Heritage Convention (WHC) is just that – a convention is designed to protect the world's outstanding heritage. The world's heritage is that related to humanities, 'creative [cultural] genius and of the rich resources of nature'.[25] Together, these categories encompass many non-tangible universal values[26] that belong to all peoples. The emphasis is upon the *world's* heritage. That is, the Convention works on the principle that, 'each and every country has a contribution to make' and collectively, all the heritage of all nations, 'together forms the patrimony of mankind'.[27] Such heritage of 'outstanding interest' needs, 'to be preserved as part of the world heritage of mankind as a whole'.[28] Despite clearly being sovereign property, some view this patrimony as a type of, 'global commons'.[29] As part of the patrimony of humankind or global commons of value to all humanity, the heritage must be safeguarded for future generations.[30] To allow otherwise, whereby the heritage is destroyed, is deemed, 'a

23 The natural resources of the Earth including the air, water, land flora and fauna and especially representative samples of natural ecosystems must be safeguarded for the benefit of present and future generations through careful planning and management as appropriate. Principle 2 of the Stockholm Declaration.

24 Recommendation 1. Conservation of Representative Ecosystems.' In Elliot, H. (ed). *Second World Conference on National Parks.* (1972, IUCN, Lausanne). 377.

25 UNESCO. (1978). 2nd Session of the WHC. CC-78/CONF.011/6. Nov 24, 1978. 2.

26 UNESCO. (1992). 16th Session of the WHC. WHC-92/CONF.002/12. Dec 14, 1992. 4.

27 UNESCO. (1980). 3rd Session of the WHC. CC-80/CONF.018/6. Oct 20, 1980. 4.

28 WHC. Preamble. Paragraph 7.

29 UNESCO. (1992). 16th Session of the WHC. WHC-92/CONF.002/12. Dec 14, 1992. 2.

30 WHC. Article 4. Each state has the obligation to achieve, 'transmission to future generations of the cultural and natural heritage' that is identified of outstanding universal importance. Also, UNESCO. (1987). 6th Session of the WHC. CC-87/CONF.013/5. Oct 31, 1987. 2.

harmful impoverishment of the heritage of all the nations of the world'.[31] As such, all Parties shall seek to, 'safeguard this unique and irreplaceable property, to whatever people it may belong'.[32] Accordingly, the WHC exists in a continual momentum for the discovery and listing of sites of outstanding universal value.

The 1979 Convention on Migratory Species obliged all of its Parties to, 'endeavor to conserve, and where feasible and appropriate, restore those habitats of the species which are of importance in removing the species from danger of extinction'.[33] This obligation has also been transferred to the entire subsidiary CMS Agreements.[34] Accordingly, obligations to create protected areas can be found with regard to Agreements on particular migratory species such as Albatross and Petrels;[35] Wadden Sea Seals;[36] African-Eurasian Migratory Birds;[37] Small Cetaceans of the Baltic and the North Seas;[38] Cetaceans of the Black Sea, Mediterranean Sea and Contiguous Atlantic Area;[39] and European Bats.[40] Similar obligations exist within the CMS Memorandum of Understandings for the Great Bustard,[41] the Slender billed Curlew,[42] the Siberian Crane,[43] and the Aquatic Warbler.[44]

In a similar vein, the Convention on the Conservation of European Wildlife and Natural Habitats (the Bern Convention) was built on the recognition that the conservation of

---

31 WHC. Preamble. Paragraph 2.

32 *Ibid.* Paragraph 5.

33 Article III. (4)(a). See also Article II (1).

34 CMS. Article V(5)(e)-(g).

35 ACAP. Article III. a. See also the ACAP Action Plan. 2.3, 2.3, 3.3 & 3.4. Resolution 1.4. International Implementation Priorities for 2000-2004. MOP 1 of the AEWA (South Africa, 1999). Available from the AEWA Secretariat. Resolution 2.4. International Implementation Priorities. MOP 2 of the AEWA (Bonn, 2002). Available from the AEWA Secretariat.

36 Wadden Sea Seals Agreement. Article VII.

37 AEWA. Preamble, and Article III. c, d & e.

38 ASCOBANS. Preamble, and Action Plan. Part 1(c).

39 ACCOBAMS. Article II.3.c. Action Plan. Section 3.

40 Resolution 4.4. Bat Conservation and Sustainable Forest Management. Report of the Fourth Session of the MOP to EUROBATS, 2003. Available from the Secretariat, at http://www.eurobats.org/. pp. 39. Resolution 4. Transboundary Programme: Habitat Proposals. Report of the Session of the MOP to EUROBATS. Resolution 4.3. Guidelines for the Protection and Management of Important Underground Habitats for Bats. Report of the Fourth Session of the MOP to EUROBATS, 2003.

41 Great Bustard Memorandum of Understanding. Available from the CMS Secretariat. Point 6. Action Plan for the Middle European Population of the Great Bustard. Section 1. See also Sections 1.2.3 & 1.2.4.

42 Slender Billed Curlew MOU. Preamble. Section 1.

43 MOU, Siberian Crane. Preamble and Principle 1.

44 Memorandum of Understanding Concerning Conservation Measures for the Aquatic Warbler. Available from the CMS Secretariat. Preamble. See also Part 1 of the Action Plan Concerning Conservation Measures for the Aquatic Warbler.

natural habitats is a vital component of the protection and conservation of wild flora and fauna.[45] Each Contracting Party agreed under the Bern Convention, (and the related European Diploma[46] and Emerald Network)[47] to take appropriate national policies, including necessary legislative and administrative measures to ensure the conservation of the habitats[48] of the wild flora and fauna species, and especially those which were endangered, vulnerable and/or migratory.[49] In furtherance of this goal, the Parties have identified both critical habitat types and the habitats of key species in need of protection.[50]

---

45 Bern Convention. Preamble.

46 European Diploma. Annex I. Criteria. Section B (2). The applicant area must taken into account in regional planning in order to prevent projects which run counter to the objectives of the area from being approved.

47 Recommendation No. 114. (2004). On the Role of the Bern Convention in the Preservation of Biological Diversity.

48 Bern Convention. Articles 1, 3 (1), 4 (2).

49 *Ibid.* Article 4 (1) and (3).

50 Recommendation No. 30.(1991). The Conservation of Species in Appendix I of the Convention. Resolution No. 6. (1998). Listing the Species Requiring Specific Habitat Conservation Measures. Recommendation No. 6. (1986). The Protection of the Mediterranean Monk Seal. Recommendation No. 11. (1988) Protection of the Common Seal. Recommendation No. 94. (2002). Urgent Measures for the Conservation of the Iberian Lynx. Recommendation No. 19. (1991). The Pardel Lynx in the Iberian Peninsula. Recommendation No. 10. (1988). Protection of the Brown Bear. Recommendation No. 53 (1996) On the Conservation of the European otter (Lutra). Recommendation No. 79 (1999). Protection of the Common Hamster in Europe. Recommendation No. 60. (1997). The Implementation of the Action Plans for Globally Threatened Birds in Europe. Recommendation No. 70. On Protection of the Great Crested Newt in the United Kingdom. Recommendation No. 31. (1991). The Protection of the European Mink. Recommendation No 7. (1987). On the Protection of Marine Turtles and Their Habitat. Recommendation No 8. (1987). On the Protection of Marine Turtles in Dalyan and Other Important Areas in Turkey. Recommendation No. 12. (1988). Concerning the Protection of Important Turtle Nesting Sites in Turkey. Recommendation No. 24 (1991). The Protection of Some Beaches In Turkey of Particular Importance to Marine Turtles. Recommendation No. 54 (1996) on conservation of Caretta caretta at Patara (Turkey). Recommendation No. 66. The Conservation Status of Some Nesting Beaches for Marine Turtles in Turkey. Recommendation No. 95. (2002). The Conservation of Marine Turtles in Kazanli Beach (Turkey). Recommendation No. 63. (1997). The Conservation of the Akamas Peninsula, Cyprus. Recommendation No. 64. (1997). The Conservation of the Caretta caretta in Kaminia, Greece. Recommendation No 9. (1987). On the Protection of Caretta Caretta in Lagasas Bay, Zakynthos (Greece). Declaration on Laganas Bay, Zakynthos, Greece (1992). Decision Concerning the Conservation of Laganas Bay, Zakynthos, Greece. Recommendation No. 23. (1991). On the Protection of the Habitat of Vipera Ursinii Rakosiensis in Hungary. Recommendation No. 84 (2000). The Conservation of Western Milos and in Particular the Milos Viper, Macrovipera Schweizeri.. Recommendation No. 104 (2003). The Conservation of the Spur-thinghed Tortoise in Spain. Recommendation No. 41. (1993). The Conservation of Freshwater Fish. Recommendation No. 12. (1988). Measures for the Protection of Critical Biotopes of Endangered Amphibians and Reptiles. Recommendation No 27 (1991). The Conservation of Some Threatened Amphibians in Europe. Guidelines Number 3. (1993). Recovery Plans for Species of Amphibians and Reptiles. Recommendation No. 29 (1991).

Despite the fact that clear progress in the facilitation of the creation of protected areas was taking place throughout the 1970s, the third World Congress on Protected Areas nevertheless, called upon governments to,

> Give high priority to the fulfillment of the ecological representiveness of their terrestrial protected areas systems by establishing new ones areas or enlarging existing ones.[51]

Five years later, the World Commission on Environment and Development (WCED), introduced a novel idea. This idea was that of a target of how many protected areas should be sought. Specifically, although the WCED noted that the number of protected areas was growing, nevertheless,

> A consensus of professional opinion suggests that the total expanse of protected areas needs to be at least tripled if it is to constitute a representative example of the Earth's ecosystems. There is still time to save species and their ecosystems. It is an indispensable prerequisite for sustainable development.[52]

The next major response of the international community to these types of recommendation came at the 1992 Earth Summit. However, one year before then, the 1991 Madrid Protocol, building on a long established practice for the South Pole,[53] came to oblige

---

The Conservation of Wetland Invertebrates. Recommendation No. 29 (1991). The Conservation of Wetland Invertebrates. Recommendation No. 12. (1988). Measures for the Protection of Critical Biotopes of Endangered Amphibians and Reptiles. Recommendation No 26 (1991). The Conservation of Some Threatened Reptiles in Europe. Guidelines Number 3. (1993). Recovery Plans for Species of Amphibians and Reptiles. Recommendation No. 42. The Conservation of Some Threatened Amphibians and Reptiles in the Areas of the Gulf of Orosei, Sardinia, Italy. Recommendation No. 52 (1996) on habitat conservation for invertebrate species. Recommendation No 47. Concerning the Conservation of European Semi-Aquatic Insectivora. Recommendation No. 22. (1991). The Conservation of the Pearl Mussel and Other Freshwater Mussels. Recommendation No. 50 (1996) on the Conservation of Margaritifera auricularia. Recommendation No. 34 (1992). The Conservation of the Flora of the Macaronesian Region. Recommendation No. 44. The Conservation of Some Threatened Plants in Central Europe. Recommendation No. 36. (1992). The Conservation of Underground Habitat. Recommendation No. 67. On the Conservation of Heathlands in Dorset, United Kingdom. Recommendation No. 83 (2000). The Conservation Status of Lake Vistonis and Lafra-Lafrouda Lagoon (Greece).

51 Recommendation 2. Global System of Representative Terrestrial Protected Areas. Recommendations of the World National Parks Congress. In McNeely, J. (ed). *National Parks, Conservation and Development.* (Smithsonian, Washington). 766.

52 World Commission on Environment and Development. (1987). *Our Common Future.* (OUP, Oxford). 165-166. The Third World Parks Congress in 1982, has earlier suggested, in passing, that a 10% target be established for the protection of different biomes.

53 See the 1964 Agreed Measures for the Conservation of Antarctic Fauna and Flora, from which all the Parties agreed to, 'exert appropriate efforts, consistent with the Charter of the United nations, to the end that no one engages in any activity in the Treaty Area contrary to the

its signatories to protect Antarctica as, 'a natural reserve, devoted to peace and science'[54] and effectively turned the location into one giant protected area. Building on from such momentum, the importance of protected areas was entrenched at the 1992 Earth Summit, in both Agenda 21 and the Convention on Biological Diversity (CBD). In the first instance, Agenda 21 iterated the importance of protected areas with regards to the conservation of forests,[55] mountains,[56] and biodiversity.[57] In the second instance, the most important document to evolve from the 1992 Earth Summit to deal with protected areas was the CBD. Article 8 of the CBD obliged each Contracting Party, 'as far as possible and as appropriate' to,

> (a) Establish a system of protected areas or areas where special measures need to be taken to conserve biological diversity;
> (b) Develop, where necessary, guidelines for the selection, establishment and management of protected areas or areas where special measures need to be taken to conserve biological diversity.

The ultimate aim of the CBD is,

> 'the establishment and maintenance of an effectively managed, ecologically representative global system of protected area networks where human activities are managed to maintain the structure and functioning of the full range of ecosystems, in order to provide benefits to both present and future generations and to achieve a significant reduction in the rate of biological diversity loss'.[58]

In large part, this CBD objective is due to their conclusion that the creation and maintenance of protected areas are 'essential' in meeting all of the broad objectives of the CBD, the 2010 target (to significantly reduce the rate of biodiversity loss) from the World Summit on Sustainable Development and the attainment of the United Nations Millennium Development Goals.[59] To achieve these goals, protected areas became incorporated within many of the thematic areas of the CBD, as well as becoming an important stand alone item on the CBD agenda, which is supplemented by active working groups.[60]

---

principles or purposes of these Agreed Measures'. Moreover, each Party was obliged ("shall') take appropriate action to carry out these Agreed Measures. Article III & X. Agreed Measures.

54 Madrid Protocol. Article 2.

55 Agenda 21. Chapter 11.14.(b)

56 *Ibid.* Chapter 13.7. (b)

57 *Ibid.* Chapter. 15.5. (g)

58 UNEP/WCWC. (2004). *Protected Areas and Biodiversity.* (UNEP: Biodiversity Series No 21). 11-12.

59 CBD. Decision VII/28. Protected Areas. Paragraph 1.

60 Decision VII/28. Protected Areas. Annex. Paragraphs 25, 26 & 28. Decision IV/16. Annex II. Decision VI/30. Preparations for the 7th COP.

The idea of targets for development in general, and sustainable development in particular, although clearly part of the international architecture dating back to the WCED, received a huge boost with the Millennium Development Goals, and goal seven in particular of seeking to achieve environmental sustainability by, inter alia, integrating the principles of sustainable development into country policies and programmes, whilst also seeking to reverse the loss of environmental resources. Soon after, the idea of targets began to filter in a number of multilateral environmental agreements. With specific regard to protected areas, a number of established conventions began to adopt soft targets.[61] This theme of targets for protected areas was strongly replicated with the Fifth World Parks Congress. This Congress called for governments and appropriate international organizations to,

> Maximize representation and persistence of biodiversity in comprehensive protected area networks in all ecoregions by 2012, focusing especially on threatened and under-exploited ecosystems and those species that qualify as globally threatened with extinction.[62]

As a series of subsidiary targets, the Congress called for all globally threatened species to be effectively conserved in-situ with the following immediate targets,

A. All critically endangered and endangered species globally confined to single sites are effectively conserved in situ by 2006.
B. All other globally critically endangered and endangered species are effectively conserved in situ by 2008.
C. All other globally threatened species are effectively conserved in situ by 2010.
D. Sites that support internationally important populations of restricted range species are adequately conserved by 2010.

They also called for 'viable representations of every terrestrial, freshwater and marine ecosystems' within protected areas with the following immediate targets,

A. A common global framework for classifying and assessing the status of ecosystems established by 2006.
B. Quantitative targets for each ecosystem type identified by 2008.
C. Viable representation of every threatened or under protected ecosystem conserved by 2010.[63]

---

61 See Taylor, D. (2002). 'The Ramsar Convention on Wetlands'. 12 (3) *Parks*. 42. Simpson, K. (2002). 'The Natura 2000 Network'. 12 (3) *Parks*. 36, 37.

62 See Recommendation 5.04. Building a Comprehensive and Effective Protected Area System. (Vth IUCN World Parks Congress).

63 IUCN Vth World Parks Congress. The Durban Action Plan. pp. 9. Box 3.

Finally, the Congress called for, 'a representative network of marine protected areas by 2012, as stated in the WSSD plan of implementation'.[64] By the time of the 7th COP of the CBD in 2004, the above targets of the Fifth World Parks Congress were being supplemented by the proposals of the working group on protected areas. The most controversial of these proposals, relating to the imposition of clear targets and timetables for the creation of more protected areas had been thoroughly square bracketed.[65] Nevertheless, after some lengthy negotiations, broad targets (subject to national priorities) were agreed.[66] These were,

> The establishment and maintenance by 2010 for terrestrial and by 2012 for marine areas of comprehensive, effectively managed, and ecologically representative national and regional systems of protected areas that collectively, inter alia through a global network contribute to achieving the three objectives of the Convention and the 2010 target to significantly reduce the current rate of biodiversity loss.[67]

Within this broad target, a series of subsidiary targets were agreed. These include that Parties, 'as a matter of urgency' by 2006 'take action to establish or expand protected areas in any large, intact or relatively un-fragmented or highly irreplaceable natural areas, or areas under high threat, as well as areas securing the most threatened species in the context of national priorities, and taking into consideration the conservation needs of migratory species'. The 2010 target was also supplemented with gap analysis for representative systems by 2006, integration of these into broad sustainable development strategies by 2008, and designation of more protected areas by 2009.[68]

3 Marine Protected Areas

A good example of the growing obligation to create protected areas is with Marine Protected Areas (MPAs). The international recognition of this obligation can be traced to the First World Conference on National Parks in 1962, which invited all governments with marine frontiers,

---

64 See Recommendation 5.04. Building a Comprehensive and Effective Protected Area System. (Vth IUCN World Parks Congress).

65 Protected Areas. UNEP/CBD/COP/7/L32. Recommendation IX/4. Protected Areas. UNEP/CBD/COP/7/4.pp.5. SBSTTA. Report of the Ad Hoc Technical Expert Group on Protected Areas. UNEP/CBD/SBSTTA/9/INF/3. 22 Sep, 2003. Annex II. Pp.89.

66 Aglionby, J. (2004). '123 Nations Throw Lifeline to Species At Risk.' *Guardian Weekly.* Feb 26.

67 CBD. Decision VII/28. Protected Areas. Paragraph 18 & Goal 1.1.

68 Decision VII/28. *Ibid.* Annex. 1.1.2.

> To examine as a matter of urgency the possibility of creating marine parks or reserves to defend underwater areas of special significance from all forms of human interference.[69]

The necessity for direct action in this area was reiterated at the World Congresses on protected areas in 1972,[70] 1982,[71] and 1994. These calls were supplemented by similar recommendations from notable and powerful national and international commissions,[72] soft international law,[73] and a large number of regional seas agreements covering, inter alia, the Mediterranean, the Caribbean, East Africa, the South East Pacific, and the North Atlantic.[74] Against this background, the Fifth World Parks Congress in 2002 suggested, targets for this area,[75] and the CBD, after long recognising the value of MPAs,[76] called for,

> The establishment and maintenance ... by 2012 for marine areas of comprehensive, effectively managed, and ecologically representative national and regional systems of protected areas that collectively, inter alia, through a global network contribute to achieving the three object-

---

69 See 'Closing Plenary Session.' In Adams, A. (ed). *First World Conference on National Parks.* (US Department of the Interior, Washington). 382. Recommendation No 15.

70 'All governments concerned to set aside appropriate marine areas as national parks and reserves and to take action to extend the boundaries of existing terrestrial national parks and reserves to include representative marine ecosystems' Recommendation 4. Marine National Parks. In Elliot, H. (ed). *Second World Conference on National Parks.* (1972, IUCN, Lausanne). 443.

71 The Third Congress in 1982 called for, 'as much as possible their territorial seas or other areas of jurisdiction' of marine and coastal protected areas, including on the high seas. Recommendation 3. Marine and Coastal Protected Areas. Recommendations of the World National Parks Congress. In McNeely, J. (ed). *National Parks, Conservation and Development.* (Smithsonian, Washington). 765.

72 Independent World Commission on the Oceans. (1998). *The Ocean Our Future.* (Cambridge University Press, Cambridge). 79. Kelleher, G. (1995). *A Global Representative System of Marine Protected Areas.* (World Bank, Washington). Volume IV. 5-6. National Research Council (2001). *Marine Protected Areas.* (National Academy Press, Washington).

73 Agenda 21. Chapter 17.7 and 17.85. Global Programme of Action for the Protection of the Marine Environment from Land-Based Activities. Section 152 (d). UNEP(OCA)/LBA/IG.2/7. 5 Dec. 1995. Finally, see the FAO Code of Conduct for Responsible Fisheries. Section 6.8

74 See the Protocol Concerning Protected Areas of Wild Fauna and Flora in the Eastern African Region. Reprinted in Austen, A. (ed). *Basic Legal Document on International Animal Welfare and Wildlife Conservation (Kluwer, London).* Article 8. The 1989 Protocol for the Conservation and Management of Protected Marine and Coastal Areas of the South East Pacific. Article 11. The Caribbean Protocol. Articles 3 and 4 of the Mediterranean Protocol,. Both of these are also in Austen, at 160, and 165. See also the OSPAR Recommendation 2003/3 on a Network of Marine Protected Areas. Sections 2 and 3.

75 IUCN 5th World Parks Congress (2003, Durban). Recommendation 5.22: Building a Global System of Marine and Coastal Protected Area Networks.

76 CBD. Decision VII/5 Marine and Coastal Biological Diversity. Section 20. CBD Decision II/10. Paragraph 11. Annex I to decision II/10. Section iv. See also CBD. Decision VII/28. Protected Areas. Paragraph 20.

ives of the Convention and the 2010 target to significantly reduce the current rate of biodiversity loss.[77]

This goal was supplemented with the suggestion, that such coverage should include marine ecosystems beyond areas of national jurisdiction in accordance with applicable international law.[78] This decision from the CBD was consistent with the WSSD goals in this area.[79] However, exactly how the high seas MPAS are to be achieved, despite clear advocacy for them[80] and tacit support for them within the CBD,[81] is less than clear.[82]

4 Transboundary Protected Areas

A second example of the success of the growth of protected areas is with transboundary protected areas (TBPAs). By 2003, there were 169 TBPAs, involving 666 individual protected areas in 113 countries. Together, these sites represent at least 10% of all the world's protected areas.[83] These numbers did not develop quickly. Rather, they represent the culmination of over seventy years of international co-operation that began in 1932.[84] Since that point, the utility of TBPAs has been consistently advocated in the World Parks Congresses,[85] and a number of soft law documents of international

77 CBD. Decision VII/28. Protected Areas. Paragraph 18 & Goal 1.1.

78 *Ibid.* Decision VII/28. Annex. 1.1.3

79 Report of the World Summit on Sustainable Development. A/CONF. 199/20. WSSD. Paragraph 32 (d).

80 IUCN, WCPA, WWF. (2003). *Towards a Strategy for High Seas Marine Protected Areas.* (IUCN, Gland). 2. IUCN 5th World Parks Congress (2003, Durban). Recommendation 5.22: Protecting Marine Biodiversity and Ecosystem Processes Through Marine Protected Areas Beyond National Jurisdiction. Operative paragraph 2.

81 CBD. Decision VII/28. Protected Areas. Paragraph 29. Annex I. Para 3. Goal 1.3. Para. 1.3.2. CBD. Decision VII/5 Marine and Coastal Biological Diversity. Section 30.

82 Report of the UNICPOLOS At its Fourth Meeting. A/58/95. (2003, June 26). Paragraph 22.

83 Zbiez, D. (2000). 'Transfrontier Ecosystems and Internationally Adjoining Protected Areas.' Available from the World Conservation Monitoring Centre. IUCN. (2003). *Transboundary Protected Areas for Peace and Cooperation.* (IUCN, Geneva). VII. See Recommendation 5.11. A Global Network to Support the Development of Transboundary Conservation Initiatives. (Vth IUCN World Parks Congress).

84 The first recorded TBPA was created in 1932, when Poland and Czechoslovakia announced their intention to have shared nature reserve. In the same year, the Waterton-Glacier International Peace Park, connecting the mountainous regions of the shared boundaries between the United States and Canada came into force.

85 The 1972 Second World Congress on National Parks called upon governments to, 'collaborate closely in the planning and management of neighboring or contiguous national parks'. Recommendation 6. International Parks. In Elliot, H. (ed). *Second World Conference on National Parks.* (1972, IUCN, Lausanne). 444. See also Recommendation 5.11. A Global

environmental law.[86] It has also been strongly mooted by the CBD,[87] as well as by a number of international regimes. Most notably, the MAB,[88] the WHC[89] (which actively encourages TBPAs[90] unless co-operation is not forthcoming between the Parties)[91] and the Ramsar[92] (which also directs Parties to cooperate in this matter).[93] Even the Global Environment Facility[94] (with 29 TBPAs under its auspice),[95] and the International Timber Trade Organisation (ITTO) are notable in this context, despite having no explicit mandate to further protected areas. Nevertheless, the ITTO has

---

Network to Support the Development of Transboundary Conservation Initiatives. (Vth IUCN World Parks Congress).

86 Agenda 21. Chapter 15.7. Section (g)

87 CBD. Decision VII/28. Protected Areas. Annex I. Para 3. Goal 1.3.

88 Seville Strategy. Objective I.2 and IV.2. UNESCO. (2002). Biosphere Reserves: Special Places for People and Nature. (UNESCO, Paris). 136-140. For a full study of these five transboundary biosphere reserves, see MAB. (2003). *Five Transboundary Biosphere Reserves in Europe.* (UNESCO, Paris).

89 *Operational Guidelines.* 2002 Edn. Paragraphs 16 & 20.

90 Guinea, Liberia and the Ivory Coast with the Nimba Strict Nature Reserve. Fifth Session (1981) of the WHC. at 4. 26th Session (2002) of the WHC, at 19. Belarus and Poland, with the Belovezhskaya National park. 16th Session (1992) of the WHC, at 30. Columbia and Panama, with the Los Katios park. 18th Session (1995) of the WHC, at 40. The Talamanca Range Reserve in Costa Rica and Panama for the La Amistad. 7th Session (1984) of the WHC, at 5. 14th Session (1990) of the WHC, at 5. India and Bhutan, with the Manas site. 25th Session (2001) of the WHC, at 40-41. 26th Session (2002) of the WHC, at 20. Zambia and Zimbabwe, with the Victoria falls. 13th Session (1989) of the WHC, at 12; and Bulgaria and its Srebarna site.27th Session (2003) of the WHC, at 16.

91 Such as with the deferred Transborder Rainforest Heritage of Borneo, Indonesia. See Decision 30 COM 8B.23.

92 Ramsar. Article 5. (1971). Resolution 4.4. Implementation of Article 5. (1990, Montreux). Resolution 7.19. International Cooperation. (1999, San Jose). Annex. The Guidelines for international cooperation under the Ramsar Convention. Resolution 8.25. The Ramsar Strategic Plan. (2002, Valencia). Annex. Operational Objective 12. Resolution 8.26. The Implementation of the Strategic Plan 2003-2008. (2002, Valencia). Annex I. Global Implementation of the Targets for the Convention.

93 Resolution 9.8. Streamlining the Implementation of the Strategic Plan of the Convention 2003-2008 (2005, Kampala). Strategy 2.5. See Peru and Bolivia, with regard to Lake Titicaca. Recommendation 6.17. Ramsar Sites in Particular Countries. (1996, Brisbane); Austria, the Czech Republic and Slovakia, Recommendation 6.17. Ramsar Sites in Particular Countries. (1996, Brisbane); Countries sharing the High Andean ecosystems, Resolution 8.39. High Andean Wetlands as Strategic Ecosystems. (2002, Valencia); And Greece and Turkey with regard to the Evros/Meric Delta transfrontier wetland. Recommendation 5.1.1. Greek Ramsar Sites. (1993, Kushiro). Note, in the last instance, Turkey was decidedly luke warm about this proposal, even insisting on a reservation to the Ramsar Guidelines for International Co-operation, which it explicitly refuses to recognise as a legally binding document. Resolution 7.19. International Cooperation. (1999, San Jose).

94 UNESCO. (2004). ICC of the MAB Programme. SC-04/CONF.204/14. pp. 5.

95 GEF. (2005). *GEF In Action: Sustaining Wilderness Areas.* (GEF, Washington). 2-3. GEF. (2005). *Making a Visible Difference in Our World.* (GEF, Washington). 12.

become actively involved of the support of a number of TBPA forest sites.[96] TBPAs, thus, have grown as a result of persistent efforts, over time, by a number of international regimes for protected areas.

5 The Number of Protected Areas

In 1958, the International Union for the Conservation of Nature (IUCN) proposed that an international list be established which contained the entire world's protected areas. Soon after, the Economic and Social Council of the United Nations, requested the Secretary General to establish, 'a list of national parks and equivalent reserves, with a brief description of each'.[97] Since this point, an international inventory has been produced every ten years, showing exactly how many protected areas are in existence. The overall number has grown from just over 1,000 in 1962,[98] to 1,204 in 1971,[99] 2,671 in 1982,[100] to 12,754 in 1997. By 2003, the numbers had increased to a remarkable 102,102 protected areas.[101] The 2003 figure is the equivalent to 12.65% of the Earth's land surface. If marine protected areas were included in the calculation, 18.8 million kilometers of the Earth fall within protected areas. If marine protected areas are excluded from these calculations, the terrestrial extent of protected areas is some 17.1 million kilometers (11.5% of the land surface). This is almost the same as the entire continent of South America.[102]

---

96 The TBPAs that the ITTO has supported include the Pulong Tau National Park in Malaysia, on the border region of Sabah and Sarawak, the Mengame-Minkebe Transboundary Gorilla Sanctuary on the Cameroon-Gabon border; the Betung-Kerihun National Park in Indonesia; the natural protected area system between Peru and Bolivia; the Condor Range between Ecuador and Peru; and the Phatam Protected Forest complex between Thailand, Cambodia and Laos. See ITTO. (2004). 'The Incredible Condor'. *ITTO Tropical Forest Update.* 14(4). 1-7.

97 ECOSOC Resolution 713 (XXVII), 1959.

98 See Monod. T. (1962). 'The United Nations List of National Parks and Equivalent Reserves.' In Adams, A. (ed). *First World Conference on National Parks.* (US Department of the Interior, Washington). 62-98.

99 *United Nations List of National Parks and Equivalent Reserves.* (1971, Hayez, Brussels). 7-10.

100 Miller, K. (1984). 'The Natural Protected Areas of the World.' In McNeely, J. (ed). *National Parks, Conservation and Development.* (Smithsonian, Washington). 20-23.

101 UN List. 2003. *Ibid.* 27.

102 UNEP. (2003). *United Nations List of Protected Areas.* (IUCN/Thanet, UK).3. UNEP/WCWC. (2004). *Protected Areas and Biodiversity.* (UNEP: Biodiversity Series No 21). 7.

6 Some International Protected Areas of Note

Aside the generic figures included in the United Nations list of protected areas, it is also possible to note that a number of these are internationally recognised sites. The 2003 list included 4,633 internationally designated sites. Within these low thousands, a number of sites are particularly notable. The first set of noticeable sites comes from the WHC. This Convention has seen its numbers (of natural and cultural sites) go from 12 in 1978, to 754 listed sites in 125 State parties in 2005. Of these, 582 were inscribed as cultural properties, 149 as natural sites and 23 as mixed properties.[103] MAB sites have increased from 56 in 1976 to 459 sites in 97 countries in 2005.[104] As of 2005, there were 1525 wetland sites, totaling 129.5 million hectares. In the Antarctic, there are 2741 square kilometers, of protected areas.[105] By 2005, there were 64 areas in receipt of the European Diploma.[106] The International Maritime Organisation also has a collection of notable areas under international protection.[107] The sheer number of internationally recognized sites illustrates the progress of the creation of protected areas of international importance.

7 The Gaps in the System

In order to understand how the system of treaties came into being, it is important to examine the historical progression of the obligation to create protected areas. But, to understand how the system for protected areas exists in its present state and identify gaps in the current system, it is necessary to undertake a thematic analysis.

---

103 IUCN. (2004). *Review of the World Heritage Network: Biogeography, Habitats and Biodiversity.* (IUCN, Gland). 5. See UNESCO. (1978). 2nd Session of the WHC. CC-78/CONF.010/10. Oct 9, 1978. pp.6.

104 UNESCO. (2004). 18th Session of the ICC Bureau Meeting. SC-04/CONF.204/14. Jan 11. 19.

105 See New Zealand (2005). A Review of the Antarctic Protected Areas System. CEP Paper WP 11 (Stockholm, 2005). 1.

106 For a detailed list and examination of some of the earlier sites, see Bauer, F. (2002). 'The European Diploma of Protected Areas'. 12 (3) *Parks.* 29, -33.

107 Note, inter alia, IMO Assembly Resolution A.284 (VIII). Routeing Measures. IMO Assembly Resolution. A.430 (XI). IMO Assembly Resolution. A. 475 (XII). IMO Assembly Resolution A.527 (13). Routeing Measures. IMO Assembly Resolution A. 619 (15). Use of Pilotage Services in the Great Barrier Reef and Torres Strait Area. IMO Assembly Resolution. 669 (16). IMO Assembly Resolution. A. 711 (17). IMO Assembly Resolution A. 768 (18). The first two PSSAs recognised were the Great Barrier Reef MEPC 44(30). See Resolution MEPC. 97 (47). Identification of the Sea Area Around the Florida Keys as a PSSA. MEPC. (2002). Report of the MEPC on its 47th Session. MEPC 47/20. Annex 4. Resolution MEPC.101 (48). Identification of the Wadden Sea as a Particularly Sensitive Sea Area. MEPC. (2004). Report of the MEPC on its 51st Session. MEPC. 51/22. 38, 40-41. MEPC Resolution on the Designation of the Western European Waters as a Particularly Sensitive Area. MEPC. (2004). Report of the MEPC on its 52nd Session. MEPC. 52/WP.17.

Although the sheer numbers of protected areas is, without doubt, impressive, the numbers are deceptive, for as the CBD noted, 'existing systems of protected areas are neither representative of the world's ecosystems, nor do they adequately address conservation of critical habitat types, biomes and threatened species'.[108] With regard to species threatened with extinction, more than 1,300 species of mammals, amphibians and threatened birds are not represented in any protected areas.[109] Similar problems exist with threatened or endangered plan species. For example, in Eastern Europe of the 796 important areas identified as containing threatened or endangered plant life, 170 had no legal protection.[110] Likewise, with regard to ecosystems by type, although some ecosystems are well represented in protected area figures, such as with tropical humid forests (with a total of 23% coverage) subtropical forests (16.9% coverage) and mixed island ecosystems, (29.7% coverage), other ecosystems, such as temperate grasslands (with only 4.59% protected area coverage of the total known area) or lake systems (at only 1.54% coverage) are vastly underrepresented.

Even within areas that appear well represented, the figures may be deceptive. For example, with over 17% of the Arctic landmass under formal protection, it may seem that the level of the protection of the Arctic is adequate. However, this statistic is problematic, as it disguises the very low protection afforded to the marine environment. It also discounts the fact that if the nearly one million kilometer Greenland national park is removed, the percentage drops by half.[111] Likewise, if looking at the figures for protected areas in the Antarctic (a tiny 0.008% of the total land area) of the sites which are protected, these are located in two clusters, on the fringes of the Antarctic, with no sites a significant distance inland. Similarly, there is a complete absence of protected areas within Marie Byrd Land in western Antarctica.[112] Even within relatively successful regimes such as the Ramsar, sites tend to be concentrated in certain regions, and of certain wetland types, much to detriment of other possible areas.[113] For example, out of 1180 Ramsar sites listed at the end of 2002, only 70 were temporary pools.[114]

---

108 CBD. Decision VII/28. Protected Areas. Paragraph 16. See also Annex. I, Para 2.

109 Secretariat of the CBD. (2004). *Biodiversity Issues for Consideration in the Planning, Establishment and Management of Protected Area Sites and Management.* (CBD Technical Series No 15). 45-52.

110 Anon. (2005). 'Plants Hotspots in Protection Peril'. *New Scientist.* June 4. 18.

111 Conservation of Arctic Flora and Fauna. (2002). *Protected Areas of the Arctic: Conserving a Full Range of Values.* (CAFF Secretariat, in Department of Foreign Affairs, Canada). Ii.

112 See New Zealand (2005). A Review of the Antarctic Protected Areas System. CEP Paper WP 11 (Stockholm, 2005). 2.

113 Recommendation 1.3. Designating More Sites for the Ramsar List. (1980, Cagliari).

114 Resolution 8.33. Guidance for Identifying, Sustainably Managing and Designating Temporary Pools as Wetlands of International Importance. (2002, Valencia). Annex. Paragraph 5.

One of the best ways of looking at the problem of under, and over-representation of types of protected areas, is by looking at them thematically, in terms of ecosystem type. In this regard, marine, forest, drylands and mountainous areas are divisible categories.

8 Thematic Gaps

A Marine

The problem of vast areas without adequate representative coverage is particularly obvious with MPAs, in that about only one fifth of all marine biogeographic types identified are encompassed within MPAs.[115] This is not surprising in that although the international protected areas network now covers about 11 per cent of Earth's land surface, less than 1 per cent of the Earth's marine area is covered. As such, marine and coastal ecosystems are severely under-represented as protected areas, and the existing MPAs only protect a very small proportion of marine and coastal environments globally. Consequently, the existing MPAs make a relatively small contribution to the overall sustainable management of marine and coastal biodiversity.[116] Moreover, the MPAs that do exist provide a very slanted picture. This is because of the 1.6 million kilometers attributed to MPAs, a few overtly large MPAs make up the lion's share of this figure, with the difference between the mean size of an MPAs being 100,000 hectares, whilst the median size is 1,584 hectares.[117] The other caveat in the MPA discussion is that MPAs tend to be disproportionately represented in only certain parts of the world. For example, as of 2006, of the 34 WHC sites with a marine component, 11 of them were in Oceania/Australasia. Even within a number of relatively progressive international regimes which deal with such questions, such as with the Antarctic regime, the creation of MPAs has proven fraught with difficulty caused by concerns of sovereignty and overlapping international organisations, taking over twenty years to achieve the pitifully small total of only 3 MPAs.[118]

---

115 Kelleher, G. (1995). *A Global Representative System of Marine Protected Areas.* (World Bank, Washington). Volume IV. 5-6. CBD. Decision VII/5 Marine and Coastal Biological Diversity. Section 13.

116 CBD. Decision VII/5 Marine and Coastal Biological Diversity. Section 14.

117 Conservation of Arctic Flora and Fauna. (2002). *Protected Areas of the Arctic: Conserving a Full Range of Values.* (CAFF Secretariat, in Department of Foreign Affairs, Canada). 15. Kelleher, G. (1995). *Ibid.* Volume IV. 5. IUCN. (2004). *Speaking A Common Language: Management Categories for Protected Areas.* (IUCN, Gland). 106.

118 Antarctic Treaty: Report of the Thirteenth Meeting. (Brussels, 1985). Paragraphs 65 and 66. Antarctic Treaty: Report of the Twelfth Meeting. (Canberra, 1983). Agenda Item 7. Recommendation XIV-6. Marine Sites of Special Scientific Interest. In Antarctic Treaty: Report of the Fourteenth Meeting (Rio de Janeiro, 1987). See Annex V, Article 6 (2) of the Madrid Protocol. Decision 4. (1998). Marine Protected Areas. In Antarctic Treaty: Report of the

This problem is particularly obvious with certain key oceanic ecosystems such as coral reefs.[119] These ecosystems are important because, inter alia, globally, nearly two thirds of all fish harvested ultimately depend on the health of them.[120] Coral reefs, (including both cold and warm water corals), are the forests of the ocean. They have vast economic, cultural and ecological importance. On the last factor alone, although coral reefs occupy less than one quarter of 1% of the marine environment, coral reefs are home to more than a quarter of all known marine fish species and cumulatively they may hold close to 1 million species (although only 93,000 are known).[121]

Although coral reefs are the hotspots of marine biodiversity, only slightly more than 400 MPAs contain them. Moreover, despite being identifiable within the listings of the WHC, MAB, Ramsar and the IMO,[122] this critical subset of marine biodiversity is largely invisible as a particular theme for protected areas. Indeed, at the turn of the century, at least 40 countries lacked any marine protected areas for conserving their coral reef ecosystems.[123] Although the MAB, the WHC, and most notably the Ramsar have recognised the category, as a subset within other areas of their overall work,[124] the only international body which explicitly deals with coral reefs, is the International

---

Twenty-Second Meeting. (Tromso, 1997). 70-71.119. Antarctic Treaty: Fourteenth Antarctic Treaty Consultative Meeting. (Rio de Janeiro, 1987). Para 88.

119 Olson, D. et al. (2000). *The Global 200: A Representative Approach to Conserving the Earth's Distinctive Ecoregions.* (WWF, Washington). 20.

120 Resolution 8.11. Additional Guidance for Identifying and Designating Under Represented Wetland Types as Wetlands of International Importance. (2002, Valencia). Annex. Identification and Designation of Mangroves.

121 Commission on Sustainable Development. (2001). Global Status of Biodiversity. E/CN.17/2001/PC/18. March 14. 5. Pain. S. (1999). 'Treasures Lost in Reef Madness.' *New Scientist.* Feb 25. 14. Freiwald, A, Fosse, J. (2004). *Cold Water Coral Reefs.* (UNEP, WCMC, Cambridge). SBSTTA. Report of the Ad Hoc Technical Expert Group on Protected Areas. Brooks, T. (2002). 'Habitat Loss and Extinction in the Hotspots of Biodiversity.' *Conservation Biology.* 16(4): 909-923. UNEP/CBD/SBSTTA/9/INF/3. 22 Sep, 2003. pp.35.

122 UNEP. (2004). *Conventions and Coral Reefs.* (UNEP, Nairobi). 5-15.

123 Commission on Sustainable Development. (2001). Global Status of Biodiversity. E/CN.17/2001/PC/18. March 14. 5.

124 See World Heritage Marine Programme. In Report of the World Heritage Centre in Implementing Strategic Objectives. WHC-05/29.COM/5. IUCN. (1997). *A Global Overview of Wetland and Marine Protected Areas on the World Heritage List.* (IUCN, Gland). UNESCO. (2002). *Proceedings of the World Heritage Marine Biodiversity Workshop.* (World Heritage Papers No. 4, UNESCO, Paris). Resolution 8.11. Additional Guidance for Identifying and Designating Under Represented Wetland Types as Wetlands of International Importance. (2002, Valencia). Resolution 8.32. Conservation, Integrated Management and Sustainable Use of Mangrove Ecosystems and Their Resources. (2002, Valencia). Resolution 9.4. The Ramsar Convention and the Conservation, Production and Sustainable Use of Fisheries Resources. (Kampala, 2005). Paragraph 35.

Coral Reef Initiative (ICRI).[125] However, despite voicing the importance of MPAs encompassing coral reefs, the ICRI has no power to designate such areas as protected.[126]

B Forests

Forests are an other obvious choice as protected areas. This is because natural forests are typically strong repositories for biodiversity, with great cultural, economic and ecological importance. This common-sense realization is part of the reason why forests are, on the whole, relatively well protected. Indeed, the Global Forest Resource Assessment by the Food and Agricultural Organisation in the year 2000 estimated that around 12% of the world's forests are included in IUCN protected areas categories.[127] This is not surprising as of the year 2000, 22 countries had already pledged to protect a minimum of 10% of their forests.[128] Central America, South America, eastern and southern Africa, Australia and New Zealand have 25% or more of their forests within some kind of protected area. However, not all categories of forest have the same level of protection, and their situation is often hidden beneath the generic figure.[129] For example, forests in North Africa, Middle East and the Pacific are particularly poorly protected with less than 5% of their area within protected sites. Freshwater swamp forests in both tropical and temperate regions, mixed needle-leaved and broad–leaved forests in tropical regions and sub-tropical thorn and sclerophyllous dry forests are also, in general, poorly protected.[130]

---

125 ICRI Decision on Cold Water Coral Reefs. In ICRI (2004). Report of the ICRI Meeting in Okinawa, Japan. 3-4 July, 2004. For the support of ICRI, see paragraph 31 (e) of the WSSD Plan of Implementation, and Chapter 17 of Agenda 21.

126 Decision on Marine Protected Areas.In ICRI (2004). Report of the ICRI Meeting in Okinawa, Japan. 3-4 July, 2004.

127 FAO. (2000). *Global Forest Resources Assessment 2000.* (FAO, Rome). xxv. Secretariat of the CBD. (2004). *Biodiversity Issues for Consideration in the Planning, Establishment and Management of Protected Area Sites and Management.* (CBD Technical Series No 15). 63-70.

128 See World Commission on Forests and Sustainable Development. (2000). *Our Forests, Our Future.* (Cambridge University Press, Cambridge). 100.

129 The most protected forests are tropical moist forests and temperate needle-leaf forests, which have over 11% of their area included in protected areas. Tropical dry forests are the least protected with less than 9% of their area included in protected areas belonging to management categories I-VI. About 10% of the temperate broad-leaved forests are included under protected area of various IUCN categories.

130 Secretariat of the CBD. (2004). *Biodiversity Issues for Consideration in the Planning, Establishment and Management of Protected Area Sites and Management.* (CBD Technical Series No 15). 63-70.

The recognition that forests should be prime candidates to be made into protected areas dates back to Second World Conference on National Parks in 1972.[131] This goal was reiterated in 1982,[132] and also within the considerably watered down[133] 1992 Non-Legally Binding Authoritative Statement of Principles for a Global Consensus on the Management, Conservation and Sustainable Development of all Types of Forests.[134] Agenda 21 emphasised the importance of enhanced protected forest areas,[135] as has the CBD,[136] and the GEF. The GEF is particularly notable due to its economic support for a number of forest protected areas, such as the Amazon Region Protected Areas programme which aims to incorporate and additional 25 million hectares to read to the goal of 37 million hectares under protection. This would triple the existing extent of Brazil's protected areas by 2012, to an area the size of Spain.[137]

Despite the utility of the above processes, the only regime in the international community, aside some thematic studies in the WHC[138] and the MAB,[139] which could effectively facilitate the establishment and management of forest protected areas, by virtue of

---

131 This conference drew attention to the, 'paucity of protected areas in the tropical forest biomes' and called upon governments as a matter of urgency, 'to take effective steps to increase protected areas of virtually untouched natural forests of the humid tropics'. Recommendation 2. Conservation of Tropical Rain Forest Ecosystems. In Elliot, H. (ed). *Second World Conference on National Parks.* (1972, IUCN, Lausanne). 377, 378.

132 The third Congress noted the 'critical situation' with regard to the biomes of tropical forests (in given selected areas). Recommendation 2. Global System of Representative Terrestrial Protected Areas. Recommendations of the World National Parks Congress. Recommendation 18. International Agreements and Protected Areas. Recommendations of the World National Parks Congress. In McNeely, J. (ed). *National Parks, Conservation and Development.* (Smithsonian, Washington). 775.

133 See Humphreys, D. (1996). *Forest Politics: The Evolution of International Cooperation.* (Earthscan, London). Annex D. Draft Text for a Convention for the Conservation and Wise Use of Forests. Articles 8 and 9. See also, World Commission on Forests and Sustainable Development. (2000). *Our Forests, Our Future.* (Cambridge University Press, Cambridge). 100.

134 A/CONF.151/26 (Vol. III). Principle 7 (b).

135 Agenda 21. Chapter 11.14. b.

136 Recommendation VII/6. Forest Biological Diversity. UNEP/CBD/COP/6/4.pp.34. Recommendation IX/6. Ecosystem Approach: Further Elaboration, Guidelines for Implementation and Relationship with Sustainable Forest Management. Annex II. pp.56. SBSTTA. Protected Areas: Report of the International Workshop of Protected Forest Areas. UNEP/CBD/SBSTTA/9/INF/39. Nov 9, 2003.

137 GEF. (2005). *GEF In Action: Sustaining Wilderness Areas.* (GEF, Washington). 2-3. GEF. (2005). *Making a Visible Difference in Our World.* (GEF, Washington). 32.

138 See IUCN. (1997). *A Global Overview of the Forest Protected Areas on the World Heritage List.* (IUCN, Gland). As discussed, at the 21st (1997) Session of the WHC at 52; and the 23rd (1999) Session of the WHC, at 8.. As of 2006, World Heritage forest sites encompassed a total surface area of 73 million hectares.

139 UNESCO. (2006). MAB ICC. 19th Session. SC-06/CONF.202/16. Nov 28. 13-14.

the fact that they are forests, is either the Montreal Process, or the ITTO. Of these two, only the latter, is a formal international organization, with real possibilities in this area. The former being largely driven by the development of sustainability indicators, of which protected areas are but one factor.[140] Although the ITTO also utilizes indicators, with an overlap into protected areas,[141] the ITTO has actually gone little further in the promotion of protected areas. This is despite the fact that although the primary instrument in this area and the International Tropical Timber Agreement,[142] places a strong emphasis upon 'sustainability', no mention of protected areas is present in the document. The only mention of protected areas, in the high level documents, appears in the 2002 to 2006 ITTO Action Plan, under which the Parties pledged themselves to maintain the integrity of the resource base, including protected area networks.[143] Since this point, the ITTO has assisted its member countries in setting aside and managing totally protected areas. Despite this support, the ITTO does not nominate or evaluate protected areas of forest. Rather, it only supports it member's decisions in this area.

In many ways, the failure of the international community to develop a specific mechanism that could encompass forest protected areas is a reflection of their larger failure to develop an effective and overall international forestry convention. Accordingly, despite a near universal recognition that forests make perfect candidates as protected areas, as it stands, forest protected areas remain tangential to the Montreal Process, only within a discussion forum of the CBD, and barely in the margins of the ITTO. The problem in this instance can be best demonstrated by the collapse of the United Nations Forest Forum (UNFF) in 2005. One of the few things that all of the participants could agree on was calling upon all countries to significantly increase the area of protected forests and sustainably managed forests.[144] However, as the UNFF collapsed, the only mechanisms left to achieve this goal were the Montreal Process, the CBD and the ITTO. Without an international forestry convention or a similar mechanism, therefore, gaps in forest protection will continue to limit the international system of protected areas.

---

140 The Montreal Process. (1997). *The First Approximation Report.* (Canadian Forest Service, Ottawa). Appendix 1. The Montreal Process. (1999). *Criteria and Indicators for the Conservation and Sustainable Management of Temperate and Boreal Forests.* (Canadian Forest Service, Ottawa). 10.

141 ITTO. (2005). *Revised ITTO Criteria and Indicators for the Sustainable Management of Tropical Forests, Including Reporting Format.* (ITTO, Yokohama, Policy Development Series No. 15).

142 ITTO. (1994). TD/TIMBER. 2/16.

143 ITTO. (2002). *ITTO Yokohama Action Plan 2002-2006.* (ITTO, Yokohama, Policy Development Series No. 11). 11.

144 Earth Negotiations Bulletin. United Nations Forum on Forests, 16-27 May, 2005. Volume 13 (133).

C *Mountains*

Mountain environments cover 27% of the world's land surface, and host about 12% of the Earth's human populations. Lowland people also depend on mountain environments for a wide range of goods and services, including water, food, timber and biodiversity. Mountains are increasingly fragile, due to being under multiple anthropogenic threats.[145] Accordingly, the conservation of mountain biodiversity and its linkage with protected areas was iterated at the WSSD,[146] the CBD,[147] Agenda 21[148] and the World Parks Congress.[149] However, aside some GEF support for this area, (one third of GEF sponsored protected area assistance goes to mountain areas, encompassing 107 projects in 64 countries),[150] and some tangential focusing on mountains within the MAB,[151] WHC,[152] and Ramsar[153] there is no specific, over-riding body directing work in this area. This is all the more disappointing given that there are a number of regional instruments which are specifically focused on the conservation of certain mountain ecosystems, such as the Alpine[154] and Carpathian Conventions.[155] However, once more, protected areas are but a small subset within a much larger sustainable management agenda, and there is no direct regional or international guidance or law by which protected areas in mountainous regions can be facilitated.

D *Drylands, Arid, Semi-arid, Grassland and Savannah Ecosystems/Dry and Semi-Humid Lands*

Natural grasslands and savannahs host very distinctive plant and animal communities where diversity tends to increase towards the tropics. All these systems hold an array

---

145 UNEP. (2002). *Mountain Watch: Environmental Change and Sustainable Development in Mountains.* (UNEP/WCMC, Cambridge).

146 WSSD. Plan of Implementation. Paragraph 43.

147 Mountain Biodiversity. UNEP/CBD/COP/7/L.29..

148 See Chapter 13.7. (b) of Agenda 21.

149 See Recommendation 5.06. Strengthening Mountain Protected Areas as a Key Contribution to Sustainable Mountain Development. (Vth IUCN World Parks Congress).

150 GEF. (2005). *Making a Visible Difference in Our World.* (GEF, Washington). 23.

151 See MAB. (2003). *Global Change Research in Mountain Biosphere Reserves.* (MAB, UNESCO). UNESCO. (2006). MAB ICC. 19th Session. SC-06/CONF.202/16. Nov 28. 10. UNESCO. (2001). MAB ICC Bureau Meeting. SC/-01/CONF.211/13. Apr 10. 19.

152 See IUCN (2002). *A Global Overview of Mountain Protected Areas on the World Heritage List.* (IUCN, Gland). UNESCO. (2000). Thematic Expert Meeting on Potential Natural World Heritage Sites in the Alps. WHC-2000/CONF.204/WEB.2.

153 Resolution 8.12. Enhancing the Wise Use and Conservation of Mountain Wetlands. (2002, Valencia). Resolution 8.39. High Andean Wetlands as Strategic Ecosystems. (2002, Valencia).

154 Anon. (2004). 'Alpine Convention: Implementation in Progress.' *Environmental Policy and the Law.* 34(5): 191-192.

155 Bilobran, I. (2003). 'Convention Signed.' *Environmental Policy and the Law.* 33(5): 203.

of native herbivores, and these, in turn, can support a high profile of mammals and avian predators. The savannah communities of East Africa, for example, are typified by large herds of ungulate herbivores including more than 70 species of antelope and other medium to large sized bovids. At very fine spatial scales, natural grasslands can be among the most species rich habitats on Earth. Up to 80 plant species have been identified in a square meter in the Central Asian Steppe, and 42 plant species in a quarter of a square meter in pine savannah on the Atlantic coastal plain of the United States. Even deserts, which are not normally associated with biodiversity, can have highly unique species within them. Collectively, analysis of global habitat distribution of threatened mammals and birds shows that drylands, scrublands and grasslands make up the second most important group of threatened species of mammals. In addition a high proportion of extinctions of continental species since 1600, occurred in dry land ecosystems.[156]

Due to such considerations, the CBD in its discussions on these areas has recommended the importance of inter alia, protected areas as part of the strategy to combat biodiversity loss in dryland associated ecosystems.[157] Despite such recommendations, the primary international instrument in this area, the United Nations Convention to Combat Desertification in Countries Experiencing Serious Drought and/or Desertification, Particularly in Africa (CCD), although developing a series of ways to combat desertification, and protect both human communities and non-human biodiversity,[158] has been largely silent on the utilization or value of protected areas. The only other convention which has dealt with a small category of grasslands (those which are wet) in passing, has been the Ramsar.[159] Likewise, the MAB has 'drylands' as one of its thematic areas.[160] In this regard, the MAB has worked with the CCD on some basic

156 CBD (2002). Thematic Programmes of Work: Biological Diversity of Dry and Sub Humid Lands. UNEP/CBD/COP/6/INF/39. Apr 4, 2002.

157 Recommendation IV/3. Assessment and Status of …Dryland, Arid, Semi-arid and Savannah Ecosystems. UNEP/CBD/SBSTTA/4/14.pp 38. Decision V/23. Consideration of Options for the Conservation and Sustainable Use of Biological Diversity in Dryland, Mediterranean, Arid, Semi Arid and Savannah Ecosystems. UNEP/CBD/COP/5/23. pp 173.

158 See Decision 8/COP.4. Declaration on the Commitments to Enhance the Implementation of the Obligations of the Convention. ICCD/COP (4)/11/Add 1.pp29. UNEP/FAO. (1996). Our Land Our Future. (UNEP, Nairobi). 42-46. Ryan, J. (1999). *Desert and Dryland Development: Challenges and Potential in the New Millennium.* (Icarda, Syria). Traylor, I. et al. (1996). *Desert Development: The Endless Frontier.* (International Center for Arid and Semiarid Land Studies, Texas). FAO. (2001). *From Farmer to Planner Back: Harvesting Best Practices.* (FAO, Rome). FAO. (1997). *Negotiating a Sustainable Future for Land.* (FAO, Rome). See UNEP (1977). *United Nations Conference on Desertification: Round Up, Plan of Action and Resolutions.* (UNEP, Nairobi).

159 Resolution 8.11. Additional Guidance for Identifying and Designating Under Represented Wetland Types as Wetlands of International Importance. (2002, Valencia).

160 UNESCO. (2006). MAB ICC. 19th Session. SC-06/CONF.202/16. Nov 28.10-12.

materials and education projects relating to desertification, but it has not got a specific drylands protected areas list (as such).

9 Priority Areas

Due to the multifaceted problems noted above, it has been suggested that there is an urgent need to take action to improve the coverage and representativeness of protected areas nationally, regionally and globally.[161] However, recognition of this problem is easier to articulate, than developing an approach to solve it by which all countries, let alone those seeking to establish protected areas, can agree. Indeed, it is not always clear what the primary conservation objectives should be, as there are a number of different approaches to consider. Moreover, these different approaches often conflict. This problem is inflamed by the difficulties of limited resources. Accordingly, it has become increasingly necessary to seek and prioritise what areas should be at the forefront of conservation efforts.[162] A number of conventions have already started this process, with the development of strategies and inventories, designed to help select key areas which they could come to protect. The process of comparative and thematic analysis (whereby sites are put forward on tentative lists, and broadly compared) is made use, as a gap-analysis tool by, inter alia, the CBD,[163] the Bern Convention,[164] and Ramsar.[165] However,

161 Decision VII/28. Protected Areas..

162 Kleiner, K. (2003). 'Conserving a Wild World.' *New Scientist.* Aug 23. 6. Drewett, J. (1988). 'Never Mind the Whale, Save the Insects.' *New Scientist.* Dec 17. 32-34. Randerson, I. (2002). 'Glamorous Animals Get All the Cash.' *New Scientist.* Aug 24. 9. Moran, D. (1996). 'Global Biodiversity Priorities.' *Global Environmental Change.* 6(2): 103-119. Ginsberg, J. (1999). 'Global Conservation Priorities.' *Conservation Biology.* 13(1): 5-12. IUCN. (2005). *Background Paper for the Special Expert Meeting of the World Heritage Convention on the Concept of Outstanding Universal Value.* (IUCN, Gland). 7-8.

163 CBD. Decision VII/28. Protected Areas. Annex. 1.1.2.

164 Recommendation No 3. (1984). On the Establishment of National Inventories of Three Types of Natural Habitat. Recommendation No 14. (1989). On Species Habitat Conservation and on the Conservation of Endangered Natural Habitat. Also, Resolution No 6, 1998.

165 Final Act of the Ramsar Conference. Annex II. Recommendations adopted by the International Conference on the Conservation of Wetlands and Waterfowl at Ramsar, Iran, 3 February 1971. Recommendation 10. African Wetlands. Recommendation 1.5. National Wetland Inventories. (1980, Cagliari). Recommendation 4.6. Establishment of National Scientific Inventories of Potential Ramsar Sites. (1990, Montreux). Resolution 12. National Wetland Inventories. (1996, Brisbane). Resolution 7.20. Wetland Inventory. (1999, San Jose). Resolution 8.6. A Ramsar Framework Inventory. (2002, Valencia). Resolution 8.26. The Implementation of the Strategic Plan 2003-2008. (2002, Valencia). Annex I. Global Implementation of the Targets for the Convention. Resolution 8.7. Gaps In and Harmonisation of Ramsar Guidance on Wetland Ecological Character, Inventory, Assessment and Monitoring. (2002, Valencia). Resolution 8.6. A Ramsar Framework Inventory. (2002, Valencia).

this process is most notable with the WHC and its extensive emphasis upon tentative lists, in addition to comparative and thematic analysis.[166]

10 The Choice of Priority Areas

Despite the utilization of tentative lists and comparative and thematic analysis, it is not always clear what the primary conservation objectives should be, as there are a number of different approaches to consider and exactly what and where the priority areas are is a matter of debate between four different (but often overlapping) schemas. These schemas are the Udvardy system, the Global 200, Species Focused Approaches, and Hotspots. To one degree or another, most regimes interested in protected areas utilize one or more of these schemas. For example, the GEF focuses on globally significant and representative ecosystems, including protected areas within the Global 200 (140 GEF projects covering 761 protected areas) and Hotspots (112 projects covering 606 protected areas)[167] lists. The schemas, which will be addressed individually below, should enable the international community to meet goals for protected areas in spite of the current gaps in the system.

166 UNESCO. (1996) Expert Review on Evaluation of General Principles and Criteria for Nominations of Natural World Heritage Sites. WHC-96/CONF.202/INF.9. Apr 15. 6. UNESCO. (1994). Expert Meeting on the Global Strategy. WHC-94/CONF.003/INF.6. Oct 13. 1994. 1. See IUCN (1996). *Earth's Geological History: A Contextual Framework for Assessment of Fossil Site Nominations.* (IUCN, Gland). IUCN (2002). *A Global Overview of Mountain Protected Areas on the World Heritage List.* (IUCN, Gland). UNESCO. UNESCO. (2000). Thematic Expert Meeting on Potential Natural World Heritage Sites in the Alps. WHC-2000/CONF.204/WEB.2. IUCN. (1997). *A Global Overview of the Forest Protected Areas on the World Heritage List.* (IUCN, Gland). IUCN. (1997). *A Global Overview of Wetland and Marine Protected Areas on the World Heritage List.* (IUCN, Gland).

167 GEF. (2005). *Making a Visible Difference in Our World.* (GEF, Washington). 32.

A The Udvardy System

In 1975, the Udvardy biogeographical system was unveiled. This was the first unified system that classified the natural ecosystems of the world into biogeographical realms, and the further divided them into biomes and showed their geographic distribution. At the top level, eight large biogeographical realms[168] which are continent or sub-continent sized areas with geography and fauna/flora/vegetation were recognised. These were subdivided into 14 biomes.[169] Biomes are groups of ecosystems that are related, and which show similarity in both appearance and internal structure, due to being influenced by the same climate, soil conditions and elevational conditions. Finally, biomes were divided into the last category of 193 (later reanalyzed as 227)[170] biogeographical provinces, which approximately correspond to floristic regions of botanists and the faunal provinces of zoologists. Although this classification has some obvious limitations, such as overall bluntness, its restriction to only terrestrial considerations[171] and focusing predominantly on vegetational components (with limited recognition of the species in them), it has the merit of being able to clearly identify the different biogeographical provinces of the Earth, and then conserve them within appropriate protected area regimes. In this regard, the approach has clearly been successful. For example, all of Udvary's Biomes are contained within some WHC Sites (with the most common being the 32 mountain systems, 26 tropical humid and 25 tropical dry forests) except with the biogeographical provinces recognised as cold winter deserts. Cold winter deserts, tundra and polar systems, and temperate grasslands (as of 2004 there are only four of each) are the least common biome classifications.[172]

---

168 Africotropical; Antarctica; Australian; Indomalayan; Nearctic; Neotropical; Oceanian & Palaearctic.

169 Mixed mountain systems; Humid Tropical Forests; Tropical Dry/Deciduous Forests; Mixed Island Systems; Subtropical/temperate rainforest; Warm desert/semi deserts; Temperate Broad Leaf Forests; Temperate Needle leaf Forests; Evergreen Forests/Scrub; Tropical Grassland/Savannah; Lake Systems; Tundra/polar desert; Temperate Grasslands & Cold Winter deserts.

170 Udvardy, M. (1984). 'A Biogeographical Classification System for Terrestrial Environments.' In McNeely, J. (ed). *National Parks, Conservation and Development.* (Smithsonian, Washington). 34-39.

171 Work on a complimentary biophysical coastal and marine classification system (around the Americas) began in the early 1980s Ray, C. (1984). 'Development of a Biophysical Coastal and Marine Classification System.' In McNeely, *Ibid.* 39-43.

172 IUCN. (2004). *Review of the World Heritage Network: Biogeography, Habitats and Biodiversity.* (IUCN, Gland). 7-8.

B The Global 200

The 'Global 200' is the mechanism of the World Wildlife Fund (WWF), and it has been actively promoted touted at the WHC.[173] This mechanism seeks to answer many of the possible deficiencies of the Udvary system, as it covers marine areas, incorporates a much greater degree of weight towards biodiversity considerations within the biomes, and provides the clear objective of the protection of major habitat types ('eco-regions'), and not just individual species or hotspots of diversity.

The Global 200 mechanism is predicated upon an analysis of the eco-regions representing the Earth's 30 terrestrial, freshwater and major marine habitat types. An eco-region is defined as a relatively large unit of land or water containing a characteristic set of natural communities that share a large majority or their species, dynamics and evolutionary conditions. This was further divided by Major Habitat Type (MHT). MHTs describe different areas of the world which share similar environmental conditions, habitat structure and patterns of biological complexity and that contain communities with similar guild structures and adaptations. MHT classifications are roughly equivalent to biomes. Each MHT was further subdivided by biogeographical realm (e.g. Nearctic, Indian Ocean) in order to represent the unique flora and fauna in each area. This resulted in a collection 867 'ecoregions.'

The ecoregions were then analysed in terms of their species richness, endemic nature, higher taxonomic uniqueness (unique genera, relict species etc), extra-ordinary ecological or evolutionary phenomena (e.g. adaptive radiations, intact large assemblages, presence of migrations of large vertebrates). The rich and endemic nature of species is not the sole defining characteristics, as a number of 'sparse' eco-regions (such as some boreal forests, tundra, and some ecoregions in very dry conditions) do not have high biodiversity counts in these regards. Accordingly, an enhanced emphasis was also given to 'extra-ordinary ecological phenomena' (i.e. ecosystem rarity) and 'unusual evolutionary phenomena' (such as uniquely adapted species to key environments). The most biologically outstanding of the 867 ecoregions, which were whittled down to 238 ecoregions. These 238 (the so called Global 200) are comprised of 142 terrestrial, 53 freshwater and 43 marine ecoregions.[174]

This clear list gives the benefit of being able to present a comprehensive strategy for conserving global biodiversity, that focuses not only on the obvious areas (such as tropical forests) but also the other distinctive ecosystems of the world (from tundra, grasslands, lakes, polar seas, mangroves etc) that hold much of the world's biodiversity.

---

173 UNESCO. (1998). 22nd Session of the WHC. WHC-98/CONF.208/18. Jan 29, 1998. 89-90.

174 Olson, D. et al. (2000). *The Global 200: A Representative Approach to Conserving the Earth's Distinctive Ecoregions.* (WWF, Washington). 1-4.

The Global 200 thesis is that all such ecosystems and habitat types need to be represented within meaningful conservation strategies. This is especially so as some of these major habitat types (i.e. biomes) such as tropical dry forests and Mediterranean climate shrublands, are on average more threatened than are tropical moist forests and require immediate conservation action, as they are not within any protected area regime.[175] For example, fifty terrestrial Global 200 ecoregions are not in any WHC site, nor are 18 Marine Global 200 ecoregions.[176]

C Species Focused Approaches

An approach that falls between the need to protect habitats and key species, is that which seeks to identify key habitat which are necessary to protect, so as to conserve the biodiversity that rely upon that habitat. This focus may be upon individual species, biodiversity in general, or species threatened with extinction. The latter is a particularly common articulation of this approach given the clear links that can be made between species survival and habitat loss. Indeed, in late 2005, an international team of scientists identified almost 600 sites around the world as 'zones of imminent extinction'. Each site contained at least one endangered species which lived no-where else. Of the 794 'trigger species' 408 are amphibians, 217 are birds and 131 are mammals.[177] Although these figures are new, the recognition of this approach is not, as this is one of the most well known and long-standing orientation strategies for protected areas.[178] This approach is well utilised within the CMS and Bern Conventions, and a secondary theme with regards to the Ramsar.

A species focused approach is also partly replicated in the IUCN/Species Survival Global Habitat Classification. This system is derived from calculations involved in the protection of the necessary habitat for species which are endangered, and listed on the IUCN Red List. These divide into a three level hierarchical system. The first level consists of 15 broad habitat categories. Of these, 11 subdivide into 78 second level habitat types, which are further subdivided into 154 third level categories. Within these divisions, it is possible to show that some first habitat sites are more protected in international protected area systems (such as forests in and wetlands). Conversely, the seven types of shrub-land

---

175 *Ibid.* 1.

176 IUCN. (2004). *Review of the World Heritage Network: Biogeography, Habitats and Biodiversity.* (IUCN, Gland). 32-34.

177 Anon. (2005). 'Going, Going…' New Scientist. Dec 17. 5.

178 See 'Closing Plenary Session.' In Adams, A. (ed). *First World Conference on National Parks.* (US Department of the Interior, Washington). 384. Recommendation No 22. The First World Conference, then went onto identify a number of threatened species in need of such protected areas. They were five species of rhinoceroses; the Mountain Tapir, Spectacled bear & Pudu deer. See Recommendations 24 & 25.

are very poorly represented, as is over half (four out of seven) of all grassland types. Finally, marine and coastal habitats have a low occurrence in all continents/regions.

A variation on the above theme was offered by Birdlife International and their recognition of Endemic Bird Areas (EBAs). The variation is that one species is alone recognised as the key species linking to a habitat that should be the placed within a protected area. An endemic bird area is defined as,

> An area which encompasses the overlapping breeding ranges of restricted range bird species, such that the complete ranges or two or more restricted range species are entirely included within the boundary of the EBA. This does not necessarily mean that the complete ranges of all of an EBA's restricted range species are entirely included within the boundary of a single EBA, as some species may be shared between EBAs.[179]

These are identified as areas that encompass the breeding ranges of two or more birds whose total breeding is restricted to 50,000 km or less. The biological importance of an EBA is measured by the number of restricted range species occurring in it, and whether they are shared with any other EBAs. Most EBAs support 2 to 10 restricted bird species. Globally, 218 EBAs have been identified. These 218 EBAs cover approximately 2% of the world's land surface.[180] Despite this relatively small area requiring protection, 144 EBAs are not within WHC sites.[181]

The final variant on focusing on key species as the basis for protected areas focuses upon Centres of Plant Diversity (CPD). This IUCN/WWF initiative identified 250 priority sites for the global conservation of higher plants.[182] Plants were identified as key species because they are often highly threatened (the estimate is that as many as 60,000 species may become extinct by 2050, or 1 in 4 plants). Accordingly, the IUCN/WWF initiative identified areas around the world which are of, 'the greatest importance for plant conservation'.[183] Sites were selected on the basis of their botanical richness, geographically defined areas with high species diversity and/or endemism (such as the Atlas Mountains), and/or vegetation types which are exceptionally rich and/or endemic (such as the Amazon rain forests). Additional considerations involved how much the site was threatened, the diversity of the habitats within a site, the proportion of species adapted to special edaphic conditions (i.e. limestone) and the potential use of the plants

---

179 Stattersfield, A. (1998). *Endemic Bird Areas of the World: Priorities for Bird Conservation (Birdlife International, Cambridge).* 24.

180 World Commission on Environment and Development. (1987). *Our Common Future.* (OUP, Oxford). 165-166.

181 IUCN et al. (2004) *Review of the World Heritage Network: Biogeography, Habitats and Biodiversity.* (IUCN, Gland). 81-82.

182 IUCN/WWF. (1995). *Centres of Plant Diversity: A Guide and Strategy for Their Conservation.* (Chiltern, London).

183 IUCN/WWF. *Ibid.* 2.

contained.[184] Despite the utility of CPDs, only 20.2% of CPDs occur within WHC sites, while 79.8% do not.[185]

D Hotspots

As noted above, protecting habitats because they are linked to species is not a new idea. However, the divergence from focusing upon individual species, to numbers of species within an area (as a justification for creating protected areas), only fully appeared on the international arena in the early 1980s.[186] By the end of the 1980s, the idea of creating protected areas to encompass areas of rich biodiversity (in terms of species numbers) has been considerably refined by Norman Myers[187] and the NGO Conservation International, with the concept of 'hotspots'. Originally, 25 hotspots were identified, but this number was later taken to 32.[188] This idea has become so influential, that the WSSD called upon all governments to, 'effectively conserve and sustainably use biodiversity, promote and support initiatives for hot spot areas and other areas essential for biodiversity'.[189]

To make the hotspot list, an area must meet the criteria of endemism and threat. Although these criteria are not necessarily absolutely robust,[190] the yardstick is that with regard to 'threat', they should have 25% or less of its original primary natural

184 IUCN/WWF. *Ibid.* 3-4.

185 IUCN et al. (2004) *Review of the World Heritage Network: Biogeography, Habitats and Biodiversity.* (IUCN, Gland). 100.

186 Recommendation 10. Conservation of Genetic Resources. Recommendations of the World National Parks Congress. In McNeely, J. (ed). *National Parks, Conservation and Development.* (Smithsonian, Washington). 771.

187 In 1988 Norman Myers identified 10 threatened hotspots in the tropical rain forests of the world, estimating they contained 13% of all plant diversity in just 0.2% of the land area of the planet. In subsequent analysis, he added four other rain forests and four Mediterranean style ecosystems and came up with a total of 18 areas that accounted for 20% of the global plant diversity in just 0.5% of the land area of the planet. Mittermeier, R & Myers, N. (2000). *Hotspots.* (University of Chicago Press, Chicago). 26-27.

188 Myers, N. (2005). *Hotspots Revisited.* (University of Chicago Press, Chicago)

189 WSSD. Plan of Implementation. Paragraph 44. (g)

190 Not all hotspots, are the same. For example, in South east Asia, although there are many areas under threat, but are not all hotspots of species numbers, or where there are large numbers, they are not always endemic. Indeed, in this area, only 2.5% of the hotspots fulfilled all three criteria, and these were all within the Andes mountains Anon. (2005). 'Some Hotspots Are Hotter than Others'. *New Scientist.* August 20. 19. In addition, many of the following options are constrained by the limitations of what is, and is not scientifically known about both species and habitat, as well as competing arguments on ecological theory. Brummit, N. (2003). 'Biodiversity: Where's Hot and Where's Not.' *Conservation Biology.* 17(5): 1442-1448. Pearce, F. (2000). 'Spread the Wealth.' *New Scientist.* Feb 26. 12.

vegetation cover remaining intact.[191] The endemism consideration is that the site has to have 0.5% of 300,000 species, or 1,500 endemic vascular plant species (roughly 0.5% of the world total) within its borders. As with the CPD approach, plants were chosen as the qualifiers as they are the basis for diversity for other taxonomic groups. Indeed, all of the hotspots also have a high correlation with endangered species. For example, 57.5% of all mammal species listed as critically endangered or endangered are found within the 25 hotspots. 82.1% of all birds listed as critically endangered, and 81.3% of all birds listed as endangered are also within the 25 identified hotspot sites.[192]

From the analysis derived from the above two considerations, 25 hotspots (plus two mini hotspots – the Galapagos and the Juan Fernandez Islands) have been identified and ranked.[193] Of these 25 hotspots, 15 are tropic rainforests and nine are islands.[194] When the number of hotspots was expanded to 32, Japan, the Madrean pine oak forests of Mexico south west United States and Eastern Melanesia were added. Cumulatively they represent only 2.1 million square kilometres (for the 25 hotspots) or 2.3 % (for the 32 hotspots). This is approximately 1.44% (for the 25) of the land surface of the planet. Together, these places contain 131,399 endemic vascular plants or 43.8% of all plants on Earth. The 32 hotspots include more than 50% of the vascular plants and 42% of all land vertebrates.[195] With the 25 when the non-endemic species are added, the total is closer to 70% of all the vascular plants on the planet in these spaces. They also contain 9,681 endemic (non-fish) species (35.5% of the global total). If the non-endemic is included, the total non-fish vertebrates on the planet are also closer to 70%.[196] A total of 56 WHC sites are situated in 21 of the 25 selected priority hotspots. Because hotspots are generally very large (an average size of 663,000, in comparison to an average WHC site size of 9,960) some 29 WHC sites are encompassed within hotspots.[197]

11 Conclusion

International and regional obligations to create protected areas can be traced to 1933. Nevertheless, a process began in 1962 which called for more protected areas to be created. The international community, over the following decades has responded with

191 Mittermeier, R. & Myers, N. (2000). *Hotspots.* (University of Chicago Press, Chicago). 29.

192 Mittermeier. *Ibid.* 58.

193 The Caribbean, the Philippines and Madagascar and the Indian Ocean Islands are the highest priority hotspots of all. Mittermeier, *Ibid.* 53.

194 Pearce, F. (2000). 'Spread the Wealth.' *New Scientist.* Feb 26. 12.

195 Holmes, B. (2005) 'Should We Seek To Save the Earth's Iconic Hotspots ?' *New Scientist.* Feb 5. 10-11.

196 Mittermeier, R. & Myers, N. (2000). *Hotspots.* (University of Chicago Press, Chicago). 30-38.

197 IUCN et al. (2004) *Review of the World Heritage Network: Biogeography, Habitats and Biodiversity.* (IUCN, Gland). 72.

a variety of instruments that facilitate the creation of protected areas in both generic and specifics senses. However, these instruments have not gone as far as they could have, and greater progress, via the creation of more protected areas needs to be achieved. This criticism was first linked in 1987 into a numerical target of exactly how many protected areas should be created. The numerical targets, have since been iterated by the World Parks Congresses and adopted by the CBD. These targets are despite the fact that there has already been substantial success in the creation of protected areas. Indeed, by 2003, there were over 102,102 registered protected areas in 191 countries. The 2003 figure is equivalent to 12.65 of the Earth's land surface, or an area greater than the combined land area of China, South Asia and Southeast Asia. If marine protected areas (which along with TBPAs are good exemplars of the push for more protected areas) are included in the calculation, 18.8 million kilometers of the Earth fall within protected areas.

Despite the broad obligations to create more protected areas, and the strong international support for this goal, there are clear gaps in the international framework of protected areas. This is most notable, at the thematic level, with regard to marine, mountain, dryland (and types of) forest protected areas. In many ways, these gaps are because unlike with wetlands, there is no thematic international regime which has proved itself willing or able to pick up protected areas with their respective ecosystems. The answer to this problem which has evolved has been one of identifying priority areas. Some regimes have utilized a series of mechanisms, such as tentative lists, comparative and thematic analysis to help identify potential priority areas, and such analysis is often assisted by the schemas of the Udvardy system, hotspots, the Global 200 or notable areas of endemic species. Although these schemas are all commendable, it is necessary to note that they are not all seeking to conserve the same areas. As such, suggesting that the existing protected areas regimes make extensive utilisation of the existing schemas is not ideal. Nevertheless, given that the differences between are philosophical in their priority setting, it is not always necessary to try to select which one is best. Rather, until the thematic gaps in the international legal architecture are filled by meaningful instruments which can directly list protected areas by specific type, the options should be fully utilised by the existing protected areas regimes, as the best way to prioritise what areas need to be saved, and thereby begin to meet the goals that the international community has set itself.

Chapter V

MANAGEMENT

All protected areas need to be managed. They need to be managed because an area which is left without appropriate supervision or oversight, is inviting failure for the protected status of the site. Despite this importance, the management of protected areas is not an area which has attracted a large amount of attention. This is surprising, as although a diversity of international forums deal with protected areas, very similar practices have evolved (often in isolation of each other) on management questions. In particular, eight considerations are common to all of the forums working with the creation or maintenance of protected areas. These considerations relate to management plans, legal status, size, boundaries, buffer zone, corridors and networks, staffing and associated resources and the utilisation of Environmental Impact Assessments (EIAs).

1 Management Plans

Having adequate plans to effectively manage the natural sites in question is a key part of most, if not all protected area regimes, and the goal is commonly articulated in, inter alia, the Mediterranean[1] and Helsinki Commissions'[2] and the OSPAR.[3] Management plans have also been emphasised with the Bern Convention,[4] the Habitats Directive[5]

---

1 Mediterranean Protocol. Annex I. D. Protection, Planning and Management Measures. Report of the 12th MOP to the Convention for the Protection of the Mediterranean Sea Against Pollution and its Protocols. UNEP (DEC)/MED IG.13/8. Dec 30, 2001. 14 and Annex II.

2 Helcom Recommendation 15/5 (1994). Guidelines for Designating Marine And Coastal Baltic Sea Protected Areas (BSPA).

3 OSPAR Recommendation 2003/3 on a Network of Marine Protected Areas. Section 4. Outline structure for a Management Plan for an MPA of the OSPAR Network. Table 1. OSPAR Recommendation 2003/3 on a Network of Marine Protected Areas. Section 8. The relevant IUCN work being, Salm, R.V., & Clark, J.R. (2000). *IUCN Marine and Coastal Protected Areas.* (IUCN, Gland). Kellerher, G. (1999). *Guidelines for Marine Protected Areas.* (IUCN, Gland). Salm, R. (1989). *Marine and Coastal Protected Areas: A Guide for Planners and Managers.* ((IUCN, Gland).

4 Recommendation No 16. (1989). On Areas of Special Conservation Interest. Section 4. Recommendation No. 83 (2000). The Conservation Status of Lake Vistonis and Lafra-Lafrouda Lagoon (Greece). Report of the 20th Meeting of the Bern Convention. T-PVS (2000). 75. Appendix 7. Recommendation No. 113. (2004). On the Installation of a New Antenna in the Sovereign Base Area (Cyprus). Report of the 24th Bern Meeting of the Bern Convention. T-PVS (2004). 16. Appendix 7.

5 Habitats Directive. Article 6.

and the European Diploma.[6] The MAB has not just emphasised the importance of management plans,[7] it has also challenged new inscriptions, or those under periodic review, if their management plans were not up to scratch.[8] Although both the MAB and the Bern Convention have developed a small corpus of decisions on the need for management plans, the foremost decisions have come from Ramsar, the WHC and the Antarctic regime.

The broad obligations for a State with WHC sites to, 'integrate the protection of that heritage into comprehensive planning programmes' is set down in the Convention.[9] Despite this clear obligation, in the early years of the Convention, many sites were inscribed with inadequate management plans. This was clearly the case with many African sites, where, despite being inscribed for over a decade, over 50% (as of 2002) did not have functional management plans.[10]

Due to such problems, the Committee has come to place an increased emphasis upon Parties nominating sites, to have finalised plans for the management of each natural site nominated, or clear evidence of operational plans that will guide the management of the site until such time when a management plan is finalized.[11] If at the time of inscription, a site does not have an adequate existing or proposed management plan, inscription may be conditional upon a suitable revised management plan first being made available to the Committee. Enhanced work on management plans, as part of the listing process have been requested from the Committee in relation to applications from Australia,[12] Madagascar,[13] Senegal,[14] Tanzania,[15] Peru,[16] Zaire,[17] India,[18] Sri

---

6 European Diploma. Annex I. Criteria. Section B (4).

7 Seville + 5 Recommendations. Recommendation Number 4.

8 Velebit in Croatia. Spreewald in Germany. UNESCO. (2003). ICC Bureau Meeting. SC/-03/CONF.217/14. July 30. 20-21. Nanda Devi, India. UNESCO. (2004). 18th Session of the ICC Bureau Meeting. SC-04/CONF.204/14. Jan 11. Cat Tien in Vietnam. UNESCO. (2001). ICC Bureau Meeting. SCI/-01/CONF.217/8. Dec 12, 2. 14. Niyka Vwaza in Malawi, Yasuni in Ecuador UNESCO. (2001). ICC Bureau Meeting. SC-01/CONF.217/8. Dec 12, 2. 15. Volzhsko in Russia. UNESCO. (2004). 18th Session of the ICC Bureau Meeting. SC-04/CONF.204/14. Jan 11. 16. Sierra Gorda in Mexico. MAB. (2000). 16th Session of the ICC Bureau. SC-00/CONF.208/13. 5. UNESCO. (2001). MAB ICC Bureau Meeting. SC/-01/CONF.211/13. Apr 10.

9 WHC. Article 5 (a).

10 UNESCO. (2002). *Periodic Report for Africa.* (World Heritage Reports Number 3). 39.

11 *Operational Guidelines.* 2002 Edn. Paragraphs 21 and 44.

12 Willandra Lakes, UNESCO. (1981). 5th Session of the Bureau for the WHC. CC-81/CONF.002/4. July 20, 1981. pp.3. UNESCO. (1981). Fifth Session of the WHC. CC-81/CONF.003/6. Jan 5, 1981. pp.3. Wet Tropics of Queensland. UNESCO. (1988). 12th Session of the WHC. SC-88/CONF.001/13. Dec 23, 1988. 14.

13 Tsiny. UNESCO. (1990). 14th Session of the WHC. CLT-90/CONF.004/13. Dec 12, 1990. 4.

Lanka[19] and the Solomon Islands.[20] Failure to produce such management plans within a reasonable period of time has resulted in strong rebuke by the Committee.[21]

The problem of inadequate management regimes has also been listed as a reason for refusing the extension in the size of a site,[22] or deferring its extension until a later date.[23] The Committee has also issued direct recommendations to countries to update or revise their existing management plans, if they do not adequately confront new challenges. At other times, the Committee has recommended that the entire management plan needs to be revised. Such recommendations have been made, at various times, to Slovakia,[24] Nepal,[25] Australia,[26] Thailand,[27] India,[28] Peru[29]and Tanzania.[30]

---

14 Nikolo-Koba National Park in Senegal. WHC UNESCO. (1981). Fifth Session of the WHC for the Protection of the World Cultural and Natural Heritage. CC-81/CONF.003/6. Jan 5, 1981. pp. 5.

15 Kilimanjaro National park. UNESCO. (1987). 11th Session of the WHC. CC-87/CONF.005/9. Jan 20, 1988. pp 6.

16 Huascaran National Park. UNESCO. (1985). 9th Session of the WHC. SC-85/CONF.008/9. Dec, 1985. pp 6.

17 Salonga National Park. UNESCO. (1984). 8th Session of the WHC. SC/84/CONF.004/9. Nov 2, 1984. pp 9.

18 Sundarbans National Park. UNESCO. (1987). 11th Session of the WHC. CC-87/CONF.005/9. Jan 20, 1988. pp 5. See also Nanda Devi. UNESCO. (1988). 12th Session of the WHC. SC-88/CONF.001/13. Dec 23, 1988. 14.

19 Sinharaha Forest reserve. UNESCO. (1993). 17th Session of WHC. WHC-93/CONF.002/14. Feb 4, 1993. 16.

20 East Rennell. UNESCO. (2003). 27th Session of the WHC. WHC-03/27.COM/24. Dec 10, 2003. 38.

21 UNESCO. (2004). 28th Session of the WHC. WHC-04/28.COM/26. Oct 29. Decision 28 COM 15B.30.8p92.

22 Western Caucus. UNESCO. (2004). 28th Session of the WHC. WHC-04/28.COM/26. Oct 29. Decision 28 COM 14B.16. pp25.

23 See Decision 29 COM 8B17 (Lope-Okanda, Gabon) and 29 COM 8B18 (Minkebe Massif, Gabon), and 29 COM 8B.20 (Chiribiquete, Columbia).

24 The Skocjan underground caves in (former) Yugoslavia. UNESCO. (1996). 20th Session of the WHC. WHC-96/CONF.201/21. Mar 10, 1997. 25.

25 Chitwan. UNESCO. (1993). 17th Session of WHC. WHC-93/CONF.002/14. Feb 4, 1993. 16.

26 Shark Bay. UNESCO. (1991). 15th Session of the WHC. SC-91/CONF.002/15. Dec 12, 1991. 18.

27 Thungyai Wildlife sanctuary. UNESCO. (1991). 15th Session of the WHC. SC-91/CONF.002/15. Dec 12, 1991. 19.

28 Kaziranga National Park. UNESCO. (2002). 26th Session of the WHC. WHC-02/CONF.202/25. Aug 1, 2002. 31.

29 UNESCO. (1997). 21st Session of the WHC. WHC-97/CONF.208/17. Feb 27, 1998. 23. UNESCO. (1998). 22nd Session of the WHC. WHC-98/CONF.208/18. Jan 29, 1998. 45-46.

30 The Ngorongoro Conservation Area. UNESCO. (1984). 7th Session of the WHC. SC/83/CONF.009/8. Jan 12, 1984. pp 10. UNESCO. (1985). 9th Session of the WHC. SC-85/CONF.008/9. Dec, 1985. pp 10.

Finally, in some instances, a revised (and acceptable to the Committee) management plan has been deemed a critical condition for the removal of a site from the Danger List.[31]

Having adequate management plan for wetlands has been a clear priority of the Ramsar, since the mid 1980s.[32] Despite this long standing commitment, by 2002 of the 1230 wetlands on List of Wetlands of International Importance only 35% had management plans.[33] This figure is regrettable, as the Ramsar has developed a very strong practice in this area. This has ranged from calling for the development of adequate management plans for specific countries (in particular with Greece),[34] through to the creation of management guidelines. These guidelines have been refined and renewed,[35] and even financial assistance to help with the creation of such management plans can be granted.[36] The conclusion of the Ramsar process in this area has been twofold. First, from the 7th COP came the Guidelines for Developing and Implementing National Wetland Policies.[37] Second, the 8th COP adopted revised Guidelines for Management planning for Ramsar sites and other wetlands.[38] It also established the 'San Jose Record.' This record consists of sites where management plans are being implemented which are models for demonstrating application of the Ramsar Guidelines for the

---

31 Such as with Srebarna. UNESCO. (2001). 25th Session of the WHC. WHC-01/CONF.208/24. Paris 8, Feb 2002. 30-31.

32 Recommendation 2.3. Action Points for Priority Attention. (1984, Groningen).

33 Resolution 8.25. The Ramsar Strategic Plan. (2002, Valencia). Annex. I.9.

34 Recommendation 5.1.1. Greek Ramsar Sites. (1993, Kushiro). When Greece responded, the 7th COP was appreciative. Resolution 7.12. Sites in the Ramsar List. (1999, San Jose). Resolution 9.15. The Status of Sites on the Ramsar List of Wetlands of International Importance. (2005, Kampala). Paragraph 27.

35 Recommendation 5.3. The Essential Character of Wetlands and the Need for Zonation Related to Wetland Reserves. (1993, Kushiro). Additional Guidance for the Implementation of the Wise Use Concept. Annexed to Resolution 5.6. Wise Use of Wetlands (1993, Kushiro). Resolution 5.7. Management Planning for Ramsar Sites and Other Wetlands. (1993, Kushiro). Guidelines on Management Planning for Ramsar and Other Wetlands Sites. Annexed to Resolution 5.7. Management Planning for Ramsar Sites and Other Wetlands. (1993, Kushiro). These guidelines set down the basic headings and detailed sections on, inter alia, Preamble, description, evaluation and objectives such as long-term management objectives, factors influencing achievement of long-term management objectives and identification of operational objectives and limits of acceptable change and the basics for Action Plan/Prescriptions, including work plans, projects work programmes and reviews. Recommendation 6.13. Guidelines on Management Planning. (1996, Brisbane). Recommendation 6.9. National Wetland Policies. (1996, Brisbane).

36 Resolution 5.7. Management Planning for Ramsar Sites and Other Wetlands. (1993, Kushiro). Note, this is a long standing target for financial assistance within the Convention. See Recommendation 2.3. Annex: Framework for Implementing the Convention. (1984, Groningen).

37 Resolution 7.6. National Wetland Policies. (1999, San Jose).

38 Resolution 8.14. New Guidelines for Management Planning for Ramsar Sites and Other Wetlands. (2002, San Jose).

Implementation of the Wise Use concept. This record is meant to display 'effective management and exemplary practices.'[39] The Ramsar target is for at least three quarters of all Ramsar sites having management plans in place in the short term future.[40]

The final regime of note with regard to management plans is that related to Antarctica. According to Article 1 of Annex V of the Madrid Protocol, a 'Management Plan' is a plan to manage the activities and protect the special value or values in an Antarctic Specially Protected Area or an Antarctic Specially Managed Area. Such plans, which supplement a number of generic environmental controls for the Antarctic,[41] establish the particular processes that management plans must follow before they are accepted,[42] and identify a number of specified details,[43] which must be addressed and accompany any proposition for a designated area within the Antarctic regime.[44] Although this policy is currently well settled within the Antarctic Treaty regime, it took over twenty years to evolve, before it covered all of the types of protected areas in the region.[45] In 1995,

---

39 Resolution 8.15. The San Jose Record for the Promotion of Wetland Management. (2002, San Jose).

40 Resolution 7.12. Sites in the Ramsar List. (1999, San Jose).

41 These controls deal with everything from waste, to the marine environment, and the ships that can visit the area, through to the pollution from them. See Annex III to the Protocol on Environmental Protection to the Antarctic Treaty Waste Disposal and Waste Management. The obligation is to generally minimise waste, safe storage and then removal (of specified wastes, from radio-active materials to plastics). Incineration of waste (but phased out in all but exceptional circumstances), land disposal for only limited amount of waste, in specific areas. Disposal into the sea, of sewage, only after treatment. Strong, regularly reviewed management plans to deal with waste mandated. Annex IV to the protocol on environmental protection to the Antarctic treaty prevention of marine pollution , (with a Strong Relationship to MARPOL), Covering Hydrocarbon Spills, Garbage, Sewage, Reception Facilities, Ship Design, And Emergency Situations. Antarctic Treaty: Report of the Twenty-Seventh Meeting. (Cape Town, 2004). Decision 4. Guidelines for Ships Operating in Arctic and Antarctic Ice Covered Waters. Antarctic Treaty: Report of the Twenty-Seventh Meeting. (Cape Town, 2004). Resolution 1. Enhancing Prevention of Marine Pollution By Fishing Activities. 222.

42 See Article 6(1) of Annex V.

43 See Annex V, Article 5 (3). Management plans shall include, inter alia, a description of the area, the value/s of the area and why it needs protection, activities which are allowed, access and structure locations, controls on activities in the area (covering everything from the protection of flora to the disposal of waste), and reporting requirements.

44 See Annex V, Article 5(1).

45 Recommendation VII-3. Sites of Special Scientific Interest. In Report of the Seventh Antarctic Treaty Meeting. (1972, Wellington). 56. Recommendation VIII-3. Sites of Special Scientific Interest. In Antarctic Treaty: Report of the Eighth Meeting. (1975, Oslo). 53. Antarctic Treaty: Report of the Fourteenth Meeting. (Rio de Janeiro, 1987). Paragraphs 85-87. Recommendation XIV-6. Marine Sites of Special Scientific Interest. In Antarctic Treaty: Report of the Fourteenth Meeting (Rio de Janeiro, 1987). 119. Recommendation XV-11. Antarctic Protected Area System: Establishment of Multiple Use Planning Areas. In Antarctic Treaty: Report of the Fifteenth Meeting (Paris, 1989). 84. Recommendation XV-10. Antarctic Protected Area System: Establishment of Specially Reserved Areas. In Antarctic Treaty: Report of the 15th

a uniform model for management plans for SPAs was adopted,[46] and in 1998, Guidelines for the Preparation of Management Plans for all of the respective protected area types in the region were issued.[47] These uniform models and guidelines have assisted a process undertaken since 1992, whereby the Consultative Parties all agreed to re-examine their existing protected areas, and revise their management plans for them as necessary.[48] This process of entering revised descriptions and new management plans continued in 1994,[49] 1997,[50] 2002,[51] 2003,[52] 2004[53] and 2005.[54] Alternately, existing management plans may be given an extension on their expiry dates.[55]

Part of the reason why the Consultative Parties have been revising their management plans for their protected areas has been in response to the Madrid Protocol, which established that management plans only have a currency of five years.[56] Accordingly, in 1998, and again in 2002,[57] the Consultative Parties identified the SPAs and the countries responsible for them in need of revised management plans, and called for

---

Meeting (Paris, 1989). 82. Recommendation XV-8. Agreed Measures for the Conservation of Antarctic Fauna and Flora: Amendment to Article VIII: Management Plans for Specially Protected Areas. In Antarctic Treaty: Report of the Fifteenth Meeting (Paris, 1989). 78. Recommendation XV-9. Development of Improved Descriptions and Management Plans for Specially Protected Areas. In Antarctic Treaty: Report of the Fifteenth Meeting (Paris, 1989). 80.

46 Resolution 9 (1995). Uniform Model for Management Plans. In Antarctic Treaty: Report of the Nineteenth Meeting. (Seoul, 1995). 125.

47 Resolution 2 (1998). Guide to the Preparation of Management Plans for Antarctic Specially Protected Areas. In Antarctic Treaty: Report of the Twenty-Second Meeting. (Tromso, 1998). 78-89.

48 See Recommendation XVII-2. Revised Descriptions and Proposed Management Plans for Specially Protected Areas. In Antarctic Treaty: Report of the Seventeenth Meeting. (Venice, 1992). 57.

49 Measure 1 (1995). Revised Descriptions and Management Plans for Specially Protected Areas. In Antarctic Treaty: Report of the Nineteenth Meeting. (Seoul, 1995). 43-60.

50 Measure 1 (1997). Revised Description and Management Plan for Specially Protected Areas. In Antarctic Treaty: Report of the Twenty-first Meeting. (Christchurch, 1997). 37.

51 Measure 1 (2002). Management Plans for Antarctic Specially Protected Areas. In Antarctic Treaty: Report of the Twenty-Fifth Meeting. (Warsaw, 2002). 33.

52 See Measure 2. Antarctic Treaty: Report of the Twenty-Sixth Meeting. (Madrid, 2003). Pages 62-240.

53 Measure 2. Antarctic Treaty: Report of the Twenty-Seventh Meeting (Cape Town). 94-166.

54 Measure 2. (2005). Antarctic Specially Protected Areas: Designations and Management Plans. Report of the 28th Consultative meeting. (Stockholm, 2005).

55 Measure 4. (2005). Antarctic Specially Protected Areas: Extension of Expiry Dates. Report of the 28th Consultative meeting. (Stockholm, 2005). 11.

56 See Article 6(3) of Annex V.

57 Measure 2 (2002). Revision of Antarctic Specially Protected Area Management Plans. In Antarctic Treaty: Report of the Twenty-Fifth Meeting. (Warsaw, 2002). 158.

the adoption of timetables for these to be completed.[58] Despite this push, a number of SPAs require updated management plans.[59] Likewise, with SSSIs, although management plans associated with these areas have been called far from the early 1970s, and designation of an SSSI or a CEMP now requires an accompanying management plan[60] compliance with these has not always been strong. Accordingly, since the mid 1980s, the Consultative Parties have had to badger their fellow members to make sure the management plans for their respective SSSIs are up to date.[61] However, this process has been slow, and in 1998, the Consultative Parties took the initiative in this area, and identified the SSSIs, and the countries responsible for them, in need of revised management plans, and called for the adoption of timetables for these to be completed.[62] The Consultative Parties reiterated this call in 2002.[63]

2 Legal Status

Every area, to qualify for its recognition as protected, must have a specific legal status guaranteeing its protection. This is important for questions of both definition and operation.[64] This rule is recognised in numerous regimes including, inter alia, the Mediterranean[65] and Caribbean[66] Protocols, the Bern Convention (which has directed

---

58 Resolution 1 (1998). Annex V, Protected Areas. In Antarctic Treaty: Final Report of the Twenty-Second Antarctic Treaty Consultative Meeting. (Tromso, 1998). 75-78.

59 See New Zealand (2005). A Review of the Antarctic Protected Areas System. CEP Paper WP 11 (Stockholm, 2005). 1-2.

60 Recommendation VIII-3. Sites of Special Scientific Interest. In I Report of the Eighth Meeting. (1975, Oslo). 53. Recommendation XIV-6. Marine Sites of Special Scientific Interest. In Antarctic Treaty: Report of the Fourteenth Meeting (Rio de Janeiro, 1987). 119. See Conservation Measure 91-01. (2004) Procedure for According Protection to CEMP Sites.

61 Recommendation XIV-4. Facilitation of Scientific Research: Sites of Special Scientific Interest: Interim Guidelines: Extensions of Designation. In Antarctic Treaty: Report of the Fourteenth Meeting (Rio de Janeiro, 1987). 77. See Measure 2 (1995). Revised Descriptions and Management Plan for Sites. In Antarctic Treaty: Report of the Nineteenth Meeting. (Seoul, 1995). 61. Measure I (1996). Revised Description and Management Plan for Sites of Special Scientific Interest. In Antarctic Treaty: Report of the Twentieth Meeting. (Utrecht, 1996). 49. Measure 3 (1997). Revised Description and Management Plan for Sites of Special Scientific Interest. In Antarctic Treaty: Report of the Twenty-first Meeting. (Christchurch, 1997). 68. Measure 1 (1999). Revised Management Plan for Site of Special Scientific Interest No 23. In Antarctic Treaty: Report of the Twenty-Third Meeting. (Lima, 1999). 41.

62 Resolution 1 (1998). Annex V, Protected Areas. In Antarctic Treaty: Report of the Twenty-Second Meeting. (Tromso, 1998). 75-78.

63 Measure 2 (2002). Revision of Antarctic Specially Protected Area Management Plans. In Antarctic Treaty: Report of the Twenty-Fifth Meeting. (Warsaw, 2002). 158.

64 IUCN. (2004). *Speaking a Common Language: The IUCN System of Management Categories.* (IUCN, Gland). 14. Kelleher, G. (ed). Guidelines for Marine Protected Areas (IUCN, Gland, 1999). 11-19.

65 Mediterranean Protocol. Article 7 (2)(a). See also Annex. I. C. Legal Status.

resolutions to particular parties to clarify legal status issues),[67] the Ramsar (again at both generic and specific levels),[68] and the European Diploma. The latter is clear, that such a Diploma can only be awarded, if the country in question has an appropriate protection system in place, which effectively guarantees its legally protected status.[69]

Other regimes, such as the WHC, refuse to inscribe a nominated site until its legal protections have been viewed to the satisfaction of the Committee.[70] If a site does not have adequate legal protection at the stage of inscription, the application will be deferred. Accordingly, between 1992 and 2002, 9 sites were deferred listing until strengthened legal regimes were in place,[71] including applications from, inter alia, Sri Lanka,[72] Cuba[73] and Ethiopia.[74]

Aside the issue of having adequate laws guaranteeing protection at the time of inscription, is the question of the viability of the existing laws, several years post inscription. The Ramsar has dealt with this potential problem by issuing Guidelines for Reviewing Laws and Institutions to promote the Conservation and Wise Use of Wet-

---

66 Report of the Working Group on the Development of Guidelines for the Listing of Protected Areas Under the SPAW Protocol. (2005). UNEP (DEC)/CAR WG.29/INF.12.

67 See Res. No. 16 of the Bern Convention. See also, Recommendation No. 83 (2000). The Conservation Status of Lake Vistonis and Lafra-Lafrouda Lagoon (Greece). Report of the 20th Meeting of the Bern Convention. T-PVS (2000). 75. Appendix 7.

68 Recommendations adopted by the International Conference on the Conservation of Wetlands and Waterfowl at Heiligenhafen, Federal Republic of Germany, 6 December 1974. Recommendation 8. Protection of Wetlands in Italy. Recommendation 2.3. Annex: Framework for Implementing the Convention. (1984, Groningen). Recommendation 4.4. Establishment of Wetland Reserves. (1990, Montreux). Recommendation 5.3. The Essential Character of Wetlands and the Need for Zonation Related to Wetland Reserves. (1993, Kushiro). Recommendation 4.10. Guidelines for the Implementation of the Wise Use Concept. Annex. Guidelines for the Implementation of the Wise Use Concept of the Convention. Resolution 8.25. The Ramsar Strategic Plan. (2002, Valencia). Annex. Operational Objective 2. Additional Guidance for the Implementation of the Wise Use Concept. Annexed to Resolution 5.6. Wise Use of Wetlands (1993, Kushiro).

69 European Diploma, Article 1 and Annex I. Criteria. Section B (1).

70 *Operational Guidelines.* 2002 Edn. Paragraph 11.

71 IUCN. (2003). *World Heritage Convention: Effectiveness 1992-2002 and Lessons For Governance.* (IUCN, Gland). 14.

72 Sinharaha Forest reserve. UNESCO. (1982). 6th Session of the WHC. CC-82/CONF.014/6. Aug 20, 1982. pp.5.

73 The Valley of Vinales Pinar in Cuba. UNESCO. (1997). 21st Session of the WHC. WHC-97/CONF.208/17. Feb 27, 1998. 38.

74 The Abiyata-Shala Lakes. UNESCO. (1981). 5th Session of the WHC. CC-81/CONF.002/4. July 20, 1981. pp.8

lands.[75] By the new century, the emphasis was shifting towards incorporation of meaningful ways to establish compliance with the requisite legal regimes for wetlands,[76] as is done in comparable international environmental arrangements.[77] The Ramsar goal was that at least 100 members review the adequacy of their national policies and laws on this question, by 2002.[78] This target was later extended to 2005,[79] and then 2008.[80]

The only other regime to confront the problem of antiquated or inadequate laws is the WHC. In this instance, the approach has been one whereby the Committee has re-examined already inscribed WHC sites and issued direct recommendations to remedy legal deficiencies that have developed over the years. This process has been most clearly demonstrated with the Galapagos, which originally narrowly avoided (although concerns continued)[81] before being listed as in Danger (in 2007), due to its new legal regime.[82] Other examples where new laws were required have involved Ha Long Bay in Vietnam,[83] Shirakami-Sanchi in Japan[84] and Dja Faunal Reserve in the Cameroon.[85]

3 Boundaries

Every protected area must have clear boundaries. This rule has been strongly pursued by the Ramsar, which aside granting a small latitude on boundary delineations with the initial designations, has come to strongly emphasise the importance of clearly marked, mapped and delimited wetlands, replete with full and correct information (hence

75 Resolution 7.7. Laws and Institutions Concerning Wetlands. (1999, San Jose). These Guidelines cover everything from the review team to the review itself, with a strong basis of removing constraints to conservation and wise use, and moving towards positive incentives in this area had been issued.

76 Resolution 8.14. New Guidelines for Management Planning for Ramsar Sites and Other Wetlands. (2002, San Jose). Annex.

77 Resolution 8.24. UNEP's Guidelines for Enhancing Compliance with Multilateral Environmental Agreements et al. (2002, Valencia).

78 Resolution 7.27. The Convention's Work Plan 2000-02. (1999, San Jose). Annex. Work Plan.

79 Resolution 8.26. The Implementation of the Strategic Plan 2003-2008. (2002, Valencia). Annex I. Global Implementation of the Targets for the Convention.

80 See Resolution 9.8. Streamlining the Implementation of the Strategic Plan of the Convention 2003-2008. (Kampala, 2005). Strategy 1.2..

81 Decision 29 COM 7B.29.

82 UNESCO. (1995). 18th Session of the WHC. WHC-94/CONF.003/16. Jan 31. 1995. 44. UNESCO. (1996). 19th Session of the WHC. WHC-95/CONF.203/16. Jan 31, 1996. 36

83 UNESCO. (1995). 18th Session of the WHC. WHC-94/CONF.003/16. Jan 31. 1995. 43. UNESCO. (1996). 19th Session of the WHC. WHC-95/CONF.203/16. Jan 31, 1996. '8. UNESCO. (1996). 20th Session of the WHC. WHC-96/CONF.201/21. Mar 10, 1997. 28.

84 UNESCO. (1993). 17th Session of WHC. WHC-93/CONF.002/14. Feb 4, 1993. 34.

85 UNESCO. (1987). 11th Session of the WHC. CC-87/CONF.005/9. Jan 20, 1988. pp 4.

detailed Ramsar information sheets)[86] that fall under its auspice.[87] It is recommended that such boundaries and information should be reviewed every six years.[88] This matter has been increasingly pursued since it became apparent that a number of Ramsar sites are without adequate information, including mapping and boundaries issues.[89] For example, in 2002, 70 countries were singled out as being in default of one or more Ramsar information sheets.[90] This is a particular problem with regard to boundaries, which may have changed from the time of original inscription, and require new and accurate re-surveying.[91] A similar approach is mirrored in the Bern Convention, although it has focused more on the need of clear boundaries around its sites,[92] and has directed resolutions to countries, such as Greece, involved with particular boundary problems.[93]

Finally, it is with the WHC, that this issue has become most pronounced, where large mistakes (or omissions) between the original inscription files and the current reality of many WHC sites has become apparent. In this regard, the Parties to the WHC have instigated what is known as the Retrospective Inventory, whereby the traditional records are being updated to reflect the modern realities of the sites.

---

86 Resolution 8.13. Enhancing the Information on Wetlands of International Importance. (2002, San Jose).

87 Resolution 6.16. Accession Procedures. (1996, Brisbane). Resolution 4.5. Accession Requirements. (1990, Montreux).

88 Resolution VI.13. Information on Ramsar Sites. (1996, Brisbane).

89 Resolution 7.12. Sites in the Ramsar List. (1999, San Jose).

90 Resolution 7.10. Improving Implementation of the Strategic Framework and Vision for the List of Wetlands of International Importance. (2002, Valencia). Annex. Resolution 9.15. The Status of Sites on the Ramsar List of Wetlands of International Importance. (2005, Kampala). Paragraph 17.

91 Resolution 8.21. Defining Ramsar Site Boundaries More Accurately in Ramsar Information Sheets. (2002, Valencia). Resolution 7.23. Boundary Definitions and Compensation. (1999, San Jose).

92 Recommendation No 16. (1989). On Areas of Special Conservation Interest. Section 4.

93 Recommendation No. 83 (2000). The Conservation Status of Lake Vistonis and Lafra-Lafrouda Lagoon (Greece). Report of the 20th Meeting of the Bern Convention. T-PVS (2000). 75. Appendix 7. Resolution 4.9.5. Greek Ramsar Sites. (1990, Montreux). Recommendation 5.1.1. Greek Ramsar Sites. (1993, Kushiro). Recommendation 6.17.1. Greek Ramsar Sites. (1996, Brisbane).

4 Size

The idea that a protected area should be of a sufficient size, so as to achieve its objectives, is one which can be traced back to the 1933 Africa Convention,[94] and has been repeated in multiple instruments thereafter. For example, according to the Madrid Protocol, the area proposed for designation should be of sufficient size to protect the values for which the special protection or management is required.[95] Thus, it is not the size of an area per-se which is the issue, but whether the size of the area allows it to fulfil its objectives, in terms of the values it is trying to preserve.[96]

They key word here is 'integrity'. Thus, as at the first UNESCO Conference on the Use and Conservation of the Biosphere in 1968 explained, 'an area may be small or large; its actual size is not its defining characteristic. It must however, have integrity'.[97] Accordingly, some regimes, such as the Ramsar have actually set out to capture, inter alia, relatively small and transitory areas such as temporary pools.[98] Conversely, other regimes have set out to capture relatively large areas. This second approach is noticeable with international and/or regional MPAs. For example, although the Mediterranean,[99] and Caribbean[100] Protocols, and the OSPAR Convention followed the traditional line that MPAs under its auspice should be of a sufficient size for the area to maintain its integrity and enable effective management,[101] the Helsinki Convention actually put a minimum figure down. That is, the minimum size of a BSPA should be preferably 1.000 hectares for terrestrial parts and/or 3.000 hectares for marine/lagoon parts.[102] Likewise, with the IMO, it is suggested that the size of a Special Area will be 'rather large'[103] and the practice of approved Special Areas, reflects the focus upon large areas. The existing Special Areas are the Mediterranean Sea Area, the Black Sea, the

94 1933 London Convention. Article 4 (3).

95 Annex V, Article 5 (2).

96 IUCN. (2004). *Speaking a Common Language: The IUCN System of Management Categories.* (IUCN, Gland). 14. Phillips, A. (2004). 'The History of the International System of Protected Area Management Categories'. 14(3) *Parks.* 4, 12.

97 UNESCO. (1968). Use and Conservation of the Biosphere. (UNESCO, Paris). 144.

98 Resolution 8.33. Guidance for Identifying, Sustainably Managing and Designating Temporary Pools as Wetlands of International Importance. (2002, Valencia).

99 Mediterranean Protocol. Article 4. Sites shall be, 'size to ensure their long-term viability and to maintain their biological diversity'.

100 Caribbean Protocol. Article 4.2.

101 Ospar Recommendation 2003/3 on a Network of Marine Protected Areas. Appendix 2. Section 1.

102 HELCOM REC.15/5 (1994). Guidelines for BSPA. See also HELCOM HOD 11/2003

103 IMO General Assembly. 17th Session. A 17/Res.720. Guidelines for the Designation of Special Areas and the Identification of Particularly Sensitive Sea Areas. Table 3.

Red Sea, the Gulfs area (which was partly expanded in 2001),[104] the Gulf of Aden, the Antarctic area and the Baltic. Similar considerations apply to PSSAs, although there is an increasing concern, as with the Western European PSSA, that they should not be so large, as to not include throughout the nominated area, all of the values that they were nominated for.

The other regime which gives an emphasis on larger, as opposed to smaller protected areas, is the MAB. This is partly due to the obvious fact that 'biospheres' (as of biosphere reserves) tend to be large interconnected ecosystems, implicitly related to biogeographical provinces.[105] The median or most common size, of a biosphere reserve in the 1980s was between 10,000 to 25,000 hectares.[106] However, although some Parties clearly envisage that biosphere reserves may be large enough to encompass entire bioregions,[107] and there has been some casual guidelines suggested,[108] there is no corresponding recognition of this in the official objectives of the programme. The only clear guidance in this area is the Statutory Framework for Biosphere Reserves, which stipulates that each site should have, 'an appropriate size' to serve the three functions of biosphere reserves.[109] In this regard, although it is agreed that each Biosphere Reserve should have enough, 'critical mass' to enable objectives of the biosphere reserve to be achieved, there is no standard definition of size requirement. This is especially so with regards to the buffer and transition zones which are more defined by political, rather than ecological considerations. With core areas within an MAB site, size is a little easier to define, in that there might be a lower limit of size beyond which it would not be possible to conserve viable populations of certain species, or for an ecosystem to function.[110] Accordingly, at various times, it has been recommended that the core

---

104 In 2001, Oman applied for an extension of the 'Special Area' of the Gulf Areas, under Annex I and V of MARPOL 73/78 to be extended to include the entire coast of Oman. However, the MEPC found that it could only be justified as a Special Area under Annex I, and bot Annex V as the threat of garbage from ships was not demonstrated. MEPC.(2001). Report of the MEPC on its 46th Session. MEPC 46/23. 44. MEPC. (2002). Report of the MEPC on its 48th Session. MEPC 48/21. 35.

105 Udvardy, M. (1975). *A Classification of the Biogeographical Provinces on the World.* (IUCN Occasional Paper No 18).

106 See Miller, K. (1983). 'Biosphere Reserves and the Global Network of Protected Areas'. In UNESCO. (ed). *Conservation, Science and Society: The 1983 International Biosphere Reserve Congress.* (UNESCO, Paris). 1, 5.

107 UNESCO. (2002). 17th Session of the ICC Bureau. SC-02/CONF.201/11. Apr 12. 4.

108 The size of biosphere reserves, need to be capable of maintaining their characteristic biodiversity, or, 'consider what might be an adequate area to maintain a healthy population of the top carnivore, and then, for safety's sake, doubling it'. Lovejoy, T. (1983). 'Biosphere Reserves: The Size Question'. In UNESCO. (1983) *Ibid.* 146, 149.

109 The Statutory Framework of the World Network of Biosphere Reserves. Article 4 (4).

110 UNESCO. (2003). ICC Bureau Meeting. SC-02/CONF.210/10. Jan 7. 22.

area of a biosphere reserve be expanded or refined.[111] However, it is not unknown that a nominated site be deferred, as the proposed area was too small to fulfil the three functions of a biosphere reserve in terms of conservation, sustainable development and logistic support.[112]

The issue of size is also a matter of concern for the WHC. Although there is a precedent whereby a site has been denied for being too small,[113] this is very unusual, and the typical practice for WHC sites is that there are no key size requirements. Accordingly, they range from 2 square kilometres (the Slovakian caves of Skocjan) through to 127,900 square kilometres (Australia's Great Barrier Reef).[114] The key requirement for the WHC is that the site must possess, 'adequate size to ensure the complete representation of the features and processes which convey the property's significance'.[115] This question is then devolved into the four separate categories. Thus, with criteria 1 (geomorphic or physiographical excellence) nominations, the recommended site should contain all or most of the key interrelated and interdependent elements in their natural relationships.[116] With criteria 2 (ecological and biological processes) sites should have suffi-

---

111 Laciana and Picos in Spain. UNESCO. (2003). ICC Bureau Meeting. SC/-03/CONF.217/14. July 30. 13. Iroise in France. UNESCO. (2001) ICC Bureau Meeting. SC-01/CONF.217/8. Dec 12. 21. Delta del Parana in Argentina, Baishuijiang in China. MAB. (2000). 16th Session of the ICC Bureau. SC-00/CONF.208/13. 19, 20. Huanglong in China. UNESCO. (2001). MAB ICC Bureau Meeting. SC/-01/CONF.211/13. Apr 10. 10. Kosciusko in Australia. UNESCO. (2003). ICC Bureau Meeting. SC/-03/CONF.217/14. July 30. 17. Cerrado IV in Brazil. UNESCO. (2003). ICC Bureau Meeting. SC-02/CONF.210/10. Jan 7. 14. Vessertal in Germany. UNESCO. (2003). ICC Bureau Meeting. SC-02/CONF.210/10. Jan 7. 19. The Statutory Framework of the World Network of Biosphere Reserves. Article 5.

112 Ant Atoll, Micronesia. UNESCO. (2006). MAB ICC. 19th Session. SC-06/CONF.202/16. Nov 28. 10.

113 The Cedars of Lebanon. UNESCO. (1993). 17th Session of WHC. WHC-93/CONF.002/14. Feb 4, 1993. 38.

114 Other notable sites under 100 square miles (sqm) in size, include the Aeolian islands (5 sqm), Keoladeo in India (11 sqm), Ngorongoro (12 sqm), Sinharaja in Sri Lanka (30 sqm), Goreme in Turkey (40 sqm), Corsica (and its four reserves at 46 sqm) and Simien park in Ethiopia (85 sqm). Even the more well known sites, are not necessarily that large. For example, Kilimanjaro only covers 291 square miles, and the Grand Canyon is only 277 miles long and 20 miles wide. Manu in Peru (arguably the protected area with the most biodiversity within it anywhere on Earth) is 5,800 square miles The largest sites terrestrial site is Canada's Glacier Bay (42,500 sqm).Cattaneo, M. & Trifoni, J. (2003). *The World Heritage Sites of UNESCO: Nature Sanctuaries* (WhiteStar, Vercelli). 28, 44, 49, 72, 97, 98, 128, 176, 181, 210, 241, 242, 247, 267, 301, 334, 344.

115 UNESCO. (2003). 6th Extra-ordinary Session of the WHC. WHC-03/6. EXT.COM/8. Paris, May 27, 2003. 9.

116 For example, an 'ice age' area should include the snow field, the glacier itself and samples of cutting patterns, deposition and colonization (e.g. striations, moraines, pioneer stages of plant succession, etc.). In the case of volcanoes, the magmatic series should be complete and all or most of the varieties of effusive rocks and types of eruptions be represented.

cient size to contain the necessary elements to demonstrate the key aspects of processes that are essential for the long-term conservation of the ecosystems and the biological diversity they contain.[117] Thus, the size of inscribed forests should be large enough so that they retain their ecological integrity.[118] With criteria 3 (aesthetics) a site should include areas that are essential for maintaining the beauty of the site.[119] Finally, with criteria 4 (threatened species of outstanding value) a site should be large enough to include the most critical habitats essential to ensure the survival of viable populations of those species.[120]

In light of the above considerations, in some instances, original listings have been deferred, so that the State Party could consider the recommendations of the Committee on how sites should be extended, to encompass certain key areas[121] (which may not even be physically adjacent to each other).[122] Extensions are often following IUCN recommendations to include additional areas so as to help maintain the integrity of a property.[123] Between 1992 and 2002, with regard to natural sites, the Committee recommended that 17 sites be deferred until additional hectares are included in the site. In some instances, these were very large increases. For example, the Central Eastern Rainforest site of Australia, increased by 30% to 108,000 hectares, Laponia of Sweden,

---

Operational Guidelines. 2002 Edn. Paragraph 44.

117 For example, an area of tropical rain forest should include a certain amount of variation in elevation above sea-level, changes in topography and soil types, patch systems and naturally regenerating patches. Similarly a coral reef should include seagrass, mangrove or other adjacent ecosystems that regulate nutrient and sediment inputs into the reef. *Operational Guidelines*. 2002 Edn. Paragraph 44.

118 See Decision 29 COM 5.2. Adopting the Recommendations from the Second International World Heritage Forest Meeting. In Report of the World Heritage Centre in Implementing Strategic Objectives. WHC-05/29.COM/5. Recommendations 2 and 3.

119 For example, a site whose scenic values depend on a waterfall, should include adjacent catchment and downstream areas that are integrally linked to the maintenance of the aesthetic qualities of the site. *Operational Guidelines*. 2002 Edn. Paragraph 44.

120 *Operational Guidelines*. 2002 Edn. Paragraph 44.

121 Lake Ohrid site by the former Yugoslavia. UNESCO. (1979). 3rd Session of the WHC. CC-79/CONF.003/13. Nov 30, 1978. pp.11. Also with Alligator river and the Kakadu National Park. UNESCO. (1981). 5th Session of the Bureau for the WHC. CC-81/CONF.002/4. July 20, 1981. pp.2. UNESCO. (1981). 5th Session of the WHC. CC-81/CONF.003/6. Jan 5, 1981. pp.2. UNESCO. (2003). 27th Session of the WHC. WHC-03/27.COM/24. Dec 10. 100.

122 It is possible for States Parties to propose in a single nomination a series of natural properties in different geographical locations, provided that they are related because they belong to, in the case of natural heritage, the same type of property which is characteristic of the geographical zone or the same geomorphological formation, the same biogeographic province, or the same ecosystem type. As such, it is the series, and not its components taken individually, which is of outstanding universal value. *Operational Guidelines*. 2002 Edn. Paragraph 19.

123 See for example, the extension to Donana. Decision 29 COM. 8B.16.

increased from 285,000 to 940,000 hectares, and the Sundarbans of Bangladesh, went from 71,500 to 140,000 hectares.[124]

There is an equally strong tradition here, in that sites which are applying to be listed have been deferred or accepted on condition that a certain piece of territory is not included in the nomination. For example, Canaima National Park was finally accepted, after a section of savannah was removed because it did not meet WHC criteria.[125] Similar reductions of sizes have occurred with listing nominations from Mauritania[126] and Vietnam.[127]

The more usual way in which the size of sites is altered, is post-facto. This is when either the Committee or the Party themselves, seek to revisit the original boundaries of a listed area, and an extension is made assuming the extended area also meets the inscription criteria.[128] The pursuit of extensions began as an ad-hoc process until the 1990s when it became a standing item on the agenda for each Committee meeting. Sometimes extension requests are at the initiative of a Party, who after a period of reflection, have come to the conclusion that the borders of a site are no longer adequate. For example, within Latin America and the Caribbean, a 2004 periodic review showed that 49.2% of the Parties were actively considering revisions of boundaries or buffer zones to existing WHC sites.[129] In some instances, the extensions can be quite large. For example, in addition to a number of extensions to other WHC sites in Australia,[130] the extension of the Eastern Rainforest Reserves increased the site by an extra 35%.[131] Other countries which have extended their sites include the Ivory Coast,[132] Peru,[133]

124 IUCN. (2003). *World Heritage Convention: Effectiveness 1992-2002 and Lessons For Governance.* (IUCN, Gland). 14.

125 UNESCO. (1995). 18th Session of the WHC. WHC-94/CONF.003/16. Jan 31. 1995. 42.

126 At the proposal time, Banc d'Arguin park. UNESCO. (1989). 13th Session of the WHC. SC-89/CONF.004/12. Dec, 22 1989. pp 12.

127 Ha Long Bay. UNESCO. (1995). 18th Session of the WHC. WHC-94/CONF.003/16. Jan 31. 1995. 43.

128 Thus, the Belovezhskaya Pushcha/Bialowieza Forest between Belarus and Poland extension not accepted. UNESCO. (1999). 23rd Session of the WHC. WHC-99/CONF.209/22. Mar 22, 2000. 25.

129 UNESCO. (2004). *The State of World Heritage in Latin America and the Caribbean: 2004 Periodic Report.* (UNESCO, Paris). 21.

130 Great Barrier Reef. UNESCO. (1981). 5th Session of the WHC. CC-81/CONF.002/4. July 20, 1981. pp.3. Uluru Park. UNESCO. (1987). 11th Session of the WHC. CC-87/CONF.005/9. Jan 20, 1988. pp 3. Kakadu. 16th Session of the WHC. WHC-92/CONF.002/12. Dec 14, 1992. 35.

131 UNESCO. (1995). 18th Session of the WHC. WHC-94/CONF.003/16. Jan 31. 1995. 43.

132 Comoe National Park. UNESCO. (1984). 7th Session of the WHC. SC/83/CONF.009/8. Jan 12, 1984. pp 5.

133 Santuario de Machu Picchu. UNESCO. (1984). 7th Session of the WHC. SC/83/CONF.009/8. Jan 12, 1984. pp 6.

the Seychelles,[134] Argentina and Malawi,[135] Canada,[136] Bulgaria,[137] Costa Rica,[138] Tanzania,[139] the United Kingdom,[140] Kenya,[141] Russia,[142] Ecuador, (despite being initially deferred)[143] and two sites in New Zealand were further extended by being collapsed into one site.[144]

In some instances, sites have been extended in one area (by an area of equal or better value), and reduced in others (at the suggestion of the Committee).[145] This has occurred in Canada[146] and Australia, with the latter involving one instance of a site reduction by 30%.[147] This process introduces the idea that in as much as territory can be added to a site, it can also be removed. With regard to removals of parts of sites after they have already been listed, the key consideration is that removal is only permissible if the already inscribed areas do not possess (and were probably mistakenly listed) out-

---

134 Vallee do Mai Nature Reserve. UNESCO. (1984). 7th Session of the WHC. SC/83/CONF.009/8. Jan 12, 1984. pp 6.

135 The Iguazu national Park Argentina, the Canadian Rockies, the Malawi national Park. UNESCO. (1984). Eighth Session of the WHC. SC/84/CONF.004/9. Nov 2, 1984. pp 7-8.

136 Canadian Rocky Mountains. UNESCO. (1990). 14th Session of the WHC. CLT-90/CONF.004/13. Dec 12, 1990. 7. Glacier bay was formed by linking the Wrangell and Kluane sites of Canada and the United States. UNESCO. (1992). 16th Session of the WHC. WHC-92/CONF.002/12. Dec 14, 1992. 35.

137 Pirin National park. UNESCO. (1991). 15th Session of the WHC. SC-91/CONF.002/15. Dec 12, 1991. 6.

138 Coco Islands National Park. UNESCO. (2002). 26th Session of the WHC. WHC-02/CONF.202/25. Aug 1, 2002. 60. Guancaste. UNESCO. (2004). 28th Session of the WHC. WHC-04/28.COM/26. Oct 29. Decision 28 COM 14B.19. pp26.

139 Kilimanjaro. UNESCO. (1987). 11th Session of the WHC. CC-87/CONF.005/9. Jan 20, 1988. pp 6.

140 Henderson Island. UNESCO. (1988). 12th Session of the WHC. SC-88/CONF.001/13. Dec 23, 1988. 14. Gough Island. UNESCO. (2004). 28th Session of the WHC. WHC-04/28.COM/26. Oct 29. Decision 28 COM 14B.17. pp25.

141 Lake Turkana. UNESCO. (2001). 25th Session of the WHC. WHC-01/CONF.208/24. Feb 8, 2002. 92-95.

142 Volcanoes of Kamchatka. UNESCO. (2001). 25th Session of the WHC. WHC-01/CONF.208/24. Feb 8, 2002. 92-95.

143 UNESCO. (2001). 25th Session of the WHC. WHC-01/CONF.208/24. Feb 8, 2002. 92-95.

144 Westland/Mount Cook National Park and the Fiordland National Park in NZ, were collapsed into the Te Wahipounamu-South West NZ site. UNESCO. (1990). 14th Session of the WHC. CLT-90/CONF.004/13. Dec 12, 1990. 4.

145 UNESCO. (1991). 15th Session of the WHC. SC-91/CONF.002/15. Dec 12, 1991. 7.

146 Ibid.

147 The Willandra Lakes. UNESCO. (1996). 19th Session of the WHC. WHC-95/CONF.203/16. Jan 31, 1996. 37. Also the Temperate and Sub Tropical Rainforest Parks on the Australian East Coast. UNESCO. (1986). 10th Session of the WHC. CC-86/CONF.003/10. Dec 5, 1986 42.

standing universal value,[148] or parts of the non-core area (where the OUV is not located), perhaps on the periphery, have become degraded.[149] However, it is clear that downsizing of the site is not possible if the reduction includes core areas which still encompass the outstanding universal values for why the site was listed in the first place. The later precedent was clear with the Mount Nimba park in the Guinea/Cote d Ivoire Park.[150]

5 Buffer Zones

Zoning is the principal method used to control uses within or next to a protected area.[151] It is designed to allocate geographical areas for specific levels and intensities of human activities and conservation. It is particularly useful in helping people understand what site values are located where, as well as establishing boundaries and associated standards to show what is acceptable or not in different locations. As such, zones are the map of management objectives. Zoning may be applied within single areas (such as core or buffer areas), or as a strategic framework for the planning of an overall group of protected areas.

The first protected area regime of note to recommend zoning was the 1933 African Convention. This instrument clearly envisaged the creation of, 'intermediate zones' around the protected areas, through which certain activities, which would otherwise be strictly controlled in the core area, would be permitted under strict controls.[152] The 'intermediate zones' of the 1933 African Convention are now known as 'buffer zones'. Buffer zones, as best described in the MAB Statutory Framework for Biosphere Reserves, as areas which are, 'clearly identified and surrounding or contiguous to the core area or areas, where only activities compatible with the conservation objectives can take place'.[153] Buffer zones should be part of a subset within an overall zoned region, of which boundaries and associated standards to show what is acceptable or not in the core, buffer and transition zones, are only parts of the picture. Collectively,

148 Such as with the reduction of parts (in particular 3 Indian reserves) of La Amistad/Talamanca range. UNESCO. (1990). 14th Session of the WHC. CLT-90/CONF.004/13. Dec 12, 1990. 11.

149 Such as with the Kenyan Natural Forest park, which excluded areas heavily impacted upon by deforestation. UNESCO. (1997). 21st Session of the WHC. WHC-97/CONF.208/17. Feb 27, 1998. 38.

150 A proposal to take out about 30% of the total area, in exchange for support of conservation programmes elsewhere. UNESCO. (1991). 15th Session of the WHC. SC-91/CONF.002/15. Dec 12, 1991. 8.

151 Zoning is required for the IUCN categories, so that at least 75% of a area is managed for its primary purpose IUCN. (2004). *Speaking a Common Language: The IUCN System of Management Categories.* (IUCN, Gland). 14.

152 1933 London Convention. Article 4 (2).

153 The Statutory Framework of the World Network of Biosphere Reserves. Article 4 (5).

they should all work towards the strong conservation of the core areas. Primarily, a buffer zone should help to protect the core area from harmful human activities, interact to provide a positive landscape features, provide diffusion to sustain natural and man-made flows in the landscape, and control human activities in areas adjacent to the protected area, whilst also enhancing compatible opportunities for the local populations in these areas.[154]

The utility, and recommendations for the creation and use of buffer zones can be found in the 1968[155] and 2003 African Convention,[156] the Caribbean,[157] South East Pacific,[158] and East African Protocols,[159] the Helsinki Convention,[160] the Arctic regime,[161] repeatedly in Agenda 21,[162] the IMO with its PSSAs,[163] the ITTO,[164] the Ramsar,[165] and the European Diploma.[166] Even the GEF has come to support buffer zones, and has financed 44 projects, covering at least 209 protected areas, to

---

154 Budhathoki, p. (2004). 'Linking Communities With Conservation in Developing Countries'. *Oryx.* 38(3). 334-341. Kelleher, G. (ed). *Guidelines for Marine Protected Areas (IUCN, Gland, 1999).* 51-53. UNESCO. (2002). *Biosphere Reserves: Special Places for People and Nature.* (UNESCO, Paris). 17.

155 African Convention (1968). Article X (2).

156 2003 African Convention. Article XII (4).

157 Caribbean Protocol, Articles 8 and 9..

158 1989 Protocol for the Conservation and Management of Protected Marine and Coastal Areas of the South East Pacific. Reprinted in Austen, A. (ed). *Basic Legal Document on International Animal Welfare and Wildlife Conservation* (Kluwer, London). Article 6.

159 Protocol Concerning Protected Areas of Wild Fauna and Flora in the Eastern African Region. Reprinted in Austen, A. *Ibid.* Article 11.

160 See HELCOM HOD 11/2003.

161 See CAFF. (1996). *The Circumpolar Protected Area Network: Principles and Guidelines.* (CAFF Habitat Conservation Report, No 4.) Principle 11.

162 See Chapters 11.14 (c) and 15.5. (j) of Agenda 21.

163 Annex 6. Guidelines for the Designation of Special Areas Under MARPOL 73/78 and Guidelines for the Identification and Designation of Particularly Sensitive Sea Areas. MEPC (2001). Report of the MEPC on its 46th Session. MEPC 46/23. Section 6.3. MEPC. (2004). Report of the MEPC on its 52nd Session. MEPC. 52/WP.13. 55.

164 The ITTO has funded a number of projects seeking to enhance buffer zones. For example, the transboundary forest site between Cambodia, Laos and Thailand contains a total of 82 villages and about 89,000 people, but no human settlements in the core area itself.

165 Recommendation 5.3. The Essential Character of Wetlands and the Need for Zonation Related to Wetland Reserves. (1993, Kushiro). Resolution 8.14. New Guidelines for Management Planning for Ramsar Sites and Other Wetlands. (2002, San Jose). Annex.

166 Note the emphasis in the Diploma is more on zoning itself, than buffer zones. The applicant area must be the subject, if possible, of a zoning, which must indicate the objectives of each sub-division described, 'The boundaries between the applicant area and the surrounding area must be clearly marked on a plan or a geographical map, particularly where there are nearby protected areas with different objectives (as is often the case in a biosphere reserve), Failing these considerations, the uses of the land which are authorised should be clearly indicated. European Diploma. Annex I. Criteria. Section B (3).

incorporate buffer zones.[167] The idea of having an added layer of protection around a site has also been utilised by the WHC.[168] Thus, as the *Operational Guidelines* explain,

> The boundaries should include sufficient areas immediately adjacent to the area of outstanding universal value in order to protect the site's heritage values from direct effects of human encroachment and impacts of resource use outside of the nominated area. The boundaries of the nominated site may coincide with one or more existing or proposed protected areas, such as national parks or biosphere reserves. While an existing or proposed protected area may contain several management zones, only some of those zones may satisfy criteria for listing a natural site. Other zones, although they may not meet the criteria set for listing a natural site, may be essential for the management to ensure the integrity of the nominated site. For example, in the case of a biosphere reserve, only the core zone may meet the criteria and the conditions of integrity, although other zones, i.e. buffer and transitional zones, would be important for the conservation of the biosphere reserve in its totality.[169]

The need for such a buffer zone has been emphasised by the Committee with regard to applications from India,[170] Peru,[171] Japan,[172] the United Kingdom[173] and Guatemala.[174]

The other regime which has developed a strong jurisprudence on buffer zones is the MAB. The MAB places buffer zones between the core area,[175] and the transition zone.[176] All three zones are obligatory for an MAB site to come into existence,[177]

---

167 GEF. (2005). *Making a Visible Difference in Our World.* (GEF, Washington). 11.

168 The area constituting the buffer zone should be determined in each case through technical studies *Operational Guidelines.* 2002 Edn. Paragraph 17.

169 *Operational Guidelines.* 2002 Edn. Paragraph 44.

170 The Kaziranga National Park. UNESCO. (1985). 9th Session of the WHC. SC-85/CONF.008/9. Dec, 1985. pp 6.

171 Manu National Park. UNESCO. (1987). 11th Session of the WHC. CC-87/CONF.005/9. Jan 20, 1988. pp 6.

172 Shirakami-Sanchi. UNESCO. (1993). 17th Session of WHC. WHC-93/CONF.002/14. Feb 4, 1993. 34.

173 St Kilda. UNESCO. (1999). 23rd Session of the WHC. WHC-99/CONF.209/22. Mar 22, 2000. 74-75.

174 Tikal park. UNESCO. (1993). 17th Session of WHC. WHC-93/CONF.002/14. Feb 4, 1993. 15.

175 According to the Statutory Framework for Biosphere Reserve, each Biosphere Reserve must have, a legally constituted core area or areas devoted to long-term protection, according to the conservation objectives of the biosphere reserve, and of sufficient size to meet these objectives. The Statutory Framework of the World Network of Biosphere Reserves. Article 4 (5).

176 According to the Statutory Framework for Biosphere Reserves, the final area of zoning required for Biosphere Reserves is, 'an outer transition area where sustainable resource management practices are promoted and developed'. The Statutory Framework of the World Network of Biosphere Reserves. Article 4 (5). These transition areas may contain a variety

and sites failing to deliver the three zones have been deferred.[178] This is especially the case with inadequate buffer zones, which have resulted in the nominated sites either being deferred,[179] or given conditional acceptance, on the consideration that their buffer zones are enhanced. Enhancement is typically in terms of legal protection, clarity of location or supplementing values to the core zone.[180]

6 Networks and Corridors

Protected areas, and the ecosystems and species within them, can rarely exist as isolated islands. Rather, they have to be integrated into the broader ecology.[181] Buffer zones, as discussed above, are the first stage of this process. The second stage is that of corridors and inter-connected networks. Corridors are various ecological features, other than core areas, which represent links that permeate the landscape, maintaining or re-establishing natural connectivity. In Europe, ecological corridors are often the result of human intervention in nature, such as hedgerows, stonewalls, landscapes with small

---

of agricultural or forestry activities (both being managed for long term conservation objectives) settlements and other uses, in which the local community and interested participants (from scientists to NGOs) work together to manage and sustainably develop the areas biological resources. UNESCO. (2002). *Biosphere Reserves: Special Places for People and Nature.* (UNESCO, Paris). 17. UNESCO. (2001) ICC Bureau Meeting. SC-01/CONF.217/8. Dec 12. 22. El Kala in Algeria. UNESCO. (2003). ICC Bureau Meeting. SC-02/CONF.210/10. Jan 7. 17. Nanda Devi in India. UNESCO. (2001). ICC Bureau Meeting. SCI-01/CONF.217/8. Dec 12, 15, 17.

177 Seville Strategy. Objective IV.1.

178 Desnyansko in the Ukraine. UNESCO. (2004). 18th Session of the ICC Bureau Meeting. SC-04/CONF.204/14. Jan 11. 17. El Tuparro in Columbia. UNESCO. (2001) ICC Bureau Meeting. SC-01/CONF.217/8. Dec 12, 20. Cat ba in Vietnam. UNESCO. (2003). ICC Bureau Meeting. SC-02/CONF.210/10. Jan 7. 16. Radom in Sudan. UNESCO. (2001) ICC Bureau Meeting. SC-01/CONF.217/8. Dec 12, 22.

179 Kenozersky in Russia. UNESCO. (2003). ICC Bureau Meeting. SC/-03/CONF.217/14. July 30. 15.

180 Foping in China. UNESCO. (2003). ICC Bureau Meeting. SC/-03/CONF.217/14. July 30. 14. Chrea in Algeria. UNESCO. (2002). ICC Bureau Meeting. SC-02/CONF.210/10. 8. Badiar in Guinea. Bogd and Dornod in Mongolia, UNESCO. (2003). ICC Bureau Meeting. SC-02/CONF.210/10. Jan 7. 10, 15. Fitzgerald in Australia. UNESCO. (2003). ICC Bureau Meeting. SC/-03/CONF.217/14. July 30. 19. Elgon in Kenya. UNESCO. (2003). ICC Bureau Meeting. SC/-03/CONF.217/14. July 30. 10. Caatinga in Brazil. UNESCO. (2001). ICC Bureau Meeting. SCI/-01/CONF.217/8. Dec 12, 2. 12.

181 Bennet, G. (2004). *Integrating Biodiversity, Conservation and Sustainable Use.* (IUCN, Gland). UNESCO. (1998). *Biosphere Reserves: Myth or Reality?.* (UNESCO, Paris). 5.

forests, canals and regulated rivers. Corridors reduce ecological fragmentation, and allow species to bypass barriers that would otherwise represent clear threats to them.[182]

Whilst a number of regimes talk of a 'network' of protected areas, such as the CBD,[183] MAB,[184] and some oceanic regimes,[185] and a number of instruments mention 'corridors' relatively few have actually tried to implement them. The notable few which have tried are the Bern Convention,[186] the Habitats Directive[187] the GEF, the MAB, and the WHC. Although the WHC,[188] and the MAB have made recommendations to some of its members to 'consider the feasibility of establishing ecological corridors between the core areas',[189] it is the Habitats Directive which has progressed the greatest distance on this topic.

The Habitats Directive is notable because it obliges its Member States to endeavour, where they consider it necessary, in particular, with a view to improving the ecological coherence of the Natura 2000 network, to encourage the management of 'features of the landscape which are of major importance for wild fauna and flora'. The Habitats Directive explains that, 'such features are those which, by virtue of their linear and continuous structure (such as rivers with their banks or the traditional systems for marking field boundaries) or their function as stepping stones (such as ponds or small

---

182 Bennett, A. (2003). *Linkages in the Landscape: The Role of Corridors and Connectivity in Wildlife Conservation.* (IUCN, Gland). Holmes, B. (2005). 'Major Highways Are a Hard Cross to Bears'. *New Scientist.* Oct 1. 10.

183 CBD Secretariat. (2005). *Towards Effective Protected Area Systems.* (CBD Technical Series No. 18). 18, 24. The language of the CBD in this area is of 'ecological connectivity and the concept, where appropriate, of ecological networks'.

184 UNESCO. (1971). *International Coordinating Council for the Programme on Man and the Biosphere.* (UNESCO, MAB Report Series No 1). UNESCO. (1998). *Biosphere Reserves: Myth or Reality?.* (UNESCO, Paris). 4.

185 OSPAR Recommendation 2003/3 on a Network of Marine Protected Areas. Appendix 1. Report of the Working Group on the Development of Guidelines for the Listing of Protected Areas Under the SPAW Protocol. (2005). UNEP (DEC)/CAR WG.29/INF.12. See Resolution on the International Coral Reef Action Network (ICRAN). In ICRI (2000). Report of the ICRI Meeting in Noumea, New Caledonia, 25-26 May, 2000.

186 The Bern convention has called for the establishment of conservation areas, outside of the protected areas proper, as designated through the Bern convention. As such, it called upon Parties to consider conservation measures for areas of special conservation interest, ecological corridors, landscape features, ecologically sensitive areas (such as coastal zones, mountains, flood plains, forests) and protected landscapes. Recommendation No.25. (1991). The Conservation of Natural Areas Outside Protected Areas Proper.

187 Note the importance of networks within the Habitats Directive. Article 3.

188 As with Simien. 'Finalise the extension… with interlinking corridors'. See Decision 30 COM 7A.9.

189 Barranca de Metztilan, Mexico. UNESCO. (2006). MAB ICC. 19th Session. SC-06/CONF.202/16. Nov 28. 10.

woods), are essential for the migration, dispersal and genetic exchange of wild species'.[190] The GEF is notable in this area because it has provided funding for 32 biodiversity projects, involving at least 207 protected areas, which include corridor components. An outstanding example in this area is the Program for the Consolidation of the Meso-American Biological Corridor, as coordinated by the Commission for Environment and Development in Central America.[191]

7 Staff and Other Resources

The First National Parks Congress in 1962 suggested that because national parks are so important, they should be, 'vested in a statutory organization charged with the duty of permanent trusteeship'.[192] Implicit within this recommendation, was that such an agency would have adequate resources, in terms of both effective human and other capital, to carry out its responsibilities.[193] The overall goal, as recently articulated by the Parties to the CBD, which was following repeated concerns all of the subsequent World Parks Congresses,[194] is that all of its Parties should,

> Ensure that protected areas are effectively managed or supervised through staff that are well-trained and skilled, properly and appropriately equipped, and supported, to carry out their fundamental role in the management and conservation of protected areas.[195]

Due to the importance of such a goal, the CBD also recommended that by 2006, 'appropriate methods, standards, criteria and indicators for evaluating the effectiveness of protected area management and governance' be established. Moreover, management

---

190 Habitats Directive. Article 10.

191 GEF. (2005). *Making a Visible Difference in Our World.* (GEF, Washington). 11.

192 See 'Closing Plenary Session.' In Adams, A. (ed). *First World Conference on National Parks.* (US Department of the Interior, Washington). 379. Recommendations No 8, 14 & 19.

193 IUCN. (2003). *Guidelines for Management Planning of Protected Areas.* (IUCN, Gland). IUCN. (2000). *Evaluating Effectiveness: A Framework for Assessing the Management of Protected Areas.* (IUCN, Gland). See 'Administration of National Parks.' In Adams, *ibid.* 178-205, 362-365.

194 See Recommendation 1. Strengthening Institutional and Societal Capacities for Protected Area Management in the 21st Century.; 5.02. Strengthening Individual and Group Capacities for Protected Area Management., 5.18. Management Effectiveness Evaluation. (Vth IUCN World Parks Congress). Also, The Durban Action Plan. pp.3-4. Miller, K. (1972). 'Development and Training of Personnel: The Foundation of National Park Programmes in the Future.' Also, Recommendation 18. Training. In Elliot, H. (ed). *Second World Conference on National Parks.* (IUCN, Lausanne). 326-347, 449. Recommendation 12. Protected Area Personnel: Training and Communication. Recommendations of the World National Parks Congress. In McNeely, J. (ed). *National Parks, Conservation and Development.* (Smithsonian, Washington). 773.

195 CBD. Decision VII/28. Protected Areas. Annex. Paragraph 1.4.6

effectiveness evaluations should be carried out for, 'at least 30% of each Party's protected areas by 2010 and of national protected area systems and, as appropriate, ecological networks'.[196]

The importance of staff and supporting resources for effective management of protected areas is clearly recognised in, inter alia, the European Diploma,[197] the Mediterranean,[198] South East Pacific,[199] and Caribbean[200] Protocols, the African,[201] and Bern Conventions,[202] Agenda 21,[203] the MAB,[204] the Ramsar Convention[205] and the WHC.[206]

Despite such recognition, the relatively clear goals in this area are not being met. For example, in the late 1990s, although the global mean staff input in protected areas was 27 persons per 1.000 square kilometres of protected areas, and the averages between the developed (26.9 per 1.000 km) and developing (27.6 per 1.000 km) were broadly similar, the discrepancies within the overall total ranged from 432 per 1.000 km in East Asia, to 4 in Central and South America. Such differences reflect the fact that whilst the global mean budget for protected areas was $893 (USD) per square kilometre in the late 1990s, the developed country mean was $2,058 per square kilometre, whereas the developing country level was $157. Within this range, the differences in budget range from $12,308 per kilometre in East Asia, through to $24 in Africa.[207] Such

196 Ibid. Annex. Paragraphs 4.2.1 & 4.2.2.

197 European Diploma. Annex I. Criteria. Section B (6).

198 Mediterranean Protocol. Article 7 (2)(f) and (4).

199 1989 Protocol for the Conservation and Management of Protected Marine and Coastal Areas of the South East Pacific. Reprinted in Austen, A. (ed). *Basic Legal Document on International Animal Welfare and Wildlife Conservation (Kluwer, London).* Article 10.

200 Caribbean Protocol. Article 6.

201 2003 African Convention. Articles XXI and XX (2). For the earlier 1968 Convention on this point, see African Convention (1968). Article XV.

202 Recommendation No 16. (1989). On Areas of Special Conservation Interest. Section 3.

203 Agenda 21, chapter 15.11. (d)

204 Seville Strategy. Objective III.4.

205 Ramsar. Article 4.1. Recommendations adopted by the International Conference on the Conservation of Wetlands and Waterfowl at Heiligenhafen, Federal Republic of Germany, 6 December 1974. Annex II. Recommendations for Criteria to be used in identifying Wetlands of International Importance.

206 The Parties 'shall' (as far as possible and appropriate for each country) inter alia, 'set up within its territories, where such services do not exist, one or more services for the protection, conservation and presentation of the cultural and natural heritage with an appropriate staff and possessing the means to discharge their functions'. WHC Convention. Article 5 (b). In addition, the Parties 'shall' (as far as possible and appropriate for each country) inter alia, 'foster the establishment or development of national or regional centres for training in the protection, conservation and presentation' of WHC sites. Article 5 (e).

207 WCMC. (1999). *A Global Review of Protected Area Budgets and Staff.* (WCMC, Cambridge). V.

considerations, of lack of staff and resources typically lead to the contention that many protected areas are only 'paper parks'. For example, in 2004, a survey of almost 200 forest protected areas in 34 countries found that less than 25% were considered well managed with good infrastructure, and only 1% were regarded as secure in the long term.[208] In a similar vein, the WHC periodic review of African sites found that the equipment of 19 sites was disparate, often limited to more or less functional vehicles or unreliable accommodation, and the data bases at 11 sites were rudimentary, old or incomplete. Only 40% of the sites were well or moderately well equipped for research purposes.[209] Likewise, the management level of MPAs in the mid 1990s revealed that of a then total of 1,306 MPAs 117 had high management (meeting management objectives), 155 had medium (partially meeting), 111 low (failed to achieve management objectives) and 923 were unknown. The recurring themes for those in the low and medium bracket was that they had insufficient technical and financial support and lacked trained staff.[210]

Despite such pressing needs in this area, only three instruments have clear policies to rectify the problem. The first is the GEF, of which capacity building is a strong theme in their protected area assistance. Over three quarters of GEF protected area projects involve capacity building, covering at least 875 sites. In particular, training is the focus of 103 projects covering 406 sites.[211] The other two instruments of note are the Ramsar and the WHC. The Ramsar is notable because it has continually reiterated the importance of manager training programmes,[212] and it has also sought to establish centres for the training of such peoples,[213] and provided financial assistance for this purpose.[214]

With regard to the WHC, although training may be considered part of technical assistance, for the purposes of this section, I have divided them into two categories. Technical assistance was one of the first agreed funding objectives of both the WHC, and the

---

208 WWF. (2004). *How Effective Are Protected Areas? (WWF, Gland).* UNEP/WCWC. (2004). *Protected Areas and Biodiversity.* (UNEP: Biodiversity Series No 21). 34. SBSTTA. Report of the Ad Hoc Technical Expert Group on Protected Areas. UNEP/CBD/SBSTTA/9/INF/3. 22 Sep, 2003. pp.25-29. CBD. (2004). *Technical Advice on the Establishment and Management of a National System of Marine and Coastal Protected Areas.* (CBD Technical Series No 13). 20-31. Secretariat of the CBD. (2004). *Biodiversity Issues for Consideration in the Planning, Establishment and Management of Protected Area Sites and Management.* (CBD Technical Series No 15). 37-45, 73-82.

209 UNESCO. (2002). *Periodic Report for Africa.* (World Heritage Reports Number 3). 44.

210 Kelleher, G. (1995). *A Global Representative System of Marine Protected Areas.* (World Bank, Washington). Volume IV. 7-8.

211 GEF. (2005). *Making a Visible Difference in Our World.* (GEF, Washington). 21.

212 Resolution 8.25. The Ramsar Strategic Plan. (2002, Valencia). Annex. Operational Objective 20.

213 Resolution 7.26. Regional Ramsar Centre for Training and Research. (1999, San Jose).

214 Recommendation 6.5. Wetland Manager Training Programmes. (1996, Brisbane). Recommendation 1.2. Developing Countries and the Convention. (1980, Cagliari).

Committee.[215] Training represents 16.8% of the World Heritage Fund.[216] The 2004 figure for this budgetary component (360,000, although the figure was actually larger as part of what was traditionally seen as technical assistance now falls within the category of capacity building)[217] was over double what it was in the late 1970s.[218] Although it was originally difficult to ascertain exactly what the 'technical assistance' grantss were for (as it was not recorded in the official records),[219] later records have shown that technical assistance included, inter alia, assistance for the purchase of anti-poaching materials,[220] motor boats,[221] motor vehicles,[222] audio visual equipment,[223] park shelters and guard posts,[224] visitor centers,[225] communications equipment, solar panels, construction of wells, donkeys for use in national parks,[226] water quality measurement tools, buffer zone development and GPS systems,[227] equipment to study the effect of various types of air pollution,[228] biodiversity inven-

---

215 Article 21(1). Also UNESCO. (1977). 1st Session of the WHC. CC-77/CONF.001/9. Oct 17, 1977. pp.8.

216 For discussion of the period 1998 to 2003, see Information on the World Heritage Fund. WHC/-05/29.COM/14 B.

217 As of 2005, technical cooperation represented 16.5% of the WH Fund, and 39.9% of International Assistance (and 31.3% if emergency assistance is counted). 236 grants were awarded, with an average grant size of 22,664. UNESCO. (2005). Information on the World Heritage Fund. WHC-05/29.COM/14B.9.

218 165,400. UNESCO. (1979). 3rd Session of the WHC. CC-79/CONF.003/13. Nov 30, 1978. pp.15. UNESCO. (2004). 7th Extraordinary Session of the WHC. WHC-04/7 EXT.COM/7. Oct 25. pp5.

219 UNESCO. (1978). 2nd Session of the WHC. CC-78/CONF.010/10. Oct 9, 1978. pp.4. UNESCO. (1990). 14th Session of the WHC. CLT-90/CONF.004/13. Dec 12, 1990. 15. UNESCO. (1996). 20th Session of the WHC. WHC-96/CONF.201/21. Mar 10, 1997. 64. UNESCO. (1980). 4th Session of the WHC. CC-80/CONF.017/4. May 28, 1980. pp.7.

220 UNESCO. (1986). 10th Session of the WHC. CC-86/CONF.003/10. Dec 5, 1986. pp 9. UNESCO. (1987). 11th Session of the WHC. CC-87/CONF.005/9. Jan 20, 1988. pp 12.

221 UNESCO. (1979). 3rd Session of the WHC. CC-79/CONF.003/13. Nov 30, 1978. pp.12. UNESCO. (1988). 12th Session of the WHC. SC-88/CONF.001/13. Dec 23, 1988. 12. UNESCO. (1989). 11th Session of the WHC. SC-89/CONF.004/12. Dec, 22 1989. pp 9. UNESCO. (1991). 15th Session of the WHC. SC-91/CONF.002/15. Dec 12, 1991. 15.

222 UNESCO. (1988). 12th Session of the WHC. SC-88/CONF.001/13. Dec 23, 1988. 12. UNESCO. (1990). 14th Session of the WHC. CLT-90/CONF.004/13. Dec 12, 1990. 15. UNESCO. (1991). 15th Session of the WHC. SC-91/CONF.002/15. Dec 12, 1991. 14.

223 UNESCO. (1989). 11th Session of the WHC. SC-89/CONF.004/12. Dec, 22 1989. pp 10. UNESCO. (1997). 21st Session of the WHC. WHC-97/CONF.208/17. Feb 27, 1998. 55.

224 UNESCO. (1991). 15th Session of the WHC. SC-91/CONF.002/15. Dec 12, 1991. 8. UNESCO. (1997). 21st Session of the WHC. WHC-97/CONF.208/17. Feb 27, 1998. 55.

225 UNESCO. (1991). 15th Session of the WHC. SC-91/CONF.002/15. Dec 12, 1991. 14.

226 UNESCO. (1993). 17th Session of WHC. WHC-93/CONF.002/14. Feb 4, 1993. 42.

227 UNESCO. (1995). 18th Session of the WHC. WHC-94/CONF.003/16. Jan 31. 1995. 49.

228 In the former Yugoslavia. UNESCO. (1987). 11th Session of the WHC. CC-87/CONF.005/9. Jan 20, 1988. pp 12. UNESCO. (1988). 12th Session of the WHC. SC-88/CONF.001/13. Dec 23, 1988. 12.

tories,[229] conservation projects,[230] new and revised management plans[231] and even assistance to help the Seychelles eradicate the feral goats on Aldabra Atoll.[232]

The provision of funds for training is difficult to trace through the WHC, as the concept is both widely interpreted (and goes well beyond traditional conceptions of staff at protected areas, practical hands-on, related management training)[233] and has fallen under a number of different categories. These categories range from being part of 'technical assistance'[234] to part of 'capacity building'.[235] Whichever way it is looked at, it is notable that since the late 1980s the demand for training assistance was growing faster than any other kind of international assistance.[236] By the new century, support from training had risen (despite a ceiling placed on the amount each training request could seek)[237] from around $200,000 (USD) per year in 1980 to close to one million per year.[238] Training workshops remains prominent in contemporary budgets[239]

229 UNESCO. (1996). 19th Session of the WHC. WHC-95/CONF.203/16. Jan 31, 1996. 52.

230 UNESCO. (2002). 26th Session of the WHC. WHC-02/CONF.202/25. Aug 1, 2002. 68.

231 UNESCO. (1996). 19th Session of the WHC. WHC-95/CONF.203/16. Jan 31, 1996. 52. UNESCO. (2002). 26th Session of the WHC. WHC-02/CONF.202/25. Aug 1, 2002. 69. UNESCO. (1986). 10th Session of the WHC. CC-86/CONF.003/10. Dec 5, 1986. pp 14. UNESCO. (1980). 4th Session of the WHC. CC-80/CONF.017/4. May 28, 1980. pp.8. UNESCO. (1980). 4rth Session of the WHC. CC-80/CONF.016/10. Sep 29, 1980. pp.11. UNESCO. (1992). 16th Session of the WHC. WHC-92/CONF.002/12. Dec 14, 1992. 38.

232 UNESCO. (1986). 10th Session of the WHC. CC-86/CONF.003/10. Dec 5, 1986. pp 14.

233 Training is defined as, 'broadly encompassing the term that includes education, training and promotion'. The purpose and objective of training is to, 'to enhance the capacity of all State parties to identify, protect, conserve and present the natural heritage'. UNESCO. (1996). 19th Session of the WHC. WHC-95/CONF.203/16. Jan 31, 1996. 49.

234 UNESCO. (1986). 10th Session of the WHC. CC-86/CONF.003/10. Dec 5, 1986. pp 14.

235 UNESCO. (2004). 7th Extra-Ordinary Session of the WHC. WHC-04/7. EXT.COM/10. Oct 10. Table 1.

236 3,000,000 of 7,465,000. UNESCO. (1989). 7th General Assembly of Parties to the WHC. CC-89/CONF.013/6. Nov 13, 1989. 1. UNESCO. (1989). 13th Session of the WHC. SC-89/ CONF.004/9. Dec 22, 1989. pp 2.

237 As of 2003, the ceiling for each application for training and research assistance was 30,000 per application. UNESCO. (2003). 6th Extra-ordinary Session of the WHC. WHC-03/6. EXT.COM/8. May 27, 2003. 12.

238 For 1979-1980, training assistance cost 204,700. This rose to 335,000 for 1981/82 before rising to 500,000 per year for 1982-84. It fell to 150,000 for 1985, before doubling to 300,000 for 1986, and then stabilizing in 1987, 1988 & 1989 at 500,000. It rose to 550,000 for 1990, before falling back to 500,000 (91), 475,000 (92) and 400,000 in 1993 before beginning to rise to 440,000 for 1994, 452,000 for 1995, before rising quickly in the late 1990s to 982,000 (1998) 981,000(1999) 980,000 (2000) and 960,000 for 2001. Note, within these figures, a component has typically been set aside for training provided by the IUCN. At the turn of the century, this was normally around 30,000 (inclusive within the overall training budget).

(especially as part of the work of the Advisory bodies)[240] and increased allowances for training were given to the IUCN in 2005.[241] Part of this growth is due to the change in funding emphasis for this area, which has gone from being largely ad-hoc one-off-requests in the 1980s,[242] to being more systematized in the 1990s, with particular regional training programmes.[243] This was taken further with the Global Training Strategy (as part of the overall goal of capacity building), which attempts to focus training into institutional teaching, individual scholarships, inventories and mapping and thematic training, such as with forest managers.[244]

8 Environmental Impact Assessments

An Environmental Impact Assessments (EIAs) is, 'a process of evaluating the likely environmental impacts of a proposed project or development, taking into account interrelated socio-economic, cultural and human health impacts, both beneficial and adverse'.[245] Such evaluations are critical management tools as they ensure that the impacts of any potential developments within, or next to a protected area, are fully assessed before approval or rejection of the development is given. The facilitation and utilisation of EIAs, is already an existing obligation for the signatories to the 1991 Convention on Environmental Impact Assessment in a Transboundary Context. However, since not all States are Parties to this instrument, and also, because most protected areas fall within domestic jurisdictions, the primary convention which has come to utilize EIAs for protected area managements is the CBD. In this regard, the CBD's basic obligation upon all Parties, with regard to proposed projects that could have significant

239 Training represents 16.8% of the WHC Fund, 40.6% of International Assistance (or 31.8% if emergency assistance is counted). 221 grants were awarded, with an average grant being 24,607. UNESCO. (2005). Information on the World Heritage Fund. WHC-05/29.COM/14B. 10.

240 UNESCO. (2004). 7th Extra Ordinary Session. Of the WHC. WHC-04/7. p5. Ext.Com/3C. 28 COM 10A.2.

241 Decision 29 COM 10.

242 UNESCO. (1995). 18th Session of the WHC. WHC-94/CONF.003/16. Jan 31. 1995. 51-52. UNESCO. (1996). 20th Session of the WHC. WHC-96/CONF.201/21. Mar 10, 1997. 64-65. UNESCO. (2003). 27th Session of the WHC. WHC-03/27.COM/24. Dec 10. 33. UNESCO. (1987). 11th Session of the WHC. CC-87/CONF.005/9. Jan 20, 1988. pp 12. UNESCO. (1991). 15th Session of the WHC. SC-91/CONF.002/15. Dec 12, 1991. 15.

243 UNESCO. (1999). 23rd Session of the WHC. WHC-99/CONF.209/22. Mar 22, 2000. 104-106. UNESCO. (2001). 24th Session of the WHC. WHC-2000/CONF.204/21. Feb 16, 2001. 115-120. UNESCO. (2003). 27th Session of the WHC. WHC-03/27.COM/24. Dec 10. 140-144.

244 Note, the thematic theme was an IUCN suggestion. UNESCO. (2001). 25th Session of the WHC. WHC-01/CONF.208/24. Feb 8, 2002. 100.

245 Decision VI/7. Identification, Monitoring, Indicators and Assessment. UNEP/CBD/COP/6/20.00.92.

adverse effects on biodiversity, is for EIAs to be undertaken.[246] To further this goal, the CBD has produced synthesis reports on the use of EIAs in this context,[247] placed the utilization of EIAs in all of its thematic work,[248] and reiterated their importance with regard to substantive (national) decision making policies.[249] Thereafter, the Parties to the CBD[250] adopted Guidelines for Incorporating Biodiversity Related Issues into Environmental Impact Assessment Legislation and/or processes,[251] and their importance has been stressed in all CBD related areas. For example, that with regard to protected areas, the Parties to the CBD have recommended that all Parties,

> Apply, as appropriate, timely environmental impact assessments to any plan or project with the potential to have effects on protected areas, and ensure timely information flow among all concerned Parties to that end, taking into account [CBD Guidelines in this area].[252]

The CBD also adopted the recommendations for the conduct of cultural, environmental and social impact assessments regarding developments proposed to take place on, or which are likely to impact on, sacred sites and on lands and waters traditionally occupied or used by indigenous communities.[253] The key parts of these recommendations pertain to the involvement of traditional and local communities in the impact assessment process (so that the cultural angle of the socio-economic impacts can be taken into account) and that both the knowledge and the holders of the knowledge are respected. These latter recommendations on indigenous peoples and EIAs became incorporated (despite strong debate at the 7th COP) as the (Akwe Kon) Voluntary Guidelines for the Conduct of Cultural, Environmental and Social Impact Assessments Regarding Developments to take Place on, Or Which Are Likely to Impact on Sacred Sites and On Lands and Waters Traditionally Occupied or Used by Indigenous and Local Communities.[254]

---

246 CBD. Article 14 (1).

247 Decision IV/10. Measures for Implementing the CBD. UNEP/CBD/COP/4/27.pp.120.

248 Recommendation IV/6. Incorporation of Biological Diversity Considerations Into Environmental Impact Assessments. UNEP/CBD/SBSTTA/4/14. pp.48.

249 Decision V/18. Impact Assessment, Liability and Redress. UNEP/CBD/COP/5/23. pp.148.

250 Recommendation VII/10. Further Development of Guidelines for Incorporating Biodiversity Related Issues into Environmental Impact Assessments. UNEP/CBD/COP/6/4. pp.87.

251 Decision VI/7. Identification, Monitoring, Indicators and Assessment. UNEP/CBD/COP/6/20.00.92. The Guidelines suggested the fundamental components (each of which was fleshed out with further specific options for inclusion) for EIA are, 1. Screening to determine which projects require an EIA. 2. Scoping to identify potential impacts, and to derive terms of reference for impacts. 3. Predictions and identifications of likely impacts. 4. Identification of mitigation measures. 5. Deciding whether to proceed or not. 6. Monitoring and evaluating, to ensure consistency with given measures.

252 CBD. Decision VII/28. Protected Areas. Annex. Section 1.5.1

253 Decision VI/10. Article 8(j) and Related Provisions. UNEP/CBD/COP/6/20.pp 151. Annex II.

254 The cultural impact assessment is a process of evaluating the likely impacts of a proposed development on the way of life of a particular group or community, with full involvement of this group or community of people and possibly undertaken by this group or community

The process which followed this, was largely modeled on the established EIA process (screening, scoping, impact analysis and assessment, mitigation options/alternatives, reporting, review, monitoring and decision making) although considerations specific to indigenous peoples and associated protocols were added.[255]

The passing notation of the utility of EIAs is clear in the 2003 African Convention,[256] the Mediterranean,[257] South East Pacific,[258] East African[259] and Caribbean Protocols,[260] the Habitats Directive[261] and Agenda 21.[262]

One of the most notable features of the discussion of EIAs over all of the other protected area regimes is how developed this area has become in terms of both the general recognition of the value of EIAs, and directed calls for their utilisation. For example, with the CMS, the utilisation of EIAs with regard to all developments that need to have their impacts anticipated and predicted due to their possible impacts on Appendix I species, has become uppermost.[263] This approach has also been directly reflected in both their Albatross and Petrel Agreement,[264] and the cetacean agreement for the Mediterranean.[265]

With the regime for the Antarctic, although the idea of EIAs can be found in a number of earlier recommendations,[266] it was not until 1987, when the scope and considerations for an 'initial environmental evaluation' were set down. In particular, such evaluations were called for to determine whether proposed activities might reasonably be expected

---

of people: a cultural impact assessment will generally address the impacts, both beneficial and adverse, or a proposed development that may affect, for example, the values, belief systems, customary laws, languages, customs, economy, relationship with the local environment and particular species, social organization and traditions of the affected community. Report of the Third Meeting of the Ad Hoc Open Ended Inter Sessional Working Group on Article 8(j) and Related Provisions. UNEP/CBD/COP/7/7. Dec 12, 2003. pp.29.

255 Article 8(j). UNEP/CBD/COP/7/L19.Rev 1.

256 2003 African Convention. Article XIV (2)(b).

257 Mediterranean Protocol. Article 17.

258 1989 Protocol for the Conservation and Management of Protected Marine and Coastal Areas of the South East Pacific. Reprinted in Austen, A. (ed). *Basic Legal Document on International Animal Welfare and Wildlife Conservation* (Kluwer, London). Article 8.

259 Protocol Concerning Protected Areas of Wild Fauna and Flora in the Eastern African Region. Reprinted in Austen, A. *Ibid.* Article 7.

260 Caribbean Protocol. Article 13.

261 With the Habitats Directive, note the (rebuttable) assumption not to proceed with a development if the EIA indicates significant impacts. Habitats Directive. Article 6 (2)- 6 (4).

262 Agenda 21. Chapter 17.8.

263 Resolution 7.2. Impact Assessment and Migratory Species. (COP 7, 2002, Bonn).

264 ACAP. Action Plan. 3.1.

265 ACCOBAMS. Conservation Plan. 1.c.

266 See Recommendations IV-4, VIII-11, VIII-13, IX-5 and XII-3.

to have a significant impact on a protected area. If this was so, a 'comprehensive environmental evaluation' was to be conducted, and shared with the other Parties, to examine the possible impacts, benefits, alternatives, and suitable monitoring regimes for the proposed activity.[267] The importance of EIAs was later incorporated into the Madrid Protocol.[268] Rules for the circulation of EIAs, with uniform formats and information they should contain, were later agreed,[269] as were guidelines (which were later renewed with a particular focus on looking at alternative options) of the potential impacts.[270]

The WHC does not mention the utilization of EIAs. However, it has become the very clear practice of the WHC Committee to request countries to get EIAs done before projects are undertaken which may have implications for WHC sites. This has been the practice with developments in the United States,[271] with pulp mills in Canada[272] and Russia,[273] helicopter flights in Peru,[274] and tourism in South Africa[275] and

---

267 Recommendation XIV-2. Human Impact on the Antarctic Environment: Environmental Impact Assessment. In Antarctic Treaty: Report of the Fourteenth Meeting (Rio de Janeiro, 1987). 71.

268 See Article 6(1)(b) and article 8 in particular. According to Article 8 of the Madrid Protocol, if proposed activities, which do not have less than a minor or transitory impact, relating to scientific research programmes, tourism and all other governmental and non-governmental activities, including associated logistic support activities, then prior assessment of the impacts of those activities must be followed in accordance with a dedicated Annex. The Annex contained a preliminary impact assessment, followed by an initial environmental evaluation (to see if it is minor or not), followed by a Comprehensive Environmental Evaluation, if it is not minor, which will look at, inter alia, the extent of the direct and indirect impacts of the proposed activity and possible mitigation measures. This evaluation shall then be forwarded to all Parties, prior to the next meeting, and the Committee shall comment (and make recommendations) on it. The final project shall be closely monitored, including with key environmental indicators.

269 See Resolution 1 (2005). Environmental Impact Assessment: Circulation of Information. Final Report of the 28th ATCM. (Stockholm, 2005). 27. Resolution 6. (1995). Environmental Impact Assessment: Circulation of Information. In Antarctic Treaty: Report of the Nineteenth Meeting. (Seoul, 1995). 121-125.

270 Resolution 4 (2005). Updating the Guidelines for Environmental Impact Assessment in the Antarctic. Final Report of the 28th ATCM. (Stockholm, 2005). 27 Resolution 1. (1999). Guidelines for EIA in Antarctica. In Antarctic Treaty: Report of the Twenty-Third Meeting. (Lima, 1999). 55.

271 Mammoth Cave National Park. UNESCO. (2002). 26th Session of the WHC. WHC-02/CONF.202/25. Aug 1, 2002. 37.

272 Buffalo Park. UNESCO. (1990). 14th Session of the WHC. CLT-90/CONF.004/13. Dec 12, 1990. 10.

273 Lake Baikal. UNESCO. (2003). 27th Session of the WHC. WHC-03/27.COM/24. Dec 10, 2003. 42. UNESCO. (2004). 28th Session of the WHC. WHC-04/28.COM/26. Oct 29. Decision 28 COM 15B.22.pp87.

274 Machu Picchu. UNESCO. (1995). 18th Session of the WHC. WHC-94/CONF.003/16. Jan 31. 1995. 23.

Australia.[276] EIAs have also been called for proposed hydro developments in the former Yugoslavia,[277] Honduras,[278] Niger,[279] China,[280] and Senegal,[281] mines in Canada[282] and Russia,[283] power lines in Venezuela,[284] wind turbines in Slovenia[285] and roads in Mauritania,[286] Ecuador,[287] Indonesia[288] and Nepal.[289] In instances where an EIA has not been utilized, the Committee has been unusually blunt. For example, with the roading projects associated with the Royal Chitwan Park in Nepal, the Committee recommended that the WHC Centre and the IUCN,

> Continue to communicate with all concerned donors to fully understand how an infrastructure project impacting World Heritage could have been financed without an EIA and how the recurrence of such practice could be prevented in Nepal and elsewhere in the future.[290]

---

275 St Lucia. UNESCO. (2003). 27th Session of the WHC. WHC-03/27.COM/24. Dec 10, 2003. 34.

276 Great Barrier Reef. UNESCO. (1995). 18th Session of the WHC. WHC-94/CONF.003/16. Jan 31. 1995. 19.

277 Durmitor National Park. UNESCO. (1991). 15th Session of the WHC. SC-91/CONF.002/15. Dec 12, 1991. 10.

278 Rio Platano Reserve. UNESCO. (1998). 22nd Session of the WHC. WHC-98/CONF.203/18. Jan 29, 1999. 23.

279 UNESCO. (2004). 28th Session of the WHC. WHC-04/28.COM/26. Oct 29. Decision 28 COM 15B.1.

280 Decision 29 COM 7B.7, and the Three Parallel Rivers.

281 UNESCO. (1980). 4th Session of the WHC. CC-80/CONF.017/4. May 28, 1980. pp.3. UNESCO. (1981). 5th Session of the WHC. CC-81/CONF.002/4. July 20, 1981. pp.5.

282 Nahanni Park. UNESCO. (2002). 26th Session of the WHC. WHC-02/CONF.202/25. Aug 1, 2002. 28. UNESCO. (2003). 27th Session of the WHC. WHC-03/27.COM/24. Dec 10, 2003. 40.

283 Kamchatka Volcanoes. UNESCO. (1997). 21st Session of the WHC. WHC-97/CONF.208/17. Feb 27, 1998. 22. Lake Baikal. UNESCO. (2004). 28th Session of the WHC. WHC-04/28.COM/26. Oct 29. Decision 28 COM 15B.22.pp87.

284 Canaima National Park. UNESCO. (1997). 21st Session of the WHC. WHC-97/CONF.208/17. Feb 27, 1998. 22-23.

285 Decision 29 COM 15B.28. UNESCO. (2004). 28th Session of the WHC. WHC-04/28.COM/26. Oct 29. Decision 28 COM 15B.22.8p91.

286 Banc d'Arguin National Park. UNESCO. (2002). 26th Session of the WHC. WHC-02/CONF.202/25. Aug 1, 2002. 33.

287 Sangay National Park. UNESCO. (1991). 15th Session of the WHC. SC-91/CONF.002/15. Dec 12, 1991. 7-18. UNESCO. (1996). 19th Session of the WHC. WHC-95/CONF.203/16. Jan 31, 1996. 9

288 Lorentz. UNESCO. (2004). 28th Session of the WHC. WHC-04/28.COM/26. Oct 29. Decision 28 COM 15B.10.pp80.

289 Chitwan. UNESCO. (2003). 27th Session of the WHC. WHC-03/27.COM/24. Dec 10, 2003. 36.

290 UNESCO. (2004). 28th Session of the WHC. WHC-04/28.COM/26. Oct 29. Decision 28 COM 15B.11.pp81.

Although the Committee will challenge a country if an EIA is slow in coming,[291] and may even ask for copies of the EIA,[292] they generally do not appear to challenge the results of the EIA, unless it was flawed in its scope, such as with Russian EIA for possible oil accidents on a bordering Lithuanian WHC site.[293] The exception to this was with a planned open pit mine in the Rockies. Here, despite the fact that the EIA concluded the project only had limited and containable impact (and the Canadian government had subsequently agreed to it) the Committee called upon the Canadian government to reconsider the decision, with a view to seeking out alternative sites with less damaging effects.[294]

Article 3 of the Ramsar convention obliges the conservation of wetlands, when change is 'likely.' To work out whether change is likely, implicitly entails a degree of anticipation that requires a means of predicting effects. The Ramsar has dealt with this through both general rules for EIAs, as well as directions for them to be utilised by certain Parties with regard to some specifically threatened wetlands. It is the target of Ramsar that all members use EIAs for all wetland decisions in the new century.[295] To further this, in 2005 one of the adopted goals from the Kampala meeting, was for the Secretariat to have identified at least 50 Parties to have in place Strategic Environmental Assessments for policies, programmes and plans impacting upon wetlands by 2008.[296]

The general rule in this area was clearly articulated in 1980 when the Ramsar COP recommended that for Ramsar Parties (and development agencies)[297] involved in cases of large scale wetland transformation, 'not to make a decision until an assessment of all the values involved has been made'. In subsequent meetings, the Parties fleshed out what an EIA should consist of. Specifically, they should be participatory and trans-

291 UNESCO. (2003). 27th Session of the WHC. WHC-03/27.COM/24. Dec 10, 2003. 36.

292 UNESCO. (1999). 23rd Session of the WHC. WHC-99/CONF.209/22. Mar 22, 2000. 62. UNESCO. (2004). 28th Session of the WHC. WHC-04/28.COM/26. Oct 29. Decisions 28 COM 15B.1, B.7 & B28. Decision 29 COM 7B.5 (on Banc d'Arguin).

293 Decision 29 COM 7B.67.Rev.

294 UNESCO. (1997). 21st Session of the WHC. WHC-97/CONF.208/17. Feb 27, 1998. 21.

295 Resolution 7.27. The Convention's Work Plan 2000-02. (1999, San Jose). Annex. Work Plan.

296 See Resolution 9.8. Streamlining the Implementation of the Strategic Plan of the Convention 2003-2008. (Kampala, 2005). Strategy 1.2.

297 The Parties to the Ramsar have recommended that development agencies, both utilise EIAs for wetland projects before funding projects in their own work Recommendation 3.4. Responsibility of Development Agencies Towards Wetlands. (1987, Regina). Development agencies were also called upon to support funding EIAs, even when they are not involved in the projects themselves.

parent,[298] buttressed by rigorous and formal legal and policy procedures,[299] and supplementary to the CBD and CMS efforts in this field.[300]

The Ramsar practice of calling for EIAs with regard to specific wetlands of international importance dates back to 1971. The initial instance (in fact, the first resolution from the first meeting) was directed to some of the key Baltic states not to proceed with planned dams or industrial activities until appropriate research has demonstrated that no harmful effects would result.[301] Subsequent recommendations for assessments before works proceed were issued to the Ukraine,[302] Iceland,[303] Jordan (repeatedly),[304] Australia,[305] and Germany (and its neighbours sharing trans-boundary sites).[306] In addition, EIAs have been recommended, generically, for most forms of coastal development and intertidal areas.[307]

In a very similar manner, the Bern Convention has developed a strong utilisation of EIAs in its work. This practice, derived from the Convention itself,[308] has lead to calls for the utilisation of EIAs for particular developments related to particular species, such as new fish farms and fresh water mussels,[309] the introduction of non-native

---

298 Recommendation 6.2. Environmental Impact Assessment. (1996, Brisbane).

299 Resolution 7.16. Impact Assessment. (1999, San Jose).

300 Ibid. Resolution 8.9. Guidelines For Incorporating Biodiversity Related Issues into Environmental Impact Assessment Legislation Adopted by the Convention on Biological Diversity. (2002, Valencia). Resolution 7.12. Sites in the Ramsar List. (1999, San Jose).

301 Final Act of the Ramsar Conference. Annex II. Recommendations adopted by the International Conference on the Conservation of Wetlands and Waterfowl at Ramsar, Iran, 3 February 1971. Recommendation 1. Conservation of the Wadden Sea, north-western Europe.

302 Resolution 9.15. The Status of Sites on the Ramsar List of Wetlands of International Importance. (2005, Kampala). Paragraph 27.

303 The recommendation was for delaying the proposal to flood until the results of research permit a re-evaluation of resources allocation in this area. Final Act of the Ramsar Conference. Annex II. *Ibid.* Recommendation 2. Conservation of Thjorsarver, Iceland. Iceland subsequently agreed to an EIA on this plan.

304 Recommendation 3.8. The Azraq Oasis, Jordan. (1987, Regina). Recommendation 4.9.3. The Azraq Oasis, Jordan. (1990, Montreux). Recommendation 6.17.3. The Azraq Oasis, Jordan. (1996, Brisbane).

305 Recommendation 6.17.4. Australian Ramsar Sites. (1996, Brisbane).

306 Resolution 7.12. Sites in the Ramsar List. (1999, San Jose).

307 Recommendation 6.8. Strategic Planning in Coastal Zones. (1996, Brisbane). Resolution 7.21. Intertidal Wetlands. (1996, San Jose). Resolution 7.21. Intertidal Wetlands. (1996, San Jose). Recommendation 6.8. Strategic Planning in Coastal Zones. (1996, Brisbane).

308 All planning and development policies, including with the generation of pollution, of the Parties must have regard to the habitats they are obliged to protect, so as to avoid or minimise as far as possible any deterioration of such areas. Bern Convention. Article 3 (2) and 4 (2).

309 Recommendation No. 22. (1991). The Conservation of the Pearl Mussel and Other Freshwater Mussels.

species,[310] wind turbines,[311] and overhead electric power cables.[312] Specific countries and the impacts of their developments on particular species, or habitats, have also been drawn out, such as with, inter alia, Greek engineering works around an area of important bird habitat,[313] and for mining activities around key snake habitat.[314] Afforestation[315] and hydro development in Iceland[316] has also lead to calls for EIAs. The Bern Convention is also notable in this area, not only because of its calls for EIAs, but also for its insistence on what they should contain, and how they should be interpreted. For example, the Parties have been quick to point out when an EIA has been inadequate and in need of further input. This has been obvious with the State Party decisions (and subsequent criticisms from the Parties to the Bern Convention) on motorways through the Kresna Gorge in Bulgaria,[317] and national parks of Poland,[318] and the proposed navigable waterway through the Bystroe estuary (Danube Delta, Ukraine),[319] by which the Parties to the Bern Convention set down very clearly all the steps that an appropriate EIA should contain. In other instances, such as with Greece,

310 Recommendation No. 57. The Introduction of Organisms Belonging to Non-Native Species into the Environment. CoE. (1997). Report of the 17th Meeting of the Bern Convention. T-PVS (97). 63. Appendix 8.

311 Recommendation No. 109. (2004). On Minimizing Adverse Effects of Wind Power Generation on Wildlife. Report of the 24th Bern Meeting of the Bern Convention. T-PVS (2004). 16. Appendix 3.

312 Recommendation No. 109. (2004). On Minimizing Adverse Effects of Above Ground Electricity Transmission Facilities (power lines) on Birds. Report of the 24th Bern Meeting of the Bern Convention. T-PVS (2004). 16. Appendix 4.

313 Recommendation No. 83 (2000). The Conservation Status of Lake Vistonis and Lafra-Lafrouda Lagoon (Greece). Report of the 20th Meeting of the Bern Convention. T-PVS (2000). 75. Appendix 7.

314 Recommendation No. 84 (2000). The Conservation of Western Milos and in Particular the Milos Viper, Macrovipera Schweizeri. Report of the 20th Meeting of the Bern Convention. T-PVS (2000). 75. Appendix 8.

315 Recommendation No. 96. (2002). The Conservation of Natural Habitats and Wildlife, Especially Birds, in Afforestation of Lowland in Iceland. Report of the 22nd Meeting of the Bern Convention. T-PVS (2002). 13. Appendix 8.

316 Recommendation No. 112. (2004). On Hydroelectric Dams at Karahnjukar (Iceland). Report of the 24th Bern Meeting of the Bern Convention. T-PVS (2004). 16. Appendix 6.

317 Recommendation No. 98. (2002). The Project to Build a Motorway Through the Kresna Gorge (Bulgaria). Report of the 22nd Meeting of the Bern Convention. T-PVS (2002). 13. Appendix 10.

318 Recommendation No. 108 (2003). The Proposed Construction of the Via Baltica (Poland). Report of the 23rd Meeting of the Bern Convention. T-PVS (2003). 24. Appendix 12.

319 Recommendation No. 111. (2004). On the Proposed Navigable Waterway Through the Bystroe Estuary (Danube Delta, Ukraine). Report of the 24th Bern Meeting of the Bern Convention. T-PVS (2004). 16. Appendix 5.

they have called for a certain position to be adopted, if the EIA reaches certain conclusions.[320]

9 Conclusion

If areas are to have effective protection, they must be managed. In this regard, there are solid core management considerations which all protected area regimes should seek to reconcile. However, not all eight considerations require the same attention in each regime, and different regimes have developed some areas more than others. For example, with regard to management plans, the foremost regimes of note are the WHC and the Antarctic regime. With the WHC, failure of having adequate management plans may result in nominations or extensions being referred, and can be part and parcel for a site being listed in Danger. The Ramsar has developed a different approach, whereby targets, models, and guidelines have been utilised to spur countries to create management plans. The Antarctic regime has also issued models and guidelines, and in addition to having a process of identifying management plans which need to be updated, also instigated a rule that each management plan only has a five year lifetime.

A strong legal status, with clear boundaries, is essential for all protected area regimes, and listings are only possible if a site has both of these requirements. Once a site is listed, if the legal protections become questionable, most regimes are quick to issue recommendations to Parties to clarify the problems. The WHC is particularly strong in this approach, but only the Ramsar has instigated a systematic review of the laws covering all of their sites.

There is no specific rule on the necessary size of a protected area, beyond the fact that a site should be big enough to preserve the integrity of the area. Although MPAs and MAB sites tend to be larger than other sites, other regimes, depending on the area in focus can be equally big. The primary regime to have developed an active policy for changing the size of sites, via extensions or reductions, is the WHC. Buffer zones, between the core site, and the surrounding areas are increasingly recognised in most protected area regimes, as an essential part of any management process. Despite this recognition, only the WHC and, in particular, the MAB have developed clear rules for buffer zones. Ecological networks and corridors are also notable in the literature, but very few regimes have actually tried to implement these. The exception to this avoidance is with the Habitats Directive, and in particular, with the GEF.

---

320 Recommendation No. 38 (1992). The Conservation of the Missolong Wetlands in Greece. Recommendation No. 64. (1997). The Conservation of the Caretta caretta in Kaminia, Greece. Report of the 17th Meeting of the Bern Convention. T-PVS (97) 63. Appendix 17.

Having adequate staff and associated resources is recognised in all protected area regimes, and is a clearly iterated goal of the CBD with regard to protected areas. However, only the Ramsar, the GEF and the WHC have developed clear policies to facilitate this area, with the GEF and the WHC particularly notable for their targeted financial assistance.

Finally, EIAs have become an intrinsic part of the protected area framework, and the calls for their utilisation have become obvious, from the generic work of the CBD, right through to the specific regimes doing the inscriptions of each protected area. Some regimes, such as that of Antarctica, have developed clear rules on what must be examined. Other regimes, such as the WHC, Ramsar and the Bern have all created clear precedents calling for the utilisation of EIAs, and at times, have even called into existence the adequacy of the EIAs, if they fear an inadequate conclusion of the process.

Chapter VI

LOCAL POPULATIONS

1 The Paradigm Shift in Protected Areas

The idea of 'popular participation' as a necessary ingredient of sustainable development was iterated in a number of important international documents leading up to the 1992 Earth Summit,[1] and at Rio itself, where the Principle 10 of the Declaration emphasised that 'environmental issues are best handled with the participation of all concerned citizens, at the relevant levels'.[2] This type of perspective was reinforced by international commissions in the 1990s,[3] the World Summit for Social Development,[4] the 1996 Habitat Conference,[5] the 1998 Convention on Access to Information, Public Participation in Decision Making and Access to Justice in Environmental Matters[6] and finally the 2002 World Summit on Sustainable Development (WSSD). The WSSD was notable as it was agreed that, 'good governance within each country and at the international level is essential for sustainable development',[7] and popular participation is the foundation of good governance.

In addition to the theme of popular participation, an equally notable ideal of sustainable development, if the goal is to conserve biodiversity, is the preservation of knowledge, innovations and practices of indigenous and local communities embodying traditional

---

1 See for example, IUCN (1990), *World Conservation Strategy for the 1990s* (IUCN, Gland), 137, 138. 156-157.

2 The Rio Declaration on Environment and Development. (1992). UNCED Doc/A. CONF.151/5/Rev/1. See also chapters 3, 11 & 14 of Agenda 21 (1992). UNCED Doc A. CONF.151/4.

3 The Independent Commission on Population and Quality of Life was forthright in its realisation that, 'the starting-point of a new social contract will be the legal and pragmatic acknowledgment that sovereignty rests with the people: it is the people who must become the subjects of the enhancement of the quality of life'. Independent Commission on Population and Quality of Life: *Caring for the Future* (1996). (Oxford University Press, Oxford) 260-261. See also the Commission on Global Governance (1995), *Our Global Neighbourhood* (Oxford University Press, Oxford), 35-37, 65-67.

4 Principle 4. Copenhagen Declaration. Supra n. 21. See also paragraphs 1.8, 16 & 71 of the Program of Action of the World Summit for Social Development.

5 See paragraphs 115-118, 165 & 180-183 of the Habitat Agenda: Global Plan of Action: Strategies for Implementation.

6 1998 Convention on Access to Information, Public Participation in Decision Making and Access to Justice in Environmental Matters. 38 *International Legal Materials*. 517 (1999).

7 Plan of Implementation of the World Summit on Sustainable Development. (2002). A/CONF.199/L.1. Paragraph 4.

lifestyles relevant for the conservation and sustainable use of biological diversity. This ideal was iterated at the WSSD,[8] following the adoption of this principle in the CBD,[9] and its thematic work.[10]

The ideals of meaningful popular participation, the active involvement of indigenous and/or local peoples, and the conservation of biodiversity all coincide with the creation and management of protected areas.[11] Although the linkages between local people, biodiversity and protected areas are multifarious, the core idea is that protected areas created in isolation of local populations, in terms of their values, participation, or sharing of benefits, risk failure. Thus, as the Director General of UNESCO stated,

> [W]ithout the understanding and support of the public at large, without the respect and daily care of the local communities, which are the true custodians of World Heritage, no amount of funds or army of experts will suffice in protecting the sites.[12]

The justification for this is not merely philanthropic. It is also self interested, in that one of the most important (but by no means definitive) factors for the long-term success of a protected area, is having the buy-in of affected local populations.[13] This support is necessary because disenfranchised traditional, indigenous and/or local communities

---

8 See the WSSD Plan of Implementation, paragraph 44, sections J, L and H.

9 CBD. Article 8 (j). See also 10 (c).

10 For some of the primary decisions in this area, see Decision III/14. Implementation of Article 8(j). UNEP/CBD/COP/3/38.pp.90. Decision IV/9. Implementation of Article 8(j). UNEP/CBD/COP/4/27. pp.111. Decision V/16. Article 8(j) and Related Provisions. UNEP/CBD/COP/5/23.pp.139. Decision VI/10. Article 8(j) and Related Provisions. UNEP/CBD/COP/6/20.pp 151. Decision VII/16. Article 8(j) and Related Provisions. UNEP/CBD/COP/7/WG2/CRP3. pp. 25.

11 See Borrini-Feyerabend, G. (2004). *Indigenous and Local Communities and Protected Areas.* (IUCN, Gland).

12 UNESCO. (1999). 12th General Assembly of the WHC. WHC-99/CONF.206/7. Nov 8, 1999. 4. For further comments on this points, see also UNESCO. (1998). 22nd Session of the WHC. WHC-98/CONF.203/18. Jan 29, 1999. 10. UNESCO. (1996). 19th Session of the WHC. WHC-95/CONF.203/16. Jan 31, 1996. 63. UNESCO. (1993). 17th Session of WHC. WHC-93/CONF.002/14. Feb 4, 1993. 45. UNESCO. (1999). Second World Heritage Global Strategy Meeting for the Pacific Islands Region. August, 2000.

13 It is important to note that local and community support is not a lone guarantor of conservation success for all protected areas. Indeed, a number of protected areas which have tried to blend conservation and development have failed from a conservation point of view. Rangerson, J. (2005). 'Biodiversity Golden Rules Do Not Work.' *New Scientist.* Feb 5. 11. IUCN. (2002). 'Local Communities and Protected Areas.' *Parks.* 12(2): 190. Bruner, A. (2001). 'The Effectiveness of Parks in Protecting Tropical Biodiversity.' *Science.* 291: 125-128. Hackel, J. (1999). 'Community Conservation and the Future of Africa's Wildlife.' *Conservation Biology.* 13: 726-734. IUCN. (2001). 'ICDPs: Working With Parks and People.' Parks. 11(2): 1-60. Robinson, G. (2004). 'Parks, People and Pipelines'. *Conservation Biology.* 18(3): 607-608.

may actively work against protected areas which do not reflect their interests, or fail to deliver on the promises and/or expectations raised, when the site was given protected status. This problem has appeared within the WHC, where between 1986 and 2004, 4 natural sites reported to the Committee that they were being threatened due to problems with local communities. For example, when the collective forests of Yuhu village were incorporated into the Yulongxueshan nature reserve in northwest China, without the full consultation and meaningful involvement of local farmers, the farmers responded by cutting down trees they had previously managed sustainably.[14]

Other examples of failure include when the local peoples have been excluded from the protected site, or the site ends up creating costs for the local communities. Instances of such costs involve, inter alia, damage caused by non-human species within the protected area to their crops or livelihoods, and/or threats to them or their families. Alternately, the benefits of the site are not equitably shared. For example, in the mid 1990s, less than 6% of the tourist income generated at some key Costa Rican national parks, accrued to the local communities.[15]

Due to such problems, it has been commonly iterated that indigenous and/or local populations should directly relate to protected areas they are connected with, and meaningfully included and 'participate'[16] in all important decisions and outcomes. This

14 IUCN. (2004). *Speaking A Common Language.* (IUCN, Gland). 133.

15 Neumann, R. (1998). *Imposing Wilderness: Struggles Over Livelihood and Nature Preservation in Africa.* (University of California Press, Berkeley). Weladji, R. (2003). 'Conflict Between People and Protected Areas'. *Oryx* 37 (1): 72-79. Gillingham, S. (2003). 'People and Protected Areas: A Case Study of Local Perceptions of Wildlife, Crop Damage and Conflict'. *Oryx* 37(3): 316-325. Adams, W. (2001). 'If Community Conservation is the Answer in Africa, What is the Question ?' *Oryx* 35(3): 193-200. IUCN. (2002). *Sustainable Tourism in Protected Areas: Guidelines for Planning and Management.* (IUCN, Gland). 25.

16 The spectrum of what 'participate' is wide. The lowest level of participation is one where groups or individuals receive information about proposed actions but have no opportunities to change them. One step above is 'consultation,' whereby information is given and the views of those consulted are sought. The third step is 'deciding together', builds on the above two steps, with the relevant stakeholders being part of the final decision making process, within established boundaries of influence. 'Acting together' is where there is both a shared decision making process and shared responsibility for implementing decisions. 'Supporting independent community interests', is the highest level of participation. It is where communities become responsible for setting their own agendas and implementing the decisions which are taken. The role of experts and other agents or investors is to support the community with information and expertise and perhaps resources to help them make informed decisions. This represents a completely 'bottom up' approach to conservation. IUCN. (2003). *Guidelines for Management Planning of Protected Areas.* (IUCN, Gland). 57-61.

is especially so in terms of access and benefit sharing, related to protected areas.[17] This theme, which has become increasingly loud (especially on the indigenous peoples' question)[18] from the World Parks Congresses, is a relatively new development.[19] It is possible to suggest there has been a substantive change in this area, with the importance of local values gaining a currency in the new century that was practically unthinkable in the earlier one. Such changes are evidenced by the large differences on this question between the African Conventions of 1968[20] and 2003.[21] To help facilitate such changes, important classification schemes, such as that advocated by the IUCN, seeking to involve indigenous peoples in practically every protected area classification

---

17 Secretariat of the CBD. (2004). *Biodiversity Issues for Consideration in the Planning, Establishment and Management of Protected Area Sites and Management.* (CBD Technical Series No 15). 94-111, 148-155.. Kelleher, G. (ed). *Guidelines for Marine Protected Areas (IUCN, Gland, 1999).* 21-37.

18 Brosius, P. (2004). 'Indigenous Peoples and Protected Areas'. *Conservation Biology.* 18(3) 609-612.

19 This was most notable at the Fifth Congress in 2003. See Recommendation 5.27: Mobile Indigenous Peoples and Conservation. Recommendation 5.13. Cultural and Spiritual Values of Protected Areas. Recommendation 5.17. Recognising and Supporting a Diversity of Governance Types for Protected Areas. Recommendation 5.24. Indigenous Peoples and Protected Areas. Brosius, P. (2004). 'Indigenous Peoples and Protected Areas'. *Conservation Biology.* 18(3) 609-612. For earlier debates on these points at the Congresses, see Dasman, R. (1984). 'The Relationship Between Protected Areas and Indigenous Peoples.' In McNeely, J. (ed). *National Parks, Conservation and Development.* (Smithsonian, Washington). 667-671. Recommendation 9. Protected Areas and Traditional Societies. Recommendations of the World National Parks Congress. Also in McNeely, *ibid.* 765.

20 The 1968 Convention placed an emphasis on the best interests of the people, whilst seeking to reconcile customary rights. African Convention (1968). Preamble, Articles II. and XI.

21 The 2003 African Convention emphasised the active participation by the local communities, protection, and authorised utilisation of indigenous and/or traditional knowledge, and access and benefit sharing for these peoples) 2003 African Convention. Article XVII (1) to (3); Article 9 (2) (h) and (j); and Article XII. (3).

have been developed.[22] Collectively, the objective in this area is now best summed up by the CBD goal, which after strong debate,[23] aimed for,

> Full and effective participation by 2008, of indigenous and local communities, in full respect of their rights and recognition of their responsibilities, consistent with national law and applicable international obligations, and the participation of relevant stakeholders, in the management of existing, and the establishment and management of new protected areas. …The establishment, management and monitoring of protected areas should take place with the full and effective participation of, and full respect for the rights of, indigenous and local communities consistent with national law and applicable international obligations.[24]

Moreover, protected areas should be established that, 'benefit indigenous and local communities' in accordance with the objectives of the CBD.[25] Annex II of the protected area agenda under the CBD, added significantly to these goals, calling for multiple aspects of governance, participation, equity and benefit sharing to be facilitated by the establishments of mechanisms for equitable sharing by 2008. Finally, any resettlement due to the need to create or maintain protected areas should only be done with prior informed consent, and in accordance with relevant domestic and international law.[26]

2 Promotion of the Local/Traditional/Indigenous Populations

The importance of active, and ecologically sustainable, participation of local, traditional, and/or indigenous peoples in protected area management is clear within MPA related

---

22 Of all the IUCN protected area categories, only one (strict nature reserves) is designed to be significantly free of direct human intervention and capable of remaining as such. All the other categories, including wilderness Areas, should permit the involvement of indigenous peoples. However, the extent of the involvement is dependent on the category. Thus, whilst Wilderness Areas should only have low-density, traditional, non-permanent, indigenous populations, national Parks (the most common protected area to encompass indigenous peoples) may include indigenous peoples practicing low-impact, sustainable subsistence resource use (as in, no industrial agriculture or other heavy use land conversions or settlement building or commercial exploitation of resources). Natural monuments should explicitly recognizes heritage significance to indigenous peoples, and species focused approaches should deliver benefits to indigenous populations practicing traditional management techniques. Multiple use areas have clear benefits for both local and indigenous populations. IUCN. (2004). *Speaking A Common Language.* (IUCN, Gland). 135, 136 and 140.

23 See in particular, the amount of square brackets around Recommendation IX/4. Protected Areas. UNEP/CBD/COP/7/4.pp.5.

24 CBD. Decision VII/28. Protected Areas. Paragraph 22 and Annex. Goal 2.2. For similar goals with regards to MPAs, see CBD. Decision VII/5 Marine and Coastal Biological Diversity. Section 21.

25 CBD. Decision VII/28. Protected Areas. Annex. 1.1.7.

26 Ibid. Annex. See sections 2.1.2; 2.1.3; 2.1.4; 2.1.5; 2.1.6; 2.2.2; 2.2.4; 2.2.5; 3.2; 3.2.2.

instruments, including, inter-alia, the OSPAR regime,[27] the ICRI,[28] the Mediterranean, Caribbean,[29] and East African Protocols. The latter is notable with its provision that,

> The Contracting Parties shall, in promulgating protective measures, take into account the traditional activities of their local populations in the areas to be protected. To the fullest extent possible, no exemption which is allowed for this reason shall be such as,
> (a). To endanger the maintenance of the ecosystem protected under the terms of the present Protocol or the biological processes contributing to the maintenance of those ecosystems.
> (b). To cause either the extinction of, or any substantial reduction in, the number of individuals making up the species of animal and plant populations within the protected ecosystems, or any ecologically connected species or populations, particularly migratory, endemic, rare, depleted, threatened or endangered species.'[30]

Similar objectives are repeated within the Arctic regime,[31] the Habitats Directive,[32] and even the GEF. The GEF is particularly interesting in this setting, as it has actively facilitated the involvement of local communities. For example, by 2005, 6 million (USD) had been invested in participatory planning processes involving local and national stakeholders in more than 100 community based protected area initiatives.[33] It also has 137 projects, focused on engaging the public (and NGO involvement in particular), covering 751 protected areas,[34] as well as supporting the involvement of indigenous communities in protected areas, from traditional knowledge, to modern management initiatives.[35] In addition to the above regimes, the MAB, Ramsar and the WHC, stand out due to their detailed work on the local participation question.

With regard to the MAB, the importance of widespread consultation before the establishment of protected areas was first articulated at the 1968 UNESCO conference on the Use and Conservation of the Biosphere.[36] The MAB went on to give emphasis to the

---

27 OSPAR Recommendation 2003/3 on a Network of Marine Protected Areas. Section 3. Management of the MPAs of the OSPAR Network. Appendix 2 Practical criteria/considerations. Section 3.Degree of acceptance.

28 See Principle 1 of the ICRI (1995) Framework for Action.

29 Mediterranean Protocol. Articles 7 and 18. See also Annex I.B. Caribbean Protocol. Articles 4 (2) and 14.

30 Protocol Concerning Protected Areas of Wild Fauna and Flora in the Eastern African Region. Reprinted in Austen, A. (ed). *Basic Legal Document on International Animal Welfare and Wildlife Conservation* (Kluwer, London). Article 12.

31 See CAFF. (1996). The Circumpolar Protected Area Network: Principles and Guidelines. (CAFF Habitat Conservation Report, No 4). Principles 10 and 12.

32 Habitats Directive. Article 2 (3).

33 GEF. (2005). *Making a Visible Difference in Our World.* (GEF, Washington). 7. GEF. (2005). People and Protected Areas. (GEF, Washington). 1.

34 GEF. (2005). *Ibid.* (GEF, Washington). 17.

35 *Ibid.* 18.

36 UNESCO. (1968). *Use and Conservation of the Biosphere.* (UNESCO, Paris). 223.

importance of substantive participation of local communities in biosphere reserves,[37] especially after its revamp in the 1990s.[38] To help facilitate this involvement, the MAB Secretariat has helped members devise guidelines for identifying relevant stakeholders,[39] whilst praising MAB site nominations with a 'high democratic process'.[40] In other instances, where the site has been approved, but 'additional engagement and involvement with local people and communities' is necessary, the Committee has been quick to make such recommendations.[41] Conversely, the MAB Bureau has rejected some new nominations, and citicised sites revisited in their periodic reviews, if they have inadequate local or public involvement. In such instances the Parties have been urged to change their approaches and actively involve local communities.[42] The MAB has even recommended the formation of biosphere reserve committees which include all key stakeholders.[43] Finally, the 1990s, the value of the participation of indigenous peoples has been parti-

37 See UNESCO. (ed). *Conservation, Science and Society: The 1983 Biosphere Reserve Conference in Minsk.* (UNESCO, UNEP). 534-610

38 The Statutory Framework of the World Network of Biosphere Reserves. Article 4 (6). Seville Strategy. Objective II.1, II.2. UNESCO. (1998). *Biosphere Reserves: Myth or Reality?.* (UNESCO, Paris). 48. Seville + 5 Recommendations. Recommendations Number 4 and 9.

39 UNESCO. (2001). MAB ICC Bureau Meeting. SC/-01/CONF.211/13. Apr 10. 16.

40 Entlebuch in Switzerland. UNESCO. (2001). ICC Bureau Meeting. SCI/-01/CONF.217/8. Dec 12, 2. 14.

41 Jebal Samhan, Oman. UNESCO. (2006). MAB ICC. 19th Session. SC-06/CONF.202/16. Nov 28. 26.

42 Southwest Nova in Canada. UNESCO. (2001). ICC Bureau Meeting. SCI/-01/CONF.217/8. Dec 12, 2. 12. Far East Marine Reserve in Russia. UNESCO. (2003). ICC Bureau Meeting. SC/-03/CONF.217/14. July 30. 11. Boatianman in China. UNESCO. (2001). ICC Bureau Meeting. SCI/-01/CONF.217/8. Dec 12, 2. 12. Nanda Devi in India. UNESCO. (2003). ICC Bureau Meeting. SC/-03/CONF.217/14. July 30. 14. Chrea in Algeria. UNESCO. (2002). ICC Bureau Meeting. SC-02/CONF.210/10. 8. Far East Marine in Russia. UNESCO. (2003). ICC Bureau Meeting. SC-02/CONF.210/10. Jan 7. 15. Barkindji in Australia. UNESCO. (2004). 18th Session of the ICC Bureau Meeting. SC-04/CONF.204/14. Jan 11. 12. Kamsky, in Russia. UNESCO. (2003). ICC Bureau Meeting. SC/-03/CONF.217/14. July 30. 15. Cabo de Hornos in Chile. UNESCO. (2004). 18th Session of the ICC Bureau Meeting. SC-04/CONF.204/14. Jan 11. 13. Apatin Monostor, Yugoslavia. UNESCO. (2001). ICC Bureau Meeting. SCI/-01/CONF.217/8. Dec 12. 16. Cat Ba in Vietnam. UNESCO. (2003). ICC Bureau Meeting. SC-02/CONF.210/10. Jan 7. 17. Cinturon Andino in Columbia. UNESCO. (2001). ICC Bureau Meeting. SCI/-01/CONF.217/8. Dec 12. 19. El Kala in Algeria, Niagara in Canada. UNESCO. (2003). ICC Bureau Meeting. SC-02/CONF.210/10. Jan 7. 17. Nyika-Vwaza in Malawi. MAB. (2000). 16th Session of the ICC Bureau. SC-00/CONF.208/13. 22.

43 Sumaco Biosphere Reserve in Ecuador, and Mulanje in Malawi. MAB. (2000). 16th Session of the ICC Bureau. SC-00/CONF.208/13. 21.

cularly highlighted,[44] welcomed and encouraged with regard to specific MAB site nominations.[45]

A pro-public participation approach is also evident with the Parties to the Ramsar Convention. The Ramsar Parties place a premium on the involvement of local communities, through what it currently identified as 'Participatory Environmental Management'.[46] This premium is, in part, due to an earlier practice that took local and/or indigenous involvement for granted. To rectify this problem, the Ramsar has come to emphasise stakeholder involvement, including local (and national)[47] communities and indigenous people, recognising good examples of where this has been achieved, such as with the joint management with Aboriginal owners in the custodianship and management of Australia's Kakadu Ramsar site.[48] Ramsar has also sought to assist State practice with its Guidelines for Management.[49] Specifically, the Guidelines have called upon all Parties,

> [T]o make specific efforts to encourage active and informed participation of local and indigenous people...and their direct involvement, through appropriate mechanisms, in wetland management... with a view to reflecting their needs and values, traditional and other knowledge and practices in national wetland policies and programmes.[50]

---

44 Seville Strategy. Objective 1.2. Seville + 5 Recommendations. Recommendation Number 4. For the earlier lack of focus on indigenous peoples in MAB reserves, See Nietschmann, B. (1983). 'Biosphere Reserves and Traditional Societies'. In UNESCO. (ed). *Conservation, Science and Society: The 1983 Biosphere Reserve Conference in Minsk.* (UNESCO, UNEP). 499-508.

45 Terras do Minos. UNESCO. (2003). ICC Bureau Meeting. SC-02/CONF.210/10. Jan 7. 13. Uluru in Australia. UNESCO. (2003). ICC Bureau Meeting. SC/-03/CONF.217/14. July 30. 18. Croajingalong in Australia. UNESCO. (2003). ICC Bureau Meeting. SC/-03/CONF.217/14. July 30. 17. Riding Mountain in Canada. UNESCO. (2001). ICC Bureau Meeting. SCI/-01/ CONF.217/8. Dec 12. 18. UNESCO. (2001). ICC Bureau Meeting. SCI/-01/CONF.217/8. Dec 12. 18. UNESCO. (2002). *Biosphere Reserves: Special Places for People and Nature.* (UNESCO, Paris). 48-55.

46 Resolution 8.36. Participatory Environmental Management (PEM) As A Tool for Management and Wise Use of Wetlands. (2002, Valencia). Note that the theme of participation is repeated in numerous Ramsar areas. Resolution 5.6. Wise Use of Wetlands (1993, Kushiro). Resolution 8.14. New Guidelines for Management Planning for Ramsar Sites and Other Wetlands. (2002, San Jose). Annex. Resolution 8.25. The Ramsar Strategic Plan. (2002, Valencia). Annex. Operational Objective 6. Resolution 8.39. High Andean Wetlands as Strategic Resources. (2002, Valencia). Resolution VI:14. The Ramsar 25th Anniversary Statement and the Strategic Plan. (1996, Brisbane).

47 As of the end of 2002, 88 Parties had national wetland committees. Resolution 8.25. The Ramsar Strategic Plan. (2002, Valencia). Annex. I.9.

48 Recommendation 6.17.4. Australian Ramsar Sites. (1996, Brisbane).

49 Resolution 8.14. New Guidelines for Management Planning for Ramsar Sites and Other Wetlands. (2002, San Jose). Annex.

50 Recommendation 6.3. Involving Local and Indigenous People. (1996, Brisbane).

The Ramsar Parties have also adopted the Guidelines for Establishing and Strengthening Local Communities and Indigenous Peoples Participation in Management of Wetlands.[51] The goal of these Guidelines is to encourage active and informed participation, and the assumption of responsibility, by local communities and people in the management of Ramsar listed sites and other wetlands at the local, watershed and national levels. 'Extensive' consultation and 'active' engagement, within transparent mechanisms that build trust, flexibility, continuity, capacity building and incentive measures are all clear goals.[52]

The final convention of note in this area is the WHC. The WHC, recognises that its Parties 'shall' (as far as possible and appropriate for each country), inter alia, 'adopt a general policy which aims to give the cultural and natural heritage a function in the life of the community'.[53] The foremost way that this goal has been furthered has been with the facilitation of local participation with WHC sites. This facilitation has become increasingly common, as it has become apparent, that local populations are usually surrounding, or within, a large number of WHC natural sites.[54] Notable indigenous/traditional/local groups exist within the WHC sites of, inter alia, Lapland, Banc d'Arguin in Mauritania, Air and Tenere reserve in Niger, Lake Turkana national park in Kenya, the Serengeti and Ngorongoro in Tanzania.[55] In many instances, these populations are deemed to be consistent with the WHC objectives.[56] Accordingly, the Committee has emphasized the importance of the sovereign authorities engaging and consulting with local peoples wherever appropriate,[57] and seeking an equitable sharing of benefits, derived from the WHC sites, where possible.[58] In some instances, such as with the Virunga in the Democratic Republic of the Congo, the Committee has urged, that the State Party 'develop a strategy to share any profits, such as from tourism related to gorillas, with the local communities, in order to improve relations'.[59]

---

51 Resolution 7.8. Local Communities and Indigenous People. (1999, San Jose).

52 *Ibid.* Annex. Guidelines for establishing and strengthening local communities' and indigenous people's participation in the management of wetlands.

53 WHC. Article 5 (a).

54 Pressouyre, L. (1992). *The World Heritage Convention, Twenty Years Later.* (UNESCO, Paris). 14-15, 22.

55 Cattaneo, M & Trifoni, J. (2003). *The World Heritage Sites of UNESCO: Nature Sanctuaries* (WhiteStar, Vercelli). 16, 66, 70, 80, 93, 100-101.

56 UNESCO. (2003). 6th Extra-ordinary Session of the WHC. WHC-03/6. EXT.COM/8. Paris, May 27, 2003. 9.

57 UNESCO. (1995). 18th Session of the WHC. WHC-94/CONF.003/16. Jan 31. 1995. 42.

58 UNESOC. (2005). Assessment and Conclusion of the Kazan Meeting. WHC-05/29. COM/9. Section 19 (g) and 20 (c).

59 See Decision 30 COM 7A.7.

Within the discussions about community involvement, the issue of local indigenous communities within WHC sites has been particularly notable.[60] These discussions have ranged from the names of the sites,[61] through to the direct management of the sites. One general theme in this area is that the Committee has commonly directed State Parties to attempt to create strong relationships with the local indigenous communities. The Committee has also been (generally) sympathetic to hearing concerns from indigenous communities involved with WHC sites in New Zealand,[62] Honduras[63] and Venezuela.[64]

In some instances, the WHC Committee has recommended direct action for the benefit of the indigenous communities, such as with calling for clearer arrangements for the governance of WH areas in terms of making the sites management plan much more accommodating of the needs of the resident indigenous community, such as with Purnululu park in Australia.[65] This recommendation, to clearly engage the indigenous community, had earlier been reflected at the Kakadu National Park and the debate over uranium mining. Although the mining was found to not cause an overt detrimental impact upon the natural heritage, it was repeatedly emphasized by the Committee that meaningful dialogue and continuing participation and negotiation, between the interested groups, especially the traditional aboriginal owners of the area, who had serious cultural concerns about the project, was essential.[66] A similar approach was adopted with

---

60 The WH Global Strategy Meeting in the Pacific, emphasized the importance of partnerships with the local communities and traditional custodians. UNESCO. (1997). *Global Strategy Meeting: Identification of World Heritage Properties in the Pacific.* (Suva, 1997).

61 Sometimes this has been at the recommendation of the Committee, such as with Australia's Fraser Island. (1992). 16th Session of the WHC. WHC-92/CONF.002/12. Dec 14, 1992. 30. It has become more commonly, an action undertaken by States. In the new century, changes of name were so common they were a standing agenda item. UNESCO. (2001). 24th Session of the WHC. WHC-2000/CONF.204/21. Feb 16, 2001. 59.

62 Reports from members of the 'local Maori community' about the use of 1080 poison to fight possums was brought to the attention of the Committee, which noted the issue but did not pass comment. UNESCO. (1996). 19th Session of the WHC. WHC-95/CONF.203/16. Jan 31, 1996. 15. Concern about logging in an area adjacent to the Te Wahiponamu National Park in NZ, by the Maori owners, was noted, but not seen as a serious concern. UNESCO. (1995). 18th Session of the WHC. WHC-94/CONF.003/16. Jan 31. 1995. 21.

63 Concern over a planned hydro development. UNESCO. (1998). 22nd Session of the WHC. WHC-98/CONF.203/18. Jan 29, 1999. 23.

64 Canaima National Park and threats to the park, including, inter alia, transmission lines. UNESCO. (1998). 22nd Session of the WHC. WHC-98/CONF.208/18. Jan 29, 1998. 37.

65 They specifically called upon the State to conduct appraisals of ethnographic, sociological and oral recordings or intangible and tangible cultural traditions. UNESCO. (2003). 27th Session of the WHC. WHC-03/27.COM/24. Dec 10. 103-05. Decision 29 COM 7B.11.

66 UNESCO. (2001). 24th Session of the WHC. WHC-2000/CONF.204/21. Feb 16, 2001. 45. UNESCO. (2002). 26th Session of the WHC. WHC-02/CONF.202/25. Aug 1, 2002. 39. UNESCO. (2003). 27th Session of the WHC. WHC-03/27.COM/24. Dec 10, 2003. 45-46. UNESCO. (1998). 22nd Session of the WHC. WHC-98/CONF.208/18. Jan 29, 1998. 43.

concerns over the indigenous peoples and Manu National Park in Peru,[67] and with the Masai in the Ngorongoro Conservation Area in Tanzania. In this later instance, the Committee emphasized the need for a management regime which shared tourist revenues, which will in turn ensure conservation of the natural environment and the welfare of the Masai people.[68]

Despite the above precedents, the Committee is not always sympathetic to indigenous peoples or their management practices. A hint of this arose with the Everglades and the Miccosukee Tribe, which was given permission by the Government of the United States to remain in the site and develop it accordingly. Although similar situations had been noted without comment in other WHC sites, such as Tatshenshini Alsek Wilderness Park in Canada,[69] the Everglades instance provoked a response by the Committee that future development from these peoples represented a possible threat in terms of the restoration of water flows, which were considered to be an essential measure for the successful restoration of into the Everglades ecosystem.[70] In other instances, such as with the East Rennell of the Solomons, a strong debate was held on the suitability of customary management practices. Although the Committee eventually endorsed the customary management practices, Thailand disassociated itself from the decision as they believed customary practices did not necessarily lead to adequate protection of the site.[71]

Most commonly, the issue of meaningful indigenous involvement in a WHC site is simply omitted. For example, in 2005 when Japan listed Shiretoko, despite being clearly noted as containing areas of utmost importance to the indigenous Ainu peoples, consideration of their involvement in the management of the site was largely absent from discussion on the floor (and the inscription notes), as the other values of the site submerged such considerations.[72] A similar situation occurred with the Mexican Islands of the Gulf of California, where the Seri involvement with a sacred site, although noted, was subsumed beneath other inscription values.[73]

Most substantively, recommendations for a permanent body to advise on indigenous issues have been roundly rejected by the Committee of the WHC. This process began in the year 2000 when representatives from Australia, Canada, New Zealand and the South Pacific attended a conference on Indigenous Peoples and World Heritage. These

Anon. (2005). 'Australian Mining Deal'. New Scientist. March 5.5.

67 UNESCO. (1987). 11th Session of the WHC. CC-87/CONF.005/9. Jan 20, 1988. pp 6.

68 UNESCO. (1995). 18th Session of the WHC. WHC-94/CONF.003/16. Jan 31. 1995. 21.

69 UNESCO. (1995). 18th Session of the WHC. WHC-94/CONF.003/16. Jan 31. 1995. 44.

70 UNESCO. (1998). 22nd Session of the WHC. WHC-98/CONF.203/18. Jan 29, 1999. 26.

71 Ibid. 60.

72 Decision 29 COM. 8B6. 264 For discussion of the Ainu in this site, see the IUCN evaluations WHC-05/29.COM/INF.8B.2. 23, 31.

73 IUCN. IUCN Evaluation of Nominations. WHC-05/29.COM/INF.8B.2. 55, 59.

representatives later made a presentation to the Committee, pleading for protection of indigenous knowledge systems, values and traditions in WHC areas, asserting that these sites were often 'ancestral lands' that had to be treated with respect, and the involvement and negotiation with the traditional owners was emphasized. The Representatives were particularly concerned with,

> The lack of involvement of indigenous peoples in the development and implementation of laws, policies and plans for the protection of their holistic knowledge, traditions and cultural values, which apply to their ancestral lands within or comprising sites now designated as World Heritage sites.[74]

The representatives put forward four recommendations, with a particular emphasis upon the creation of a World Heritage Indigenous Council of Experts, to supplement the existing advisory bodies. The objective of the Council was to provide advice on effective and efficient consultation, involvement and negotiation in the development, implementation and management of laws, policies and plans with all matters related to indigenous peoples and WHC sites.[75] Although the Committee recognized that, 'indigenous peoples have a special role with respect to certain WHC properties and that a network could provide a positive forum for an exchange of information' the Committee recommended that this be done on the initiative of State Parties, and the proposal, for a new consultative body on indigenous issues, was not accepted. The Committee refused further funding for meetings on the topic.[76]

Despite these earlier knock-backs on the indigenous question, subsequent Committee members, such as New Zealand, have sought to reinvigorate the debate on this issue. Accordingly, in 2006 when the Committee called for the creation of two compendiums to help elaborate what was meant by 'outstanding universal value', part of the criteria for investigation was examination of 'the utilization of, or obvious omission of the values of minorities, indigenous and/or local peoples'.[77]

---

74 UNESCO. (2001). Report of the World Heritage Indigenous Peoples Council of Experts. WHC-2001/CONF.205/WEB.3. June 14, 2001. 2.

75 UNESCO. (2000). 24th Session of the WHC. WHC-2000/CONF.204/21. Feb 16, 2001. 5. UNESCO. (2001). Report of the World Heritage Indigenous Peoples Council of Experts. WHC-2001/CONF.205/WEB.3. June 14, 2001. 3.

76 The exact reasons for the refusal were difficult to gauge (as they were not specifically recorded) although some members had clear difficulties with any possible definition of indigenous peoples and the relevance of such a distinction in different regions of the world. UNESCO. (2001). 25th Session of the WHC. WHC-01/CONF.208/24. Feb 8, 2002. 105-106.

77 See Decision 30 COM 9. Paragraph 7 (e).

3 On-the-Ground Non-Governmental Organisations

A clear subset of the popular participation issue relates to non-governmental organizations (NGOs) which have 'grass roots'. That is, NGOs who get actively involved with local topics and 'on-the-ground' work in protected areas. In these instances, the contributions of NGOs working in particular areas range from small to large. The smallest contributions may be volunteers replanting sections of a site. The largest contributions may be paying 35 million (USD) for the Palmyra atoll – one of the world's richest coral reef systems – and then turning it into a protected area.[78]

The way that the various regimes facilitate grass-roots NGOs differs with each instrument. One of the more interesting processes involves the Antarctic regime, which, in part due to the unique situation that the Consultative Parties govern NGO activities on the continent of Antarctica. In particular, the Consultative Parties actively control NGO access to the region via overseeing how the NGOs are operating,[79] insistence upon adequate insurance coverage for their possible recovery from Antarctica,[80] and adherence to a broad set of guidelines deemed necessary to protect the Antarctic environment.[81]

Other regimes, such as the WHC, MAB and Ramsar have a much more facilitative approach. For example, with the WHC, in addition to the work of its Partner organizations[82] the WHC has lavished praise on a number of NGOS for their strong, on the ground work in a number of WHC natural sites,[83] especially those in danger.[84] Accordingly, the Director General of the WHC has called upon Parties to, 'establish partnerships with NGOs and grassroots organizations' in order to meet the challenge of protecting

78 Anon. (2000). 'Richest of Reefs.' *New Scientist.* May 13. 17.

79 All operations must be run through a single contact point with each Consultative party, and this information should be shared between parties. Final Report of the XXVII ATCM. Cape Town. 2004. Resolution 3. Tourism and NGO Activities: Enhanced Cooperation Amongst Parties. 226.

80 Final Report of the XXVII ATCM. Cape Town. 2004. Measure 4. Insurance and Contingency Planning for Tourism and NGO Activity in the Antarctic Treaty Area. 167.

81 Final Report of the XXVII ATCM. Cape Town. 2004. Resolution 4. Guidelines on Contingency Planning, Insurance and Other Matters for Tourist and Other Non-Governmental Activities in the Antarctic Treaty Area. 227-229.

82 See chapter IX.

83 Especially Greenpeace and the WWF. UNESCO. (1996). 19th Session of the WHC. WHC-95/CONF.203/16. Jan 31, 1996.35. UNESCO. (1996). 20th Session of the WHC. WHC-96/CONF.201/21. Mar 10, 1997. 15, 17. UNESCO. (1997). 21st Session of the WHC. WHC-97/CONF.208/17. Feb 27, 1998. 11, 13. UNESCO. (1998). 22nd Session of the WHC. WHC-98/CONF.208/18. Jan 29, 1998. 60. UNESCO. (2001). 25th Session of the WHC. WHC-01/CONF.208/24. Feb 8, 2002. 36. UNESCO. (2003). 27th Session of the WHC. WHC-03/27.COM/24. Dec 10. 99.

84 UNESCO. (2002). 26th Session of the WHC. WHC-02/CONF.202/25. Aug 1, 2002. 19.

world heritage.[85] In some instances, this was furthered with (repeated)[86] directives to specifically include NGOs in national processes, such as with formal NGO representation on the independent monitoring committee with the Kakadu uranium project.[87]

In addition, a less targeted, but still clearly supportive initiative of the WHC to enhance relationships with, inter alia, NGOs, began to emerge early in the new century,[88] before being formally unveiled in 2002 as the Partnerships for Conservation Initiative (PACT).[89] The PACT was linked to performance indicators, such as increasing the numbers of NGOs involved in WHC work, and increasing the funds generated by them. Within the PACT, a large and diverse number of initiatives have been concluded, to the appreciation of the Committee, with regards to conservation, capacity building and communication.[90] Support for this initiative was reiterated in 2005.[91]

The Ramsar Parties have also been direct in encouraging the, 'strong support ... to the development and functioning of national and international NGOs that aim for the conservation and wise use of wetlands'. In particular, consultation, provision with relevant information and opportunity to contribute to national policies has been consistently urged.[92] Parties have been encouraged to include NGOs in National Committees[93] and other less formal domestic arrangements, such as publicity of the Convention and its goals.[94] To assist this process, the 7th COP adopted the target for enhanced NGO involvement within the Ramsar of NGO involvement in at least 100 parties by 2002.[95]

---

85 UNESCO. (1992). 16th Session of the WHC. WHC-92/CONF.002/12. Dec 14, 1992. 4.

86 UNESCO. (2004). 28th Session of the WHC. WHC-04/28.COM/26. Oct 29. Decision 28 COM 15B.35.pp95.

87 UNESCO. (2001). 25th Session of the WHC. WHC-01/CONF.208/24. Feb 8, 2002. 54. This recommendation was followed, and reemphasised in future years. See Decision 29 COM 7B.30.

88 UNESCO. (2001). 25th Session of the WHC. WHC-01/CONF.208/24. Feb 8, 2002. 20.

89 UNESCO. (2002). 26th Session of the WHC. WHC-02/CONF.202/25. Aug 1, 2002.15. The PACT was previously known as the Partnership Initiative (WHPI).

90 UNESCO. (2004). 7th Extra-Ordinary Session of the WHC. WHC-04/7 EXT.COM/12. Oct 25 & Decision 7 EXT.COM 12.

91 Decision 29 COM 13.

92 Recommendation 5.6. The Role of Non Governmental Organisations in the Ramsar Convention. (1993, Kushiro).

93 Recommendation 5.7. National Committees. (1993, Kushiro).

94 Recommendation 6.12. Private and Public Funded Activities. (1996, Brisbane). Resolution 6.21. Assessment and Reporting on the Status of Wetlands. (1996, Brisbane).

95 Resolution 7.27. The Convention's Work Plan 2000-02. (1999, San Jose). Annex. Work Plan.

The Bern Convention has also sought to promote community and NGOs participation in their work.[96] The 'catalytic role' played by NGOs, has been highlighted with the implementation and follow up of Species Action Plans,'[97] as well as areas of general concern, such as with wind-turbines.[98] NGO involvement has also been recommended, with identified Bern concerns that involve Bern sites in Greece,[99] Portugal,[100] Bulgaria[101] and Poland.[102]

4 Conclusion

Since the early 1990s, there has been a paradigm shift in the way that public participation has been viewed. What was once seen as a subsidiary issue has, in international environmental law, moved to the centre stage. This shift is particularly noticeable with

---

96 The role of NGOs in the case-files system is often decisive. Frequently, it is often only via these organisations that it is possible to gauge how provisions of the convention are being applied in specific cases and indeed, the majority of cases which have led to the opening of files have been notified by national or international NGOs. Such organisations, carrying out their own on-the-spot investigations are a key source of information for processing files. They also often play a major role in informing public opinion (awareness-raising campaigns) which in many cases has led to a de facto resolution to the problem, and ensured that the Standing Committee's recommendations are applied through constant pressure on the competent authorities.

97 As specifically noted with Birdlife International and globally threatened birds in Europe. Recommendation No. 59. The Drafting and Implementation of Action Plans of Wild Fauna Species. CoE. (1997). Report of the 17th Meeting of the Bern Convention. T-PVS (97). 63. Appendix 10. Section 6. Recommendation No. 60. (1997). The Implementation of the Action Plans for Globally Threatened Birds in Europe. Report of the 17th Meeting of the Bern Convention. T-PVS (97) 63. Appendix 11. Terms of Reference for the Group of Experts on Bird Conservation. Report of the 17th Meeting of the Bern Convention. T-PVS (97) 63. Appendix 14.

98 Recommendation No. 109. (2004). On Minimizing Adverse Effects of Wind Power Generation on Wildlife. Report of the 24th Bern Meeting of the Bern Convention. T-PVS (2004). 16. Appendix 3.

99 Recommendation No. 38 (1992). The Conservation of the Missolong Wetlands in Greece. Recommendation No. 84 (2000). The Conservation of Western Milos and in Particular the Milos Viper, Macrovipera Schweizeri. Report of the 20th Meeting of the Bern Convention. T-PVS (2000). 75. Appendix 8. Recommendation No. 64. (1997). The Conservation of the Caretta caretta in Kaminia, Greece. Report of the 17th Meeting of the Bern Convention. T-PVS (97) 63. Appendix 17.

100 Recommendation No. 107. The Odelouca Dam (Portugal). Report of the 23rd Meeting of the Bern Convention. T-PVS. (2003). 24. Appendix 11.

101 Recommendation No. 98. (2002). The Project to Build a Motorway Through the Kresna Gorge (Bulgaria). Report of the 22nd Meeting of the Bern Convention. T-PVS (2002). 13. Appendix 10.

102 Recommendation No. 108 (2003). The Proposed Construction of the via Baltica (Poland). Report of the 23rd Meeting of the Bern Convention. T-PVS (2003). 24. Appendix 12.

protected areas, and is reflected in multiple bodies from the GEF to the CBD. The protected area regimes which have the most developed jurisprudence in this area are the WHC, Ramsar and the MAB. The MAB is particularly notable, as its Parties are quite willing to refuse inscription of potential sites if they have inadequate public participation. The Parties to the Ramsar steer a more middle ground, preferring to emphasise the importance of public participation at a thematic level, rather than on a site by site basis. The Parties to the WHC and their practice is somewhere between the Ramsar and the MAB.

With regard to the question of indigenous peoples, although the Ramsar is supportive of the meaningful involvement of indigenous peoples, the WHC is most notable (but with ambiguous outcomes) protected area organisation in this area. A relatively strong support for grass-roots NGOs is also notable in the WHC and Bern Conventions. Conversely, the Parties to the Ramsar have, consistent with their approach on public participation, adopted a more thematic approach. Finally, the Antarctic regime has, partly due to its unique position, a more constraining approach to NGOs seeking to work 'on the ground' under their auspice.

Chapter VII

THREATS

The goal to create and effectively manage protected areas of global significance has been resolutely adopted by the international community.[1] Despite the clear merits of this goal, the need to maintain and conserve these protected areas from any number of threats has not been systematically advanced and it is becoming increasingly obvious that a large number of protected areas of international significance are under threat.[2] Despite the clear and emerging threats there is no overall schema showing how these threats are being dealt with. The aim of this chapter is to provide a framework, by which the primary threats can be shown, and responded to (or ignored) by the governing international bodies in question. Once these foundations have been laid, it may be possible for a much greater, and synchronized international attempt to comprehensively mitigate these threats to begin.

1 The Integrity of a Protected Area

Theoretically, every protected area has an 'integrity'. Although philosophers and politicians have long debated about what the 'integrity' of a protected area is,[3] and some regimes use different languages,[4] the goal is always the same, namely, that the integrity or character of the site, must be protected.[5] For example, with WHC sites the goal is

---

1 See chapters IV and V.

2 See National Geographic (2006). 'Places We Must Save: World Parks at Risk'. *National Geographic*. October.

3 UNESCO. (1996) Expert Review on Evaluation of General Principles and Criteria for Nominations of Natural World Heritage Sites. WHC-96/CONF.202/INF.9. Apr 15. 4. For an early discussion of this, see UNESCO. (1981). 5th Session of WHC. CC-81/CONF.003/6. Jan 5, 1981. 9.

4 Such as the Ramsar talking of the 'ecological character' Ecological character is the combination of the ecosystem components, processes and benefits/services that characterise the wetland at a given point in time'. Resolution 9.1. Additional Scientific and Technical Guidance for Implementing the Ramsar Wise Use Concept. (2005, Kampala). Annex A, paragraph 15. For earlier definitions, see Resolution 7.10. Wetland Risk Assessment. (1999, San Jose) For discussion of the earlier term, see Recommendation 5.2. Guidelines For the Interpretation of Article 3. (1993, Kushiro). Resolution 6.1. Working Definitions of Ecological Character. (1996, Brisbane). And Resolution 8.25. The Ramsar Strategic Plan. (2002, Valencia). Annex. Operational Objective 11.

5 Recommendation 11. The Integrity of National Parks and Equivalent Reserves. In Elliot, H. (ed). *Second World Conference on National Parks*. (1972, IUCN, Lausanne). 445.

that any utilization of that area 'does not adversely impact upon the outstanding universal value, of the site that was recognized when it was originally inscribed.'[6] If such values are irretrievably lost, as nearly happened twice before finally delisting the Arabian Oryx Site in Oman in 2007,[7] the threatened site can be removed from the WHC List.[8] The idea of the inscription values being irretrievably lost is the best way to understand the integrity of a protected area. That is, the integrity of an area is related to the reasons it was inscribed in the first place.

The integrity of a protected area may be challenged by any number of threats. Indeed, as the WHC recognised in the first sentence of its founding document, 'natural [and cultural] heritage [is] increasingly threatened with destruction not only by the traditional causes of decay, but also by changing social and economic conditions which aggravate the situation with even more formidable phenomena of damage or destruction'.[9] Such threats are not particular to the WHC. Rather, they may threaten many protected areas. Accordingly, the international community, through the CBD, has pledged itself to 'prevent and mitigate the negative impacts of key threats to protected areas'.[10] Although this is a laudable goal, there are dozens of different threats to protected areas, and what may be threatening one, may not be threatening another. Accordingly, it is very difficult, if not impossible to speak about types of threats which are applicable to all protected areas, all of the time.[11] Despite this limitation, the objective of this chapter is to outline the most commonly recognized threats to protected areas in the applicable international

---

6 UNESCO. (2003). 6th Extra-ordinary Session of the WHC. WHC-03/6. EXT.COM/8. Paris, May 27, 2003. 10. UNESCO. (1998). *Report of the World Heritage Strategy Natural and Cultural Heritage Expert Meeting.* (UNESCO, Amsterdam).4, 9, 11-13. *Operational Guidelines.* 2002 Edn. Paragraph 58.

7 With regard to the Srebarna Biosphere, seeUNESCO. (1992). 16th Session of the WHC. WHC-92/CONF.002/12. Dec 14, 1992. 18; and Ichkeul National Park. UNESCO. (1996). 20th Session of the WHC. WHC-96/CONF.201/21. Mar 10, 1997. 26.

8 *Operational Guidelines.* 2002 Edn. Paragraphs 6, 46 and 50. Paragraph 22 stipulates, where the intrinsic qualities of a property nominated are threatened by action of man and yet meet the criteria and the conditions of authenticity or integrity set out in paragraphs the listing paragraphs, an action plan outlining the corrective measures required should be submitted with the nomination file. Should the corrective measures submitted by the nominating State not be taken within the time proposed by the State, the property will be considered by the Committee for delisting in accordance with the procedure adopted by the Committee. Note, this justification for delisting is a long standing one. See UNESCO. (1979). 3rd Session of the WHC. CC-79/CONF.003/13. Nov 30, 1978. pp.20. UNESCO. (1992). 16th Session of the WHC. WHC-92/CONF.002/12. Dec 14, 1992. Annex II.

9 WHC. Preamble. Paragraph 1.

10 Specifically, by 2008, the target is to have, 'effective mechanisms for identifying and preventing, and/or mitigating the negative impacts of key threats to protected areas are in place'. CBD. Decision VII/28. Protected Areas. Annex. Goal 1.5.

11 See Brandon, K. (1998). *Parks in Peril. People, Politics and Protected Areas.* (Island Press, Washington DC). Dayton, L. (1990). 'World Chart Reveals Endangered Parks.' *New Scientist.* Dec 15. 8.

and regional regimes, and illustrate how these are being dealt with. The following list of threats is not in any particular order.

2 Permanent Human Populations

Human populations can represent a potential threat, as either permanent inhabitants or temporary (typically tourist) visitors to protected areas from a number of angles.[12] Despite the clear threat that permanent human populations may pose to protected areas, only the WHC, has developed material in this area. This material has developed because although the majority of WHC natural sites have no resident human populations in them (73 out of 126 sites in 1998), 47 sites did possess resident populations. The sizes of these populations ranged from a low of 38 individuals (Willandra lakes) to a high of 50,000 (Lake Baikal). The average population of the 47 sites was 6,268 people, and with only a few exceptions, most of the WHC sites with human populations in them were in non- OECD countries.[13] The largest human population in a natural site in Africa is with the 4,500 inhabitants of Air Tenere, but due to its vast area, the population density is only 0.06 humans per square kilometer.[14]

The WHC response to situations involving resident human populations has been where uncontrolled population expansion has occurred in the buffer zones and/or problems of illegal colonization and conflicts within the zone have arisen. In such instances, some sites have been refused inscription.[15] In other instances, once a site has already been inscribed, the Parties to the WHC have called for information on trends of numbers of people living inside the sites. This is especially so if the populations are living in the core areas, or they are living adjacently in the buffer zones. Explicit recommendations to WHC Parties to control human population levels have also been directed with

---

12 UNEP/WCWC. (2004). *Protected Areas and Biodiversity.* (UNEP: Biodiversity Series No 21). 34. WWF. (2004). *How Effective Are Protected Areas ?* (WWF, Gland). SBSTTA. Report of the Ad Hoc Technical Expert Group on Protected Areas. UNEP/CBD/SBSTTA/9/INF/3. 22 Sep, 2003. pp.25-29. CBD. (2004). *Technical Advice on the Establishment and Management of a National System of Marine and Coastal Protected Areas.* (CBD Technical Series No 13). 20-31. Secretariat of the CBD. (2004). *Biodiversity Issues for Consideration in the Planning, Establishment and Management of Protected Area Sites and Management.* (CBD Technical Series No 15). 37-45, 73-82. Recommendation 17. Human Populations and Biosphere Reserves. Recommendations of the World National Parks Congress. In McNeely, J. (ed). *National Parks, Conservation and Development.* (Smithsonian, Washington). 774.

13 IUCN. (1998). *Human Use of World Heritage Natural Sites: A Global Overview.* (IUCN, Gland). 3.

14 UNESCO. (2002). *Periodic Report for Africa.* (World Heritage Reports Number 3). 50.

15 IUCN. (2005). Evaluation of Nominations. WHC-05/29.COM/INF.8B.2. 67-69. Also decision 29 COM B8.13.

regard to Ha Long Bay,[16] the Galapagos,[17] Ngorongoro[18] and the Serengeti.[19] In 2004, the issue of permanent human populations within WHC natural sites was most notable with the Simien park in Ethiopia, as a core part of the benchmarks set for removing the site from the Danger List, included realignment of the Park's boundaries to exclude villages along the boundary, and a, 'significant and sustainable reduction in the human population density within the Park, especially within the core area'.[20] Efforts undertaken to control population in this park were supported by the Committee in 2005, which also recommended measures to control agricultural encroachment, domestic livestock, domestic dogs, and called upon systems to monitor population, beginning with a census in the area.[21] The following year, the Committee called for 'the realignment of the boundary to exclude certain villages'.[22] In other instances, decisions to change the boundaries of WHC areas, so as to exclude human populations have been warmly welcomed by the Committee.[23]

3 Temporary (tourist) Human Populations

It has long been realized that nature tourism is a double edged sword. Although it is correct that tourism can bring lucrative financial rewards, it has been recognized since 1962[24] that if badly managed, tourism can also have far reaching environmental and social impacts on the site and its surrounding areas.[25] For one example among many,

---

16 In Vietnam. UNESCO. (2003). 27th Session of the WHC. WHC-03/27.COM/24. Dec 10, 2003. 38.

17 See Decision 30 COM 7B.29. Also, UNESCO. (1990). 14th Session of the WHC. CLT-90/CONF.004/13. Dec 12, 1990. 1.

18 Decision 29 COM 7B.1.

19 UNESCO. (1995). 18th Session of the WHC.WHC-94/CONF.003/16. Jan 31. 1995. 21.

20 UNESCO. (2004). 28th Session of the WHC. Oct 29. Decision 28 COM 15.A.4.pp55. UNESCO. (2001). 25th Session of the WHC. WHC-01/CONF.208/24. Paris 8, Feb 2002. 35-36.

21 Decision 29 COM7A.5.

22 Decision 30 COM 7A.9.

23 Decision 29 COM 8B.15.

24 See 'Smith, A. (1962). 'Problems of Visitation and Preservation.' In Adams, A. (ed). *First World Conference on National Parks.* (US Department of the Interior, Washington). 169-176. Also, Fisher, J. (1972). 'Population and Economic Pressures on National Parks.' In Elliot, H. (ed). *Second World Conference on National Parks.* (IUCN, Lausanne). 102-108.

25 Broadly speaking there are four ways by which the impact of tourists upon protected areas can be reduced. These relate to controlling the overall numbers of tourists visiting an area, restricting the times or types of visits, hardening the resource via the development of more resilient facilities, or managing the impact of use (such as by breaking up concentrations or dispersing impacts). IUCN. (2002). *Sustainable Tourism in Protected Areas: Guidelines for Planning and Management.* (IUCN, Gland). 31-39, 88-98. Recommendation IV/7. Development of Approaches and Practices for the Sustainable Use of Resources, Including Tourism. UNEP/CBD/SBSTTA/4/14.pp.50-63.

nature tourism, whereby people go to see gorillas in their natural surroundings, is the second biggest killer of gorillas (due to the transmission of respiratory diseases) only slightly below the impact of civil war.[26]

Due to such concerns, and spurred on by the World Summit on Sustainable Development,[27] the World Parks Congress,[28] the IUCN,[29] and the CBD have actively examined this area.[30] Accordingly, in 2004 the CBD adopted the voluntary Guidelines on Biodiversity and Tourism Development.[31] A number of the international or regional regimes including, inter alia, the Helsinki Convention (and Baltic Marine Protected Areas),[32] the South East Pacific Protocol,[33] the Convention on Migratory Species

---

26 See Anon. (2005). 'Gorilla Deaths Show Eco-Tourist Should Keep Their Distance'. *New Scientist.* July 9. 17. Ananthaswamy, A. (2004). 'Beware the Ecotourist.' *New Scientist.* Mar 6. 6-7.

27 WSSD. Plan of Implementation. Paragraph 44 (b).

28 Such as respecting the primacy of the role of conservation for protected areas; make tangible and equitable contributions to the conservation of the area; contribute to local economic development and poverty reduction; encourage appropriate behaviour of visitors; use ecologically and culturally appropriate technologies; monitor impacts, etc. See Recommendation 5.12. Tourism as a Vehicle for Conservation and Support of Protected Areas. (Vth IUCN World Parks Congress).

29 IUCN. (2002). *Sustainable Tourism in Protected Areas: Guidelines for Planning and Management.* (IUCN, Gland). See also Wood, M. (2002). *Ecotourism: Principles, Practices and Policies for Sustainability.* (UNEP, Nairobi). IUCN. (1999). *Guidelines for Public Use Measurement and Reporting at Parks and Protected Areas.* (IUCN, Gland).

30 Decision V/25. Biological Diversity and Tourism. UNEP/CBD/COP/5/23.pp.185. Decision V/25. Biological Diversity and Tourism. UNEP/CBD/COP/5/23.pp.185. Recommendation IV/7. Development of Approaches and Practices for the Sustainable Use of Resources, Including Tourism. UNEP/CBD/SBSTTA/4/14.pp.50-63. Report of the 4th COP to the CBD. UNEP/CBD/COP/4/27. June 15. pp.40.

31 The Guidelines were designed to provide a framework for managing all tourism and biodiversity, notification processes in relation to such a management framework, and public education, capacity building and awareness raising. The core considerations within this matrix were baseline information and review, vision and objectives, review of legislation and control measures, impact assessment, impact management and mitigation, decision making, implementation, monitoring and reporting and adaptive management. Notably, the COP also placed an emphasis upon involvement of indigenous peoples and local communities in this area, and seeking consistency with the Akwe Kon Guidelines. Decision VII/14. Biological Diversity and Tourism. UNEP/CBD/COP/7/L10. For some of the build-up to these Guidelines, see Recommendation VII/5. Sustainable Tourism. UNEP/CBD/COP/6/4. pp.33. Decision VI/14. Biological Diversity and Tourism. UNEP/CBD/COP/6/20.pp.178. Recommendation VIII/5. Biological Diversity and Tourism. UNEP/CBD/COP/7/3. pp.72.

32 See the Guidelines for Sustainable and Environmentally Friendly Tourism in the Coastal Zones of the Baltic Sera Area. See Helcom Recommendation 21/3.

33 1989 Protocol for the Conservation and Management of Protected Marine and Coastal Areas of the South East Pacific. Reprinted in Austen, A. (ed). *Basic Legal Document on International Animal Welfare and Wildlife Conservation.* (Kluwer, London). Article 5 (b).

and the Antarctic regime have mirrored the approach of voluntary Guidelines. With regard to the CMS, the importance of controlling tourism around protected areas is clearly recognised in its subsidiary arrangements such as the African-Eurasian Waterbird Agreement (AEWA),[34] the Agreement on the Conservation of Albatross and Petrels (ACAP),[35] the Memorandum of Understanding for the Slender Billed Curlew,[36] and most notably the Agreement for the Conservation of Cetaceans in the Black Sea, Mediterranean Sea and Contiguous Atlantic Area (ACCOBAMs). The ACCOBAMS is notable because in addition to urging restraint in this area, the Parties have actually issued Guidelines for the tourist (whale-watching) interaction with the cetaceans of the area.[37] The Antarctica regime has adopted a highly advanced regime, in that the Consultative Parties are obliged to actively monitor tourist activities in the region, and should only allow tourism if it is conducted (with adequate insurance for full recovery) in accordance the Guidance for Visitors to the Antarctic.[38] Parties to other regimes, such as the MAB programme, whilst encouraging eco-tourism within biosphere reserves, have been quick to point out where such practices need to be better controlled.[39]

The Parties to the Ramsar have a practice of identifying unsustainable tourist developments, such as those in the Dollart (Netherlands and Germany),[40] the Donana site in

---

34 AEWA. Action Plan. Point 4.2.

35 ACAP. Action Plan. 3.4.

36 Slender Billed Curlew. Action Plan. Sections 4.

37 ACCOBAMS. Resolution 1.11. Guidelines for Commercial Cetacean Watching in the ACCOBAMS Area. See also ACCOBAMS. Resolution 1.9. International Implementation Priorities for 2002-2006.. Also, section 2 of the Conservation Plan.

38 See Measure 3 (1995). Reporting of Tourism and Non-Governmental Activities. In Antarctic Treaty: Report of the Nineteenth Meeting. (Seoul, 1995). 98. Antarctic Treaty: Report of the Twenty-Seventh Meeting. (Cape Town. 2004). Resolution 3. Tourism and NGO Activities: Enhanced Cooperation Amongst Parties. 226. Antarctic Treaty: Report of the Twenty-Seventh Meeting. (Cape Town. 2004). Measure 4. Insurance and Contingency Planning for Tourism and NGO Activity in the Antarctic Treaty Area. 167. Resolution 4. Guidelines on Contingency Planning, Insurance and Other Matters for Tourist and Other Non-Governmental Activities in the Antarctic Treaty Area. Also from the Twenty-Seventh meeting, at 227-229. These obligations built on Article 15 of the Madrid Protocol. Recommendation XVIII-1. Tourism and Non-Governmental Activities. In Antarctic Treaty: Report of the Eighteenth Meeting. (Kyoto, 1994). 35-39.

39 Wudalianchi in China. UNESCO. (2003). ICC Bureau Meeting. SC/-03/CONF.217/14. July 30. 9. Selva Pisana in Italy. UNESCO. (2004). 18th Session of the ICC Bureau Meeting. SC-04/CONF.204/14. Jan 11. Amboseli in Kenya. UNESCO. (2003). ICC Bureau Meeting. SC/-03/CONF.217/14. July 30. 22. UNESCO. (2001) ICC Bureau Meeting. SC-01/CONF.217/ 8. Dec 12, 24.

40 Recommendations adopted by the International Conference on the Conservation of Wetlands and Waterfowl at Heiligenhafen, Federal Republic of Germany, 6 December 1974. Recommendation 9. Protection of the Dollart.

Spain,[41] and Cuare in Venezuela,[42] and issuing direct calls for remedying the situation. Likewise, the Parties to the Bern Convention which recognised the threat of uncontrolled tourism to natural habitats as its very first resolution,[43] have gone on to directly challenge countries with regard to tourist related habitat disturbance related to marine turtles,[44] in Turkey,[45] Cyprus,[46] and Greece – and the highly controversial instance of the Greek island of Zakynthos[47] in particular. Similar concerns have been reiterated with regard to the lynx and tourism,[48] and the Bald ibis in Morocco.[49]

The problem of tourism and WHC sites is particularly heightened due to the fact that WHC sites usually attract large numbers of visitors. These large numbers may, if badly managed, represent a clear threat to the integrity of the site. This has clearly been the case with many cultural listings. However, despite the obvious risk, a surprising number of WHC sites, both natural and cultural, have no plans to manage tourism. This was particularly obvious with sites in Africa, when it became apparent in 2002, that only one in three sites had a tourism development plan.[50] Likewise, within Latin America and the Caribbean, a 2004 periodic review showed that 41% of all sites in this region were without specific tourist management plans.[51]

To confront such problems, aside some general discussions and dedicated workshops on the topic, the main approach of the WHC has been to address the problem in a site specific context.[52] To do this, the Committee has dealt with considerations of tourism at both the inscription of new sites to the WHC List, and post-inscription. With regard to the inscription stages, in some instances, applications have been deferred, such as

---

41 Recommendation 4.9.1. Donana National Park. (1990, Montreux). Recommendation 5.1. Ramsar Sites in Specific Contracting Parties. (1993, Kushiro).

42 Recommendation 5.1.2. Cuare, Venezuela. (1993, Kushiro).

43 Recommendation No. 1. (1982). Concerning the Protection of Gran Sasso (Italy).

44 Recommendation No 7. (1987). On the Protection of Marine Turtles and Their Habitat.

45 Recommendation No 8 (1889). On the Protection of Marine Turtles in Dalyan and Other Important Areas in Turkey.

46 Recommendation No. 63. (1997). The Conservation of the Akamas Peninsula, Cyprus. Report of the 17th Meeting of the Bern Convention. T-PVS (97) 63. Appendix 16.

47 Recommendation No 9. (1987). On the Protection of Caretta Caretta in Lagasas Bay, Zakynthos (Greece).

48 Recommendation No. 19. (1991). The Pardel Lynx in the Iberian Peninsula.

49 Recommendation No. 97. (2002). The Conservation of the Bald ibis and the Tourism Development Project in Tifnit (Morocco). Report of the 22nd Meeting of the Bern Convention. T-PVS (2002). 13. Appendix 9.

50 UNESCO. (2002). *Periodic Report for Africa.* (World Heritage Reports Number 3). 38.

51 UNESCO. (2004). *The State of World Heritage in Latin America and the Caribbean: 2004 Periodic Report.* (UNESCO, Paris). 23.

52 UNESCO. (1993). *Managing Tourism in Natural World Heritage Sites.* UNESCO/UNEP. 3-5. Pressouyre, L. (1992). The World Heritage Convention, Twenty Years Later. (UNESCO, Paris). 49-52.

with a New Zealand application, until the Committee was satisfied that tourist development was under control.[53] Alternatively, applications have proceeded, conditional on the Party controlling various tourist problems, such as with the Tikal national park in Guatemala.[54]

More commonly, the Committee has had to deal with considerations of tourism once the site has become established, and the former controls with regard to the new influx of human numbers have proven inadequate. Accordingly, the Committee has had to make recommendations to State Parties to control tourism with regard to the natural sites of Iguaçu,[55] Machu Picchu,[56] the Serengeti,[57] Peninsula Valdes,[58] specific sites within China (such as the Wulingyuan Scenic Area,[59] Jiuzhaigou Scenic Valley[60] and Mount Huangshan),[61] South Africa,[62] Giant's Causeway and Causeway Coast in the United Kingdom,[63] Kaziranga National Park in India,[64] Australia's Great Barrier Reef,[65] as well as sites in Vietnam,[66] Mali,[67] Iceland[68] and the Galapagos.[69] In

53 Tongariro. UNESCO. (1987). 11th Session of the WHC. CC-87/CONF.005/9. Jan 20, 1988. pp 8. UNESCO. (1990). 14th Session of the WHC. CLT-90/CONF.004/13. Dec 12, 1990. 5. Note also the Westland and Mount Cook National Parks in NZ, was only accepted with satisfaction after management plans were concluded to control aircraft flights. UNESCO. (1986). 10th Session of the WHC. CC-86/CONF.003/10. Dec 5, 1986. pp 5.

54 UNESCO. (1979). 3rd Session of the WHC. CC-79/CONF.003/13. Nov 30, 1978. pp.10.

55 With up to 8 helicopters over the waterfalls at the same time ! UNESCO. (1991). 15th Session of the WHC. SC-91/CONF.002/15. Dec 12, 1991. 6.

56 UNESCO. (1995). 18th Session of the WHC. WHC-94/CONF.003/16. Jan 31. 1995. 23. UNESCO. (1996). 20th Session of the WHC. WHC-96/CONF.201/21. Mar 10, 1997. 30. UNESCO. (1997). 21st Session of the WHC. WHC-97/CONF.208/17. Feb 27, 1998. 23. UNESCO. (1998). 22nd Session of the WHC. WHC-98/CONF.208/18. Jan 29, 1998. 45-46. UNESCO. (1999). 23rd Session of the WHC. WHC-99/CONF.209/22. Mar 22, 2000. 78. UNESCO. (2002). 26th Session of the WHC. WHC-02/CONF.202/25. Aug 1, 2002. 39. UNESCO. (2003). 27th Session of the WHC. WHC-03/27.COM/24. Dec 10, 2003. 46.

57 UNESCO. (1995). 18th Session of the WHC. WHC-94/CONF.003/16. Jan 31. 1995. 21.

58 UNESCO. (1999). 23rd Session of the WHC. WHC-99/CONF.209/22. Mar 22, 2000. 18.

59 UNESCO. (1992). 16th Session of the WHC. WHC-92/CONF.002/12. Dec 14, 1992. 31.

60 UNESCO. (1996). 20th Session of the WHC. WHC-96/CONF.201/21. Mar 10, 1997. 27.

61 Ibid. 30.

62 St Lucia Wetland Park. UNESCO. (2003). 27th Session of the WHC. WHC-03/27.COM/24. Dec 10, 2003. 34.

63 UNESCO. (2003). 27th Session of the WHC. WHC-03/27.COM/24. Dec 10, 2003. 43.

64 UNESCO. (2002). 26th Session of the WHC. WHC-02/CONF.202/25. Aug 1, 2002. 31.

65 UNESCO. (1995). 18th Session of the WHC. WHC-94/CONF.003/16. Jan 31. 1995. 19.

66 UNESCO. (1996). 19th Session of the WHC. WHC-95/CONF.203/16. Jan 31, 1996. '8. UNESCO. (1996). 20th Session of the WHC. WHC-96/CONF.201/21. Mar 10, 1997. 28. UNESCO. (2004). 28th Session of the WHC. WHC-04/28.COM/26. Oct 29. Decision 28 COM 15B.13.pp72.

67 Cliff of Bandiagara. UNESCO. (1989). 13th Session of the WHC. SC-89/CONF.004/12. Dec, 22 1989. pp 12.

some instances, the Committee has recommended moratoriums or strict limits on further tourist developments in or around sites, such as with Ngorongoro[70] and Sian Ka'an in Mexico.[71] With the sites of Ngorongoro and the Serengeti, both in Tanzania, the Committee has called for EIAs for tourist accommodation plans and vehicle congestion, and other measures to mitigate the negative impacts of tourism on the sites.[72] Overt failure to control problematic tourism, as with Bulgaria's Pirin National Park almost lead to it being inscribed on the Danger List.[73]

4 Alien Species

An alien species is a species which is new to the region and has a negative impact on the new environment, either ecologically, economically or socially. In some ways, this is a difficult area to navigate, as humanity and Nature have been mixing biota on the global scale, at a massive level, for thousands of years and consequently, all ecological communities have been invaded to a greater or lesser degree. This mixing has been both purposeful and accidental, and biotic enrichment as well as impoverishment has resulted from this mixing. Invasive species are widespread in the world and can be found in most taxonomic groups. Invasive species include bacteria, protozoans, phytoplankton and zooplankton. Invasive plant species have been reported among, inter alia, sea weeds, trees, shrubs, vines and grasses. In the animal kingdom, a number of invertebrates (including sponges, sea squirts, mollusks, insects, crustaceans and worms), fish, amphibians, reptiles, birds and mammals have been reported as invasive species. At present, plants, mammals and insects (such as ants) are the most common taxa on the lists of invasive species in terrestrial environments. Invertebrates, especially molluscs, crustaceans and algae predominate among invasive alien species in marine and coastal

---

230 Anon. (2005). 'Arctic Reprieve'. *New Scientist.* Nov 19. 5. Anon. (2005). 'Alaska Waits for Oil Outcome'. *New Scientist.* Nov 12. 6. Anon. (2002). 'Reprieve For Wildlife Refuge'. *New Scientist.* Apr 27. 5. Anon. (2005). 'Setback For Alaska Reserve'. *New Scientist.* Mar 26. 7.

231 1989 Protocol for the Conservation and Management of Protected Marine and Coastal Areas of the South East Pacific. Reprinted in Austen, A. (ed). *Basic Legal Document on International Animal Welfare and Wildlife Conservation.* (Kluwer, London). Article 5 (b).

232 Madrid Protocol. Article 7.

233 Mining, Minerals and Sustainable Development/Business Council for Sustainable Development. (2002). *Breaking New Ground.* (Earthscan, London). 161-166.

234 Especially when compared to earlier times. For example, following earlier World Parks Congress precedents in this area for compromise, rather than an outright prohibitive approach, they called for strong management regimes, including EIAs, to make sure that the integrity of protected sites is not destroyed. Recommendation 6. Threats to Protected Areas. Recommendations of the World National Parks Congress. In McNeely, J. (ed). *National Parks, Conservation and Development.* (Smithsonian, Washington). 769.

areas while fish, aquatic weeds and other invertebrate's top lists of invasive species of freshwater areas.[74]

Depending on the type of ecosystems and the species within them, invasive alien species can alter evolutionary trajectories, disrupt community and ecosystem processes. They can also cause large scale economic losses and be threats to human health and welfare. Invasive species can lead to a decrease of genetic diversity through the loss of genetically distinct populations, loss of genes and gene complexes, and hybrization of introduced species with native ones. At the species and community levels, invasive alien species can compete with native biota, displace them, prey upon them, and transmit or causes diseases, reduce growth and survival rates, cause decline, extirpation or populations or total extinction. They can form mono-specific stands, thereby altering community structure, uproot and break off parts of plants, affect growth and survival of other organisms at both the micro, and ultimately the macro level for some local ecosystems. They can stimulate fire, deplete water, cause disease, decimate crops and/or forest, fisheries, grazing lands and human habitats. They can impede navigation, clog water works, and destroy or severely impede other species. Collectively, alien invasive species are a directly impacting 30% of all threatened birds, 15% of all threatened plants and 10% of all threatened mammals.[75]

The broad obligation upon all countries, as echoed at the WSSD,[76] but specifically contained in the CBD, is for every country to prevent the introduction of, control or eradicate those alien species which threaten ecosystems, habitats or species.[77] To facilitate this, the CBD has created some guiding principles for the prevention, intro-

74 SBSTTA. (2001). Invasive Alien Species: Status, Impacts and Trends. UNEP/CBD/SBSTTA/6/INF/11. Feb 26. 5-6. CBD Secretariat. (2001). *Assessment and Management of Alien Species That Threaten Ecosystems, Habitats and Species.* (CBD Technical Series No 1, Montreal). 1-2. SBSTTA. (2000). The Global Strategy on Invasive Alien Species. UNEP/CBD/SBSTTA/6/INF/9. 10-13. Commission on Sustainable Development. (2001). Global Status of Biodiversity. E/CN.17/2001/PC/18. March 14. 4.

75 CBD Secretariat. (2001). *Assessment and Management of Alien Species.* Ibid. SBSTTA. (2001). Invasive Alien Species. Ibid. SBSTTA. Pilot Assessments: The Ecological and Socio Economic Impact of Alien Species on Island Ecosystems. UNEP/CBD/SBSTTA/9/INF/33. Nov 5, 2003. McNeely, J. (2004). 'Strangers in Our Midst'. *Environment.* July/August. 15, 21-22. Generally, Mooney, H. (ed). *Invasive Species in a Changing World.* (Kluwer, Netherlands). National Research Council. (1996). *Stemming the Tide: Controlling the Introduction of Non-Indigenous Species By Ships Ballast Waters.* (National Academy Press). Pearce, F. (1996). 'Species Invasions Are Beyond Our Control.' *New Scientist.* July 6. 4. Anderson, I. (1992). 'Pests In the Post Threaten Crops in Hawaii.' *New Scientist.* Nov 21. 10. Brooke, M. (2004). 'Birds in Decline Around Globe.' *New Scientist.* Mar 13. 14.

76 WSSD. Plan of Implementation. Paragraph 44. (i).

77 CBD. Article.8. (h)

duction and mitigation of alien species,[78] whilst also keeping the issue on their agenda.[79] With particular regard to protected areas, one of the CBD (and World Parks Congress)[80] goals is for all Parties to adopt measures to control risks associated with invasive alien species in protected areas.[81] This goal is assisted by the GEF which, as of 2005, was running projects covering at least 125 sites, aimed at eradicating alien species.[82]

The goal of controlling alien species in protected areas can be traced to the 1933 African Convention on the Conservation of Nature and Natural Resources, by which the Parties pledged themselves to, inter alia,[83] 'give consideration to the desirability of preventing the introduction of exotic trees or plants into national parks or reserves'.[84] Since this point, the obligation has become one of attempting to strictly control the accidental or deliberate introduction of alien species, and other pests and/or animal or plant diseases both generally and with regard to protected areas in particular. This obligation is solidly reflected in most, if not all, instruments which deal with protected areas. With MPAs, although the United Nations Convention on the Law of the Sea,[85] Mediterranean[86] and Caribbean Protocols[87] are notable with regard to the general need to control alien species, the foremost instrument in this area is the International Maritime Organisation's Ballast Water Convention, which sets both a universal standard for ballast water management and ballast water control areas ('certain areas') to be designated where additional measures, to control the possible entry of alien species, are required.[88]

---

78 Recommendation IV/4. Development of Guiding Principles for the Prevention of Impacts of Alien Species and Identifying Priority Areas of Work. UNEP/CBD/SBSTTA/4/14. pp40-41. Annex I. Recommendation V/4. Alien Species: Guiding Principles for the Prevention, Introduction and Mitigation of Impacts. UNEP/CBD/COP/5/3. pp.43. Annex I. Recommendation VI/4. Alien Species That Threaten Ecosystems, Habitats or Species. UNEP/CBD/COP/6/3.pp.38. Decision VI/23. Alien Species That Threaten Ecosystems, Habitats or Species. UNEP/CBD/COP/6/20.pp.240.

79 Alien Invasive Species. UNEP/CBD/COP/7/L18.

80 See Recommendation 1. Strengthening Institutional and Societal Capacities for Protected Area Management in the 21st Century. (Vth IUCN World Parks Congress). IUCN Vth World Parks Congress. The Durban Action Plan. pp.3-4.

81 CBD. Decision VII/28. Protected Areas. Annex. Paragraph1.5.4.

82 GEF. (2005). *Making a Visible Difference in Our World.* (GEF, Washington). 25.

83 They also promised to exchange between themselves, in the future, 'information relating to infectious or contagious diseases of importance for the preservation of fauna or flora, or capable of affecting men as well as animals'. 1933 Africa Convention. Protocol attached to the Convention, Article 1.

84 1933 Africa Convention. Article 7 (5).

85 UNCLOS. Article 196.

86 Mediterranean Protocol. Article 13.

87 Caribbean Protocol. Article 12.

88 MEPC. (2000). Report of the MEPC on its 45th Session. MEPC 45/20. 10. MEPC.(2001). Report of the MEPC on its 46th Session. MEPC 46/23. 23-29. MEPC. (2002). Report of the MEPC on its 47th Session. MEPC 47/20. 6-8.

Other instruments which have a broad recognition of this problem include the MAB regime,[89] and the 2003 African Convention,[90] the CMS, Ramsar and the Antarctica regime. With Antarctica, the obligation to prohibit the bringing into the Treaty Area any species of animal or plant not indigenous to that Area, except with regard to a few listed exceptions,[91] in accordance with a permit,[92] dates back to 1964. They also agreed to take 'all reasonable precautions shall be taken to prevent the accidental introduction of parasites and diseases into the Treaty Area' with particular regard to poultry and certain dogs.[93] Very similar restrictions were later included into the Madrid Protocol,[94] with the addition, that all dogs were to be completely removed from the continent.[95] The existing restriction on poultry was increased (to even include inspections of dressed poultry being shipped to the Antarctic) and its careful removal if not consumed. The importation of non-sterile soil was also to be avoided to the maximum extent practicable.

With the CMS, given that alien species have the potential to destroy the habitats that the migratory species depend upon, the Parties to the CMS have agreed, as a general principle, that all Range States of a highly endangered migratory species shall, inter alia, strictly control the introduction of, control or eliminate, alien species which threaten the endangered migratory species.[96] The Parties to the CMS have also mirrored this commitment in a number of subsidiary CMS agreements,[97] such as those pertaining to the Great Bustards,[98] the ACAP[99] and the AEWA.[100] The AEWA is of interest

---

89 UNESCO. (2002). *Biosphere Reserves: Special Places for People and Nature.* (UNESCO, Paris). 43, 91. UNESCO. (1968). *Use and Conservation of the Biosphere.* (UNESCO, Paris). 203.

90 2003 African Convention. Article 9 (2) (h) and (i).

91 Including, sledge dogs, domestic animals and plants, and laboratory animals and plants including viruses, bacteria, yeasts and fungi. Annex C of the 1964 Agreed Measures.

92 See Article IX of the Agreed Measures.

93 Annex D. Precautions to Prevent Accidental Introduction of Parasites and Diseases Into the Treaty Area.

94 See Article 4 of Annex II.

95 See Appendix B of the Madrid Protocol which allowed entry on to the continent, if with a permit, for (a) domestic plants; and (b) laboratory animals and plants including viruses, bacteria, yeasts and fungi.

96 Article III. (4)(c).

97 Each Agreement should provide for, inter alia, protection of such habitats from disturbances, including strict control of the introduction of, or control of already introduced, exotic species detrimental to the migratory species. CMS. Article V.(5)(e).

98 The Action Plan of the MoU on GBs called for all foxes and dogs to be controlled in areas where Great Bustards occur regularly. Action Plan for the Middle European Population of the Great Bustard. Section 2.3.1.

99 ACAP. Article III. b. The Action Plan reinforced the necessity to, 'take all feasible action to prevent the introduction to habitats, deliberately or otherwise, of non-native taxa of animals, plants or hybrids of disease causing organisms that may be detrimental to the population of albatrosses or petrels.' In addition, measures should be undertaken to the extent feasible,

as in addition to the broad commitment to control alien species in AEWA habitats, is recognised within its Agreement,[101] its associated Action Plan[102] and Guidelines.[103]

Somewhat surprising, given the overt risk that alien species can represent to wetlands, the Ramsar was relatively late in coming to address this threat. The issue was not considered until the mid 1990s, when the Ramsar recommended EIAs before the release of live exotic species which have the potential for a significant impact on wetlands.[104] It was not until 1999 that Ramsar called upon all of its Parties to, wherever possible, address the environmental, economic and social impacts of invasive species on wetlands within their jurisdictions.[105] This issue, which was deemed a 'high priority' resulted in calls for information sharing between the Parties, greater collaboration with other organisations working on this question, as well as the formation of Guidelines for confronting the problem.[106] The development of guidance and promotion of protocols and actions to prevent, control or eradicate invasive alien species in wetland systems is a clear goal for future Ramsar work.[107]

The two conventions which have moved away from the broad-brushed approach, and have come to pinpoint particular problem areas involving alien species are the Bern

---

to control and, 'where possible, eradicate non-native taxa of animals or plants or hybrids thereof, that are, or may be, detrimental to populations of albatrosses or petrels.' ACAP. Action Plan. 1.4.

100 African-Eurasian Waterbird Agreement. (1999, March 18, Bonn). See Resolution 1.12. Tribute to the Organisers. MOP 1 of the AEWA. (South Africa, September 16, 1999). Available from the AEWA Secretariat.

101 AEWA covers alien species, in that under general conservation measures, the parties agreed to prohibit the deliberate introduction of non-native waterbird species into the environment and take all appropriate measures to prevent the unintentional release of such species if this introduction or release would prejudice the conservation status of wild flora and fauna. In addition, when non-native waterbird species have already been introduced, the Parties shall take all appropriate measures to prevent these species from becoming a potential threat to indigenous species. AEWA. III.2. (g)

102 The Action Plan suggests that non-native species be prohibited, if necessary, if such introductions would be detrimental to populations listed on Table 1. Likewise, the Action Plan notes the possibility of controlling such introduced species already in the wild, and taking precautions to prevent accidental escapes of captive birds belonging to non-native species. AEWA. Action Plan. Point 2.5.

103 The Guidelines on Alien Species were accepted as interim guidance for Contracting Parties in the implementation of the Action Plan at the 2nd MOP in 2002. Resolution 2.3. Conservation Guidelines. 2nd MOP (2002, Bonn). Available from the AEWA Secretariat.

104 Recommendation 6.17.4. Australian Ramsar Sites. (1996, Brisbane).

105 Resolution 7.14. Invasive Species and Wetlands. (1999, San Jose).

106 Resolution 8.18. Invasive Species and Wetlands. (2002, Valencia).

107 Resolution 9.8. Streamlining the Implementation of the Strategic Plan of the Convention 2003-2008 (2005, Kampala. Strategy 1.6. Resolution 8.25. The Ramsar Strategic Plan. (2002, Valencia). Annex. Operational Objective 5.

Convention and the WHC. With regard to the former, after building upon the general obligation for each Party to the Bern Convention (and the related Habitats Directive)[108] to strictly control the introduction of non-native species,[109] the Parties have gone on to issue general guidelines in this area for the introduction of non-native species into new areas,[110] and with regard to particular thematic areas, such as highly endangered species,[111] birds,[112] islands,[113] underground habitat,[114] forests and original habitat areas relied upon by threatened species[115] and transboundary situations.[116] They have also issued recommendations with regard to particular species, as being either threatened by alien species, or in need of direct assistance, including crayfish,[117] Mink,[118] ornamental plants,[119] or tropical seaweed,[120] fresh-water fish,[121] ducks,[122] squirrels[123] and tortoise.[124]

---

108 Habitats Directive. Article 22 (b).

109 Bern Convention. Article 11 (2) (b).

110 Recommendation No. 57. The Introduction of Organisms Belonging to Non-Native Species into the Environment. CoE. (1997). Report of the 17th Meeting of the Bern Convention. T-PVS (97). 63. Appendix 8.

111 Recommendation No. 30.(1991). The Conservation of Species in Appendix I of the Convention.

112 Recommendation No. 77 (1999). On the Implementation of New Action Plans for Globally Threatened Birds in Europe. Report of the 19th Meeting of the Bern Convention. T-PVS (99) 30. Appendix 8.

113 Recommendation No. 91. Alien Invasive Species That Threaten Biological Diversity in Islands and Geographically and Evolutionary Isolated Ecosystems. Report of the 22nd Meeting of the Bern Convention. T-PVS (2002). 13. Appendix 3.

114 Recommendation No. 36. (1992). The Conservation of Underground Habitat.

115 Recommendation No. 96. (2002). The Conservation of Natural Habitats and Wildlife, Especially Birds, in Afforestation of Lowland in Iceland. Report of the 22nd Meeting of the Bern Convention. T-PVS (2002). 13. Appendix 8. Recommendation No. 10. (1988). Protection of the Brown Bear. Guidelines on the Conservation of the Wildcat. (1992).

116 Recommendation No. 99 (2003). The European Strategy of Invasive Alien Species. Report of the 23rd Meeting of the Bern Convention. T-PVS (2002). 13. Appendix 3.

117 Recommendation No. 18. (1989). On the Protection of Indigenous Crayfish In Europe.

118 Recommendation No. 31. (1991). The Protection of the European Mink.

119 Recommendation No. 34 (1992). The Conservation of the Flora of the Micronesian Region.

120 Recommendation No. 45. Controlling the Proliferation of Caulerpa taxifolia in the Mediterranean. CoE (1995). Report of the 14th Meeting of the Bern Convention. T-PVS (95) 26. Appendix 8.

121 Recommendation No. 41. (1993). The Conservation of Freshwater Fish.

122 Recommendation No. 61. (1997). On the Conservation of the White Headed Duck. Report of the 17th Meeting of the Bern Convention. T-PVS (97) 63. Appendix 12.

123 Recommendation No. 78 (1999). The Conservation of the Red Squirrel in Italy. Report of the 19th Meeting of the Bern Convention. T-PVS (99) 30. Appendix 9.

124 Recommendation No. 104 (2003). The Conservation of the Spur-thinghed Tortoise in Spain. Report of the 23rd Meeting of the Bern Convention. T-PVS (2003). 24. Appendix 8.

With particular regard to WHC sites, the purity of biodiversity and ecosystems, in terms of their being free from alien species (or similar species with threatening diseases)[125] is sometimes highlighted in inscription nominations.[126] However, the typical WHC practice involves dealing with alien species that have subsequently threatened the integrity of a site already listed. Such threats, and the need to confront them, have been noted with regard to sites in Argentina,[127] Tanzania,[128] the United States,[129] Nepal,[130] New Zealand,[131] Australia,[132] South Africa[133] and Ecuador with the Galapagos.[134] In some instances, the alien species may be so problematic, that the site may be inscribed as in Danger. For example, with the Djoudj National Bird Sanctuary in Senegal, alien species became so difficult that the overall integrity of the site was deemed threatened.[135] Likewise, with the Keoladeo Park in India, the invasion of paspalum grass, as linked to a decline in the number of migrating Siberian cranes and failure to control this alien species was listed as a catalyst which would otherwise result in the site being listed as in Danger.[136] In terms of sites already listed as in Danger, the Yellowstone site was notable, as dealing with its invasive species (43,000 predatory trout were removed from the site) was an important factor in its eventual removal from the Danger List.[137]

---

125 See the discussions on Diseased bison in Wood Buffalo National Park. UNESCO. (1990). 14th Session of the WHC. CLT-90/CONF.004/13. Dec 12, 1990. 10. See also the debate about the cattle drive through Selous Game reserve. UNESCO. (1991). 15th Session of the WHC. SC-91/CONF.002/15. Dec 12, 1991. 10.

126 UNESCO. (1997). 21st Session of the WHC. WHC-97/CONF.208/17. Feb 27, 1998. 36.

127 The European Hare in Los Glaciares. UNESCO. (1981). 5th Session of the WHC. CC-81/CONF.002/4. July 20, 1981. pp.2.

128 Ngorongoro, and the 'Mexican poppy' weed. Decision 29 COM 7B.1.

129 Introduced mountain goats in Olympic park. UNESCO. (1981). 5th Session of the WHC. CC-81/CONF.002/4. July 20, 1981. pp.6. And exotic species in the Hawaii Volcanoes National Park. UNESCO. (1987). 11th Session of the WHC. CC-87/CONF.005/9. Jan 20, 1988. pp 6.

130 Chitwan. UNESCO. (2003). 27th Session of the WHC. WHC-03/27.COM/24. Dec 10, 2003. 36.

131 The Sub Antarctic Islands. UNESCO. (1998). 22nd Session of the WHC. WHC-98/CONF.208/18. Jan 29, 1998. 58.

132 Cane toads in Kakadu. Decision 29 COM 7B.30.

133 The Cape Floral Region. See Decision 30 COM 7B.5.

134 Decision 30 COM 7B.29. UNESCO. (1990). 14th Session of the WHC. CLT-90/CONF.004/13. Dec 12, 1990. 1.

135 Decision 29 COM. 7A. UNESCO. (2001). 24th Session of the WHC. WHC-2000/CONF.204/21. Feb 16, 2001. 39. UNESCO. (2001). 25th Session of the WHC. WHC-01/CONF.208/24. Feb 8, 2002. 42. UNESCO. (2003). 27th Session of the WHC. WHC-03/27.COM/24. Dec 10, 2003. 13. UNESCO. (2004). 28th Session of the WHC. Oct 29. Decision 28 COM 15.A.7.pp56.

136 UNESCO. (1990). 14th Session of the WHC. CLT-90/CONF.004/13. Dec 12, 1990. 11. UNESCO. (1995). 18th Session of the WHC. WHC-94/CONF.003/16. Jan 31. 1995. 20.

137 UNESCO. (2001). 25th Session of the WHC. WHC-01/CONF.208/24. Feb 8, 2002. 44-45.

5 Air Pollution and Climate Change

Although air pollution has been linked to impacts in a number of protected areas, there has been no systematic response to the issue by any of the international or regional bodies which cover protected areas.[138] This is despite the fact that air pollution has been recognised as a problem under the Bern Convention (with regard to some plant species[139] and freshwater Pearl Mussels),[140] the MAB (with regard to some forests in the Carpathians),[141] and the WHC (in terms of America's Great Smokey Mountains).[142]

Conversely, climate change has been recognized by inter alia, the World Parks Congress,[143] as a formidable threat to the overall existence of protected areas. Although some climate change may already be impacting upon protected areas, this problem is largely one of future impacts.[144] Due to such potential risks, some forums, such as the CBD have gone so far as to recommend that Parties should, 'integrate climate change adaptation measures in protected area planning, management strategies, and in the design of protected area systems'.[145] Despite this broad recommendation, the respective regimes have adopted a diversity of responses.

The strongest response has emerged from the International Coral Reef Initiative (ICRI), which has gone from classifying climate change as a 'potential' problem of large implications for coral reefs,[146] to one which was already having a 'significant im-

---

138 UNEP/WCWC. (2004). *Protected Areas and Biodiversity.* (UNEP: Biodiversity Series No 21). 34.

139 Recommendation No. 44. The Conservation of Some Threatened Plants in Central Europe. CoE (1995). Report of the 14th Meeting of the Bern Convention. T-PVS (95) 26. Appendix 7.

140 Guidelines on the Taking of the Pearl Mussel and Pearl Fishing (1992).

141 UNESCO. (2001). MAB ICC Bureau Meeting. SC/-01/CONF.211/13. Apr 10. 5.

142 UNESCO. (2002). 26th Session of the WHC. WHC-02/CONF.202/25. Aug 1, 2002. 37.

143 IUCN Vth World Parks Congress. The Durban Action Plan. 3. Accordingly, the Vth IUCN World Parks called upon Governments to act meaningfully through their domestic and international responses (i.e. the Kyoto Protocol) to the problem. See Recommendation 5.05. Climate Change and Protected Areas. (Vth IUCN World Parks Congress).

144 UNEP/WCWC. (2004). *Protected Areas and Biodiversity.* (UNEP: Biodiversity Series No 21). 34. SBSTTA. Report of the Ad Hoc Technical Expert Group on Protected Areas. UNEP/CBD/SBSTTA/9/INF/3. 22 Sep, 2003. pp.25-29. CBD. (2004). *Technical Advice on the Establishment and Management of a National System of Marine and Coastal Protected Areas.* (CBD Technical Series No 13). 20-31. Secretariat of the CBD. (2004). *Biodiversity Issues for Consideration in the Planning, Establishment and Management of Protected Area Sites and Management.* (CBD Technical Series No 15). 37-45, 73-82.

145 CBD. Decision VII/28. Protected Areas. Annex. Section 1.4.5

146 In 1999, the ICRI noted that, 'the rise in sea temperature and consequent coral bleaching and morality events pose a significant threat to coral reef ecosystems and the human populations which depend upon them'. Moreover, 'the geographical extent, increasing frequency,

pact'.[147] Accordingly, the ICRI has sought to ingratiate itself in the pivotal international forums examining this problem such as the United Nations Framework Convention on Climate Change, (UNFCCC), the CBD and the Intergovernmental Panel on Climate Change (IPCC) so as to get the matter of coral reefs particularly focused upon.[148] They have also called upon all Parties to 'consider reducing their outputs of greenhouse gases' as such 'increases are linked with global climate change with resulting damage to coral reefs'.[149]

The one protected areas regime which has actively engaged the UNFCCC on this matter is the Ramsar. The Ramsar has been examining the possible impacts and vulnerabilities of wetlands to climate change since 1990.[150] This ongoing scientific work has links to the IPCC.[151] Although all of the science on this issue is not yet concluded, the Ramsar is clearly of the opinion that climate change and its predicted impacts represent a major threat to wetlands of international importance.[152] At the same time, ill managed climate mitigation strategies, such as with the creation of carbon sinks, may also damage wetland ecosystems. Accordingly, the Ramsar called upon its Parties, when implementing the UNFCCC or Kyoto Protocol through revegetation, forest management, afforestation and reforestation, to ensure that, 'this implementation does not lead to serious damage to the ecological character of the wetlands'.[153] The overall goal in the face of such threats, is that wetlands should be managed so as to, inter alia, increase their resilience to climate change and extreme climatic events.[154] However, realising also that the solution to the problem of climatic change will be found in the UNFCCC and Kyoto Protocol (and not the regime on wetlands), the Ramsar signatories have noted the WSSD recommendation to Parties to ratify the Kyoto Protocol.[155]

Next to the implications of climate change on wetlands, there is the issue of the contribution of greenhouse gas emissions from wetlands, to the problem of climate change. This

---

and regional severity of mass bleaching events are likely a consequence of a steadily rising baseline of marine temperatures in combination with climate change'.

147 Resolution on Priority Actions. In ICRI (2000). Report of the ICRI Meeting in Noumea, New Caledonia, 25-26 May, 2000.

148 See Resolution on Coral Bleaching and Climate Change to the UN Framework Convention on Climate Change. In ICRI. (1999). Report of the ICRI Meeting in Guadeloupe, France, 27-28 Oct, 1999.

149 See ICRI. (2001). Report of the ICRI Meeting in Maputo, Mozambique, 29-30 Nov, 2001.

150 Recommendation 4.1. Wetland Restoration. (1990, Montreux).

151 Resolution 6.13. Information on Ramsar Sites. (1996, Brisbane). Resolution 8.1. Allocation and Management of Water. (2002, Valencia). Paragraph 20.

152 Resolution 8.25. The Ramsar Strategic Plan. (2002, Valencia). Annex. I.12.

153 Resolution 8.1. Allocation and Management of Water. (2002, Valencia). Paragraph 18.

154 Resolution 8.3. Climate Change and Wetlands: Impacts, Adaptation and Mitigation. (2002, Valencia). Resolution 8.32. Conservation, Integrated Management and Sustainable Use of Mangrove Ecosystems and Their Resources. (2002, Valencia).

155 Resolution 8.1. Allocation and Management of Water. (2002, Valencia). Paragraph 22.

problem was becoming apparent by the end of the 1990s when the strong overlap between wetlands and climatic change, with regard to their capacity to both emit and sequester climatic gases became apparent. Although emissions from peat fires is a recognised Ramsar concern,[156] it is the sequestration potential of peatlands which has occupied most of the Ramsar Parties attention. This attention is because 'peatlands globally have been identified as a major storehouse of the world's carbon, exceeding that of forests'.[157] Thus, they are, 'vital to the world's climate system'.[158] Accordingly, special attention should be given to, inter alia, 'the capacity to act as a carbon store and the presence of a carbon sequestration function'.[159] In furtherance of this sequestration capacity, the Ramsar has developed two lines of approach. First, it has endorsed the idea of a Memorandum of Understanding with the UNFCCC.[160] This is partly due to ensure that considerations surrounding wetland carbon sinks and sequestration are adequately built within the Kyoto Protocol.[161] Second, the Ramsar has created and adopted Guidelines for the Global Action on Peatlands.[162] The priority areas for these Guidelines are the inventory, status, trends and public awareness of the role of wetlands in the climate change matrix.[163] This is buttressed by strong recommendations to Parties to minimise the degradation, and improve the management practices of peatlands and other wetland types that have significant sequestration potential.[164]

The final convention of note in this area is the WHC. Within its ambit, it has been suggested that a number of Parties are failing in their obligations to protect the world's heritage, by not adequately confronting the problem of climatic change.[165] Accordingly, in 2005, the WHC was strongly lobbied to classify as in Danger, the Sagamartha (Everest) National Park in Nepal, the Huascaran National Park in the Peruvian Andes, and the Belize Barrier Reef, because of the threat of climatic change. Although the Committee decided against such inscription, it did agree to an expert working group to review the nature and scale of the risks posed to WHC sites arising from climate change.[166] This duly reported, and in 2006 a further workshop was called for to look

---

156 Recommendation 7.1. The Wise Use of Peatlands. (1999, San Jose).

157 Resolution 8.17. Guidelines for Global Action on Peatlands (GAP). (2002, Valencia). Annex. Paragraph 14.

158 Ibid.

159 Resolution 8.11. Additional Guidance for Identifying and Designating Under Represented Wetland Types as Wetlands of International Importance. (2002, Valencia). Annex. Identification and Designation of Peatlands. Paragraphs 15-16.

160 Recommendation 7.2. Small Island Developing States. (1999, San Jose).

161 Recommendation 7.1. The Wise Use of Peatlands. (1999, San Jose). Annex. Draft Global Action Plan for the Wise Use and Management of Peatlands. Para. 2.

162 Resolution 8.17. Guidelines for Global Action on Peatlands (GAP). (2002, Valencia).

163 Ibid.

164 Resolution 8.1. Allocation and Management of Water. (2002, Valencia). Paragraphs 15 & 18.

165 Anon. (2004). 'Lawsuits Over Reef Damage.' *New Scientist.* Oct 2. 7.

166 See Decision 29 COM 7B.aRev.

at, inter alia, 'legal questions on the role of the World Heritage Convention with regard to suitable responses to climate change' and 'alternative mechanisms, other than the List of World Heritage in Danger, to address concerns of international implication, such as climatic change'.[167]

Exactly how far the WHC will go on the topic of climate change is a matter of speculation, as the WHC has treaded cautiously in this area. Apart from some notations that some sites are important for the monitoring of climate change[168] and that some sites may become 'species refuges' from the impacts of climate change,[169] the matter has not advanced greatly. In fact, in a number of instances, the WHC has noted that some climate friendly technologies, such as wind turbines may have detrimental aesthetic implications for some sites.[170] The concern about wind-turbines has also been echoed by the CMS[171] and the Bern Convention,[172] although with the latter two, the concern is over their impact on wildlife, not aesthetics.

6 Water Supply and Large Dams

Having an adequate water supply to a protected area is essential for the ecological integrity of many protected areas.[173] Although this is a threat to the sites under all international or regional regimes, and has been noted in the WHC,[174] it is, unsurprisingly, most pronounced with the Ramsar, which considers the diversion of water as one

---

167 For a report of the Committee, see Gibson, M. (2006). 'World Heritage and the Challenge of Climate Change'. 42 *World Heritage* 2006, June. 3-9. For the 2006 decision, see 30 COM 7.1.

168 The Uvs Nuur Basin shared between Mongolia/Russia has been chosen as a site for the International Geosphere-Biosphere Programme (IGPB) site for monitoring global warming. UNESCO. (2003). 27th Session of the WHC. WHC-03/27.COM/24. Dec 10. 102. The Virgin Komi Forests of the Russian Federation is also recognised as an important site for scientific research including climate change. UNESCO. (1996). 19th Session of the WHC. WHC-95/CONF.203/16. Jan 31, 1996. 35.

169 Sumatra. UNESCO. (2004). 28th Session of the WHC. WHC-04/28.COM/26. Oct 29. Decision 28 COM 14B5. pp. 17. As also argued with the Cerrado in Brazil. UNESCO. (2001). 25th Session of the WHC. WHC-01/CONF.208/24. Feb 8, 2002. 90.

170 UNESCO. (2004). 28th Session of the WHC. WHC-04/28.COM/26. Oct 29. Decision 28 COM 15B.22.8p91.

171 Resolution 7.5. Wind Turbines and Migratory Species. (COP 7, 2002, Bonn).

172 Recommendation No. 109. (2004). On Minimizing Adverse Effects of Wind Power Generation on Wildlife. Report of the 24th Bern Meeting of the Bern Convention. T-PVS (2004). 16. Appendix 3.

173 See for example, Young, E. (2005). 'East African Parks Face Bleak Future'. *New Scientist*. Sept 24. 11.

174 Water extraction at Te Wahipouamu. UNESCO. (1992). 16th Session of the WHC. WHC-92/CONF.002/12. Dec 14, 1992. 24.

of the primary threats to the conservation of wetlands in the 21st century.[175] To begin to confront this potential problem, the Ramsar Parties have adopted, and refined, guidelines for a precautionary, sustainable, equitable, transparent and flexible management of water for maintaining the ecological functions of wetlands.[176] At all points in this debate, the Ramsar Parties have emphasised that even in situations of adversity, all efforts, as far as practicable, should seek to allow the continued allocation of water to Ramsar wetlands in accordance with their natural hydrological regimes, so as to ensure that they can continue to provide their full range of functions and values.[177] Despite the simplicity of this goal Ramsar Parties have had to issue recommendations to rectify water related problems to Spain,[178] Senegal,[179] the United States,[180] Greece[181] and Australia.[182] The most direct example of Ramsar concern in this area is with Jordan, where direct resolutions were issued from the late 1980s to the late 1990s calling upon the Jordanian authorities to set clear limits on how much water could be taken from the Azraq oasis to provide drinking water for their capital.[183]

The foremost example dealing with the control of fresh water and protected areas is with regard to large dams. In addition to their potentially vast social costs, large dams generally have a range of extensive impacts on rivers, watersheds and aquatic ecosystems. The evidence suggests that to date, these impacts are more negative than positive and, in many cases, have lead to irreversible loss of species and ecosystems. Efforts to counter these impacts have met with limited success. Accordingly, as the World Commission on Dams concluded, avoiding ecological impacts through good site selection and project design (such as ensuring that adequate water flows pass through

---

175 Resolution 8.25. The Ramsar Strategic Plan. (2002, Valencia). Annex. I.12. Resolution VI.23. Ramsar and Water. (1996, Brisbane).

176 Resolution 9.1. Additional Scientific and Technical Guidance for Implementing the Ramsar Wise Use Concept. (2005, Kampala). Annex C. Guidelines for the Management of Groundwater to Maintain Wetland Ecological Character. Resolution 8.1. Allocation and Management of Water. (2002, Valencia). See also Resolution 8.40. Guidelines for Rendering the Use of Groundwater Compatible with The Conservation of Wetlands. (2002, Valencia).

177 Resolution 8.35. The Impact of Natural Disasters, Particularly Drought, on Wetland Ecosystems. (2002, Valencia).

178 Recommendation 4.9.1. Donana National Park. (1990, Montreux).

179 Recommendation 2.7. Djoudj National Bird Park. (1984, Groningen).

180 Recommendation 4.9.2. The Everglades. (1990, Montreux).

181 Recommendation 6.17.1. Greek Ramsar Sites. (1996, Brisbane).

182 Recommendation 6.17.4. Australian Ramsar Sites. (1996, Brisbane).

183 The 3rd COP called upon Jordan to reduce the then current rate of extraction of 16 million cubic meters of water per annum by 50% and the 4th COP followed up, recommending a total extraction rate that should not exceed the 'safe yield' of 20 million cubic tonnes annually. Recommendation 3.8. The Azraq Oasis, Jordan. (1987, Regina). Recommendation 4.9.3. The Azraq Oasis, Jordan. (1990, Montreux). Recommendation 5.1. Ramsar Sites in Specific Contracting Parties. (1993, Kushiro). Recommendation 6.17.3. The Azraq Oasis, Jordan. (1996, Brisbane).

the dam to the downstream ecosystems) is a priority.[184] The potential problems that large dams may present to protected areas have been evident since 1962, when the First World Conference on National Parks recommended,

> Structures such as dams and reservoirs for hydro-electric and other purposes which would in any way [be] prejudicial to the purpose of a park should not be allowed in a national park, and that buildings and other tourist facilities should, wherever possible, be made outside of the parks, in order to preserve those values for which the parks were established.[185]

The protected area forums that have had to deal with large dams have never adopted this recommendation. Rather, the Ramsar, Bern and WHC have all, implicitly, accepted that large dams may be within their respective sites, provided their impacts are containable. For example, with the Bern Convention, the typical approach of the Parties has been to recommend to the countries contemplating large dams in important habitat areas to have full EIAs, cost-benefit analysis, and careful studies to make sure that the species and ecosystems that may be impacted upon by the projects are within acceptable limits. This approach has been with the planned Iruena dam in Salamanca in Spain,[186] the Odelouca dam in Portugal,[187] and hydro-dams in Iceland.[188] Only once, with the Vidrieros dam project in Spain, did the Parties request Spain to 'reconsider' the project, due to its impact on the habitat of the Cantabrian bear.[189]

Dams and water diversion have been a clear threat to Ramsar wetlands since the inception of the Convention. Their threats have ranged from transboundary impacts between Afghanistan and Iran,[190] through to plans by Greece (which did not eventuate)[191] for river diversion projects which would have reduced the amount of water entering listed wetlands of international importance from 1.1 billion to 600 million m^3

---

184 World Commission on Dams. (2000). *Dams and Development: A New Framework for Development.* (Earthscan, London). Xxvii. For the Ramsar support of this Commission, see Resolution 8.2. The Report of the World Commission on Dams and it Relevance to the Ramsar Convention. (2002, Valencia). for some additional critiques on large dams; see Pearce, F. (2003). 'Replumbing the Planet'. *New Scientist.* June 7. 30-34. Also by Pearce, in *New Scientist.* March 22, 2003 at 9 and 27.

185 See 'Closing Plenary Session.' In Adams, A. (ed). *First World Conference on National Parks.* (US Department of the Interior, Washington). 380. Recommendation No 11.

186 Recommendation No. 46. (1995). On the Proposed Iruena Dam Site, Salamanca, Spain. Report of the 14th Meeting of the Bern Convention. T-PVS (95) 26. Appendix 10.

187 Recommendation No. 107. The Odelouca Dam (Portugal). Report of the 23rd Meeting of the Bern Convention. T-PVS. (2003). 24. Appendix 11.

188 Recommendation No. 112. (2004). On Hydroelectric Dams at Karahnjukar (Iceland). Report of the 24th Bern Meeting of the Bern Convention. T-PVS (2004). 16. Appendix 6.

189 Recommendation No. 37. (1992). The Conservation of the Cantabrian Bear.

190 Recommendation 4.9. Sites in the Territories of Specific Contracting Parties. (1990, Montreux).

191 Resolution 7.12. Sites in the Ramsar List. (1999, San Jose).

per year.[192] From the very first Ramsar conference, recommendations[193] were urging that any planned dams or dikes on the drawing board for Denmark, the Netherlands and West Germany (a concern which was to reappear for West Germany again in the early 1990s with the Leybucht sector of the Wadden sea)[194] should not be undertaken until appropriate research has demonstrated that no harmful effects to their wetlands would result. Similar pleas were directed to Iceland, with regard to the Thjorsarver wetland.[195] Even with disputes over wetlands and dams between its Parties that ended up at the International Court of Justice, such as with the 1997 *Case Concerning the Gabcikovo-Nagymaros Project*,[196] the Ramsar response was only to encourage them to accept the ICJ ruling (to continue talking to resolve the dispute in good faith),[197] and to work with the international community towards a satisfactory resolution of ecological concerns such as the safeguarding of the best wildlife sites along the lower Danube.[198]

The most direct approach to large scale dams the Ramsar has adopted was with the various hydro-agricultural development projects planned for the Senegal valley.[199] Specifically, although Ramsar did not call for an end to the projects, they did recommend, and retained on the Ramsar agenda,[200] a call for the respective governments (Mali, Mauritania and Senegal) to,

> Take all necessary steps to prevent adverse consequences via plans for an adequate network of wetland reserves and to ensure the continued value of the Djoudj National Park as a

192 Recommendation 6.17.1. Greek Ramsar Sites. (1996, Brisbane).

193 Final Act of the Ramsar Conference. Annex II. Recommendations adopted by the International Conference on the Conservation of Wetlands and Waterfowl at Ramsar, Iran, 3 February 1971. Recommendation 1. Conservation of the Wadden Sea, north-western Europe.

194 Recommendation 4.9.4. Leybucht, Germany. (1990, Montreux). Recommendation 5.1. Ramsar Sites in Specific Contracting Parties. (1993, Kushiro).

195 Final Act of the Ramsar Conference. Annex II. *Ibid.* Conservation of Thjorsarver, Iceland.

196 *Case Concerning The Gabcíkovo-Nagymaros Project* (Hungary/Slovakia). 1997 , 25 September, General List No. 92.

197 Hungary/Slovakia. Ibid. Paragraph 141, 143, 155 (2)(b). See Eckstein, G. (1995). 'Application of International Water Law to Transboundary Groundwater Resources, and the Slovak-Hungarian Dispute Over Gabcikovo-Nagmaros'. 19 *Suffolk Transnational Law Review.* 67, 72, 78-79.

198 Recommendation 5.1.3. The Lower Danube Basin. (1993, Kushiro).

199 Recommendations adopted by the International Conference on the Conservation of Wetlands and Waterfowl at Heiligenhafen, Federal Republic of Germany, 6 December 1974. Recommendation 10. Conservation of the Senegal Valley.

200 The Ramsar meeting in 1984, continued recommendations in this area, calling specifically for an artificial estuary be protected in Mauritania to complement the Djoudj Park in Senegal (as otherwise all natural habitat in the lower Senegal delta would disappear after the Diama Dam would come into operation). Recommendation 2.8. Establishment of a Protected Area in the River Senegal Basin in Mauritania. (1984, Groningen).

> wetland of international importance which this development would have for the natural wetlands of the Senegal valley.[201]

Hydro development can be found within 15% of all WHC natural sites.[202] Such development, especially when at the proposal stage, has been recorded with a note of caution due to potential impacts on WHC areas with sites in the United States,[203] Brazil,[204] Honduras,[205] Serbia and Montenegro,[206] Thailand,[207] Niger,[208] Zimbabwe[209] and the shared Victoria Falls.[210] The test, as clearly stated with regard to the Djoudj site in Senegal,[211] Manas Reserve in India[212] and Wood Buffalo in Canada, is that the integrity of the site must not be compromised by the development. In some instances, such as with the Canadian one, the yardstick of integrity was whether the dam altered the nesting of the whooping crane in the park.[213] If the integrity of the site was compromised by the dam, it is likely that the site would be inscribed as in Danger. This type of warning was made very clearly to Australia[214] and Niger.[215] Also, in 2004,

201 Recommendation 10. Conservation of the Senegal Valley. *Ibid.*

202 IUCN. (1998). *Human Use of World Heritage Natural Sites: A Global Overview.* (IUCN, Gland). 6-7.

203 Yosemite National Park. UNESCO. (1984). 8th Session of the WHC. SC/84/CONF.004/9. Nov 2, 1984. pp 9.

204 Decision COM 7B.28.

205 Rio Platano. UNESCO. (1998). 22nd Session of the WHC. WHC-98/CONF.203/18. Jan 29, 1999. 22-23.

206 Durmitor National Park. This concern originally arose in 1985. UNESCO. (1985). 9th Session of the WHC. SC-85/CONF.008/9. Dec, 1985. pp 11-12. In 2005, the Committee congratulated Serbia and Montenegro to halt the hydro project. See Decision 29 COM 7B.201.

207 Thungyai Wildlife Sanctuary. UNESCO. (1991). 15th Session of the WHC. SC-91/CONF.002/15. Dec 12, 1991. 19.

208 Decision 29 COM 7B.4, welcoming Niger's decision to forgo the planned dam. For earlier discussion, see Decision 28 COM 15B.1.

209 Mana Pools & Chewore Safari Areas. UNESCO. (1984). 8th Session of the WHC. SC/84/CONF.004/9. Nov 2, 1984. pp 9.

210 UNESCO. (1992). 16th Session of the WHC. WHC-92/CONF.002/12. Dec 14, 1992. 27. UNESCO. (1993). 17th Session of WHC. WHC-93/CONF.002/14. Feb 4, 1993. 17. UNESCO. (1995). 18th Session of the WHC. WHC-94/CONF.003/16. Jan 31. 1995. 22.

211 UNESCO. (1981). 5th Session of the WHC. CC-81/CONF.002/4. July 20, 1981..5. UNESCO. (1981). 5th Session of the WHC. CC-81/CONF.003/6. Jan 5, 1981.4.

212 Manas Wildlife Sanctuary. UNESCO. (1985). 9th Session of the WHC. SC-85/CONF.008/9. Dec, 1985. pp 6.

213 Wood Buffalo National Park. UNESCO. (1984). 7th Session of the WHC. SC/83/CONF.009/8. Jan 12, 1984. pp 5. UNESCO. (1985). 9th Session of the WHC. SC-85/CONF.008/9. Dec, 1985. pp 11-12. UNESCO. (1990). 14th Session of the WHC. CLT-90/CONF.004/13. Dec 12, 1990. 10.

214 The Western Tasmania Wilderness National Parks. UNESCO. (1983). 6th Session of the WHC. CC-83/CONF.015/8. Jan 17, 1983. pp.3-4. UNESCO. (1984). 7th Session of the WHC. CLT/83/CONF.021/8. Aug 1, 1983. pp 9.

2005,[216] and 2006,[217] the Committee gave a clear warning to China over its Three Parallel Rivers of the Yunnan Protected Areas, by expressing,

> [I]t's gravest concerns on the impacts that the proposed construction of dams could have on the outstanding universal value of [what]… may be the most biologically diverse temperate ecosystem in the world.[218]

Likewise, when the Sichuan Giant Panda sanctuary was inscribed in 2006, not only were effective mitigation measures required for the existing or already approved dams, the Committee also clearly stated that 'no additional dams are built within the property'.[219] A similar request to the State Party of Brazil 'to deny authorisation' for a proposed dam which would impact upon the Iguacu National Park, was also made by the Committee in 2006.[220]

In some instances, a site proposed for inscription is deferred until demonstration by the State Party of its commitment that the integrity of the site will be protected, such as by maintaining water flow or control pollution.[221] In other instances, once a site has been inscribed on the WHC List, it may become necessary to prompt a State to maintain adequate flows of water. This has been the practice with sites in Madagascar,[222] Tanzania and Kenya,[223] India,[224] and Nepal.[225] Occasionally, Parties have been congratulated for securing greater inputs of water into sites that were under stress, such as with the Everglades.[226] However, in three instances, sites were listed as in Danger because the water quantity (and/or quality) deteriorated to such a point, that the integrity of the site was directly threatened. This was the case with the Ichkeul

215 The Western National Park. UNESCO. (2003). 27th Session of the WHC. WHC-03/27.COM/24. Dec 10, 2003. 34.

216 Decision 29 COM 7B.7.

217 Decision 30 COM 7B.11.

218 UNESCO. (2004). 28th Session of the WHC. WHC-04/28.COM/26. Oct 29. Decision 28 COM 15B.9.pp79. Also, Marshall, J. (2006). 'The Three Gorges Dam'. *New Scientist.* Feb 25. 18-19.

219 Decision 30 COM 8B22.

220 Decision 30 COM 7B. 30.

221 Such as with the Steppe and Lakes of Kazakhstan. UNESCO. (2003). 27th Session of the WHC. WHC-03/27.COM/24. Dec 10. 100.

222 Tsingy. UNESCO. (1992). 16th Session of the WHC. WHC-92/CONF.002/12. Dec 14, 1992. 24.

223 With regard to water flows into the Serengeti. UNESCO. (2002). 26th Session of the WHC. WHC-02/CONF.202/25. Aug 1, 2002. 36.

224 Keoladeo in India. 29 COM 7B.8.

225 UNESCO. (1990). 14th Session of the WHC. CLT-90/CONF.004/13. Dec 12, 1990. 9. UNESCO. (1991). 15th Session of the WHC. SC-91/CONF.002/15. Dec 12, 1991. 9.

226 UNESCO. (1989). 11th Session of the WHC. SC-89/CONF.004/12. Dec, 22 1989. pp 5.

National Park in Tunisia,[227] the Srebarna Biosphere reserve[228] and the Djoudj National Bird Sanctuary.[229]

7 Mineral and/or Hydrocarbon Exploration and/or Extraction

Mineral and/or hydrocarbon exploration and/or extraction within protected areas produce high level public debates. This problem is noticeable in both domestic (such as with the American Arctic National Wildlife Refuge)[230] and international settings. Although some regimes, such as the South East Pacific Protocol expressly prohibit any mining activities in the protected areas,[231] the most known example of this approach is with the Antarctic regime. In particular, the Parties to the Antarctic Treaty, after a high profile international debate, opted to expressly prohibit, not regulate, any activity related to mineral/hydrocarbon extraction.[232]

Feelings run-high because mineral and/or hydrocarbon exploration and/or extraction can impact on protected areas in any number of ways. When it is illegal, by its nature it is likely to be unregulated and damaging. In such instances, both the legitimate mining industry and environmental NGOs are in general agreement, that such illegal activities in protected areas must be stopped. The policy on which there is less agreement relates to legal and well regulated extraction within protected areas. Although legal exploration or extraction within an area is often a highly visible intrusion, dramatically changing the landscape, if well managed, the visual impacts may not last more than a few decades. Conversely, badly regulated exploration and/or extraction, may permanently destroy the integrity of a site.

---

227 See also, Lac Ichkeul. UNESCO. (1978). 2nd Session of the WHC. CC-78/CONF.010/3. Sep 5, 1978. pp.4.

228 UNESCO. (1991). 15th Session of the WHC. SC-91/CONF.002/15. Dec 12, 1991. 6.

229 Decision 29 COM 7A. UNESCO. (1981). 5th Session of the WHC. CC-81/CONF.002/4. July 20, 1981. pp.6. UNESCO. (1981). 5th Session of the WHC. CC-81/CONF.003/6. Jan 5, 1981. pp.5. UNESCO. (1984). 7th Session of the WHC. SC/83/CONF.009/8. Jan 12, 1984. pp 10. UNESCO. (1985). 9th Session of the WHC. SC-85/CONF.008/9. Dec, 1985. pp 6. UNESCO. (1986). 10th Session of the WHC. CC-86/CONF.003/10. Dec 5, 1986. pp 8. UNESCO. (1987). 11th Session of the WHC. CC-87/CONF.005/9. Jan 20, 1988. pp 10. UNESCO. (1988). 12th Session of the WHC. SC-88/CONF.001/13. Dec 23, 1988. 6, 15. UNESCO. (1992). 16th Session of the WHC. WHC-92/CONF.002/12. Dec 14, 1992. 25.

230 Anon. (2005). 'Arctic Reprieve'. *New Scientist.* Nov 19. 5. Anon. (2005). 'Alaska Waits for Oil Outcome'. *New Scientist.* Nov 12. 6. Anon. (2002). 'Reprieve For Wildlife Refuge'. *New Scientist.* Apr 27. 5. Anon. (2005). 'Setback For Alaska Reserve'. *New Scientist.* Mar 26. 7.

231 1989 Protocol for the Conservation and Management of Protected Marine and Coastal Areas of the South East Pacific. Reprinted in Austen, A. (ed). *Basic Legal Document on International Animal Welfare and Wildlife Conservation.* (Kluwer, London). Article 5 (b).

232 Madrid Protocol. Article 7.

Due to such potential impacts of legal exploration and/or extraction, a number of NGOs have actively campaigned against such activities within protected areas. These campaigns have run directly into to the goals of a number of industry groups that claim that mineral and/or hydro-carbon exploration and/or extraction within protected areas need not be mutually exclusive as such operations can contribute to biodiversity conservation, while minimizing environmental impacts. In addition, it is contended, that well managed extraction can help reduce poverty and produce positive economic feedbacks for local communities.[233] This conflict between the two opposing views came to a head in 1998 when the World Commission on Protected Areas, in a clear hardening of positions,[234] issued a policy position that called on governments to exclude all forms of mineral extraction from all protected areas that would fall within the IUCN categories[235] I to IV (the relatively pristine protected areas, encompassing about 6% of the global land areas from mineral activity), and strict controls over mineral extraction in Categories V to VI (the more sustainable use areas). This policy position was confirmed at the fourth[236] and fifth[237] World Parks Congresses. However, due to a number of problems with this proposal, not least the robustness of the IUCN categories,[238] the mineral and/or hydrocarbon industries have not pledged themselves to this goal. Indeed, some transnational corporations, such as British Petroleum continue to possess 49 units operating near or adjacent to protected areas, with 5 of these units operating in areas categorized between I to IV. However, some notable transnational corporations, such as Shell,[239] and some other members of the International Council on Mining and Metals,[240] have promised not to explore or mine in WHC sites, and to take all possible steps to ensure that their operations are not incompatible with the outstanding universal values of the sites in question.

---

233 Mining, Minerals and Sustainable Development/Business Council for Sustainable Development. (2002). *Breaking New Ground.* (Earthscan, London). 161-166.

234 Especially when compared to earlier times. For example, following earlier World Parks Congress precedents in this area for compromise, rather than an outright prohibitive approach, they called for strong management regimes, including EIAs, to make sure that the integrity of protected sites is not destroyed. Recommendation 6. Threats to Protected Areas. Recommendations of the World National Parks Congress. In McNeely, J. (ed). *National Parks, Conservation and Development.* (Smithsonian, Washington). 769.

235 See chapter II.

236 See Recommendation 2.82. 'In categories V and VI, exploration and localized extraction would be accepted only where the nature and extent of the proposed activities of the mining project indicates the compatibility if the project activities with the objectives of the protected areas'.

237 IUCN 5th World Parks Congress (2003, Durban). Recommendation 5.28: Protected Areas: Mining and Energy. Last preambular paragraph and Operative Paragraph 1.

238 See IUCN. (2004). *Speaking A Common Language.* (IUCN, Gland). 159.

239 Kaipla, S. (2004). 'Shell's Perspective on the IUCN Protected Areas Management Category System'. 14(3) *Parks.* 46-50.

240 Richards, D. (2004). 'International Council on Mining and Metals Perspective on the IUCN Protected Areas Management Category System'. 14(3) *Parks.* 39-45.

Concerns with mineral and/or hydrocarbon extraction and/or exploration have also arisen in the Bern Convention,[241] and the Ramsar with regard to gas exploration in the Wadden Sea[242] and mining in South Africa.[243] They have also arisen with the MAB,[244] where in 2006 the Bureau ruled very clearly that mining activities within a core area were not compatible with core area status.[245] However, it is the WHC which has developed the most extensive jurisprudence on this area. This is not surprising, given the fact that mineral and/or hydrocarbon extraction and/or exploration occurs in 26% of all WHC natural sites.[246] In response to such threats, a number of influential position papers have been issued and workshops on the topic have been held[247] from which the Parties to the WHC have adopted a complicated response to the issue.

First, the Parties have targeted the big mining companies (as noted above). Second, the Committee have sought to work directly with the interested Parties, and finally, the Committee developed a strong jurisprudence on the issue, which can be broken down into two areas. The first area deals with substantial mining within or adjoining a WHC site. In these instances the Committee has sent strong signals to countries, such as Zimbabwe,[248] Panama,[249] Cameroon,[250] Australia[251] and Niger,[252] whom were all at

241 They were particularly concerned over the collapse of mine tailing dam at Doanna in southern Spain.

242 Final Act of the Ramsar Conference. Annex II. Recommendations adopted by the International Conference on the Conservation of Wetlands and Waterfowl at Ramsar, Iran, 3 February 1971. Recommendation 1. Conservation of the Wadden Sea, north-western Europe. Recommendation 4.9.4. Leybucht, Germany. (1990, Montreux). Recommendation 5.1. Ramsar Sites in Specific Contracting Parties. (1993, Kushiro). The 6th COP welcomed measures introduced by the Netherlands to counter the threat posed by gas exploration in the Wadden sea. Recommendation 6.17. Ramsar Sites in Particular Countries. (1996, Brisbane).

243 Recommendation 4.9. Sites in the Territories of Specific Contracting Parties. (1990, Montreux). Recommendation 5.1. Ramsar Sites in Specific Contracting Parties. (1993, Kushiro). Recommendation 6.17. Ramsar Sites in Particular Countries. (1996, Brisbane).

244 UNESCO. (2002). *Biosphere Reserves: Special Places for People and Nature.* (UNESCO, Paris). 45.

245 Huascaran, Peru. UNESCO. (2006). Meeting of the Bureau of the International Coordinating Committee. SC-05/CONF.210/16. Aug 18. 15.

246 IUCN. (1998). Human Use of World Heritage Natural Sites: A Global Overview. (IUCN, Gland). 6-7.

247 UNESCO. (1999). 23rd Session of the WHC. WHC-99/CONF.209/22. Mar 22, 2000. 90-91. UNESCO. (2001). 24th Session of the WHC. WHC-2000/CONF.204/21. Feb 16, 2001. 55-56.

248 Mana pools. UNESCO. (1985). 9th Session of the WHC. SC-85/CONF.008/9. Dec, 1985. pp 4.

249 Talamanca La Amistad National Park. UNESCO. (1991). 15th Session of the WHC. SC-91/CONF.002/15. Dec 12, 1991. 7. UNESCO. (1992). 16th Session of the WHC. WHC-92/CONF.002/12. Dec 14, 1992. 20.

250 UNESCO. (2004). 28th Session of the WHC. WHC-04/28.COM/26. Oct 29. Decision 28 COM 15B.2.pp76.

various points contemplating allowing mineral or hydrocarbon exploration within some of their WHC sites. In each instance, the Committee clearly pointed out that any such activities could quickly lead to the site being placed on the Danger List. Conversely, when any small scale existing mining within a proposed site has been stopped, the Committee has always voiced its strong approval.[253] Second, the Committee has expressed direct concern about possible mining in the vicinity (typically adjacent to or close by) WHC sites, and the need to control such activities, so as to not threaten the outstanding universal value of WHC sites. Such expressions of concern have been forwarded to Mauritania,[254] Russia,[255] Yugoslavia,[256] Spain,[257] Canada[258] and Peru.[259] In 2006, the Committee continued forwarded their extreme concern to interested Parties, such as Oman, due to their plan to explore for oil in the Arabian Oryx Sanctuary, and threatened that such explorations could create the case (as it eventually did) for having the site as being listed as in Danger.[260] However, it has been most clearly dealt with in the cases of Australia's Kakadu, Cote d Ivoire's Mount Nimba, the Rwenzori Mountains in Uganda and Italy's Aeolian islands.

With regard to the Kakadu site, the extension to the original site was only designated in the mid 1980s, when it was clear that mining would not be allowed in the actual property (the mining site was actually an enclave which was subsequently incorporated

---

251 Great Blue mountains and the proposed sand and clay mine. UNESCO. (2004). 28th Session of the WHC. WHC-04/28.COM/26. Oct 29. Decision 28 COM 15B.15.pp83.

252 The Western National Park. UNESCO. (2003). 27th Session of the WHC. WHC-03/27.COM/24. Dec 10, 2003. 34.

253 Such as with the Western Tasmanian Wilderness National Park. UNESCO. (1989). 13th Session of the WHC. SC-89/CONF.004/12. Dec, 22 1989. pp 11.

254 Banc d'Arguin National Park.UNESCO. (2003). 27th Session of the WHC. WHC-03/27.COM/24. Dec 10, 2003. 35.

255 The Kamchatka Volcanoes. Decision 29 COM 7B.20. UNESCO. (1997). 21st Session of the WHC. WHC-97/CONF.208/17. Feb 27, 1998. 22.

256 Durmitor National Park. UNESCO. (1996). 20th Session of the WHC. WHC-96/CONF.201/21. Mar 10, 1997. 29.

257 Donana National Park, noted for toxic spill in neighbouring mine that nearly effected the WH site. UNESCO. (1998). 22nd Session of the WHC. WHC-98/CONF.208/18. Jan 29, 1998. 37.

258 Despite an EIA showing limited impact for this mine proposal 2km away from the Rockies site, the Committee called upon the Canadian government to reconsider the decision, with a view to seeking out alternative sites with less damaging effects. UNESCO. (1997). 21st Session of the WHC. WHC-97/CONF.208/17. Feb 27, 1998. 21. See also the debate about Nahanni Park. UNESCO. (2002). 26th Session of the WHC. WHC-02/CONF.202/25. Aug 1, 2002. 28. UNESCO. (2003). 27th Session of the WHC. WHC-03/27.COM/24. Dec 10, 2003. 40. For Jasper park in the Rockies, see Decision 29 COM 7B.16.

259 Manu Park. UNESCO. (1989). 11th Session of the WHC. SC-89/CONF.004/12. Dec, 22 1989. pp 4.

260 See Decision 30 COM 7B.10.

into the WHC property) and its overall integrity would remain intact.[261] However, when a uranium mine was opened up on the outskirts of the site, a strong debate occurred over its possible ecological and cultural impacts and whether the site needed to be listed as in Danger.[262] An independent review of the mine came to the conclusion that if the highest environmental standards were followed (which meant that in this instance, public participation, monitoring and compliance all needed to be enhanced), then the mining would not threaten the overall health of people or the biological and ecological systems of the site.[263] Nevertheless, the Kakadu mines remained a standing concern for the Committee.[264]

The Mount Nimba site is inscribed upon the Danger List. Although it is listed as in Danger for numerous reasons, the fact that there is mining close to the border of the site, and that site boundaries have been amended to accommodate the mining leases, the Committee adopted a number of unusual approaches.[265] In particular, it requested foreign States to not directly encourage any mining in this area, indirectly warning off international investment/aid agencies such as the World Bank[266] and working closely with other UN agencies and NGOs, to form Memorandum's of Understanding with the mining companies, so as to ensure rigorous environmental management standards are met.[267]

---

261 UNESCO. (1987). 11th Session of the WHC. CC-87/CONF.005/9. Jan 20, 1988. pp 3. UNESCO. (1986). 10th Session of the WHC. CC-86/CONF.003/10. Dec 5, 1986. pp 7.

262 UNESCO. (1998). 22nd Session of the WHC. WHC-98/CONF.203/18. Jan 29, 1999. 9, 39-45.

263 UNESCO. (2001). 24th Session of the WHC. WHC-2000/CONF.204/21. Feb 16, 2001. 42, 45. UNESCO. (2001). 25th Session of the WHC. WHC-01/CONF.208/24. Feb 8, 2002. 54. See also the debate on Purnululu National Park in Australia. UNESCO. (2003). 27th Session of the WHC. WHC-03/27.COM/24. Dec 10. 104-105.

264 Thus, in 2004, the Committee of the WHC expressed their concern to Australia over the continued contaminated water problems from the Ranger uranium mine and the apparent failure of international management systems of the site. UNESCO. (2004). 28th Session of the WHC. WHC-04/28.COM/26. Oct 29. Decision 28 COM 15B.35.pp95.

265 UNESCO. (2004). 28th Session of the WHC. Oct 29. Decision 28 COM 15.A.5.pp55.

266 UNESCO. (1989). 11th Session of the WHC. SC-89/CONF.004/12. Dec, 22 1989. pp 4.

267 *Ibid.* UNESCO. (1990). 14th Session of the WHC. CLT-90/CONF.004/13. Dec 12, 1990. 10. UNESCO. (1991). 15th Session of the WHC. SC-91/CONF.002/15. Dec 12, 1991. 9. UNESCO. (1992). 16th Session of the WHC. WHC-92/CONF.002/12. Dec 14, 1992. 23. UNESCO. (1993). 17th Session of WHC. WHC-93/CONF.002/14. Feb 4, 1993. 18. UNESCO. (1995). 18th Session of the WHC. WHC-94/CONF.003/16. Jan 31. 1995. 18. UNESCO. (1996). 19th Session of the WHC. WHC-95/CONF.203/16. Jan 31, 1996. 10. UNESCO. (1996). 20th Session of the WHC. WHC-96/CONF.201/21. Mar 10, 1997. 14. UNESCO. (1997). 21st Session of the WHC. WHC-97/CONF.208/17. Feb 27, 1998. 12. UNESCO. (1999). 23rd Session of the WHC. WHC-99/CONF.209/22. Mar 22, 2000. 61. UNESCO. (2001). 24th Session of the WHC. WHC-2000/CONF.204/21. Feb 16, 2001. 31-32. UNESCO. (2001). 25th Session of the WHC. WHC-01/CONF.208/24. Feb 8, 2002. 37-38. UNESCO. (2003). 27th Session of the W.H. Committee. WHC-03/27.COM/24. Dec 10, 2003. 11-12.

Finally, with the Rwenzori Mountains, the site was removed from the Danger list in 2004 after three areas were brought under effective State control. Next to a new demarcation line and tourism management, 'the removal of mines from the property' was seen as pivotal.[268] Likewise, with Italy's Aeolian Islands, the Committee, whilst welcoming the news that no new pumice quarries would be opened or extended within the existing WHC site, the Committee urged the Party to, 'seek a long term solutions towards a closure of the existing quarries to stop all mining activities in the WHC property'.[269] The slow progress in stopping all the mining in this WHC site remains a 'great concern' for the Committee.[270]

8 Traffic and Routing

Traffic and routing issues through protected areas can be divided into roading and vehicular traffic, and ocean vessels and marine traffic. The initial recognition that vehicular traffic and its associated roading may present a problem to protected areas occurred in 1972 at the Second World Congress on National Parks. This Congress called upon governments to, wherever possible, have systems of transport in national parks that discouraged or banned automobiles and that great care should be taken in the allowance of roads in protected areas. The Congress also emphasized the need for controls on boats and planes in protected areas.[271] Although the Third World Parks Congress was not as dogmatic on this question, the necessity for strict management control, so as to ensure that the integrity of the site was not damaged from any proposed roading, was emphasized.[272] This strict management approach, although noted in the Ramsar,[273] is more in line with the practice of the Bern Convention which has issued directed recommendations to various governments, to control traffic and roading that threatened endangered species within their natural habitats.[274] The Parties to the Bern

---

268 UNESCO. (2004). 28th Session of the WHC. Oct 29. Decision 28 COM 15.A.8.pp57.

269 WHC-04/28.COM/26. Oct 29. Decision 28 COM 15B.26.pp90.

270 Decision 30 COM 7B.23.

271 Recommendation 12. Usage of national Parks, and Recommendation 13, Detrimental Effects of Land Vehicles, Boats and Aircraft. In Elliot, H. (ed). *Second World Conference on National Parks*. (1972, IUCN, Lausanne). 446-47.

272 Recommendation 6. Threats to Protected Areas. Recommendations of the World National Parks Congress. In McNeely, J. (ed). *National Parks, Conservation and Development*. (Smithsonian, Washington). 769.

273 Recommendations adopted by the International Conference on the Conservation of Wetlands and Waterfowl at Heiligenhafen, Federal Republic of Germany, 6 December 1974.Recommendation 7. Conservation of the Europe Reserve Riddagshausen-Weddeler Teiche.

274 Recommendation No. 84 (2000). The Conservation of Western Milos and in Particular the Milos Viper, Macrovipera Schweizeri. Report of the 20th Meeting of the Bern Convention. T-PVS (2000). 75. Appendix 8.

Convention have also called for full EIAs on proposed motorways in Poland[275] and recommended planned motorways in Bulgaria be routed around, not through, protected unique habitats.[276]

With the WHC, the practice is whereby Parties are typically requested to provide reports and/or EIAs with planned roads through natural sites so as to make sure that the integrity of the site is not threatened. This approach has been requested with roads planned in relation to WHC sites in Vietnam,[277] Cameroon,[278] Zaire,[279] Costa Rica,[280] Egypt,[281] Mauritania,[282] Spain,[283] Peru,[284] Australia,[285] Canada,[286] Indonesia,[287] Vietnam,[288] Ecuador,[289] Senegal[290] and Niger.[291]

---

275 Recommendation No. 108 (2003). The Proposed Construction of the Via Baltica (Poland). Report of the 23rd Meeting of the Bern Convention. T-PVS (2003). 24. Appendix 12.

276 Recommendation No. 98. (2002). The Project to Build a Motorway Through the Kresna Gorge (Bulgaria). Report of the 22nd Meeting of the Bern Convention. T-PVS (2002). 13. Appendix 10.

277 Decision 29 COM 7B.14. Phong Nha Ke Bang. UNESCO. (2003). 27th Session of the WHC. WHC-03/27.COM/24. Dec 10. 101.

278 Dja Faunal Reserve. UNESCO. (1987). 11th Session of the WHC. CC-87/CONF.005/9. Jan 20, 1988. pp 4.

279 Kahuzi National Park. UNESCO. (1990). 14th Session of the WHC. CLT-90/CONF.004/13. Dec 12, 1990. 12. UNESCO. (1991). 15th Session of the WHC. SC-91/CONF.002/15. Dec 12, 1991. 11.

280 Talamanca La Amistad. UNESCO. (1992). 16th Session of the WHC. WHC-92/CONF.002/12. Dec 14, 1992. 20. UNESCO. (2003). 27th Session of the WHC. WHC-03/27.COM/24. Dec 10, 2003. 44. UNESCO. (2004). 28th Session of the WHC. WHC-04/28.COM/26. Oct 29. Decision 28 COM 15B.33.pp94.

281 Decision 29 COM. 8B5 (Whale Valley).

282 Banc d'Arguin National Park. UNESCO. (2002). 26th Session of the WHC. WHC-02/CONF.-202/25. Aug 1, 2002. 33. UNESCO. (2003). 27th Session of the WHC. WHC-03/27.COM/24. Dec 10, 2003. 35.

283 With Donana National Park. UNESCO. (2002). 26th Session of the WHC. WHC-02/CONF.202/25. Aug 1, 2002. 35. See also Garajonay National Park. UNESCO. (1991). 15th Session of the WHC. SC-91/CONF.002/15. Dec 12, 1991. 10.

284 Huascaran National Park. UNESCO. (1996). 19th Session of the WHC. WHC-95/CONF.203/16. Jan 31, 1996. 16.

285 The Great Barrier Reef. UNESCO. (1986). 10th Session of the WHC. CC-86/CONF.003/10. Dec 5, 1986. pp 8.

286 Hood Buffalo National Park. UNESCO. (2002). 26th Session of the WHC. WHC-02/CONF.202/25. Aug 1, 2002. 28. UNESCO. (2003). 27th Session of the WHC. WHC-03/27.COM/24. Dec 10, 2003. 40. UNESCO. (2004). 28th Session of the WHC. WHC-04/28.COM/26. Oct 29. Decision 28 COM 15B.25.pp90.

287 Lorentz. UNESCO. (2004). 28th Session of the WHC. WHC-04/28.COM/26. Oct 29. Decision 28 COM 15B.10.pp80.

288 Phong Nha Ke Bang. UNESCO. (2004). 28th Session of the WHC. WHC-04/28.COM/26. Oct 29. Decision 28 COM 15B.7.pp85.

The favored response in such situations is an alternative route with substantively less impact on the site. For example, in the mid 1990s there was strong concern about a planned road through Redwood National Park in the United States, which would have resulted in the felling of between 200 and 750 large trees.[292] Soon after, the United States, to the appreciation of the Committee, adopted an alternative route that would only result in the removal of five large trees.[293] Conversely, failures by a Party to seriously consider alternatives to original roading proposals have been reproached by the Committee. This was the case with Nepal[294] and Senegal.[295] It is rare that proposed roads, by themselves, can lead to a possible Danger listing.[296] The only clear instance of roading directly leading to a site being classified as in Danger is from the Iguaçu National Park. Of note, the roading in this instance was illegal, and when Brazil took measures to stop the road the site was removed from the Danger List.[297] Likewise, when Ecuador came to, inter alia, carefully control the road development in Sangay National park, the park was removed from the Danger List.[298]

289 Sangay National Park. UNESCO. (1991). 15th Session of the WHC. SC-91/CONF.002/15. Dec 12, 1991. 7-18. UNESCO. (1993). 17th Session of WHC. WHC-93/CONF.002/14. Feb 4, 1993. 15. UNESCO. (2003). 27th Session of the WHC. WHC-03/27.COM/24. Dec 10, 2003. 18.

290 See Decision 30 COM 7B.1.

291 Air and Tenere. Note, this was more a concern with the planned routing of the Paris-Dakar rally than an actual road. UNESCO. (1996). 20th Session of the WHC. WHC-96/CONF.201/21. Mar 10, 1997. 16.

292 Greater than 36 inches in diameter.

293 UNESCO. (1995). 18th Session of the WHC. WHC-94/CONF.003/16. Jan 31. 1995. 22. UNESCO. (1996). 19th Session of the WHC. WHC-95/CONF.203/16. Jan 31, 1996. 17.

294 Chitwan. UNESCO. (2003). 27th Session of the WHC. WHC-03/27.COM/24. Dec 10, 2003. 36.

295 Note, the World Bank eventually withdrew support for the project. Niokolo-Koba. UNESCO. (1989). 11th Session of the WHC. SC-89/CONF.004/12. Dec, 22 1989. pp 4. UNESCO. (1990). 14th Session of the WHC. CLT-90/CONF.004/13. Dec 12, 1990. 10. UNESCO. (1992). 16th Session of the WHC. WHC-92/CONF.002/12. Dec 14, 1992. 25. UNESCO. (1993). 17th Session of WHC. WHC-93/CONF.002/14. Feb 4, 1993. 12-13.

296 Typically, the roading was only part of a package of detrimental issues. See Simen. UNESCO. (1996). 20th Session of the WHC. WHC-96/CONF.201/21. Mar 10, 1997. 24. UNESCO. (1998). 22nd Session of the WHC. WHC-98/CONF.203/18. Jan 29, 1999. 21-22.

297 UNESCO. (1997). 21st Session of the WHC. WHC-97/CONF.208/17. Feb 27, 1998. 20. Such measures as destroying bridges, ferry boats, placing guards along the road and replanting damaged areas.
UNESCO. (2001). 25th Session of the WHC. WHC-01/CONF.208/24. Feb 8, 2002. 29-30. Note the remaining concern on this road in 2004. UNESCO. (2004). 28th Session of the WHC. WHC-04/28.COM/26. Oct 29. Decision 28 COM 15B.32.pp94.

298 Decision 29 COM 7A.11.

With regard to shipping vessels and marine protected areas, it has been long recognized that large vessels[299] can threaten such areas (and the marine environment in general) by accidents,[300] physical damage[301] and standard operational practices.[302] Within the work of the IMO on this area, and their various protected area measures, as guided by the UNCLOS,[303] the risk posed by 'the particular character of its traffic' and the 'vessel traffic characteristics'[304] are all carefully noted in the debate about the merit of creating an area by which international shipping, or parts thereof, are excluded.[305] The objective of the IMO analysis is to show the existing maritime regulations are not sufficient, in light of the existing ecological and oceanographic conditions in the area, and the risks posed by the vessel traffic and its routing.[306] Thus, with the Great Barrier Reef application, the fact that it was a significant shipping route, with around 2,000 ships passing through an incredibly vulnerable and valuable ecosystem each year was drawn out.[307] Conversely, failure to draw out the risks posed by international maritime traffic, as with the original applications by Columbia (with regard to the Malpelo

299 Over 400 tons, and therefore under the auspice of the IMO.

300 Such as oil, noxious liquid substances, packaged harmful substances, and solid bulk substances.

301 Such as the mechanical destruction of habitats, or the smothering of habitats.

302 Such as pollutants involving oil, noxious liquid substances, sewage, garbage, solid substances carried in bulk, air pollution, anti-fouling paints, alien organisms, noise.

303 Article 211 of UNCLOS is conscious of 'the particular character of its traffic'.

304 Such as the types of vessels, and what they are carrying, in addition to previous evidence of foreseeable risks to the area, including historical accidents, and the vulnerability of the area.

305 IMO General Assembly. 17th Session. A 17/Res.720. Guidelines for the Designation of Special Areas and the Identification of Particularly Sensitive Sea Areas. Table 3. Annex 6. Guidelines for the Designation of Special Areas Under MARPOL 73/78 and Guidelines for the Identification and Designation of Particularly Sensitive Sea Areas. MEPC (2001). Report of the MEPC on its 46th Session. MEPC 46/23. Section 5.

306 This area is known as 'Other Considerations'. The focus is upon the extent the area is influences by non-maritime sources of pollution, and how well these other sources are being managed. In short, the goal is to make sure shipping is not being blamed for a problem it did not cause, and cannot solve acting alone. IMO General Assembly. 17th Session. A 17/Res.720. Guidelines for the Designation of Special Areas and the Identification of Particularly Sensitive Sea Areas. 24-27, and Table 3. Annex 6. Guidelines for the Designation of Special Areas Under MARPOL 73/78 and Guidelines for the Identification and Designation of Particularly Sensitive Sea Areas. MEPC (2001). Report of the MEPC on its 46th Session. MEPC 46/23. Sections 2.8 to 2.10. MEPC. (2004). Report of the MEPC on its 51st Session. MEPC. 51/22. 35.

307 Annex 6. Guidelines for the Designation of Special Areas Under MARPOL 73/78 and Guidelines for the Identification and Designation of Particularly Sensitive Sea Areas. MEPC (2001). Report of the MEPC on its 46th Session. MEPC 46/23. Summary of Existing PSSAs. 17,

island),[308] and Peru,[309] led to both applications for protected area status being deferred until this omission was rectified.

9 General Industrial Development

General industrial developments have been a concern with all of the major international regimes governing protected areas. Sports complexes in Italy,[310] golf courses in Ireland,[311] housing projects in the United Kingdom,[312] and infrastructure projects in France,[313] have all been criticized by the Bern Convention for threatening the integrity of important protected areas and/or key habitats. The Ramsar has followed a similar path, warning of the risks of general developments putting internationally significant wetlands at risk in, inter alia, Iceland,[314] Ireland,[315] the United Kingdom,[316] Germany[317] and Senegal.[318] However, unlike the Bern Convention, the Ramsar has taken

308 MEPC. (2000). Report of the MEPC on its 44th Session. MEPC 44/20. 30-31.

309 MEPC. (2002). Report of the MEPC on its 48th Session. MEPC 48/21. 34.

310 Recommendation No. 32 (1991). The Protection of the Sources of the River Pescara.

311 Recommendation No. 33 (1991). The Conservation of the Natterjack Toad.

312 Recommendation No. 70. On Protection of the Great Crested Newt in the United Kingdom. Report of the 18th Meeting of the Bern Convention. T-PVS (98). 62. Appendix 11.

313 Recommendation No. 55 (1996) On Giving Consideration to ZNIEFF (Nature Reserves Of Ecological Interest For Fauna And Flora) In the Development of Projects for the Biltzheim Forest and the Areas of Niffer and the Petit Landau (France).

314 The Thjorsarver area was the breeding ground of more than half the world population of Anser brachyrhynchus. Final Act of the Ramsar Conference. Annex II. Recommendations adopted by the International Conference on the Conservation of Wetlands and Waterfowl at Ramsar, Iran, 3 February 1971. Recommendation 2. Conservation of Thjorsarver, Iceland.

315 North Bill Island. Final Act of the Ramsar Conference. Annex II. *Ibid.* Recommendation 3. Conservation of North Bull Island, Ireland.

316 The proposed airport development in Kent, in the UK, was highlighted as an area of concern due to its potential impact on migratory waterfowl and could well become critically important as a wintering ground for part of the fifth of the world population of the dark-bellied race of the Brent goose, Branta bernicla, that would be displaced if Foulness became the site for London's third airport. Final Act of the Ramsar Conference. Annex II. *Ibid.* Recommendation 5. Conservation of the Medway Estuary, England.

317 The Lower Elbe estuary, which is of high international importance for both migrating and nesting waterfowl and waders, and in particular that during migration it supports approximately half of the world population of the Bewick's Swan, Cygnus columbianus bewickii. Recommendations adopted by the International Conference on the Conservation of Wetlands and Waterfowl at Heiligenhafen, Federal Republic of Germany, 6 December 1974. Recommendation 4. Development Threat to Marshes of the Lower Elbe Estuary in Lower Saxony. Recommendation 5. Conservation of the Lower Elbe Estuary Marshes in Schleswig-Holstein. See also Recommendation 7. Conservation of the Europe Reserve Riddagshausen-Weddeler Teiche.

the interesting approach of warning off foreign investment into development projects, both with regard to multinational development banks development agencies[319] and even private foreign investment,[320] which may have been considering investing in industrial developments which may have been of direct detriment to wetlands of international importance.

Generic industrial development, of the types not noted above, occurs in 54% of the WHC natural sites.[321] Accordingly, the Committee of the WHC has kept a watching eye on this area, and come to view issues including, inter alia, proposed pulp and paper mills near the Royal Chitwan National Park in Nepal,[322] prawn harvesting near or in the Sundarbans Park in India[323] and Ha Long Bay in Vietnam,[324] pumice ex-

---

318 The Senegal valley. Recommendations adopted by the International Conference on the Conservation of Wetlands and Waterfowl at Heiligenhafen, Federal Republic of Germany, 6 December 1974. Recommendation 10. Conservation of the Senegal Valley. See also Recommendation 2.7. Djoudj National Bird Park. (1984, Groningen).

319 In 1987 the Ramsar COP called upon Development Agencies, to formulate and adopt coherent, co-ordinated, wetland policies directed at sustainable utilisation, wise management and conservation within their development policies. Recommendation 3.4. Responsibility of Development Agencies Towards Wetlands. (1987, Regina). However, this recommendation failed to make an impact, and in 1987, the Ramsar noted, 'there are still too many instances of MDB financed projects leading directly or indirectly to the loss of critical wetlands and that MDBs are not generally promoting the wise use and conservation of wetlands in developing countries'. Accordingly, the COP not only called upon the 1987 recommendations to be applied in a more rigorous and systematic way, but also urged contracting parties, 'to ensure that their representatives to the MDBs adopt voting standards in support of the conservation and wise use of wetlands'. Recommendation 4.13. Multilateral Development Banks and Wetlands. (1990, Montreux). Although the force of such recommendations to MDBs softened over subsequent years, the necessity for such agencies to give greater priority to wetland conservation, was reiterated at the 5th (Recommendation 5.5. Multilateral and Bilateral Development Cooperation Programmes. 1993, Kushiro) 6th (this COP welcomed the OECD Guidelines for Aid Agencies for Improved Conservation and Sustainable Use of Tropical and Sub Tropical Wetlands Recommendation 6.16. Bilateral and Multilateral Development Co-Operation Programmes. 1996, Brisbane) and 8th COPs. Resolution 8.25. The Ramsar Strategic Plan. (2002, Valencia). Annex. I.12.

320 Although the Ramsar has not identified any specific companies as direct threats to wetlands of international importance, the 7th COP recommended the Guidelines for International Co-operation Under the Ramsar Convention. These Guidelines emphasised regulation of foreign investment to ensure wetland conservation and wise use. The regulation envisaged with the utilisation of EIAs, and voluntary Codes of Conduct for foreign interests and financial measures, to help aim at the sustainable use of wetlands. Resolution 7.19. International Cooperation. (1999, San Jose). Annex. The Guidelines for international cooperation under the Ramsar Convention.

321 IUCN. (1998). (IUCN, Gland). 6-7.

322 UNESCO. (1984). 8th Session of the WHC. SC/84/CONF.004/9. Nov 2, 1984. pp 9.

323 UNESCO. (2002). 26th Session of the WHC. WHC-02/CONF.202/25. Aug 1, 2002. 30.

324 UNESCO. (2003). 27th Session of the WHC. WHC-03/27.COM/24. Dec 10, 2003. 38.

traction from Italy's Aeolian Islands[325] and proposed engineering to prevent natural hazards within a WHC site in New Zealand.[326] Aesthetic concerns related to development in terms of radio tracking facilities,[327] telecommunications towers[328] are also notable.

It is only in two instances, that concerns related to industrial development have been deemed especially serious. These involved Mexico's El Viscaino whale sanctuary and Russia's Lake Baikal. With the former, the planned project involved converting part of the lagoon into salt ponds for industrial salt production. When the evidence of the project was finally concluded, it was shown that the whale population was not endangered by the current salt production, and it was allowed to continue. This was buttressed by strong conservation measures of the Mexican government.[329] Since the core of why the site was inscribed (the whales) were not detrimentally impacted upon, it was not inscribed as in Danger. The second example in this area involves Russia's Lake Baikal, and its existing pulp and paper mill. The operation of this mill, and its pollution potential in particular, lead to strong debate about whether the site should be inscribed on the Danger List. This debate swung back and forth, before the Committee warned that crossing the oil and gas pipeline over the watershed of Lake Baikal, 'would make the case for inscription' on the Danger List.[330] Russia subsequently adopted an alternative route for the pipeline (much to the satisfaction of the Committee)[331] although very similar concerns continued to exist with other Russian sites.[332]

10 Pollution

The WHC Committee keeps a watchful eye on industrial pollution. The general rule is that a site will be accepted only if does not have significant pollution problems, or what pollution problems it has are under control, such as with the industrial pollution

---

325 UNESCO. (2002). 26th Session of the WHC. WHC-02/CONF.202/25. Aug 1, 2002. 32.

326 UNESCO. (2001). 25th Session of the WHC. WHC-01/CONF.208/24. Feb 8, 2002. 54.

327 On St Kilda of the UK. UNESCO. (1986). 10th Session of the WHC. CC-86/CONF.003/10. Dec 5, 1986. pp 6.

328 The Lord Howe Island Group. UNESCO. (1983). 6th Session of the WHC. CC-83/CONF.015/8. Jan 17, 1983. pp.4.

329 UNESCO. (1996). 19th Session of the WHC. WHC-95/CONF.203/16. Jan 31, 1996.15. UNESCO. (1996). 20th Session of the WHC. WHC-96/CONF.201/21. Mar 10, 1997. 25. UNESCO. (1999). 23rd Session of the WHC. WHC-99/CONF.209/22. Mar 22, 2000. 73. UNESCO. (1999). 23rd Session of the WHC. WHC-99/CONF.209/22. Mar 22, 2000. 73. UNESCO. (2001). 24th Session of the WHC. WHC-2000/CONF.204/21. Feb 16, 2001. 39.

330 Decision 29 COM 7B.19.

331 See Decision 30 COM 7B.18.

332 As with the Golden Mountains. See Decision 30 COM 7B.19.

going into the Skocjan underground caves in the former Yugoslavia.[333] With regard to existing sites, the Committee has expressed a range of opinions from noting their concern over no- fault accidents and their impact upon WHC sites, such as with the 70,000 gallon oil spill on America's Olympic National Park,[334] through to the need to prepare for possible oil spills.[335] More often than not, the Committee expresses their concern about various fault-based pollution problems which impact upon WHC sites.[336] The extreme situation, where the site may actually be listed as in Danger, occurred with the Everglades, after nutrient pollution from agriculture and mercury contamination of wildlife (in addition to a dropping water table) were deemed of sufficient threat that the site was inscribed.[337]

Pollution of protected areas has also become a notable source of concern in the Bern Convention. Although generic types of pollution have been referred to be threatening key marine species,[338] and lead pollution caused by shotgun pellets,[339] (which is a clear concern with the AEWA)[340] by far the most commonly iterated recommendation has been to control agricultural pollution, (typically pesticides) due to their impact on key habitats and the protected species within them. Although this problem has been noted in the MAB,[341] the primary forum to deal with this problem has been the Bern Convention which has connected the issue of agricultural pollutants to their detrimental impacts upon insects such as ants, wasps and bees,[342] tortoises,[343] mink,[344] otters,[345] turtles[346] and underground habitats[347] in general. The Ramsar has also

333 UNESCO. (1986). 10th Session of the WHC. CC-86/CONF.003/10. Dec 5, 1986. pp 7. UNESCO. (1987). 11th Session of the WHC. CC-87/CONF.005/9. Jan 20, 1988. pp 10. UNESCO. (1996). 19th Session of the WHC. WHC-95/CONF.203/16. Jan 31, 1996. 16.

334 UNESCO. (1991). 15th Session of the WHC SC-91/CONF.002/15. Dec 12, 1991. 10. UNESCO. (1992). 16th Session of the WHC. WHC-92/CONF.002/12. Dec 14, 1992. 26.

335 As with the Banc d'Arguin National Park of Mauritania. See Decision 30 COM 7B.9.

336 UNESCO. (2002). 26th Session of the WHC. WHC-02/CONF.202/25. Aug 1, 2002. 37.

337 UNESCO. (1993). 17th Session of WHC. WHC-93/CONF.002/14. Feb 4, 1993. 18-19.

338 Recommendation No. 11. (1988) Protection of the Common Seal.

339 Recommendation No. 28. (1991). On the Use of Non-Toxic Shot in Wetlands.

340 Resolution 1.14. Phasing Out of Lead Shot in Wetlands. MOP 1 of the AEWA (South Africa, 1999). Available from the AEWA Secretariat. Resolution 2.4. International Implementation Priorities. MOP 2 of the AEWA (Bonn, 2002). Available from the AEWA Secretariat. Resolution 2.2. Phasing Out Lead Shot for Hunting In Wetlands. MOP 2 of the AEWA (Bonn, 2002). Available from the AEWA Secretariat.

341 Delta del Parana in Argentina. MAB. (2000). 16th Session of the ICC Bureau. SC-00/ CONF.208/13. 19.

342 Recommendation No 21. (1991). The Conservation of Insects of the Hymenoptera and Their Habitats.

343 Recommendation No. 104 (2003). The Conservation of the Spur-thinghed Tortoise in Spain. Report of the 23rd Meeting of the Bern Convention. T-PVS (2003). 24. Appendix 8.

344 Recommendation No. 31. (1991). The Protection of the European Mink.

345 Recommendation No. 53 (1996) on the conservation of the European Otter (Lutra lutra).

dealt directly with agricultural pollutants. Apart from some passing concerns about oil pollution from oceanic sources on coastal wetlands,[348] their overt focus has been upon the detrimental impact that pesticides have upon wetlands.[349] This has been a long-standing concern for the Ramsar Parties, who have from the outset, recognised the worst types of pesticides as 'a grave danger' to wetlands, that need to be strictly (and equitably between countries) controlled,[350] whilst all possible efforts towards finding alternatives are undertaken.[351] They have facilitated controls in this area by the development of good pesticide management practices and links to appropriate international organisations to accelerate their work in the development of assessment protocols for more understanding the effects of pesticides upon wetlands and those who depend upon them.[352]

11 Legal Agriculture, Forestry and Fishing

As pointed out above, the primary pollutants evident in protected areas are pesticides, or persistent organic pollutants. The importance of these chemicals is their common linkage with agriculture. Unfortunately, unsustainable agriculture can also impact upon protected areas in a number of other ways, ranging from the demands it may place upon water, its consumption of arable land, and most notably, its by-products, such as nutrient pollution.[353] In terms of Ramsar decisions, this was most notable with the Everglades, with which it was recommended to the United States that they, inter alia, eliminate the

---

346 Recommendation No. 95. (2002). The Conservation of Marine Turtles in Kazanli Beach (Turkey). Report of the 22nd Meeting of the Bern Convention. T-PVS (2002). 13. Appendix 7.

347 Recommendation No. 36. (1992). The Conservation of Underground Habitat.

348 The Ramsar called for strict international and domestic compliance with the International Convention for the Prevention of the Pollution of the Sea by Oil. Final Act of the Ramsar Conference. Annex II. Recommendations adopted by the International Conference on the Conservation of Wetlands and Waterfowl at Ramsar, Iran, 3 February 1971. Recommendation 6. Oil Pollution.

349 The only direct recommendation to a specific government to control pesticides in relation to the wetlands came from the 4th COP which called upon the Spanish government to, inter alia, control the use of agricultural chemicals effecting the Donana National Park. Recommendation 4.9.1. Donana National Park. (1990, Montreux).

350 Final Act of the Ramsar Conference. Annex II. Recommendations adopted by the International Conference on the Conservation of Wetlands and Waterfowl at Ramsar, Iran, 3 February 1971. Recommendation 7. Pesticides. The Parties deplored, 'an apparent tendency for such pesticides, although often banned or restricted in the countries of manufacture, to be exported in quantity and even offered for sale at reduced prices to less developed countries, which may lead to the degradation of natural areas including wetlands of international importance'.

351 Recommendations adopted by the International Conference on the Conservation of Wetlands and Waterfowl at Heiligenhafen, Federal Republic of Germany, 6 December 1974. Recommendation 14. Use of Biocides.

352 Recommendation 6.14. Toxic Chemicals. (1996, Brisbane). Resolution 7.25. Measuring Environmental Quality in Wetlands. (1999, San Jose).

353 Resolution 8.34. Agriculture, Wetlands and Water Resource Management. (2002, Valencia).

nutrient enrichment that was threatening this globally important wetland.[354] Given the ubiquitous nature of agriculture and its management, Ramsar has restricted itself to recommending that its Parties accord with the CBD guidelines on sustainable agricultural practice[355] whilst emphasising that agricultural practices should be compatible with the conservation and sustainable use of wetlands.[356] To further this last goal, the Parties to Ramsar directed their scientific body to establish a framework for identifying good practices for agriculture,[357] and aquaculture[358] with regard to wetlands. The only other regimes to express concern over agricultural practices are the MAB[359] and the Bern Convention. In the latter instance, the Parties have tended to focus on particular agricultural methods, and their direct impact upon particular risk species, such as with threatened birds,[360] tortoises,[361] hamsters[362] and snakes.[363]

The last body which should have a particular interest with regard to agricultural questions is the WHC. This interest should be due to the fact that agricultural practices (of one degree or another) are practiced in 37% of all WHC natural sites.[364] However, the WHC is silent on this topic. Conversely, the Committee of the WHC has expressed concern with regard to unsustainable fisheries around Banc d'Arguin National Park in Mauritania,[365] (commercial fisheries occurs in 24% of all WHC sites)[366] and official

354 Recommendation 4.9.2. The Everglades. (1990, Montreux).

355 Decision III/11. Conservation and Sustainable Use of Agricultural Biological Diversity. UNEP/CBD/COP/3/38. pp 72. Decision IV/6. Agricultural Biological Diversity. UNEP/CBD/COP/4/27. pp.96.

356 Resolution 8.34. Agriculture, Wetlands and Water Resource Management. (2002, Valencia).

357 Ibid. Paragraph 25.

358 Resolution 9.4. The Ramsar Convention and the Conservation, Production and Sustainable Use of Fisheries Resources. (Kampala, 2005).

359 Bosque Mbaracayu in Paraguay. MAB. (2000). 16th Session of the ICC Bureau. SC-00/CONF.208/13.21.

360 Recommendation No. 60. (1997). The Implementation of the Action Plans for Globally Threatened Birds in Europe. Report of the 17th Meeting of the Bern Convention. T-PVS (97) 63. Appendix 11.

361 Recommendation No. 104 (2003). The Conservation of the Spur-thinghed Tortoise in Spain. Report of the 23rd Meeting of the Bern Convention. T-PVS (2003). 24. Appendix 8.

362 Recommendation No. 68. (1998). On Protection of the Common Hamster in Alsace, France. Report of the 18th Meeting of the Bern Convention. T-PVS (98). 62. Appendix 9. Recommendation No. 79 (1999). Protection of the Common Hamster in Europe. Report of the 19th Meeting of the Bern Convention. T-PVS (99) 30. Appendix 10.

363 Recommendation No. 84 (2000). The Conservation of Western Milos and in Particular the Milos Viper, Macrovipera Schweizeri. Report of the 20th Meeting of the Bern Convention. T-PVS (2000). 75. Appendix 8.

364 IUCN. (1998). *Human Use of World Heritage Natural Sites: A Global Overview.* (IUCN, Gland). 6-7.

365 UNESCO. (2002). 26th Session of the WHC. WHC-02/CONF.202/25. Aug 1, 2002. 33.

366 IUCN. (1998). *Ibid.* 6-7.

logging (forestry and logging occur in 26% of the all WHC natural sites)[367] in the buffer zones around sites in Australia[368] and Cameroon[369] and with regard to Mount Athos in Greece.[370] The only other regime to substantively address the issue of forestry within a protected area is the European Diploma, and the case of the Poloniny National Park in Slovakia. In this instance, Poloniny only just had its diploma renewed, on the condition that the forest reserves were increased, forest categories had to be reclassified (so as to restore the woodlands necessary for the protection of the waters of the reservoir catchment area) and clear-cutting throughout the National Park was prohibited.[371]

12 Illegal Logging, Mining and Poaching

The illegal extraction of resources from protected areas is typically in the form of logging, mining, and/or poaching of wildlife. The recognition of this problem dates back to 1982, when the Third World's Park Congress in 1982 identified poaching as, 'the most important threat to the integrity of some protected areas'.[372] Unfortunately, this remains the case in the 21st century,[373] as the CBD has confirmed.[374] Even within

367 Ibid.

368 The Tasmanian Wilderness. UNESCO. (1996). 19th Session of the WHC. WHC-95/CONF.203/16. Jan 31, 1996.12.

369 UNESCO. (1997). 21st Session of the WHC. WHC-97/CONF.208/17. Feb 27, 1998. 20. UNESCO. (2001). 25th Session of the WHC. WHC-01/CONF.208/24. Feb 8, 2002. 50.

370 UNESCO. (1992). 16th Session of the WHC. WHC-92/CONF.002/12. Dec 14, 1992. 27-28. UNESCO. (1995). 18th Session of the WHC. WHC-94/CONF.003/16. Jan 31. 1995. 20.

371 See CM(2003)66 30 April 2003. Resolution ResDip(2003) on the renewal of the European Diploma of Protected Areas awarded to the Poloniny National Park (Slovakia). Bauer, F. (2002). 'The European Diploma of Protected Areas'. 12 (3) *Parks.* 29, 34.

372 Recommendation 770. Combating Poaching. In McNeely, J. (ed). *National Parks, Conservation and Development.* (Smithsonian, Washington). 765.

373 UNEP/WCWC. (2004). Protected Areas and Biodiversity. (UNEP: Biodiversity Series No 21). 34.WWF. (2004). *How Effective Are Protected Areas ?* (WWF, Gland). SBSTTA. Report of the Ad Hoc Technical Expert Group on Protected Areas. UNEP/CBD/SBSTTA/9/INF/3. 22 Sep, 2003. pp.25-29. CBD. (2004). *Technical Advice on the Establishment and Management of a National System of Marine and Coastal Protected Areas.* (CBD Technical Series No 13). 20-31. Secretariat of the CBD. (2004). *Biodiversity Issues for Consideration in the Planning, Establishment and Management of Protected Area Sites and Management.* (CBD Technical Series No 15). 37-45, 73-82.

374 The 7th CBD COP in 2004 urged, concerned Parties, individually and collectively, to take further steps in curbing the illegal exploitation and trade of resources, particularly from existing protected areas and from areas of ecological importance for biodiversity conservation'. CBD. Decision VII/28. Protected Areas. Paragraph 21 & Paragraph 1.5.6 of the Annex.

relatively well resourced protected areas, such as those under the WHC, poaching remains a clear problem in many instances.[375]

The WHC has recognized illegal logging as a clear problem with regard to Kenya,[376] the Central African Republic,[377] the Philippines,[378] Indonesia,[379] Honduras,[380] Cameroon,[381] the Philippines,[382] India,[383] Tanzania,[384] Ethiopia,[385] Zaire,[386] Vietnam,[387] Niger,[388] Cote d'Ivoire,[389] Ivory Coast (at Tai National park[390] and Mount Nimba)[391] Costa Rica,[392] and the shared forest between Belarus

375 With regard to WHC sites in OECD countries, commercial hunting and/or poaching was evident in 24% of the sites, and 57% of the sites for non-OECD WHC sites. IUCN. (1998). *Human Use of World Heritage Natural Sites: A Global Overview.* (IUCN, Gland). 6-7.

376 Sibiloi Park. UNESCO. (1997). 21st Session of the WHC. WHC-97/CONF.208/17. Feb 27, 1998. 38. By 2004, Kenya was being congratulated on progress in this area. UNESCO. (2004). 28th Session of the WHC. WHC-04/28.COM/26. Oct 29. Decision 28 COM 15B.3.pp77.

377 Parc National du Manovo-Gounda St Floris UNESCO. (1988). 12th Session of the WHC. SC-88/CONF.001/13. Dec 23, 1988. 14.

378 Tubbataha. UNESCO. (2004). 28th Session of the WHC. WHC-04/28.COM/26. Oct 29. Decision 28 COM 15B.18.pp84.

379 Sumatra. UNESCO. (2004). 28th Session of the WHC. WHC-04/28.COM/26. Oct 29. Decision 28 COM 14B5. pp. 17.

380 Rio Platano. UNESCO. (1988). 12th Session of the WHC. SC-88/CONF.001/13. Dec 23, 1988. 7. UNESCO. (1989). 11th Session of the WHC. SC-89/CONF.004/12. Dec, 22 1989. pp 4.

381 Dja Faunal Reserve. UNESCO. (2003). 27th Session of the WHC. WHC-03/27.COM/24. Dec 10, 2003. 30.

382 Tubbataha Reef Marine Park. UNESCO. (2003). 27th Session of the WHC. WHC-03/27.COM/24. Dec 10, 2003. 37.

383 The Manas Wildlife sanctuary. UNESCO. (1990). 14th Session of the WHC. CLT-90/CONF.004/13. Dec 12, 1990. 10.

384 The Serengeti. UNESCO. (1995). 18th Session of the WHC. WHC-94/CONF.003/16. Jan 31. 1995. 21.

385 Abihatta Shalla Lakes. UNESCO. (1980). 4th Session of the WHC. CC-80/CONF.017/4. May 28, 1980. pp.2.

386 Garamba & Kahuzi-Biega. UNESCO. (1980). 4th Session of the WHC. CC-80/CONF.017/4. May 28, 1980. pp.4.

387 Phong Nha Ke Bang. UNESCO. (2004). 28th Session of the WHC. WHC-04/28.COM/26. Oct 29. Decision 28 COM 15B.7.pp85.

388 Decision 29 COM 7A.6. Rev.

389 Comoe National Park. UNESCO. (2003). 27th Session of the WHC. WHC-03/27.COM/24. Dec 10, 2003. 32.

390 UNESCO. (1984). 8th Session of the WHC. SC/84/CONF.004/9. Nov 2, 1984. pp 14. UNESCO. (1985). 9th Session of the WHC. SC-85/CONF.008/9. Dec, 1985. pp 11. UNESCO. (1988). 12th Session of the WHC. SC-88/CONF.001/13. Dec 23, 1988. 7. UNESCO. (2003). 27th Session of the WHC. WHC-03/27.COM/24. Dec 10, 2003. 31-32.

391 UNESCO. (1984). 8th Session of the WHC. SC/84/CONF.004/9. Nov 2, 1984. pp 14.

and Poland.[393] In the case of Rio Platano in Honduras, the necessity to control illegal logging (and poaching), were identified as part of the package for getting the site removed from the Danger List.[394] With the proposed Transborder Rainforest Heritage of Borneo, Indonesia and Malaysia, failure to control illegal logging, was one of the primary reasons for deferring its inscription on the World Heritage List.[395] Meanwhile, failure to control illegal logging in the Tropical Rainforest Heritage of Sumatra was also a 'great concern' to the 2006 WHC Committee.[396] Illegal fishing has also been noted as a clear concern with a number of WHC sites,[397] such as Tubbataha Reef Marine Park in the Philippines,[398] and the Galapagos.[399]

The importance of rehabilitating species which are threatened (by issues other than illegal extraction) has had a clear importance to the WHC. The general process is that a flagship species of a site is identified, its population verified, and its decline is then monitored.[400] From these processes, once it can be shown that if a key population is declining, the Committee will highlight its concerns. This has been the case with sites in New Zealand,[401] Australia[402] and India.[403] In extreme cases, the loss of key species can be part of the reason for a site being listed as in Danger or fully delisted. This was clearly demonstrated with the Keoladeo National Park in India, in which the number of migrating Siberian cranes annually visiting the park fell from 41 in 1985

392 Talamanca La Amistad. UNESCO. (2003). 27th Session of the WHC WHC-03/27.COM/24. Dec 10, 2003. 44.

393 Belovezhskaya Pushcha/ Biaowieza. Decision 29 COM 7B.15.

394 UNESCO. (2004). 28th Session of the WHC. WHC-04/28.COM/26. Oct 29. Decision 28 COM 15A.13. pp.60-61.

395 See Decision 30 COM 8B.23.

396 Decision 30 COM 7B.12.

397 Decision 29 COM 7B.5 (on Banc d'Arguin).

398 Decision 29 COM 7B.13.

399 UNESCO. (2004). 28th Session of the WHC. WHC-04/28.COM/26. Oct 29. Decision 28 COM 15B.31.8p93. UNESCO. (1990). 14th Session of the WHC. CLT-90/CONF.004/13. Dec 12, 1990. 1.
UNESCO. (1995). 18th Session of the WHC. WHC-94/CONF.003/16. Jan 31. 1995. 44. UNESCO. (1996). 19th Session of the WHC. WHC-95/CONF.203/16. Jan 31, 1996. 36. Anon. (2004). 'Eco-Blockade.' *New Scientist.* June 12. 5.

400 See for example, the way this debate has been dealt with concerning the Arabian Oryx Sanctuary. UNESCO. (1995). 18th Session of the WHC. WHC-94/CONF.003/16. Jan 31. 1995. 40-41. UNESCO. (1996). 19th Session of the WHC. WHC-95/CONF.203/16. Jan 31, 1996.15. UNESCO. (1996). 20th Session of the WHC. WHC-96/CONF.201/21. Mar 10, 1997. 27. UNESCO. (1999). 23rd Session of the WHC. WHC-99/CONF.209/22. Mar 22, 2000. 76.

401 Fiordland National Park and the Takahe. UNESCO. (1986). 10th Session of the WHC. CC-86/CONF.003/10. Dec 5, 1986. pp 5.

402 Uluru. UNESCO. (1987). 11th Session of the WHC. CC-87/CONF.005/9. Jan 20, 1988. pp 3.

403 Sundarbans National Park and its tigers. UNESCO. (1987). 11th Session of the WHC. CC-87/CONF.005/9. Jan 20, 1988. pp 5. UNESCO. (2002). 26th Session of the WHC. WHC-02/CONF.202/25. Aug 1, 2002. 30.

to none in the mid 1990s.[404] Although the Keoladeo was not inscribed in the Danger List, in other instances, the decline of key species has been a defining characteristic. This was notable (along with other reasons) with Yellowstone,[405] but most specifically with the Simen National Park in Ethiopia. In the latter instance, the site was listed as in Danger, primarily over threat to a number of key mammal species, such as the Walia ibex and Simien fox.[406] A similar process has been followed with the European Diploma, where the drastic decline in bird numbers (in the Kuscenneti Manyas National Park – the 'bird paradise' – in Turkey) was the primary reason that Turkey was warned that its Diploma would not be renewed unless its ornithological value was restored.[407]

Most commonly, the reason that key numbers of species experience a critical decline in population numbers is because of poaching. Although this has been noted with some MAB sites,[408] the problem is most pronounced with the WHC. This problem was well shown with the Air and Tenere Nature Reserves in Niger, which were placed on the Danger List in 1992, following the advent of the civil war, along with widespread poaching. Indeed, by 2001 ostrich had totally disappeared from the site and gazelle were rarely seen.[409] Tanzania's Ngorongoro experienced similar concerns before being removed from the Danger List after confronting its difficulties.[410] Aside these two examples, in terms of chronology, the first site to experience this problem was the Garamba in mid 1980s, which was inscribed on the Danger List, due to poaching taking the white rhino population down to less than 15 individuals.[411] After this situation stabilized and the population more than doubled (to 32) in the early 1990s, it was removed from the Danger List.[412] The site was re-inscribed as the site became embroiled in civil war in the Congo, and the rhino population began to fall again, with only between 17 and 22 individuals alive in 2004, and the northern white rhino was,

---

404 UNESCO. (1990). 14th Session of the WHC. CLT-90/CONF.004/13. Dec 12, 1990. 11. UNESCO. (1995). 18th Session of the WHC. WHC-94/CONF.003/16. Jan 31. 1995. 20.

405 UNESCO. (1996). 19th Session of the WHC. WHC-95/CONF.203/16. Jan 31, 1996. 18.

406 UNESCO. (1996). 20th Session of the WHC. WHC-96/CONF.201/21. Mar 10, 1997. 24. UNESCO. (2001). 25th Session of the WHC. WHC-01/CONF.208/24. Feb 8, 2002. 35-36. UNESCO. (1984). 8th Session of the WHC. SC/84/CONF.004/9. Nov 2, 1984. pp 14. UNESCO. (1991). 15th Session of the WHC. SC-91/CONF.002/15. Dec 12, 1991. 8.

407 See Bauer, F. (2002). 'The European Diploma of Protected Areas'. 12 (3) *Parks*. 29, 34.

408 With regard to the need to control the illegal hunting of snow leopard, see Issyk Kul in Krygyz. UNESCO. (2001). ICC Bureau Meeting. SCI/-01/CONF.217/8. Dec 12, 2. 13.

409 UNESCO. (1992). 16th Session of the WHC. WHC-92/CONF.002/12. Dec 14, 1992. 24. UNESCO. (1993). 17th Session of WHC. WHC-93/CONF.002/14. Feb 4, 1993. 16. UNESCO. (2001). 25th Session of the WHC. WHC-01/CONF.208/24. Feb 8, 2002. 40-41.

410 UNESCO. (1988). 12th Session of the WHC. SC-88/CONF.001/13. Dec 23, 1988. 6. But note, UNESCO. (1993). 17th Session of WHC. WHC-93/CONF.002/14. Feb 4, 1993. 12-16.

411 UNESCO. (1984). 8th Session of the WHC. SC/84/CONF.004/9. Nov 2, 1984. pp 12.

412 UNESCO. (1985). 9th Session of the WHC. SC-85/CONF.008/9. Dec, 1985. pp 10. UNESCO. (1992). 16th Session of the WHC. WHC-92/CONF.002/12. Dec 14, 1992. 27.

'threaten[ed] with extinction'.[413] In 2005, it was feared that continued poaching might lead to the 'imminent extinction of the northern white Rhino,' and the Committee clearly warned this could result in the loss of the outstanding universal value of the Garamba site.[414] Likewise, in 2005, it was noted elephants had fallen from 15,000 to 4,000 and the Congo giraffe from 200 to less than 60.[415] A similar situation, with a site being inscribed as in Danger, due to poaching occurred with Mana Pools in Zimbabwe, where its ten remaining rhinos were moved from the park to an intensive protection zone. The Committee saw this as the park losing one of its 'flagship species.'[416] A similar dire prognosis, whereby sites have been inscribed as in Danger, linked to, inter alia, illegal extraction has also been evident with the Virunga National Park[417]and the Manovo-Gounda in the Central African Republic[418] where heavy poaching accounted for up to 80% of the Park's wildlife. For example, within Virunga, the hippo population fell from 20,000 in 1990 to about 1,300 in 2003. In Kahuzi-Beiga, the gorilla population of 8,000 in the late 1970s has fallen by over 50%.[419]

13 War

Peace is an essential prerequisite for any kind of sustainable development. War destroys both cultural and natural heritage without discrimination, and often with little restraint. With regard to protected areas, war and conflict is often the primary facilitator for many of the problems noted above, with only large influxes of refugees into protected areas, and physical attacks by combatants upon protected area and their staff and their infra-

---

413 UNESCO. (2004). 28th Session of the WHC. Oct 29. Decision 28 COM 15.A.3.pp53. UNESCO. (1996). 20th Session of the WHC. WHC-96/CONF.201/21. Mar 10, 1997. 26. UNESCO. (2001). 25th Session of the WHC. WHC-01/CONF.208/24. Feb 8, 2002. 32. Anon. (2004). 'Surge in Poaching.' *New Scientist.* Aug 14. 5.

414 Decision 29 COM 7A.4. Rev. Anon. (2005). 'Congo Risks Ejection'. *New Scientist.* July 23. 5.

415 Decision 29 COM 7A.4. Rev.

416 UNESCO. (1995). 18th Session of the WHC. WHC-94/CONF.003/16. Jan 31. 1995. 22. UNESCO. (1986). 10th Session of the WHC. CC-86/CONF.003/10. Dec 5, 1986. pp 9. UNESCO. (1987). 11th Session of the WHC. CC-87/CONF.005/9. Jan 20, 1988. pp 11. UNESCO. (1987). 11th Session of the WHC. CC-87/CONF.005/9. Jan 20, 1988. pp 11.

417 UNESCO. (1993). 17th Session of WHC. WHC-93/CONF.002/14. Feb 4, 1993. 17. UNESCO. (1995). 18th Session of the WHC. WHC-94/CONF.003/16. Jan 31. 1995. 19, 45. UNESCO. (1996). 19th Session of the WHC. WHC-95/CONF.203/16. Jan 31, 1996.11. UNESCO. (1996). 20th Session of the WHC. WHC-96/CONF.201/21. Mar 10, 1997. 18.

418 UNESCO. (1990). 14th Session of the WHC. CLT-90/CONF.004/13. Dec 12, 1990. 9. UNESCO. (1997). 21st Session of the WHC. WHC-97/CONF.208/17. Feb 27, 1998. 19. Decision 29 COM 7A.1.

419 Huart, J. (2004). 'Survival of the Major Natural Sites of the Democratic Republic of the Congo.' 37 *World Heritage.* 4-24.

structure, being the additional problems, thrown into the mix.[420] This last factor alone can be thought provoking. For example, between the outbreak of war in the Congo in the mid 1990s and its end in 2004, over 50 park guards lost their lives in the cause of their employment.[421]

The rules of destruction of the environment are dealt with in the laws of armed conflict. Accordingly, as this area is dealt with elsewhere, very few regimes actually give this theme much consideration. The exception to this is the WHC, which is the only regime to attempt to deal with the issue of war and protected areas.[422] This is not surprising as between 1986 and 2004, 22 sites (including 14 natural) were reported to the Committee, as being threatened by war.

The response of the WHC to the threat of conflict is twofold. First, the Committee tries to maintain a restraining influence on the belligerents, even in times of conflict. As such, they typically urge all possible efforts to protect the sites from all destructive activities, related to the conflict. In some instances, such as with the Garamba in the Democratic Republic of the Congo, they urged, inter alia, that the guard force 'is properly equipped and, in particular, has adequate arms and ammunition'.[423] Second, the sites in question, including those in Honduras,[424] Cote d'Ivoire (Comoe National Park[425] and Mount Nimba,),[426] the Rwenzori Mountains of Uganda,[427] the Manas wildlife reserve in India,[428] as well as the sites within the Democratic Republic of the Congo[429] (Virunga[430] Okapi[431] Kahuzi Biega,[432] Garamba[433] and Salonga),

420 Oglethorpe, J. (2004). 'Parks in the Crossfire: Strategies for Effective Conservation in Areas of Armed Conflict'. 14(1) *Parks.* 2-7.

421 Bandarin, F. (2004). 'Protecting Heritage.' *Our Planet.* 14(2): 11.

422 See Debonnet, G. (2005). 'Supporting Protected Areas at a Time of Political Turmoil'. In UNESCO. (ed) *World Heritage at the Vth IUCN World Parks Congress.* (Paris, World Heritage Report No. 16). 28-31.

423 See Decision 30 COM 7A.4.

424 Rio Platano had 50,000 refugees and settlers invaded the park and its threatened integrity. UNESCO. (1988). 12th Session of the WHC. SC-88/CONF.001/13. Dec 23, 1988. 7. UNESCO. (1989). 11th Session of the WHC. SC-89/CONF.004/12. Dec, 22 1989. pp 4.

425 Decision 29 COM 7A.2. UNESCO. (2003). 27th Session of the WHC. WHC-03/27.COM/24. Dec 10, 2003. 32. Also, Fischer, F. (2004). 'Status of Comoe National Park, Cote d' Ivoire and the Effects of War'. 14(1) *Parks.* 17-26.

426 Decision 29 COM 7A3. UNESCO. (2003). 27th Session of the WHC. WHC-03/27.COM/24. Dec 10, 2003. 11-12.

427 UNESCO. (2001). 24th Session of the WHC. WHC-2000/CONF.204/21. Feb 16, 2001. 34.

428 Decision 29 COM 7A.9.

429 Debonnet, G. (2004). 'Supporting Protected Areas n a Time of Political Turmoil: The Case of World Heritage Sites in the Democratic Republic of the Congo'. 14(1) *Parks.* 9-17.

430 UNESCO. (1993). 17th Session of WHC. WHC-93/CONF.002/14. Feb 4, 1993. 17. UNESCO. (1995). 18th Session of the WHC. WHC-94/CONF.003/16. Jan 31. 1995. 19, 45. UNESCO. (1996). 19th Session of the WHC. WHC-95/CONF.203/16. Jan 31, 1996.11. UNESCO. (1996).

are inscribed on the Danger List because of the conflict within and around them.[434] Likewise, Plitvice National Park in the former Yugoslavia was inscribed for the duration of the former Yugoslavian conflict.[435] Once the conflict has ended (or at least stabilized), the Committee urges that all armed groups be evacuated from the site as soon as possible.[436] However, even with the evacuation of armed groups from the site, it may still be troubled, even if removed from the Danger List. For example, when the Rwenzori was removed from the Danger List, anti-personnel mines remained a distinct problem in the park for years to come.[437]

14 Conclusion

All protected areas have an integrity. The integrity of each area is related to the values for why it was originally inscribed. The integrity of each area may be threatened by at least 12 different threats. The first threat is permanent human populations. However, only one regime, the WHC, recognises this as a potential threat to their sites. With regard to non-permanent populations (the second threat), such as tourism, all of the protected area regimes have recognised the damaging potential of the influx of uncontrolled and unlimited visitors to a site. Some regimes such as the Bern, Ramsar, and WHC have gone further, and issued specific recommendations to individual countries to control particular tourism problems. The third threat is alien species. The control of alien species has become a well recognised goal in most biodiversity forums, and the CBD in particular. This goal is continually repeated with regard to protected areas. The two regimes with the strongest, generic, controls in this area are the Antarctic regime and the IMO. The Bern and the WHC are also notable in this area, but due to their individualised response to sites threatened by alien species. The WHC is of particular interest as alien species have been recognised as such clear threats that they can lead to a site being listed as in Danger.

Pollution and climate change are the fourth threats. Air pollution is a relatively small scale problem in sites under the MAB, Bern and WHC. Conversely, climate change

---

20th Session of the WHC. WHC-96/CONF.201/21. Mar 10, 1997. 18.

431 UNESCO. (1997). 21st Session of the WHC. WHC-97/CONF.208/17. Feb 27, 1998. 19. UNESCO. (2001). 25th Session of the WHC. WHC-01/CONF.208/24. Feb 8, 2002. 32.

432 Ibid.

433 UNESCO. (1996). 20th Session of the WHC. WHC-96/CONF.201/21. Mar 10, 1997. 26. UNESCO. (2001). 25th Session of the WHC. WHC-01/CONF.208/24. Feb 8, 2002. 32

434 Decision 29 COM 7A.4. Rev. UNESCO. (2004). 28th Session of the WHC. Oct 29. Decision 28 COM 15.A.3.pp53.

435 UNESCO. (1991). 15th Session of the WHC. SC-91/CONF.002/15. Dec 12, 1991. 10.

436 As with the Kahuzi-Biega in the Congo. See Decision 30 COM &A.6. Also, noted with the Virunga,Decision 30 COM 7A.7; and the Salonga. Decision 30 COM 7A.5.

437 See State of Conservation Reports. WHC-05/29.COM/7B.Rev. Section 4.

is recognised as a potentially large scale problem. Despite this possibility, only the ICRI and the Ramsar have become actively involved in this debate. Other forums, such as the Bern and CMS have been relatively silent. The response of the WHC as the question of climate change is currently evolving. The fifth threat relates to inadequate or disrupted supply of water into a protected area, as most commonly evidenced with large dams. This has long been recognised as a clear threat to protected areas. However, none of the various regimes have an outright prohibition against large dams. Rather, the Ramsar, Bern and WHC have all continually warned that if the integrity of a site is substantially damaged by the activities of large dams or similar water disruptive processes, then the sites may be listed as in Danger.

The sixth threat is mineral and/or hydro-carbon extraction and/or exploration this is one of the most prominent public debates about threats to protected areas. These debates are both domestic and international, and a number of high level NGO resolutions have been issued calling for restrictions on such activities in most protected areas. The foremost regime to follow such an approach in the Antarctic regime, which prohibits all mining on the continent of Antarctica. Most other regimes have preferred to take a case by case approach, with each activity assessed against the impacts it is making on the integrity of the site. In this regard, the WHC has shown clearly in three separate instances, that poorly regulated mineral and/or hydrocarbon extraction can lead a site as being inscribed as in Danger.

Traffic and routing and general industrial developments are the seventh and eighth threats. These have been long standing issues in a number of protected area forums, with the Bern and the WHC in particular. It is however quite rare, for roading or industrial developments alone to directly lead to a site being classified as in Danger, although this has happened. Rather, these threats are typically part of a package of larger concerns. This approach is unlike the IMO, of which (maritime) traffic, in terms of both type and quantity, going near vulnerable areas is a key consideration on the need for protected areas. The ninth threat to protected areas is pollution. Pollution is a general concern in all of the regimes, but agricultural pollution, is particularly highlighted in the Ramsar and the Bern. However, legal agriculture, as the source of the pollution, and despite infringing into numerous protected areas, has not been the source of detailed discussion outside of the Ramsar, and to a lesser degree, the Bern Convention. A similar situation exists with legitimate forestry in internationally protected areas, with only the European Diploma passing strong recommendations on the need to dramatically control most forms of logging in some of the sites under their auspice. When the focus turns to the threat of illegal extraction, all of the regimes have a similar, steadfast approach, in that it must be controlled. In extreme situations, such extractions, typically poaching, can lead to a site being classified as in Danger. This is a particular problem with a number of African WHC sites. Such illegal activities are commonly associated with times of armed conflict, which is the final threat to protected areas, but only one regime, the WHC, has any recognition of this problem.

Chapter VIII

COMPLIANCE

The principle that all nations will comply with their commitments to ensure the conservation of their listed protected areas can be traced to the 1933 African Convention.[1] The word 'compliance', however, is rarely seen within protected area forums, and debates about how to implement compliance, such as with regard to the precautionary principle or not,[2] are nascent. Nevertheless, a clear practice which attempts to achieve compliance is in evidence with regard to the way each regime attempts, in an obvious overlap with CBD goals,[3] to protect and restore any internationally recognised sites from becoming in danger, and ultimately de-listed, struck off or removed from any internationally accredited list of protected areas.

Being de-listed from an inscribed list, is the ultimate sanction in this area, as the site loses any international standing that it once possessed. Theoretically, most, if not all, of the regional or international regimes that inscribe protected areas, have the potential power to de-list areas as well as inscribe them. In as much as inscription is at one end of the spectrum of the management of sites of international significance, de-listing is at the other end of the spectrum of what may happen to sites in extreme cases.

Before such extreme conclusions can be reached, in most cases, there are a number of steps that have to be taken first, before alleged non-compliance with the conservation needs of a protected area can be substantively addressed.

---

1 1933 London Convention. Articles 1 and 9 (2). And those that came after it in 1968, See the African Convention (1968). Article XVI and the 2003 African Convention, Article XXIII.

2 Only the Ramsar and the 2003 African Convention (article 4) have adopted the precautionary principle. With regard to the Ramsar, the precautionary principle, as defined in principle 15 from the Rio Declaration, has been subsequently identified as a key part of any successful management regime for Ramsar sites. Resolution 8.14. New Guidelines for Management Planning for Ramsar Sites and Other Wetlands. (2002, San Jose). Annex. The specific gloss for Ramsar sites is that while comprehensive understanding of the ecological constraints of a wetland system should be sought, activities affecting wetlands need to be governed by the 'precautionary principle' when such knowledge is not available. Accordingly, if the impact of specific actions is not clearly understood, then these actions should be prohibited even if there is insufficient evidence to prove a direct link between the activities and resulting wetland degradation. Additional Guidance for the Implementation of the Wise Use Concept. Annexed to Resolution 5.6. Wise Use of Wetlands (1993, Kushiro).

3 CBD. Decision VII/28. Protected Areas. Annex. Section 1.5.3.

1 Discovering Sites Threatened with Danger

A Monitoring

Monitoring means the keeping track of things in time, or perhaps more rigorously, a time-series of systematic observations of a system which should permit statistical inferences designed to reduce uncertainty in knowledge of the functioning of the system. It is about data collection which helps to produce information which is necessary and sufficient to understand and manage wisely whatever system is being monitored. There are two functions of monitoring. First, to detect changes and trends by comparing measurements taken or estimates made at different times. The second function of monitoring is to help understand how things work through correlations between the environmental variables being managed. Evidence of change can be useful in assessing not only the success or failure of each respective protected area, but also assessing changes which have implications beyond the boundaries of the specific area of either regional and/or international trends. The importance of this evidence cannot be underestimated, and the CBD places a premium on its collection.[4]

The importance of a comprehensive monitoring of protected areas, is recorded in the 2003 African Convention,[5] a number of regional seas programmes,[6] with MPAs in particular,[7] the Mediterranean[8] and Caribbean Protocols,[9] and the Helsinki regime for the Baltic Sea Protected Areas.[10] The ICRI places a premium upon the monitoring (and restoration)[11] of coral reefs and other critical coastal habitats such as seagrasses and mangroves. To assist this goal, the Parties to the ICRI created the Global Coral Reef Monitoring Network (GCRM).[12]

---

4 CBD. Decision VII/28. Protected Areas. Annex. Section IV.

5 2003 African Convention. Article XIV (2)(c).

6 UNEP. (2000). Report of the Third Global Meeting of Regional Seas Conventions and Action Plans. Available from the UNEP Regional Seas Programme. Paragraphs 60-68. UNEP. (2004). Report of the Sixth Global Meeting of Regional Seas Conventions and Action Plans, Istanbul. Available from the UNEP Regional Seas Programme. 5.

7 See IMO (1990). *Proceedings of the International Seminar on Protection of Sensitive Sea Areas.* (IMO, London). Annex 1. Paragraph 19.

8 Mediterranean Protocol. Articles 5, 7 (2)(b) and Annex I. 8.

9 Caribbean Protocol. Articles 6 and 19.

10 Helcom Recommendation 15/5 (1994). Guidelines For Designating Marine And Coastal Baltic Sea Protected Areas (BPSA).

11 Resolution on Artificial Coral Reef Restoration and Rehabilitation. In ICRI (2004). Report of the ICRI Meeting in Okinawa, Japan. 3-4 July, 2004. Decision on Reef Restoration. Report of the ICRI Meeting in the Philippines, 5-6 April, 2001.

12 Recommendation on Expanded and Sustained Support for the Global Coral Reef Monitoring Network. In ICRI (2000). Report of the ICRI Meeting in Noumea, New Caledonia, 25-26 May, 2000. Decision on Global Monitoring of Seagrasses and Mangroves. In ICRI (2001). Report of the ICRI Meeting in the Philippines, 5-6 April, 2001.

Environmental monitoring[13] at the local, regional and international levels is one of the primary justifications for Biosphere Reserves.[14] The MAB monitoring, which is carried out under the Biosphere Reserve Integrated Monitoring (BRIM) programme, devolves into a series of thematic areas such as mountains, climate change, and flora and fauna.[15]

The importance of co-operative long term monitoring programmes of the human impact on the Antarctic environment is also a strong theme running through the ATS.[16] These monitoring objectives were formalised in the Madrid Protocol,[17] which required its signatories to undertake regular and effective monitoring to allow assessment of the impacts of ongoing activities. Such monitoring is meant to facilitate early detection of detrimental impacts of activities carried on both within and outside the Antarctic Treaty area on the Antarctic environment and dependent and associated ecosystems.[18]

Maintaining the ecological character of all Ramsar sites is a clear objective of the Ramsar and its Parties.[19] Accordingly, the prevention of any detrimental anthropogenic changes to the ecological character of such wetlands is desired. However, before this goal is possible, it is necessary to be able to detect such changes. With this need in mind, the Parties have long agreed to inform the Secretariat, at the earliest possible time of any change in the ecological character of any of their listed wetlands.[20] Despite this long standing commitment, lack of adequate monitoring by the Ramsar Parties (only 37% were monitoring in 1999), resulted in the Ramsar re-emphasising the importance

---

13 Note a 'human dimension' of monitoring, encompassing social and economic considerations, was added. See Seville Strategy. Objective III.2. MAB. (2000). 16th Session of the ICC Bureau. SC-00/CONF.208/13. 18. UNESCO. (2002). 17th Session of the ICC Bureau. SC-02/CONF.201/11. Apr 12. 9.

14 See UNESCO. (ed). *Conservation, Science and Society: The 1983 Biosphere Reserve Conference in Minsk.* (UNESCO, UNEP). 360-449. For its current importance, see Seville Strategy. Objective III.2.

15 UNESCO. (2002). *Biosphere Reserves: Special Places for People and Nature.* (UNESCO, Paris). 80-91, 168-169. UNESCO. (2004). 18th Session of the ICC Bureau Meeting. SC-04/CONF.204/14. Jan 11. 11, 21.

16 Recommendation XV-5. Human Impact on the Antarctic Environment: Environmental Monitoring in Antarctica. In Antarctic Treaty: Report of the Fifteenth Meeting (1989, Paris). 57.

17 See Article 3 (2).

18 See Article 3 (2)(d) & (e). Resolution 1 (2005). Practical Guidelines for Developing and Designing Environmental Monitoring Programs in Antarctica. Final Report of the 28th ATCM. (Stockholm, 2005). 28.

19 Resolution 8.25. The Ramsar Strategic Plan. (2002, Valencia). Annex. Operational Objective 11.

20 As caused by of technological developments, pollution or other human interference. Ramsar. Article 3.2.

of reliable monitoring of all Ramsar sites, developing refined monitoring methods,[21] (and even providing indicators of what to monitor[22] in addition to rapid assessment guidelines)[23] and financial assistance[24] so as to be able to detect ecological changes in wetlands of international significance. To assist this process, the Ramsar Parties adopted the target of, by 2005, 20 Parties having undertaken vulnerability assessments, and 50 Parties to have undertaken water quality and quantity assessments.[25]

The Bern Convention, and the associated Habitats Directive[26] is also concerned with monitoring at both the generic level (encompassing all protected areas)[27] and specifically, in terms of both particular countries (such as Poland,[28] and Cyprus)[29] and distinct-

21 Resolution 8.8. Assessing and Reporting the Status and Trends of Wetlands and the Implementation of Article 3.2. of the Convention. Resolution 8.14. New Guidelines for Management Planning for Ramsar Sites and Other Wetlands. (2002, San Jose). Annex. Resolution 8.6. A Ramsar Framework Inventory. (2002, Valencia). Resolution 7.10. Wetland Risk Assessment. (1999, San Jose). Annex. Wetland Risk Assessment Framework. Recommendation 4.7. Improved Application of the Convention. Annex 1, The Monitoring Procedure. (1990, Montreux). Recommendation 2.3. Annex: Framework for Implementing the Convention. (1984, Groningen). Recommendation 4.10. Guidelines on the Implementation of the Wise Use Concept. (1990, Montreux). The emphasis of all the information sheets, is establishing a baseline describing the functions, products and attributes of the site (from which measurement can occur), information on human induced factors, information on monitoring and survey methods and information on the natural variability and amplitude of changes (including natural ones). Resolution 8.13. Enhancing the Information on Wetlands of International Importance. (2002, San Jose). Annex II. Explanatory Note. Recommendation 4.10. Guidelines for the Implementation of the Wise Use Concept. Annex. Guidelines for the Implementation of the Wise Use Concept of the Convention. Resolution 7.12. Sites in the Ramsar List. (1999, San Jose).

22 Resolution 9.1. Additional Scientific and Technical Guidance for Implementing the Ramsar Wise Use Concept. (2005, Kampala). Annex D. Ecological Outcome Orientated Indicators for Assessing the Implementation Effectiveness of the Ramsar Convention. These cover aspects ranging from trends in bird populations to nutrient content.

23 Resolution 9.1. Additional Scientific and Technical Guidance. *Ibid.* Annex E i. Guidelines for Rapid Assessment of Inland, Coastal and Marine Wetland Biodiversity.

24 Resolution 5.7. Management Planning for Ramsar Sites and Other Wetlands. (1993, Kushiro). Note, this is a long standing target for financial assistance within the Convention. See Recommendation 2.3. Annex: Framework for Implementing the Convention. (1984, Groningen). Resolution 5.2. Financial and Budgetary Matters. (1993, Kushiro).

25 Resolution 8.26. The Implementation of the Strategic Plan 2003-2008. (2002, Valencia). Annex I. Global Implementation of the Targets for the Convention.

26 Habitats Directive. Article 11.

27 Recommendation No 16. (1989). On Areas of Special Conservation Interest. Section 4. Resolution No. 5 (1998) Concerning The Rules For The Network of Areas of Special Conservation Interest (Emerald Network). Report of the 18th Meeting of the Bern Convention. T-PVS (98) 62. Appendix 3. Article 4.

28 Recommendation No. 108 (2003). The Proposed Construction of the Via Baltica (Poland). Report of the 23rd Meeting of the Bern Convention. T-PVS (2003). 24. Appendix 12.

ive threats (such as with wind-turbines[30] and hydro-dams).[31] In addition, the Bern Convention sets aside a significant portion of their budgetary allocations (and have done so since 2000), for the dedicated monitoring of sites (and species) at risk.[32]

The term 'monitoring' does not appear within the text of the WHC.[33] However, the Parties are of the view that a number of the articles of the Convention clearly imply it, and accordingly, have created a positive obligation for the Convention (for all Parties, in conjunction with the Advisory Bodies) to establish a comprehensive monitoring system.[34] The roots of this issue date back to the early 1980s when the Advisory Bodies were directed to independently monitor, on an ad-hoc basis, the progress of work undertaken for the preservation of WHC sites.[35] Although overall proposals for more comprehensive monitoring systems were deemed 'premature',[36] due to political concerns relating to the monitoring of cultural properties,[37] the monitoring of natural sites was not met with the same reticence.[38] Accordingly, the IUCN began ad-hoc monitoring and reporting soon after.[39] This process grew with the increasing realization that effective monitoring was an essential part of the WHC,[40] before becoming a standing

29 Recommendation No. 113. (2004). On The Installation of a New Antenna in the Sovereign Base Area (Cyprus). Report of the 24th Bern Meeting of the Bern Convention. T-PVS (2004). 16. Appendix 7.

30 Recommendation No. 109. (2004). On Minimizing Adverse Effects of Wind Power Generation on Wildlife. Report of the 24th Bern Meeting of the Bern Convention. T-PVS (2004). 16. Appendix 3.

31 Recommendation No. 112. (2004). On Hydroelectric Dams at Karahnjukar (Iceland). Report of the 24th Bern Meeting of the Bern Convention. T-PVS (2004). 16. Appendix 6.

32 Appendix 9. Bern Convention Budget for 2005. Report of the 24th Bern Meeting of the Bern Convention. T-PVS (2004). 16.

33 It is however, arguably, implied through Article 29.

34 UNESCO. (1995). 10th General Assembly of the WHC. WHC-95/CONF.204/8. Nov 22. 1995. 13. See in particular, the Operational Guidelines. 2002 Edn. Paragraphs 54 and 55.

35 UNESCO. (1981). 5th Session of the WHC. CC-81/CONF.003/6. Jan 5, 1981. pp.9.

36 UNESCO. (1982). 6th Session of the WHC. CC-82/CONF.014/6. Aug 20, 1982. pp.7.

37 Cultural sites which presented, 'extremely complex problems, not only of a juridical and financial nature, but aesthetic and ethical ones as well'. UNESCO. (1984). 7th Session of the WHC. CLT/83/CONF.021/8. Aug 1, 1983. pp 12. UNESCO. (1986). 10th Session of the WHC. CC-86/CONF.003/10. Dec 5, 1986. 11. Nevertheless, in the mid 1980s, the Committee was moving towards the acceptance that a monitoring-cum-reporting system was an integral part of the process of maintaining a World Heritage List for cultural properties.

38 UNESCO. (1984). 7th Session of the WHC. SC/83/CONF.009/8. Jan 12, 1984.10.

39 UNESCO. (1985). 9th Session of the WHC. SC-85/CONF.008/9. Dec, 1985.3.

40 UNESCO. (1993). Expert Meeting on Approaches to Monitoring of World Heritage Properties. WHC-93/CONF.002/INF.5. Nov 23. 1993. 2-3. UNESCO. (1996). 19th Session of the WHC. WHC-95/CONF.203/16. Jan 31, 1996. 7, 31-33.

item on the WHC agenda by the late 1980s,[41] and a stand alone budget item in 1992 (it has since more than trebled in cost).[42] At this point, it was agreed that monitoring should be continuous, flexible, participatory and adaptable to national and regional needs.[43] Importantly, monitoring was not to be seen as a sanction.[44] To achieve these goals, the Committee set up a three level (systematic, ad-hoc and administrative) monitoring system.

Systematic monitoring is a continuous process of monitoring WHC sites via periodic reporting obligations. The primary responsibility for this type of day-to-day monitoring, (and reporting thereof) rests on the State Parties,[45] which monitor their own sites, with the guidance of the WHC.[46] From time to time, external and independent professionals, such as the Advisory Bodies or the Centre, may be required to be involved in systematic monitoring.[47] This is often necessary as in many instances, national monitoring of sites is not sufficient. For example, within Latin America and the Caribbean, a 2004 periodic review showed that 52.5% of sites did not have formal monitoring systems.[48]

---

41 UNESCO. (1988). 12th Session of the WHC. SC-88/CONF.001/13. Dec 23, 1988. 1, 6.

42 UNESCO. (1993). 17th Session of WHC. WHC-93/CONF.002/14. Feb 4, 1993. 41. And grew from 189,000 in 1993 (including 34,000 for the advisory bodies who were assisting with monitoring functions). By 2002, it was 540,000. This budget breaks down into reactive monitoring (of which the advisory bodies get a cut) and periodical regional monitoring. The total 2002 budget for monitoring was 540,000.

43 UNESCO. (1992). 16th Session of the WHC. WHC-92/CONF.002/12. Dec 14, 1992. Annex II. UNESCO. (1993). Expert Meeting on Approaches to Monitoring of World Heritage Properties. WHC-93/CONF.002/INF.5. Nov 23. 1993. 1. UNESCO. (2001). 24th Session of the WHC. WHC-2000/CONF.204/21. Feb 16, 2001. 24. UNESCO. (1995). 10th General Assembly of the World Heritage Convention. WHC-95/CONF.204/8. Nov 22. 1995. 8.

44 UNESCO. (1996). 20th Session of the WHC. WHC-96/CONF.201/21. Mar 10, 1997. 12. UNESCO. (1997). 11th Session of the WHC. WHC-97/CONF.205/7. Paris 18, 1997. 5-8.

45 UNESCO. (1995). 18th Session of the WHC. WHC-94/CONF.003/16. Jan 31. 1995. 58-59. UNESCO. (2001). 24th Session of the WHC. WHC-2000/CONF.204/21. Feb 16, 2001. 24.

46 This involves monitoring from an adequate baseline of the sites, which was created when the site was originally inscribed. From such baseline information, change can be monitored and benchmarks and indicators established. The information is fed into a WHC data base, and is assisted by a specific format for the monitoring report. See UNESCO. (2002). *Monitoring World Heritage.* (UNESCO, World Heritage Paper No 10). 118-123. For earlier discussion on this, see UNESCO. (1998). 22nd Session of the WHC. WHC-98/CONF.203/18. Jan 29, 1999. 14. UNESCO. (1997). 21st Session of the WHC. WHC-97/CONF.208/17. Feb 27, 1998. 8. UNESCO. (1993). 17th Session of WHC. WHC-93/CONF.002/14. Feb 4, 1993. 12-13. UNESCO. (1999). 23rd Session of the WHC. WHC-99/CONF.209/22. Mar 22, 2000. 52.

47 UNESCO. (1999). 23rd Session of the WHC. WHC-99/CONF.209/22. Mar 22, 2000. 51. UNESCO. (2001). 24th Session of the WHC. WHC-2000/CONF.204/21. Feb 16, 2001. 24. UNESCO. (1995). 18th Session of the WHC. WHC-94/CONF.003/16. Jan 31. 1995. 13.

48 UNESCO. (2004). *The State of World Heritage in Latin America and the Caribbean: 2004 Periodic Report.* (UNESCO, Paris). 23.

Administrative monitoring is related to follow up actions via the Centre to ensure implementation of the recommendations and decisions of the Committee. Ad-hoc monitoring involves reports by the Centre, other UNESCO sectors and/or the Advisory bodies. Ad-hoc monitoring is typically done in response to exceptional circumstances (such as when a site may become, or is, in danger), and is primarily 'reactive' whereby missions are sent to investigate the site for independent assessment of the risks the site is presented with, or progress made in rectifying such risks. Ad-hoc monitoring has a strong relationship to previous Committee recommendations.[49]

B Reporting

Timely and correct national reports allow regimes to critically assess their own success and failures, and develop strategies to confront the problems before them. Without such information, all such regimes are effectively operating in the dark. This recognition, with regards to protected areas, dates back to the 1933 African Convention, which required Parties to provide information to the Depository (which would subsequently pass on the information to the other Parties), of measures taken for the purpose of carrying out the obligations of the Convention, (such as the creation and management of protected areas).[50] Similar obligations were also mandated in the 1940 Western Hemisphere Convention[51] and the 1968 African Convention.[52] Later instruments such as the Antarctic regime,[53] the European Diploma,[54] the 2003 African Convention,[55]

49 Decision 29.COM/DD/7A and 7B. UNESCO. (1993). 17th Session of WHC. WHC-93/CONF.002/14. Feb 4, 1993. 12-13. UNESCO. (1995). 18th Session of the WHC. WHC-94/CONF.003/16. Jan 31. 1995. 10, 13, 58-59.

50 Specific reporting requirements included measures to control the trade in trophies, hunting measures on species listed in the Annex, notification of the protected areas of either strict nature reserves or national parks, they created (along with their location, governing legislation and methods of administration), including reserves, and also all other information, 'relevant to the purposes of the present Convention and communicated to them by any national museums or by any societies, national or international, established within their jurisdiction and interested in those purposes'. See Articles 5(1) & (2), 7 (4), 8 (6), 9 (9) and 12 of the 1933 London Convention.

51 This obliged its Parties to notify the Depository of their establishment of any national parks, national reserves, nature monuments, or strict wilderness reserves. In addition, they were required to provide information on the governing legislation, including the methods of administrative control. 1940 Western Hemisphere Convention. Article II (3).

52 The Contracting States were obliged to provide the depository with copies of relevant laws, decrees and instructions, as well as applicable reports and documentation, to show how the Convention was being applied. African Convention (1968). Article XVI.

53 See Article 17 of the Madrid Protocol, and Articles 9 and 10 of Annex V.

54 European Diploma. Article 7 (2).

the MAB regime,[56] the Habitats Directive,[57] the Mediterranean[58] and Caribbean Protocols[59] and the Helsinki Convention,[60] have all increased the frequency of the reports, and the details needed to be reported upon.

Although non-reporting is a common problem for many international environmental organisations,[61] the problem was particularly acute with the Ramsar, with less than 25% of all the Parties reporting on time.[62] Even fewer adequately reporting on changes, or likely changes in the ecological character of their listed wetlands.[63] To help rectify these problems, the Ramsar Parties have attempted to make the reporting process easier by standardising and harmonising reporting requirements with comparable international environmental regimes,[64] and simplifying the process by detailing exactly what has to be reported upon.[65]

---

55 Each Party to the 2003 African Convention has reporting obligations on the measures adopted by them in the implementation of this Convention and the results thereof, in addition to some other standard information, such as related laws, focal points, overlapping conventions. See Article XXIX (2). The Secretariat can comment on national reports, in particular regarding failure to report, adequacy of the report and of the measures described therein. Article XXIX (2).

56 Bridgewater, p. (2002). 'Biosphere Reserves: A Network for Conservation and Sustainability'. 12 (3) *Parks.* 15.

57 As due every six years. Habitats Directive. Article 17.

58 Mediterranean Protocol. Article 23.

59 Caribbean Protocol. Article 19.

60 Three yearly reports. Helcom Recommendation 15/5 (1994). Guidelines For Designating Marine And Coastal Baltic Sea Protected Areas (BPSA).

61 For example, with the Bern Convention, in the mid 1990s, only 60% of the Parties were providing reports. Report of the 18th Meeting of the Bern Convention. T-PVS (98) 62. 8.

62 Recommendation 4.3. National Reports. (1990, Montreux).

63 Resolution 9.15. The Status of Sites in the Ramsar List of Wetlands of International Importance. (2005, Kampala).

64 Resolution 9.5. Synergies With Other International Organisations Dealing With Biological Diversity, Including Collaboration on, and Harmonisation of, National Reporting, Among Biodiversity Related Conventions and Agreements. (Kampala, 2005). Resolution 7.4. Cooperation With Other Conventions. (1999, San Jose). Resolution 7.27. The Convention's Work Plan 2000-02. (1999, San Jose).

65 Such as wetland status, threats facing them, involvement of local communities and indigenous peoples, utilisation of incentive measures etc. Resolution 8.26. National Reports for Ramsar COP 9. (2002, Valencia). Resolution 7.8. Local Communities and Indigenous People. (1999, San Jose). Resolution 7.15. Incentive Measures. (1999, San Jose). Recommendation 6.15. Restoration of Wetlands. (1996, Brisbane). Resolution 6.21. Assessment and Reporting on the Status of Wetlands. (1996, Brisbane). Recommendation 2.1. National Reports. (1984, Groningen).

Within the WHC, national reports (also known as State of Conservation or SOC reports)[66] as clearly envisaged in the Convention,[67] and facilitated by the Committee,[68] are treated as, non-coercive and 'part of a consultative process'.[69]

Despite the foundations, and good-intentions with regard to the utilization of national reports, the system has commonly needed to be supplemented, due to the insufficient nature of some national reporting. Accordingly, the Parties to the WHC have attempted to supplement this area with periodic regional reports (which are commonly made up of a series of sub-regional reports). These periodic reports are based on a revolving cycle of between 4 to 6 years.[70] This process, of an initial, substantive and follow-up reports and the formation of Action Plans to address the identified problems, allows groups of countries to address the reporting requirements collectively, whilst also introducing a degree of objectivity into the process, as Parties are not just reporting about themselves. The first periodic report was from Arabia (18 Arab Parties covering 41 sites)[71] was completed in 2000. The follow-up report (on progress made since the substantive report) was in 2004.[72] The substantive periodic report for Africa (53 sites

---

66 See Decision 29 COM 7C. Submission of State of Conservation Reports of World Heritage Properties by February 2006.

67 The Parties shall provide, 'information on the legislative and administrative provisions which they have adopted and other action which they have taken for the application of this Convention, together with details of the experience acquired in this field'. WHC. Article 29.

68 The UNESCO General Assembly called upon parties, in accordance with Article 29, through the Committee, to provide reports on their sites (on legal, administrative and conservation issues). UNESCO. (1997). 21st Session of the WHC. WHC-97/CONF.208/17. Feb 27, 1998. 8. The Committee recommended that parties keep them informed, 'of their intention to undertake or to authorize in an area protected under the Convention major restorations or new constructions which may affect the World Heritage value of the property'. The ideal is that notice should be given as soon as possible (for instance, before drafting basic documents for specific projects) and before making any decisions that would be difficult to reverse, so that the Committee may assist in seeking appropriate solutions to ensure that the world heritage value of the site is fully preserved. *Operational Guidelines.* 2002 Edn. Paragraph 56.

69 UNESCO. (1996). 19th Session of the WHC. WHC-95/CONF.203/16. Jan 31, 1996. 7, 31-33.

70 UNESCO. (1995). 18th Session of the WHC. WHC-94/CONF.003/16. Jan 31. 1995. 13-14. The first project to undertake pilot monitoring in Latin America and the Caribbean was in 1991.

71 The initial report presented a dismal state of affairs in the region (lack of strategy, documentation, professional and technical skills, non-involvement of civil society, absence of indicators, ill understood values). UNESCO. (1999). 23rd Session of the WHC. WHC-99/CONF.209/22. Mar 22, 2000. 49-50. UNESCO. (2001). 24th Session of the WHC. WHC-2000/CONF.204/21. Feb 16, 2001. 23.

72 The progress was mainly in terms of expert missions and enhanced financial assistance UNESCO. (2004). 7th Extraordinary Session of the WHC. WHC-04/7 EXT.COM/5B. Decision 7 EXT.COM 5B.

in the territories of 18 Parties) was concluded in 2001,[73] and adopted when the associated Action Plan was concluded.[74] The progress report on the Periodic Report for Africa was presented in 2005.[75] The periodic report for Europe and North America was, after being deferred and split,[76] was presented in 2005.[77] The periodic report for the Asia-Pacific region[78] was concluded in 2002, and the periodic report for Latin America and the Caribbean was concluded in 2003 (and noted in 2004).[79] 2007 was designated as a Reflection Year, as no periodic reports fell for completion in this year.

C Independent Visits

The Antarctic regime has the potentially strongest regime for independent inspections of protected areas. This regime is derived from Article VII of the Antarctic Treaty. This provision, which has been supplemented by resolutions,[80] was designed to promote the objectives and ensure the observance of the provisions of the Treaty. It provides the right to Contracting Parties to designate observers to carry out inspections of stations, installations and all other facilities of other Contracting Parties. In addition, Article 14 of the Madrid Protocol provided that inspections shall be arranged in order to promote the protection of the Antarctic environment and, to ensure compliance with the Protocol. However, the clear practice of the Parties to the Antarctic Treaty is that stations, as opposed to protected areas, are the preferred choice of inspection.[81]

---

73 This revealed lack of policy and legislative measures for heritage conservation, lack of involvement of local communities and NGOs, inadequate professional personnel, skills and equipment; lack of scientific information, financial resources, education and public awareness; poorly defined and understood WHC values; and lack of mechanisms for addressing threats. The report emphasized the need for mainstreaming WHC protection within the public and private sectors, establishing long term conservation programmes; promoting transparency and proactive environmental assessment tools and effective management regimes. UNESCO. (2001). 25th Session of the WHC. WHC-01/CONF.208/24. Paris 8, Feb 2002. 22-25.

74 UNESCO. (2002). 26th Session of the WHC. WHC-02/CONF.202/25. Aug 1, 2002. 16.

75 UNESCO. (2005). Progress Report on the Implementation of the Recommendations of the Periodic Report. WHC-05/29.COM/11C.

76 UNESCO. (2004). 7th Extraordinary Session of the WHC. WHC-04/7 EXT.COM/5A. Decision 7 EXT.COM 5A.1 & 7 EXT.COM 5A.2.

77 UNESCO. (2005). Periodic Report for North America. WHC-05/29.COM/11A. UNESCO. (2005). Periodic Report for Europe. WHC-05/29.COM/11B.

78 UNESCO. (2004). 7th Extraordinary Session of the WHC. WHC-04/7 EXT.COM/5D. EXT.COM 5D.

79 UNESCO. (2004). 7th Extraordinary Session of the WHC. WHC-04/7 EXT.COM/5A. 7 EXT.COM 5E. The Action Plan is reprinted in WHC-04/7 EXT.COM/INF.5E. Nov 24.

80 Without prejudice to their rights under the Treaty, the Parties also agreed to adopt checklists to assist in the structuring of inspections. See Resolution 5/1995: Antarctic Inspection Checklists.

81 See for example, the Final Report of the Twenty-Eighth Antarctic Treaty Consultative Meeting. (Stockholm, 2005). Paragraphs 181-198.

The Antarctic Treaty Parties also provided (as originally agreed in 1987)[82] that after reports have been circulated to the Parties, and have been considered at their annual meeting, the reports of such inspections will be made publicly available. Although the checklists adopted by the Parties[83] have been largely tangential to protected areas, it is possible that these could be extended in time to also directly protected these areas. Indeed, when reviewing the overall effectiveness of the protected areas in the Antarctic, the SCAR recommended (in 1987), inter alia, that periodic 'visits' be made to such areas, at such intervals as are necessary to in order to determine whether the objectives of the their designation are being met, and if not, what steps could be taken to improve the situation.[84] However, despite the advocacy of certain countries, such as Russia, that effective monitoring of protected areas needs to be enhanced, the inspection of protected areas within the Antarctic regime remains ad-hoc.[85]

With regard to the WHC, if there is a possible concern over a protected area, the ideal situation is that the State Party on whose territory the site is situated shall inform the Secretariat over its concerns.[86] The Secretariat may also receive such information, 'from a source other than the State Party concerned'.[87] In such situations, the Secretariat will, as far as possible, verify the source and the contents of the information in consultation with the Party concerned and request its comments. The Advisory Bodies may also comment on the information received.[88] As part of this process, 'a fact-finding mission or the consultation of specialists'[89] may be dispatched to the site in question. Thereafter, all of the information received from the Advisory Bodies, the Party in which the site

---

82 See Antarctic Treaty: Report of the Fourteenth Meeting. (Rio de Janeiro, 1987). Paragraphs 75-84. The information required (especially information of physical or biological change, evidence of activity contrary to the Agreed Measures or its management plan, and evidence of whether it is continuing to serve the purpose for which it was designated) from such proposed visits, was set in paragraph 98.

83 These being, permanent Antarctic Stations and Associated Installations; Vessels within the Antarctic Treaty Area; Abandoned Antarctic Stations and Associated Installations and Waste Disposal Sites.

84 See Antarctic Treaty: Report of the Fourteenth Meeting. (Rio de Janeiro, 1987). Paragraphs 75-84. The information required (especially information of physical or biological change, evidence of activity contrary to the Agreed Measures or its management plan, and evidence of whether it is continuing to serve the purpose for which it was designated) from such proposed visits, was set in paragraph 98.

85 See Russian Federation. (2004). On the Need of Environmental Monitoring of Antarctic Specially Protected Areas. CEP Paper IP 044 (Cape Town, 2004).

86 *Operational Guidelines*. 2002 Edn. Paragraph 47.

87 *Ibid.* Paragraph 48. UNESCO. (1992). 16th Session of the WHC. WHC-92/CONF.002/12. Dec 14, 1992. Annex II.

88 *Operational Guidelines*. 2002 Edn. Paragraph 49.

89 *Ibid.* Paragraph 50. This importance of this fact-finding need in these situations was established at the 3rd Committee meeting. UNESCO. (1979). 3rd Session of the WHC. CC-79/CONF.003/13. Nov 30, 1978. pp.4.

is located, and even the original source, is brought to the attention of the WHC Committee, if appropriate.[90]

The MAB and the European Diploma, both utilise appraisals (in accordance with specific conditions) by independent experts. This is especially so when there is the possibility that a site may be in danger.[91] On-site assessments are also utilised by the Bern Convention, with matters of alleged non-compliance. In the event of difficulty or doubt as to the measures to be taken in a particular case and if further information is required, an expert appointed by the Secretary General of the Council of Europe can be directed (with a member of the Secretariat and a representative of the Party concerned) to carry out an on-the-spot appraisal. As of 2005, there had been eleven on-the spot visits since the process began. Laganas Bay on Zakynthos has been visited twice.

2 Recognition of the Danger

Once a site is recognised as being threatened, each regime will attempt to develop methods by which that danger can be mitigated. More often than not, there is no specific record, which recognises which sites need to be assisted. The common practice is that since there are only a few threatened sites, the issue does not need an elaborate procedure, as the facts speak for themselves. For example, the Bern Convention runs a 'case-file' system, which deals with sites which are threatened. However, with the Ramsar and the WHC, a particular record is created which explicitly recognises and publicises the threats to the particular sites.

Wetlands of international importance which are undergoing (or are likely to undergo) an anthropogenically induced change in their ecological characteristics are, aside general national monitoring processes,[92] inscribed upon the Ramsar list of threatened sites. This list, known as the 'Montreux Record' was formally created in 1990,[93] after six years of debate.[94] The purpose of the record is 'to identify priority sites for positive national and international conservation attention' and to guide 'implementation of the Monitoring Procedure' and 'allocation of resources available under the financial mechan-

---

90 *Operational Guidelines*. 2002 Edn. Paragraph 50. On the changing of the List, see Paragraph 53.

91 European Diploma. Articles 7 (2), 8 and 9.

92 The 7th COP called upon parties to document the loss of their intertidal wetlands, giving priority to those sites which are important to local communities and indigenous peoples, and those holding globally threatened wetland species. Resolution 7.21. Intertidal Wetlands. (1996, San Jose).

93 Recommendation 4.8. Change in Ecological Character. (1990, Montreux). Recommendation 4.7. Improved Application of the Convention. (1990, Montreux).

94 Recommendation 2.3. Action Points for Priority Attention. (1984, Groningen).

ism'.[95] There were 57 sites in 2005, from 30 countries on the record.[96] However, this number may be deceptive, due to the lack of reporting from many Parties on the issue of ecological change. Even with the minority of (28) Parties that did adequately address this issue in 2005, at least 102 Ramsar sites where human induced changes in ecological character have occurred or may occur, were identified.[97] To help assist the utilisation of the Montreux process, the Parties to the Ramsar formulated the Wetland Risk Assessment Framework. This framework provides guidance on how to go about predicting and assessing change in the ecological character of wetlands and promotes, in particular, the usefulness of early warning systems.[98]

If a site is placed on the Montreux Record, the goal of the Ramsar Parties is to have the threat mitigated and the values for why it was originally inscribed restored. Such restoration of threatened protected areas was first recognised by the Ramsar Parties in 1974, when waterfowl returned to the Thames in London, due to reduced pollution of the river.[99] Such restoration processes have continued over the following decades. As of 2005, 23 sites had been entered onto the record and subsequently removed due to successful restoration.[100] However, the rate of removal from the record appears to be slowing. At the 2005 Kampala meeting it was noted that of the 57 Ramsar sites included on the Montreux record, only three had been removed since 2002, and all of these removals were in the Ukraine.[101]

Despite slowing removal rates, restoration successes have resulted in the Ramsar recognising wetland restoration as one of its clear strategic objectives,[102] and accordingly the Ramsar Parties have encouraged restoration at both the generic level[103] and

95 Resolution 5.4. The Monteux Record. (1993, Kushiro). Resolution 8.8. Assessing and Reporting the Status and Trends of Wetlands and the Implementation of Article 3.2. of the Convention.

96 Ramsar. (2005). Key Documents of the Ramsar Convention: The Montreux Record.

97 Resolution 9.15. The Status of Sites on the Ramsar List of Wetlands of International Importance. (2005, Kampala). Paragraph 17.

98 Resolution 7.10. Wetland Risk Assessment. (1999, San Jose). Annex. Wetland Risk Assessment Framework.

99 Recommendations adopted by the International Conference on the Conservation of Wetlands and Waterfowl at Heiligenhafen, Federal Republic of Germany, 6 December 1974. Recommendation 3. Return of Waterfowl to the Inner Thames in London, England.

100 Ramsar. (2003). *Key Documents of the Ramsar Convention: The Montreux Record.* (Ramsar, Gland).

101 Resolution 9.15. The Status of Sites on the Ramsar List of Wetlands of International Importance. (2005, Kampala). Paragraph 17.

102 Resolution 8.25. The Ramsar Strategic Plan. (2002, Valencia). Annex. Operational Objective 4.

103 Recommendation 4.1. Wetland Restoration. (1990, Montreux). Recommendation 6.15. Restoration of Wetlands. (1996, Brisbane). Resolution 7.17. Wetland Restoration. (1999, San Jose).

with specifically identified sites.[104] Principles and guidelines for wetland restoration[105] have been adopted in addition to a series of targets with regards to this goal. Specifically, it was hoped that restoration inventories by at least 50 Parties would be undertaken by 2002,[106] and 100 Parties by 2008.[107]

Finally, the WHC has maintained a 'List' of WHC sites, natural and cultural, 'in Danger' since 1978. The 'Danger List' encompasses sites which are 'threatened by serious and specific dangers' and require 'major' conservation operations.[108] Although the Convention originally noted the types of dangers that may cause such deterioration,[109] the Committee has come to view the problem with regard to what the threats represent to the integrity of the site, rather than the types of threats in themselves. The key idea of why a site is entered on the Danger List is whether it has, 'deteriorated to the extent that it has lost those characteristics which determined its inclusion in the World Heritage List'.[110] Although a site may have deteriorated, a pivotal assumption is that if the threat can be defeated, and restoration of the site is possible,[111] then all possible efforts should be expended on the attempt.

104 Recommendation 3.9. Change in Ecological Character of Ramsar Sites. (1987, Regina). For an early example of this, see Recommendation 4.9.4. Leybucht, Germany. (1990, Montreux). See also Recommendation 6.17. Ramsar Sites in Particular Countries. (1996, Brisbane).

105 Resolution 8.16. Principles and Guidelines for Wetland Restoration. (2002, San Jose). The importance of applying these principles as a means to address vulnerability to floods and droughts was highlighted. Linking them into the level of catchment and river basin level was emphasised, as was the need to pay particular attention to peatlands in this context. The key principles were the need for a national programme, with clear understanding and goals; careful planning; compatibility with RAMSAR goals; stewardship, local involvement and strong consideration of water allocation principles.

106 Resolution 7.27. The Convention's Work Plan 2000-02. (1999, San Jose). Annex. Work Plan.

107 See Resolution 9.8. Streamlining the Implementation of the Strategic Plan of the Convention 2003-2008. (Kampala, 2005). Strategy 1.5. The original target date was 2005. See Resolution 8.26. The Implementation of the Strategic Plan 2003-2008. (2002, Valencia). Annex I. Global Implementation of the Targets for the Convention.

108 WHC. Article 11 (4).

109 Such as 'the threat of disappearance caused by accelerated deterioration, large- scale public or private projects or rapid urban or tourist development projects; destruction caused by changes in the use or ownership of the land; major alterations due to unknown causes; abandonment for any reason whatsoever; the outbreak or the threat of an armed conflict; calamities and cataclysms; serious fires, earthquakes, landslides; volcanic eruptions; changes in water level, floods and tidal waves'. WHC. Article 11 (4).

110 *Operational Guidelines.* 2002 Edition. Paragraph 6.

111 *Ibid.* Paragraph 50.

Sites may be added,[112] and removed, from the Danger List.[113] The early emphasis of the Danger List was with high profile cultural sites, such as Jerusalem,[114] and natural properties did not originally feature prominently on the List. However, by the mid 1990s, there were 9 natural sites on the Danger List,[115] and by 2006 there were 16 (out of a total of 31).[116] Although the 2006 figure was lower than earlier years,[117] the goal of the Parties to the WHC was to reduce the number of sites on the Danger list by at least 20% by 2007.[118]

3 Mitigating Threatened Sites

Once it is established that a site is threatened, the question becomes what can be done to entice, or force, a State Party to protect it? The ultimate question is, can actions be taken with regard to that site, such as inscribing it on a danger list, or even de-listing it from its original inscription list, without State consent? This is a particularly difficult issue, as its conclusion may have a number of implications of both domestic and international importance.[119]

There are two methods which the international community has adopted in this area. The first option involves automatic review by which, all sites which are inscribed under a particular regime. The background to the regular review is a presumption that if a site is no longer up to scratch, it will be removed from the list. State consent to such possible de-listings is not paramount. The second, more common, option is whereby sites are presumed to remain on the list, until they are shown to be in danger. If in danger, the site can only be removed from the list, with or without State consent.

It is possible in such instances where State consent cannot be obtained, that the debate could lead to a formal dispute between countries, and the dispute would have to be dealt with through an agreed dispute settlement procedure. Although a number of

---

112 The Committee may at any time, in case of urgent need, make a new entry in the List of World Heritage in Danger and publicize such entry immediately. WHC. Article 11 (4).

113 UNESCO. (1978). 2nd Session of the WHC. CC-78/CONF.010/10. Oct 9, 1978. pp.4.

114 UNESCO. (1983). 6th Session of the WHC. CC-83/CONF.015/8. Jan 17, 1983.3-4.

115 UNESCO. (1996). 20th Session of the WHC. WHC-96/CONF.201/21. Mar 10, 1997. 12.

116 UNESCO. (2004). 28th Session of the WHC. WHC-04/28.COM/26. Oct 29. Decision 28 COM 15C.2. pp149-151.

117 UNESCO. (2003). 27th Session of the WHC. WHC-03/27.COM/24. Dec 10. 94.

118 UNESCO. (2004). 28th Session of the WHC. WHC-04/28.COM/26. Oct 29. Decision 28 COM 13.1. Point 13 C. pp. 13.

119 Pressouyre, L. (1992). *The World Heritage Convention, Twenty Years Later.* (UNESCO, Paris). 8-10.

protected area regimes contain such dispute settlement procedures,[120] other forums, such as the WHC and the Ramsar have a noticeable absence of dispute resolution provisions. Despite these possibilities, with the exception of the Bern Convention and the Zakanthos file (see below), none of the regimes have recognised possible disputes over protected areas. Rather, all high-level inter-state and all of the disputes have been dealt with inside of the forums.

A Automatic Review

The European Diploma is only one regime, whereby inscriptions are automatically reviewed every five years, as each site has to have its diploma renewed. Accordingly, remaining inscribed is conditional upon the receipt of positive annual reports, and fresh (and positive) appraisals by independent experts.[121] This necessity for renewal is unlike other international conventions, as the threat of non-renewal acts as a deterrent to letting an area slip in standards.[122]

A similar approach whereby sites are automatically reviewed is with the Antarctic. In this instance, the earlier practice was that some protected areas were delisted,[123] reclassified (to a lesser standing)[124] or remodelled to accommodate other needs in the area (such as the construction of a scientific base).[125] These practices are particularly pronounced with historic sites and monuments, where the Consultative Parties have called upon the responsible governments to visit the sites under their auspice, to make sure site still exists, check if it meets the guidelines for the sites, and consider whether it requires additional protection, or whether it should be de-listed.[126] With such concerns in mind, in 2004, 2 historic sites were removed from the list.[127] With regard to conservation based protected areas, the principle is clear that not all sites are inscribed permanently. That is, although ASPAs are for an indefinite period, unless the management plan states otherwise (and the management plans themselves may have to be renewed),[128] all SSSIs have to apply for extensions, and are thus renewed at set

---

120 Including, inter alia, African Convention (1968). Article XVIII. 2003 African Convention. Article XXX, Bern Convention. Article 18 (1), (2) and (3). Article 18 of the Madrid Protocol.

121 European Diploma. Article 9.

122 See Bauer, F. (2002). 'The European Diploma of Protected Areas'. 12 (3) *Parks*. 29, 33.

123 Recommendation XV-7. Antarctic Protected Area System: Redesignation of Specially Protected Area No. 11. In Antarctic Treaty: Report of the Fifteenth Meeting (Paris, 1989). 73.

124 See Recommendation VIII-2.

125 See Recommendation V-5.

126 Resolution 4 (2001). Historic Sites and Monuments. In Antarctic Treaty: Report of the Twenty-Third Meeting. (St Petersburg, 2001). 52.

127 Antarctic Treaty: Report of the Twenty-Seventh Meting. (Cape Town. 2004). Measure 3. 166.

128 See Annex V, Article 6(3).

periods. This renewal is because the values for which they are inscribed, – scientific investigation – are not presumed to be permanent.[129] Accordingly, a number of SSSIs have come into existence, only to later disappear when they were not renewed.[130]

B Selective Review and the Question of State Consent

A Contracting Party may request inclusion of a site on Ramsar's Montreux Record, because of the potential or actual adverse change in its ecological character of that site. Alternatively, the Bureau, on receipt of information on actual or possible adverse change from partner organizations, other international or national NGOs, or other interested bodies, may draw to the attention of the Contracting Party, the status or threat to the wetland in question, and enquire whether a Ramsar site should be included in the Montreux Record. Although the Bureau may make such an enquiry, a site can only be included on the Record with the approval of the Contracting Party concerned.[131] The same logic applies with regard to de-listing of Ramsar sites. With regard to this consideration, a Party may, because of its urgent national interest, unilaterally delete

---

129 Recommendation VIII-3. Sites of Special Scientific Interest. In 1 Report of the Eighth Meeting. (1975, Oslo). 53. Recommendation XIV-6. Marine Sites of Special Scientific Interest. In Antarctic Treaty: Report of the Fourteenth Meeting (Rio de Janeiro, 1987). 119. See also Conservation Measure 91-01. (2004) Procedure for According Protection to CEMP Sites.

130 The first 6 sites listed in 1975, set to expire in 1981 were the first to get extensions until mid 1985, whilst the seventh site only had an extension until 1983. Recommendation X-6. Sites of Special Scientific Interest. In Antarctic Treaty: Report of the Tenth Meeting. (Washington, 1979). 47. In 1983, all of these sites, along with the additional site listed in 1979, were given extensions until the end of 1985. Recommendation XII-5. Sites of Special Scientific Interest. In Antarctic Treaty: Report of the Twelfth Meeting. (Canberra, 1983). 43. Seven sites (but not the original site Number 1, which lapsed in late 1985) later had extensions granted for between 1987 and 1995. Recommendation XIII-7. Sites of Special Scientific Interest: Interim Guidelines: Extensions of Designation. In Antarctic Treaty: Report of the Thirteenth Meeting. (Brussels, 1985). 42. One site, set to expire in 1987, extended to 1997. Recommendation XIV-4. Sites of Special Scientific Interest: Interim Guidelines: extensions of Designations. In Antarctic Treaty: Report of the Fourteenth Meeting. (Rio de Janeiro, 1987). 52. Further extensions for SSSIs were approved in 1996, Resolution III (1996). Extension of the Expiry Dates for Sites of Special Scientific Interest. In Antarctic Treaty: Report of the Twentieth Meeting. (Utrecht, 1996). 41; and 2001. Measure 3 (2001). Extension of Expiry Dates for Certain Sites of Special Scientific Interest. In Antarctic Treaty: Report of the Twenty-Third Meeting. (St Petersburg, 2001). 43.

131 Resolution VI.1. Guidelines for Operation of the Montreux Record, (Brisbane 1996). Annex, section 3.

or restrict the boundaries of its wetlands of international importance,[132] but they should compensate such a removal by listing other wetlands in its place.[133]

No Ramsar sites have ever been 'de-listed', although three early sites were later removed from the List, in coordination with the Contracting Party, when it was found that they did not meet the listing criteria. On a further three occasions, Parties have invoked the 'urgent national interest' clause to restrict the boundaries of some of their sites. These instances involved Belgium in the 1980s, Australia in 1997 (although in this case the restriction of boundaries did not in fact occur) and Germany in 2000.

In furtherance of this concern, in 2002, the Parties to the Ramsar provided guidance on what was an 'urgent national interest'[134] and began to examine different scenarios in such situations.[135] The Parties concluded this area in 2005 with guidance for addressing Ramsar sites, or parts of sites, which no longer meet the criteria for designation. In this guidance, the Parties to Ramsar clarified the importance of a Party with a listed wetland that was losing its ecological character to 'consider' the utility of seeking advice from the STRP, adding the site to the Montreux record, or requesting a Ramsar Advisory Mission. The only obligation upon the Party is to report the situation to the Ramsar Secretariat. The only possible response for the Ramsar members is to make recommendations to the Party concerned.[136] The Parties followed this approach in 2005, making

---

132 Ramsar. Article 2 (5). Article 4.2 provides, however, that such deletions or restrictions should be compensated for by the creation of additional nature reserves or by the protection, either in the same area or elsewhere, of a suitable portion of the original habitat.

133 The Ramsar Convention was unique in its time, for stipulating that where a Contracting Party in its urgent national interest, deletes or restricts the boundaries of a wetland included in the List, it should as far as possible compensate for any loss of wetland resources, and in particular it should create additional nature reserves for waterfowl and for the protection, either in the same area or elsewhere, of an adequate portion of the original habitat. Ramsar. Article 4.2. Despite this clear articulation, aside from some directed recommendations to parties to examine 'initiatives for compensatory measures' (Recommendation 4.9.4. Leybucht, Germany, 1990). The issue remained largely unexamined until the late 1990s. At this point, the 7th COP reiterated the compensatory ideal for wetland loss (in size or quality) caused by human activities. The preference of the COP was for compensation for wetland loss with wetlands of a similar type and in the same local water catchment. Resolution 7.24. Compensation for Lost Wetland Habitats. (1996, San Jose). Note, the Standing Committee were directed to develop some criteria and guidelines for the compensation of wetland habitats.

134 Resolution VIII.20. General guidance for interpreting urgent national interests under Article 2.5 of the Convention and considering compensation under Article 4.2 (Valencia, 2002).

135 Resolution 8.22. Issues Concerning Ramsar Sites That Cease To Fulfil or Never Fulfilled the Criteria for Designation of Wetlands of International Importance. (2002, Valencia).

136 Resolution 9.6. Guidance for Addressing Ramsar Sites or Parts of Sites Which No Longer Meet the Criteria for Designation. (Kampala, 2005).

recommendations to both Chile, to consider listing a site on the Montreux Record, and Greece, to consider removing a site from the Montreux Record.[137]

The facilitation of periodic reviews of all biosphere reserves, every ten years, was agreed in the Seville Strategy,[138] confirmed in the 1995 Statutory Framework,[139] and re-iterated in the Seville + 5 Strategy. The latter document explained,

> The main purpose of the review is to ensure that each biosphere reserve effectively fulfils all three functions of a biosphere reserve, or has the potential to do so, *inter alia* through an effective and robust institutional arrangement.[140]

The review, which is carried by the Advisory Committee for Biosphere Reserves, may involve field visits. The Committee provides recommendations to the International Co-ordinating Council (ICC), based on a report prepared by the concerned authority and forwarded to the MAB Secretariat by the State concerned. If the ICC concludes that a site no longer satisfies the biosphere reserve criteria, it may recommend that the State concerned take measures to ensure conformity with the said provisions,[141] and restore the qualities of the site.[142] If adequate change is not recognised within a 'suitable time', then 'the area will no longer be referred to as a biosphere reserve which is part of the Network'.[143]

Within this context, it is important to note that periodic review is voluntary, and soft. Aside the fact that it is relatively difficult to place an MAB site in danger (due to their very nature),[144] if this is achieved, and an MAB site has had its original inscription values destroyed,[145] the clear preference for the MAB is that the State voluntarily remove sites from the MAB list[146] rather than have it removed by the Council.[147] The ICC adopted this approach, after it became clear when the review process demonstrated that a number of sites would fail to meet the inscription objectives if resubmitted.

---

137 Resolution 9.15. The Status of Sites on the Ramsar List of Wetlands of International Importance. (2005, Kampala). Paragraph 27.

138 Seville Strategy. Objective IV.2.

139 The 1995 Statutory Framework of the World Network of Biosphere Reserves. Article 9 (4).

140 Seville + 5 Recommendations. Recommendation Number 8.

141 The 1995 Statutory Framework of the World Network of Biosphere Reserves. Article 9(5).

142 Restoration and rehabilitation, an important idea for biosphere reserves. UNESCO. (2002). *Biosphere Reserves: Special Places for People and Nature.* (UNESCO, Paris). 70-71.

143 The 1995 Statutory Framework of the World Network of Biosphere Reserves. Article 9(6).

144 Bridgewater, p. (2002). 'Biosphere Reserves: A Network for Conservation and Sustainability'. 12 (3) *Parks.* 15.

145 Due to an overexploitation of water, lack of management and limited protection of core area, as with Mancha Humeda in Spain. UNESCO. (2003). ICC Bureau Meeting. SC-02/CONF.210/10. Jan 7. 21.

146 The 1995 Statutory Framework of the World Network of Biosphere Reserves. Article 9(8).

147 UNESCO. (2001). MAB ICC Bureau Meeting. SC/-01/CONF.211/13. Apr 10. 17.

Rather than forcefully remove these sites, the ICC, which places a great emphasis upon the national sovereignty of any MAB site,[148] decided that direct recommendations were the most fruitful way forward. Suggestions for the creation of a 'Red List' of threatened MAB sites were not adopted due to their 'coercive line of reasoning'.[149] The difference between the MAB and other conventions, such as the WHC, on dealing with sites clearly threatened, was clearly evidenced in 2005 with regard to Lake Baikal (which is both a WHC and an MAB site). Whereas the Chairperson for the WHC Committee got directly involved in a high-profile dispute with the State Party over the proposed pipeline, the approach of the MAB was simply one of questions being put to the State Party, and calls for clarification.[150]

Unlike the Ramsar and the MAB, the European Diploma is clear that if the danger to a site proves real, and the State concerned does not implement the recommended changes to safeguard that site within a given timeframe, the Committee and/or its Bureau has the authority to decide whether or not to recommend to the Council of Ministers that the Diploma be withdrawn[151] before the end of the five-year period.[152] This practice has only occurred once, when the Diploma was not renewed for the Pyrenees National Park in France, because the authorities had not taken into account the concerns of the Council of Europe with regard to the development of a ski resort.[153]

The Bern Convention has similar powers, in that a designated site may be considered for declassification where the threat is proven and verified.[154] However, due to the relatively new auspice of coverage (with regard to ASCIs) the Parties to the Convention have not yet had time to fully explore its powers in this area. Nevertheless, the Parties have dealt with a number of very similar matters under its well established compliance regime, which encompasses monitoring, reports, independent verification and case-files.[155] Whilst not a strictly legally binding system, as there are no legal remedies in the event of infringements, other than with regard to formal disputes between coun-

148 The Statutory Framework of the World Network of Biosphere Reserves. Article 2 (3).

149 UNESCO. (2002). 17th Session of the ICC Bureau. SC-02/CONF.201/11. Apr 12. 7. MAB. (2000). 16th Session of the ICC Bureau. SC-00/CONF.208/13. 12. UNESCO. (2001). MAB ICC Bureau Meeting. SC/-01/CONF.211/13. Apr 10. 17.

150 See UNESCO. (2005). MAB ICC Bureau Meeting. SC-05/CONF.210/16. August 18. 5.

151 The decision requires a two third majority vote. European Diploma. Article 8 (2).

152 European Diploma. Articles 7 (3) and 8 (1).

153 See Bauer, F. (2002). 'The European Diploma of Protected Areas'. 12 (3) *Parks*. 29, 33.

154 Resolution No. 5 (1998) Concerning The Rules For The Network of Areas of Special Conservation Interest (Emerald Network). Report of the 18th Meeting of the Bern Convention. T-PVS (98) 62. Appendix 3. Article 5.

155 Recommendation No. 114. (2004). On the Role of the Bern Convention in the Preservation of Biological Diversity. Report of the 24th Bern Meeting of the Bern Convention. T-PVS (2004). 16. Appendix 8.

tries,[156] the Bern Convention acts as a forum where decisions are made (typically by consensus, rarely by voting). Within the Bern Convention, diplomacy, flexibility and publicity are the key tools to addressing non-compliance.

The Bern Convention utilises 'case-files' whereby sites are verified in regard to their application of the provisions of the Convention by the respective Parties.[157] As of 2005, the Committee had dealt with over 400 alleged cases of non-compliance, and established 76 case-files since 1982. Many cases placed on the Committee's agenda never lead to the official opening of a case-file or, therefore, to a recommendation. Often the initiation of the procedure by the Secretariat (an official request for information) has been enough to prompt an appropriate response from the implicated Parties and the case-file has not been opened.

A file is opened, if evidence, which may come from NGOs or private individuals, is presented to the Secretariat, and the Secretariat decides that there is enough merit in the information for further investigation. If so, the Party is informed of the matter, and invited to respond to the allegations. In light of this response and the information at hand, it is decided, by the Secretariat and the Bureau, whether the matter should be put before the Committee. If the Committee comes to examine the issue, they may call for an on-the spot investigation for the purposes of eliciting further information, or they may issue directed recommendations to the Party concerned.[158] The recommendations adopted are communicated to the Contracting Parties for implementation and the Party must duly report on how it is responding to these recommendations. The recommendations are made in public.

Of the 76 files dealt with by the Bern Convention, 47% have been resolved (or no longer discussed) and closed within two years of appearing on the agenda, 37.5 % were closed after four years, and 15.5 % were closed after six years. Only two files remained open and unresolved for longer than this. Both of these were in Greece. These are the Missolonghi Wetlands which remains an open file, and Laganas Bay, Zakynthos which was closed after 14 years with no positive result. Greece also possesses the largest number (11) of case-files against it since 1982.[159] The Zakynthos file is the nadir of the Bern Convention, as it ended up with the Committee issuing two declarations[160] following two on-the-spot visits, concerning the failure of recommended conservation measures relating to the nesting beaches for the marine turtle (*Caretta caretta)* on the Greek island.

156 See Article 18 of the Bern Convention.

157 Resolution No. 7. Medium Term Strategic Development of the Bern Convention. Report of the 20th Meeting of the Bern Convention. T-PVS (2000). 75. Appendix 3.

158 The recommendations must be passed by at least a two thirds majority.

159 Spain and United Kingdom have both had 9 case-files, France 8, Turkey 7, Italy and the Netherlands 6, Cyprus, Ireland and Germany 3, Austria had 2, and Hungary, Luxembourg, Norway, Poland, Portugal, Senegal, Sweden and Switzerland all had one case-file.

160 Declaration on Laganas Bay, Zakynthos, Greece (1992).

The two declarations were followed by two decisions. The first gave a solemn warning that the Greek government had been, and was continuing to commit a serious and repeated infringement against the Bern Convention,[161] and the second closed the file and handed over the case to the Court of Justice of the European Communities.[162] The Court found, in support of the Bern Convention, that Greece had failed to fulfil its obligations.[163] The European Community then set a deadline, and forwarded to Greece an opinion of the situation, before requesting ECJ punitive financial penalties.[164] As of the end of 2005, these had not yet been requested.

Unlike the above conventions, which are either receptive, or not, to State consent, the WHC is ambiguous. It is ambiguous for two reasons. First, the WHC places a large amount of the burden to protect sites of outstanding universal value (and even provides emergency funding for such purposes,)[165] on both the countries which hold the site[166]

---

161 Decision Concerning the Conservation of Laganas Bay, Zakynthos, Greece. In CoE. (1995) 14th Meeting of the Bern Convention. T-PVS (95) 26. Appendix 9.

162 Decision of the Standing Committee on the Lack of Appropriate Conservation of Laganas Bay, Zaknthos, Greece. Report of the 19th Meeting of the Bern Convention. T-PVS (99) 30. Appendix 11.

163 Judgment of 30-1- 2002, Commission/Greece, Case C-103, European Court Reports 2002: 1147.

164 EC Press Release IP/02/1923 19.12.2002.

165 Emergency assistance for sites already inscribed on the WHC List, with a priority for those already inscribed as in Danger. The total allowable budget for emergency funding in 2005 was 400,000. UNESCO. (2003). 6th Extra-ordinary Session of the WHC. WHC-03/6. EXT.COM/8. Paris, May 27, 2003. 12. For general background on the Emergency Fund, see UNESCO. (1977). 1st Session of the WHC. CC-77/CONF.001/9. Oct 17, 1977. pp.4. UNESCO. (1992). 16th Session of the WHC. WHC-92/CONF.002/12. Dec 14, 1992. Annex II. UNESCO. (2004). 7th Extra Ordinary Session of the WHC. WHC-04/7. p6. Ext.Com/3C. 28 COM 10B. UNESCO. (1979). 3rd Session of the WHC. CC-79/CONF.003/13. Nov 30, 1978. pp.16. UNESCO. (1984). 7th Session of the Bureau. CLT/83/CONF.021/8. Aug 1, 1983. pp 10. UNESCO. (1993). 17th Session of the WHC. WHC-93/CONF.002/14. Feb 4, 1993. 5. UNESCO. (1978). 2nd Session of the WHC. CC-78/CONF.010/10. Oct 9, 1978. pp.10. See Decision 29 COM 16. Annex I, Table 3.

166 Each State Party to this Convention recognizes that the duty of ensuring the identification, protection, conservation, presentation and transmission to future generations of the cultural and natural heritage [recognised as outstanding universal value] and situated on its territory, belongs primarily to that State. It will do all it can to this end, to the utmost of its own resources and, where appropriate, with any international assistance and co-operation, in particular, financial, artistic, scientific and technical, which it may be able to obtain. WHC. Article 4. These broad obligations, are buttressed by additional obligations upon States to, 'develop scientific and technical studies and research and to work out such operating methods as will make the State capable of counteracting the dangers that threaten its cultural or natural heritage' (article 5.c) as well as taking 'the appropriate legal, scientific, technical, administrative and financial measures necessary for the identification, protection, conservation, presentation and rehabilitation of this heritage'. WHC. Article 5 (d).

and the international community in general.[167] In addition, although State sovereignty clearly applies, the division line between which side should have precedence in dictating what course of action should be followed if a site is in danger, is not always clear. Second, the WHC has a practice which in some exceptional instances results in state consent not being required,[168] However, in most instances, the consent of the Party concerned is required.

State consent for the inclusion of any sites within its territory on the WHC list of sites of outstanding universal value is paramount.[169] Although this is mainly a problem with cultural sites[170] it has also occasionally appeared with natural sites, where the exact sovereign of the disputed site is not clear, such as with Antarctica,[171] and the Central Karakorum national park.[172] In such instances, the practice of the Committee is to have the issue deferred until the controversial question of sovereignty can be resolved.

However, when dealing with the issue of state consent for a Danger Listing, the primacy is not so clear. In many instances, this is not a problem as the interested Parties consent to the inscription of their sites on the Danger List. The list of consensual inscriptions

---

167 WHC. Preamble. Paragraphs 5 and 7. See also articles 4, 5 & 29. Accordingly, all Parties promise not to take any deliberate measures which might damage directly or indirectly WHC. See. Article 6 (3). They specially agreed to help each other and the nations within inadequate resources in particular. Preamble. Paragraph 3 and Article 6 (2). It is incumbent on the international community as a whole to participate in [its] protection ... by the granting of collective assistance which, although not taking the place of action by the State concerned, will serve as an efficient complement thereto. WHC. Preamble. Paragraph 8. For the purpose of the WHC, international protection of world heritage is, 'understood to mean the establishment of a system of international co-operation and assistance designed to support States Parties to the Convention in their efforts to conserve and identify that heritage'. Article 7.

168 Although the State in which the site is located must first be contacted and consulted on the issue, and informed of any subsequent decisions. *Operational Guidelines.* 2002 Edn. Paragraphs 51 and 52. Also, UNESCO. (2002). 26th Session of the WHC. WHC-02/CONF.202/INF.15. Mar 11, 2002. 45-48, 61.

169 WHC. Article 11. (3).

170 Most obviously Jerusalem, which was listed without the consent of the occupying Israeli military forces. UNESCO. (1980). 4th Session of the WHC. CC-80/CONF.016/10. Sep 29, 1980. pp.5. UNESCO. (1981). 1st Extra-Ordinary Session of the WHC. CC-81/CONF.008/2/Rev. Sep 30, 1981. pp.1-5. UNESCO. (1982). 6th Session of the WHC. CC-82/CONF.014/6. Aug 20, 1982. 5.

171 UNESCO. (1991). 15th Session of the WHC. SC-91/CONF.002/15. Dec 12, 1991. 13.

172 As nominated by Pakistan, but India disputed its ownership. UNESCO. (1997). 21st Session of the WHC. WHC-97/CONF.208/17. Feb 27, 1998. 6-7, 35. But note Los Glaciares. This was nominated and accepted by the Committee by Argentina despite Chile disputing their ownership. UNESCO. (1981). 5th Session of the WHC. CC-81/CONF.003/6. Jan 5, 1981. Annex III.

on the Danger List include Tanzania's Ngorongoro Conservation Area,[173] the Ichkeul National Park in Tunisia;[174] Senegal's Djoudj National Bird Sanctuary;[175] Zaire's Garamba;[176] Bulgaria's Srebarna;[177] Cote d'Ivoire; Comoe National Park;[178] Uganda's Rwenzori Mountains,[179] as well as Yellowstone and the Everglades in the United States.

In a number of other instances, State consent for the listing was not obtained and a number of sites have been inscribed, 'even though there were no requests from the State Parties concerned'.[180] These have included the Manas Wildlife Reserve in India (India had failed to respond to requests for two years),[181] Simen National Park in Ethiopia (which lead to much controversy),[182] Sangay National Park in Ecuador (following repeated delays in the Ecuadorian responses),[183] Rio Platano in Honduras (where the Committee originally waited for the Honduran responses, but these were clearly inadequate),[184] Plitvice National Park in the former Yugoslavia (the question of who was sovereign to grant their consent was tied into the conflict),[185] and all of the sites in the Democratic Republic of the Congo, as the country descended into civil war (although Virunga was listed with the help of neighbouring Zaire and Uganda),[186] and Mount Nimba in Guinea and the Ivory Coast.[187]

---

173 UNESCO. (1985). 9th Session of the WHC. SC-85/CONF.008/9. Dec, 1985. pp 10. Note the importance of the independent inquiry preceding the consent.

174 Ibid. pp 11. UNESCO. (1987). 11th Session of the WHC. CC-87/CONF.005/9. Jan 20, 1988. pp 10. Note the importance of the independent inquiry preceding the consent.

175 UNESCO. (1984). 8th Session of the WHC. SC/84/CONF.004/9. Nov 2, 1984. pp 11.

176 UNESCO. (1984). 8th Session of the WHC. SC/84/CONF.004/9. Nov 2, 1984. pp 12.

177 UNESCO. (1991). 15th Session of the WHC. SC-91/CONF.002/15. Dec 12, 1991. 6.

178 UNESCO. (2003). 27th Session of the WHC. WHC-03/27.COM/24. Dec 10, 2003. 32.

179 UNESCO. (2001). 24th Session of the WHC. WHC-2000/CONF.204/21. Feb 16, 2001. 34.

180 UNESCO. (1992). 16th Session of the WHC. WHC-92/CONF.002/12. Dec 14, 1992. 37.

181 UNESCO. (1991). 15th Session of the WHC. SC-91/CONF.002/15. Dec 12, 1991. 9. UNESCO. (1992). 16th Session of the WHC. WHC-92/CONF.002/12. Dec 14, 1992. 23.

182 UNESCO. (1997). 21st Session of the WHC. WHC-97/CONF.208/17. Feb 27, 1998. 12. UNESCO. (1998). 22nd Session of the WHC. WHC-98/CONF.203/18. Jan 29, 1999. 21-22. UNESCO. (1999). 23rd Session of the WHC. WHC-99/CONF.209/22. Mar 22, 2000. 59-60.

183 UNESCO. (1992). 16th Session of the WHC. WHC-92/CONF.002/12. Dec 14, 1992. 21.

184 UNESCO. (1990). 14th Session of the WHC. CLT-90/CONF.004/13. Dec 12, 1990. 12. UNESCO. (1991). 15th Session of the WHC. SC-91/CONF.002/15. Dec 12, 1991. 1. UNESCO. (1996). 19th Session of the WHC. WHC-95/CONF.203/16. Jan 31, 1996.14-15. UNESCO. (1996). 20th Session of the WHC. WHC-96/CONF.201/21. Mar 10, 1997. 24. UNESCO. (1997). 21st Session of the WHC. WHC-97/CONF.208/17. Feb 27, 1998. 13. UNESCO. (1999). 23rd Session of the WHC. WHC-99/CONF.209/22. Mar 22, 2000. 62. UNESCO. (2001). 24th Session of the WHC. WHC-2000/CONF.204/21. Feb 16, 2001. 32. UNESCO. (2001). 25th Session of the WHC. WHC-01/CONF.208/24. Feb 8, 2002. 40.

185 UNESCO. (1991). 15th Session of the WHC. SC-91/CONF.002/15. Dec 12, 1991. 10.

186 UNESCO. (1993). 17th Session of WHC. WHC-93/CONF.002/14. Feb 4, 1993. 17.

187 UNESCO. (1992). 16th Session of the WHC. WHC-92/CONF.002/12. Dec 14, 1992. 23.

In most of the above instances, the State concerned had simply not bothered to object, or if they did, their responses to the Committee's concerns were feeble, and they did not attempt to actively block the inscription of their site onto the Danger List. However, in some instances, the State Parties did vigorously object. The first time this happened was in 1982,[188] when the Australian government refused a WHC request to propose entering the Western Tasmania Wilderness for inclusion on the Danger list. In doing so, they clearly argued that any such listing, without their consent, would be fruitless as only they, the State Party at the centre of the debate, could ultimately guarantee the protection of the threatened site.[189] The second instance involved the Galapagos. In the latter instance, the IUCN recommended that this site be put on the Danger List. However, Ecuador objected to this possible listing, arguing that they were taking measures to protect the site and that this was a matter to be resolved by the Ecuadorian government. The Committee decided that the Director of the Centre would visit the Ecuadorian authorities to discuss the issues and report back to the Committee.[190] It was duly reported that although considerable efforts where being made, serious problems remained and that immediate remedial actions were essential. Ecuador promised to address these problems, whilst requesting that the site not be inscribed. The Committee took the exceptional step and warned they would place the property on the Danger List, unless a substantive and suitable response, which the met the Committees concerns, was obtained from Ecuador by a set date.[191] The 'pioneering legislation' prepared (and finally implemented) by Ecuador pleased the Committee, and the Galapagos was not inscribed on the Danger List,[192] despite clear concerns about the site remaining.[193]

The key point of the Galapagos example is that the Committee was willing to inscribe the Galapagos, contrary to Ecuador's wishes, if the Ecuadorian response was not sufficient. Although some countries and the Advisory Bodies were content with this approach,[194] a number of countries (notably, the United Kingdom, Australia and

---

188 And was repeated in subsequent years with other threatened sites in Australia, as with the Kakadu debate and uranium mining. UNESCO. (1998). 22nd Session of the WHC. WHC-98/CONF.203/18. Jan 29, 1999. 9, 39-45.

189 UNESCO. (1984). 7th Session of the Bureau. CLT/83/CONF.021/8. Aug 1, 1983. pp 9. UNESCO. (1984). 7th Session of the WHC. SC/83/CONF.009/8. Jan 12, 1984. pp 10, 19.

190 UNESCO. (1996). 19th Session of the WHC. WHC-95/CONF.203/16. Jan 31, 1996. 14.

191 UNESCO. (1996). 20th Session of the WHC. WHC-96/CONF.201/21. Mar 10, 1997. 9, 22-23.

192 UNESCO. (1997). 21st Session of the WHC. WHC-97/CONF.208/17. Feb 27, 1998. 21. UNESCO. (1998). 22nd Session of the WHC. WHC-98/CONF.208/18. Jan 29, 1998. 34. UNESCO. (1999). 23rd Session of the WHC. WHC-99/CONF.209/22. Mar 22, 2000. 75. UNESCO. (2001). 25th Session of the WHC. WHC-01/CONF.208/24. Feb 8, 2002. 50. UNESCO. (2002). 26th Session of the WHC. WHC-02/CONF.202/25. Aug 1, 2002. 29. UNESCO. (2003). 27th Session of the WHC. WHC-03/27.COM/24. Dec 10, 2003. 44.

193 Anon. (2005). 'Trouble In Darwin's Paradise'. *New Scientist* Apr 16. 7. Nordling, L. (2004). 'Crisis In Darwin's Paradise'. *New Scientist* Nov 27. 6.

194 UNESCO. (2002). 26th Session of the WHC. WHC-02/CONF.202/INF.15. Mar 11, 2002. 49.

China)[195] were clearly dissatisfied in the way that State consent was being bypassed. Accordingly, legal advice on the question was sought.[196] The Legal Advisor to the Convention responded by pointing out that there was a clear dichotomy within the Convention, 'between State sovereignty on the one hand and the safeguarding of values which transcend individual State interests, on the other'.[197] The broad problem was that although the Convention, 'fully respect[s] the sovereignty of States on whose territory the recognised world heritage is situated' it is also recognised that, 'such heritage constitutes a world heritage for whose protection it is the duty of the international community as a whole to co-operate'.[198] In this instance, the dichotomy was a clear preference for state consent in normal situations[199] as opposed to (undefined) 'urgent' situations. The Advisor suggested that the WHC practice was that 'urgent' was akin to 'exceptional circumstances,' in that, sites have been inscribed without State consent, but this was only done without explicit State objection to the process. The Committee accepted this analysis, and concluded that in cases of urgent need, the property may be inscribed on the Danger list without state consent. If however, the Party expressly objects, the Committee should envisage an appropriate mechanism for obtaining the co-operation of the Party in the interest of safeguarding the property in question. It was also decided that the Committee should establish clear criteria for 'urgent need.'[200]

Since this time, the Committee has been reluctant to inscribe sites on the Danger List without State consent, if it is a non-urgent situation. Rather, in situations of concern, a more indirect, but still forceful approach has been adopted to achieve very similar ends. Thus, with Russia's Lake Baikal, despite clear cause for concern, decisions about inscription on the Danger List were deflected and the Committee chose to deal with the issue through regular meetings between Russia, the Chairperson to the Convention, the Advisory Body and UNESCO, with regard to clear identifications of what needed to be done, by when.[201] However, in 2005, when new information came to light that the proposed developments (crossing the oil and gas pipeline over the watershed of Lake Baikal) may be in contradiction to what is required to protect the site, and accordingly the Committee warned Russia, that such developments 'would make the case for

195 Ibid. 54-60.

196 UNESCO. (2001). 25th Session of the WHC. WHC-01/CONF.208/24. Feb 8, 2002. 21-22.

197 UNESCO. (2002). 26th Session of the WHC. WHC-02/CONF.202/INF.15. Mar 11, 2002. 35.

198 WHC. Article 6 (1).

199 See Article 11.(3) & 11.(4). In addition, the Convention is relatively clear that 'consultation' is an important part of the danger listing debate. Specifically, before refusing a request for inclusion on the WH in Danger List, the Committee shall consult the State Party in whose territory the property in question is situated. WHC. Article 11 (6). Likewise, when drawing up studies and research related to the Danger List, the Committee shall do so 'with the agreement of the States concerned.' WHC. Article 11 (7).

200 UNESCO. (2002). 26th Session of the WHC. WHC-02/CONF.202/INF.15. Mar 11, 2002. 61.

201 UNESCO. (2002). 26th Session of the WHC. WHC-02/CONF.202/25. Aug 1, 2002. 35.

inscription' on the Danger list.[202] This warning was amplified by the Chairperson through a series of high-level press conferences, before the Russian's formally changed their mind about the direction of the proposed pipeline, and the threat to this site was removed (much to the satisfaction of the Committee),[203] although very similar concerns continued to exist with other Russian sites.[204]

4 Removal of Threatened Status

All of the protected area regimes seek to restore any protected areas which have been inscribed on their lists, but subsequently threatened or damaged. In most instances, the goal is axiomatic, in that they seek to counter the problem which caused the danger in the first place, and restore the site to its original condition and thereby preserve any values of the site that were threatened. The only regime which has not followed this general approach is the WHC, which has a clear process for removing any WHC sites placed upon their Danger List.

Placement on the WHC Danger List publicises the threats to the site, creates a framework from which direct, measurable and restorative action, within a set time period, can be advanced, and allows access to special assistance.[205] Collectively, the results of being inscribed on the Danger List should assist the overall goal of the WHC that, 'all possible measures should be taken to prevent the deletion of any property from the [WHC] List [of sites of outstanding universal value]'.[206] To further this goal, the WHC has set itself the target of having at least five properties removed from the Danger List between 2003 and 2009.[207]

Although some sites have been inscribed on the Danger List and later removed from it, until the late 1990s, the exact process that this followed was unclear.[208] For example, the Tanzanian Ngorongoro Conservation Area was no longer considered in danger after a series of years showing 'marked improvement'.[209] Likewise, the Djoudj

---

202 Decision 29 COM 7B.19.

203 See Decision 30 COM 7B.18.

204 As with the Golden Mountains. See Decision 30 COM 7B.19.

205 UNESCO. (1983). 6th Session of the WHC. CC-83/CONF.015/8. Jan 17, 1983.6. Operational Guidelines. 2002 Edn. Paragraphs 50 and 51.

206 Operational Guidelines. 2002 Edn. Paragraph 54.

207 UNESCO. (2004). 7th Extra-Ordinary Session of the WHC. WHC-04/7. EXT.COM/10. Oct 10. Table 1.

208 UNESCO. (2001). 24th Session of the WHC. WHC-2000/CONF.204/21. Feb 16, 2001. 35.

209 UNESCO. (1984). 8th Session of the WHC. SC/84/CONF.004/9. Nov 2, 1984. pp 11. UNESCO. (1986). 10th Session of the WHC. CC-86/CONF.003/10. Dec 5, 1986. pp 8. UNESCO. (1987). 11th Session of the WHC. CC-87/CONF.005/9. Jan 20, 1988. pp 10. UNESCO. (1988). 12th Session of the WHC. SC-88/CONF.001/13. Dec 23, 1988. 6.

National Bird Sanctuary was also removed after conditions 'improved'.[210] The only other site of note, that did not have specific improvement markers that were linked to its reclassification (as no longer being in danger) was the Plitvice National Park in the former Yugoslavia. This site was removed from the Danger List, once the area had stabilized and the new authority (Croatia) put strong conservation efforts into its rehabilitation.[211]

The above examples presented a problem, in that although the sites were removed from the Danger List, the exact reasons why this was so, was not always clear. This is no longer the case with the WHC, which has now developed a clear procedure for dealing with such situations. First, there must be engagement with the State concerned. If it is a civil war or external conflict situation, then although the Committee will have its concerns expressed to the appropriate authorities, the Committee will wait until peace and safety returns, before an evaluation mission will be sent to the site. This was the practice with the Air and Tenere Nature Reserves in Niger,[212] Manovo-Gounda St Floris in the Central African Republic,[213] Plitvice National Park in the former Yugo-

---

UNESCO. (1989). 13th Session of the WHC. SC-89/CONF.004/12. Dec, 22 1989. pp 13.

210 UNESCO. (1985). 9th Session of the WHC. SC-85/CONF.008/9. Dec, 1985. pp 6. UNESCO. (1986). 10th Session of the WHC. CC-86/CONF.003/10. Dec 5, 1986. pp 8. UNESCO. (1987). 11th Session of the WHC. CC-87/CONF.005/9. Jan 20, 1988. 10. UNESCO. (1988). 12th Session of the WHC. SC-88/CONF.001/13. Dec 23, 1988. 6, 15.

211 UNESCO. (1992). 16th Session of the WHC. WHC-92/CONF.002/12. Dec 14, 1992. 21.UNESCO. (1993). 17th Session of WHC. WHC-93/CONF.002/14. Feb 4, 1993. 18. UNESCO. (1995). 18th Session of the WHC. WHC-94/CONF.003/16. Jan 31. 1995. 13-14. UNESCO. (1996). 19th Session of the WHC. WHC-95/CONF.203/16. Jan 31, 1996. 9. UNESCO. (1996). 20th Session of the WHC. WHC-96/CONF.201/21. Mar 10, 1997. 13. UNESCO. (1997). 21st Session of the WHC. WHC-97/CONF.208/17. Feb 27, 1998. 10-11. UNESCO. (1998). 22nd Session of the WHC. WHC-98/CONF.203/18. Jan 29, 1999. 33.

212 UNESCO. (1995). 18th Session of the WHC. WHC-94/CONF.003/16. Jan 31. 1995. 18. UNESCO. (1996). 19th Session of the WHC. WHC-95/CONF.203/16. Jan 31, 1996. 11. UNESCO. (1996). 20th Session of the WHC. WHC-96/CONF.201/21. Mar 10, 1997. 16.

213 The sites being, Virunga, Okapi Faunal Reserve, Kahuzi Biega, Garamba and Salonga. UNESCO. (1992). 16th Session of the WHC. WHC-92/CONF.002/12. Dec 14, 1992. 19. UNESCO. (1998). 22nd Session of the WHC. WHC-98/CONF.203/18. Jan 29, 1999. 19. UNESCO. (1999). 23rd Session of the WHC. WHC-99/CONF.209/22. Mar 22, 2000. 54. UNESCO. (2001). 24th Session of the WHC. WHC-2000/CONF.204/21. Feb 16, 2001. 28-29. UNESCO. (2001). 25th Session of the WHC. WHC-01/CONF.208/24. Feb 8, 2002. 30-31. UNESCO. (2003). 27th Session of the WHC. WHC-03/27.COM/24. Dec 10, 2003. 9. UNESCO. (2004). 28th Session of the WHC. Oct 29. Decision 28 COM 15.A.1.pp51.

slavia,[214] Comoe in Cote d'Ivoire[215] and the sites of the Democratic Republic of the Congo.[216]

After an independent assessment has taken place, the State must also assess the situation themselves, and explain to the Committee how they intend to restore the site in question. This was the clear practice with the sites in Tunisia[217] and India.[218] These self-assessments are then juxtaposed against the visits by the Advisory Bodies. The Advisory Bodies may be directed, in conjunction with the State Party, to the site when there is a general cause for concern, independent of a danger listing. This was the practice with, inter alia, Shark Bay in Australia,[219] the Wet Tropics of Queensland,[220] Pirin park in Bulgaria,[221] Lorentz park in Indonesia,[222] Iguacu Park in Brazil,[223] Canaima Park in Venezuela,[224] Rio Platano in Honduras,[225] the Rockies in Canada,[226] the Kamchatka Volcanoes in Russia,[227] Tai National Park,[228] Manas in India,[229] the Belovezhskaya Pushcha/Bialowieza Forest,[230] and Durmitor National Park in the former Yugoslavia.[231]

---

214 UNESCO. (1992). 16th Session of the WHC. WHC-92/CONF.002/12. Dec 14, 1992. 21.UNESCO. (1993). 17th Session of WHC. WHC-93/CONF.002/14. Feb 4, 1993. 18.

215 UNESCO. (2004). 28th Session of the WHC. Oct 29. Decision 28 COM 15.A.2.pp52.

216 UNESCO. (1997). 21st Session of the WHC. WHC-97/CONF.208/17. Feb 27, 1998. 11, 19-20. UNESCO. (2001). 25th Session of the WHC. WHC-01/CONF.208/24. Feb 8, 2002. 31. UNESCO. (2002). 26th Session of the WHC. WHC-02/CONF.202/25. Aug 1, 2002. 18.

217 UNESCO. (1996). 20th Session of the WHC. WHC-96/CONF.201/21. Mar 10, 1997. 26.

218 Ibid. 15. UNESCO. (1997). 21st Session of the WHC. WHC-97/CONF.208/17. Feb 27, 1998. 13. UNESCO. (1998). 22nd Session of the WHC. WHC-98/CONF.203/18. Jan 29, 1999. 23.

219 UNESCO. (1995). 18th Session of the WHC. WHC-94/CONF.003/16. Jan 31. 1995. 20.

220 UNESCO. (1992). 16th Session of the WHC. WHC-92/CONF.002/12. Dec 14, 1992. 16.

221 UNESCO. (2002). 26th Session of the WHC. WHC-02/CONF.202/25. Aug 1, 2002. 28. Note the slow failure of response by Bulgaria to the recommendations. See UNESCO. (2004). 28th Session of the WHC. WHC-04/28.COM/26. Oct 29. Decision 28 COM 15B.21.pp87.

222 UNESCO. (2002). 26th Session of the WHC. WHC-02/CONF.202/25. Aug 1, 2002. 31. UNESCO. (2003). 27th Session of the WHC. WHC-03/27.COM/24. Dec 10, 2003. 35.

223 UNESCO. (2001). 25th Session of the WHC. WHC-01/CONF.208/24. Feb 8, 2002. 29-30. UNESCO. (2003). 27th Session of the WHC. WHC-03/27.COM/24. Dec 10, 2003. 43.

224 UNESCO. (1998). 22nd Session of the WHC. WHC-98/CONF.208/18. Jan 29, 1998. 37.

225 UNESCO. (2004). 28th Session of the WHC. WHC-04/28.COM/26. Oct 29. Decision 28 COM 15A.13. pp.60.

226 UNESCO. (1996). 19th Session of the WHC. WHC-95/CONF.203/16. Jan 31, 1996. 12.

227 UNESCO. (2003). 27th Session of the WHC. WHC-03/27.COM/24. Dec 10, 2003. 42.

228 UNESCO. (2002). 26th Session of the WHC. WHC-02/CONF.202/25. Aug 1, 2002. 29. UNESCO. (2003). 27th Session of the WHC. WHC-03/27.COM/24. Dec 10, 2003. 31-32.

229 UNESCO. (2004). 28th Session of the WHC. WHC-04/28.COM/26. Oct 29. Decision 28 COM 15A.10. pp.58.

230 UNESCO. (2003). 27th Session of the WHC. WHC-03/27.COM/24. Dec 10, 2003. 39.

231 UNESCO. (1992). 16th Session of the WHC. WHC-92/CONF.002/12. Dec 14, 1992. 26.

The other option for the Committee is whereby the Advisory Bodies will be independently directed to sites (obviously, with the state consent of the Party concerned), so as to make assessments and recommendations on the necessary restoration required. The Manas,[232] Sangay,[233] Rwenzori Mountains,[234] and the sites of the Democratic Republic of Congo are all clear instances of this other approach.[235]

In some instances (such as with Ichkeul National Park)[236] the Advisory Body and the Centre identified the existing problems, and correspondingly, the necessary actions for successful restoration of the site in question. The State was then requested to respond to the diagnosis and suggested remedy. In other, more common, instances, the State is requested to work with the Centre/Advisory Body. The goal is that each site in danger will then be given a clear analysis and evaluation of the threats that face it, robust targets and benchmarks indicating the corrective measures to be taken, and buttressed by effective and comprehensive monitoring and reporting regime (from the Centre, Advisory Bodies and especially the State Party), so as to achieve an effective restoration of the site.[237] In some instances, such as with the Galapagos, special missions are organized just to agree to benchmarks (in this instance, to keep the site from the Danger List).[238]

The above practice is best demonstrated with the Yellowstone inscription on the Danger List. After a burst of initial improvements in mitigating the threats to the Yellowstone site, the Committee requested the United States, in conjunction with the Centre and the Advisory Body, to outline the benchmarks and an associated timetable, in addition to a robust monitoring and reporting considerations, by which restoration could be shown, and thereafter, the site could be removed from the Danger List.[239] These were

---

232 UNESCO. (1993). 17th Session of WHC. WHC-93/CONF.002/14. Feb 4, 1993. 15. UNESCO. (1995). 18th Session of the WHC. WHC-94/CONF.003/16. Jan 31. 1995. 18. UNESCO. (1996). 19th Session of the WHC. WHC-95/CONF.203/16. Jan 31, 1996. 10.

233 UNESCO. (1993). 17th Session of WHC. WHC-93/CONF.002/14. Feb 4, 1993. 15. UNESCO. (1995). 18th Session of the WHC. WHC-94/CONF.003/16. Jan 31. 1995. 17. UNESCO. (1996). 19th Session of the WHC. WHC-95/CONF.203/16. Jan 31, 1996. 9. UNESCO. (1996). 20th Session of the WHC. WHC-96/CONF.201/21. Mar 10, 1997. 14.UNESCO. (1997). 21st Session of the WHC. WHC-97/CONF.208/17. Feb 27, 1998. 11. UNESCO. (1998). 22nd Session of the WHC. WHC-98/CONF.203/18. Jan 29, 1999. 20-21.

234 UNESCO. (2001). 24th Session of the WHC. WHC-2000/CONF.204/21. Feb 16, 2001. 34. UNESCO. (2001). 25th Session of the WHC. WHC-01/CONF.208/24. Feb 8, 2002. 44.

235 The sites being Virunga, Okapi Faunal Reserve, Kahuzi Biega, Garamba and Salonga. UNESCO. (1999). 23rd Session of the WHC. WHC-99/CONF.209/22. Mar 22, 2000. 54-58. UNESCO. (2001). 24th Session of the WHC. WHC-2000/CONF.204/21. Feb 16, 2001. 29-30.

236 UNESCO. (1997). 21st Session of the WHC. WHC-97/CONF.208/17. Feb 27, 1998. 14.

237 Decision 29 COM C. See also COM 7A and 7B.

238 See Decision 30 COM 7B.29.

239 UNESCO. (1996). 20th Session of the WHC. WHC-96/CONF.201/21. Mar 10, 1997. 17. UNESCO. (1997). 21st Session of the WHC. WHC-97/CONF.208/17. Feb 27, 1998. 15. UNESCO. (1998). 22nd Session of the WHC. WHC-98/CONF.203/18. Jan 29, 1999. 27.

duly established and the site was removed from the list in 2003, after all the key issues that had originally justified to the listing of the danger listing, were verifiably mitigated.[240] Similar processes to the Yellowstone example can also be seen with the Everglades,[241] the sites in the Democratic Republic of the Congo,[242] Simien park,[243] Sangay,[244] the Rwenzori Mountains,[245] Mount Nimba,[246] Rio Platano,[247] Manas[248] and Comoe National Park in Cote d'Ivoire.[249]

A clear example of benchmarks and indicators being successfully utilized and leading to the eventual removal of a site from the Danger List was with the Srebarna Biosphere. This was placed on the Danger List because all of the large colonies of migratory water-

---

UNESCO. (1999). 23rd Session of the WHC. WHC-99/CONF.209/22. Mar 22, 2000. 66.
UNESCO. (2001). 24th Session of the WHC. WHC-2000/CONF.204/21. Feb 16, 2001. 35.
UNESCO. (2001). 25th Session of the WHC. WHC-01/CONF.208/24. Feb 8, 2002. 44-45.
UNESCO. (2002). 26th Session of the WHC. WHC-02/CONF.202/25. Aug 1, 2002. 22.

240 UNESCO. (2003). 27th Session of the WHC. WHC-03/27.COM/24. Dec 10, 2003. 17.

241 UNESCO. (1993). 17th Session of WHC. WHC-93/CONF.002/14. Feb 4, 1993. 18-19.
UNESCO. (1995). 18th Session of the WHC. WHC-94/CONF.003/16. Jan 31. 1995. 18.
UNESCO. (1996). 19th Session of the WHC. WHC-95/CONF.203/16. Jan 31, 1996. 11.
UNESCO. (1996). 20th Session of the WHC. WHC-96/CONF.201/21. Mar 10, 1997. 16.
UNESCO. (1997). 21st Session of the WHC. WHC-97/CONF.208/17. Feb 27, 1998. 14-15.
UNESCO. (1998). 22nd Session of the WHC. WHC-98/CONF.203/18. Jan 29, 1999.25-26.
UNESCO. (1999). 23rd Session of the WHC. WHC-99/CONF.209/22. Mar 22, 2000. 65.
UNESCO. (2001). 24th Session of the WHC. WHC-2000/CONF.204/21. Feb 16, 2001. 34.
UNESCO. (2001). 25th Session of the WHC. WHC-01/CONF.208/24. Feb 8, 2002. 44-45.
UNESCO. (2002). 26th Session of the WHC. WHC-02/CONF.202/25. Aug 1, 2002. 21.
UNESCO. (2003). 27th Session of the WHC. WHC-03/27.COM/24. Dec 10, 2003. 16.
UNESCO. (2004). 28th Session of the WHC. WHC-04/28.COM/26. Oct 29. Decision 28 COM 15A.11. pp.59.

242 UNESCO. (2001). 25th Session of the WHC. WHC-01/CONF.208/24. Feb 8, 2002. 33-35.
UNESCO. (2002). 26th Session of the WHC. WHC-02/CONF.202/25. Aug 1, 2002. 19.

243 UNESCO. (2001). 24th Session of the WHC. WHC-2000/CONF.204/21. Feb 16, 2001. 31.
UNESCO. (2001). 25th Session of the WHC. WHC-01/CONF.208/24. Feb 8, 2002. 35-36.
UNESCO. (2003). 27th Session of the WHC. WHC-03/27.COM/24. Dec 10, 2003. 11.

244 Decision 29 COM 7A.11. UNESCO. (1999). 23rd Session of the WHC. WHC-99/CONF.209/22. Mar 22, 2000. 58-59. UNESCO. (2001). 24th Session of the WHC. WHC-2000/CONF.204/21. Feb 16, 2001. 31. UNESCO. (2001). 25th Session of the WHC. WHC-01/CONF.208/24. Feb 8, 2002. 35. UNESCO. (2003). 27th Session of the WHC. WHC-03/27.COM/24. Dec 10, 2003. 18.

245 UNESCO. (2003). 27th Session of the WHC. WHC-03/27.COM/24. Dec 10, 2003. 14.

246 UNESCO. (2001). 25th Session of the WHC. WHC-01/CONF.208/24. Feb 8, 2002. 37.

247 UNESCO. (2003). 27th Session of the WHC. WHC-03/27.COM/24. Dec 10, 2003. 19.

248 UNESCO. (1999). 23rd Session of the WHC. WHC-99/CONF.209/22. Mar 22, 2000. 63.
UNESCO. (2001). 24th Session of the WHC. WHC-2000/CONF.204/21. Feb 16, 2001. 32-33.

249 UNESCO. (2003). 27th Session of the WHC. WHC-03/27.COM/24. Dec 10, 2003. 32.

birds, (the original justification for its inscription as a WHC site) had gone.[250] However, direct action helped a small colony of Dalmatian pelicans be re-established. In conjunction with other rehabilitation measures, such as measurable improvements in the quality and quantity of water, the site began to become reinvigorated.[251] These improvements were verified by the Advisory Body via an on-site visit, and the site was removed from the Danger list (in 2003).[252] This removal, reflected the earlier removal of the Garamba from the Danger List (it was later reinscribed) because the white rhino population had doubled (to 32) and civil stability had returned to the country.[253] Conversely, with the Air & Tenere site, until, inter alia, ostrich and addax (gazelle) populations have been reintroduced, the site is not allowed off the Danger List.[254] Although in the above wildlife instances, the primary benchmarks to be obtained are fairly obvious, in other instances, it has been explicitly set down. For example, with the Manas wildlife site in India, the benchmarks included rebuilding the park's infrastructure, a full compliment of park staff, a timely release of funds to the park, and a comprehensive wildlife survey, as a baseline for monitoring recovery of the property.[255] In a similar vein, with the Ichkeul site, the agreed benchmark was a sustained waterflow of an average, and ongoing, 80-120 million cubic meters per year into the site.[256]

Finally, in 2006 the Committee introduced a further layer to this process, when although it agreed that a site (Ichkeul) could be removed from the Danger List as it had met the agreed benchmarks, the Committee clearly warned that, 'if there is no continued satisfactory progress, the property shall be reinscribed on the List of World Heritage in Danger at [the next session]'.[257]

---

250 UNESCO. (1991). 15th Session of the WHC. SC-91/CONF.002/15. Dec 12, 1991. 6. UNESCO. (1992). 16th Session of the WHC. WHC-92/CONF.002/12. Dec 14, 1992. 18.

251 UNESCO. (1996). 19th Session of the WHC. WHC-95/CONF.203/16. Jan 31, 1996. 8-9. UNESCO. (1996). 20th Session of the WHC. WHC-96/CONF.201/21. Mar 10, 1997. 12-13. UNESCO. (1997). 21st Session of the WHC. WHC-97/CONF.208/17. Feb 27, 1998. 10.

252 UNESCO. (1999). 23rd Session of the WHC. WHC-99/CONF.209/22. Mar 22, 2000. 52-54. UNESCO. (2001). 24th Session of the WHC. WHC-2000/CONF.204/21. Feb 16, 2001. 28. UNESCO. (2001). 25th Session of the WHC. WHC-01/CONF.208/24. Feb 8, 2002. 30-31. UNESCO. (2002). 26th Session of the WHC. WHC-02/CONF.202/25. Aug 1, 2002. 18. UNESCO. (2003). 27th Session of the WHC. WHC-03/27.COM/24. Dec 10, 2003. 16.

253 UNESCO. (1985). 9th Session of the WHC. SC-85/CONF.008/9. Dec, 1985. pp 10. UNESCO. (1989). 13th Session of the WHC. SC-89/CONF.004/12. Dec, 22 1989. pp 13. UNESCO. (1990). 14th Session of the WHC. CLT-90/CONF.004/13. Dec 12, 1990. 1. UNESCO. (1992). 16th Session of the WHC. WHC-92/CONF.002/12. Dec 14, 1992. 27.

254 UNESCO. (2001). 25th Session of the WHC. WHC-01/CONF.208/24. Feb 8, 2002. 40-41.

255 Decision 29 COM 7A.9.

256 Decision 29 COM 7A.8. UNESCO. (2003). 27th Session of the WHC. WHC-03/27.COM/24. Dec 10, 2003. 14. UNESCO. (2004). 28th Session of the WH Committee. WHC-04/28.COM/26. Oct 29. Decision 28 COM 15A.9. pp.58.

257 See Decision 30 COM 7A.12.

5 Conclusion

Compliance is an uncommon word, when dealing with protected areas of international significance. However, most of the key regimes in this area have developed, without using the word 'compliance', effective compliance mechanisms to ensure that all internationally listed sites are not overtly threatened, to the point that they are in danger. The first step in this process has been the creation of effective monitoring regimes. In this regard, the Antarctic, Bern, Ramsar and WHC have all developed elaborate, guided, and at times assisted, monitoring, reporting and independent visits to sites in question. Moreover, the Bern, Ramsar and WHC have also established effective lists of sites which they consider to be in danger, from which remedial action must be taken if the site is to be removed from the Danger list.

Once it established that a site is in danger, the question becomes what can be done about it, and most importantly, whether the consent of a State needs to be involved in such deliberations. Some regimes, such as with the European Diploma and the Antarctic regime (to a degree) have bypassed the question of State consent, as all of their areas must be periodically reviewed. However, these are the exception, as most regimes support the presumption that a site must be proven to be in danger, and then dealt with. In such settings, the divergence between the regimes, on the critical question of whether the consent of a Party is required for de-listing is vast. Thus, whilst some regimes, such as the Ramsar and the MAB, will not de-list a site which has lost its values, without the consent of the Party in whose territory the site is in, others, such as the Bern, will consider delisting without state consent. The WHC is between these two extremes, although it prefers to utilize State consent whenever possible. Moreover, all attempts to 'rescue' the threatened site will be made, and clear markers of what must be achieved to reach success will be set down.

Chapter IX

FINANCIAL ASSISTANCE, COMMUNICATION, CONSTITUENTS AND FINAL ISSUES

1 Financial Assistance

According to the Global Environment Facility, without stable and sustainable sources of financing, protected areas will deteriorate and the values they protect will not be maintained.[1] This applies to all protected areas. For example, at least 34% of all WHC sites in Africa are dependent on financial assistance from bilateral, European or intergovernmental funding.[2] The recognition of the problem of inadequate financial support for protected areas can be traced to the 1968 UNESCO Conference on the Use and Conservation of the Biosphere.[3] This problem and the need to rectify it via financial assistance have been reiterated in numerous forums, such as the World Parks Congresses,[4] the CBD[5] and the WSSD.[6] The CBD is particularly notable, as it has adopted the goal of ensuring the financial sustainability of all protected areas by 2008.[7] Moreover, in 2006, the CBD added that the issue of financial mobilisation in this area was critical. This was especially so with regards to developing countries, and the least developed and small island States in particular.[8] Despite such needs, only two regimes, the Ramsar and the WHC, have successfully developed internal mechanisms to provide financial assistance. All of the other regimes of note, as well as the Ramsar and the WHC, have come to place an increased reliance on the GEF, which has come to represent the premier international instrument for the financial support of protected areas.

---

1 GEF. (2005). *Making a Visible Difference in Our World.* (GEF, Washington). 29.

2 UNESCO. (2002). *Periodic Report for Africa.* (UNESCO, Paris). 42.

3 UNESCO. (1968). *Use and Conservation of the Biosphere.* (UNESCO, Paris). Recommendations 18 and 19. 230-232.

4 See for example, Recommendation 17. Technical and Financial Assistance. In Elliot, H. (ed). *Second World Conference on National Parks.* (1972, IUCN, Lausanne). 449. Recommendation 11. Development Assistance and Protected Areas. Recommendations of the World National Parks Congress. In McNeely, J. (ed). *National Parks, Conservation and Development.* (Smithsonian, Washington). 771

5 CBD. Decision VII/28. Protected Areas. Paragraphs 4, 8, 9, 29 and section 3.4.7 of the Annex.

6 World Summit on Sustainable Development. Plan of Implementation. Paragraph 44 (f).

7 Decision VII/28. Protected Areas. Annex. Goal 3.4. Also, CBD Secretariat. (2005). *Towards Effective Protected Area Systems.* (CBD Technical Series No. 18). 18.

8 CBD Decision VIII/24. Protected Areas. Paragraphs 17 to 22.

A Financial Assistance from Internal Sources

In some regions, such as the European Community, financial assistance for environmental purposes and protected areas in particular, is linked through the overall governing mechanisms, such as with the Habitats Directive.[9] In such instances, considerations of assistance are dealt with outside of the bodies overseeing the protected areas. Alternatively, assistance may be obtained by an independent global facility, such as the GEF, which seeks to support sustainability across a large number of sectors. This approach is different to other regimes, such as the African Convention,[10] the MAB, Ramsar and the WHC whereby assistance is generated, distributed or facilitated by the governing bodies directly.

Although the GEF is not a body which designates protected areas, its financial support for them, is second to none. Indeed, support for new and existing parks, wildlife refuges, heritage sites and other protected area places accounts for 60% of the GEFs biodiversity portfolio. As of 2004, GEF support encompassed some 1,432 protected areas covering over 279 million hectares. The support from GEF has included more than $1.2 billion (USD) in direct investment, and it has helped leverage an additional $3.1 billion in co-financing from project partners.[11] In Africa, 37% of all protected areas receive GEF assistance.[12]

Despite the paramount position of the GEF when it comes to economic assistance, the WHC was clearly unique, given its time in history, for the emphasis it placed upon financial assistance. This assistance has proved long standing and wide reaching, although there is evidence that the amount of requests received by WHC has been falling since the end of the twentieth century. Nevertheless, between 1978 and 2001, more than 1,200 requests for assistance were dealt with.[13] The success and width of this programme is because, in part, the WHC actively facilitates requests, within a given

---

9 Habitats Directive. Article 8.

10 This point is merely a note of intention, with regard to the 2003 African Convention, which declared, a 'conservation fund' constituted from voluntary contributions of Parties, for activities relating to the conservation of the environment and natural resources, may be established. African Convention. Article XXXVIII.

11 GEF. (2005). *The GEF and the World Wilderness Congress.* (GEF, Washington). 1.

12 GEF. (2005). *Making a Visible Difference in Our World.* (GEF, Washington). 3, 9.

13 The basic division for this period (based on 2002 figures for sites and Party numbers) was 27% went to Africa (36 parties with 53 properties), 13 % to Arab Parties (18 parties and 52 properties); Asia-Pacific obtained 21% (35 state parties and 135 sites); Lain America and the Caribbean gets 24% (29 parties and 98 sites) and Europe and North America gets 15% (49 parties and 352 properties). UNESCO. (2001). 25th Session of the WHC. WHC-01/CONF.208/24. Feb 8, 2002. 114.

format,[14] for supplementary assistance[15] for the protection, conservation, presentation to, or rehabilitation of, sites related to the WHC List or the WHC Danger List.[16] Such help is channelled through the categories of emergency, preparatory, and conservation and management assistance.[17] If assistance is granted, it is likely that a series of non-political conditions[18] will be attached to the grant.[19] All requests are prioritised,[20]

---

14 'The purpose of such requests may be to secure any State Party to the Convention, after providing certain base information'. The Party shall submit with its request such information and documentation provided including the operation contemplated, the work that is necessary, the expected cost thereof, the degree of urgency and the reasons why the resources of the State requesting assistance do not allow it to meet all the expenses. Such requests must be supported by experts' reports whenever possible) in accordance with the Committee's directions, which will enable the Committee (which shall carry out such studies and consultations as it deems necessary) to come to a decision. Article 21 (1) & (2). International assistance on a large scale must be preceded by detailed scientific, economic and technical studies. These studies shall draw upon the most advanced techniques for the protection, conservation, presentation and rehabilitation of the natural heritage and should be consistent with the objectives of this Convention. The studies should also seek means of making rational use of the resources available in the State concerned. Article 24.

15 Specifically, the WHC Committee 'shall' receive and study requests for international assistance, which is generally meant to be supplementary to State funds, not in exchange of such funds. As a general rule, only part of the cost of work necessary shall be borne by the international community. The contribution of the State benefiting from international assistance should constitute a substantial share of the resources devoted to each programme or project, unless its resources do not permit this. Article 25.

16 Articles 13 (1), 19 and 20.

17 Decision 29 COM 14B. For discussion of the period 1998 to 2003, see Information on the World Heritage Fund. WHC/-05/29.COM/14 B.

18 'No political conditions may be attached to contributions made to the Fund'. WHC. Article 15. Such as ongoing state responsibility for the conservation of the site, and satisfactory accounting for how the funds are utilised. UNESCO. (2002). 26th Session of the WHC. WHC-02/CONF.202/25. Aug 1, 2002. 20-21. UNESCO. (2003). 27th Session of the WHC. WHC-03/27.COM/24. Dec 10, 2003. 12.

19 Article 26. In addition, States Parties to this Convention which receive international assistance under the Convention, 'shall take appropriate measures to make known the importance of the property for which assistance has been received and the role played by such assistance'. Article 28.

20 'Bearing in mind the respective importance for the world natural heritage of the property requiring protection, the need to give international assistance to the property most representative of a natural environment, the urgency of the work to be done, the resources available to the States on whose territory the threatened property is situated and in particular the extent to which they are able to safeguard such property by their own means'. Article 13 (2). Requests based upon disasters or natural calamities should, by reasons of the urgent work which they may involve, are given immediate, priority consideration by the Committee. Article 21 (2). The debate about how to order the priorities within the Committee was originally a strong one. UNESCO. (1977). 1st Session of the WHC. CC-77/CONF.001/9. Oct 17, 1977. pp.7.

and in accordance with guidance from the Committee, are signed off by the Chairperson of the Committee.[21]

Financial assistance is also available under the Ramsar. Although there are some regional wetland assistance funds,[22] the primary (and successful)[23] funding for non-OECD countries[24] from the Ramsar comes from their Small Grants Fund for Wetlands Conservation and Wise Use.[25] This carefully regulated[26] fund was financed by voluntary contributions,[27] before the Parties agreed to find a 'more vigorous method to support the Small Grant Fund' in 2005.[28] Between 1990 and 2002, the Small Grants Fund assisted (with an average grant of 40,000 SFR) 156 projects in 86 countries.[29] The annual target is $1 million (USD) per year for distribution.[30] The small grants are used for, inter alia, public education, inventories, monitoring, training and management plans.

---

21 'Decisions of the Committee shall be taken by a majority of two-thirds of its members present and voting. A majority of the members of the Committee shall constitute a quorum'. Article 13 (5).

22 The 7th COP, in endorsing Wetlands for the Future Initiative for Capacity Building in the Western Hemisphere (supported by the United States to the level of 250,000 $ per year). Since 1995, this funded 60 projects in 14 countries. Recommendation 7.4. Wetlands for the Future. (1999, San Jose).

23 The fund is recognised within the Ramsar as an, 'extremely valuable mechanism for facilitating the implementation of the Convention'. Resolution 8.29. Evaluation of the Small Grants Fund for Wetland Conservation and Wise Use. (2002, Valencia).

24 Resolution 6.6. The Wetland Conservation Fund. (1996, Brisbane). Assistance for countries in economic transition is believed to be better suited to bilateral contributions or via assistance from multilateral institutions. Resolution 5.8. The Wetland Conservation Fund. (1993, Kushiro).

25 This was earlier known as the Wetland Conservation Fund. Resolution 4.3. A Wetland Conservation Fund. (1990, Montreux). Note also, Recommendation 2.3. Action Points for Priority Attention. (1984, Groningen).

26 Funding of new projects is conditional upon satisfactory compliance with reporting requirements for previous grants. Resolution 7.5. Small Grants Fund. (1999, San Jose).

27 Resolution 8.29. Evaluation of the Small Grants Fund for Wetland Conservation and Wise Use. (2002, Valencia).

28 Resolution 9.13. Evaluation of the Ramsar Endowment Fund as a Mechanism to Resource the Small Grants Fund. (2005, Kampala).

29 Resolution 8.25. The Ramsar Strategic Plan. (2002, Valencia). Annex. I.9. Resolution 5.8. The Wetland Conservation Fund. (1993, Kushiro).

30 Resolution 5.8. The Wetland Conservation Fund. (1993, Kushiro). Resolution 6.6. The Wetland Conservation Fund. (1996, Brisbane). Resolution 7.28. Financial and Budgetary Matters. (1999, San Jose).

B Generating Mechanisms

As noted above, with the Ramsar, all assistance is generated by voluntary contributions. This situation is different to the WHC, whereby all requests to the WHC are ultimately drawn from the World Heritage Fund (the 'Fund').[31] The Fund was created by Article 15 of the Convention. The Fund consists of compulsory and voluntary contributions made by State Parties and other entities.[32] The lion's share of the Fund is made up of regular payments, every two years, of an, 'amount of which, in the form of a uniform percentage applicable to all States'. The amount is set by the General Assembly of the WHC.[33] Although the General Assembly has some flexibility in this area, it is clear that, 'in no case shall the compulsory contribution of States Parties to the Convention exceed 1% of the contribution to the regular budget of the UNESCO'.[34] This 1% figure was adopted at the first session of the Parties,[35] and was subsequently reiterated. However, by 2003, it was being argued that this approach was 'outdated'[36] and Parties were encouraged to (voluntarily) give more.[37] Nevertheless, the 1% figure has remained, and although 9 countries make additional voluntary contributions to the Fund, the vast majority of others have accepted the 1% figure as obligatory. The Fund has grown from $838,234 (USD) in 1980/81[38] to $6,656,836 for 2006.[39]

Despite the apparent clarity and cohesion of the Fund system, it is important to note that it has been plagued with difficulties. The core of these difficulties is some countries refusing to recognize their contribution as compulsory, and only making what they deem

31 Article 13 (3). Note however, the Committee is also obliged to seek ways of increasing their available resources and shall take all useful steps to this end (i.e. outside of the Fund).

32 Some countries made voluntary contributions, even though not members (such as Austria and the Netherlands in the mid 1980s) and additional voluntary contributions because they wanted to. UNESCO. (1987). 6th General Assembly of States Parties to the WHC. CC-87/CONF.013/5. Oct 31, 1987. 4. Contributions, gifts or bequests which may also be collected from non-state parties, organisations within the UN system (particularly the UNDP), or other intergovernmental organizations, public or private bodies or individuals. WHC. Article 15. Fund-raising campaigns under he auspice of UNESCO are to be encouraged, as are, 'national public and private foundations or associations whose purpose is to invite donations for the protection of the cultural and natural heritage'. Articles 17 & 18.

33 Article 16 (2). Note, States may make a declaration refusing to be bound by such decisions, if they had signalled their intention at the time of depositing their instrument.

34 Article 16 (1).

35 UNESCO. (1977). 1st Session of the WHC. SHC/76/conf.014/COL.9. Feb 15. 4.

36 UNESCO. (2001). 13th Session of the WHC. WHC-01/CONF.206/8 Rev. July 29, 2003. 5.

37 UNESCO. (2003). 14th Session of the WHC. WHC-03/14.GA/10. Feb 2, 2003. 23.

38 UNESCO. (1979). 3rd Session of the WHC. CC-79/CONF.003/13. Nov 30, 1978. pp.15.

39 Decision 29 COM 16. Note, the 2006 figure excludes promotional funds, which are typically in the range of 500,000.

as voluntary contributions.[40] The difficulty with voluntary payments is their arbitrary nature. This was particularly apparent in the early to mid 1980s when UNESCO, the home of the WHC, became entangled in ideological politics and a number of prominent Western countries refused to commit themselves to payments to the WHC on a regular basis. This situation became so 'critical' that the overall implementation of the Convention was threatened.[41] Although the WHC survived these ideological debates, the problem of arrears continued in subsequent decades, with (at the turn of the century) large arrears (in the millions) owed by a number of countries.[42] The response of the Committee to such non-payment is that a defaulting Party may not be a member of the Committee[43] and unless it is an exceptional circumstance, the defaulting Party may not be able to obtain assistance from the Fund.[44]

C Financial Assistance from External Sources

In 1971, at the first Ramsar meeting, it was recommended that the Afghani government, 'seek financial or other assistance from international organizations if this is required'[45] for the conservation of some of their wetlands. A similar plea was made with regard to the threatened wetlands in Senegal in 1974[46] and the Sahel in 1984.[47] In most other instances, the suggestions for seeking bilateral and/or international financial assistance have been with more generic wetlands issues relating to science and research,[48] in-

40 UNESCO. (1980). 3rd General Assembly of WHC. CC-80/CONF.018/6. Oct 20, 1980. 2.

41 UNESCO. (1984). 7th Session of the WHC. SC/83/CONF.009/8. Jan 12, 1984. pp 2. UNESCO. (1984). 8th Session of the WHC. SC/84/CONF.004/9. Nov 2, 1984. pp 2. UNESCO. (1985). 9th Session of the WHC. SC-85/CONF.008/9. Dec, 1985. pp 9. UNESCO. (1983). 4th General Assembly of the WHC. CC-83/CONF.022/6. Nov 28, 1983. 2. UNESCO. (1985). 5th General Assembly of States Parties to the WHC. CC-85/CONF.009/5. Nov 6, 1985. 2.

42 UNESCO. (2001). 13th General Assembly of the WHC. WHC-01/CONF.206/8 Rev. July 29, 2003. 2, 5, 6. UNESCO. (2001). 25th Session of the WHC. WHC-01/CONF.208/24. Feb 8, 2002. 107, 109.

43 WHC. Article 16 (4).

44 UNESCO. (1990). 12th Session of the WHC. CLT-90/CONF.004/12. Dec, 12 1990. pp 18.

45 Final Act of the Ramsar Conference. Annex II. Recommendations adopted by the International Conference on the Conservation of Wetlands and Waterfowl at Ramsar, Iran, 3 February 1971. Recommendation 4. Conservation of Lakes Ab-i-Istada and Dasht-e-Nawar, Afghanistan.

46 Recommendations adopted by the International Conference on the Conservation of Wetlands and Waterfowl at Heiligenhafen, Federal Republic of Germany, 6 December 1974. Recommendation 10. Conservation of the Senegal Valley.

47 Recommendation 2.6. Sahel Wetlands. (1984, Groningen).

48 Final Act of the Ramsar Conference. Annex II. *Ibid.* Recommendation 8. Promotion of wetlands research. Recommendations adopted by the International Conference on the Conservation of Wetlands and Waterfowl at Heiligenhafen, Federal Republic of Germany, 6 December 1974. Recommendation 12. Publication of Numerical Data on Waterfowl Distribution.

ventory programmes,[49] institutional development, capacity building and training of staff,[50] public education,[51] environmental impact assessments,[52] the wise use of wetlands[53] and specific international wetland initiatives, such as the Asia Pacific Migratory Waterbird Conservation Strategy.[54] These calls have all been buttressed by repeated Ramsar suggestions for Parties to earmark their bilateral and multilateral aid programmes to giving enhanced prominence to the conservation of wetlands.[55]

In addition a series of general calls for enhanced cooperation among development assistance agencies with regard to wetlands issues, in terms of both awareness[56] and funding,[57] are prominent. From this history, the Ramsar has sought to establish strong links with the GEF. This drive has been consistently advocated since 1993,[58] and in 2002 the Ramsar set itself a target of helping at least 15 countries in preparing wetland projects for submission to the GEF.[59] The Ramsar COPs have also highlighted the suitability of some specific wetlands for GEF support, such as the Azraq wetland in Jordan[60] and those associated with the African/Eurasian Migratory Waterbird Flyways Project.[61]

---

49 Resolution 7.20. Wetland Inventory. (1999, San Jose). Resolution 8.6. A Ramsar Framework Inventory. (2002, Valencia).

50 Recommendation 5.1. Ramsar Sites in Specific Contracting Parties. (1993, Kushiro).

51 Resolution 8.31. The Convention's Programme on Communication, Education and Public Awareness. (2002, Valencia).

52 Recommendation 1.6. Assessment of Wetland Values.

53 Resolution 7.19. International Cooperation. (1999, San Jose). Annex. The Guidelines for international cooperation under the Ramsar Convention. Resolution 8.25. The Ramsar Strategic Plan. (2002, Valencia). Annex. Operational Objective 15.

54 Resolution 8.37. International Cooperation on Conservation of Migratory Waterbirds and Their Habits in the Asia Pacific. (2002, Valencia).

55 Recommendation 1.2. Developing Countries and the Convention. (1980, Cagliari). Recommendation 2.3. Annex: Framework for Implementing the Convention. (1984, Groningen). Recommendation 5.5. Multilateral and Bilateral Development Cooperation Programmes. (1993, Kushiro).

56 Resolution 7.19. International Cooperation. (1999, San Jose). Annex. The Guidelines for international cooperation under the Ramsar Convention.

57 Resolution 7.27. The Convention's Work Plan 2000-02. (1999, San Jose).

58 Recommendation 5.4. The Relationship Between the GEF and the CBD. (1993, Kushiro). Resolution 6.10. Co-Operation with the GEF and its Implementing Agencies. (1996, Brisbane). Resolution 8.6. A Ramsar Framework Inventory. (2002, Valencia).

59 Resolution 8.26. The Implementation of the Strategic Plan 2003-2008. (2002, Valencia). Annex I. Global Implementation of the Targets for the Convention. Resolution 8.6. A Ramsar Framework Inventory. (2002, Valencia).

60 Recommendation 5.1. Ramsar Sites in Specific Contracting Parties. (1993, Kushiro). Recommendation 6.17.3. The Azraq Oasis, Jordan. (1996, Brisbane).

61 Resolution 8.38. Waterbird Population Estimates and the Identification and Designation of Wetlands of International Importance. (2002, Valencia).

The MAB has developed a very similar approach to the Ramsar with regard to external funding options, with a strong focus on bilateral and multilateral agencies, and the GEF in particular.[62] In such instances, the Secretariat, has attempted to act as a type of 'broker' in identifying and helping submit proposals to donors/financing agencies.[63] This approach has begun to show success, as a number of MAB sites in Africa,[64] Central America,[65] and Russia[66] have all been recipients of GEF grants.

The other regime which has been developing strong relationships with the GEF is the WHC. The WHC work in this area can be traced to their (ad-hoc) co-operation with the World Bank,[67] (which is a partner institution of the GEF) which also has a long standing commitment to protected areas.[68] With regard to safeguarding some WHC sites,[69] the World Bank has obliged the WHC in a number of instances and they have refused to fund a number of specific developments that would be contrary to the outstanding universal values of the sites.[70] With regard to the GEF, as of 2005, at least 50 GEF projects encompassed 65 WHC sites.[71] The GEF assistance is often leveraged against other financial sources. For example, the United Nations Foundation provided over $32 million (USD) to more than 50 WHC sites between 1999 and 2004. The GEF has also provided more than $45 million in parallel funding to the Foundation.[72] In a number of other instances, these projects are done in co-operation with assistance

62 Seville Strategy. Objective IV.2. Seville + 5 Recommendations. Recommendation Number 2.UNESCO. (2001). ICC Bureau Meeting. SC/-01/CONF.211/13. Apr 10. 13-14.

63 UNESCO. (2003). ICC Bureau Meeting. SC/-03/CONF.217/14. July 30. 1.

64 See UNESCO. (2004). ICC Bureau Meeting. SC-04/CONF.204/14. 5. Note GEF funding for Capacity and Management Concerns with Dryland Biosphere Reserves in Africa. (For 2001-2006), UNESCO. (2001). ICC Bureau Meeting. SC/-01/CONF.211/13. Apr 10. 2. UNESCO. (2001). ICC Bureau Meeting. SCI/-01/CONF.217/8. Dec 12, 2. Note also the GEF linkage to Dinder in Sudan. UNESCO. (2001) ICC Bureau Meeting. SC-01/CONF.217/8. Dec 12. 22; and sites in Cameroon. UNESCO. (2001). ICC Bureau Meeting. SC/-01/CONF.211/13. Apr 10. 2

65 Such as Sierra Gorda and the Gulf of Mannar, both are in Mexico. UNESCO. (2001). ICC Bureau Meeting. SC/-01/CONF.211/13. Apr 10.11. UNESCO. (2001). ICC Bureau Meeting. SCI/-01/CONF.217/8. Dec 12, 2. 13.

66 The Commander Islands.UNESCO. (2003). ICC Bureau Meeting. SC-02/CONF.210/10. Jan 7. 11.

67 UNESCO. (2002). 26th Session of the WHC. WHC-02/CONF.202/25. Aug 1, 2002. 17.

68 Goodland, R. (1984). 'The World Bank and Protected Areas.' In McNeely, J. (ed). *National Parks, Conservation and Development.* (Smithsonian, Washington). 698-705.

69 UNESCO. (2004). 28th Session of the WHC. WHC-04/28.COM/26. Oct 29. Decision 28 COM 15B.7.pp78. Decision 28 COM 15B20. pp86.

70 Such as the proposed highway across the Niokolo-Koba park in Senegal. See UNESCO. (1989). 11th Session of the WHC. SC-89/CONF.004/12. Dec, 22 1989. pp 4. And Iron Ore mining at Mount Nimba in Cote d Ivoire. UNESCO. (1989). 11th Session of the World Heritage Committee. SC-89/CONF.004/12. Dec, 22 1989. pp 4.

71 GEF. (2005). *Making a Visible Difference in Our World.* (GEF, Washington). 33.

72 Wirth, T. (2004). 'Common Inheritance.' *Our Planet.* 14(2): 8.

from the WHC Fund,[73] such as with the sites of Mount Nimba,[74] Air and Tenere,[75] Ichkeul,[76] Kamchatka[77] and the Three Parallel Rivers in China.[78]

The final organization which has very strong links to the GEF with regards to protected areas is the CBD. The strong links are derived from direct recommendations by the CBD Parties to the GEF, over exactly what areas of their protected areas programme need financial support.[79]

2 Education and Communication

The period between 2005 and 2014 has been designated as the United Nations Decade for Education for Sustainable Development. Within this rubric of overall education, the section of protected areas is particularly notable, as the vast majority of regimes have active programs designed to promote the values of such sites. This practice is in full accord with the CBD, which places a premium on the promotion and encouragement of the understanding of the importance of, and measures required for the conservation of biological diversity, both nationally and internationally.[80] The CBD has built on this goal by continually reiterating the importance of such education and public awareness,[81] with specific initiatives on Communication, Education and Public Awareness (CEPA)[82] with regard to biodiversity in general, and protected areas in particular.[83]

Although the CBD goal is laudable, it was nearly six decades behind the development of this practice with regards to protected areas regimes. For example, the 1933 African Convention obliged its Parties, to communicate with the depository information, 'relevant to the purposes of the present Convention and communicated to them by any national museums or by any societies, national or international, established within their jurisdiction and interested in those purposes'.[84] This was one of the first recognitions of

73 UNESCO. (1992). 16th Session of the WHC. WHC-92/CONF.002/12. Dec 14, 1992. 7.
74 UNESCO. (2001). 25th Session of the WHC. WHC-01/CONF.208/24. Feb 8, 2002. 37.
75 Ibid. 42.
76 UNESCO. (2003). 27th Session of the WHC. WHC-03/27.COM/24. Dec 10, 2003. 14.
77 Ibid. 42.
78 Ibid. 99.
79 See for example, CBD Decision VIII/24. Protected Areas. Paragraph 22.
80 CBD. Article 13.
81 Decision IV/10. Measures for Implementing the CBD. UNEP/CBD/COP/4/27.pp.118. Decision V/17. Education and Public Awareness. UNEP/CBD/COP/5/23. pp.147.
82 Decision VI/19. Communication, Education and Public Awareness. UNEP/CBD/COP/6/20.pp.197. Communication, Education and Public Awareness. UNEP/CBD/COP/7/L.22.
83 Decision VII/28. Protected Areas. Annex. Paragraph 3.5.1. See also IUCN 5th World Parks Congress (2003, Durban). Recommendation 5.32: Strategic Agenda for Communication, Education and Public Awareness for Protected Areas.
84 1933 London Convention, Article 5 (2).

the importance of 'societies, national or international' with regard to international environmental policy, let alone the law and practice of protected areas. Since that point, it has become standard practice to include provisions for the facilitation of conservation education and publicity about the values of the targeted protected areas. Such provisions and/or practices can be seen in the 1940 Western Hemisphere Convention,[85] the 1968 African Convention,[86] the Mediterranean[87] and Caribbean Protocols,[88] the Bern Convention,[89] the Habitats Directive,[90] the ICRI,[91] the East African Protocol[92] and the 2003 African Convention.[93]

In addition to the above instruments, three regimes stand out due to their particular developments in this area. They are the MAB, the Ramsar and the WHC. The MAB is unique because it has, since 1968, consistently placed a high premium on the publicity of the values of their biosphere reserves[94] in both its foundation documents[95] and with regard to individual sites.[96] The WHC shares very similar publicity goals,[97] and it has been largely successful (apart from a few glitches)[98] with the help of

85 1940 Western Hemisphere Convention. Article III.

86 African Convention (1968). Article XIII.

87 Mediterranean Protocol. Article 19.

88 Caribbean Protocol. Article 16.

89 Bern Convention. Article 3 (3).

90 Habitats Directive. Article 22 (c).

91 Resolution on the International Coral Reef Information Network. In ICRI (2000). Report of the ICRI Meeting in Noumea, New Caledonia, 25-26 May, 2000. Decision on the Formation of an Information Coordination Committee. Report of the ICRI Meeting in the Philippines, 5-6 April, 2001.

92 Protocol Concerning Protected Areas of Wild Fauna and Flora in the Eastern African Region. Reprinted in Austen, A. (ed). *Basic Legal Document on International Animal Welfare and Wildlife Conservation.* (Kluwer, London). Article 15.

93 2003 African Convention. Article XVI, and XX (1)(c).

94 UNESCO. (1968). *Use and Conservation of the Biosphere.* (UNESCO, Paris). Recommendations 9,10,11, 12 and 13. 209-214. The Statutory Framework of the World Network of Biosphere Reserves. Article 6.

95 Seville Strategy. Objective III.3. and IV.1. Seville + 5 Recommendations. Recommendation Number 10. See also UNESCO. (ed). *Conservation, Science and Society: The 1983 Biosphere Reserve Conference in Minsk.* (UNESCO, UNEP). 565-610.

96 Oasis du sud Marocain in Morocco. MAB. (2000). 16th Session of the ICC Bureau. SC-00/CONF.208/13. 21.

97 The WHC has an obligation upon its Parties to, 'endeavour by all appropriate means, and in particular by educational and information programmes, to strengthen appreciation and respect by their peoples' of the world's heritage of outstanding universal value. Article 27.

98 Such as advertising sites which were not actually on the WHC List. UNESCO. (1986). 10th Session of the WHC. CC-86/CONF.003/10. Dec 5, 1986. pp 12.

UNESCO,[99] and a budgetary allocation which has gone from $48,000 USD in the late 1970s to over $1 million (USD) per year in the new century[100] (depending on what is counted) or $230,000 (USD) for public awareness (alone) in 2005.[101] The long-standing success of the WHC in this area is likely to continue, as education, communication and the increasing of public awareness of the Convention is currently identified as one of its four strategic objectives. This objective is linked to a series of performance indicators which range from the number of press releases through to partnerships with the media.[102]

Public education and communication of the values and importance of wetlands to the public is recognised as a key part of successful management regimes within the Ramsar.[103] This recognition with regard to the values of wetlands dates back to 1974.[104] Ten years later, the Ramsar COP came to emphasise the importance of education and public awareness within a framework for implementing the Convention in domestic settings.[105] In the early 1990s, these goals were developed into a strong thematic ob-

---

99 The publicity activities have ranged from stamp issues to seminars for journalists. See UNESCO. (1978). 2nd Session of the WHC. CC-78/CONF.010/10. Oct 9, 1978. pp.5. UNESCO. (1979). 3rd Session of the WHC. CC-79/CONF.003/13. Nov 30, 1978. pp.6. UNESCO. (1985). 9th Session of the WHC. SC-85/CONF.008/9. Dec, 1985. pp 13. UNESCO. (1988). 12th Session of the WHC. SC-88/CONF.001/13. Dec 23, 1988. 9. UNESCO. (2001). 25th Session of the WHC. WHC-01/CONF.208/24. Feb 8, 2002. 100-01.

100 In 1978/79, 48,000 was allocated for public information. The following year, this was changed to 'promotional activities' and fell to 36,900, before rising to 86,000 (1981/82), 100,400 (1982/83) and 150,000 (1984/85) before falling to 70,000 per year for the next two years. It rose back to 142,000 in 1987, and remained at 150,000 for 1988 and 1989 budgets. It then rose to 200,000 (1990) before falling back to 150,000 (1991) and then doubling to 300,000 (1992). It fell back to 210,000 (1993) and 270,000 (1994), and then plummeted to 40,000 in 1995 (now under the bracket of educational and promotional activities). In the late 1990s, this budget item became difficult to track as parts of it mingled with technical assistance, and then became 'documentation and education.' With regard to this category, 579,333 was allocated in the late 1990s, followed by 385,000 in 2000, and 336,000 in 2001. However, by 2003, the category had changed back to 'public awareness' (very similar to where it began 30 years earlier) and was allocated the budgetary amount of 1,277,600.

101 See Decision 29 COM 16. Annex I, Table 3.

102 UNESCO. (2002). 26th Session of the WHC. WHC-02/CONF.202/25. Aug 1, 2002. 14. UNESCO. (2001). 24th Session of the WHC. WHC-2000/CONF.204/21. Feb 16, 2001. 99-101. UNESCO. (2003). 27th Session of the WHC. WHC-03/27.COM/24. Dec 10. 126.

103 Resolution 8.14. New Guidelines for Management Planning for Ramsar Sites and Other Wetlands. (2002, San Jose). Annex.

104 Recommendations adopted by the International Conference on the Conservation of Wetlands and Waterfowl at Heiligenhafen, Federal Republic of Germany, 6 December 1974. Recommendation 15. Observation Facilities to Promote Conservation Education.

105 Recommendation 2.3. Annex: Framework for Implementing the Convention. (1984, Groningen).

jective of the Convention[106] as it became apparent that a well informed public is central to achieving the strategic goals of the Convention.[107] The Ramsar Parties have consistently reiterated their support for the CEPA,[108] established a CEPA oversight panel,[109] and created a separate voluntary fund[110] which was linked into a series of targets in terms of audiences to reach (in relation to the CEPA objectives).[111] Original targets for CEPA in 2002 called for 50 Parties to have CEPAs and 75 Parties to have at least one wetland education center.[112] Although progress was being made in this area,[113] the target date was later moved to 2008.[114] The foremost example of practical public education within the Ramsar context is through the facilitation of, 'modern techniques for enabling the wariest of waterfowl to be observed at close quarters by large numbers of people without disturbance to the birds'. The need to facilitate suitable observation facilities within wetland protected areas, dates back to 1974.[115] This idea continued to be emphasised over the following decades,[116] and as of 2002, there were at least 480 wetland education centres in 68 countries.[117]

106 Recommendation 5.8. Public Awareness of Wetland Values in Wetland Reserves. (1993, Kushiro).

107 Resolution 6.19. Education and Public Awareness. (1996, Brisbane).

108 Resolution 8.25. The Ramsar Strategic Plan. (2002, Valencia). Annex. Operational Objective 9.

109 Resolution 9.18. Establishment of an Oversight Panel for the CEPA Activities of the Convention. (2005, Kampala).

110 Resolution 7.28. Financial and Budgetary Matters. (1999, San Jose).

111 Resolution 8.31. The Convention's Programme on Communication, Education and Public Awareness. (2002, Valencia). Annex I: The CEPA Programme. Appendix II. Resolution 7.9 The Convention's Outreach Programme. (1999, San Jose).

112 Resolution 8.26. The Implementation of the Strategic Plan 2003-2008. (2002, Valencia). Annex I. Global Implementation of the Targets for the Convention.

113 By the end of 2002, 26 parties had national CEPA Task Forces, 86 parties had designated focal points for CEPA and 69 parties had identified national NGO focal points. In addition, of the 119 reports submitted for COP 8, it was shown that in 18 countries wetlands are addressed at all levels informal education curricula, and that in a further 58, wetlands are addressed at some level in formal education curricula. Resolution 8.31. The Convention's Programme on Communication, Education and Public Awareness. (2002, Valencia).

114 Resolution 9.8. Streamlining the Implementation of the Strategic Plan of the Convention 2003-2008 (2005, Kampala). Strategy 1.6.

115 Recommendations adopted by the International Conference on the Conservation of Wetlands and Waterfowl at Heiligenhafen, Federal Republic of Germany, 6 December 1974. Recommendation 15. Observation Facilities to Promote Conservation Education.

116 Recommendation 4.5. Education and Training. (1990, Montreux).

117 Resolution 8.31. The Convention's Programme on Communication, Education and Public Awareness. (2002, Valencia).

3 Constituents and Final Issues

A Secretariats

It is typical of most international or regional regimes, that they have a Secretariat with a permanent base. Moreover, the Secretariat usually has a long list of accompanying duties related to the servicing of the Convention.[118] In many instances, the Secretariats are connected to larger organizations. Thus, the Secretariat for the MAB is UNESCO,[119] for the Bern Convention it is the Council of Europe, and for the 2003 African Convention, it is the Chairperson of the African Union.[120] In some instances, such as with the ICRI, and originally the Antarctic regime, the Secretariat is a revolving job, shared between the State Parties. In other instances, the Secretariat has evolved into a stand-alone position. For example, although the Ramsar dates back to 1971, it was not until 1980 that it was suggested that a permanent Secretariat (as opposed to the more informal IUCN support based model),[121] be established.[122] Although this proposal took seven years to gestate before a permanent structure, with a dedicated Secretary General, was achieved,[123] it became apparent in 2005, that a number of outstanding issues over its official status as Secretariat had to be resolved.[124]

One of the more interesting practices of Secretariats relates to the WHC. In particular, although UNESCO[125] was the original interim Secretariat to the WHC, a strong debate developed over, inter alia, questions of assistance to the Secretariat, utilisation of this funding and broader political issues relating to UNESCO.[126] The situation was resolved in 1992, when the Strategic Operational Plan for the Convention was adopted. This recommended that UNESCO provide sufficient funds for the operation of the Convention, as required by the WHC, and that the 'Centre' be given temporary assistance for

---

118 See for example, 2003 African Convention. Article XXVII.

119 The 1995 Statutory Framework of the World Network of Biosphere Reserves. Article 10.

120 2003 African Convention. Article XLI. Note, this is to be interim Secretariat, until the COP establishes a new and independent one.

121 Recommendation 1.8. Proposed Amendments to the Convention. (1980, Cagliari).

122 Recommendation 1.10. A Permanent Secretariat. (1980, Cagliari).

123 Resolution 3.1. Secretariat Matters. (1987, Regina). Resolution 6.8. Secretary General Matters. (1996, Brisbane).

124 Resolution 9.10. Use of the Term and Status of the 'Ramsar Secretariat'. (2005, Kampala). It was not actually a Secretariat of an International Organisation, as such, and although it was permitted to continue to utilise the nomenclature of Secretariat, a series of options had to be examined before the transformation of the Ramsar Secretariat towards an International Organisation or other status could be completed.

125 In addition to a number of other WHC functions, the Director-General of UNESCO performs depository functions. WHC. Article 36. Nevertheless, the Convention is registered with the Secretariat of the UN, at the request of UNESCO. WHC. Article 38.

126 UNESCO. (1980). 4th Session of the WHC. CC-80/CONF.016/10. Sep 29, 1980. pp.12. UNESCO. (1983). 6th Session of the WHC. CC-83/CONF.015/8. Jan 17, 1983. pp.9.

this purpose.[127] Although budget concerns for the Centre appeared in 2004/05, this assistance, in conjunction of that offered by individual State Parties (such as the United States)[128] has increased over time.[129] Although the Centre performs all of the Secretarial duties of the WHC,[130] the question of its overall relationship with UNESCO (it is physically located in the UNESCO grounds in Paris) and how much autonomy it possesses, have been ongoing. This is despite providing clearly demarcated services to the Committee of the WHC, the WHC remains under the direct authority of the Director General of UNESCO.[131]

B Standing Bodies

Most international regimes have Standing Committees, or other forms of subsidiary bodies, which act on behalf of all of the Parties, when the rest of the Parties cannot be assembled. This is particularly notable with inter alia, the Ramsar[132] and the Bern

---

127 UNESCO. (1992). 16th Session of the WHC. WHC-92/CONF.002/12. Dec 14, 1992. Annex II.

128 UNESCO. (1993). 17th Session of WHC. WHC-93/CONF.002/14. Feb 4, 1993. 8-9.

129 Ibid. 11-12. UNESCO. (1995). 18th Session of the WHC. WHC-94/CONF.003/16. Jan 31. 1995. 1. UNESCO. (1999). 12th Session of the WHC. WHC-99/CONF.206/7. Nov 8, 1999. 12. UNESCO. (2004). 28th Session of the WHC. WHC-04/28.COM/26. Oct 29. Decision 28 COM 12.

130 Such as acting as a clearing house for information sharing between the Committee and other conventions and overseeing training, monitoring and technical assistance. It is also tasked to be the primary instrument for facilitating the implementation of the decisions of the Committee including; inscription on the list, assistance and coordination of requests for training and technical assistance; coordination of monitoring; organizing regular meetings; preparation of reports and draft proposals. UNESCO. (1993). 17th Session of WHC. WHC-93/CONF.002/14. Feb 4, 1993. 9-11.

131 UNESCO. (1998). 22nd Session of the WHC. WHC-98/CONF.208/18. Jan 29, 1998. 85. UNESCO. (2002). 26th Session of the WHC. WHC-02/CONF.202/25. Aug 1, 2002. 13. UNESCO. (1995). 18th Session of the WHC. WHC-94/CONF.003/16. Jan 31. 1995. 12. UNESCO. (1996). 20th Session of the WHC. WHC-96/CONF.201/21. Mar 10, 1997. 70-71.

132 The 1987 COP created a Standing Committee. This Committee has the tasks of carrying out the interim activities (such as making recommendations, providing guidance, making reports etc) on behalf of the COP, as necessary. The Committee was limited to 9 members (although observers from all signatories were welcome) with at least 7 of those being based on proper geographical distribution (Africa, Asia, North America, Oceania, Southern America and Eastern and Western Europe – which was rolled into one region in 1999) with due regard to proper representation from developing countries. The importance of rotating representation and limited tenure (two terms) for the Standing Committee was emphasised in 1999. Resolution 3.3. Establishment of a Standing Committee. (1987, Regina). Resolution 7.1. Regional Categorisation. (1999, San Jose).

Conventions.[133] However, it is the Intergovernmental Committee for the Protection of the Cultural and Natural Heritage of Outstanding Universal Value,[134] (or simply, 'the Committee') of the WHC that has attracted most of the attention.

The Committee is ultimately the engine room of the WHC, through which a select group of countries get to vote (non-elected countries may still attend the meetings as observers)[135] on a number of major decisions (aside direct budgetary concerns, which are decided at the General Assembly) which get their most detailed examination and resolution. Given the importance of this role, the need for the complete independence of the Committee has been repeatedly emphasized and good practice recommendations, such as a State Party which is serving on the Committee, not being able to have nominations for the WHC List have been long mooted (so as to avoid any possible conflict of interest between nomination and acceptance), but never resolved. The high tide mark for this self denial of nominations is that some countries have voluntarily refrained from nominating their own sites whilst on the Committee.[136]

The WHC requires[137] that the Committee membership reflects, 'an equitable representation of the different regions and cultures of the world'.[138] The geographical distribution of members of the Committee is part of this mix.[139] The original number of members of the Committee was 15, but this was increased as the number of signatories to the WHC expanded.[140] However, there have always been more applicants for the seats on the Committee, than available seats. As such, a number of alternative methods to facilitate 'equity' in this area have been debated, and continually 'reflected upon'[141]

133 Bern Convention. Article 13. Non-members may be invited to attend. See Article 14. Such as review the provisions of this Convention, including its Appendices, and examine any modifications necessary; make recommendations to the Contracting Parties concerning measures to be taken for the purposes of this Convention etc.

134 WHC. Article 8 (2).

135 UNESCO. (1989). 7th General Assembly of Parties to the WHC. CC-89/CONF.013/6. Nov 13, 1989. 4.

136 UNESCO. (2004). Item 4B of the Provisional Agenda. Legal Implications Relating to the Abstention From Proposing Nominations by Members of the WHC. WHC/-04/7 Ext.Com/4B.Add. 2004, Nov 26. UNESCO. (1977). 1st Session of the WHC.. CC-77/CONF.001/9. Oct 17, 1977. pp.4. UNESCO. (1980). 4th Session of the WHC. CC-80/CONF.016/10. Sep 29, 1980. pp.5. UNESCO. (1984). 7th Session of the WHC. SC/83/CONF.009/8. Jan 12, 1984. pp 17-18. UNESCO. (1980). 4th Session of the WHC. CC-80/CONF.016/10. Sep 29, 1980. pp.8.

137 UNESCO. (2000). 24th Session of the WHC. WHC-2000/CONF.204/21. Feb 16, 2001. 13-16.

138 WHC. Article 8.

139 UNESCO. (1977). 1st Session of the WHC. SHC/76/conf.014/COL.9. Feb 15. 1.

140 WHC. Article 8 (1).

141 See Decision 30 COM 14A.

but without successful conclusion.[142] Nevertheless a number of restrictions on membership application to the Committee have appeared. Some of these have been voluntary, such as the magnanimous gestures of some States to stand aside for others,[143] and for countries to 'bear in mind the moral obligation to achieve an equitable distribution'.[144] Other restraints have been non-voluntary. For example, applicants for the Committee must not be in financial arrears to the Convention.[145] Some seats 'may' be reserved for Parties with no sites on the WHC List,[146] and Parties are urged to desist from seeking consecutive terms of office in the WHC.[147]

The term of office for members of the Committee was set by the Convention,[148] although in subsequent years a number of countries have voluntarily reduced their term of office (from 6 to 4 years).[149] The selection process (via secret voting),[150] works on a phased rotation (i.e. only a section of the Committee is voted in at each meeting, and accordingly there is never a complete turnover of Committee members). The voting process has been increasingly streamlined over the subsequent decades.[151]

---

142 UNESCO. (1977). 1st Session of the WHC. SHC/76/conf.014/COL.9. Feb 15. 2, 3. UNESCO. (1987). 11th Session of the WHC. CC-87/CONF.005/9. Jan 20, 1988. pp 15. UNESCO. (1987). 6th General Assembly of the WHC. CC-87/CONF.013/5. Oct 31, 1987. 3-4. UNESCO. (1989). 13th Session of the WHC. SC-89/CONF.004/9. Dec 22, 1989. pp 3. UNESCO. (1993). 9th General Assembly of the WHC. WHC-93/CONF.003/6. Nov 2, 1993. 6-7.

143 UNESCO. (1999). 12th General Assembly of the WHC. WHC-99/CONF.206/7. Nov 8, 1999. 11.

144 UNESCO. (1978). 2nd General Assembly of the WHC. CC-78/CONF.011/6. Nov 24, 1978. 3.

145 Ibid.

146 UNESCO. General Assembly to the WHC, Rules of Procedure. WHC-03/GA/1. Rev. 2. Rule 14. See also UNESCO. (2001). 13th General Assembly of the WHC. WHC-01/CONF.206/8 Rev. July 29, 2003. 13.

147 UNESCO. (2000). 24th Session of the WHC. WHC-2000/CONF.204/21. Feb 16, 2001. 13-16.

148 WHC Convention. Article 9. From the end of the ordinary session of the General Conference during which they are elected until the end of its third subsequent ordinary session.

149 UNESCO. (2001). 13th General Assembly of the WHC. WHC-01/CONF.206/8 Rev. July 29, 2003. 14-31. UNESCO. (2000). 24th Session of the WHC. WHC-2000/CONF.204/21. Feb 16, 2001. 13-16.

150 UNESCO. (1977). 1st General Assembly of States Parties to the WHC. SHC/76/conf.014/COL.9. Feb 15. 3.

151 Ibid. Annex I. UNESCO. (2003). 27th Session of the WHC. WHC-03/27.COM/24. Dec 10. 139. UNESCO. General Assembly of the WHC. (Available from UNESCO, 2004). Rules 13 & 14.

C Non-Governmental Organisations

NGOs have a very long standing in international environmental law, with regard to the creation and respect of protected areas.[152] Arguably, the organizations which have the greatest international recognition in this area, of which the CBD was aware (in 2006) of their 'substantial contributions' are Conservation International, the World Wildlife Fund (WWF), the Nature Conservancy and the Wildlife Conservation Society.[153] However, it is the IUCN/World Conservation Union which is, arguably, the most influential NGO with regard to international debates about protected areas. Indeed, even within the work of the CBD, it is the IUCN and its World Commission on Protected Areas that are singled out for 'enhanced collaboration'.[154]

The World Conservation Union was founded in October 1948 as the International Union for the Protection of Nature following an international conference in Fontainebleau, France. The organization changed its name to the International Union for Conservation of Nature and Natural Resources in 1956. Use of the name 'World Conservation Union' began in 1990, but the full name and the acronym are often used together as many people still know the Union as the IUCN. The World Conservation Union is a multicultural, multilingual organisation with over 1000 staff located in 62 countries. Its headquarters are in Gland, Switzerland.

The objective of the IUCN is to influence, encourage and assist societies throughout the world to conserve the integrity and diversity of nature and to ensure that any use of natural resources is equitable and ecologically sustainable.[155] This objective, which is buttressed by research related to the conservation of nature and natural resources,[156] is sought in both national and international settings.[157] As of 2006, there were 1,086 members of the IUCN. 775 of these were national NGOs and 84 were international NGOs.[158] 113 were government agencies, 81 were State members, and 33 were affiliate members. All members must share the IUCN's objectives, and successful membership bids require a two thirds positive vote[159] by the Council.[160] Collectively, this mix

152 See Pough, R. (1962). The Role of Non-Governmental Organisations in Park Activities.' In Adams, A. (ed). *First World Conference on National Parks.* (US Department of the Interior, Washington). 351-357.

153 CBD Decision VIII/24. Protected Areas. Paragraph 1.

154 CBD Decision VIII/24. Protected Areas. Paragraph 14.

155 IUCN. (2004). *Statutes and Regulations.* (IUCN, Geneva). Section 2.

156 Ibid. Section 3 (h).

157 Ibid. Section 2.

158 The IUCN has distinct rules for NGOs seeking membership. Independent boards, periods of existence and non-profit status are key for national, whilst these and 'substantial records of influence' in two or more countries are required for international ones. See Rules 5 and 6 of the IUCN Regulations.

159 IUCN. (2004). *Statutes and Regulations.* (IUCN, Geneva). Sections 7 and 8.

of government and non-governmental organizations form a body of unparallel influence in international environmental law and policy. A large part of this influence and research comes from the IUCN's six Commissions,[161] which collectively unite over 10,000 volunteer experts from a range of disciplines. Each Commission is composed of members selected by the Chair of the Commission, following a process of 'appropriate consultation' with members of the Commission, and the Steering Committee of the Commission, in particular. The Steering Committee is made of members, who reflect 'technical qualification, geographic representation, a diversity of points of view and gender equity'.[162]

The IUCN World Commission on Protected Areas (WCPA) is one of the six IUCN Commissions. Its mission is to promote the establishment and effective management of a world-wide representative network of terrestrial and marine protected areas, as an integral contribution to the IUCN mission. It also seeks to assist in the planning of protected areas and their integration into all sectors by providing strategic advice to policy makers. Strengthening the capacity and effectiveness of protected area managers, and investment for protected areas are also the goals of the WCPA. The WCPA has some 1,300 members from over 140 countries. WCPA is centrally coordinated by a steering committee and supported by the Programme on Protected Areas (PPA). It is organised geographically, thematically and functionally. WCPA membership is by invitation, on the basis of individual experience in relation to protected areas as well as a willingness to assist in a voluntary capacity with the work of WCPA.[163]

In addition to the IUCN, dozens, if not hundreds of smaller NGOs attend the various meetings of the protected area regimes. The numbers of NGOs at these forums range

---

160 The 32 member Council is elected every four years at the World Conservation Congress. The Council is composed of, the President; the Treasurer; three Regional Councillors from each of IUCN's eight Statutory Regions (Africa, Meso and South America, North America and the Caribbean, South and East Asia, West Asia, Oceania, East Europe, North and Central Asia and West Europe); a representative of IUCN's Host Country – the Swiss Confederation; the Chairs of IUCN's six Commissions; and five additional Councillors chosen by Council on the basis of diverse qualifications, interests and skills.

161 These are the Species Survival Commission, the World Commission on Protected Areas, the Commission on Environmental Law, the Commission on Communication and Education, the Commission on Ecosystem Management, and the Commission on Environmental, Economic and Social policy.

162 IUCN. (2004). *Statutes and Regulations.* (IUCN, Geneva). Regulations, rules 69 to 80.

163 In general, five types of people are members of the Commission. These are managers of protected areas, typically senior officials of protected areas agencies, but also field practitioners, experts in relation to the fields of WCPA's interests, academic specialists in areas relating to protected areas, resource economics, biogeography wildlife management, marine conservation and other related fields, officials from relevant non-government organisations involved with protected areas; and ex-officio members from key partner organisations.

from only five NGOs at the Antarctic regime in 2004,[164] eight at the third COP of the Caribbean Protocol in 2004,[165] twenty-three at the thirteenth meeting of the Mediterranean Protocol in 2003,[166] and twenty-one at the Bern Convention in 2004.[167] Assessing NGO numbers in the WHC is deceptive, as the split objectives of the Convention (natural and cultural heritage) means that a large number of the NGOs attending are focused on cultural and not natural heritage. Nevertheless, it is possible to show that at the first WHC meeting in 1977 only four NGOs attended.[168] The numbers of environmental NGOs attending the WHC grew slowly over the following years,[169] until some high profile meetings with strong domestic debates (such as uranium mining in Kakadu Park) were held in liberal countries, and the number of attending environmental NGOs rose to seven.[170] Numbers continued to increase in the late 1990s,[171] reaching twenty-nine NGOs of which nine were environmental in 2000,[172] before falling again[173] to when there were only eleven NGOs, with only one (Birdlife) environmental NGO.[174] Six environmental NGOs were part of the total of twenty in

---

164 Final Report of the XXVII ATCM. Cape Town. 2004. 6.

165 3rd Meeting of COP to the SPAW in the Wider Caribbean Protocol (2004). UNEP (DEC)/CAR IG.23/4. Oct 15, 2004. Annex IV. There were 10 at the 2001 meeting.

166 Report of the 13th MOP to the Convention for the Protection of the Mediterranean Sea Against Pollution and its Protocols. UNEP (DEC)/MED IG.15/11. Dec 30, 2001. Annex I.

167 Report of the 24th Meeting of the Bern Convention. T-PVS (2004). 16. Appendix 1. The high point was 28 in 1998. See Report of the 18th Meeting of the Bern Convention. T-PVS (98) 62. Appendix I.

168 UNESCO. (1977). General Assembly of States Parties to the Convention Concerning the Protection of the World Cultural and Natural Heritage. SHC/76/conf.014/COL.9. Feb 15. 1. Note, this point is with regard to the Committee, not the General Assembly. Indeed, within the General Assembly, the numbers of environmental NGOs was a small blip before becoming non-existent until the mid 1980s, when the IUCN began to attend meetings.

169 Note, in the late 1970s, sometimes 'other NGOs' attended who were not identified. UNESCO. (1977). 1st Session of the WHC. CC-77/CONF.001/9. Oct 17, 1977. pp.1. UNESCO. (1978). 2nd Session of the WHC. CC-78/CONF.010/10. Oct 9, 1978. pp.1. For example, in the mid 1990s, the WCMC, along with IUCN were the only environmental ones present at the 1995 meeting. UNESCO. (1996). 19th Session of the WHC. WHC-95/CONF.203/16. Jan 31, 1996. 1.

170 At the 22nd Session meeting in 1998, IUCN, IFAW, WWF, the Wilderness Society, and the Natural Resources Defense Council, FoE, the Environmental Diplomacy Institute, and a number of cultural NGOs. UNESCO. (1998). 22nd Session of the WHC. WHC-98/CONF.203/18. Jan 29, 1999. 5.

171 In addition to the advisory bodies, there were 17 NGOs at the 1999 meeting, including 3 environmental NGOs. UNESCO. (1999). 23rd Session of the WHC. WHC-99/CONF.209/22. Mar 22, 2000. 4.

172 UNESCO. (2000). 24th Session of the WHC. WHC-2000/CONF.204/21. Feb 16, 2001. 1.

173 In 2001 it was 14 in addition to the advisory NGOs, of which some were IOs (such as UNEP) but no obviously environmental NGOs. UNESCO. (2001). 25th Session of the WHC. WHC-01/CONF.208/24. Feb 8. 2002. 4.

174 UNESCO. (2002). 26th Session of the WHC. WHC-02/CONF.202/25. Aug 1, 2002. 4.

2003.[175] The special meeting of 2004 had only eleven observers, of which only one was possibly an environmental NGO.[176] The 2005 meeting had twenty-nine observers (ranging from individual academics to Friends of the Earth).[177]

D NGOs as Partners

A number of the international regimes dealing with protected areas allow NGOs to become 'Partners'. 'Partner organisations' have a much higher level of influence and responsibility than that possessed by non-partners. Although Partner status is obtainable within a number of protected area regimes, ranging from the Mediterranean Protocol[178] through to the MAB, it is with the WHC and the Ramsar, that the partner question is most developed.

The WHC stipulated that a representative from the International Centre for the Study of the Preservation and Restoration of Cultural Property (ICCROM), a representative of the International Council of Monuments and Sites (ICOMOS) and a representative of the IUCN, at the request of States Parties to the WHC, may attend both the General Assembly of all of the Parties to the WHC, and the sessions of the Committee.[179] ICOMOS, ICCROM and the IUCN are the officially recognised 'Advisory Bodies' which provide (compensated) services to the WHC.[180] The arrangements between the World Heritage Centre and the Advisory Bodies were formalized in 1996.[181]

---

175 UNESCO. (2003). 27th Session of the WHC. WHC-03/27.COM/24. Dec 10, 2003. 3-4.

176 UNESCO. (2004). Requests for Observer Status. WHC/-04/7 Ext.COM/2. 2004, Nov 30.

177 UNESCO. (2005). Requests for Observer Status. WHC-05/29.COM/2.

178 The Mediterranean Protocol had ten Partner NGOs by 2003. See Report of the 12th MOP to the Convention for the Protection of the Mediterranean Sea Against Pollution and its Protocols. UNEP (DEC)/MED IG.13/8. Dec 30, 2001. Annex IV. Report of the 13th MOP to the Convention for the Protection of the Mediterranean Sea Against Pollution and its Protocols. UNEP (DEC)/MED IG.15/11. Dec 30, 2001. Annex III.

179 WHC. Article 8.

180 The first budget approved by the WHC committed 18,000 for the technical review of nominations by the IUCN and ICOMOS. By 2004 the total figure for the IUCN services was just over 600,000 per year for their advisory services, alone. Additional costs include reactive monitoring and training activities. Note, although the IUCN and the other advisory NGOs get paid for their work, they maintain that they put much more back into the Convention, in financial terms, than they take out. See UNESCO (2004). WHC-04/7 EXT.COM/INF.7 Dec 2. Analysis by the Advisory Bodies of the Funds Required For Their Services. The total IUCN budget, as derived from the WH Fund for 2006, was 908,870. See Decision 29 COM 16. Annex I, Table 3.

181 As dealt with by MoUs, which clarify and define their respective roles, requirements and responsibilities UNESCO. (1996). 20th Session of the WHC. WHC-96/CONF.201/21. Mar 10, 1997. 61-62.

Although the WHC recognises that other intergovernmental or NGOs, with similar objectives, may also participate or contribute to the WHC work,[182] the Advisory Bodies clearly have a privileged role. Specifically, the WHC stipulated that the Committee, shall utilise, 'to the fullest extent possible the services' of the Advisory Bodies, 'in their respective areas of competence and capability'[183] and the Advisory Bodies have a series of listed responsibilities.[184] The responsibilities are assistance in the preparation of the Committee's documentation and the agenda of its meetings, responsibility for the implementation of some of the Committee's decisions,[185] monitoring sites (as directed),[186] and providing the background assessments of site nominations, to assist the Committee's examination of them.[187] The IUCN is responsible for natural properties, and the natural component of mixed or cultural landscapes.[188] In all instances, the Committee 'takes note' of the advice offered to it by the Advisory Bodies,[189] and practice suggests that the advice given is often followed (but not always)[190] by the Committee, which is typically appreciative of the advice proffered.[191]

The Advisory Bodies are entrusted with their tasks because of their expertise, integrity, independence and transparency.[192] The Advisory Bodies have even self-censored, so as to avoid entering into debates within the WHC, of which they would normally enter

182 WHC. Articles 8 & 10.

183 See also UNESCO. *Committee Rules of Procedure for the World Heritage Convention.* Available from UNESCO, 2004. Rule 43.2.

184 UNESCO. *Committee Rules of Procedure. Ibid.* 2004. Rule 6.

185 WHC. Article 14.

186 UNESCO. (1981). 5th Session of the WHC. CC-81/CONF.003/6. Jan 5, 1981. pp.9. UNESCO. (1985). 9th Session of the WHC. SC-85/CONF.008/9. Dec, 1985. pp 3. UNESCO. (1988). 12th Session of the WHC. SC-88/CONF.001/13. Dec 23, 1988. 10. UNESCO. (1991). 15th Session of the WHC. SC-91/CONF.002/15. Dec 12, 1991. 1. UNESCO. (1993). Expert Meeting on Approaches to Monitoring of World Heritage Properties. WHC-93/CONF.002/INF.5. Nov 23. 1993. 4-6.

187 UNESCO. (2004). 28th Session of the WHC. Oct 29. Decision 28 COM 14B.57.

188 *Operational Guidelines.* 2002 Edn. Paragraph 57. For a discussion of this role, see UNESCO. (1977). First Intergovernmental WHC meeting. CC-77/CONF.001/9. Oct 17, 1977. pp.4, 6. UNESCO. (1996). 19th Session of the WHC. WHC-95/CONF.203/16. Jan 31, 1996. 65.

189 UNESCO. (1983). 6th Session of the WHC. CC-83/CONF.015/8. Jan 17, 1983. pp.3-4.

190 Such as when the Western National Park of Niger was inscribed on the List, despite the IUCN being clear it did not meet any of the listed criteria. UNESCO. (1996). 20th Session of the WHC. WHC-96/CONF.201/21. Mar 10, 1997. 41.

191 UNESCO. (1977). 1st Session of the WHC. CC-77/CONF.001/9. Oct 17, 1977. pp.1.

192 *Operational Guidelines.* 2002 Edn. Paragraph 61. UNESCO. (1980). 4rth Session of the WHC. CC-80/CONF.016/10. Sep 29, 1980. pp.8.

outside of the WHC, such as with mining in sites of high international significance.[193] However, on the areas they are entrusted with, they speak freely,[194] although occasionally their comments have been strongly rebuked by State Parties.[195] Applications by other large international NGOs, with a long-track record of active support for the WHC, such as the WWF[196] to become additional Advisory Bodies have been declined.[197]

According to the Ramsar Parties, a small number of international NGOs (Birdlife International, WWF, the IUCN and IWRB) had played an, 'instrumental role ... in the creation of the Ramsar Convention'.[198] This was asserted because although NGOs had not been formally written into the Convention text (unlike the FAO and UNESCO) Ramsar nevertheless made explicit provision for (Secretariat type) assistance. This assistance was provided by the IUCN on an interim basis[199] until the 1980s, when UNEP, in conjunction with the IUCN, became directly involved in assisting the Bureau of the Ramsar.[200] When the new permanent Secretariat was finally established, the IUCN and the IWRB were written into the new structure, through a formal MoU, in which they guaranteed the provision of specific services.[201] The IUCN and the IWRB have also continued their long standing practice of giving considerable financial support to the Bureau.[202]

---

193 For example, the IUCN took its role of independence so seriously at the WHC, that it refused to participate or provide expert witnessed in a national debate in Australia over the proposed listing of the Wet Tropics of Queensland. UNESCO. (1989). 11th Session of the WHC. SC-89/CONF.004/12. Dec, 22 1989. 5.

194 See for example, where the IUCN spoke freely about a series of new developments. UNESCO. (1978). 2nd General Assembly of the WHC. CC-78/CONF.011/6. Nov 24, 1978. 5. UNESCO. (1983). 4th General Assembly of the WHC. CC-83/CONF.022/6. Nov 28, 1983. 2. UNESCO. (1999). 23rd Session of the WHC. WHC-99/CONF.209/22. Mar 22, 2000. 89.

195 UNESCO. (2002). 26th Session of the WHC. WHC-02/CONF.202/INF.15. Mar 11, 2002. 57-58.

196 Despite the fact that the WWF had contributed between 1.5-2 million to the conservation of natural World Heritage Properties. IUCN. (2003). World Heritage Convention: Effectiveness 1992-2002. (IUCN, Gland). 3,5,7. UNESCO. (1989). 13th Session of the WHC. SC-89/CONF.004/12. Dec, 22 1989. pp 14. UNESCO. (1998). 22nd Session of the WHC. WHC-98/CONF.208/18. Jan 29, 1998. 89-90.

197 For earlier examples of this, see UNESCO. (1977). 1st Session of the WHC. CC-77/CONF.001/9. Oct 17, 1977. pp.9.

198 Recommendation 5.6. The Role of Non Governmental Organisations in the Ramsar Convention. (1993, Kushiro).

199 Ramsar. Article 8. Such as convening COPs, maintaining the Wetlands list, and general Secretariat duties.

200 Recommendation 1.10. A Permanent Secretariat. (1980, Cagliari).

201 As also directed by the COP. Resolution 3.1. Secretariat Matters. (1987, Regina).

202 Resolution 3.2. Financial and Budgetary Matters. (1987, Regina).

The approach of having a formalised document, which recognises the 'special' relationship of some NGOs with the Ramsar, was taken to its furthermost point with the creation of 'International NGO Partner' status. The 'International NGO Partner' status emerged as a consequence of the historical relationships with the IUCN, IWRB, Birdlife International and WWF. All four of these organisations have obtained International NGO Partner status with the Ramsar.[203] The International Water Management Institute obtained International Partner status in 2005.[204]

Partners have special privileges such as observer status in the Standing Committee,[205] the STRP[206] and the respected provision of policy, technical and financial assistance.[207] Given these enhanced privileges, the COP attaches rules for conferring of the status of International NGO Partner. Specifically, Partners may be International Organisations or NGOs. The status shall be conferred, taking into account the following characteristics,

1. A programme of activities that is global or at least covers many countries in one or more regions of the world.
2. Have a statement of purpose that explicitly, or by clear implication, includes the conservation and sustainable use of wetlands.
3. Have a track record or experience in providing support and/or implementing on the ground projects that contribute to wetland conservation or sustainable use.
4. Have demonstrated experience in implementing partnership ventures such as training and education, technical and/or scientific expertise, policy development and/or evaluation and assessment. Particularly where such ventures would bring additional benefits to the functioning of the Ramsar partnership.
5. Have a positive reputation for being willing and able to co-operate on a regular basis with national and international bodies, including both governmental and NGO ones, to further the policies of the Convention. This is particularly so by assisting Contracting Parties to meet their Ramsar obligations.[208]

203 Resolution 7.3. Partnerships with International Organisations. (1999, San Jose).

204 Resolution 9.16. The Convention's International Organisation Partner's. (2005, Kampala).

205 Resolution 7.1. Regional Categorisation. (1999, San Jose).

206 Resolution 7.2. The Scientific and Technical Review Panel. (1999, San Jose).

207 Resolution 7.27. The Convention's Work Plan 2000-02. (1999, San Jose). Resolution 8.25. The Ramsar Strategic Plan. (2002, Valencia). Annex. Operational Objective 19.

208 Resolution 7.3. Partnerships with International Organisations. (1999, San Jose). Annex. Rules for Conferring the Status of International Organisation Partner of the Convention on Wetlands.

NGOs which are not international partners[209] have also been actively involved in the work of some of its subsidiary bodies of Ramsar, such as the scientific bodies.[210] When the scientific research panel of Ramsar was solidified into the STRP, a process for limited access within the STRP for 2 long standing NGOs was set.[211] This was later expanded to a maximum of 12 (partner and non-partner) NGOs[212] so that the, 'technical and scientific review capacity' of NGOs on the work topics of the STRP could be brought to bear.[213]

E NGOs within Official Forums

The typical position for the Ramsar,[214] Africa,[215] and Bern Convention[216] is that any NGO, domestic or international, may be admitted to observe the meeting, unless one third of the members object. The exception to this approach is with the Antarctica regime, by which entry may be barred if one country objects.[217]

---

209 Resolution 7.2. The Scientific and Technical Review Panel. (1999, San Jose). Resolution 8.25. The Ramsar Strategic Plan. (2002, Valencia). Annex. Operational Objective 7.

210 The second meeting of the Ramsar signatories in 1974, recommended that waterfowl research, should, as far as possible, be co-operative at the regional level (using the services of the ICBI). Recommendations adopted by the International Conference on the Conservation of Wetlands and Waterfowl at Heiligenhafen, Federal Republic of Germany, 6 December 1974. Recommendation 11. The Need for Regional Cooperation in the Conservation of Wetlands and Waterfowl and Related Research.

211 The STRP is made up of seven members with two observers. Traditionally these have been from the IUCN and the IWRB. Resolution 5.5. Establishment of the Scientific and Technical Review Panel. (1993, Kushiro).

212 Resolution 7.2. The Scientific and Technical Review Panel. (1999, San Jose).

213 Resolution 8.28. Modus Operandi of the Scientific and Technical Review Panel. (2002, Valencia).

214 The 1980 COP recognised the need to amend the Convention, so as to adopt rules of procedure to govern the attendance of observers, especially from international NGOs, along the lines of the CMS. Recommendation 1.8. Proposed Amendments to the Convention. (1980, Cagliari). The directive to review the Rules of Procedure at the COP, with a view to providing some revised Rules, 'in harmony with those of other international environmental conventions' was reiterated, again, at the 1996 meeting. Resolution VI.15. Rules of Procedure. (1996, Brisbane). Resolution VI.15. Rules of Procedure. (1996, Brisbane). Those desiring to attend the meetings must submit the names of the observers to the Bureau at least one month prior to the meeting. The one-third exclusion clause has never been invoked. However, at COP8 in 2002 some 'direct action' groups attended the meeting and there were some murmurs amongst the Parties' about abusing their abuse of the attendance privilege. Nevertheless, there was no exclusion of any NGO.

215 2003 African Convention. Article XXVI (4).

216 Bern Convention. Article 14 (3).

217 Final Report of the XXVII ATCM. Cape Town. 2004. Decision 1. Revised Rules of Procedure. Rule 38 (m).

Theoretically, all of the protected area regimes only allow entry for NGOs to the official meetings, which are qualified in one area or another. For example, with wetlands, the NGO must be, 'qualified in fields relating to the conservation and sustainable use of wetlands',[218] or with Antarctica, they must possess a 'scientific or technical interest'.[219] NGOs seeking entry to the WHC must be working in, 'activities in the fields' covered by the Convention.[220] With the Bern Convention, the NGOs must be 'technically qualified in the protection, conservation or management of wild fauna and flora and their habitats.[221]

The Antarctica regime, obviously, only deals with international NGOs. The WHC has traditionally favoured international NGOs,[222] and national only NGOs have often been denied access, especially when dealing with contentious domestic considerations.[223] The Bern Convention has no preference for international or domestic NGOs, but all domestic NGOs seeking entry, must have been approved for this purpose by the State in which they are located.[224]

NGOs can 'participate' but not vote in the WHC,[225] Ramsar, Antarctica,[226] and the Bern Convention.[227] However, in the ICRI, NGOs can vote, as equals with the Parties.[228] Oral contributions, if time allows and cleared by the Chair, are permissible with the WHC,[229] Ramsar, and the sub-committees within the Antarctic regime.[230]

---

218 Resolution VI.15. Rules of Procedure. (1996, Brisbane). Those desiring to attend the meetings must submit the names of the observers to the Bureau at least one month prior to the meeting.

219 Final Report of the XXVII ATCM. Cape Town. 2004. Decision 1. Revised Rules of Procedure. Rule 38 (1). (the Consultative Parties, deliberate on this point)

220 UNESCO. *Committee Rules of Procedure for the World Heritage Convention.* Available from UNESCO, 2004. Rule 8.3. And having 'objectives similar to those of this Convention'. See Article 13 (4) of the WHC.

221 Bern Convention. Article 14 (3).

222 UNESCO. *General Assembly of State Parties to Convention Concerning the Protection of the World Cultural and Natural Heritage.* (Available from UNESCO, 2004). Rule 2.2.

223 The refused NGOs were invited to contact their national delegations. UNESCO. (1981). 5th Session of the WHC.. CC-81/CONF.003/6. Jan 5, 1981. pp.3.

224 Bern Convention. Article 14 (3).

225 UNESCO. *General Assembly of State Parties. Ibid.* Rule 2.2.

226 See Article 12 of the Madrid Protocol.

227 Note, in the Bern Convention they can make a proposal for a vote if supported by at least one delegation.

228 Decision on Organisation and Management Procedures for the ICRI. In ICRI (2004). Report of the ICRI Meeting in Okinawa, Japan. 3-4 July, 2004. Articles 1 & 7. Resolution on the International Coral Reef Action Network. In ICRI (2000). Report of the ICRI Meeting in Noumea, New Caledonia, 25-26 May, 2000.

229 'the consent of the Chairperson must be obtained whenever an observer wishes to address the assembly'. UNESCO. *General Assembly of State Parties to Convention Concerning the Protection of the World Cultural and Natural Heritage.* (Available from UNESCO, 2004). Rule 7.3.

With the latter, they can also submit documents, but these must first go through the Secretariat.[231]

F Science and Technical Bodies

It is not uncommon for most international environmental conventions to have an independent scientific arm. This practice, which has been replicated in a number of protected area regimes.[232] However, some regimes, such as the WHC, despite having the capacity to create such bodies,[233] have effectively out-sourced this responsibility to their Advisory Bodies, which in the case of conservation, is the IUCN. Other regimes, such as the Ramsar and the Antarctic regime, have kept their scientific advice in-house, although the IUCN, as a member of the scientific bodies of both of these bodies, continues to have a large influence.

With the Ramsar, although the IUCN and IWRB had provided scientific advice to the Convention since its outset, in 1980 it was recommended that the Convention be amended to create a new subsidiary body which provided scientific advice.[234] Over a decade later, this came out as the Scientific and Technical Review Panel (STRP). The STRP is made up of one member from each Ramsar region, and six further members are nominated. A further list of bodies (a combination of other international environmental secretariats, organisations and NGOs) is given to each COP, which are invited to be observers to the STRP. These 'extras' are invited to establish working cooperative relationships with the STRP on matters of common interest. The system is also connected via national focal points.[235]

The Secretariat makes recommendations for appointment in accordance with the STRP objectives and needs. Its individual members are elected by the Standing Committee, based upon nominations from the Parties, on the same regionally proportionate basis that is used for electing the Standing Committee itself. The members serve in their own

---

230 See Article 12 of the Madrid Protocol.

231 Final Report of the XXVII ATCM. Cape Town. 2004. Decision 1. Revised Rules of Procedure. Rule 38 (n) –(q).

232 See for example, the Caribbean Protocol. Article 20. See Decision 1. Report of the First COP to the SPAW in the Wider Caribbean Region Protocol (2001). UNEP(DEC)/CAR IG.20/7. Annex II.

232 Recommendation 1.8. Proposed Amendments to the Convention. (1980, Cagliari).

233 WHC. Article 10.

234 Recommendation 1.8. Proposed Amendments. *Ibid.*

235 National Focal Points are invited to make nominations of candidates for appointment as members of the STRP, identify their thematic areas of STRP study, be invited to join any relevant STRP Working Groups and be invited to contribute to the peer review of reports and other documents being considered for publication in the Ramsar Technical Report series.

capacities as experts in the scientific areas required by the STRP's work plan and not as representatives of their countries.[236] Each of the four partner organisations may also have a member in the STRP.[237]

The STRP is tasked to give authoritative scientific and technical advice, on all directed matters,[238] to the necessary Ramsar bodies (but the Standing Committee and the Bureau in particular). The STRP was given a revised modus operandi in 2005 and an Oversight Committee. The Oversight Committee, on the recommendation of the Secretariat, is made up of one suitably qualified member from each Ramsar region and a further six Panel members (any Party may attend as an observer) shall be appointed as wetlands experts (based in different Ramsar countries or regions and/or from Northern and Southern parts of the world). A final member is a CEPA specialist.[239] A core part of the Oversight Committee is their determination of Working Groups and their respective Chairs. Such Chairs may be from within the STRP, from the Parties, or the Partners or other observer organizations.

The Madrid Protocol crated the Committee on Environmental Protection (CEP).[240] The CEP has the role of providing advice and formulating recommendations to the Consultative Parties, in connection to the implementation of the Protocol.[241] The CEP is a body, of which each Party which is a member of the Protocol is entitled to membership. SCAR (Scientific Committee on Antarctic Research) and CCAMLR are invited observers at the CEP. SCAR also provides scientific advice to the CCAMLR and the ACAP.

The SCAR was formed in 1958 as an inter-disciplinary committee of the International Council for Science (ICSU). The SCAR, which seeks to be 'the leading non-governmental organisation for facilitating and coordinating research in Antarctica',[242] began

---

236 Resolution 8.28. The Modus Operandi of the STRP. (2002, Valencia). Paragraph 1.

237 Resolution 9.11. Revised Modus Operandi for the Scientific and Technical Review Panel (2005, Kampala). For earlier versions of these rules, see Resolution 5.5. Establishment of the Scientific and Technical Review Panel. (1993, Kushiro).Refinements (on alternates at meetings) and nominations for the STRP were secured at the 6th COP. Resolution 6.7. The Scientific and Technical Review Panel. (1996, Brisbane). This was revised again at the 8th COP. Resolution 8.28. Modus Operandi of the Scientific and Technical Review Panel. (2002, Valencia).

238 Including, inter alia (review of the Bureau's annual scientific programme, review of the criteria for listing; review of the Montreux record; identification of priorities for the Monitoring procedure; review of the Wetland Conservation Fund; evaluation of the guidelines of wise use etc). Resolution 5.5. Establishment of the Scientific and Technical Review Panel. (1993, Kushiro).

239 Resolution 9.11. Revised Modus Operandi for the Scientific and Technical Review Panel.

240 See Article 11 of the Madrid Protocol.

241 See Article 12 of the Madrid Protocol.

242 SCAR Constitution. Section 2.1.

providing advice to the Antarctic Treaty as soon as the treaty came into being in 1961. It is guided by the principles of, inter alia, 'to provide objective and independent scientific advice to the Antarctic Treaty Consultative Meeting' and 'to facilitate free and unrestricted access to Antarctic scientific data and information'.[243] The scientific business of SCAR is conducted by its Standing Scientific Groups which represent the scientific disciplines active in Antarctic research and report to SCAR. SCAR's Standing Scientific Groups are responsible for sharing, identifying, coordinating scientific research within their respective areas, and also Expert Groups to address specific research topics. The SCAR currently has three Standing Scientific Groups,[244] and five research programmes.[245]

Membership of SCAR is comprised of full members,[246] associate members,[247] union membership,[248] and honorary members.[249] National membership was later added to the types of membership.[250] Unlike other members, national members must explicitly agree with the SCAR Principles for the Protection of the Antarctic Environment (which is largely reflected in the Madrid Protocol). Observers can be invited to the meetings.[251] Membership reflects voting rights (only full members can vote on all issues)[252] and financial contributions.[253]

---

243 SCAR Constitution. Sections 2.3 (b) and (c).

244 These are the Groups on Life Sciences, GeoSciences and Physical Sciences.

245 These are Antarctic Climate Evolution, Subglacial Antarctic Lake Environments, Evolution and Biodiversity in the Antarctic, Antarctica and the Global Climate Systems

246 National organisations adhering to the ICSU or nominated by such a national organisation adhering to the ICSU that represents the scientific community of that country. The country must maintain an active and continuing programme of research in the Antarctic, and must have formed a National Committee to communicate with SCAR.

247 Must have the ICSU links, as above, but do not qualify for full membership.

248 A member of the ICSU Union, related to the objectives of SCAR and wishes to contribute.

249 Past members of SCAR.

250 National membership nominations should go through the ICSU linkages, of if not appropriate, consultation with the SCAR Secretariat. National membership rules are found in the SCAR Rules of Procedure, not the SCAR Constitution.

251 Invited observers from other governmental and non-governmental organizations may be invited to attend meetings of the Delegates. SCAR Constitution. Section 6 (e).

252 SCAR Constitution. Sections 4 and 5. The only other members who can vote are Union Member who can vote on everything except financial matters.

253 SCAR financing is obtained from annual contributions from its national members according to the scale determined by the meeting of delegates, as well as from grants and income obtained from the ICSU and other sources. Contributions are obtained from the category of membership. Full members have four possible categories, and are encouraged to contribute annually, 'according to their own assessment of the scale of their national scientific activity in the Antarctic'. Associate members have a separate category, at a lower level than full members. SCAR only funds expenses of members of the Executive Committee, Chief Officers, and persons appointed by SCAR who are required at the meetings.

G *Submission Procedures*

In theory, all sites nominated to be protected, should be done so via a verifiable, robust, and transparent process.[254] These goals are typically achieved by a common submission process. The pattern is typically a site is nominated by a sovereign government, that site is then reviewed first by a desk officer of the particular regime. The first review tends not to look at the merits of the application, but makes sure all of the components for its assessment are in place. Second, the nomination is independently reviewed by a specialist body. The review is conducted via previously agreed criteria. The independent review (either by in-house advisory bodies, or out-house experts) then makes recommendations to the governing part of the regime in question. Finally, the Parties to the regime make a decision (typically by consensus or entrenched majority) on whether the site should be inscribed on their list of protected areas. The exception to this approach is with the Ramsar.[255] In some instances, additional considerations, as voiced by overlapping international organizations are taken into account. These broad processes are well developed with the Antarctic regime,[256] the MAB,[257] the IMO,[258]

254 CBD. Decision VII/28. Protected Areas. Annex. Section IV. Goal 4.4. Noting the importance of science in selection.

255 Ramsar sites are placed on their List after being submitted by State Parties, which should follow their own (guided) processes, before the nomination is reviewed by the STRP and the Bureau, and collectively, they make the decision about inscription – not the conference of the Parties). Resolution 5.3. Initial Designation of Ramsar Sites. (1993, Kushiro). Review Procedure for Listed Sites Which May Not Qualify Under any of the Criteria Established By Recommendation 4.2. This is annexed to Resolution 5.3. Initial Designation of Ramsar Sites. (1993, Kushiro).

256 See Articles 6 and 12 of the Madrid Protocol. Recommendation VII-3. Sites of Special Scientific Interest. In Report of the Seventh Meeting. (1972, Wellington). 56.Recommendation VIII-3. Sites of Special Scientific Interest. In Final Report of the 8th Antarctic Treaty Meeting. (1975, Oslo). 53. Recommendation XIII-5. Man's Impact on the Antarctic Environment: Additional Protective Arrangements. Recommendation XV-10. Antarctic Protected Area System: Establishment of Specially Reserved Areas, and Recommendation XV-11. Antarctic Protected Area System: Establishment of Multiple Use Planning Areas. Antarctic Treaty: Report of the Fifteenth Meeting (Paris, 1989). 82 and 84. Recommendation XIV-6. Marine Sites of Special Scientific Interest. In Antarctic Treaty: Report of the Fourteenth Meeting (Rio de Janeiro, 1987). 119.

257 The Statutory Framework of the World Network of Biosphere Reserves. Article 5. Bridgewater, p. (2002). 'Biosphere Reserves: A Network for Conservation and Sustainability'. 12 (3) *Parks*. 15.

258 MEPC. (2002). Report of the MEPC on its 48th Session. MEPC 48/21. 34. IMO General Assembly. 17th Session. A 17/Res.720. Guidelines for the Designation of Special Areas and the Identification of Particularly Sensitive Sea Areas. Table 7.

the Mediterranean[259] and Caribbean Protocols,[260] and the ASCIs, Diplomas and Emeralds of the European regime.[261]

Although all of the above regimes have their own robust submission procedures, arguably, the strongest of all of the regimes is the WHC, which attempts to select sites, 'in accordance with modern scientific methods'.[262] This goal is sought to as to ensure that sites are not inscribed on the WHC List, which do not have outstanding universal value as such inscriptions could lead to a dilution of the value of the WHC List.[263]

This is not only a theoretical problem, as a number of sites have been inscribed, such as the West National Park of Niger,[264] the Djoudj national bird sanctuary in Senegal,[265] and the Pitons in St Lucia, against the Advisory Body recommendations.[266]

Although such instances may have occurred, a far greater number of examples exist where sites have failed to meet the WHC standards for inscription and are either deferred or referred back to the State Party. In such instances, if possible, the file is put on hold until the Party can satisfactorily address the outstanding issues. In other instances, the nominations may be refused outright as the sites are not judged to be of outstanding universal value. Such rejections have encompassed nominations of natural sites from,

---

259 Mediterranean Protocol. Article 9. Da Cruz, H. (2002). 'The Barcelona Convention and its Impact on Biodiversity'. 12 (3) *Parks*. 7-14.

260 Report of the Working Group on the Development of Guidelines for the Listing of Protected Areas Under the SPAW Protocol. (2005). UNEP (DEC)/CAR WG.29/INF.12.

261 European Diploma. Articles, 4, 5 and 6. Resolution No. 5 (1998) Concerning The Rules For The Network of Areas of Special Conservation Interest (Emerald Network). Report of the 18th Meeting of the Bern Convention. T-PVS (98) 62. Appendix 3. Article 2 (1).

262 WHC. Preamble. Paragraph 9

263 UNESCO. (1979). 3rd Session of the WHC. CC-79/CONF.003/13. Nov 30, 1978. pp.6. UNESCO. (1980). 3rd General Assembly of States Parties to the WHC. CC-80/CONF.018/6. Oct 20, 1980. 2. Hales, D. (1984). 'The World Heritage Convention: Status and Directions.' In McNeely, J. (ed). *National Parks, Conservation and Development.* (Smithsonian, Washington). 744, 746-48.

264 UNESCO. (1996). 20th Session of the WHC. WHC-96/CONF.201/21. Mar 10, 1997. 41.

265 UNESCO. (1979). 3rd Session of the WHC. CC-79/CONF.003/3. Aug 27, 1979. pp.4.

266 UNESCO. (1996) Expert Review on Evaluation of General Principles and Criteria for Nominations of Natural World Heritage Sites. WHC-96/CONF.202/INF.9. Apr 15. 3, 6.

inter-alia, Costa Rica[267] China,[268] Croatia,[269] Malawi, Pakistan, Zaire,[270] Australia,[271] Brazil,[272] India and Vietnam.[273]

Although failure to achieve inscription for a nominated site should not be viewed as an implicit rejection of the values of that site,[274] the fact remains that States which fail in this process are undoubtedly disappointed. Accordingly, from the outset the Parties to the WHC have tried to soften the blow and seek ways to avoid such high level disappointments from occurring in the first place.[275] Accordingly, a number of processes have been established which hope to short-circuit this possible conclusion for sites which do not meet the agreed criteria. These processes have, since 1977, attempted to simplify, clarify and assist countries seeking to get sites inscribed on the WHC Lists.[276] At core, each nomination should be presented in the form of a well-argued case for listing.[277] It should be submitted on the appropriate form,[278] and should

---

267 The Coco Island National Park. UNESCO. (1985). 9th Session of the WHC. SC-85/CONF.008/9. Dec, 1985. pp 7. Note, this site was later listed.

268 The Jixian Conservation Area. UNESCO. (1987). 11th Session of the WHC. CC-87/CONF.005/9. Jan 20, 1988. pp 8.

269 Kopacki in Croatia. UNESCO. (2001). 24th Session of the WHC. WHC-2000/CONF.204/21. Feb 16, 2001. 68.

270 The Nyika park of Malawi, the Kirthar National Park of Pakistan and the Maiko National Park of Zaire. UNESCO. (1984). 8th Session of the WHC. SC/84/CONF.004/9. Nov 2, 1984. pp 10.

271 Macquarie Island nature reserve was initially rejected from the list for a failure to meet the biological criteria, although it was noted that it might be enhanced if it included some of New Zealand's neighbouring island groups. UNESCO. (1992). 16th Session of the WHC. WHC-92/CONF.002/12. Dec 14, 1992. 34. Although this never happened, as NZ and Australia presented separate nominations, Australia was eventually successful in getting this site listed under geological – not the originally suggested biological- criteria.

272 Serra da Capivara. UNESCO. (2003). 27th Session of the WHC. WHC-03/27.COM/24. Dec 10. 106.

273 The Wild Ass Sanctuary of India, and the Cuc-Phong National Park of Vietnam. UNESCO. (1993). 17th Session of WHC. WHC-93/CONF.002/14. Feb 4, 1993. 38.

274 The fact that a property belonging to natural heritage has not been included in the WHC List, 'shall in no way be construed to mean that it does not have an outstanding universal value for purposes other than those resulting from inclusion" on the List'. WHC. Article 12.

275 Before refusing a request for inclusion on the WHC List, the Committee shall consult the State Party in whose territory the property in question is situated. WHC. Article 11 (6).

276 At the 1977 Committee meeting, the IUCN & ICOMOS were directed to prepare model files, to be reviewed by the Secretariat, of what a model application would look like. UNESCO. (1977). 1st Intergovernmental Committee for the WHC. CC-77/CONF.001/9. Oct 17, 1977. pp.5. This was later rejected by the Committee, who opted instead, for a booklet (prepared by the IUCN & ICOMOS) on how to prepare World Heritage List Nominations. UNESCO. (1978). 2nd Session of the WHC. CC-78/CONF.010/10. Oct 9, 1978. pp.9.

277 *Operational Guidelines.* 2002 Edition. Paragraph 10.

provide all the information to demonstrate that the property nominated is truly of outstanding universal value. The Advisory Body in question (in this instance the IUCN) will then make an independent evaluation of the nominated site, and deliver its recommendations to the Committee. The Committee will then decide (typically by consensus, but a minimum of two thirds approval)[279] on the submitted inscription, and limited procedures exist for preventing undue Party influence in the nomination process.[280] Former nomination dossiers, IUCN evaluations and the final recommendations of the Committee on each inscribed site are available for consultation by States Parties which may wish to use such information as guides for identifying and elaborating nomination of sites within their own territories.[281] These processes were re-examined and changed following the high profile failure en-masse of five nominations from the Ukraine in 2001. The core of the changes was a preliminary vetting process (which enhanced the long-standing[282] traditional informal consultation process with the Secretariat and/or

278 Identification of the Property. Maps and/or plans showing boundary of area proposed for inscription and of any buffer zone, area of site proposed for inscription and proposed buffer zone if any). Justification for inscription (statement of significance, possible comparative analysis including state of conservation of similar sites; authenticity / Integrity; criteria under which inscription is proposed and justification for inscription under these criteria). Description (of property, history and development; form and date of most recent records of site; present state of conservation, policies and programmes related to the presentation and promotion of the property). Management (ownership, legal status, protective measures and means of implementing them; agency / agencies with management authority, level at which management is exercised (e.g., on site, regionally) and name and address of responsible person for contact purposes, agreed plans related to property e.g., regional, local plan, conservation plan, tourism development plan); sources and levels of finance; sources of expertise and training in conservation and management techniques; visitor facilities and statistics. Site management plan and statement of objectives (copy to be annexed); staffing levels (professional, technical, maintenance). Factors affecting the site (development pressures e.g., encroachment, adaptation, agriculture, mining; environmental pressures e.g., pollution, climate change; Natural disasters and preparedness such as earthquakes, floods, fires, etc; visitor / tourism pressures; number of inhabitants within site, buffer zone; other monitoring (key indicators for measuring state of conservation; administrative arrangements for monitoring property; results of previous reporting exercises. Documentation (photographs, slides and, where available, film / video copies of site management plans and extracts of other plans relevant to the site bibliography; address where inventory, records and archives are held signature on behalf of the State Party. The Committee adopted at its twentieth session substantive explanatory notes to the above nomination considerations. These notes relate to the above headings and are made available as an annex to the nomination form to the States Parties in order to provide guidance to those nominating properties for inclusion on the World Heritage List.

279 UNESCO. *Committee Rules of Procedure for the World Heritage Convention.* Available from UNESCO, 2004. Rule 50 & 51. UNESCO. (1977). 1st Session of the WHC. CC-77/CONF.001/9. Oct 17, 1977. pp.2.

280 Decision 29 COM 18 B.

281 *Operational Guidelines.* 2002 Edn. Paragraph 45.

282 UNESCO. (1981). 5th Session of the WHC. CC-81/CONF.003/6. Jan 5, 1981. pp.8.

the advisory bodies) to make sure all of the information is in order and greater assistance in demonstrating WHC requirements.[283]

H The Relationships between Organisations

The importance of promoting synergies and avoiding unnecessary duplications between the complimentary organizations, with regards to protected areas is well recognised by, inter alia, the CBD,[284] Ramsar,[285] WHC[286] and the MAB.[287]

Within this broad area of overlapping organizations, the most commonly sought connection is with the CBD. In this regard, the MAB has a particular attraction to the CBD,[288] seeing itself as being able to implement the objectives of the CBD through its biosphere reserves.[289] Accordingly, it is represented at the relevant SBSTTA meetings,[290] and the MAB is recognized by the CBD, as one of its global partners with regard to the CBD's portfolio on protected areas.[291] A similar relationship with the Bern Convention and the CBD also exists, based on their shared Memorandum of Understanding (MoU).[292] The Ramsar also shares an MoU with the CBD.[293] Although

283 *Operational Guidelines*. 2002 Edn. Paragraph 13. UNESCO. (2001). 25th Session of the WHC. WHC-01/CONF.208/24. Feb 8, 2002. 96. UNESCO. (2002). 26th Session of the WHC. WHC-02/CONF.202/INF.15. Mar 11, 2002. 72.

284 CBD. Decision VII/28. Protected Areas. Paragraph 34.

285 Resolution 9.5. Synergies With Other International Organisations Dealing With Biological Diversity, Including Collaboration on, and Harmonisation of, National Reporting, Among Biodiversity Related Conventions and Agreements. (Kampala, 2005). Resolution 8.5. Partnerships and Synergies With Multilateral Environmental Agreements. (2002, Valencia). Resolution 8.25. The Ramsar Strategic Plan. (2002, Valencia). Annex. Operational Objective 13. Resolution 8.26. The Implementation of the Strategic Plan 2003-2008. (2002, Valencia). Annex I. Global Implementation of the Targets for the Convention. Resolution 7.27. The Convention's Work Plan 2000-02. (1999, San Jose). Resolution 7.19. International Cooperation. (1999, San Jose). Annex. The Guidelines for international cooperation under the Ramsar Convention.

286 WHC. Preamble. Paragraph 4.

287 Seville Strategy. Objective 1.2. UNESCO. (2001). MAB ICC Bureau Meeting. SC/-01/CONF.211/13. Apr 10. 13.

288 The Statutory Framework of the World Network of Biosphere Reserves. Article 2 (2). Seville Strategy. Objective 1.1, 1.2, II.1. MAB. (2000). 16th Session of the ICC Bureau. SC-00/CONF.208/13. 2.

289 UNESCO. (1998). *Biosphere Reserves: Myth or Reality?'* (UNESCO, Paris). vii.

290 UNESCO. (2001). MAB ICC Bureau Meeting. SC/-01/CONF.211/13. Apr 10. 6.

291 UNESCO. (2004). 18th Session of the ICC Bureau Meeting. SC-04/CONF.204/14. Jan 11. 4.

292 Draft Memorandum of Cooperation Between the Secretary General of the Council of Europe in his Capacity as Secretary of the Convention on the Conservation of European Wildlife, and the Executive Secretary of the Convention on Biological Diversity Report of the 19th Meeting of the Bern Convention. T-PVS (99) 30. Appendix 12. Report of the 18th Meeting of the Bern Convention. T-PVS (98) 62. 6-7. Resolution No. 7. Medium Term Strategic

the CBD is noted in the WHC's work, the relationship is less formal than with the other organizations noted above.[294] Other organizations, such as the ICRI, have long desired relationships with the CBD.[295] The other instrument which emerged from the 1992 Earth Summit, with which protected area regimes have increasingly been seeking links, is the United Nations Framework Convention on Climate Change (UNFCCC). In this regard, in the general context of protected areas, the WHC,[296] the MAB,[297] have sought to establish relationships, whilst in a specific context (with regard to peatlands[298] and small island States),[299] the Ramsar has sought the same goal. Even the Regional Seas Programme[300] has sought links with the UNFCCC. The other linkage of note with one of the emerging 'big areas' is with regard to water resources. In this context, only the Ramsar has sought an engagement process with the ongoing multilateral processes.[301]

Species conventions which are linked to protected area regimes which are notable are the CMS and the Convention on International Trade in Endangered Species of Fauna

---

Development of the Bern Convention. Report of the 20th Meeting of the Bern Convention. T-PVS (2000). 75. Appendix 3. CoE (1995). Report of the 14th Meeting of the Bern Convention. T-PVS (95) 26. See the Monaco Declaration on the Role of the Bern Convention in the Implementation of Worldwide International Instruments for the Protection of Biodiversity. Appendix 4.

293 Recommendation 5.4. The Relationship Between the GEF and the CBD. (1993, Kushiro). Resolution 6.10. Co-Operation with the GEF and its Implementing Agencies. (1996, Brisbane). Resolution 8.6. A Ramsar Framework Inventory. (2002, Valencia). Recommendation 5.4. The Relationship Between the GEF and the CBD. (1993, Kushiro). Resolution 6.9. Cooperation With the CBD. (1996, Brisbane).

294 UNESCO. (1992). 16th Session of the WHC. WHC-92/CONF.002/12. Dec 14, 1992. Annex II. UNESCO. (1995). 18th Session of the WHC. WHC-94/CONF.003/16. Jan 31. 1995. 4. UNESCO. (1989). 13th Session of the WHC. SC-89/CONF.004/9. Dec 22, 1989. pp 2. UNESCO. (1991). 15th Session of the WHC. SC-91/CONF.002/15. Dec 12, 1991. 1.

295 See Resolution on Coral Bleaching and Climate Change to the Convention on Biological Diversity. In ICRI. (1999). Report of the ICRI Meeting in Guadeloupe, France, 27-28 Oct, 1999.

296 Decision 29.COM/7B.a.Rev.

297 MAB. (2000). 16th Session of the ICC Bureau. SC-00/CONF.208/13. 9.

298 Resolution 8.11. Additional Guidance for Identifying and Designating Under Represented Wetland Types as Wetlands of International Importance. (2002, Valencia). Annex. Identification and Designation of Peatlands. Paragraphs 15-16. Resolution 8.17. Guidelines for Global Action on Peatlands (GAP). (2002, Valencia). Annex. Paragraph 14.

299 Recommendation 7.2. Small Island Developing States. (1999, San Jose).

300 UNEP. (1999). Second Global Meeting of Regional Seas Conventions and Action Plans. The Hague, 5-8 July. Available from the UNEP Regional Seas Program. Paragraph 107.

301 Resolution 9.3. Engagement of the Ramsar Convention on Wetlands in Ongoing Multilateral Processes Dealing with Water (Kampala, 2005).

and Flora (CITES). The MAB has an ad-hoc relationship with the CMS,[302] as does the Bern Convention, although the latter is very focused on particularly migratory species which they share in common.[303] Conversely, the Ramsar has a particularly strong relationship with the CMS by which the two organizations share a number of developments, such as the Brisbane Initiative, which seeks to establish and link wetlands of international importance for migratory shorebirds along the East Asian Australasian Flyway.[304] Ad-hoc relationships with CITES are also evident with the WHC,[305] Ramsar,[306] the Caribbean Protocol[307] and the Regional Seas Programme.[308]

Strong relationships are also common between the large protected area regimes. The strongest relationship is probably between the Antarctic Treaty System and CCAMLR with regard to MPAs, with extensive consultation procedures, and the consent of CCAMLR being required before any MPA under the auspice of the Antarctic Treaty System being designated.[309] Strong collaborative relationships also exist between the

---

302 MAB. (2000). 16th Session of the ICC Bureau. SC-00/CONF.208/13. 9. UNESCO. (2002). 17th Session of the ICC Bureau. SC-02/CONF.201/11. Apr 12.

303 Recommendation No. 72. (1999). On the Implementation of the Action Plan for the Conservation of the Greater Horseshoe Bat. Report of the 19th Meeting of the Bern Convention. T-PVS (99). 30. Appendix 3. Recommendation No. 75. On the Implementation of New Action Plans for Globally Threatened Birds in Europe. Report of the 19th Meeting of the Bern Convention. T-PVS (99) 30. Appendix 6. Recommendation No. 86 (2001). The Conservation of the Black Sea Bottle Nosed Dolphin. Report of the 21st Meeting of the Bern Convention. T-PVS (2001). 89. Appendix 4.

304 Recommendation 6.4. The Brisbane Initiative. (1996, Brisbane). Recommendation 2.3. Annex: Framework for Implementing the Convention. (1984, Groningen). Recommendation 4.12. Co-Operation Between Contracting Parties for the Management of Migratory Species. (1990, Montreux). Resolution 4.4. Implementation of Article 5. (1990, Montreux). Recommendation 7.3. Migratory Birds of the Asia Pacific Region. (1999, San Jose). Resolution 8.37. International Cooperation on Conservation of Migratory Waterbirds and Their Habitats in the Asia Pacific. (2002, Valencia).

305 This is particularly noticeable when some areas of mutual concern overlap. See for example, the 2006 decisions relating to Garamba 30 COM 7A.4; and Kahuzi 30 COM 7A.6. For some historical decisions on this, see UNESCO. (1986). 10th Session of the WHC. CC-86/CONF.003/10. Dec 5, 1986. pp 9. UNESCO. (1987). 11th Session of the WHC. CC-87/CONF.005/9. Jan 20, 1988. pp 11. UNESCO. (1989). 13th Session of the WHC. SC-89/CONF.004/9. Dec 22, 1989. pp 2. UNESCO. (1995). 18th Session of the WHC. WHC-94/CONF.003/16. Jan 31. 1995. 22-23. UNESCO. (1986). 10th Session of the WHC. CC-86/CONF.003/10. Dec 5, 1986. pp 9. UNESCO. (1987). 11th Session of the WHC. CC-87/CONF.005/9. Jan 20, 1988. pp 11.

306 Recommendation 5.13. The Neotropical Region. (1993, Kushiro).

307 Caribbean Protocol. Article 25. See Decision II. Report of the First COP to the SPAW in the Wider Caribbean Region Protocol (2001). UNEP(DEC)/CAR IG.20/7. Annex II.

308 UNEP. (1999). Second Global Meeting of Regional Seas Conventions and Action Plans. The Hague, 5-8 July. Available from the UNEP Regional Seas Program. Paragraphs 81-84..

309 See Madrid Protocol. Annex V, Article 6 (2). Decision 4. (1998). Marine Protected Areas. In Antarctic Treaty: Report of the Twenty-Second Meeting. (Tromso, 1997). 70-71.

Ramsar, and the WHC,[310] MAB[311] and Bern Convention.[312] The WHC also has partaken in collaborative exercises with the European Landscape[313] and Alpine[314] Conventions, and the IMO.[315] It also maintains strong relations with the MAB.[316] Meanwhile, the MAB is unique in its relationship with the Convention to Combat Desertification (CCD).[317] Finally, the Bern Convention is closely linked to the Habitats (and other related) Directives, Natura 2000 and the Emerald Network.

The MPA forums, are typically inter-linked (although often in a very ad-hoc manner) through the MPA protocols,[318] the various oceans commissions,[319] the CBD, the UNICPOLOS[320] and the IMO.[321] Lesser connections involve the Regional Seas Programme and the ICRI.[322] In the more MPA focused regimes, such as the ICRI, strong relationships with Regional Fisheries Bodies and the FAO in particular are sought.[323]

---

310 Resolution 7.4. Cooperation With Other Conventions. (1999, San Jose).

311 Final Act of the Ramsar Conference. Annex II. Recommendations adopted by the International Conference on the Conservation of Wetlands and Waterfowl at Ramsar, Iran, 3 February 1971. Recommendation 11. Wetlands and the Man and the Biosphere Programme. MAB. (2000). 16th Session of the ICC Bureau. SC-00/CONF.208/13. 1-2, 10.

312 Recommendation No. 32 (1991). The Protection of the Sources of the River Pescara. Recommendation No. 83 (2000). The Conservation Status of Lake Vistonis and Lafra-Lafrouda Lagoon (Greece). Report of the 20th Meeting of the Bern Convention. T-PVS (2000). 75. Appendix 7.

313 UNESCO. (1997). 21st Session of the WHC. WHC-97/CONF.208/17. Feb 27, 1998. 53.

314 UNESCO. (2000). Thematic Expert Meeting on Potential Natural World Heritage Sites in the Alps. WHC-2000/CONF.204/WEB.2.

315 UNESCO. (2004). 28th Session of the WHC. WHC-04/28.COM/26. Oct 29. Decision 28 COM 15B.31.8pp93. Decision 29 COM 7B.5 (on Banc d'Arguin).

316 UNESCO. (2004). 7th Extraordinary Session of the WHC. WHC-04/7. EXT.COM/9. Nov 25. Annex II.

317 MAB. (2000). 16th Session of the ICC Bureau. SC-00/CONF.208/13. 5. 9. UNESCO. (2001). MAB ICC Bureau Meeting. SC/-01/CONF.211/13. Apr 10. 7.

318 See Decisions III and V. Report of the First COP to the SPAW in the Wider Caribbean Region Protocol (2001). UNEP(DEC)/CAR IG.20/7. Annex II.

319 HELCOM REC.15/5 (1994). Guidelines for BSPA. Section 1.2.

320 CBD. Decision VII/28. Protected Areas. Annex I. Para 3. Goal 1.3. Para.1.3.2.

321 Report of the 13th MOP to the Convention for the Protection of the Mediterranean Sea Against Pollution and its Protocols. UNEP (DEC)/MED IG.15/11. Dec 30, 2001. Annex III. HELCOM REC.15/5 (1994). Guidelines for BSPA. Section 1.2.

322 UNEP. (1999). Second Global Meeting of Regional Seas Conventions and Action Plans. The Hague, 5-8 July. Available from the UNEP Regional Seas Program. Paragraphs 89. UNEP. (2000). Report of the Third Global Meeting of Regional Seas Conventions and Action Plans. Available from the UNEP Regional Seas Programme. Paragraph 141.

323 Resolution on Fisheries. In ICRI (2000). Report of the ICRI Meeting in Noumea, New Caledonia, 25-26 May, 2000. See Recommendation for Coral Reef Sustainable Fisheries. In ICRI (2000). Report of the ICRI Meeting in Noumea, New Caledonia, 25-26 May, 2000. Resolution on Sustainable Fisheries and Food Security. In ICRI (2001). Report of the ICRI Meeting in the Philippines, April 5-6, 2001. Decision in Support of APEC Strategy on

In many instances, the MPA forums also seek synergies with the larger forums, such as the WHC,[324] MAB,[325] Ramsar and/or the sections of the Bern regime such as Natura 2000 and the various EU Directives.[326]

I Financing the Regimes

Given that the Ramsar Bureau was effectively run by the IUCN until it was agreed that a permanent secretariat would be developed, the Convention originally had no financial provisions. Thus, aside the considerable financial support from the IUCN and the IWRB,[327] the only other support for the Bureau came from voluntary contributions towards the costs.[328] However, the voluntary contributions were not sufficient,[329] and the Ramsar Convention had to be amended to create a funding arrangement to finance the COPs and a permanent Secretariat.[330] These amendments were concluded in 1987.[331] These amendments, whilst setting down some basic due process rules[332] adopted the UN scale of contributions,[333] and despite some misgivings,[334] the regime

Destructive Fishing. In ICRI (2001). Report of the ICRI Meeting in Cebu, Philippines, 5-6 April, 2001. UNEP. (2000). Report of the Third Global Meeting of Regional Seas Conventions and Action Plans. Available from the UNEP Regional Seas Programme. Paragraph 129.

324 MEPC. (2004). Report of the MEPC on its 51st Session. MEPC. 51/22. 38.

325 Annex 6. Guidelines for the Designation of Special Areas Under MARPOL 73/78 and Guidelines for the Identification and Designation of Particularly Sensitive Sea Areas. MEPC (2001). Report of the MEPC on its 46th Session. MEPC 46/23. Section 6.2.

326 Report of the 12th MOP to the Convention for the Protection of the Mediterranean Sea Against Pollution and its Protocols. UNEP (DEC)/MED IG.13/8. Dec 30, 2001. Annex IV. See HELCOM HOD 11/2003.

327 Resolution 3.2. Financial and Budgetary Matters. (1987, Regina).

328 Recommendation 1.10. A Permanent Secretariat. (1980, Cagliari).

329 Recommendation 2.4. Support for the Interim Secretariat. (1984, Groningen).

330 Recommendation 1.8. Proposed Amendments to the Convention. (1980, Cagliari).

331 These are known as the 1987 (Regina) Amendments. Convention On Wetlands Of International Importance Especially As Waterfowl Habitat. Extraordinary Conference of the Contracting Parties. 28 May to 3 June 1987. Regina, Saskatchewan, Canada.

332 Such as although the budgets require at least a two thirds majority. Ramsar. 1987 Amendments. Article 6.5. Also, Terms of Reference for the Financial Administration of Ramsar. Recommendation C.3.2. Attachment 3. (1987, Regina). Change to the scale of contributions requires unanimity. Ramsar. 1987. Amendments. Article 6.6. A dedicated sub group in Ramsar on finance was formed in 1996. See Resolution VI.17. Financial and Budgetary Matters. (1996, Brisbane).

333 Resolution 3.2. Financial and Budgetary Matters. (1987, Regina).

334 There has been repeated calls to look at 'alternatives' to the UN scale. Resolution 5.2. Financial and Budgetary Matters. (1993, Kushiro). Resolution VI.17. Financial and Budgetary Matters. (1996, Brisbane).

has remained in place.[335] Although the Ramsar has tried to increase efficiencies,[336] and a number of costs are passed onto individual Parties (such as paying for their own scientific experts, unless they are from developing or economic transition countries,[337] or regional initiatives)[338] the Ramsar budget has grown to 3,978,735 (SFR) for 2005.[339]

J Entry Into Force

For the respective agreements to come into force, a certain number of instruments needed to be deposited. The more regional conventions required relatively small numbers. The 1940 Western Hemisphere Convention required only three deposits,[340] and the Bern[341] and earlier African Conventions only required four[342] (although the 2003 convention required 15).[343] Ramsar required seven deposits,[344] whilst the WHC needed 20.[345] The Madrid Protocol was most notable, as it required the deposit of instruments of ratification, acceptance, approval or accession by all States which are Antarctic Treaty Consultative Parties. Conversely, in as much as countries can join all of the above Conventions, they can also denounce them.[346] However, the amount of time needed for the denunciation varies between the regimes, going from 6 months for the Bern,[347] 12 months for the WHC,[348] and five years for the Ramsar.[349]

---

335 It has been tinkered with a little, via the setting of a minimum payment of SFR 1,000. Resolution 7.28. Financial and Budgetary Matters. (1999, San Jose). This was reiterated at the 8th COP. Resolution 8.27. Financial and Budgetary Matters. (2002, Valencia).

336 Resolution VI.22. Overall Cost Reduction. (1996, Brisbane).

337 Resolution 5.5. Establishment of the Scientific and Technical Review Panel. (1993, Kushiro).

338 Resolution 8.29. Evaluation of the Small Grants Fund for Wetland Conservation and Wise Use. (2002, Valencia). Annex II. Coordination Budget.

339 Resolution 8.27. Financial and Budgetary Matters. (2002, Valencia). Annex I.

340 1940 Western Hemisphere Convention. Article XII (2).

341 Bern Convention. Article 19 (2).

342 1933 Convention. Article 18. African Convention (1968). Article XXI.

343 2003 African Convention. Article XXXVIII.

344 Ramsar Convention. Article 10.

345 WHC. Article 33.

346 1933 London Convention. Article 19. 1940 Western Hemisphere Convention. Article XII (1). African Convention (1968). Article XXIII.

347 Bern Convention. Article 23.

348 WHC. Article 35.

349 Ramsar Convention. Article 11.

CONCLUSION

The goal of this book is to help with the creation and successful management of protected areas pf international significance. This goal reflects a realization that the international framework by which this objective may currently be achieved is very difficult to navigate due to its fragmented and ad-hoc nature, and what may be seen as an increasing antipathy towards protected areas under international or regional auspices. There is no single solution to the goal of this book in the face of these difficulties, but the following considerations are part of the answer.

The first area in which improvements can be made is with regards to the definitions of protected areas. International and regional institutions, in addition to national governments and the local communities within them, should be much more flexible in understanding that protected areas can take many forms. The IUCN categories, with their six divisions of possible types of protected areas are the exemplars of this process. If these categories were adopted on a much greater scale within the current international frameworks, it is likely that a greater number, and variety of protected areas could be created as they would not be restricted to any one type of protected area. Such an adoption would also allow the international or regional managing bodies to become much more syncronised with each other, in terms of both the opportunities and threats that they face, as they would be dealing with similar categories although in different regions. This would be a very complimentary overlap for the regimes learning from each other, as they would be able to compare problems which are of comparable.

The second improvement that can be made is the adoption of a more flexible approach to understanding the values of protected areas. In particular governments and international organisations need to understand that the values of protected areas are multifaceted, and evolving. This evolution does not mean that the traditional values for protected areas are disappearing, but rather, they are being supplemented. Despite these changes, the way values are being dealt with is very different in each regime. For example, although the scientific values of protected areas are commonly recognized in all regimes, only the MAB and the Antarctic regime have fully developed this area. Conversely, with the economic values of protected areas, the MAB and the Ramsar have begun to come to grips with the new methods of economic valuation and their application to protected areas. With regard to traditional economic values, such as tourism, only the MAB actively seek to capture this value. The value of protected areas for endangered species is notable with most regimes, and the species related regimes, such as the Bern and the CMS in particular. With regard to the more generic regimes, the most notable for its thematic endangered species work is the Ramsar, which has evolved to value avian, and non-avian species which rely upon wetlands. The other notable regimes, such as the MAB, and the WHC in particular, have tended to focus more on flagship species or megafauna. The protection of ecosystems is found within all protected area regimes. However, there is a diversity of ways in which this has been approached. The work of the Bern convention, in identifying sites by existing type, Ramsar by expanding type, the IMO by quality of ecosystems, and the WHC with its attraction towards hotspots are all notable. Geomorphic or Physio-graphical protected areas are notable in that whilst some regimes have actively excluded them from consideration, newer ones have come to embrace them. However, it is only the WHC which has developed a systematic listing and understanding of such values. Although intangible values common within the philosophical debates relating to protected areas, only two of these values have gained any traction. The first is aesthetics, but this has had a tightly hemmed in development, and only within the WHC. The second is 'cultural values'. Cultural values are recognized in many regimes, and the Ramsar is notable for actively pronouncing their support for such values. However, it is the WHC, which has most obviously began to grapple with this area, although it has, to date, sent out contradictory messages when dealing within its traditional categories. Nevertheless, the development of the new value of cultural landscape, in a number of other regimes, but the WHC in particular, may help resolve some of the current difficulties. There is no answer to the 'values' question beyond recognition of the fact that the values of protected areas are energing, and what may be valuable in one regime, may be valueless in another.

The obligations and gaps surrounding the creation of protected areas is the third area of difficulty with regard to the international management of protected areas. International and regional obligations to create protected areas can be traced to 1933. Nevertheless, a process began in 1962 which called for more protected areas to be created. The international community, over the following decades has responded with a variety of instruments, that facilitate the creation of protected areas in both generic and specifics senses. However, it has been argued in a number of international meetings that these instruments have not gone as far as they could have, and greater progress, via the creation of more protected areas needs to be achieved. This criticism, was first linked in 1987 into a numerical target of exactly how many protected areas should be created. The numerical targets, have since been adopted by the CBD. These targets are despite the fact that there has already been substantial success in the creation of protected areas. Indeed, by 2003, there were over 102,102 registered protected areas in 191 countries. The 2003 figure is equivalent to 12.65 of the Earth's land surface, or an area greater than the combined land area of China, South Asia and Southeast Asia. If MPAs and TBPAs are included in the calculation, 18.8 million kilometers of the Earth fall within protected areas.

Despite the broad obligations to create more protected areas, the clear successes in this area and the strong international support for this goal (as evidenced by the above figures), there are clear gaps in the international framework of protected areas. This is most notable, at the thematic level, with regard to marine, mountain, dryland and forest protected areas. In many ways, these gaps are because unlike with wetlands, there is no thematic international regime which has proved itself willing or able to pick up protected areas with their respective ecosystems. The answer to this problem which has evolved has been one of identifying priority areas. Some regimes have utilized a series of mechanisms, such as tentative lists, comparative and thematic analysis to help identify potential priority areas. Such analysis is often assisted by the schemas of the Udvardy system, hotspots, the Global 200 or notable areas of endemic species. Although these are all commendable schemas, the recognition of the priority areas are being forced through the existing protected area regimes. Whilst this is fine in some contexts, the extent that these priorities, and lesser but still valuable potential areas may become protected under an international auspice is limited by the thematic gaps in the international environmental framework of law and policy which is trying to govern this area. Part of the solution to this problem is with the international community developing new mechanisms, or strenghening and co-ordinating existing ones, so that new approaches can be pursued on a greater basis, and linked in with the flagship areas, from the hotspots to the Global 200.

The management of protected areas, and mitigation of threats facing them is the fourth and fifth areas of concern, as unless all the sites are well managed, and protected from all threats, there is minimal point in even bothering to get them inscribed as protected.

The overall problem here is that the regimes are not learning from each other. Accordingly, the best practice examples should be shared and leant from. In this regard there are a eight management considerations which all protected area regimes must reconcile. However, not all eight considerations require the same attention in each regime, and different regimes have developed some areas more than others. For example, with regard to management plans, the foremost regimes of note are the WHC and the Antarctic regime. With the WHC, failure of having adequate management plans may result in deferment of nominations, extensions, and can be part and parcel for a site being listed in Danger. The Ramsar has developed a different approach, whereby targets, models, and guidelines have been utilised to spur countries to create management plans. The Antarctic regime has also issued models and guidelines, and in addition to having a process of identifying management plans which need to be updated, also instigated a rule that each management plan only has a five year lifetime. A strong legal status, with clear boundaries, is essential for all protected area regimes, and listings are only possible if a site has both of these requirements. Once a site is listed, if the legal protections become questionable, most regimes are quick to issue recommendations to Parties to clarify the problems. The WHC is particularly strong in this approach, but only the Ramsar has instigated a systematic review of the laws covering all of their sites.

There is no specific rule on the necessary size of a protected area, beyond the fact that a site should be big enough to preserve the integrity of an area. Although MPAs and MAB sites tend to be larger than other sites, other regimes, depending on the area in focus can be equally big. The only regime to have developed an active regime for changing the size of sites, via extensions or reductions, is the WHC. Buffer zones, between the core site, and the surrounding areas are increasingly recognised in most protected area regimes, as an essential part of any management process. However, despite this recognition, only the WHC and, in particular, the MAB have developed rules for buffer zones. Ecological networks and corridors are also notable in the literature, but very few regimes have actually tried to implement these. The exception to this avoidance, is with the Habitats Directive, and in particular, with the GEF. Having adequate staff and associated resources is recognised in all protected area regimes, and is a clearly iterated goal of the CBD with regard to protected areas. However, only the Ramsar, the GEF and the WHC have developed clear policies to facilitate this area, with the GEF and the WHC particularly notable for their targeted financial assistance in this area. Finally, EIAs have become part of the protected area framework, from the work of the CBD down. Some regimes, such as that of Antarctica, have developed clear rules on what must be examined. Other regimes, such as the WHC, Ramsar and the Bern have all created clear precedents calling for the utilisation of EIAs, and at times, have even called into existence the adequacy of these.

A final management issue of note is the paradigm shift in the way that public participation has been viewed. What was once seen as a subsidiary issue, has, in international environmental law moved to the centre stage. This shift is particularly noticeable with protected areas, and is reflected in multiple bodies from the GEF to the CBD. The protected area regimes which have the most developed jurisprudence in this area are the WHC, Ramsar and the MAB. The MAB is particularly noticeable, as the Parties to the MAB framework are quite willing to refuse inscription of potential sites if they have inadequate public participation. The Ramsar Parties steer a more middle ground, preferring to emphasise the importance of public participation at a thematic level, rather than on a site by site basis. The Parties to the WHC are somewhere between the Ramsar and the MAB. However, with regard to the question of indigenous peoples, although the Ramsar is supportive of the meaningful involvement of indigenous peoples, the WHC is most notable (but with ambiguous outcomes) protected area organisation in this area. A relatively strong support for grass-roots NGOs is also notable in the WHC and Bern Conventions. Conversely, the Ramsar has, consistent with its approach on public participation, adopted a more thematic approach, whilst the Antarctic regime has, partly due to its unique position, a more constraining approach to NGOs seeking to work 'on the ground' under their auspice. The point of these developments, is that although there is still strong case of 'people free' protected aras, protected areas cannot, and should not, be made or managed in isolation from the communities around them.

The threats to protected areas all relate to the idea that each protected area has its own 'integrity'. The integrity of each area is related to the values for why it was originally inscribed. The integrity of each area may be threatened by at least 12 different threats. The first threat is permanent human populations. However, only one regime, the WHC, recognises this as a potential threat to their sites. With regard to non-permanent populations, such as tourism, all of the protected area regimes have recognised the damaging potential uncontrolled visitors. Some regimes such as the Bern, Ramsar, and WHC have gone further, and issued specific recommendations to individual countries to control particular tourism problems. The third threat is alien species. The control of alien species has become a well recognised goal in most biodiversity forums, and the CBD in particular. This goal is continually repeated with regard to protected areas. The two regimes with the strongest, generic, controls in this area are the Antarctic regime and the IMO's Ballast Water Convention. The Bern and the WHC have are also notable in this area, but due to their individualised response to sites threatened by alien species. The WHC, is of particular interest as alien species have been recognised as such clear threats, that they alone can lead to a site being listed as in Danger. Air pollution and climatic change are also clear threats to a number of protected areas. Air pollution is a relatively small scale, ad-hoc, problem in sites under the MAB, Bern and WHC. Conversely, climate change is recognised as a potentially large scale problem. Despite this possibility, only the ICRI and the Ramsar have become actively involved in this debate. Other forums, such as the WHC, Bern and CMS have been relatively silent, or are still evolving their responses.

The fifth threat relates to inadequate or disrupted supply of water into a protected area, as most commonly evidenced with large dams. This has long been recognised as a clear threat to protected areas. However, none of the various regimes have an outright prohibition against large dams. Rather, the Ramsar, Bern and WHC have all continually warned that if the integrity of a site is substantially damaged by the activities of large dams or similar water disruptive processes, then the sites may be listed as in Danger. The sixth threat is mineral and/or hydro-carbon extraction and/or exploration. This is one of the most prominent public debates about threats to protected areas. These debates are both domestic and international, and a number of high level NGO resolutions have been issued calling for restrictions on such activities in most protected areas. The foremost regime to follow such an approach in the Antarctic regime. In this context, the Parties to have prohibited all mining on the Continent. Most other regimes have preferred to take a case by case approach, with each activity assessed against the impacts it is making on the integrity of the site. The WHC has shown clearly in three separate instances, that poorly regulated mineral and/or hydrocarbon extraction can lead a site as being inscribed as in Danger.

Traffic and routing and general industrial developments are the seventh and eighth threats. These have been a long standing issues in a number of protected area forums, with the Bern and the WHC in particular. It is however quite rare, for roading or industrial developments alone to directly lead to a site being classified as in Danger, although this has happened. Rather, these threats are typically part of a package of larger concerns. This approach is unlike the IMO, of which (maritime) traffic, in terms of both type and quantity, going near vulnerable areas is a key consideration on the need for protected areas. The ninth threat to protected areas is pollution. Pollution is a general concern in all of the regimes, but agricultural pollution, is particularly highlighted in the Ramsar and the Bern Conventions. However, legal agriculture – as the source of the pollution, and despite infringing into numerous protected areas, has not been the source of detailed discussion outside of the Ramsar, and to a lesser degree, the Bern Convention. A similar situation exists with legitimate forestry in internationally protected areas, with only the European Diploma passing strong recommendations on the need to dramatically control most forms of logging in some of the sites under their auspice. When the focus turns to the threat to protected areas of illegal extraction, all of the regimes have a similar, steadfast approach, in that it must be controlled. In extreme situations, such extractions, typically poaching, can lead to a site being classified as in Danger. This is a particular problem with a number of African WHC sites. Such illegal activities are commonly associated with times of armed conflict, which is the final threat to protected areas, but only one regime, the WHC, has any recognition of this problem. The conclusion of the issue of threats is that protected areas are facing a bewildering array of threats. These are all diverse and what may threaten one site may not threaten another. Nevertheless, many are at risk of losing their integrity from one threat to another.

Compliance, as the sixth substantive area of this concern if areas of international importance are to be successfully managed. However, most of the key regimes in this area have developed, without using the word 'compliance', effective compliance mechanisms to ensure that all internationally listed sites are not overtly threatened, to the point that they are in danger. The first step in this process has been the creation of effective monitoring regimes. In this regard, the Antarctic, Bern, Ramsar and WHC have all developed elaborate, guided, and at times assisted, monitoring, reporting and independent visits to sites in question. Moreover, the Bern, Ramsar and WHC have also established effective lists of sites which they consider to be in danger, of which remedial action must be taken.

Once it established that a site is in danger, the question becomes what can be done about it, and most importantly, whether State consent needs to be involved in such deliberations. Some regimes, such as with the European Diploma and the Antarctic regime (to a degree) have bypassed the question of Party consent, as all of their areas must be periodically reviewed. However, these are the exception, as most regimes have the presumption that a site must be proven to be in danger, and then dealt with. In such settings, the divergence between the regimes, on the critical question of whether the consent of a Party is required for de-listing is vast. Thus, whilst some regimes, such as the Ramsar and the MAB, will not de-list a site which has lost its values, without the consent of the Party in whose territory the site is in, others, such as the Bern will. The WHC is between these two extremes, although it prefers to utilize State consent whenever possible. Moreover, all attempts to 'rescue' the threatened site will be made, and clear markers of what must be achieved to reach success will be set down. Despite the developing clarity of the question of compliance, the fact needs to be faced that the issue is not taken that seriously, and the international community should be willing to delist sites which have been substantively damaged in as much a it is willing to inscribe good examples of protected areas.

The final areas of note in this book is with regard to financial assistance and constituents within each regime. Financial assistance for protected areas is crucial. However, only two regimes, notably the Ramsar and the WHC have developed internal mechanisms to provide such assistance. All of the other regimes of note, as well as the Ramsar and the WHC have come to place an increased reliance on external forms of finance. However, despite a growing number of places from which assistance is available, it is the GEF, which has come to easily represent the premier international instrument for the financial support of protected areas. With regard to constituents, the key point to note is the overt importance of NGOs. These organizations are indispensable to the creation and enhancement of protected areas in international law. However, despite merit worthy NGO's operating in a number of regimes, their numbers are noticably small.

In short, in the 21st century, if the international community wishes to have a successful engagement with protected areas in international environmental law, it is necessary for them to come to terms with the debates of what areas to protect. They must also reconcile the definitions and values of protected areas. Finally, the nations of the global community, acting through their respective regimes, must achieve successful management of protected areas, including in terms of the threats facing them, and ensuring State compliance with the obligations they have already undertaken to protect areas of international significance within their boundaries. Greater financial assistance must be forthcoming, and civil society and local communities must be fully integrated into the debates.

INDEX

H

I

J

K